MW00450519

WHO AM I

The Story of Rosita Jovani Bustos

JERRY MARTINEZ

NEWMAN SPRINGS PUBLISHING
320 Broad Street
Red Bank, NJ 07701

First originally published by Newman Springs Publishing 2019

ISBN 978-1-64096-683-3 (Paperback)
ISBN 978-1-64096-684-0 (Digital)

Printed in the United States of America

Acknowledgments

THE ORIGIN OF THIS BOOK is based on the most profound moments of my life. My faith in my Diosito, my Lord and Savior, is the reason I'm still with life. My life's journey has been blessed by individuals who have assisted me during hardships and after suffering convulsions.

Special thanks to my grandmother Sinforosa. I learned about my Diosito (God) and the prayers from her. She taught me the virtues of life. She gave me the love I desired from my own mother but never got.

Special thanks to my sister Ana Lidia Reza. She was the replacement mother. My other replacement mother was Mama Lucia. She took care of me, fed, and clothed me. She gave me a place to work, enabling me to pay for my medicine.

To Don Felipe, the mailman of the pueblo. Without his help, this book would—in all probability—be nothing but a dream. He wrote my diary until I learned to read and write. By the age of six, I had learned to read and write from him.

To the people of my beautiful pueblo: Tetipec, thank you for caring and helping me during my convulsions. Thank you for the blankets you provided that protected me from the cold, for the nutrition in the plates of beans and other foods you gave me. Thank you, Tetipec, for every corner was my shelter, my home.

Special thanks to Sister Sarita and Sister Adoración. Because of their efforts, I was able to leave the jail called home for Tlapa, where the orphanage was located. They protected me from my abusive mother and her lecherous male companion.

Sister María del Mar deserves special thanks for taking me into the orphanage. She befriended me and gave me shelter until the age of eighteen.

To the people of Tlapa de Comonfort, especially Don Abel and Doña Amparito Barrera, the Porres family, Victor Superumy, Don José Luis Barrera, and all the people who helped me and the orphanage.

To my friends who showed me how the real world differs from the one I was raised in, the orphanage. I learned the true meaning of being free. Trini, Esmeralda, Magda, and Paloma, thank you for teaching me how to survive in the real world. The moral restrictions I adhered to was because of my faith in God.

When I came to this country, the people of the United States were very generous. Melchor Arreola, the father of my child, helped me in numerous ways. Mr. Francis Casey, my court-appointed foster father, showed me how generous this country is. He also introduced me to many wonderful people living in Orange County, California.

Dr. Richard Kim, neurologist at UC Irvine hospital, deserves my thanks and prayers. He led a staff of international doctors when he performed the operation to cure me of my sickness. I came to this country with the hope that my Diosito would place an expert in the path of my life to cure my illness. Dr. Kim was that doctor.

Introduction

My Mexican birth certificate shows that I was born in March 1981 in Tetipac, a pueblo in the state of Guerrero. As I look back at the calendar, I was born during Holy Week. However, after thirty-five years of studying my notes and diaries, among other research, I discovered that there is a strong possibility that I was born in Dallas, Texas. Reyna, my mother, and Jorge Bustos, my father, lived together in Dallas during 1980 and early 1981. It was during this time that she became pregnant with me.

When I started writing this book, I knew that I had a family in Dallas. My paternal grandmother, several uncles and aunts, and two half brothers reside in Dallas. Two years ago I went to Dallas and met the paternal side of my family. The information I got from my paternal side of the family is how I discovered that I was born in the United States.

The mystery is, did she register my birth in Dallas? Did she in fact register my birth and later sell my papers? In my search for the truth, I learned that selling papers of Mexican babies born here in the United States was not unusual. The obstacle I'm faced with is that the midwife who assisted with my birth is dead and the clinic mother went for treatments during the time she was pregnant is gone. Reyna, my mother, left my father and went back to Mexico and took me with her. In Mexico, Reyna did not register my birth until I was five years old. The law required a birth certificate of all eligible children entering school. She had to comply with the law and registered my birth. She had, however, baptized me; and the baptismal certificate shows my birth as a day in March 1981.

Why Reyna returned to México with a newly born baby—me—is a mystery. I have heard several stories, but I can't be sure. I've asked her that question several times only to be scolded and sometimes beaten with a belt. The fact is that she did move back to México with me. I have been diagnosed with epilepsy, which was caused by Reyna; I was not born with it. I suffered a broken skull when Reyna dropped me in a pile of rocks under a tree and abandoned me there to die. My skull was damaged that day, and I have suffered from epilepsy ever since.

I have my life in spite of fighting in the womb of my mother. Since the moment I took my first breath and gave my first cry, God has shown me His love.

In the darkness of the dawn hours, while the moon was fading into the morning light and the stars shining bright, Mama Lucia heard my cry for help. Puzzled at the sound of a baby's cry for help, she followed my cries. She noticed movement nearby, looking up to see a person hiding in the bushes. Startled, the person ran away from the cover of the bushes. Mama Lucia recognized my mother running away from the scene of the crime.

Mama Lucia didn't know what to do; finally she took off to my maternal grandmother's house. She told *Mamacita* that she'd heard a baby crying somewhere near the bushes and wanted my mamacita to accompany her. Mama Lucia didn't tell mamacita that she'd seen Reyna running away from the scene. My grandma saw me wrapped in a blanket and ever so gingerly picked me up. She recognized the blanket because she'd given it to her daughter, Reyna. My mamacita, my grandma, took me home with her.

I was probably four or five years of age when Don Felipe wrote my first memoir for me. That's a very young age to write memoirs, but I did. Don Felipe, the mailman of the pueblo, inspired me and helped me write daily notes. He was my neighbor, and it was convenient to meet whenever I had something I wanted him to write. In time he taught me how to write and read. If it wasn't for Don Felipe, I wouldn't have any information for this writing nor would I have known that I could write my own life story.

I spent my days mostly alone accompanied by the rays of the sun, playing with my shadow, or with darkness setting in talking with the stars; and when the moon gave me light, I would sleep under the trees watching *el lucero* (planet Venus). The hours passed me by, whether I was sleeping under some staircase or under a tree, always asking the heavens full of stars, but mostly Venus, the same questions. Why does my mother punish me? Who is my father? Will I ever be healthy? I never received answers. In time, my grandmother Sinforosa taught me about God. She taught me to pray, told me about the Virgin Mary, the mother of God.

Eventually I started running into the church to speak with God and the Virgin Mary. I gained a lot of faith in God and the Virgin Mary because I didn't feel alone; they were always with me. From that I became very confident within myself. As a child, at night, alone, looking at the heavens, I would speak to God, "In Your hands are all my questions, Diosito (God), and I will be waiting for Your response."

I've crossed doors after doors of life, always asking question after question, but no one answers. My Diosito is the only one listening, yet I don't have answers, but my faith grows stronger and stronger in Him.

I have confidence that I will succeed that I will arrive at whatever awaits me, because my Diosito will give me the strength. Santa Cruz Catholic church is my refuge. Day after day, barrier after barrier, I continue searching for the answer to my being. During the five years of living, many ask, "Who are you?" Now I wonder the same, in front of my Diosito and the Virgencita Maria inside the church. I ask them, "Who am I?"

The notes of my childhood, the diaries of my days in the orphanage, and the diaries that I continue to write— these account for almost 100 percent of the information in this book. The research that has followed and conversations with friends in México and here in the United States and my newly discovered family in Dallas, Texas, enhance what my notes contained in this book.

This book is written how I thought as a young girl. I didn't change it to how I feel today. No, my notes depict how and what

I lived through and how my words poured through my young and immature self.

I experienced loneliness as a child, and I still do. I have always had my Diosito and my Virgencita Maria at my side. I had my sisters—Ana, Blanquita, Beni—and my mamacita Sinforosa, Mama Lucia, Don Felipe, and many friends growing up in Tetipac. What I lacked was the love, a hug, a kiss, a kind word from my proper mother.

I survived my struggles with life here in the norte of the United States. I survived because of the kindness shown to me by people here in this country. Mr. Francis Casey, my adoptive American father; the doctors who performed the operation to cure me of my epilepsy; the policemen who helped me through many domestic abuses and helped me when I was homeless.

My desire to write this book goes back to my childhood. My notes filled several notebooks, ready to be transformed to a real book. How to proceed was a problem that I wasn't sure how to continue. I was afraid to confide in just anybody. People that knew a little of my life encouraged me to write it, but none knew or could understand fully what I wanted, what I had lived through, nor could I confide in just anybody.

I truly believe that my Diosito has put my adoptive father, my doctors, and others in my path of life. I believe that my Diosito has a role for me, and these people were placed in my path of life enabling me to accomplish whatever that might be. That is how I believe my author became part of my life. How we met is a mystery, how I was able to confide in him is a bigger mystery. Yet why God placed him in my path of life is another mystery. Mr. Martinez knows more about my life than anybody else other than myself. He has guided and advised me how much personal information is pertinent and what is not. But the ultimate decision of what is to be included is mine and mine alone. He has written two books, one of which received an award at the Latin book fair held at USC. That is one reason I decided to trust him with my life story.

Now my lifelong dream of writing my autobiography is a reality, a dream come true. I hope it inspires others like me to continue your quest. "Don't give up on Diosito, He is at your side. Be patient, He hears your cries and in time," He answers.

My life enters another chapter. I have but this life to share with others. God is with me guiding my free will to be the best person, the best ambassador that I can be for Him.

Early Childhood

I RUN WITHIN MY OWN shadow, illuminated by the moon, guided by *el lucero* in the dawn hours. Full of confusion, my eyes full of tears, with fear because I cannot control my convulsions. I fall when my body feels faint, and I convulse; I lie on the ground or wherever I fall. After time lapses, I pick myself up, quenching my thirst with the blood dripping from my knees. I wrestle with my feelings, with my soul, in my path of life.

I regret going home, regret going to face more abuse, spankings, and sometimes whippings. I sleep where I can, except at somebody's home. To do so would be inviting another whipping, so I wander seeking my little corner where I can speak with the stars, the moon, and even a stray cat. I am alone in this beautiful pueblo. I wait for dawn, wait for the church to sound its bells. That is my cue; I run to the Santa Cruz Church to talk with my Diosito.

I leave the church full of faith and anticipation that someday I will have my answer. Hurriedly I leave the church, running to leave my shadow behind; stride after stride my companion stays with me. I laugh. My laughter is short-lived as I reach Don Felipe's small single room he calls home. The expression on the old man's face reads like so many times before. He doesn't speak, only points to the corner. My clothes are strewn in the corner of his small and untidy room. Reyna's habit of leaving the pueblo without informing me or my older sister Ana is all too familiar. At least this time she left my clothes, unlike other times.

I am relieved that for a time I will be spared the abuse I suffer at her hands. At the same time, I am happy to be alone. Don Felipe can't hold back his tears; he feels sorry for me. I run to my house, which is nearby. Soon I come back with a cup of coffee for him. He tells me that Reyna left without saying where she was going nor did she tell Don Felipe when she'd be back. All she said was for Don Felipe to hand clothes over to me. The *viejito* (old man) still had tears in his eyes. I said, "Don Felipe, please don't cry, remember you are the only mailman in the pueblo, and we all need you."

I run to the *puesto* (food stand) where Mama Lucia sells her tacos, enchiladas, and other goodies to her clients. "Rosita, it's so good to see you so early, mija. Tell me why you are so happy, but of course, it seems that you are always happy."

"Mama Lucia, I am happy and sad at the same time. My mother is gone again, that's why I'm happy. But sad because I don't really have a mother. She left without telling anybody where she was going nor when she will be back. But Diosito tells me that the Virgin Mary is my mother, and she does love me and my sister Ana, and you too, Mama Lucia. Mama Lucia, I wish my grandmother Sinforosa returns to the pueblo and takes me away with her to her llano." I hug Mama Lucia, look up at her with teary eyes. I ask her, "And you, Mama Lucia, are you my mother, and will you permit me to call you Mama forever and ever?"

"Of course, you can call me Mamá." She gave me a hug full of love, a hug I wish Reyna would find it in her heart to give me.

"Mama Lucia, thank you for accepting me as your make-believe daughter. Mamá," I said, taking advantage of the opportunity to call her *Mamá*, "can I leave? I want to go to the church."

Before she can answer, I dart through the doorway and stop running when I reach the church that awaits me with open doors. I reach the statues of my Diosito and my Virgencita Maria, and my tears flow. I kneel with tears still flowing. I look up and say, "Diosito, even though the lady who carried me in her womb and gave me life doesn't love me, I love her very much. But now I have three moms, one who doesn't love me and two who love me, Mama Lucia and the Virgencita Maria."

Virgin Mary is the mother who loves me; although she doesn't answer my prayers, she listens. My other mother is Mama Lucia. She accepts me as a daughter. She feeds me, she takes care of me when

I have an epileptic convulsion. She takes care of me when Reyna leaves. She really loves me. I thank my Diosito for listening, tell Him I'm leaving, I make the sign of the cross before leaving. I am happy as I depart the church.

I run as fast as my little legs are able to carry the rest of me, trying to stay ahead of a convulsion. My second mother was busy selling tacos and other Mexican foods when I arrived. I cleaned myself up. Later when the later customers came, I helped Mama Lucia feed them. As the day was coming to a close, Mamá saw me dancing about, singing. I approached Mamá and asked her for a hug. "Mamá, from this day forward, I have two more moms."

She looked at me with a puzzled look. "Mija, how can it be that you have two moms, and who are they?" I took a few steps as though I was dancing.

I said, "Mama, it's getting late. After I help you clean the puesto and while you are frying tomorrow's carnitas, I will tell you who my mothers are." We finished cleaning the puesto. I readied myself for the trip to my grandmother's hacienda where Mama Lucia rented a *cuarto* (room) from mamacita (Grandmother Sinforosa). Her room was built behind the bath and bathroom and near the outdoor oven often used for baking bread and other foods. We entered her cozy room.

I went outside where I lit the wood under the three rocks neatly arranged with a grill atop. I placed the frying pan atop the grill; it was ready for my second mama to fry her carnitas. I arranged a nice seat for us where we, Mama Lucia and myself, could enjoy the early evening. The two of us sat outside, the early stars beginning to shine, the carnitas sizzling, and me anxious to share with Mama Lucia my secret.

"Okay, mija, tell me who your mothers are."

I placed my hands on my chin, my elbow on my knees, looking at the fire, tears slowly starting to flow, and then I finally spoke. "My first mother is the Virgin Mary, I know that she loves me. She is the mother of the whole world and the mother of my Diosito."

Mama Lucia got up to stir the meat. "Now, Rosita, tell me, who is the other mother?"

"You, Mama Lucia, is the other mother that I have." She stopped stirring the carnitas, approached me, and with tears in her eyes, gave me the hug that I've desired from my proper mom.

"Thank you, Rosita, for choosing me as your mother, I will always be at your side. Rosita, being a mother has its responsibilities. I worry and it hurts me to tell you this. Rosita, I can't provide you with your necessities of life. I am especially talking of money to buy you your medicine or money to take you to a doctor. I can help take care of you. I am here to help you confront your convulsions, and I can provide you shelter and food. Rosita, I want you to know that I love you but don't have the kind of money required for your illness."

"Mama Lucia, don't worry about money. Today, as many other days, you helped me, and you're always helping me. So please don't tell me that you can't be my mother. I am a hard worker and will always work and will never ask you for money to buy my medicine. Mama Lucia, I only ask that of what you can give me, love and hugs that a mother gives her child. When I asked you to be my mother, that is all I wanted."

"Rosita, come here." She gave a big hug saying, "I accept to be your mother, Lucia." I slept very comfortably that night.

The next morning, I leapt out of bed, ran to my house, and made coffee for Don Felipe. He was very happy, unlike yesterday. Maybe getting his first cup of coffee will make him happy. I cleaned his tiny room and dumped his urinal basin. Afterward, we sat down, and he wrote the information for my diary. I left the old man's house and headed for Doña Tolita's house.

My older sister Ana is working in the federal district and doesn't come home on a regular basis. It is difficult to reach her, but she communicates periodically with Doña Tolita, one of our neighbors. She gives me the information I want. I dash to Mama Lucia's puesto to help her out with the customers. That's how I spend my days, working with Mama Lucia and always visiting my Diosito and the Virgin Mary.

I can't complain about the customers, they treat me with respect and usually give me handsome tips. In fact, many propose marriage. But I know that they are just playing with me; besides, I'm too young for any of them. My convulsions continue; I've asked God for a cure, but He doesn't answer me. I thank Him for putting Mama Lucia in my path of life to help me cope with this illness that I have.

I'm in church praying when my mind starts to close on me, I feel a convulsion coming, I brace myself. I wake up under the heavy wooden church bench. I don't know how long I was passed out, all I can feel is an enormous headache, nausea and dizziness. I manage to make the sign of the cross before getting back on my feet. The gates of the church weren't locked yet, I crossed the gates and ran to Mama Lucia's puesto.

She was cleaning up when I arrived; seeing me, she asked, "You got sick, didn't you?" I didn't have to answer, she'd seen me in this condition many times before. Mama Lucia told me to sit. She came over to where I sat, placed a cold wet cloth over my head and another on the back of my neck. The cold wet towels felt good; she told me to rest. I felt horrible that she didn't allow me to help her clean up. Soon we were on the way to her room. I took a cold, cold shower, dried up, and took a nap. I felt a lot better after the shower and short nap. I walked to the back where Mama Lucia was preparing the meat for the following day's menu. She anticipated a big day, so I helped her through the night until two o'clock in the morning. During that time, we talked, and I sang. In time the conversation between us turned into questions that I always wanted to ask. I wanted answers, so I asked her questions.

I Learn about My Early Life

"Mama Lucia, do you know where I was born?"

"Rosita, why do you ask, don't you know?"

"I want to know because some lady told me not to play with her son because I was the daughter of the pueblo's crazy lady. Now I think that everybody believes her, and I don't want to go to school anymore. Many times instead of going to kindergarten, I go to the lakes or to my godmother's house. Mama Lucia, you know Socorro, don't you? She was my godmother when I was baptized."

"Yes, Rosita, I know your godmother.

"Rosita, what do you do at Doña Socorro's house all day?"

"Uuhh, Mama, I feed her pigs, and I give them baths. But first I clean out their sty. Yuck, it always smells horrible. Also she has a nice garden, and I pick some of the fruit, and I help her make juices." My godmother Socorro is very generous, many times the fruit or vegetables that we pick, she donates to the poor people that needs food. Through my godmother, I have met other kids that are cousins of mine. That's what my godmother tells me.

But I have met other boys and girls who have told me that their mother is my aunt. They come and play with me in the sty while I wash the pigs. When I finish, she serves me some of the most delicious food, and always she eats with me. I look at Mama Lucia's expression; I say, "Her food is almost as good as yours, Mama Lucia." She smiles. My godmother is very kind to me. She tells me to help myself to any goodie in the store, but—"

"What, mija, why the but?"

"Ay, Mamá, her daughter is extremely jealous of me. Very sad that she doesn't like me. Just the other day, she pulled me from my

16

hair, but I didn't say anything to my *madrina*. Instead I asked my Diosito to forgive her.

"Mama Lucia, tell me where I was born. Also tell me what happened to me when I was born."

"Rosita, mija, your early life is a very sad one, very sad. I never saw when you were born, I'm not even sure that you were born here in the pueblo. It's probable that you were born away from here, but I can't say where. I know very little about your early days of your life. Your grandma Sinforosa knows much more than I do. What I know is that Doña Sinforosa left the pueblo because she was having a lot of problems with your mother, Reyna.

"For over three years I didn't know much about your life. The one who knows is Don Felipe. He has been living in the same place he rents from your grandma forever. He knows more than anybody what goes on in your house."

"But you, Mama Lucia, you know a lot. Please tell me what you know. I promise not to have a convulsion, and I promise not to be saddened by what you tell me. I want to know the truth about my life—my being, please. Also I want to know where my grandma Sinforosa has her ranch."

"Okay, I will tell you what I know, but you must see Don Felipe, he knows much more. First, your grandmother's ranch is a place far away, a place she calls her llano. I visited her ranch the time that I went with her. It's a beautiful place, bigger than any I've seen around here. She has cows, horses, and a donkey or two, chickens and dogs and heaven knows what else. The closest city is Piedras Negras.

"Rosita, don't you remember that she took you to the llano with her, when you were very sick? Do you remember anything about her ranch and how good she treated you?"

"I always remember how well she treated me, but I don't remember much about the ranch. I do think about it all the time, especially her dogs and the chickens. Ah, I also remember a donkey, he was very loud and stubborn. I wish I was there with her now.

"Mama Lucia, now tell me when my mother, Reyna, returned from el Norté."

"Okay, mija, I will, but promise me you will be strong. When your mother returned to the pueblo from the United States, she was a little chubby. Your mother was the subject of a lot of gossip. Rumors about her started the first day she set foot back here in the pueblo."

I wanted to ask Mama Lucia questions, but I held back and allowed her to continue. "People used to say, 'Look at Reyna, appears that life was good up North, so why did she come back?' Your mother had gone to el Norte and left her five daughters here alone. Many people despised her for doing that."

When she mentioned that, I had to ask, "Mama Lucia, you mean to tell me that I have five sisters besides Ana?"

"Yes, mija, you do, but let me finish telling you now about your mother. As I said before, your mother arrived back here in March 1981. She was a little plump, a little heavier, and that's about the time that you were born. Now only your mother knows for sure when you were born and whether you were born in the United States, and she brought you here or that you were born here in the pueblo. If you were born here, somebody would know, but nobody knows or aren't saying. Nobody around here knew that she was pregnant.

"Reyna used to say that she gained weight because of the good life she lived in el Norte. After you were born, Reyna disappeared for a while. Your sisters didn't tell anybody where she'd gone to either because they didn't know or because she ordered them not to say. Your grandma Sinforosa took you with her and took care of you. Reyna is your mother. Even if she denied that she was pregnant, there is no doubt that she is your mother. I'm not sure when you were born, but I'm certain that your older sister knows."

I just stood starry-eyed, thinking, *Sisters, I have sisters in el Norte, and one of them knows the truth of my birth?* Mama Lucia placed her soft motherly hands on my shoulders and asked me if I heard enough. I hugged her, I said, "No, no, I want to learn more."

"Are you strong enough?" she asked. I smiled, holding back my tears. "I'm strong."

"Rosita, those eyes never lie, I see a little fib, are you sure you want to hear more?"

"Please continue, tell me, when did you first know that I was Reyna's baby?"

"Mija, I will tell you, but if your Reyna knows that I gave you this information, she will evict me, Don Felipe, and others, and since Reyna is Sinforosa's daughter, she will kick me out. However, I'm going to tell you anyway.

"It was late one night, I had prepared my carnitas for the following day. I could hear the leaves of the trees nearby, rustling with the gentle breeze. I had finished plucking the feathers of the chicken. I walked to the pile of trash to discard the feathers. Suddenly I heard a different sound, the sound of a baby crying. I dropped the feathers and walked to the edge of the patio. I saw a woman that resembled your mother running away from where the baby was crying. I kept looking at the woman, she ran toward the patio of your home. She didn't see me.

"I walked toward the cries of the baby, and that baby—now we know that it was you. I ran to Doña Sinforosa's house, I entered without knocking. Your grandma was really shocked to see me enter her house the way I did. I was short of breath and couldn't speak right away. 'Lucia, Lucia, what's the matter? Talk to me.' Doña Sinforosa was worried. Finally I said, 'Doña Sinforosa, come with me, there's an abandoned baby in the woods.'

"Doña Sinforosa calmly got dressed and followed me to where we could hear the cries of a baby. Another lady that rented from your grandma heard the commotion. She happened to be Isabela, a teacher. Your grandma told her not to worry, so she went back inside her room. We reached the place where you were abandoned. Of course at the time we didn't know that it was you. You were covered in a blanket, your head atop a rock that was lying on top of a stone wall."

I couldn't hear any more. I sat on the floor, crossed my legs, placed my hands on my forehead, elbows on my knees, and cried. The stream of tears were shed for the loneliness I felt. The tears flowed for the hurt, for the pain I felt in my heart, for the heartless mom who bore me. I felt Mama Lucia when she put a blanket underneath me. I lay there for a while. I stood up and sat on a chair. "Mama Lucia, please continue, I want to know more."

"Mija," Doña Lucia said, "I don't think that you're in a condition to hear more."

"Mama Lucia, forget my tears, I want to know why Reyna abandoned me, please continue."

"Rosita, you are absolutely sure that you want me to continue? Fine, then I will continue. Sinforosa picked you up not knowing it was her granddaughter that she was rescuing. We took you to her house. When she saw the blanket in the dim glow of light, she recognized the blanket. It was the same one she had given her daughter, your mother, Reyna. She looked at me and asked, 'Why is this babe covered in this blanket?' She kept looking at me. 'Lucia,' she asked me, 'what do you know about this?' 'Sinforosa, I saw Reyna run away from here, she abandoned this baby.' Your grandma was so angry, she screamed, 'Reyna, daughter of the damned, for sure you wanted to kill this innocent child of God. You son of a dog, I'm going to inform your brothers. You will be cast into the dungeon of criminals where you belong.' Your grandma was on her way to see Reyna, but I stopped her. I told her that Reyna had left the house shortly after she abandoned you. Your grandma shouted toward Reyna's house.

"One of your sisters came out of the house wanting to know why Sinforosa was shouting. Your sister noticed that Sinforosa was holding a baby, now you know that it was you she was holding. 'Mamacita, why are holding that baby?' she asked. Your grandma told her the truth, that Reyna had abandoned the baby she was holding. She also told your sister that you were injured. Mija, you were so beautiful, but at the moment that you started to cry, you also started to tremble. Your body became very stiff and cold, and your body started to turn a purplish color.

"After we took you to your grandma's house, she told me, 'I will kill Reyna with my own two hands if this little angel dies.' I went for the *curandero* (healer, medic) that I knew. When the healer saw you, she apologized because she didn't have a remedy that would help you. Instead she advised us to take you to the doctor.

"Doña Sinforosa stated, 'I will not permit this little soul of God to die. No, Doña Lucia, it's not possible, for this child will die.' Your grandma took you in her arms and ran to the doctor's house. Doña

Sinforosa prayed all the way asking Diosito not to take you with Him." Mama Lucia looked at me, saying, "See, mija, her prayers helped because here you are full of life.

"We got to the doctor's house. His wife, followed by a bunch of barking dogs, opened the door when she heard the doorbell. While the doctor was examining you, we prayed and prayed. Doña Sinforosa said out loud—I remember it well when she prayed, 'This soul will be saved, Diosito, this child's life is in Your hands.' The doctor finished examining you, he told us that you had a fever and wanted to know why you had a terrible bruise in your head.

"I let Doña Sinforosa do the talking. When she finished telling how you had gotten that bruise in your head, the doctor was going to call the officials. Somehow your grandma convinced him not to call the police. That's when the doctor informed us that you had suffered an epileptic attack. We looked at each other, we didn't know what that was. He explained what epilepsy was and how we had to take care of you. He examined your bruise in your head again.

"The doctor advised your grandma to take you to the hospital. He told her that if you died, he was going to press charges against your mother, Reyna. Doña Sinforosa asked what the charges were. The doctor told her to pay for the injections only. He didn't charge for his services, rather saying that seeing you alive was his reward. He insisted that you be taken to the hospital so that a neurologist could examine you. Your grandma agreed.

"Your grandma paid the doctor for the injections and signed the papers with her fingerprint. Your mamacita didn't know how to write, so that was her way of signing the papers. Papers were required so that we could take you to the hospital. All this time I held you in my arms. I looked at your beautiful face and told you that from that day on I would love you. I told you then that you would be my priority and that I would always take care of you."

"Thank you for always taking care of me, Mama Lucia. You said that my mamacita doesn't know how to write."

"Yes, mija, that's true. The doctor knows her and knows that she doesn't know how to sign her name. He accepts her fingerprint as a legal signature. She may not know how to write, but she is very intelligent, and nobody takes advantage of her. We took off to your house, Doña Sinforosa was still fuming at your mother for abandoning you.

"Your older sister Victoria answered the door. Your sister was happy to see her grandma, but Doña Sinforosa was in no mode for greetings. She yanked Victoria outside the house by her shoulder. 'Where's your —— mother.' Victoria didn't know what to say. Your grandma continued yelling at Victoria, 'Tell me, Victoria, who is the father of this innocent soul, this child your mother bore then abandoned? Don't look like you don't know, tell me, who is the father?'

"Victoria denied knowing who your father was. Doña Sinforosa asked Victoria if your mother had borne other children and abandoned them like she left you for dead. Victoria sounded surprised, and this is what she told your grandma. Victoria opened her arms, placed her hands on her head. She said, 'No wonder Mama disappeared, we don't know where she went to. Really, *Abuelita*, I don't know where she went to.' Your grandma was not satisfied.

"Again she grabbed Victoria, this time by her collar, and told her, 'Tell me everything you know about Reyna.' 'Abuelita, I don't know what you want to know.' 'Listen to me, Victoria, and listen good, I've heard that Reyna has done this before, and I'm sure that you know something.' 'Señora, please don't ask me to say anything, Reyna will kill me.'

"Rosita, when your mamacita heard that, she pulled Victoria closer to her by the collar. She told your sister Victoria, 'This is not your lucky day, because if you don't tell me, I will tell Reyna that you did. So tell me what you know.' 'Okay, yes. Reyna has borne other babies before this baby. She has buried them here in the grounds under the floor bush near the bathrooms. She buried others in San Gregorio, where she lived with my father.'

"Your grandmother almost fainted, she cried and almost fell to her knees. Victoria tried to help her, but Doña Sinforosa pushed her away. She walked away with tears flowing. I heard her mutter, 'Diosito, please forgive me for giving birth to that monster. Domingo, why did our daughter turn out to be such a horrible person, how can a mother kill her own children?' Rosita, your grandma felt as though

Reyna had taken a knife and pierced her heart. She took you in her arms, crying and crying, she couldn't speak. I went home and left you two alone.

"The following day I took some clothes for you, including the baby blanket you always carry with you. That blanket I knitted myself. That night, according to your mamacita, you perspired a lot. I fed you, changed your diaper, and dressed you real nice. Your grandma was making arrangements to take you to the hospital when your sisters came wanting to see the new baby. Your grandma took your sisters aside and talked to them. She told them to be very careful with Reyna. She instructed them to say nothing to Reyna in the event that she returned anytime soon. 'When Reyna comes back, I will have a meeting with her and her brothers. Reyna will hear what I and my sons have to say.' She gave them money, told them to visit later, but now she was taking you to the hospital.

"When you and your mamacita came back, I visited to get an update on your condition. She showed me a bunch of papers the doctor gave her. The papers described what epilepsy was. But she said, since she didn't know how to read, she confided in what they told her. 'Lucia,' your mamacita said, 'if you could have seen what they did to this innocent soul, you would've fainted. They strapped cables all over her little head, stuck her with a huge needle full of medicine. I couldn't take it anymore. I left the room. I found a waiting room and prayed and prayed. I waited about three hours, then the doctor finally talked to me.'

"The doctor told your grandma that epilepsy has no cure currently and that you will have convulsions. All of this was caused because Reyna dropped you and broke your skull. The doctor told Doña Sinforosa not to return you, God's innocent child, to Reyna. He feels that if she didn't succeed in killing you this time, she will eventually. The doctor prescribed the medicine you are currently taking. You have to take this medicine, as you know, for six years, at which time you will be examined again. Your grandma did remember the doctor saying that it was possible that your epilepsy might go away when you start your menstruation or when you have a baby."

I was amazed at all the information I had learned about my mother. All I could do or say was to ask Mama Lucia what she meant by menstruation. When I asked her that, she looked at me with a smile before replying, "Rosita, listen, at the moment, you are too young and innocent to know. In a few more years, I'll explain what menstruation is, okay?"

"Mama Lucia, I don't intend on having babies. I'm going to be a nun. What do you think that my mamacita told Reyna when they met?"

"You know, mija, I asked her the same question. What your grandma told me is that she told Reyna that you were going to stay with her and that the world would end before she gave you up. She also wanted Reyna to tell her who your father was.

"They had a big fight. Her brothers had to separate them. If Reyna would have revealed who your father was, Doña Sinforosa intended on finding him. If that didn't happen, your grandma was going to register you as her own daughter. But here you are with Reyna. She threatened your grandma, and since she was alone without Domingo to protect her, she wanted to leave the pueblo, but she didn't. Rosita, Reyna never revealed that she was pregnant with you. But if she is your mother, she got pregnant in el Norte, where she lived during the time you were born. Also, it's possible that you were born there and not here in Mexico. A few days after the confrontation with your mamacita, Reyna took off again."

I just listened to Mama Lucia talk about a little girl that which happened to be me. It was strange; it seemed like a dream, or more like a nightmare. *What kind of mother treats a child the way Reyna treats me?* I continued to listen to Doña Lucia speak, wanting to interrupt, but I didn't. When I heard the words *pregnant* and *el Norté*, I spoke up. I asked what *pregnant* and *el Norte* meant. Mama Lucia told me that I was too young to know about pregnancy, but within a few years, she would tell me what it meant.

"El Norte is the United States and a very big nation. Your uncles and many people from Mexico move to el Norté to work. That's where your mother worked when she got pregnant with you."

"Aha, then it's possible that the stork brought me to my mother in el Norté."

"Rosita, that is the same feeling that your grandma has, she believes that you were born in the United States. Someday when you grow up, Rosita, you have to investigate as to whether you were born there. If you were, then you are a citizen of the United States."

"Señora, you tell me a lot that I don't understand, but I like living in my pueblo."

"Doña Sinforosa took care of you all those months Reyna was away from the pueblo. When she returned, your grandma and Reyna had another big fight. Then Reyna came to my house and got in a fight with me. Rosita, someday you will understand what I just told you. Mija, you are probably wondering why you didn't stay with Doña Sinforosa. Reyna took your grandma to court, and being that she is your mother, the court ruled in Reyna's favor. That's when Doña Sinforosa told your mother that it was her fault you were epileptic. Reyna denied ever having abandoned you and refused to admit fault for your epilepsy.

"Now you should go see Don Felipe and write everything down. He has more information about your mother. Ask him to write everything that he knows about Reyna." I could hear what Mama Lucia was saying. But to hear all that I learned about my life with my mother was painful. My mind started to drain. I closed my eyes; I was having a convulsion. Mama Lucia was at my side when I came to. She look worried and told me to rest. She didn't want to continue telling me more for fear that I couldn't cope with any more information. I told her that convulsions were part of my life and not to worry about me. I needed to know all the information she had about my life. It was very important to me and to please continue.

Uncle Santos Comes Looking for Me

SHE CONTINUED, "ROSITA, AFTER YOUR grandma lost the lawsuit to Reyna, she came to visit me. She told me that she could no longer stay in the pueblo. She left for her llano, and every month she would come check on your condition and then leave. Soon after she left the pueblo, two men arrived at my puesto in a beautiful car. I'd never seen them before. One of the men asked me if I knew Reyna Bustos. I could tell that they were not from here. Anyway, I wasn't going to give them any information until I knew more about them.

"He offered me money and promised to eat if I gave them Reyna's address. I asked them if they were related to Reyna. At the same time, he put a green hundred-dollar bill in front of me. 'Señora,' he said, 'appears to me that you know Reyna, why don't you tell me where I can find her?' I spoke up, 'Yes, I know Reyna. What business do you have with her?' 'Tell me, señora, do you know if she had a baby recently?' I didn't say anything about the baby and that I didn't want his money. But I gave him the direction to Reyna's house.

"I was curious and wanted to find out more about them. I watched as they walked toward Reyna's house. When they were out of sight, I ran to your house. I hid under the window. From there I could hear their whole conversation. I was curious, probably nosy, but I wanted to know what they wanted with Reyna. I felt a presence in my heart and just had to know. I could see most of the room, but they couldn't see me. When Reyna heard the knock on the door, she peeked out the window. She didn't answer the door right away. Reyna ran to Ana and ordered her to take you out the back door. Ana saw me for an instant as she ran out the door with you.

arms, not saying a word until I had finished. 'Lucia,' she asked, 'how did you get all this information?'

"'Aye, Doña Sinforosa, I was wondering when you were going to ask me that question. Don't start thinking that I spy on people all the time, okay? These two men, Santos and his friend, came to my puesto asking for Reyna. After I told them where she lived, I followed them like a spy, hiding all the way. I stood under the window, and I heard every word. I even saw when Santos placed the money on the table.' 'Lucia, you heard Santos say that Jorge Bustos is the father of this innocent child?' 'Yes, señora, I heard him say that. Santos believes that this innocent was born in Tejas.'

"Doña Sinforosa knows the family of Jorge Bustos. She told me, 'I know Jorge, he is the son of Feliz Bustos. That tells me that that no-good Ruben Reza is not the father of this Alma de Dios. Ah, that is very good, now this Alma de Dios has a paternal family.' Rosita, let me tell you, your mamacita looks at me and says, 'Lucia, with everything that has happened to this child, who is she? For sure she is an Alma de Dios.'

"Your mamacita wanted to know more about Santos and the other man. I told her that Santos believed that the child Ana was holding in her arms as she ran away was Jorge's daughter. He told Reyna that he was sure that she was the child he came looking for. That's why he left Reyna money. That money was for the baby, and Reyna took it and ran from the pueblo. 'Oh my Lord, why did I have a daughter so cruel, so heartless?'

"Reyna eventually returned to the pueblo, but she never told any of us where she'd gone to. Your mamacita was obligated by law to hand you over to Reyna. You continued to have epileptic attacks. Of course your mother didn't know how to cope with them. During one of your convulsions, Reyna was scared, apparently she thought that the people were going to blame her for abuse. She ran out her house screaming for help. She ran to your mamacita's house, but she didn't open the door. Reyna then ran to Don Rafa's house for help. Reyna told Don Rafa that you were dying. He told your mama to go for the priest and have you baptized before you died.

"Rosita, I have to give her credit, she actually went and got your *padrinos* (godparents) and went for the priest. That's how Don Martín Castañeda and his wife, Socorro, became your godparents. The priest preformed an emergency baptismal service for you. Everybody thought you were dying. The moment the holy water touched your forehead, you let out a big healthy cry."

"Mama Lucia, you know so much about my life, I really appreciate you telling everything you know. Tell me, how did you know that Reyna had me baptized?"

"Well, Rosita, one day I went for groceries at Don Martin's store. He wanted to know how you were doing. That's when he told me that Reyna had asked him and Socorro to be your padrinos, that you were dying and you had to be baptized immediately. He told me about you reviving the moment the holy water touched your forehead. Everybody there was astonished when you cried. The priest said, 'This child is truly blessed by the Lord.' He said that Reyna was more shocked than surprised, he wanted to say more about her but stopped. But Don Martin did say, 'We are now the godparents of Alma de Dios. Socorro and I are so happy to be her godparents and that she continues to have life.'

"I paid for my groceries. As I was leaving, it dawned on me to ask what name they had given you. I returned and asked. 'Reyna told us to give her the name *Rosa Maria Jovani Reza Bustos*.' I was totally surprised, your mother ignored the name we had given you—being *Alma de Dios*. I asked him why the surname of *Reza* and very upset that they hadn't named you *Alma de Dios*. He asked me why I was asking about the surname. I told him, 'Don Martin, this child has suffered so much in such a young life, now she has to face life with that surname, which is not real. Reza is not the father, Jorge Bustos is the real father. This child will someday know who her real father is, and it is not Reza.'

"'Doña Lucia, you know for a fact that Reza is not the father?' Don Martin asked me. I felt sorry for Don Martin and Socorro because Reyna had deceived them. He wanted Socorro to hear what I had to say. Your madrina wanted to be sure that what I was telling them was the truth. I told them I heard it from Santos,

Jorge Bustos's own brother, claim that Jorge was the father. 'Reyna had gotten pregnant with she lived in Texas with Jorge. Santos, his brother, knows that.'"

"Mama Lucia, then it is true, Jorge Bustos is my father."

"Yes, mija, that's what I believe, but only your mother knows for sure. What I know is that Reza is not your father. He is the father of Ana, Victoria, and the other girls, but not yours. I know because Reza has been in el Norté in California, and Reyna was in Texas when she got pregnant with you.

"I thought, how could Reyna give you those names and not *Alma de Dios*? Worse yet, why did she give you that surname? I prayed for you, and finally I knew that I had to move away from there. I couldn't take Reyna anymore, I couldn't intervene in the abusive life you were living under that woman. I packed my bags and was about to head out to rent another place. Your mamacita arrived at my house just as I was about to leave.

"She placed her hands on her hips and asked me, 'Lucia, where do you think you are going with those cartons full of your clothes?' I told her that I could no longer live near Reyna and witness the way she was abusing you, Rosita. She invited me to her house to talk. Once we got to her house, she wanted to know what Reyna did this time to force me to move.

"I started by telling Doña Sinforosa that you had to be baptized because you were close to dying. When I told her that Reyna had named you *Rosita Jovani Reza Bustos*, your mamacita almost fainted. She was so angry because Reyna had given you the surname of her first husband, *Reza*. Mija, I will not use the exact words your mamacita used because you are too young to hear them. She said, 'Why — did Reyna give my Alma de Dios the surname of that worthless first husband? She doesn't know where in el Norté he went to. Lucia, in reality, I don't know what to do with her anymore. I only wish that she would let me take Alma de Dios with me, but she won't, and I don't understand why.'

"That's when your mamacita told me she was leaving the pueblo. She would stay until after the Santa Cruz fiesta. That fiesta was a very busy time for her, she rented rooms to the people that came for the fiesta. She asked me not to leave. Well, mija, as you can see, I'm still here. Thanks to God that I stayed because I have you close to me."

I hugged Mama Lucia. "Tomorrow," I told her, "I will go to Don Felipe's house, and he can write all the information you have shared with me. Thank you, Mama Lucia." Both of us were exhausted; we went to bed.

Next morning, I visited Don Felipe; he was waiting for his coffee. With coffee in hand, I told him everything I'd learned from Mama Lucia. He had much more information. All that went into my diary. From his little unkempt room, I ran to the church. I talked to my Diosito and the Virgin Mary. I wanted them to know all the information I had learned about myself, and I thanked them for watching over me. On my way out the main gates, I saw my elderly aunt Feliz with her ankle-length dress, her braids hanging down to her waist. She was walking slowly with the aid of her cane toward the church. Her dog, Oso, knew me and allowed me to help her. I grabbed her hand and helped her walk inside the church. After she thanked me, I ran to the puesto.

Doña Lucia was busy preparing her place; the aroma permeated her little puesto. While I was helping her get the place ready for the patrons, I happened to mention that I saw Aunt Feliz going to early Mass. "You know your aunt Feliz?" Mama Lucia asked; before I answered, she said, "But of course you do, and I'm not surprised because you know half of the people in the pueblo." I just laughed. "Mama Lucia, Aunt Feliz showed me where she has a treasure buried."

"What? Your aunt showed you where the treasure is buried? She always told me about a treasure hidden in her hacienda. Other people had heard about it, but nobody believed her. Mija, are you sure? Do you really know where it's buried?"

"Yes, Mama Lucia, I met my aunt Feliz at mamacita's house. One day when I was at mamacita's house, my aunt Feliz was there too. They were talking. I was listening, and soon I started to sing. My aunt was very surprised with my singing. She wanted to give me money, but I hesitated. Mamacita told me not to be shy and to take it. I could hear both of them talking about me, but I just smiled. When my aunt was leaving, she told me that she wanted me to visit her.

"One day I went to visit her. She was very happy to see me. I remember she gave me a glass of a real sweet drink. She said, 'Alma de Dios, help me walk to the back of the house, I want to show you something.' We walked to the other side of her chicken coop. She said, 'Mija, what I'm going to show you is a secret. I'm showing you before my granddaughters discover where it's hidden. When they find it, they will take it to el Norte and become very rich.' With a cane on one side and me holding her hand on the other, we slowly made it to the place where the treasure was hidden. Her trusty dog, Oso, always behind. We reached the little corner, my aunt opened the lid covering a hole. She took out a brilliant yellow rock from the hole. 'Mija,' she told me, 'come look at the box inside the hole.'

"I remember seeing plenty of other brilliant yellow rocks inside the box. She said, 'This is a treasure, a real good treasure. Alma de Dios, whenever you want a little rock, tell me, and I'll come with you. This treasure is mine. My husband became the owner when my in-laws gave it to him when he lived somewhere up in the mountains. My in-laws claimed that the treasure belonged to the Spaniards that came to Tetipac in the year of our Lord 1495.' She told me that *Tetipac* means 'Sobre las Piedras.' I asked, 'Who are these Spaniards? Aunt, the president of the pueblo, said we are Mexicans, others speak of el Norté, and now you tell me that the people that owned the treasure are Spaniards? I am confused, please tell me again.'

"'Okay, mija, the Spaniards are blond gringos from another nation farther away than el Norte. Look, mija, the United States is what we call el Norte, because it is north of us.' She pointed in the direction of what I thought was toward el Norte. 'The Spaniards wanted to become owners of the best lands in the Republic of Mexico. They were lost, and they didn't know in what part of the world they were in.'

"Aunt Feliz told me that I have much to learn about our beautiful pueblo. She told me that I have a natural divine opportunity in this world and that my destiny was that I would be a mystery to the whole world. She told me that it was already happening in the pueblo, and, Mama Lucia, I have no idea what she was saying. You know what else she told me?"

"What else did Doña Feliz tell you?"

"Mama Lucia, have you seen the arches that are near the Eagle's Hole? Well, my aunt Feliz told me that the Spaniards started to construct them to guard the treasures they hid near the arches.

"They had to terminate when the Chichimecas moved during the fifteenth century. The Chichimecas entered the pueblo from the northern part of the state. They currently live in Chontales. From 1533–35, the blondes from New Spain divided for political reasons Tetipac and the city of Taxco. They took into account that we were two municipalities. We that live in the pueblo along with the ranchers from around can govern ourselves.

"Mama Lucia, I have a lot of new information in my head, and I don't think I can hear any more." I went to sleep. The next morning I ran to Don Felipe's room with his coffee. He wrote every word I remembered that Mama Lucia shared with me. Don Felipe confirmed what Mama Lucia had told me. He had been taking note of my life as well. He added a lot more information that I'm sure only he and of course Reyna knew. He told me that when I was able to read, he would show me his notes. But at the moment, I was not ready.

"Mama Lucia, I am tired, but I remember having more sisters. But I haven't seen them anymore. Only Ana, and she works. Are they away in the Norté working too?"

"Jovani, you remember your other sisters, eh? Your sisters also went to el Norté." I heard what she said, and I wondered what was so important in el Norté. My pueblo is very beautiful, why do they want to go North? I couldn't imagine what it was like. Mama Lucia was telling me of the time that Reyna left without disclosing where she was going. "Reza came to the pueblo to visit his daughters. He went to the house where his daughters lived with Reyna. When Reza found out that Reyna often left his daughters all alone, he told them to pack their belongings. He took four of them to the United States, to el Norté. Ana was not home, she was working at the time, or maybe she would have gone with him too. When your mother came home, she was really angry with Reza. That anger turned to sadness, she cried for days."

"Mama Lucia, wait, I remember when Reza took my sisters with him."

"Rosita, you remember? Tell me what you remember, I want to know in case people ask me. What I told you is all I know."

"Yes, Mama Lucia, I remember, but I didn't realize that Reza had taken them until now. I knew where Reyna had gone to. She went to the ranch for lumber, that's where she was when Reza came and took my sisters away.

"Mother did what she could to support us, according to her. This I remember, she left for the property her father, Domingo, had left her. She went for lumber to sell. Like other times when she was gone, she would leave without saying where she was going. After Reyna left and Ana went to work, I was left alone. I also remember this, Mama Lucia, that Reyna should have taken me with her. I wanted to spend time with Reyna, and I could take care of myself while she worked, so why not take me?

"Mama Lucia, I came here to be with you the day she left. But I was anxious to be me, to be free for a while. I told you, Mama Lucia, that I was going out. I didn't mention where, I just left not knowing where. I ran the open fields surrounding the pueblo not worrying about my epilepsy. I knew that my Diosito is watching over me. Later that day, I came home. My sisters, except Ana, were home. Reyna had been gone for days.

"That day again, I was here at the puesto. When I went home, the door was locked, and I couldn't get in, and my sisters weren't home. But I didn't think that they were gone for good. That same day she came back, I was sitting on the edge of the stairs at mamacita's house when I saw a truck loaded with lumber heading toward our house.

"I waited, and when I saw that it was Reyna, I ran to the house. I ran for what appeared an eternity before I reached the place. I ran into the house out of breath. My uncle Chucho was there with Mom, both crying. I ran over to hug her, she avoided me. Instead she then told me to get my dirty face out of the house. She told me to go, just go where the —— I wanted to. I was about to ask why, but then when she gives me that certain mean stare, I do as she tells me. 'Go see your padrinos and stay there, and don't go to Lucia's,' she told me.

"My padrino was happy to see me. I told him that my mother had kicked me out of the house. I said, 'Padrino, I don't know what's happening in my house.' 'Come in, mija, tell me what's troubling you?' I say, 'Padrino, because Mama and my uncle Chucho are crying.' 'Rosita, go talk to your madrina, she'll help you. She's in the laundry washing clothes, you know where it is.' My godmother

"Yes, Ana, I do. When I entered the house, I heard when she told uncle Chucho that their father had stolen our sisters and probably took them to live with him in el Norté."

"Did she mention the name of the father?"

"No, Ana, but this morning, I saw a truck with a shell that reminded me of a big inflated loaf of bread. I couldn't see anything inside. But I saw my sisters getting in and a man in the steering wheel."

"Vani, that man was my father. I'm an idiot, I should have been here. He has always wanted to take me to el Norte. But I knew that my mother would never allow that to happen. I never thought that he would take all of us. I'm sure he took them to the United States. Stupid me, I'm still here when I could be in el Norté with my sisters."

"Ana, what can I say, that man didn't even acknowledge me."

"Vani, that man is not your father." I looked at Ana. I thought she knew that Reza is not my father. Then Jorge is my father for sure. My Diosito will guide me, and someday I will know for sure. Ana started to cry. "Vani, he might still come for me. He wouldn't leave without me." We waited for Reza to show up for her. Finally we went to bed, Ana couldn't sleep, she cried throughout the night. I prayed the rosary for all my sisters asking Diosito to watch over them the way he watches over me.

We got up early the next day. Ana noticed that Reyna's suitcase was gone. She said, "Vani, looks like Reyna intends to stay away for some time."

"Don't worry, Ana, she is probably hoping to stop your father from taking our sisters to the United States. You see, Ana, I am not important to her. She doesn't care about me nor that I'm sick, but she will do anything for the other daughters." We ate a poor but delicious breakfast of beans, green chili, and freshly made corn tortillas. We talked about our sisters while we ate. Ana mentioned that in a way it was better that our sisters went North. After we ate and cleaned up, Ana left for work. We hugged before she left. When Ana gives me a hug, I feel very happy. I only wish that Reyna would give me love the way Ana does. I watched her walk away until I could see her no more.

I took a bath, got dressed, and went to do others' laundry. I went three days without a convulsion, and I felt good. Ana worries about me as though she was my mother. To my mother, I am not important, I mean nothing to her. Ana worries when I do laundry for others; she worries when I wash cars or windshields. But I have to work to pay for my medicine, which happens to be very expensive. But I always happen to have the money to pay for it. People who know me give me money for my birthday. I clean cars, and I wash the windshields of cars that park near the puesto. Don Felipe, my friend and mentor, pays me to clean his room. Ana thinks that I am too small to be working.

I asked Ana if she would take care of my money. She told me she didn't want that responsibility and that I should find a nice hiding place to keep it. I did, and now I have my own bank, as I call my hiding place. Only my Diosito and I know where I have my money hidden.

I follow my daily routine before I go to kindergarten. This morning when I took Don Felipe his coffee, he told me he'd pay me additional pesos to empty his trash. I accepted on the condition that he would pay me weekly instead of daily. I also volunteered to empty his urinal. He made a face. "You will empty that stinky can? If you do, I will pay you more." I thought, *Well, I do need the money*, so I accepted. "Okay, now," I asked, "how much are you going to pay me?" We settled on three pesos a day, twenty-one a week, and he agreed to pay me weekly.

I cleaned his room, emptied the trash and urinal, and told him I was leaving. Then I thought of something. I said, "Don Felipe, when the old man people refer to as the tinaja (man that resembles a potbellied barrel) of Ahualulco comes to visit you, promise to pay me before you start drinking with him." My mentor started to laugh. When he stopped, he asked me why I was asking that of him. "Because if he comes, you won't have any money left to pay me."

"Tell me, Rosita, what you know."

"Señor, when tinaja comes to your house, he invites you to drink with him. He never pays for anything, you always pay for everything. When you get drunk, he takes your pesos and buys good tequila and drinks it by himself. That isn't right. But, Don Felipe, if you can't pay me because he takes advantage of you, I will still bring you coffee."

"Rosita, you have such a good heart. I believe that's one reason Diosito watches over you and keeps you among the living, my innocent child of God. I will continue to be your maestro, teach you how to write your diary, and above all, I will pay you every week."

"That's good, señor, but now I must be on my way to kinder. We will talk later and give more information for my diary."

At kinder, I'm not alone, for I have a lot of friends and my teacher. She is Sister Sarita, a nun, like I desire to be when I'm of age. I'm early, the school is not open, so I go into the church. My Diosito, the señor of the main altar, looks at me when I enter; my tears flow down my cheeks. I make the sign of the cross; it gives me strength as I value the time that He allows me to be living. I talk to Him some more. When I'm through, I thank Him for being with me during my night and day, I clean my running nose and my tears, I make the sign of the cross as I genuflect looking at my Diosito, I leave the church.

The doors of the kinder are still closed. I run to my madrina's house. She is outside, sweeping her front yard. "Child, where are you coming from so early in the morning?"

"Good morning, madrina, I'm going to kinder, but I'm too early, or maybe there is no class today."

"Rosita, wait until I finish sweeping, then we go inside for a little breakfast, okay? How does that sound?"

"Godmother, did you hear my stomach rumble again? I ate some with Ana before she went off to work. Maybe I have a bottomless stomach." I made my madrina laugh. "Rosita, you are a growing girl and need to eat so that you can continue to grow."

After we ate, I followed Doña Socorro to the pigsty. We fed her pigs, and then we gave them a good bath. After we finished the day's chores, she invited in for a cold drink and a snack. I told my godmother that I was going to the puesto to be with Mama Lucia. "Why did Doña Lucia move to Doña Delfa's place? I thought she was happy where she was at."

"Madrina, I am not sure, but I think she was having problems with Reyna." I was ready to leave her house; she asked me to wait.

She approached me and gave me money, a big hug, and her blessing. I hesitated in taking the pesos, but she insisted. I had to choose between going to my "bank" and to take a bath and get rid of the stink of pigsty. I hid my pesos. Quickly I went home and got some clean clothes. I went to the bathhouse, took off my stinky clothes, and soaked myself in cold water. Feeling clean, I put on my old shoes with soles full of holes, and good clean clothes. I ran to Mama Lucia's house. I opened the iron gate, looked through the corridor, but I couldn't see anybody. I hollered for Mama Lucia. A neighbor, one who was a stranger to me, came out.

"Good afternoon, niña, who are you looking for?"

"I'm looking for Doña Lucia, and, sir, what are you doing here?"

"Look at you," the stranger said, "are you an investigator?" He laughed.

"I live here. I'm renting a room from the same lady that rents to Doña Lucia."

"I'm glad for you, sir, and what is your name?"

"For such a little girl, you ask a lot of questions. But if you tell me your name, I will tell you mine, okay?"

"My name is *Rosita Jovani Vani 'Alma de Dios' Reza Bustos*."

"Whew, what a long and interesting name you have. My name, young lady, is *Cesar*. I am a teacher at Nicolas Bravo School."

Just then, Mama Lucia opened the iron gate. I ran to her, and we embraced. The schoolteacher went inside his room. "Mija, what are you doing here?"

"Mama Lucia, I came to help you move."

"Jovani, it is not necessary, I already finished moving. I paid a couple of kids, and they helped me. Come in anyway. I know that you have your little corner you liked to sleep in. Well, I will show you a little corner you can use here as well. It will have the same kind of love the other corner has." She showed me her room. It was much smaller than the one she rented from my mamacita.

I thought of my grandmother living alone in that big house of hers. I know that she gets sad at times. But being human, some value life different. The life that we form depends with whom we share our life with in our little corner. I think of my own life, always alone. But then I see Doña Lucia's crucifix hanging on the wall, and I know that I am not entirely alone. Mama Lucia breaks my line of thought when she asks me, "What are you thinking, mija?"

I answer, "I feel happy, and I feel good for you in your new place."

"Okay, mija, but I'm about to leave for my puesto. Do you want to go with me and help me sell my carnitas?" I accompanied her to the zócalo where the puesto was located.

There were businesses close to her puesto including a cantina. The owner of the bar offered me a job, not a very good one but paid me ten pesos to clean his bathroom. I asked Mama Lucia if it was okay with her. Since the bar was close to her puesto and it wouldn't take me long to clean the bathroom, she allowed me to only if I thought I could do the work. I accepted the work. The owner provided me the material I needed. The stench in the bathroom was horrible, and even though I vomited a couple of times, I cleaned the bathroom.

I had just finished when a lady walked into the bar. She saw me putting the mop and other cleaning material; she asked me if I worked there. I told her that the owner had offered me a job, and yes, I was working there. I asked her, "Is it okay if I work here?"

"That man is man my husband, and he is taking advantage of you. What does he have you doing?"

"Señora, don't worry, the job he gave me will serve me as experience, besides, I need the money."

"Young lady, wait for me here, I'm going to have a talk with my husband." I continued to clean the filthy and smelly bathroom. I finished, and I called the owner so that he would approve the work I had done. He liked the clean walls and the whole bathroom. He praised my work, gave me ten pesos for cleaning, and a five-peso tip.

I was happy with my earnings, and I extended my hand. "My name is *Rosita Jovani*." He held my hand in his.

"My name is *Rodolfo*. What is your name, tell me again."

"Señor, my name is *Rosita Jovani*, and you should wash your ears good so you can hear me better and I won't have repeat myself."

"Are you the little girl people know as Alma de Dios or the innocent child of God? If that's you, I know your mother and father. But if you are Alma de Dios, why do you tell me that your name is *Rosita Jovani*?"

"Señor, all I can tell you is that my mother, Reyna Bustos, decided to name me. Do you know her?"

"Reyna is your mother? Reyna, Reyna, when is she ever going to take the responsibility of a mother?" Don Rodolfo thanked me. I left his cantina as fast as I could. I was about to run to the puesto when Don Rodolfo's wife came out of the side door of the cantina. She was carrying a big package.

"Your name is Rosita, right?"

"Yes, señora, but why do you ask? First Don Rodolfo asked me what my name is, and now you."

"One day, Rosita, I saw when you became ill and fell in the street. I was hoping you would open your eyes, but you didn't. I picked you up, put you in my arms, and carried you to your house. You opened your eyes before we got to our house. That's how I knew who you were, and I admire your courage."

"Thank you, señora, for helping me and for your kind words."

"Rosita," she said, "come let me show what I have for you." She opened the package. I asked, "All of these things are for me?" She had packed a couple of beautiful blankets that she had made. Also included in the package was lots of food. How can I thank señora for being so charitable? "Nina, this is but a grain of sand from my heart to help you, not charity.

"Rosita, can I invite you to eat supper with us? I want my sons to meet you. They are grown-up, and they hate to clean their own bedroom. Now look at you, Rosita, I wish that I could be a mother-in-law to someone like you."

"Someone like me? How am I? Señora, I'd like to know who I am, this way I can find out who my real father is."

"Well, let me tell you, Rosita. What I see is that you are intelligent and very pretty, you're a hard worker and very strong-willed. Nowadays you don't find too many persons like you."

"Señora, don't worry about your sons. Show them how to be independent, and they will appreciate you more. I value my life, señora, even though I don't have what your sons have—parents. My mother is never home, and my father, who knows? You see me struggling through life, but I put value in the time that my Diosito is giving me."

The señora looked at me; she asked, "Rosita, really, who are you? So young, but your words are not those of a child. In my heart I feel that you are someone very special. Rosita, would you give me your blessing?" I gave her my blessing, and she hugged me.

Mother Returns Home

I TOOK MY PACKAGE AND went to the puesto to help Mama Lucia. We finished selling, cleaned up, I went home in the dark. I know the path—every pebble, every rock, and I'm not afraid of the dark. *The light is on, Reyna is home,* I thought. My heart beat faster with the thought of Mother being home. I entered the house running. "Mama, you're home! Mama," I shouted, "you're home." She looked at as though I didn't exist, as though I wasn't her daughter.

I tried to give her a hug, but she ignored me. "Where were you, snot nose?" Whatever she said, I didn't care. I was happy that she was home, and I love her like a daughter loves a mom. I would sleep well tonight, I'm not alone anymore. I wanted to talk to her, tell her how much I missed her. I couldn't stop looking at Reyna, I thought how beautiful she was. *Why doesn't she love me, why does she ignore me?* "Hija," she said to me, "it's getting late, go to bed, and don't wake me up in the morning." I tried to give her a hug; again she ignored me. That night I fell asleep happy that she had actually referred to me as "daughter."

Reyna constructed an eatery close to the main gate of her property. Originally she offered posolé, tamales, and refreshments. I spent time helping her, even though she treated me like a helper rather than her own daughter, I was happy just being close to her. In time her business grew. The federal police that patrolled the ranches around the pueblo became her regular customers. They were very nice to me, and without fail, they rewarded me with nice tips. One of them was always talking with Reyna and laughing with her. I was curious why they would disappear for a while when he came to her eatery. Eventually I asked his name, without Reyna knowing. He told me his

person. But I assure you, ma'am, Alejo is not my father. I would be very happy if he was my father because he is a good man.

"Now tell me, where is your mother? I want to talk to her, she has to listen to what I have to say. I told you that I am the wife of Alejo, the man that is going with your mother. He and I have three sons, and I don't want your mother messing around with my husband." I smirked somewhat, thinking the baby the one Reyna is carrying will be his fourth.

"Ma'am, believe me, at this moment, I really don't know where she is. They left early this morning, but I don't know where they went to. Please save your words for when Mother comes home, but right now she is not here. Would you like to come and see for yourself?" Alejo's wife didn't know how to react. "I will be back," she said, "and your mother is going to hear what I have to say."

Ana arrived about the same time Alejo's wife was leaving. "Vani, who was that lady?"

"Ana, she is the wife of Alejo, she was looking for Reyna."

"Really? That was Alejo's wife? What did she tell you?"

"Ana, that lady told me that they have three children. I wanted to tell her that now he was going to have four, but I didn't."

"Vani, I'm glad you didn't tell her that, I'm sure her heart is hurting and doesn't need more reminders. Is that all she asked you?"

"Well, she wanted to know if this is the place where Reyna Bustos lives. She said that she will be back to speak with Mother."

"Vani, tell me, do you know where Mother went to?"

"No, Ana, I really don't. I didn't lie to that woman, I really don't know. Day before yesterday early in the morning, she and Alejo took off for Taxco and haven't returned."

"Ah, so you do know where they're at?"

"Well, they are in Taxco, but Taxco, it's too big. Maybe they went to Taxco, I don't know. Ana, you know that I don't tell lies. Don't worry, Ana, if she doesn't come back, I'll help with food and other costs."

"Vani, just don't say anything, you take care of your medicine. I can take care of the costs, okay?

"Vani you are saving your money, right?"

"Yes, I told you that I have my own hiding place, I call it my bank, remember? Nobody will ever know where I have my hiding place. But I'll tell you that my hiding place will scare everybody because of the big white worms that surround my hiding place. Ana, you aren't paying attention."

"What? Oh, Vani, please forgive me, I just remembered that I have to meet Rene. You are going out with your boyfriend?"

"Yes, Vani, he is taking me out to eat. Vani, so you want to come with us?"

"No, Ana, I better go see Don Felipe."

"Okay, Vani, don't be late, did you hear me?"

"Yes," I shouted as I was going out the door.

My friend the mail carrier of the pueblo was half asleep. He opened his eyes when he heard my footsteps. "Rosita, thank you for not scaring me. I can hear your footsteps a mile away."

"Hey, Don Felipe, you always tell me that."

"What are you doing here, mija?"

"Well, Don Felipe, my mother is gone, and Ana is getting ready to take off with Rene."

"Where is Reyna, do you know?"

"No, señor, I don't know, she and Alejo left a few days ago."

"Uujale, she is probably taking off her shoes somewhere out there."

"Don Felipe, please don't talk about Mother like that."

"Rosita, you are right.

"Now, do you have information for your diary?"

"No, not today. Señor, what I want is work to earn money. I need money to buy a present for the baby Mother has in her stomach. I have money, but that is for my medicine. Don Felipe, let me tell you where I have my money hidden, okay? I am going to trust you like the palm of my hand. My hiding place is the third walnut tree that's in the orchard. I save it there because of the big golden worms that surround the tree, and nobody gets close to it."

"What!" He dropped his coffee, cupped his face, turned pale, like mine does when I have diarrhea. "Are you okay, Don Felipe?"

"Yes, don't worry, I'm okay. But you shouldn't hide your pesos under that tree. Rosita, I'm telling not to hide your money there because there are some innocent babies buried there."

"What? Why would anybody bury babies there?"

"Yes, Rosita, that's the reason you see so many worms."

"Don Felipe, I'm going to get those babies out of there and take them to the cemetery. Don Felipe, who is the mother of those babies buried in that hole? I will tell the mothers to take those babies and to bury them in the cemetery."

"Rosita, forget the babies that are buried there. Someday you will uncover all that has happened in that house."

I thought that burying babies there and not in the cemetery was horrible. I started to leave Don Felipe's room. "Mija," Don Felipe asked, "where are you going? We haven't written your diary."

"Señor Felipe, I don't want my pesos hidden there anymore, I am going to hide them someplace else." I ran to my banking place. Once there, I prayed for the souls that were buried under the walnut tree. I took the can containing my pesos to the attic of mamacita's house. I placed the can inside a plastic bag, tied it up, and hid it where nobody would steal it. I returned to the old man's house, did my chores to the delight of Don Felipe. I sat next to him while he wrote my latest notes.

I returned home. Reyna was inside waiting. "Where have you been, snot-nose vagabond?" That was her greeting. I was so happy to see her that nothing bothered me at the moment. She continued, "For sure you just wait for the moment I leave to take to the streets." I wanted to hug her, to feel the baby the stork had left in her stomach, but held back. "No, Mama, I was at Don Felipe's doing my chores."

"Mama, what Vani says is true," Ana vouched for me. "Go ahead, Ana, and cover for your snot-nosed sister like you always have. You and I have to settle this issue soon, I'm tired of you covering up her lies."

"Mother, please believe me, I don't fib, I want you to trust me. Mama, while you were gone, a señora came looking for you."

"What woman? Come on speak, what did she want?"

"She was very angry, she told me that Alejo was her husband. That they have three children and for you to leave him alone so that they can live in peace. I almost told her that now he would have four children, but I didn't out of respect. Maybe I will tell her that when she comes back." Reyna laughed, I made her laugh! "Well, I guess we will clear things, this lady and I because I am not his woman. Speaking about Alejo, come, let me show you the food he bought for us."

I went to my little corner feeling happy that Mom was home. I fell asleep. I woke up real early, made Don Felipe his coffee, did my chores; afterward, I took off for kindergarten. The doors were closed. Thinking that there was no classes, I went back to Don Felipe's room. I was learning to read and write from him. I learned to write my name first. He showed me the diary he'd written that morning and taught me how to read it. After I'd had enough, I told Don Felipe that I was leaving. I hesitated, not wanting to go home. I decided that visiting Sister Sarita was better.

She was working in her garden. She was happy to see me. "Jovani, what are you doing here so late?"

"Kindergarten class is over for today. I was surprised, Sister Sarita, I came to class early this morning, and the doors were closed."

"Jovani, don't you know that class doesn't start until 9:00, if you come earlier than 8:30, the doors will be closed."

"Sister Sarita, I don't have a way to tell time, so I come early."

"Okay, Jovani, let me tell you, when you are at Doña Lucia's, ask the men for the time. Jovani, I know your desire to learn. I will do everything to help you learn to read and to write. But you have to attend class, okay?

"I know that Don Felipe writes the notes that you give to your Diosito."

"Sister," I interrupted, "those pages that Don Felipe writes for me aren't notes, they are gifts for my Diosito. Sister, I dream of Him all the time, and He loves me a lot."

"Jovani, what Don Felipe writes are notes. Don Felipe is the mailman for the pueblo."

"Sister Sarita, Don Felipe doesn't deliver my gifts to Diosito because heaven doesn't have an address. I give them directly to my Diosito."

"Jovani, God visits with you?"

"Yes, Sister, He is always with me, and He will always be with me. He watches and takes care of me. When I'm alone in church, I ask Diosito, 'Why is it that a wealthy person with a big house doesn't come to visit you? Then when they lose their job or encounter personal problems, they say, "Oh dear God, help me."' He helps them, and they forget about Him again. Really, Sister, I don't like it when people do that. We should always be grateful to God."

"Jovani, how is it that you have so much faith in God? Who taught you about God?"

"My mamacita Sinforosa, she has a lot of faith in my Diosito, also Don Felipe, he also has a lot of faith in God."

"So, Jovani, do you want to learn more about God? I teach a catechism class every day at 4:00. If you attend class, you will learn more about God."

"Catechism, what is it?" I questioned my own ignorance because nobody had mentioned that word to me before. However, I decided to attend and find out for myself. "Jovani, don't come to class before 3:30 because the doors will be closed." I laughed. "I promise, and I will ask the men at the puesto for the time. Madre Sarita, can I invite my friends to catechism? I can help you too."

"Jovani, you have such a kind and beautiful heart, yes, you can bring your friends."

"Really, *madre*, you think that I have a beautiful heart? I can feel it move when I run, but I can't see it. You can see my heart?"

"Jovani, you are so innocent, I said that because you want to bring your friends to catechism and help me with them. That indicates that you have a beautiful heart."

"Madre, I can sweep the classroom and empty the trash, my mamacita taught me how to do all that."

"Come, my child." She gave me a hug. "Jovani, that's why I love you. You are always helping others."

"Madre Sarita, you make me very happy when you say that I'm a good worker and that I have a beautiful heart, thank you."

Kindergarten Class

LATER THAT SAME DAY, I shared my day with Don Felipe; all that while he wrote everything on paper. The following day I went to kinder on time. Actually I was early and able to talk to Madre Sarita. I told her that I desired to be a nun and wanted to how much older I had to be to be accepted into the convent. "Jovani, I am not surprised that you want to be a nun. So you want to devote your time to God and serve His people?"

"Yes, I want to be a nun and to better serve my Diosito."

"Well, let me see, Jovani, in a few months, you will finish kinder. You will attend middle and junior school for another six years. Following those years, you will attend the secondary for a few more years of study. With all those years of studying, you will be ready to commence studies to be a nun. Although it's possible that you can be accepted into the monastery. There you will be taught how to be a nun. Niña, you have many years to decide for sure. When that day comes, I will be here to help you."

"Sister Sarita, do you get lonely being a nun? I'm asking because sometimes, especially in the mornings, I feel sad. When the other students start to arrive for kinder with their parents, I feel sad. I am always alone. I don't have anybody to bring me to school. When class is over, fathers and mothers are waiting for them. The parents hug and kiss their children, and I don't have anybody. That's the reason that you see me get out of class early. Sometimes I stay in class helping you until everybody is gone. Madre, why do you think that I'm at Mama Lucia's all the time?"

"Jovani, now I understand why you're there most of the time. What I don't understand is why do you call her *Mama*?"

66

"I call her Mama because she has taken care of me since I was born. I wish my mother would show me a fraction of love that Mama Lucia has for me."

"Then that señora is like an angel to you and shouldn't feel sad. True you don't have anyone waiting for you when class ends, but you have your Mama Lucia. Listen to me, Jovani, you have me and the other sisters, you don't have to feel lonely or sad. We are here for you."

"I do have a mother, but a father, who knows, so I don't know what to say."

"Again, I say to you don't feel sad, we are here for you."

"Thank you for those kind words. I dream that someday I will have a big family. Someday I am going to be somebody very important and with an honorable job where I can help the people."

"Jovani, I feel that you will be a very important lady. You are still very young, but your manner of being and the faith that you have in God will elevate you beyond my imagination." My head started to spin, my eyesight was getting cloudy, that's the last thing that I remember. I was in a strange room when I gained my consciousness. I looked around the room where I caught sight of a beautifully decorated small altar. Still I was not aware of my surroundings. Then I saw a picture of a nun. I then realized that I was in the home of the nuns. I got up from the bed, I felt nauseous wanting to vomit. Madre Sarita entered the room; she noticed that I was about to vomit. She talked to me in a soothing voice, told me to relax. "Madre Sarita, thank you for helping me, I had one of those bad attacks again, but

I can't help it. I hadn't had a convulsion in ten days, I was so happy. Madre, I have to go."

"Go? Go where? You are in no condition to go anywhere, stay and rest."

"No, madre, I can't stay, this is the day that I help my godmother Socorro, she depends on me."

"Jovani, you are in no condition to do any kind of work, I'm sure your madrina will understand." I could hear the nun mumbling something when I started to leave the room. I stopped before I left the room. "Madre, I will be here for catechism, I don't want you to worry."

"Oh, Jovani, really, who are you? I know everything that happens to you, and you continue being Jovani. Go with God, He truly loves you. Look, He picks you up when you fall, and you continue living in a carefree and loving manner."

I ran to my godmother's house—headache or not, I ran. For a moment I thought of going home and visiting with Reyna. Then I asked myself, *Why? She doesn't pay attention to me, so why go?* My madrina noticed the bump on my forehead the moment she saw me. I told her that I had another convulsion and that Madre Sarita had taken care of me. "But you know what, Madrina, I'm alive, I have my two feet, my body, and above all, Diosito's love. Without His love, I probably wouldn't be here to help you feed and bathe your pigs."

"Ah, my child, just look at you, with all that happens to you, you manage to have a sense of humor. Really, Rosita, who are you? Look, Rosita, go to my store, tell your padrino to send me some tea. I'm going to fix you a good cup of tea to make you feel better, then I want you to take a nap."

"Madrina, thank you, but I don't like to go into your store."

"Why? You've never told me that before. Now tell me why you don't like going into my store."

"Godmother, your daughter Rosely wants to fight and hits me every time I go in there."

"My daughter hits you, but why?"

"I don't know, Madrina, maybe she's jealous of the way you treat me."

"Mama Lucia, my heart gets sad when you cry." She cleaned her tears with the apron. "I can't help it, mija, you are special, what else can I do?"

"Well, you can tell me why you say that my heart is God-given."

"Mija, look what you have endured in such a young age, and you're very intelligent. That's why I ask, who are you?"

"Did God give you your heart, Mama Lucia? You have given me your love, shelter, tacos, and more important your time. You say that I have a beautiful heart, señora, your heart is beautiful too. Tell me, what kind of heart do the bad people have?"

"Mija, they have a heart as well, but they don't even know who they are. Those people have no faith in God, they are driven by wickedness because they have no faith in Diosito."

"Mama Lucia, I wonder if my father has a good heart. Do you think that he would be looking for me if he had a good heart?" When she didn't answer, I turned to face her. The look in her eye said a lot, but nothing came out of her mouth, only tears from her eyes. I didn't say another word, I kept thinking of my father. *Would he be looking for me? Someday I will know the truth. Reyna knows the truth but won't tell me. Others including my sisters, Mama Lucia, and probably Don Felipe know who my father is but won't tell me. All of them fear that Reyna will know who the snitch is.*

My mind wondered from Reyna to others with good and with bad hearts. "Mama Lucia, if a baby is born without a heart, where do the doctors get one to give him one? I know Don Arce, the butcher, and he sells hearts. He should donate those hearts to the hospital for the children that need one."

"Rosita, sometimes you say something that makes me laugh."

"What did I say this time to make you laugh?"

"Look, the heart of an animal doesn't work on a human, they are very different."

"Mama Lucia, the more questions I ask, the more I learn, and I don't wreck my brain."

"Well, Rosita, if that's the case, I will ask you a question. Have you eaten?"

"No, but I'm not hungry."

73

"Mija, I can hear your stomach grumbling, you have to eat something. Sit down, I will not take no for an answer."

We sat down to eat and talk. She was happy that the business for the past few days had been very good. "Yesterday I had a customer who I believe is your mother's boyfriend."

"Señora, was Alejo here? He is a very nice man. I hope he stays to live with Reyna, maybe then she won't treat me so bad. Alejo is very good to me. When he comes to visit, Reyna experiences nausea, similar to how I feel after I have a convulsion. The difference is that my mother's stomach keeps getting bigger, and my head doesn't after I suffer a convulsion." I finished eating, and off I went ready to sell my candy.

My first customer paid with a fifty-peso bill. I told him that I didn't have the change, but if he waited, I would get the change from Mama Lucia. "No, young lady, don't bother, I want you to keep the change." I thanked him and made the sign of the cross. I went all over selling my candy until I reached the office of the president of the pueblo. Several men congregating near a big table motioned me over. One asked me whether I was the daughter of Reyna Bustos. I answered, "Yes, sir, at your service and to sell you candy. To whom do I owe this question?" The man said, "Nobody important. I was just wondering."

"Any of you señores want to buy candy?" The same man handed me money. "Go buy yourself some shoes or clothes."

"Mister," I said with a frown, "I'm not asking for a handout. I'm working to earn my pesos. My tennis are worn-out, but the sole is good, and so are my clothes."

"Young lady, please forgive me if I offended you, but tell me, what is your name?"

"My name is *Rosita Jovani Bustos*, and others call me Alma de Dios."

"Okay then, Rosita, please accept this money that I'm giving you with all my heart. You can buy whatever you need." I hesitated for a moment thinking of the cost of my medicine, of my unborn sister and my desire to buy her a present when she comes home. "Señor, I appreciate your offer, it's just that I don't like for people to feel sorry for me. You see, I also work for Don Felipe, I go to kinder, and I help Mama Lucia."

"You work for Don Felipe, the mail carrier?"

"Yes, I work for him, do you know him?"

"Rosita, who doesn't know Don Felipe. He fixes my wristwatch, and he delivers all the mail that my sons send me from the United States."

"Well, señor, I bring him coffee every morning and clean his house before I go to kinder."

"Okay, Alma de Dios, you are a nice young girl, can I give you a hug?"

"Why? I don't like for any man to hug me unless I know him, and I don't know you."

"Well, then let me introduce myself, I am Juan Arce. I am married to Zoila. We know your mother and all your uncles and your grandmother Sinforosa. We used to help your sisters before they moved to the North. Alma de Dios, would you accompany me to my house and meet my wife, Zoila? She wants to meet you."

"Your wife wants to meet me, how does she know who I am?"

"Alma de Dios, she sees you going to church, and she has seen you in many other places around the pueblo. The last time she saw you is when you fainted and we took you to the house of Madre Sarita. She told us about your epilepsy and that you suffer convulsions."

"Thank you for taking care of me, I will say a novena for you and your wife. Before I can go with you, I have to ask Mama Lucia if I can go with you."

"Come on, Alma de Dios, I will go with you. I myself will ask Doña Lucia if she will allow you to go with me to my house."

"Mr. Arce," I asked him on the way to Mama Lucia's, "do your children like candy?"

"Alma de Dios, all my children left us, they are all grown-up. But what if I buy all your candy and you can give the candy to the kids in your catechism class?"

"Señor Arce, how do you know that I attend catechism class?"

"Alma de Dios, the pueblo is not that big, news gets around, besides, I have seen you going to class."

We arrived at Mama Lucia's. "What is Rosita up to now? Did you bring me a customer?"

"Good afternoon, Doña Lucia. No, not this time, but if Alma de Dios helps you, then we will come to eat here. You have quite a saleslady, yes, ma'am, she sold me all her candy."

"Good afternoon, Don Juan. Oh, yes, Rosita is quite a person."

"Doña Lucia, I came to ask your permission so that I can take Alma de Dios with me to my house. My wife, you know Zoila, she wants to meet Rosita. Señora Lucia, I want to pay you for the candies, and you can pay Rosita. She is taking all of the candies to the kids in catechism class."

"Mija, go with Don Juan," Mama Lucia told me, "it's okay, go."

Doña Zoila didn't recognize me. She asked her husband, "Who is this little girl?"

"Zoila, you don't remember this little girl? Remember the little girl that we found fainted near the church, and I carried to the house of Madre Sarita?" Before she could answer, I said, "I don't have a father, but my mother is Reyna Bustos."

"Oh, now I remember, you are the same girl we took to the nun's house. How is your epilepsy, mija? You look a little tired, that's why I'm asking about your sickness. Maybe a nice bath will help, would you like to take a bath?"

"I won't say no to a bath, especially if I don't have to warm the water like I do at home. Señora, I took a bath last night, so I'm not too dirty, but it's been a long time since I took a bath with warm water, I accept your warm water bath."

I enjoyed the bath; afterward Doña Zoila combed my hair wishing that someday my mother would comb me. I closed my eyes and pretended for a split second that Reyna was combing me. I started to sob thinking the impossible, that being that Reyna would someday comb my hair much less give me a mother's hug. Señora Arce asked, "Am I pulling your hair too hard?"

"No, señora, it's that my mother has never combed me, and I was thinking that it would nice if she did at least once."

"What, Reyna has never combed your hair?"

"No, ma'am, she never has."

"Rosita, I will comb your hair any day, visit me whenever you need anything."

"Señora Arce, what time is it? I have to ring the bell for my catechism class."

"You do that too? Mija, you are one busy young lady, aren't you?" It was time for me to leave, I thanked Mrs. Arce for being so nice. I rang the bell then I went to the puesto for the candy. Madre Sarita was waiting for me. I usually arrived at her classroom soon after I rang the bells. This time it took me a little longer, so she was worried about me. After exchanging greetings, I showed her the candy. "Jovani, what's all that candy for?"

"Madre, it's for the kids in catechism. Don Juan Arce bought them from me and donated them to the class. So what is given to me is shared with others."

The class started with the Morning Prayer; afterward, we sat down. Madre Sarita motioned me to stand up. "I have a surprise for all of you," she told the class. "You all know Rosita, or some of you know her as Jovani. Well, she brought candy for all of you." Sister Sarita and I distributed the candy. The joy I saw in the kids' faces made me feel especially happy. I made many friends that day. Madre Benigna was the catechism teacher, whereas Madre Sarita was head mother of the nuns. Madre Benigna could barely walk because of her age and swollen legs that restricted her ability to walk. I helped her out of her wheelchair during class. After the class, I would wheel her back to the house where another nun was always waiting for her. Besides catechism, I learned from Madre Benigna to value my life more. From her I realized that she would not get up if she fell down, whereas I could after every time I had a convulsion. She would laugh at her wrinkled face, remembering the days where she had none. I told her, "Madre Benigna, your wrinkles are not the result of old age, but rather, because of the life of honesty that you have lived." When I told her that, she looked at me. "Jovani, I have never heard anybody say that to me before. Jovani, who are you?"

After I left Madre Benigna, I thought of going to the puesto. No, it was a beautiful day, I didn't want to go there. Thought of going home—no, not today, Reyna is cranky, as always. Maybe go visit Don Felipe, no. I headed to toward the house of my madrina. "Rosita, what a surprise, I'm so happy to see you." I returned her greeting with a hug. "Madrina, I don't want to go home until I help you with the pigs."

"Oh, mija, how did you know? I haven't had time to feed them this afternoon."

"Madrina, I can hear the pigs squealing their hungry squeal, I'll go feed them."

"Rosita, don't worry, my son will feed them."

"Madrina, they are hungry, I'll go feed them right away."

"Okay, Rosita, go ahead, you know where I keep everything."

Her son Gabriel helped me carry the can of slop for the pigs. After they ate, I turned the hose on them. Some kids gathered around the pigsty to watch me. "Jovani," one of them yelled at me, "can I help you?" It was a warm afternoon, and the water from the hose apparently was very inviting. He jumped into the sty to help me, and before long, several others joined in. We had a good time washing the pigs and getting soaked in the process. Afterward we picked some sweet lemons from my madrina's tree.

I Meet My Cousins

We sat near the tree enjoying the lemons and conversation. Lolis, one of the girls, told me that she and I were cousins. I looked at her. "We are cousins? How do you know?"

"Because my mother told me, and my mother, Rosa, is your aunt, just like your mother, Reyna, is my aunt." Lolis introduced me to her sisters—Nene, Gaby, and Gisela. Lolis invited me to wash off the pigsty smell at her house. I was happy that I had met my cousins and that I was going to take a shower. Well, it wasn't a shower or a bath, but rather a shower system from where water flows through the tubes attached to the wall of the house. When I first saw the system, it reminded me of Don Felipe's leaky room when it rains.

My cousin Lolis and I became good friends. She invited me to her house, where I met my aunt for the first time. "Good afternoon, Doña Rosa."

"Good afternoon, little girl, and to whom am I speaking?"

"My name is *Rosita Reza Bustos.*"

"You are a Bustos?"

"Yes, ma'am, I am a Bustos on mother's side and don't know my father."

"Who are your parents?"

"My mother is Reyna Bustos, and I don't know my father."

"Rosita, if what you tell me is true, then you are the sister to Marcelo."

"Mrs. Martinez, I think you are confused because I don't have any brothers."

"Rosita, don't pay attention to me. But being your aunt, that I'm sure of, so please don't call me *Mrs. Martinez,* call me *Aunt.* My sons Javier, Carlos, and the other blond skinny boy you see running about are all your cousins." She called them over and introduced them to me. She told them that I was a cousin on the Bustos side and to watch over me and to respect me as their cousin. One by one they came over and hugged me. Then we ran out to the sprinkler system to take a shower. I couldn't believe that I had so many cousins. After the shower, my aunt called us over to eat. After the meal, we all gave thanks to Diosito for the food.

We were left alone in the kitchen. "Rosita, don't stay in here, go out and play with your cousins," she told me. "Aunt, I don't want you to eat alone."

"Rosita, that's so thoughtful of you. Mija, I want you to have confidence in us and that you can come and visit anytime you want. If you need a place to sleep, my door is always open to you." I looked at my aunt thinking, *Why can't my mother be like other mothers?* While we were talking, her older daughter Irene walked in. My aunt introduced us. Irene told me that she sees me always running all over the pueblo and sees me selling candies. I told her, "Irene, I see you with your curly-haired boyfriend. Sometimes I see both of you kissing like two little birds when they put their beaks together."

"No, Rosita, that is not me. That's my sister Rosi and her boyfriend."

"Tell me, Rosita, where do you see them?"

"Irene sometimes when I'm close to the big gate I can see them like two little birds."

I was anxious to know more about my father. I felt that my aunt knew who my father was. I had to ask. I started, "Aunt, pardon me for being inquisitive, but you mentioned that I am related to you on the Bustos side. My mother is related to you?"

"No, mija, your father is related to me, not your mother."

"I'm really confused, Reyna tells me that Rubén Reza is my father."

"No, Rosita, Rubén is not your father. But, Rosita, pretty soon you will have another cousin that's on the way."

"Aunt, we didn't leave any food for him."

"No, mija," she said laughing, "I'm pregnant."

"Oh, Aunt, that stork really gets around delivering babies." She couldn't stop laughing. "Rosita, the stork isn't bringing me my baby. The one responsible is your uncle, I got pregnant when he came to see us from the North." Then the stork didn't bring the baby that my mother has inside her stomach? I was too confused. I left my aunt and went outside to play with my cousins.

Blanquita and Beni Are Born

THE DAY STARTED LIKE ANY other day. I gave Don Felipe his coffee; after cleaning his place, I ran to the church. I didn't want to disturb Reyna because she'd been feeling strange. I went to Mama Lucia. I stayed there for a while, I felt like going home. Something about Reyna kept bothering me. I saw Alejo and Reyna leaving the house. I wanted to run toward the car, wanting to know where they were going, but I didn't. Ana was home, but Reyna was gone. I asked Ana if she knew where Reyna had gone to. Ana didn't tell me, although I felt that she knew. All she said was not to worry about Mother. I was persistent, I just had a feeling and wanted to know where Reyna was. Finally Ana said, "Vani, if you want to help Mom, help me clean the house. Soon Mother will come home with a baby, and I want the house to be clean." Mamacita Sinforosa heard that her daughter Reyna was in the hospital having a baby. How grandmothers know the latest news is a mystery, but there she was helping us clean the house.

Early the next morning, Alejo came to the house alone. I asked him for my mother, wondered why he'd come alone. Alejo, looking very happy, said, "I'm a father, and you have a little sister." I was so happy that I had a baby sister. Alejo continued talking; I heard him say, "Your sister is very beautiful, so we named her Blanca Estrella."

"Señor Alejo, take me with you, I want to be with my mother and see my baby sister." Alejo agreed to take me with him. He prepared a travel bag with items for the baby. When I saw Blanca, she was crying. She was the most beautiful baby I'd ever seen. I was so happy to see my mother giving a mother's love to her newborn

82

baby. A few days after Blanca was born, Alejo, mother, and Blanca left the pueblo.

Reyna and Blanca returned to the pueblo, but not Alejo. Reyna started selling gold and other items of value. I took care of Blanca. I didn't see Alejo for a long time. Ana told me that he would come around, but Reyna refused to see him. Reyna began to change. For about a year after Blanca was born, she didn't mistreat me. "Snot nose, come here," she ordered me. She hadn't talked to me like that in quite a while, and that's when I noticed the change. I didn't like being called names, especially *snot nose*. "My name is *Rosita*, not *snot nose*," I talked back to her. "What? You dare to speak back to me in that tone of voice, snot nose. Your name is what I say it is. Your name is *Jovani Reza*. Get in here and help me pack my suitcase." I helped her, and she told me to get lost.

I went to the safest place I knew, Mama Lucia's. We greeted each other. Now she said, "I'm going to teach you how to greet your elders." I looked at her not fully understanding what she meant. Apparently she felt that I wasn't showing the proper respect to my elders. She showed me how to properly greet them if it was morning, in the afternoon, and in the evening. "Rosita, your mother must be going someplace, otherwise you wouldn't be here this time of the day."

"Mama Lucia, how do you know so much? But yes, you are right, Reyna told me to get lost.

"Mama Lucia, I met my aunt Rosa Martinez and all my cousins. She told me that I am related to her on the part of my father, Bustos." She stopped what she was doing, looked at me, and all she said was, "WHAT! She told you that?"

"Yes, she told me that she is not related to Reyna but to my father, Bustos."

"Rosita, you are starting to learn the truth."

"But, Mama Lucia, why does Reyna tell me that I'm Reza?"

"Don't forget what your aunt Rosa told you, someday you will understand it better. My advice to you, mija, is always be careful with whom you share this information." I ran from the puesto toward Don Felipe's. I had to write all of this information down.

I spent my days going to kinder, helping Mama Lucia, and selling my candies. Reyna would come and go from the pueblo never telling me where she was going. I felt that Ana knew where Reyna was, but she kept it to herself. From what I remember and some of my notes, Ana and I used to take care of Blanquita, my baby sister. When Ana was off to work, I was responsible for Blanquita. Mama Lucia was always there helping me with Blanquita. Being alone with her was difficult, but I never complained, at least I had company. Being alone without her was easier. I had more freedom, but my epilepsy interfered with my living.

Reyna began to put weight on; Ana and I noticed that her stomach was growing, and I believe that Ana knew that Reyna was pregnant again, but it never crossed my mind. When Reyna started to vomit and became nauseous, I remembered that Reyna acted the same way when she was pregnant with Blanquita. I told Ana that I thought Reyna was going to have another baby. Ana shrugged it off, telling me, "This way Blanquita and the baby will grow up together." I thought, *Yes, that is good, but who is going to take care of them when Reyna leaves the pueblo?*

A few weeks later, we heard Mother scream with pain asking for help. Ana and I rushed to the laundry place where she was washing clothes. She was lying on the floor where she had slipped and fell down. We picked her up and helped her to the bed. I sat on the bed with her and told her not to eat so much because it appeared like she had a big ball stuck inside her stomach. "Vani, shut up, don't bother Mom. Vani, go visit Doña Lucia. I'll watch over Mom." I didn't hesitate. I ran out of the house toward the puesto. "Rosita, what brings you here at this time of the day?"

"Mama Lucia, can I stay here? Nobody wants me at the house, Reyna doesn't feel good. She feels sick again because the stork is bringing another baby."

"Rosita, I told you before, it's not the stork that brings the babies. Someday you will know the truth. But sure you know that you can stay here anytime."

I slept real good, didn't miss Blanquita's crying at all. The following day I woke up with a lot of energy. I went home to fix Don Felipe his coffee. When I entered the house, I heard a baby crying, but it wasn't Blanquita. Ana stopped me from entering the room to see who was crying. I responded to Ana's request by standing in the middle of the room not moving, just listening to the baby crying. "Vani, we have a new baby sister."

"Ana, the stork came last night, Mother has another baby?"

"Yes, Vani, Mother gave birth to another beautiful baby girl.

"Vani, Mother wants to be alone, but pretty soon you can go in and see the new baby." I sat on the patio waiting for the moment that I could see the baby. I was startled out of my daydreaming when I heard a strange voice greeting me. I looked up to see a stranger that belonged to the strange voice. I thought, *Where did this stranger come from?* He asked me, "Is this the house where Reyna lives?" Before I could answer, Ana came out of the house and greeted the gentleman. I asked him, "Sir, who are you?"

"Vani, don't ask so many questions, this gentleman is here to see his baby."

"She is right, young lady, I am the father of the baby that Reyna gave birth to." I asked him, "You are the father?" Ana grabbed me by my arm. "Vani, be quiet, don't ask so many questions, why don't you go play with the other kids."

"Ana, wait." I turned to see the baby's father. "Sir, what is your name?"

"I am Noel Pedrosa. I live in Amatitlan. Now I ask you, young lady, what is your name?"

"My name is *Rosita Jovani*, and many people know me as Alma de Dios."

Noel Pedrosa entered the room to visit with Reyna and his new daughter. I heard Reyna tell Noel, "Pardon my daughter for being so inquisitive." He told her not to worry. "It's all right for her to ask me questions." I started to feel weak; the emotions from having a new baby sister apparently triggered another convulsion. When I came to, Ana was close to me. She had placed a pillow under my head and covered me with a blanket. I was home on the floor, but I was home and not in a strange place, like so many other times I had experienced a convulsion.

My head was throbbing with a terrible headache, but I had to get up. Against Ana's objections, I helped her prepare food for Reyna, Noel, and for ourselves. I started the fire in the outside pits we used as the cooking area. The fresh air felt good. We left Reyna and Noel to converse while she and I prepared the meal. Outside Ana asked me where I had the energy to do the things I do. I asked Ana how she knew what I do during the day. "Ana, are the little birds telling you what I do?"

"Vani, you don't realize it, but when I'm home, I watch over you. I talk to people, to Madre Sarita, your madrina Socorro, Doña Lucia, and others. Vani, you'd be surprised how many people in the pueblo know who you are. They all have something nice to say about you and are concerned with your sickness."

"Ana, you go talk to Madre Sarita?"

"Sometimes I do, but I usually run into her at the market."

"I know that Madre Sarita is concerned with my sickness. But I become sad when I see the children being picked up by their parents and I'm always alone." I made Ana cry with my sad story. "Vani, you know that Reyna is not feeling well. It's possible that she will accompany you to kinder when she feels better."

"Ana, I've been waiting for that moment and for the moment that Reyna gives me a motherly hug." We set the table, but I was more anxious to talk to my *Chuchin* than I was hungry.

Entering the church, I felt that my Diosito was waiting for me. I dipped my fingers in the holy water and made the sign of the cross. I approached the altar, looked up to where my Chuchin was waiting. "Diosito, I know you know everything, so can you explain to me why I didn't see the stork when he brought my little sister? Is the stork invisible? I didn't see the stork when he brought Blanquita either." I felt that Diosito was smiling. But He didn't respond. "You know that my mother had another baby. Now I have to help her with the new baby and with Blanquita. But I'm going to teach Blanquita how to walk faster, how to eat, and train her to use the bathroom." I looked at the altar, and for an instant, I could see a slight smile from the lips of Diosito and the Virgin Mary.

My new sister was baptized. The godparents were from Amatitlán, Guerrero, the same place that Noel Pedrosa lived. The name chosen for the new baby was Beneralda Pedrosa Bustos. Noel and Reyna made a big feast to celebrate the baptism. Ana met her boyfriend, Muñeco, at the baptismal feast.

I helped Mom keep the house clean and helped with my two sisters. One day when I was tidying up the house, we had a strange visitor. I heard somebody knock on the window. *Must be a drunkard*, I thought, *nobody knocks on the window.* With broom in hand I stepped out to see who the drunk was. It was a woman, and she wasn't drunk, only upset and very angry. "Ma'am, who are you looking for?" I asked. The angry lady, moving her hands back and forth, answered, "I am looking for Reyna Bustos. This time she is going to hear me out. She had a child with my husband."

"Ma'am, I remember you, you came once before singing the same old tune."

"What do you mean, little girl? This isn't the same tune, call your mother."

"Ma'am, you should be talking with your husband, not with my mother. If you allow him to go around with other women, he might have other children somewhere out there. I believe the stork obeys the men to avoid embarrassments, so you should talk to your husband. This way you don't go around picking fights with the women your husband has affairs with."

"Little girl, this is none of your business, I want to speak with Reyna."

"Jovani, who is it?" Mother yelled. The lady pushed me aside and walked inside to where Reyna was resting. I don't know what happened between the two. The battle was between two grown-ups and didn't involve me. Not wanting to be nosy and feeling that Reyna didn't want me around, I left the house. I didn't want to forget what I had just witnessed, so I ran to the room of Don Felipe.

In time, Reyna opened a small eatery to make ends meet. I helped her with my baby sisters and to sell the food. I saved all the tips the customers gave me. Every time I bought diapers or baby food for my little sisters, Reyna wondered where I was getting the pesos. I didn't want her to know that I had a stash, so I told her a fib for fear that she would take it away from me. Without the stash, I wouldn't be able to purchase my medicine.

Cleaning the house, helping Mother sell her food, and taking care of the two babies was a full-time job for me. In addition I had to keep a supply of clean diapers. My little sisters usually cried at night when they were hungry or wet. One night I was sound asleep when Reyna yelled for me to wake up. "Jovani, come here," Reyna shouted. "Take these diapers and wash them, the babies don't have any clean ones." It was a beautiful night with the moon providing some light outside. Ana told Reyna not to send me out to wash diapers. "Besides," Ana told Reyna, "how are we going to dry them?"

Lady in White

I GOT UP FROM MY corner, took the tin pail full of diapers. The light from the moon lit my way to the outside laundry. To wash the dirty diapers, I was required to draw water from the water hole. I tied the rope to the pail, dropped it down to the hole, filled it with water, then I pulled it up. I hadn't finished the laundry when suddenly I saw the figure walking near the baths. It was the figure of a woman dressed in white. She walked around a plant of red roses sobbing as she walked. I stood up; she stopped walking when she noticed me. She raised her hand as though she was greeting me. Just then, Ana came out to check on me.

"Vani, it's too late for you to be put here, let's go inside, you can wash the diapers tomorrow. Don't pay attention to Doña Reyna."

"But, Ana, Mama will be mad at me and will probably give me a trashing."

"Don't worry, little sister, it's almost 1:00 a.m." Ana noticed the water hole. "Vani, I don't know how you manage to get the water out of that hole, especially at night." I smiled and briefly told her how I manage. I asked Ana if she had noticed the lady in white who was walking near the rose bush. "What? You saw a lady walking out here? Did you recognize her?"

"No, Ana, I have never seen her before. She appeared to be a pretty lady, with straight black hair so long that it covered her hips."

"Vani, you are scaring me, let's go inside."

"Ana, I better stay out here, if I go inside, Reyna will give me a whipping for not washing the diapers. Besides, I'm not sleepy."

"No, Vani, you can't stay out here, the lady you saw appears to be mean and scary."

"Ana, how do you know that she is mean?"

"Vani, I'm not going to argue with you, you want to stay, then stay. But I'm going inside." I stayed to wash the diapers all the while singing the chant of the morning rooster. I watched the stars bid farewell as the dawn started to shine its light. I finished the diapers, went to my corner, and took a pencil and paper with me to bed. The rooster's crowing awoke me. I made the coffee for Don Felipe. Always happy to see and smell the coffee when I entered his room, Don Felipe thanked me. "Rosita, you have work for me so early this morning, must be very important. Am I right?"

"You really know me, don't you, Don Felipe?"

"Yes, I have something important to write about." I told him about the lady in white. I asked him if he would write it down in my diary. I gave my pencil and paper. He wrote:

Lady in White

Brilliant is your courage past midnight
Your aimless soul full of pain
Your hair shines like the look in your face
A transparent white
Your dress resplendent white
With long black hair
Your presence blossoms in me
Contemplating yourself
With each step of your journey
Swallowing the tears
With courage in your eyes

When he finished writing "Lady in White," Don Felipe looked at me. "Rosita," he said, "how is it possible that a girl so young can write such a beautiful poem? Your thoughts are so beautiful, and how you form the words into the poem is incredible." I laughed. "My mind thought of my Diosito. I thanked Him, for He gave me the ability to think and to transform words in my mind." I was in admiration of myself, but quietly. I asked Don Felipe to save the pages with the other ones. "Rosita, he said, "I've known you since you were born, and I still ask you, *who are you?*"

It was still early, I went home briefly to tell Ana that I would be with Mama Lucia until I went to my kinder class. I wasn't feeling well on my way to class. Madre Sarita was preparing the classroom when I entered. I remember greeting the madre, and no more, I had a convulsion. When I came to, Madre Sarita was kneeling at my side where I lay on the floor. Madre Sarita told me to go home and rest. Usually I would have stayed, but not this time. With a terrible headache, I made my way to Mama Lucia's puesto. When Mama Lucia saw me, she knew that I had experienced another of my convulsions. She held me close to her, trying to console me. She sat me down while she fetched some cold water to clean the bump and cut I had on my forehead. I cried from the pain. Mama Lucia tried to console me while she cleaned my wounded forehead.

I fell asleep from exhaustion. When I woke up, Madre Sarita was there checking up on me. Madre thanked Mama Lucia for all that she does for me. Mama Lucia answered, "Just look at Rosita, she has a convulsion and remains strong at heart and will continue to be a strong person." Madre Sarita left once she was sure I was okay. Mama Lucia continued to rub some kind of ointment with warm towels on my forehead. Again I fell asleep. I woke up to the sound of voices. For an instance or so, I didn't remember where I was. I was in my little corner of the puesto. Mama Lucia was serving her customers. I made my way to the eating area to help her. She was surprised that I was up and willing to help. At first she balked, not wanting me to work. When I assured her that I was okay, she accepted my help.

One of the customers noticed the bump and cut on my forehead. "What happened to you? Young girl, in your condition, you should be resting instead of working."

"Sir, I fell flat on my forehead, that's why I have this bump." The man told me he was so sorry I had banged my head. Then he wanted to know who my parents were. "Sir," I said, "I don't have a father, and my mother is Reyna Bustos." The man got up from his seat and introduced me to his family. Mama Lucia came to greet the man's family. I left to attend others. After a while, the man called me over to the table.

"Rosita, can we talk to you?" I nodded my approval. "Rosita, Doña Lucia told us a lot about you. We want to ask if you would be willing to go live with us in Taxco." I was really surprised, I never expected to live anywhere else but here in my pueblo. "Sir, we just met, and I don't know anything about you or your family. I have my family here, I work and go to school here. I can't go live with you."

"Rosita, I understand. However, we are really serious in having you go live with us. We also heard about you from others living here in the pueblo, and I was really surprised to see you helping Doña Lucia. We want to help you, please reconsider and come live with us."

I thought about having a family, I thought about not being alone anymore. I had to learn more about this family. I asked him, "Mister, what brings you to our pueblo?"

"We came to visit your beautiful Santa Cruz Church because we've heard that the Crucifix with Christ in the main altar has performed some miracles." That's when I truly understood that I could not leave my pueblo. I answered the man, "Sir, you are right about my Diosito in the main altar. Thanks be to Him that I continue living. Sir, that's the reason that not even a team of mules could pull me out of this pueblo."

His wife smiled. "Rosita," she said, "I admire the way you express yourself. It appears to me that you really know how to take care of yourself. I would love you like a true mother, I would treasure you, but I respect your decision." She handed me a piece of paper with her name and address. "Rosita, whenever you decide to visit us, you will know where we live." When the family finished eating, the lady approached me. "Rosita, I want you to accept this small gift from us." I looked at Mama Lucia; she gave me an affirmative nod, saying, "Accept it, mija, they are giving it to you with all their hearts." I took the money thinking of my stash, my own little bank hidden away in my grandmother's house. I thanked the family for being so generous,

I accompanied them to the edge of the puesto, and from there, I bade them goodbye. The family kept waving their goodbyes until they disappeared around the corner. At the same time I saw Madre Sarita coming around the same corner. I waited for her until she reached the puesto. "Rosita, I came to check on you. Are you feeling better?"

"Madre, I feel better, and thank you for checking up on me. Don't worry about me."

"Niña, I'm not the only person worrying about you. Some of the mothers saw when you suffered your convulsion this morning, and they are very concerned. But I'm here for another reason besides to see how you feel."

"Really, Madre, what other reason brings you to my puesto?" asked Mama Lucia. "Well, I want to tell Rosita that she has been selected to carry the flag during this year's ceremony. This is Rosita's last year in kindergarten, and it's customary for the most outstanding student to carry the flag at the end of the year's ceremony. We all agreed that Rosita is that person."

"Madre Sarita, I'm going to carry the flag that represents our pueblo and country?" She bent over, looked at me eye to eye, and said, "Yes, Rosita, you are the one. The ceremony will include a small program for all of the kinder class." The thought of me carrying the flag was a big honor, and it was gonna be in front of all the people; at the same time, it was going to be a problem for me.

"Rosita, I can tell that something is troubling you, tell me what's on your mind."

"Madre Sarita, I can't carry the flag."

"Rosita, don't say that, now tell me what's bothering you."

"Madre, I don't have good clothes. The parents aren't going to be pleased if I carry the flag in these ragged old clothes. I prefer to write a poem that bids goodbye to my little corner where I took my first learning step."

"Oh, Rosita, you worry for nothing. You will be wearing the same uniform that everyone else is wearing. But don't worry, I will make your uniform." The nun left the puesto, leaving me thinking about the poem. I will write a poem where I reflect back to my first days at kinder.

"Rosita, when was the last time you ate? I know that you are hungry, and don't lie to me, I can hear your stomach growling."

"Yes, Mama Lucia, I am a little hungry, sell me a taco to quiet my stomach."

"Oh, child, you are stubborn. Why don't you tell me when you're hungry? Look at the time of day, and you haven't eaten." She served me a huge plate. I asked if I could have an extra plate. "You want to split your food with Don Felipe, don't you?"

"No, Mama Lucia, I want to take food to my mother so that she can have enough breast milk for my baby sister." I ate what I could and took the rest to Mother.

Reyna saw me when I walked into the house. I greeted her. She didn't acknowledge me. "Mom, I brought you a plate of warm food, I hope you're hungry."

"Put it on the table. Now tell me where you were. Out walking the streets, giving the people more to talk about me?"

"Mother, I don't do anything or say anything bad about you. I pray for good health so that I can be constructive and be able to help. Did you notice that I laundered all the diapers last night? Mother, can you have compassion for me?"

Ana walked in; she noticed the bump and cut on my forehead. "Vani, what happened to you? I feel that you got sick again, tell me, little sister, what happened?"

"I had a convulsion during kinder class and got this bump and cut in my forehead. But I'm okay now." Reyna, hearing what I told Ana, said, "What a coincidence that you got sick, you look okay to me. What you need is another beating for being such a liar." Those words hurt, and I started to cry. "Ana, you know that I don't tell tall tales about my convulsions, please tell that to Mother. I fell because of my sickness. In reality this epilepsy is very difficult on me. I can't predict when I'm going to have a convulsion. One minute I'm feeling fine, and next moment I wake up on the ground, always someplace different, with knots or worse on my head. With all my heart I ask my Diosito to enlighten anyone that offends me because of my epilepsy. Those persons will experience some kind of sickness, so they will know what it is to be sick."

Ana hugged me. "Vani, don't think like that. I feel that someday Diosito will cure you of that sickness. God has you here for some reason and will always be at your side."

"There is no doubt about that," said Reyna, "formerly she has been declared dead, only to revive."

"Mother, leave Vani alone, she doesn't need this, she needs peace in her life." Reyna replied, "Ana Lidia, remember I am your mother and in charge around here."

"Vani, let's get out of here." She grabbed my hand and led me out of the house. "Vani, continue being the strong person that you are. Don't pay attention to Mother, she hasn't been feeling well since giving birth to Beni."

Tio Taurino Pays Us a Visit

"ANA, I BROUGHT REYNA FOOD, but I see that she isn't going to eat it."

"Vani, you are always thinking of others, including Mom. But for now, think of you. I don't want you getting sick, okay? Vani, have you been taking your medicine?"

"Yes, I have, even if it tastes horrible. But thanks to my Diosito and the awful medicine for my being with life.

"But, Ana, why doesn't she appreciate me or anything that I do for her?"

"I know what you do for Mom, and I see how she continues to mistreat you. Vani, try to forget it. If she is hungry, she'll eat. I'm sure she appreciates it but doesn't know how to tell you."

"In my case, I cook for the people I work for, and look, they give all the leftover food to their dogs. They don't allow me to bring any of it home."

"Vani, I have good news, I found out that Uncle Taurino is coming to visit us."

"Who is Uncle Taurino?"

"Well, we call him *Uncle*, but he's really a cousin. I was at the store with my boss Don Ramón and his wife, when I ran into Tio José, and he told me. Tio Taurino will be here tomorrow, he is coming from the el Norte." Reyna was listening to our conversion; she stuck her head through the door. "Listen to me, Ana Lidia, you keep your mouth shut when Taurino comes to visit. I don't want you to tell him anything about me. I will leave the house while he is here because I don't want to see that man. I will be staying with Doña Eulalia, tell me when he leaves."

She packed a few things in a bag and started to leave. She was leaving the babies behind. I said, "Mother, you forgot the babies." She looked at me with eyes full of rage. "As for those two snot-nosed babies, don't tell him that I'm the mother, Ana, and you are responsible for them." She took off, left without the babies. I thought, *I'm the one who is now responsible for Blanquita and Beni, not Ana, she works during the day.* Ana entered the house, I remained seated outside. With elbows on my knees and my hands on my chin, I thought of the responsibility forced on me. *How am I going to accomplish this? What do I feed them? Did Reyna leave enough food for them? I know she breastfeeds Beni, so what do I feed her? What about Tio Taurino, what do I feed him?*

I stood up and entered the house. I walked up to Ana and asked, "How am I supposed to take care of these two babies? You work during the day, so that leaves them under my care." When Ana didn't respond, I said, "Well, don't worry, I will take care of them." Later that evening after we put Blanquita and Beni to bed, I went outside and sat on the stairs. I fell asleep waiting for the mysterious lady dressed in white. I was awakened by the glaring sound of one of the babies cry. It was early in the morning. I could see the sky starting to lighten up with the dawn light. I stretched my body before I entered the house. Ana was getting up because she also was awakened by the sound of our little baby sister's. "Vani, did you sleep outside?" I smiled. "Yes, I was waiting for the lady in white and fell asleep."

Soon after Ana left for work, Mama Lucia came to visit. "Rosita, I saw your mother entering Doña Eulalia's house with a small suitcase. I see that she left the babies in your charge. That woman has no heart, how can she do this to you? If she wants children, she should take care of them and not pawn them off on you. Oh, Reyna, how can you do this to your children? She is very irresponsible. Rosita, I will help you to take care of them." Mama Lucia made sure that we had enough food then left. As soon as Mama Lucia left, Don Felipe shouted, "Rosita, come over."

Making coffee for Don Felipe was easy. Packing Blanquita and Beni for the trip to Don Felipe's was an ordeal. I managed to tie Beni around my midsection. Blanquita walked reluctantly beside me. Don

Felipe couldn't wait to tell me, "Rosita, I saw your mother leave the house. In the past, she would leave you all alone, later with Blanquita, but now she leaves you with two baby sisters. What is wrong with your mother?" I was a little annoyed when I answered, "Don Felipe, is that why you called me over, to tell me that about my mother?"

"Rosita, I didn't know that you were in charge of your sisters. Otherwise, I wouldn't have called you."

"Don Felipe, tell me, why did you call?"

"Okay, Rosita, I was going to ask if you could bring me water from the water hole because I need to take a bath." The old-timer watched my sisters while I got his bathwater. I stayed around the house not wanting to walk all over with my sisters. When Ana came home, I mentioned that we were short of petroleum and couldn't start the heater. We were preparing supper, but a knock on the window interrupted our conversation. I ran to answer before Ana could.

I was startled to see what seemed to be an American gringo standing at the doorstep. I stood as though frozen for a moment, wondering who this blond man wanted. I greeted the stranger, then I asked him his business at our house. "Niña, open the door, I'm your uncle Taurino." I was happy to see my uncle, the stranger, for the first time. I let him in the house. He greeted me with a big hug. "Which of Reyna's daughter are you?"

"Uncle, I'm Jovani Reza Bustos." Ana greeted Uncle Taurino. He looked around the house. "Where's Reyna and your other sisters?" he asked.

Ana and Uncle went to the kitchen where she was finalizing supper. Ana called me that supper was ready.

During supper, we found out that Uncle was single and didn't have any children. He came to visit Tetipac with the main purpose of meeting his future wife. He has been to the pueblo before but still hasn't found that beautiful future wife. He planned to stay at the pueblo, hoping to meet a señorita during the festival at the end of May. We talked for a long time. Uncle Taurino looked at Ana then at me. "You two are really wonderful young ladies, but it's a pity you are living such a difficult life."

Our conversation was interrupted suddenly by Bolita, a very small man, running to the bathroom. "That was Bolita," said Uncle Taurino. "Uncle, you know that little man."

"Yes, Ana, I know Bolita, he is your uncle."

"What!" Ana said, "I want to meet him. Vani, do you know Bolita?"

"Yes, I know Bolita, but I didn't know that he is our uncle."

"Vani, go tell Bolita to come in." I waited for Bolita to come out of the bathroom. "Bolita, what are you doing here?"

"Rosita, I needed a quick bath."

"Good for you, Bolita, because it's about time, I'm sure that even your wives can't stand you, they are going to be very happy. Bolita, come into the house, my sister wants to meet you."

I went back inside. "Bolita will be here shortly," I told Ana. Bolita entered the house; he recognized Uncle Taurino. They exchanged greetings. I introduced him to Ana. Bolita looked at me. "Rosita, I haven't seen you in a long time."

"Come on, Bolita, we've seen each other many times. Just the other day, I saw you at the house of Doña Zoila. Then I saw you coming out of the carpenter's shop with a load of wood. Then I saw you last Sunday drunk and singing in the middle of the road. I helped you to the sidewalk before you were run over. You were singing, 'Qué diran los de tu casa...' That is what you sing when you get drunk." Ana and Uncle Taurino were laughing, enjoying the life of Bolita.

"Oh my god, I was really soused, wasn't I? And you helped me off the street?" Bolita couldn't take any more; he left, but not alone. I saw him pull a bottle from his hip pocket. The night was setting in, and we didn't have kerosene for the lamps. "You girls don't have petro for your lamps?" I shook my head. "No, sir, we don't."

"Okay, Ana, come with me, show me where I can buy the kerosene." I babysat my sisters while they went off to buy petro. I was lying on the floor with Blanquita and Beni when they came back with petro and groceries. "Rosita, is this where all of you sleep?" Taurino asked. I just shook my head, not saying a word. He filled the lamps with the petro and lit them.

I saw Tío Taurino pacing the floor. The way he was acting reminded me of the cat that moves about before approaching me. "Ana and Rosita, sit with me, we need to talk." He hugged both of us before we sat at the table to talk. "Tomorrow I'm taking all of you to Taxco. We are going shopping for groceries. I will also give you money to buy anything for yourselves." Ana couldn't hold back the tears. I tried to be strong, but I too got emotional. That's when I realized that I hadn't taken my medicine. I went to my hiding place where I had my medicine. Tio Taurino kept on talking all the while probably wondering what I was up to.

"Rosita, why are you taking medicine?"

"Oh, Tío, you don't know that I'm sick?" He looked at me. "No, mija, tell me about your sickness." I told him that I suffered from epilepsy. I told him about my convulsions, showed some of my scars on my head caused by the falls when I got sick. I shared with him that I buy my own medicine with money that I make selling candies, cleaning for Don Felipe, and tips I earn working with Mama Lucia. By the time I finished talking, Ana, Tio Taurino, and my little sisters were crying.

Tio Taurino took his handkerchief from his pocket, wiped away his tears, and looked at me. "Rosita, I can't believe what you told me, you look so healthy, so happy, and so full of life."

"Tío, my Diosito is always with me, I continue living by His grace and His kindness."

Ana changed Beni's diaper, and I cleaned Blanquita. Tío paced the floor until we finished. We sat down to continue with our conversation. Tío Taurino began to speak; the tone of his voice was serious. "Mijas," he said, "¿do you want to go live with me in the United States?" Ana and I looked at each other. We didn't expect that. I didn't know what to say. Ana did; she said, "Oh, Tío, I would love to go to el Norte where my father and sisters live." She got very emotional. "But these two little sisters and Vani depend on me, I can't leave them. Vani should go, maybe there the doctors have a cure for her illness."

"Ana, can you explain how Vani got this illness, was she born with it?"

"Vani, let me talk with Tio alone, okay?" I left the room, went outside, and sat on the steps, alone.

My thoughts were interrupted when Tío came and sat with me. He put his arm around me. I felt love coming from his heart. His huge hand on my right cheek, he turned my face toward his face. With tears in his eyes, he said, "I'm going to do everything possible to take you with me to el Norte. It's possible that the doctors from up North can cure your illness. Mija, meanwhile, I will pay the doctors here in the pueblo to care for you when you get hurt."

I cleaned his tears. "Tío, please don't cry. Others cry when they realize that I am epileptic and, like you, see my way of living. Tío, I don't want to see you this way, please don't cry anymore."

"Okay, niña, I won't cry anymore. Tell me, the thing that you desire more than anything is what?"

"Tío, I wish that Reyna would love me like a mother loves a daughter. I also would like to know who my real father is." He asked, "¿You don't know who your father is?"

"No, Tio, I don't."

"Okay, then I'm going to take you to Tejas—ah, Texas, where your grandmother and your aunts and uncles live."

"What? Tío, my abuelita Sinforosa lives in *el llano*, not in *tejas*, and she lives in a house, not in the roof. Tío, I know that *tejas* is the material that covers the roof of a house." He laughed. "Oh, niña, you are so innocent. Tejas, or Texas, is a place up North where your father's side of the family live, not *tejas*, a roof."

"Sorry, Tio, I didn't understand you. But Mamacita Sinforosa doesn't live in Texas." Ana was listening to our conversation; she came out and whispered something to Tío Taurino. He turned to me and said, "Rosita, forget the conversation about your grandma, I was mistaken."

Once again, why won't anybody tell me who my real father is? Well, someday I will uncover the truth. Diosito will show me the way. We went back inside the house. Tio opened his suitcase where he had some gifts for us. He brought us clothes and shoes and a pair of men's pants. Immediately I thought of Don Felipe and Bolita. I asked Tio if he would let me have the pants. "Rosita, these pants don't fit you," he joked with me. "No, Tío, I want to give a pair to Don Felipe and one to Bolita."

"For Bolita? He is too small, this pair of pants is too big for him."

"Tio, it is better than the rags he wears, the poor man doesn't have decent clothes."

"Okay, Rosita, and who is this Don Felipe?"

"Tío, he is the postman of the pueblo. He is the man I work for, and not only that, but he is teaching me how to write. He writes my diary for me, that is until I learn to write, then I will write my own notes."

"You are writing your diary, why?"

"Tío, with these notes and diary, I plan on writing a book. You, Tío, are going to be in my book. What you have done for us will go in my book."

"Rosita, are you really planning to write a book and I will be in it?"

"Believe me, Tío, someday I will write a book, and you will be the grandest tío of all." He looked at me for a moment, shook his head, and said, "Rosita, really, who are you? I noticed that you didn't ask for anything for you, but you did for Bolita and Don Felipe. You hide your sickness by working, you are always happy, you get banged up when you get sick, and now you tell me that your ambition is to write a book. I will no longer ask 'who are you?' I now know that you truly are an Alma de Dios."

"Tio, thank you for those wonderful words." I walked up to him and gave him a hug. "Tío, I have to go to bed, I'm tired, please excuse me." He gave me a hug and his blessing. "Rosita, that man Don Felipe appears to be a nice person, I'd like to meet him."

"Okay, Tío, I can take you to his room tomorrow morning." The night went by fast. I had a very restful sleep. I prepared coffee for my friend. He was happy when I arrived with his morning brew. "Rosita, I'm not nosy, you know, but you have company, don't you?"

"No, Don Felipe, you are not nosy, but you seem to know everything that goes on around here." He laughed, took a sip of coffee. "Who's your company?"

"He is my uncle Taurino, he came to visit us. He lives in the Norte in a place called Tejas. He wants to meet you, is that okay with you?"

"He wants to meet me?" He sounded annoyed. "Why, what does he know about me?"

"My uncle had some men's clothes that he brought with him to give out as gifts. I asked for a pair for you, that's why he wants to meet you. I also told him that you are my mentor and friend and are writing my journals." I was standing in the doorway when I saw my uncle approaching.

Uncle Taurino and I exchanged greetings. Don Felipe was sitting in his wheelchair. Tío walked over and introduced himself. "Señor, I had to come and meet you. Last night Rosita spoke very highly of you. I want to thank you for all you do for my niece. I have come to know quite a bit about her, and mostly is that she truly is an Alma de Dios. Again thank you for being her friend and mentor."

"Señor Taurino, she is much more than that. Taurino, Rosita tells me that you are visiting."

"Yes, Don Felipe, I came to visit family here in the pueblo, and more important, I'm here looking for a wife. In Texas, where I live, all the girls are too Americanas. I want to find me a real *mejicana*, marry her, and take her with me to el Norté."

"Oh, Señor Taurino, be very careful, a woman like that is protected by her father and brothers."

"Señor Felipe, do you know such a woman?"

"Señor Taurino, there are many señoritas in the pueblo, but it's best that you find one. I don't get involved in a matching game."

"Thanks for the advice, Don Felipe. I brought the clothes Rosita wants to give you." The old man was very happy with his new clothes. Tio Taurino asked me if I was ready for the trip to Taxco. "You are going to Taxco?" asked Don Felipe. "Yes, señor, I'm taking my nieces shopping." I jumped in and asked Don Felipe if he needed anything from the city. He needed batteries for the watches he fixes; he gave me the money to buy them.

Tío Taurino and all of us four sisters packed into his car for the trip to Taxco. He bought food to go at his favorite restaurant. We ate at a very touristy park full of beautiful flowers and shrubbery called El Huisteco. Tío took many pictures of us. We shopped most of the day. Tío was very generous. Ana and my little sisters were so exhausted that they fell asleep on the way home. Me, I preferred to look at the scenery and speak with Tío Taurino. He wasn't satisfied with the clothes he'd bought me. He told me that he and I were going shopping at the pueblo, that I needed more clothes. I said, "Tío, you tell me that I'm pretty, so if that is true, I don't need more clothes. Besides, Tío, you have bought so much for us already." We were happy with all the clothes and groceries Tío bought for us.

We Learn How to Use a Camera

HE WAITED UNTIL WE RETURNED to the pueblo to buy the goat's meat from María Casteñada. He left us alone while he went for the goat's meat. She prepared goat's meat to his liking, and he wanted to share it with us four sisters.

I grabbed the apparatus my uncle was taking pictures with. Ana told me to take the camera and to take her picture with it. She dressed up in the clothes Uncle Taurino had bought her. She looked beautiful. I grabbed the apparatus to take her photo. "Ana, what do I do?" She said, "Do you see me?"

"Ana, of course I see you."

"No, Vani, look through that little glass." I did as she told me. "Now, Vani, do you see me?"

"Yes, I see you now, but you look too small."

"Vani, that's okay."

"Ana, what now?"

"Vani, take the picture."

"But how, Ana?"

"Vani, see that red button on top, look through the glass. When you see me, press the red button." I pressed the button and actually took her picture, and we laughed. "Ana, it's my turn take my picture. I too want to be inside that apparatus." We laughed and laughed until Uncle returned. "Oh, señoritas I'm so glad to see you laughing and having a good time. What happened, why are you two laughing?" I said, "Tio, we got your apparatus, and looks like we are captured inside it." My tio couldn't stop laughing. Finally when he could talk, he said, "Señoritas, how I wish I could take you to live with me."

"Tio, excuse my response, but I must stay here. Maybe someday I will go to the United States. If my Diosito allows me more time living, He will send me to the place where I can be cured."

"Niña, I understand you perfectly, and remember that my offer is always open to you." After we finished eating the well-prepared goat's meat, I cleaned the table. Uncle Taurino admired the way I was cleaning and arranging the kitchen. "Where did you learn all that?" he asked. I told him that Mama Lucia had taught me.

"Your Mama Lucia, who is that lady? Can I take her with me to the United States?" I laughed at my uncle. I told him, "You are joking, Tio, you don't want to take a lady that is twice as old as you to be your wife, do you? Mama Lucia is a nice lady with a beautiful heart, she takes care of me."

"Rosita, I'd like to meet la Señora Lucia before I leave, but first I want to take you to see a doctor." He took me to the doctor but didn't have time to meet Doña Lucia. Before he left, he told me that he was sure that Diosito was watching over me. I answered that God loves everybody, but it is a person that doesn't seek God.

We walked him to the car. "Ana and Rosita, I never expected to meet two wonderful girls like both of you. Especially the way you live. As for your mother, well, I don't know whether to send my regards or not. Reyna knows that I'm here, but I know that she is hiding from me." I didn't hear him anymore, I had a convulsion. My uncle had me in his arms; his green eyes were full of tears when I came to. I wondered why he was crying.

"Mija, you got sick and fainted. When I saw you fall, my heart shattered into pieces. Now more than ever I want to take you with me." He picked me up and took me to bed. "Don't cry, Tio." I got hold of the rosary I had around my neck and gave it to him. "My Chuchin will protect you, and the rosary will remind you of me."

"Rosita, I have to go now. If you change your mind, call me, and I will come for you." I managed to walk with him and Ana to the car. He got in it and drove off. We watched the car until it disappeared from our view.

Ana turned to go inside the house; she gave me a hard pull. "Vani, Vani," she sounded scared, "Mother is coming, and she is mad."

"Ana, how can you be sure that she is angry?"

"Vani, look at her hands, see how they are closed into a fist." When she has her fists like that, she is bellowing fire, prepare yourself.

Reyna shouted, "You ungrateful jackasses. Did you forget that you have a mother? You forgot to send me something to eat. Now look at both of you, did you get stung by a wasp?" I stayed quiet, concentrating on her fists. She stared at me. "I'm talking to you, snot-nosed jackass." I don't know why I didn't stay quiet, but I answered, "Please, Doña Reyna, don't call me a jackass. A donkey understands more than most."

She moved swiftly like a cat; before I knew it, Reyna planted a solid slap on my face. I was shocked! "Why did you hit me?" I screamed at her. "Why are you so mean with me? You treat me as though I'm not your daughter. If that's the case, tell me, but don't hit me anymore. Your disdain as a mother hurts more than all the beatings I have felt from you."

"Who taught you to speak like that, snot nose? Clearly I'm your mother." Ana grabbed my arm. "Mother, leave her be, she needs peace and quiet. Vani had a convulsion a few moments ago, and now you are trying to hurt her." I hugged Ana and sobbed. We walked back into the house. Reyna followed us. Reyna bellowed, "I'm hungry like a dog, what's there to eat?" I said, "Mom, we have some barbequed goat for you." I fixed her a plate. She started to eat and pointed to Ana. "What a beautiful dress you have on. Did your uncle bring it to you from the Norte? Did your uncle bring anything for me?"

Reyna turned to face me. "And you, snot nose, I hope you didn't have a loose tongue and told him everything about me."

"No, Mother, he didn't even mention your name once."

"Then why in the —— did he come?" I cleaned the kitchen and washed the dishes. I told Ana that I was going to visit Mama Lucia. Doña Reyna heard what I told Ana. "Come here, snot nose, who are you going to see? Remember that I am your mother and nobody else, especially that lazy old hag along with your grandmother Sinforosa." She grabbed me by my arms. I thought, *A daughter needs love always. If you can't give me a mother's love, give me my freedom to find that love elsewhere.* I stared at her face, and my tears started to flow.

She released me; immediately I ran out of that house. I ran through the street with no destination in mind. I saw kids from the neighborhood playing. I wiped my eyes clean and approached them. They were happy to see me; they asked me to join them. I wanted to, but I needed the bathroom. Ruby, one of my friends, invited me to her house. After I did what was necessary, Ruby was waiting for me. "Rosita," said Ruby, "my mother wants to meet you."

Ruby's mother was a very beautiful lady. I saw a señora with long black hair like a moonless night, not a single gray hair. "Come get closer to me," she asked me. "Who is your family? I see you walking by here always real early, sometimes with Don Felipe. I hear people talking about you. Some call you Alma de Dios, others say your name is Rosita or Jovani. Now you tell me what your name is and who your parents are." I smiled and couldn't stop admiring the beautiful lady. "I am Rosita Reza Bustos, and my grandmother Sinforosa named me Alma de Dios before I was baptized. My mother is Reyna Bustos, and who my father is, well, only my Diosito knows."

"Rosita, I know your mother, Reyna. I understand that she has a daughter that is epileptic. Don't tell me that you are the daughter with epilepsy." I felt uneasy having to answer that I am the one with epilepsy. The look in her face, when I didn't answer, said it all. "Oh my lord," she said, "I don't mean to pry. I'm sorry, Rosita."

"Señora, I should be going, my friends are waiting for me."

"Rosita, promise that you will come back when you finish playing, I have something for you." Ruby, Rafa, Israel, and Mauricio were waiting for me. We played a game called *rehata* (tag) and finished with a game called avion (hopscotch). The missus was waiting for me when we finished playing. She gave me a bag full of clothes, which I wasn't ready to accept. I told Ruby's mother that I didn't like to receive something without me returning the favor. I volunteered to wash diapers or to help her clean her house. She smiled at me. "Rosita, who are you? Really I'm surprised that you have such a beautiful heart after all that you go through."

"Señora, don't worry about me, Diosito is always with me." She handed me the bag and a $50 bill.

I struggled with the heavy bag full of clothes. Along the way I ran into an old man that I'd seen somewhere before. "Alma de Dios, where are you going with such a big bag?" I put the bag on the ground and asked him, "Señor, how is it that you me?"

"You don't remember me, eh? I am the butcher."

"Forgive me, Señor Rafael Arce, now I remember where I've seen you." Don Rafael handed me some money. "Señor, why are you handing me these pesos? I don't work for you." He laughed. "Please accept the money." I thanked him for the pesos, made the sign of the cross with the money, picked up my bag, and continued on home.

To avoid a confrontation with Reyna, I entered the house very quietly. I didn't want Reyna to know that I was home. I reached the safety of my little corner, made the sign of the cross, and thanked God. "Chuchin," I prayed, "thank You for all that You grant me day after day. Please grant me what I ask for, and I will continue to ask to rid these attacks that I suffer." Ana was listening; she had snuck up on me. "Vani, what do you have in that bag?"

"Ana, you startled me, I didn't know you were listening. You know Ruby Arce, don't you? Her mother gave this bag full of clothes."

"Vani, let's go in the kitchen, don't be afraid of Reyna."

The clothes were really nice; we were making enough fuss that Reyna heard us. She shouted, "What are you two doing? Come here, tell me what the fuss is all about." I looked at Ana. "I don't want to go. I'm going to Mama Lucia's." I left the house as rapidly as I could. Mama Lucia was busy with customers. I started to help. The customers were always nice to me. I usually knew each customer, but not the one that was seated alongside another man with a big sombrero. I took him his order; he said to me, "You are a beautiful little girl and quite a worker, aren't you? What is your name?"

I smiled at him. "Señor, before I tell you my name, thank for saying that I am a beautiful little girl." I extended my right arm to the gentleman. "*Rosita* is my name, and I'm glad to meet you."

"Señorita, the pleasure is mine." The other señor asked, "And you are the daughter of whom?"

"Well, señor, naturally of my mother, and you?" Both men smiled at my response. The men paid for their meal and handed me some money as well. Mama Lucia told me to accept it. "It is a tip," she told me, "for being a good worker." I wrote in my diary: "Today I learned two things: *tip* and *pleasure is mine.*"

Walking home on Sundays was not that safest time to walk alone. The streets are full of drunks, so I was being very aware of my surroundings going home that night from Mama Lucia's. I was walking near the store of my padrino Martin, when I heard somebody shout my name. I stopped and turned in the direction where the shout had come from. I saw a person lying on his stomach in the middle of the street. I walked closer to the man lying in the street, thinking that maybe he had the same sickness like me and had a convulsion. Another person was walking by. "Little girl, be careful, he is Bolita, the pueblo drunkard."

Drunk again, I thought, *but this time I'm not going to help him to the curb.* Instead I stayed close to him to make sure he wasn't run over by a car. Finally he came to. "Alma de Dios, do you remember me?"

"Sure I remember you, I saw you just a few days ago. But you, Bolita, are not drunk. I know because you remembered who I am." He started to sing his favorite song, "Que diren los de tu casa..."

"Bolita, you should sing instead of getting drunk." He laughed.

"Alma de Dios, come sit where we can talk." Away from the street we sat. "I am going to tell you something that nobody else besides me knows. I live far from here in a house that nobody can enter but me. My house doesn't have doors, and I live with several sweethearts."

"Oh, Bolita, how is it possible for a drunkard like you to have so many sweethearts?"

"Alma de Dios, someday I will show you where I live, and even show some of them to you." I started to laugh at what he said. "Bolita, why don't you tell one of your girlfriends to come and help you?"

"Rosita, it's not possible, but someday I will show them to you." I left him on the side of the street and headed to my hiding place. I took my tips I'd earned and put them in my hiding place.

Everybody but Ana was asleep when I got home. The night was being lit by the light of the moon. I waited for Ana to also go to bed. I went outside, sat on the steps, put my hands on my chin, and arms on my crossed legs. I sighed a deep breath while admiring the moon. It was a beautiful tranquil night, until I heard steps. Somebody was coming around the house. I grabbed a clay pot with the intent of whacking the intruder. It was Bolita struggling to stay on his feet by holding on to the wall. He didn't see me, but before I said anything to him, he fell on the dirt floor. I approached him to see if he was okay. He was passed out. I went for a small blanket to cover him. I forgot about the moon and went to bed.

Early the next morning, I brewed coffee for Bolita and Don Felipe. Bolita was already up and washing his face. He was grateful for the coffee. "Bolita, the coffee will help you with your hangover."

"Rosita, I only get drunk on Sundays. But didn't I see you last night?"

"Yes, Bolita, we talked last night, before you came here and passed out drunk." He laughed; he said, "You and I talked last night?"

"Yes, Bolita, we talked, and you told me that your house has no doors and that you have many sweethearts living with you. Bolita, if you have so many sweethearts, you should tell them to come and help you get home."

"Rosita, I live with snakes, they are my sweethearts, but nobody knows but you."

"Bolita, you also told me to enter through the roof using a rope ladder, and you kept on mumbling."

"Rosita, did I scare you?"

"Bolita, I don't know what a snake is. But when you invite me over, you can show me your snakes, okay?"

"Rosita, I will bring you my Alicia, my favorite snake, so you can meet her. I'll be here early tomorrow morning with her."

Don Felipe was happy, as usual, with his coffee. I cleaned his room and took off to the house. Reyna was up, I greeted her. Her response was, "Don't bother me, I'm getting ready to go out." Ana was waking up, and the babies were asleep. I said, "Ana, can I talk to you?"

"Yes, Vani, what is it?"

"Did you know that Reyna is going someplace?"

"Vani, let her go wherever she wants to go, just let me sleep." I thought, *Ana is right, forget about Reyna. I don't want to get a beating for being nosy.*

Reyna came to the room. "Jovani," she said, "if your mamacita comes to the pueblo, go with her." I was so surprised, I ran outside and thanked Diosito. My tears flowed from happiness and not because I'm a crybaby. Don Felipe motioned me over to his place. I approached him with tears watering my eyes. "Mija, why are you crying?"

"Señor Felipe, never will I tire of the countless doubts that I have. I must value my health and wait for the elusive mother's hug. Don Felipe, try not to laugh, but if Reyna is not my mother, she should tell me."

He smiled. "Rosita, she is your mother. Pray to your Diosito, ask Him to forgive Reyna." The old man invited me to go to church with him. I hesitated because I wanted to see Reyna when she left. I wanted to know where she was going.

Bolita and Isabela

BOLITA RETURNED; HE SAID, "LOOK, Rosita, I brought Alicia." He opened a big enclosed cage, told me to peek inside. I did, and what I saw was the biggest and ugliest worm I'd set my set my eyes on. I screamed and jumped. "Bolita, she's not going to bite me, is she?"

"No, she won't bite you. She bites when she is angry. If she gets angry, she is liable to bite or even choke you." I took another peek; she had two heads! "Bolita, your snake has two heads." I didn't have the nerve to see any more of the multicolored worm with skin that resembled a rough tree trunk. Bolita took a small container with milk and gave it to Alicia, the snake. He took the snake and wrapped it around his neck. "Do you like my woman?" he asked. My knees were shaking from fear watching that ugly worm so big. He knew that I was scared, so he put her back in her cage and took off with his friend.

I decided to follow Bolita and find out where he lived. He walked toward a place called San Pedro. Every time he looked back, I hid from his sight. He was not aware of me when he reached the place he called home. It was an old adobe home, hidden on the west side by a nice inviting hill, and a big tree next to his house. He climbed the tree, untied a rope from the tree. He looked around as though sensing that he was not alone. He opened the aluminum cover on top of the house. After a while, he took the rope and slid down the opened roof into the house. I waited a short while before deciding to climb the tree. What I saw inside the house shocked me. Nothing but snakes! Some were wrapping around Bolita, others moving making hissing sounds. There was a snake much bigger than Alicia. I climbed down the tree and ran as fast as I could until

I couldn't run anymore. I was exhausted and thirsty when I arrived at my kinder class.

"Jovani, you look frightened, what happened? Niña, come here, tell me what is troubling you." I looked at the nun, thinking, *This lady doesn't miss anything.* "Jovani, you look pale, and your face is all red. Tell me, what's troubling you?" I smiled and said nothing about the snakes. She handed me a glass of water. "Don't want to talk, Jovani? I'll wait. In time you will tell me." As I entered the classroom, there was a group of boys talking near my desk. They broke up when they saw me coming in. One of them, Josecito, approached me; he said, "Jovani, is it true that you are an orphan, that you don't have any parents?" It took me by surprise. I thought, *I wonder how many people think that I'm an orphan. I'm always alone, and Reyna never comes to my school.*

I stared at the scrawny kid standing in front of me, smiling waiting for an answer. The others behind were also smirking, wanting to know my answer. I wanted to scream, but I held back, but I couldn't hold back my tears. I walked out of the room full of emotion; sadness engulfed me. I sat at a nearby bench and cried. Sister Sarita followed me. "Jovani, ignore what Josecito said, continue being who you are." I looked at her, tried to smile, wiped my tears, and went back to class. I didn't quite understand what she meant by her advice.

After class was over, I walked to Mama Lucia's, playing with my shadow that never leaves me, looking up at the sky hoping for a glance of the Almighty. I arrived at the puesto, Mama Lucia was busy preparing the usual menu for the day. She noticed a difference in me. "Mija, are you okay? Tell me. I know you too well to know that something is bothering you." I smiled, not saying a word, just thought, *What's with these ladies? First Madre Sarita, and now Mama Lucia realize that something is bothering me.* "Rosita, your eyes speak for you, but you say nothing." I couldn't help myself, I ran to and hugged her. I said, "Mama Lucia, I am not an orphan, I have you."

"Yes, mija, you have me."

Mama Lucia had the carton full of candies ready for me. I took my candies first to church. I entrusted myself to my Diosito and to the Blessed Virgin hoping for a good day. I walked through the terrace into what looked like a class in session. Little children were sitting on the floor listening to a teacher. The teacher had a long stick in his hand pointing to a drawing on a blackboard perched atop a simple chair. The teacher hesitated the moment he saw me; all the students turned around to see why their teacher had stopped. The teacher invited me over to the front of the class. "Little girl," he said, "would you like to join my class?" I told him that I went to kinder with the nuns. He introduced himself as David, the teacher. I extended my hand, simultaneously saying my name is *Rosita Jovani Reza Bustos.*

"Rosita, I see you around the pueblo all the time. Now I see you selling candies."

"Yes, Señor David, I have to work. Otherwise, I don't eat." I excused myself from him and the class. Usually Mondays is a very slow day. The taxi drivers are regular customers, so that's where I usually start my Monday sales. After a few sales to the chauffeurs, I went around the pueblo looking for customers. I ran into Rede, the daughter Doña Castañeda. She invited me to her house. Being that the sales were slow, I accepted my friend's invitation. Doña Castañeda had prepared lunch and invited me to eat with them. After I ate, I told Mrs. Castañeda that I'd like to help clean up. She refused my help. "No," she said, "you go about your business, I'll clean up."

Doña Castañeda handed me a bag with tacos to take home. I wasn't hungry being that I had just finished eating; she smiled and insisted that I take them. "Alma de Dios, promise that if you are ever hungry, you will come here, or if you need a place to sleep, my door's always open to you." She gave me a hug; I thought of Reyna. I walked with no sense of direction, just lost in the moment. I realized that I was close to Don Felipe's little room. I took him the tacos that Doña Castañeda had given me.

The sound of the church bells reminded me that it was time to go to my kinder class. I was really anxious and prepared to recite my poem to Madre Sarita. Madre Sarita was preparing the room when I arrived. We greeted each other and talked some before she asked me about the status of the poem. I smiled, thinking, *Finally she asked me about the poem.* "Remember, Rosita, we have but a few days before you will be carrying the flag, and then you are to recite your poem."

"Madre, do you want to hear my poem?"

"Yes," she sounded excited, "do you have a copy?"

"No, Madre Sarita, it's all in my head."

"Well, then wait until I get some paper, I want to write it down."

My poem:

Lovely Mexican Flag

Displaying three colors proud
Rosita my given name
Named like the wild rose
Like the beautiful flower
I endure what I have endured
Always wrestling for my life
Wrestling for a living
Like the flower sprouting for life
Day by day I continue my path
Always where I wander in loneliness
Recalling my wonderful people
My lovely pueblo that I love
Tetipac with its splendor
With all the flowering hills
With beautiful people with golden hearts

Ana wasn't too surprised to see me in a torn dress with a bandaged leg. I had come home in worse shape before after one of my convulsions, so she assumed that I'd had another epileptic attack. Yes, I had suffered a different attack this time. After telling her the truth, she was still not convinced. I showed her the bite mark and told her that my madrina had cleaned and dressed my wound. All she said was, "Vani, if it isn't one bad thing, it's another." She glanced at my dressed-up wound and continued knitting.

I felt very tired, told Ana that I was going to bed. I walked to my little corner of the room where I feel safe. I made the sign of the cross, closed my eyes, and talked to my Diosito. I told Him about the dog, my madrina. I woke up realizing that I had fallen asleep talking to my Chuchin. It was real early; all my sisters were still asleep. Not having eaten since yesterday, I woke up hungry; my stomach was making all kinds of noises. I warmed a tortilla, some leftover goat meat, and some salsa. The salsa was bad; I'd forgotten to store it atop a place in the roof where it would stay cool.

Later that morning after Ana left for work, I walked outside to dump the dirty dishwater. I dumped the water near the woodpile and was startled to see movement around the wood. I was looking at a snake bigger than Alicia but with only one head. I thought of Bolita and his sweethearts. I thought, *Should I get it and take the snake to Bolita?* I remembered how Bolita handled Alicia and thought that I could handle this one. I got a big bag and, with some corn, lured the snake into the bag. I dragged the bag and hid it near the bougainvillia.

My sisters were crying. I fed Blanquita and Beni, dressed and took them to the puesto. I told Mama Lucia that I would give her all my tips if she would care for my two sisters for a while. I couldn't tell her about the snake, so I told her a little fib. She didn't but my excuse; she knew me too well and knew that I wasn't being truthful with her. I had to tell her about the snake and that I was taking it to Bolita. "Rosita," she said, "of all that happens to you, and now you trapped a snake. Don't you know that snakes are very dangerous?"

"Mama Lucia, don't worry, Bolita showed me how to handle snakes."

"But why Bolita?"

"Mama Lucia, Bolita has many snakes, he lives with them."

"Rosita, how do you know all that?"

"Mama Lucia, I followed him to his house, I saw all the snakes inside."

"Oh, niña, I ask, who are you? I guess that I can't hold you back. Go on, I'll take care of your sisters."

I struggled with the snake, but I made it to his house. I tied a rock to the rope I had with me, I flung the end with the rock over a branch. I climbed the tree with the snake in the bag. From there I threw the bag with the snake into the house. As I was coming down the tree, I met Bolita. He was surprised to see me. "What are you doing here?" he asked. I told him that I had captured a snake for him. "I just threw the snake into your house," I told him. "Oh, Rosita, I hope the other snakes don't eat your snake. They don't like strangers."

I ran back to the puesto. Mama Lucia was relieved to see me. I gave her a complete account of my trip to the house of snakes and Bolita. "Rosita, how is it that you know that Bolita has lots of snakes living with him?"

"Well, señora, one day I found him lying on the street, he was drunk. That's when he told me about his girlfriends, as he calls them. Now he has another one."

I started helping with the customers. I happened to glance down the street and saw Bolita walking toward the puesto. "Rosita, thanks for the snake. Here, this is for bringing me the snake." He handed me ten pesos. I refused to take it, and he insisted. "Tell you what, Bolita, let's have a footrace, just you and I. If I win, then I will take the money. If I lose, I pay you." One of the customers heard us. He shouted we are having a footrace. Pretty soon a small crowd gathered near the race site.

I could hear people making bets; some wagered on me, and many others on him. Mama Lucia heard all the commotion; she approached me. "Niña, what are you up to now?"

"Señora Lucia, I'm going to race Bolita for ten pesos. But don't worry, I run all over the pueblo, whereas he can barely walk." The distance of the race was set, from the puesto to the church. We lined up near a makeshift starting line. As soon as Bolita said *go*, I ran like the wind. I left Bolita behind eating my dust. The poor man couldn't run. The men in the audience shouted at Bolita to run faster; he was no match. I ran to the church and back; he barely made it to the church.

A few men that witnessed the race applauded as they came up to me and handed me pesos for winning the race. Others challenged me to race against them. I just laughed, didn't accept any challenges. Bolita made it back to the puesto and handed me the ten pesos in front of others.

I helped Mama Lucia close her puesto. After I cleaned my two sisters, we headed for the church. The lady in charge of cleaning the church was busy going about her duties. I sat my sisters on a bench and asked the lady if I could help her. She was more than happy to have me help with the janitorial work. I worked my way up to where my Diosito was looking at me. I looked up at Him and said, "Do you know why I am cleaning the church? Because the church is always open to those of us that come in to confide in You their sins and ask for forgiveness."

I turned my head when I heard the lady call me, "Alma de Dios, thank you for helping me clean. When you are through here, come by the house. I have some goodies to give you."

"Thank you, señora, but forgive me, I forgot your name."

"That's okay, Alma de Dios, my name is *Carmela Bustos*." I finished mopping the floor, put the mop and pail away. I strapped Beni on my back, grabbed Blanquita, and took off to Doña Carmela's house. Poor Blanquita, she wanted to be carried, but instead she wrestled with her baby steps.

Doña Tolita, Blanquita's Godmother, and Her Loving Story

ON OUR WAY TO DOÑA Carmela's house, Doña Tolita caught up with us. She didn't greet us, which I thought unusual, but she did talk to us. "You are the daughters of Reyna Bustos, aren't you?" I was a little tired, and I don't think that I responded in a friendly manner. "Yes, Doña Tolita, we are Reyna's daughters. You should remember I am Rosita Jovani, also known as Alma de Dios, and you, Señora Tolita, are the godmother of Blanquita." I turned to my little sister Blanquita. "Say hello to your godmother." Blanquita came forward and got her wish. Doña Tolita picked her up in her arms and carried her.

"Amparo," Doña Tolita shouted to her sister, "look what I have in my arms." I saw this good-looking, tall lady as she walked toward us. "This is my godchild, I baptized her," she told Amparo, "and her name is Blanquita."

"What a beautiful godchild you have, Tolita, and this other little child is very beautiful also." I was very happy for Blanquita; now she had her godmother's love. "Amparo," Doña Tolita said, "this 'little mother,' I call her that because she is always taking care of her two sisters, is Rosita Jovani." Amparo looked at me. "Rosita," she said, "I have seen you with these two little girls all over, and I didn't realize that you were Reyna's daughters." The two ladies faced each other to talk probably about us three orphaned girls.

Doña Tolita turned to talk to me; she asked, "Do you still suffer from epileptic attacks?"

"Yes, I still have convulsions, but someday my Diosito is going to cure me." She looked at me. "Ah," she said, "you are a true blessed child of God, and I believe you. Your grandmother Doña Sinforosa asked me to look after you and your sisters."

"My mamacita did that?"

"Yes, Alma de Dios, she did. She also has told me a lot about you, how you take care of your sisters. I can see that you take good care of them. Alma de Dios, my house is always open to you and your sisters. If you need a place to stay or if you need anything, please let me know."

"Thank you, but we have a home. I take care of them with the help of Mama Lucia. She helps me during the time I'm working." Doña Tolita looked surprised. "You work as well as taking care of these two niñas? You are an incredible girl for being so young." She spoke as she put her hands on my shoulders. "Alma de Dios, I want you to bring my goddaughter to my house while you work. My sister Amparo and I will take good care of her." She gave me a hug, like one I've longed from my mother; I felt love in that embrace. I was about to leave, but they insisted that we visit with them.

I accepted because my sisters were tired and needed their nap. Once inside their house, Amparo took them into the bedroom. Doña Tolita offered me fruit. "Alma de Dios," she asked, "do you want to talk with Roberto?"

"Señora, who is Roberto?" I looked around the room trying to see Roberto. "I don't see anybody here, señora." She answered, "Roberto is quite a talker, but be careful with him, he likes to bite."

"Señora, you have a son that likes to bite?" She laughed. "No, niña, I don't have any children, I'm talking about my parrot. Come, let me show you Roberto."

She led me to her patio; there inside a huge cage was a very big beautiful parrot. I was amazed when the parrot said, "Hola, hola." I got closer to the cage, and the parrot flapped his wings across the plate full of water and splattered water all over me. The parrot then whistled at me and shouted, "Tolita, Tolita." I couldn't hold back my laughter. Then this big dog comes up to me wanting to play ball. "His name is Oso," the owner told me. She showed me around her beautiful backyard. I marveled at the beautiful flowers and all the shrubbery. She looked at my eyes, saying, "You love nature, don't you? I can tell by the way you smile, and the sparkle in your eyes tell a lot about you."

I felt so comfortable in that garden, I started to hop and skip and even took some of her berries. I sang one of my favorite songs, and soon the parrot joined in. He kept singing and shouting, "Viva México." We sang, "Alla en el rancho grande…" The parrot and I were having a great time. I enjoyed the way the parrot talked, and Doña Tolita was entertained as well by the parrot and me. Amparo asked us to join her. As soon as I walked in the house, I could smell the freshly baked bread. The table was set with all kinds of freshly cooked goodies ready for us to eat.

Doña Tolita went into the bedroom for my sisters. Blanquita and Beni were wearing beautiful new clothes. One of them reminded me of the one that awful dog had destroyed when he attacked me. Amparo showed me where I could wash my hands. Before we ate, Amparo and Doña Tolita blessed the food. All of us said grace before eating. I noticed how the two ladies handled the silverware while they ate. Very carefully I followed what they were doing while they ate. After we ate, I asked to be excused. I started to clean the table where my sisters ate. Doña Tolita was surprised that I knew what I was doing. Of course I had learned from Mama Lucia. I do this every time at her place, when I help her.

It was time to go; as Doña Tolita was helping to strap Beni on my back, we discussed the days I would bring Blanquita to her house. Before we left, the señora picked Blanquita in her arms, looked at me, and glanced at Beni. "Alma de Dios, do you think that your mother would consider allowing me to adopt these two niñas?" So many thoughts entered my mind. *Would be nice having my sisters in a place where they are not alone, and they would be close to me. But no, they are my sisters. I will take care of them.* I just smiled at Ms. Tolita; she knew that it would not be possible. Doña Tolita handed me a bag with food for Ana; we left.

Ana came home tired. I had the table and the warmed food waiting for her. She told me about her day, and I shared with her the discussions I had with Doña Tolita and the parrot. After we cleaned up, I asked Ana if I could go back to Doña Tolita's. My sister looked at me. "Vani, didn't you just spend most of the day at her house?" I answered, "Yes, but she is so nice and very interesting. I want to learn more from her, especially about Mamacita Sinforosa."

"Fine, Vani, you can go, just don't come late, okay?"

Doña Tolita was very happy to see me. "Did you come alone?" She poked her head out the door, looked around to see if I had brought Blanquita with me. "Yes, I came alone, I want to speak with you if that's okay with you."

"Of course, mija, come in." She offered some atole, a porridgelike goodie made of blue ground corn. We sat on the sofa. "Okay, mija, tell me what is on that curious mind of yours."

"Señora, I hear that Reza is not my father, others say that Jorge Bustos is my real father. The first time I asked my mother, she scolded me for asking. Next time I asked her if Jorge Bustos was my father, she gave me a severe spanking for asking. That is why I'm here to see if you know the truth."

"Mija, I have known your mother, Reyna, since she was a little girl. I knew your grandpa Domingo and your mamacita Sinforosa also."

"Señora, you knew my abuelito Domingo?"

"Yes, I did, your grandpa Domingo was a very kind man and a gentleman. When he walked, his stride was that of a caballero, always dressed like one too. When he looked at you, his face spoke volumes, you knew what was on his mind. Before he and Sinforosa, your mamacita, were married, Sinforosa and her first husband, your uncle Rubén's father, came into the pueblo regularly."

"Mamacita was married before she married my abuelito Domingo? And my uncle Rubén is not my mother's brother?"

"Wait, Alma de Dios, your mother and your uncle Rubén are related through your mamacita, she is their mother." She waited to continue, allowing the information to sink into my young and innocent brain. "Doña Tolita, what happened to mamacita's first husband?"

"I heard that one day he and your mamacita were caught in a torrential downpour, and he was swept by the flood into the river and drowned. Your mamacita was helpless, she watched as her husband was swept by the rushing muddy river." Tears started to flow as she told me that story; I thought of my poor mamacita.

"Alma de Dios, so you want to hear more?"

"Yes, señora, please continue, I'm okay."

"Your grandfather had never been married until he met Sinforosa. After her husband died, Domingo hired her as a maid. In time they fell in love and got married." More tears from my teary eyes; I couldn't hold them back. She smiled and continued, "The people in the pueblo talked, but neither cared. Some would mention the difference in their age, others that she was once a maid and now married to one of the richest men in the area."

I was anxious to ask the Doña a question, but I didn't know how she would take it. Finally I asked in my innocence, "Doña Tolita, did you ever fall in love?" She paused for several moments. I could see her eyes watering a little bit. "Yes, mija, I did, I was in love once, but I never married." I didn't say anything, waiting for more information. Then she spoke very quietly. "I was in love with Domingo, your grandfather." I was speechless; I acted instantly without thinking and gave her a hug. A few moments passed while she cleaned her tears; looking at me, she said, "Alma de Dios, your eyes say a lot about yourself, just like your grandfather Domingo. But you're more like Sinforosa, she was strong-willed, always working, and very religious. So no, niña, I never fell in love again, now you see me an old lady with nothing but memories of what could have been.

"Your grandparents loved your mother, she had everything, and that's why I can't understand why she treats you so bad." Again my tears started to flow. "Doña Tolita, the pain I suffer is not so much from my falls when I have a convulsion but from the rejection of a mother's love. I love my mother, but the times when she rejects my love or when she beats me with a belt, it feels as though a sword is piercing my heart." This time she gave me a hug with these words. "Mija, don't feel sad, and someday your mother will show her love for you.

"Alma de Dios, can I call you Rosita?" I nodded yes. "Rosita, let me share this with you: what you feel in your heart is to feel the love within your body. The stomach is the part that your body feels hunger, and in your brain is that part that guides you into the person you want to be in your life. The sad thing is sometimes we don't take into consideration our personal self-esteem. Niña, you are very sentimental."

"Señora, forgive me for asking, but if I want to learn, I have to ask, what is sentimental?"

"Ah, mija, you are right. If you don't ask, you don't learn. Well, in your case, *sentimental* means this—that a person like you is very loving and cares for all the people."

Before I left her house, Doña Tolita went to her jewelry chest, took out some jewelry. I just watched from the sofa. She showed me several of the most beautiful earrings I'd ever seen. "Rosita, I've had these earrings since I was a young girl. I want to give you a set, pick the ones you like." I loved all of them, but I couldn't just take a set without giving something in return. "Señora, why are you giving these away, don't you use them?"

"Rosita, I used to when I was young, but as you can see, I'm no longer young."

"Señora, don't say that, the wrinkles not only show age, but reveal the life of honesty a person has lived." When I finished talking, she looked at me and asked, "Rosita, *who are you*? I marvel how you speak at such a young age." I selected a pair of earrings. I started to put them on, but I couldn't. "Rosita, you must have your ears pierced," she told me. "Rosita, those earrings were given to me by your abuelito Domingo when we were young." She took them from me with a big sigh; she kissed them and gave them back to me.

Amparo walked into the room with a couple of dirty diapers my sisters had left behind. Doña Tolita told me to wash them in her laundry, she didn't want me to take them home all dirty. I was real happy, not because I was washing dirty diapers, but by the manner that Doña Tolita and Amparo had treated me. I was washing and singing at the same time. Being that the laundry was outside, my voice carried beyond the walls. "What a beautiful voice you have, you should be a professional singer." I looked around to where the voice was originating from. It was the brother-in-law of Doña Tolita. The parrot let loose and sang along with me.

I had to laugh at the way that parrot was singing. I heard applause coming from some boys who were standing near the fence. I turned to face them. "What are you boys doing back there?"

"Sing another, please sing another song." I approached them. "So you boys want to hear me sing another, huh?"

"Yes, we like your voice, you sing very pretty," one boy said. "Tell you boys what I'll do. If you boys go to catechism, I will sing a lot of songs." They looked at one another. "What's that cata…something? Catechism?"

"Don't you know that in catechism we learn about our Diosito?" I explained everything we did in that class. They promised to go to catechism class.

I was about to leave the comfort of Doña Tolita's when she asked me to wait. She gave me a bag full of fruit from her place. Ana was so happy when she saw the bag full of fruits. "Vani, you are truly remarkable, all these people are always giving you something." She pulled out a guayaba from the bag and ate it. I took all the bananas, avocados, plums, and the rest of the guayabas. "Vani, you are so lucky but, so am I for having you as my sister."

"Ana, I feel like going to the church, is that okay? If you want, you can go with me." She made a funny face. "Vani, you go, but be careful."

I cut some flowers to take to Diosito sitting atop the altar. I stayed inside the church until the caretaker, Don Luis Landa, began to close the doors. I exited the side door near the fountain; I had a convulsion. When I came to, I was inside the fountain. I didn't hurt myself; for once, I didn't have a knot on my head. Thanks to God, the fountain was bone-dry and the bottom was full of soft sand. I walked to the main gate; it was locked with a chain and lock. *How am I getting out of here?* I thought. *My Diosito will send help to get me out of here.*

Sergio, the son of Doña Tere, the owner of the bakery in the pueblo, was passing by. "Sergio, Sergio," I shouted. Finally he turned and saw me inside the church property. "Jovani, what are you doing inside? Don't tell me that you're locked in and can't get out?"

"I can't get out, will you help me?"

"Jovani, I will help you, but it's going to cost you."

"Sergio, what is your price?"

"You know the chewing gum that I like, well, you will have to give me one."

"Sergio, if you help me, I will not only give you one, I will give you two." He jumped over the wall. "Jovani, I'm going to help you to the top, okay? You wait for me there while I go for a ladder, I don't want you to jump, you promise?"

"Yes, Sergio, I will wait, I promise not to jump." He picked me up, put me on his shoulders, and I was able to climb to the top. He climbed with no problem. "Jovani, remember not to jump. I'll be back with a ladder." While I was waiting, I noticed a man taking pictures of me.

He got me out of the church grounds. "Now tell me, Jovani, how did you manage to get locked up?"

"Sergio, I left the church through the back door because the caretaker had locked the front door. I was close to the fountain when I had a convulsion. When I came to, all the gates were locked."

"Jovani, I am going to walk you home, I want to make sure that you get home safe."

"Thank you, Sergio, but you don't have to."

"I know, but I'm taking you home anyway."

Ana was waiting for me. "Vani, you had another convulsion, didn't you?" I told Ana everything that had happened to me, including my conversion with Doña Tolita. "Ana, I have seen a man taking pictures of me. I don't know why, but next time I see him, I'm going to tell him to stop."

"Vani, if he is taking pictures of you, then starting tomorrow, comb your hair and start wearing the pretty clothes that Doña Tolita gave you." I didn't like the way my sister was talking to me. "Ana, the clothes she gave me are too big. My clothes are old, but they are always clean. I mean they are clean when I leave the house, but they always get dirty when I have a convulsion.

"I hope that photographer is good at taking pictures, but I'm going to tell him not to take my picture anymore."

"Vani, he takes your picture maybe because he sees you as a very interesting person."

"But, Ana, you know that I don't presume to be anybody other than who I am. Now whoever wants to see me for who I am, fine. If not, he shouldn't see me."

I walked out of the house, walked toward the gate. I heard the sound of kittens. I looked under a big wooded pile; there underneath was a litter of kittens. I reached for one of the beautiful little kittens, but the mother snarled at me. I backed away real quick; I didn't want any part of her sharp teeth. The cat's growl was heard by Ana; she came out to investigate. "Vani, leave those kittens alone. If you don't, the mother is liable to kill them." I was thinking about what Ana said as I followed her back inside the house. The following day I went looking for the kittens, and as Ana had warned me, the mother killed all her kittens. For many days after that, I cried for and couldn't sleep thinking about those poor kittens.

That first night when the kittens were slain, I had an interesting dream. I dreamt that I was running to the church, but I was stopped by two men all dressed up. They told me that the doors were locked. They told me that a wedding was taking place and I couldn't go in. They told me that the daughter of the mayor was getting married. In my dream they informed me that the wedding was between two honorable people. He called me a snot-nosed kid and told me to leave. "Look at you, your hair is a mess, and look at those ugly pants you're wearing. Where did you come from, ugly little girl, look at those torn tennis shoes." They laughed at me. "Laugh all you want, but I will not leave." I sat on the steps waiting until the people of means came out of the church.

To my surprise, the two well-dressed men guarding the entrance left. I entered the church, inching myself toward the altar along the interior wall. A well-dressed lady saw me; she shouted, "Get this filthy girl out of here." The bride and groom and everybody turned to face me. The bride ran to where I was, grabbed me by my hair. The people were surprised at what they saw. My Diosito emerged from the cross, stretched his hands at the bride; He said, "Leave her be, for every pain she suffers at your hand, I also suffer the same pain." She let go of my hair and ran out of the church along with the rest of the people.

I stayed with my Diosito; He told me, "You are with Me, and you will always be loved."

"Thank You, Diosito, for being with me when I feel slighted by others." Diosito told me, "Feel loved by Me, walk straight always, now leave through the front door." I woke up happy in my little corner from my incredible dream. I feel it in my heart that my dreams are very real. If they weren't real, does my Diosito defend me? Why does He talk to me if my dreams weren't real? Now I ask myself what others have asked me: Who am I? It was still dark when I woke from my dream. I got up, went outside, sat on the stairs from where I could talk to the moon.

I noticed movement beyond the bushes. It was the lady in white. Even though I'd seen her before, I still got chills when I saw her. She looked beautiful dressed in a fine white fabric. The ray from the moon showed the brilliance of the dress she had on. She looked at me, but didn't speak. She made a gesture with her hands, moving them and down. I didn't understand what she was trying to convey. I confess she was scaring me; I promptly left the light of the moon and went inside. I fell asleep thinking, *Why was the lady in white so serious this time?* I fell asleep wondering, with no answer possible answer.

At daybreak I was fixing Don Felipe his favorite morning brew. I anxiously took the coffee to him because I was just as anxious to have everything written that I had gone through since the last time I wrote my diary. My old friend took out paper, including the carbon paper, and wrote everything just like I remembered it. He hid the original notes in his cabinet and the carbon copies in another cabinet. I knew where he kept both the originals and the copies. He was my keeper; he was saving them for me.

Ana was waiting for me when I got home. "I see that you have been busy already this morning, Vani."

"Yes I already took Don Felipe his coffee, and he wrote what I have been through the past few days."

"Vani, we have a busy morning ahead of us. We have to clean our side of the street, and it's especially more important because of the parade that's going to be passing by here." I put on the full-length apron Doña Tolita gave me. I spoke loud enough for Ana to hear; I said, "I will put my good hands to work." Ana looked at me. "What? What do you mean, and where did you learn to speak like that?"

"Ana, I hear that in the street, the laborers say that all the time." With my good hands, I finished sweeping our side of the street.

Aunt Pina saw me working too much and offered me some tea. Ana gave me permission, and I went for my tea.

I went across the street where Tía Pina lives with my other tia, Feliz Martínez. Aunt Pina had a chicken all cut up and fresh eggs for me to take home with me. She gave me a nice cup of lemonade instead. Her son Marcelo entered the kitchen. She told us, "Marcelo, you and Alma de Dios are siblings. Marcelo, I want you to take care of her, you hear me? She is your sister, and brothers should take care of their sisters."

"Tía, how is that possible? I have nothing but sisters, I don't have any brothers."

"Niña, Marcelo is your brother on your father's side."

"Tía, you know who my father is?"

"Niña, don't you know that Jorge Bustos is your father? Marcelo knows that his father is Jorge." My aunt looked at me with a puzzled look on her face. "Alma de Dios, forget what I said, someday you will discover the truth."

I went home with the cut-up chicken and the fresh eggs. Ana was taking a bath, and my two sisters were asleep. I started the fire in the oven and placed the chicken in a skillet to fry. In the meantime, I washed some diapers then made tortillas. Before we sat down for breakfast, Ana fed her boss's dogs. Both little sisters were nice and clean. During breakfast I told Ana that I had met Marcelo. She wasn't surprised when I told her that Tía Pina told me that Marcelo was my brother, that both of us are related through our father, Jorge Bustos. I thought, *Why doesn't Ana say a thing? Would it be because she knows who my biological father is?*

She changed subject on me. "Vani, it's that time of the year when we have to take our sisters for their vaccination." I thought, *I was right. Ana knows but doesn't want to tell me. I think she is afraid of our mother and doesn't dare tell me the truth.* I didn't say anything. "Vani, did you hear me? We have to take our sisters to the clinic."

"Ana, I have an idea."

"What are you up to now, my little sister?"

"Let's pack a lunch, and on the way back, we'll go swimming in the somersault hole located in the river Ahualulco."

"Vani, that is a great idea." We packed some leftover chicken, some soup, and other goodies for our picnic. The nurse vaccinated my sisters. She said it was okay to take them swimming.

I was real happy because we were going on a picnic as a family. "Vani, I want you to relax, you know what happens when you get too excited."

"Ana, don't worry, my Diosito won't let anything bad happen to me." It was a long ways to the river, and my little sister Blanquita was having a hard time. Beni was having a better time of it because Ana and I took turns carrying her. As soon as we got to the somersault hole, Ana told me to go ahead and jump in the water; she knew how anxious I was. Ana built a fire to the delight of my sisters. After some time, Ana called me to eat with them. I was getting out of the water when I noticed the nosy photographer taking pictures.

"Vani, this was a very good idea," she said, "it was good to get away."

"I love it here, Ana. Many times when I am lonely, I come here just to hear the water and the birds."

"Vani, it's dangerous to come here by yourself." I smiled. "Ana, my Diosito watches over me. Changing the subject…Ana, can I ask you about your boyfriend?" She looked at me with a surprised look on her face. "Hmm, sure, what do you want to know, and why?"

"Ana, I see the look on his face when he is with you, I think he likes you, Ana, but why does he put his mouth in your mouth?"

"Vani, how do you know that he does that?"

"How do I know? Because I see you and him doing that, and I always wanted to ask you."

"Okay, Vani, what you see is called a kiss."

"A kiss. That's called a kiss? Yuck!"

"Come on, Vani, it's not bad. Let me explain, it's very easy, my boyfriend puts his lips on mine."

"Yeea," I jumped up and began to dance, "I know about kissing, I know about kissing." Ana stood up smiling, with hands on her hips, watched me do my dance. When I stopped, she put her hands on my shoulders. "Vani," she said, "you have to be old enough before you can have a boyfriend." I asked her, "How old?"

"Vani, you should be at least fifteen years of age. But no matter how old you are, be careful of boys."

"Ana, I'm always careful of them, especially when they want to boss me around, they don't have a right to do that. Besides, I intend on being a nun and marry my Diosito. I know that He will always treat me good and will never try to kiss me." I thought for a moment, *The priest is a man, and he marries my Diosito, I'm going to ask Sister Sarita.* "Oh, Vani, I can sense that you are thinking about something. Want to share your thoughts with me?" I smiled at her and shook my head, indicating that I had nothing to share.

"Vani, help me with our sisters, we must go home, it's getting late." On the way home I asked Ana if she noticed the photographer taking pictures of us when we were swimming. She looked at me and asked, "He was? I guess I was too busy, and no, I didn't notice him." We were so tired when we got home.

The following day started like so many others; the coffee to Don Felipe was delivered, Ana took off for work, and I took Beni to Mama Lucia's and Blanquita to Doña Tolita. I readied myself for kinder class. On my way to school, running as usual, I met up with a lady I'd seen many times but didn't know her name. We saluted each other. I was about to take off again, but the lady stopped me. "Niña, look at your tennis shoes, they are all torn up." I shrugged my shoulders, what could I say, she was right. She asked, "What number of shoe do you wear?"

"Señora," I replied, "I didn't know that shoes have numbers."

"You are so innocent, niña, let me show you, take off your shoe."

"Señora, you are going to show me that my shoe has a size number?"

I took both of them off. "Aaw, niña, these poor shoes are so worn-out that I can't tell what size of shoe you wear. Niña, tell me what's your name."

"Some people call me *Alma de Dios*, others *Jovani*, and my sister calls me *Vani*, but I like my other name, *Rosita*." The lady said, "Then I will call you *Rosita*. Come with me to my house, I have some new shoes that I'm sure will fit you."

"Señora, I can't go with you, I have to go to kinder class."

"Okay, Rosita, go to your class, and afterward, stop by my house for the shoes." She told me where she lived, and since I knew the pueblo, I knew exactly where she lived.

When I arrived at kinder, Sister Sarita told everyone to go to the main hall because she wanted to meet with all the parents. Going into the lecture hall, a girl about my age asked how come my parents never came with me to the school. She asked me, "Don't you have a mother or a father?" Those questions tore into my heart; they hurt more than the whippings my mother administers to me. I couldn't answer; rather, with tears flowing, I ran out of the school. I didn't stop running until I came to my favorite mango tree. Mamacita Sinforosa had planted that tree many years ago. I thought of her, and the more I thought of her, the more I cried, accompanied by my shadow. I blanked out. When I awoke, my head was exploding with a terrible headache. I touched it; my head was full of dirt from the fall.

I was angry for having this sickness. I cried from the pain in my head and the frustration from having this epilepsy sickness. "Diosito, I wish this sickness was like Reyna, who never wants me around. Then my sickness would leave me like Mother does, but this darn epilepsy strikes me everywhere I'm at. Diosito, I know that someday my faith will cure me of this illness."

I looked at my dirty dress and my torn tennis shoes. *Ah,* I thought, *I should go for the shoes the nice lady promised me.* The nice lady was waiting for me; she had the shoes ready. "Rosita, just look at your hair, it's all dirty, what happened?"

"Señora, I had an epileptic convulsion and fell. But don't worry, it happens all the time, I'm okay." She told me to put the shoes on. They fit, and I loved them. I thanked the nice lady and went home. I went home for some soap and a towel; I had to clean up. After I was all cleaned up, I went for Blanquita, brought her to the little café Mama Lucia ran. Later we went home to wait for Ana. She loved my new shoes. "Good, now that you have new shoes, you can throw those old worn-out tennis shoes away."

"No, Ana, they are still good, and I intend on wearing them." Ana had to smile.

"Wait, Ana, that's not all. Sister Sarita is going to make me a dress to wear because I will be reciting poetry that I'm going to write."

"You are going to recite poetry?" I straightened up, put my hands on my hips, and lifted my chin up. "Sure, I am going to recite poetry. Ana," I said in a very confident manner, "so you want to hear it?" Ana sat down. "I am ready," she said, "recite it for me." Then she noticed the bump on my forehead; she touched it and asked me, "What happened?"

"Ana, don't ask, you know that I have convulsions all the time and get all banged up every time."

I wet my lips with my saliva, started to recite, but just as sudden, I stopped. "Vani, why did you stop, is that all?" I dropped my head down and stooped my shoulders. "No, Ana, I don't want to recite it because then you won't want to come to my graduation. I would rather have your company at my graduation. I don't have anybody else."

"Vani, of course I will be with you at your graduation."

The following day after my kinder class, Ana and I went to the river to do our laundry. Our resting point was under a guayaba tree. I climbed the tree and picked us some very delicious guayabas. We arrived at the river with plenty of time to do the laundry and take a dip. First we strung a rope between two trees so that we could hang the clothes to dry. We did our laundry on top of the rocks. I was enjoying the day, washing at the same looking at my face in the river and smiling at the funny faces I was making. I poked at the reflection of my face once too many times, and *whacala*, I fell in. The water was nice, so I stayed in thinking I might as well give myself a bath. Ana saw me fall in; she shouted, "Vani, are you okay?"

"Ana, this is the first time I fell without getting a bump on my head, don't worry, I'm okay."

Some boys arrived for a swim; they took off all their clothes. They climbed the tree hanging over the water hole. One by one they jumped into the hole. Soon they dressed and left. I thought that jumping off that tree would be an exciting thing to do.

As soon as we had finished the laundry, I went to the tree, which was so inviting. I climbed to the jumping part of the tree. From there I could see several men plowing and working the nearby fields. For some precious moments, I enjoyed the natural beauty of the river, the fields, and the farmworkers. *Should I jump or not?* I thought. I saw Ana standing on the bank looking up at me; she looked worried. *Pum!* I did a belly flop right into the river. Ana ran toward the tree.

"Vani, I didn't think that you were going to jump. What kind of sister are you? Don't ever scare me like that again, Vani, do you hear me?"

As I was leaving the water, another bunch of boys arrived at the river. They took off all their clothes right in front of us. I said to Ana, "How can these boys be so shameless, undressing in front of us like that? They have no manners."

"Vani, let them be, boys will be boys. Besides, what can you do? Close your eyes when they come out of the water, this way you don't see them."

"Ana, I'll show you and those boys what I can do." I walked over and shouted at them, "Boys, would you please do me a favor and put shorts on. I don't want to see you naked." The oldest one looked at me. "Okay, little girl, we will do that. Turn around when we come out of the water, okay?"

They all dressed and invited me to swim with them. I accepted and jumped in. They showed me how to do a proper dive and not a belly flop. All the while, Ana and my sisters were sleeping under the shade of a tree. Three of the boys snuck unto a cornfield and brought some corn. We started a fire and had some freshly roasted corn. We had enough corn for everybody, including Ana and Blanquita and Beni. The hard part was leaving all of that behind. We packed our laundry, my two little sisters, and headed for home.

"Vani, next time we come to the river, I will show you the rest of the swimming holes. This hole is called somersault hole because the swimmers jump like you did. Another is called bomb hole because it is very deep. Another is called eagle hole, that one I don't know why they gave that name." I was listening to her when suddenly her voice started to fade; I had a convulsion. I woke up in Ana's arms. "Little sis, do you feel better?"

"Ana, I feel weak, but I have to value every moment that Diosito grants me." I got up. "Vani, we still have a ways to go, and I'm afraid that you will have another convulsion."

No, I thought, *I am not going to give into my sickness.* I quietly recited my poem. Still walking, I finished my poem and sang my favorite song, "Quien diren los de tu casa cuando..."

Like somebody was listening to our cry for help, a señor and his burros caught up to us where we stopped to rest. "Señoras," he said, "looks like you need some help. If you permit me, I can give all of you a ride."

"Ah, señor, you are a godsend. Yes, we want a ride." He helped load our laundry, assisted me with Beni by strapping her on my back. I rode atop one donkey with Blanquita in front and Beni strapped to my back. Ana and the señor walked. He took us all the way to our house and did not accept our offer to pay him. Ana helped me to bed. I was so tired that I fell asleep as soon as my head hit the pillow.

The rooster signaled that it was time to get up. The sun had not yet broken through, but the moon and the stars were brilliant. I washed the dirty diapers and my clothes. The water was cold, but it felt good on my face. It felt so good that I washed my hair as well. My shadow was visible in the water, but it doesn't feel anything. I stopped washing when I saw movement beyond the brush. It was the lady in white. She smiled at me, but didn't stop, just continued her walk. She waved with her white wings that protruded from her back shoulders. I prayed the magnificent prayer for the lost souls. I finished by the time the sun started lighting my little part of the world. I bade goodbye to the moon and the stars and welcomed the sun and its warmth.

Primary Graduation Day

I THOUGHT OF MY GRADUATION day. Today I will experience what will be the first step in my education process. Don Felipe was waiting for his coffee. I told him that today was my graduation, not to forget. He assured me that nothing would keep him away. Next I went to the Mama Lucia's shop to remind her of my graduation. My invitees were Don Felipe, Mama Lucia, and Ana. Reyna, who knows? I went to the church before going home. Ana was getting ready to leave for work. I reminded her about my graduation. She left. I was again alone with my two responsibilities, Blanquita and Beni. I talked to Doña Tolita, but she still wasn't able to take care of Blanquita. I left them with Mama Lucia; she would take care of them.

The nuns, Sister Sarita and Adoración, helped me get ready for the big day. They put a dress and shoes that were donated by one of the families from the pueblo. It was beautiful and fit me real nice. My hair was combed, and the shoes fit and matched the dress. The church bells rang indicating it was almost time for the Holy Mass to start. Sister Sarita led me to the door and told me to go wait in line. I wanted to run but remembered my own words: "Relax, Rosita, be calm." Walking to the front of the church, I kept looking at my new black shoes and my dress. I felt real happy. When I got to the front of the church, the students were not in line; rather, they were bunched into little groups. I gathered all of them, and soon they formed two lines: one for boys, the other the girls.

I could hear ladies talking among themselves wondering who I was. One that I could hear said, "She is the daughter of Reyna Bustos. That little girl is always by herself taking care of her two baby sisters." Another one I heard said, "How can Reyna live with her conscience?"

Another replied, "Because Reyna has no conscience. This little girl's life is a mystery." My heart started to pound faster and faster, and I kept telling myself to relax. My tears didn't listen; they begin to water my eyes. They got even worse when I looked around and saw all the parents, except mine; I was alone.

Sister Sarita arrived, saw the two lines ready to enter the church. I was happy to see a friendly face, and she was happy with me for getting the children ready to enter the church. The priest was not Father Alfonso, my friend; it was a priest I was not familiar with. He went along the lines formed by the students with holy water, giving us his blessing. As we entered the church, I felt alone; I couldn't see any of my invitees. I looked up at the altar where my Diosito waited for all of us. I felt less alone and was able to relax. He was looking at me. During the sermon, the new priest asked the kinder students, "Tell me which one of you was the best student during class and never got into a fight and obeyed Sister Sarita."

I turned around, as did all the other students, looking for that one student. Finally most of them turned toward me. "Rosita," they shouted, "Father, Rosita is the only one that doesn't fight with anybody." The priest walked to my pew; he stretched his hand to take mine, and we stood in the aisle. "Rosita, I congratulate you for being well-mannered and obedient to the sisters."

"Father, I have to tell you, one time I got in an argument with a señora, and when I had enough, I walked away, not willing to discuss the issue anymore with her. I also have disobeyed Sister Sarita, I keep coming to kinder before the doors to the school open, and she keeps telling me not to. I would come, if the doors were closed, I'd go back home then come back to school. I finally learned how to tell time in the watch that Don Felipe gave me." I heard laughter. I even had to laugh at myself.

"Now, Rosita my child, it appears to be true that you are the most educated student. What you have just told me are tiny sins."

"Oh, Father, I recall that a sin no matter how small is still a sin and is disobeying God."

"They are not bad sins, only sins of innocence. Rosita, your life had been a mystery. I've had many conversations with Father Alfonso about you and your illness. He has told me about your baptism and other problems, but here you are among us." The priest turned to the congregation and asked them to pray for my health and the mysterious life I lead. The priest went back to the altar. I sat down wondering what had just transpired.

After Mass was over, all the kids ran to their parents; me I walked around trying to spot any of my invitees. I did run into the photographer. He was busy taking pictures of families. I was glad for him. Mama Lucia came up so suddenly that I didn't see her until she gave me a big loving hug. All my worries were gone with that hug, then I saw Blanquita and Beni smiling at me. I hugged them with the love that a mother should give. Then I saw Don Felipe standing as erect as he could, smiling with pride. My first teacher had come to see his student get her first graduation certificate. I saw Javier walking around waiting for his next customer. I called him over, and he took several pictures of us.

Mama Lucia handed me a beautiful bouquet of flowers; she said, "For you, my niña. I have another gift for you at home." Don Felipe told me that he also has a gift and will present it when we get home. He said, "It's a small gift that I give to you with all the love my heart can give you."

"Don Felipe, the best gift from you is your presence at my side here today." I was getting too emotional. I had to relax. I had to control myself. Many of the kids and their parents came by asking me to join them at their houses, which made me even happier. Mama Lucia noticed that I was getting too excited. She said, "Jovani, come with me to my place, you need to rest." I felt dizzy and became scared; that is all I remember. I had a convulsion.

When I came to, I was lying on a piece of carton. I felt nauseous and weak and very cold. It was very noisy, and there were many voices. People were asking, "What happened to her? Why is she lying on that carton? Where is her mother?" I just wanted to get up, to get away, to run away, like I do when I have a convulsion and there's nobody around to help me. I tried to get up, but I was too dizzy and couldn't. Mama Lucia held me down. "Relax, Rosita, we are here to help take care of you." In time she helped me sit up. One of the mothers touched my hand, gave me words of encouragement. Another lady told me, "Niña, I truly believe that you are someone very special, but I ask you truly, *who are you*? I see you day after day, and I notice that your presence in this life sets a grand example on the rest of us. Everybody here today has witnessed how your illness limits what you can do, but you don't allow it, always helping others."

I started to feel better. I thanked everyone for being at my side and encouraging me. I managed to stand up. I remembered that I was scheduled to present my poem at the graduation ceremony. I thought, *Oh no, I missed the ceremony.* I apologized to those near me for not presenting my poem. A lady told me that they had delayed the ceremony because of what happened to me. I smiled at the good news; for a moment, my headache left me, but headache or not, I was ready. Before we took off to the ceremony, Mama Lucia and others combed my hair and made me presentable. One of the ladies, Doña Mari Verdallez, asked, "Did anybody tell Sister Sarita that we would be late? She is probably worried or desperate." Doña Verdallez sent her daughter ahead to inform Sister Sarita that we were coming.

Sister Sarita was pacing the grounds worried and wondering all possible situations that could be preventing us from being at the ceremony. When she saw us coming, she ran up to the group. Before we got to the ceremony, she knew the reason we were late. She was so gracious, asked me if I felt well enough to recite my poetry. I assured her that nothing would stop me from presenting my poetry. "Rosita, the president of the pueblo couldn't wait, he had to leave. He really wanted to hear you present it." The presentation of the certificates started. When my name was called, I could have run up the steps, and I almost did, but my inner self told me to relax.

I remember very little of the moment when I walked to accept my certificate. I calmly walked to my seat. Sister Sarita got close to me, and in a low voice again asked if I was okay to give my presentation. I answered, "Sister Sarita, my Diosito has granted me this day, and I might never have this opportunity again, I am ready." When all the students had received their certificates, Sister Sarita took the microphone, thanked the students and the families. The moment came, the one I'd waited a long time. She introduced me, "Let's give Rosita a big hand. She is going to recite a poem that she wrote." I looked up to heaven, smiled. I wanted to run up to the stage, but I remained calm. I sashayed up to the microphone to a great applause. Sister Sarita handed me the microphone. The voices in the audience were blocked from my mind. I wet my lips.

Méxican Flag

Tricolored Méxican flag
Flying so proud and high
Rosita I am named
Like the flower I resemble
I struggle to survive
My living is a struggle
Like the sprout of a rose
Day after day I fall
I collide with earth uncontrolled
I survive wherever I fall
Dirty and bruised I awaken
In many different places
I survive with their generosity
With help from beautiful people
My Diosito placed in my path
I live in the pueblo Tetipac
Enriched with gorgeous hills
Thank you, Tetipac

I closed my eyes for a few seconds as I waited for the applause to die down. I opened them, lifted my arms, and thanked them, then I threw kisses at the people. The tears were ready to explode, but I held them back. The music started, the people started to dance, the celebration was not to be denied. My dance partner was Sergio, the son of Señor Chacha. I didn't think that he could. He surprised me; we danced to "Las Golondrinas," and Sergio danced very well.

Javier, the photographer, was all over the place snapping pictures. I thought he was taking too many pictures of me. I went up to Javier to tell him not to take anymore pictures of me because he was going to run out of film. "Hey, little girl, you flatter yourself," he replied, "I'm taking pictures of everybody."

One of the students went with her mother because she wanted her mother to meet me. She introduced us. "Mother," she said, "Rosita is the girl I have been telling you about. She is the one that saved me when I fell from the tree. Rosita, do you remember that day that I was playing in the tree that rises above our terrace? You were walking by the house, you looked up at me and told me to be careful."

"Yes, I remember.

"When I saw you, I prayed to my Diosito to keep you safe, to watch over you."

"Rosita, when I started to fall, it's as though you were my guardian angel and saved me. I didn't get hurt, don't you remember?"

"All I remember is praying to my Diosito. As I walked away, I heard a noise, I thought, 'She fell!' I turned around, and I saw you standing on the ground. Please give thanks to God, not to me. I didn't do anything other than to pray to my Diosito."

"Rosita, many times since that day, I dream that Diosito plays with me, right, Mother?"

The mother grabbed my hand. "Thank you anyway. Now you must accompany us to our house and eat with us." We joined them; we ate some delicious cooking. The señora told me that she was the godmother of one of my sisters, and she knew my mother well. In time, we left for the puesto, where Mama Lucia had her fast-food place.

On the way, Don Felipe told me that his gift to me was very simple, but it came with love for the most beautiful person in the world. We arrived at the puesto; he handed me my present. He gave me a pen and a notebook. The pen was an ink pen with a long point. "I'd never seen one like this one before."

"Now I will be teaching you how to write so that you will be able to write your own notes."

"Yes! Now I can write letters for the children in catechism class and read them to the class. Now I can show them what faith in God is." Next I opened Mama Lucia's gift. It was a set of beautiful little dishes. I was really happy with my gifts.

I took leave of Mama Lucia, Don Felipe, and my sisters and ran off to the church. I wanted to check on the bouquet of flowers I'd left for my Diosito and the Virgin Mary. The altar was full of beautiful flowers; the people of the pueblo made me proud. I prayed for my sisters, for Mama Lucia, and Don Felipe—my invitees. I prayed for Ana because I knew that she wanted to be with me. I went to the puesto for my little sisters. They were in need of a good bath and looked tired, but they were not hungry. It had been a very nice day, but I was happy to be home with my sisters. I bathed them, put on clean clothes.

After graduation, Sister Sarita shared with me that she had a gift for me. But she said, "Please keep it between you and me. You are the only student I have a gift for. The other students might resent us if they find out." In time I went to visit her. We talked about my situation and also about my vocation in wanting to be a nun. She told me how important it was that I continue my education. "Education is very important in any profession," she told me. "Sister, how old do I have to be, and how many years of schooling do I need to be married to my Diosito and be a nun?"

"Oh, my Rosita, you are truly an Alma de Dios, I will pray and pray so that you will become a nun."

"Madre Sarita, I want to show you this little doll that I made. The dress I made out of old discarded rags. The little head, the hands, and feet I took from an old doll that I found in the dump." Sister Sarita loved it; she was so emotional that a few tears were visible in her dark eyes. She took her hankie and cleaned her eyes. She took leave of me. I think that seeing the little doll had an effect on her.

I had the responsibility of a mother for my sisters. Yes, young as I was, I took care of them. Granted I had help from others, like Mama Lucia and Ana, but many times I was alone. Reyna, where was she, who knows? Certainly not us, her own children. I went to Mama Lucia's for them.

In all my years, neither I nor my little sisters have felt a mother's love. I hear Blanquita and Beni laughing, playing with their hands, pointing at the sunlight coming through the holes in the roof of the puesto. Mama Lucia made supper for us. She fed Blanquita and Beni a bowl of cereal that consisted of white corn with milk and honey. Beni had to settle for the cereal being that a mother's breast milk was nowhere near. We went home. I prepared my sisters for bed. My days pass taking care of my sisters.

I made coffee for my mentor, Don Felipe, cleaned his little shack room while my sisters slept. I cleaned Don Felipe's room then went home. I carried Beni while Blanquita was getting better at walking; in fact, she ran ahead to the puesto. Mama Lucia was busy cooking for a crew that was starting to pave the roads. The crew was from San Gregorio. They were starting to pave the road around the zócalo.

She brought an old table for me. "Rosita, I'm fixing this table for you, use it to sell your candies so you won't be going around the pueblo selling them." From that vantage point, I could see my sisters while Mama Lucia tended to her customers. We decided to place it near the gate. Ana came home the day I started selling my candies from that location. Desirous to speak with Ana, I took the candies with me.

"Vani," she said, "please forgive me for not being here with you on your graduation."

"That's okay, sister, I understand!" I answered. "But I didn't forget you. Here," she said, "try this on." She handed me a package. Ana didn't forget our two little sisters; she gave each one of them a gift. She gave me a dress of my favorite color. I put it on and started to dance, wearing my pretty new dress. I danced and sang. I have three new dresses I can wear to Mass. Ana was smiling seeing how happy I was. "Vani, don't get too excited. Remember what happens, and you have candies to sell." My happy moment will live with me forever, and yes, Ana is right, I thought, moments like this never last. I changed my clothes, took my candies to my new selling spot.

My new location was a big hit with the neighborhood kids. Most of them I knew, but there were some that I had seen but didn't know them by name. My cousins, sons of my aunt Rosa Martinez, were some of the first ones to buy some of my goodies. Kike and Gilberto, the nephews of Doña Mito, were customers also. Soon all the boys got together and started to play childhood games of marbles and spin the top. Selling candies was not fun, at least not as much fun as the boys were having. I got close to the action.

One of the boys asked, "Rosita, want to play with us?" I accepted to join the fun. Kike says, "Yes, Rosita, but it's going to cost you a few pesos to play." The others, thinking that a girl couldn't compete with them, shouted, "Yes, Rosita, play. Yes, Rosita, play." They didn't realize that I knew how to play boys' games. My half brother, Marcelo, told them that I was good; he warned them. They didn't believe them. I won 160 pesos from them. After that, I had customers and had to leave them. That didn't sit too well with them; they were upset that I wouldn't continue. I promised that when they had another game to let me know. But the invite never came.

With the money hot in my pocket, I ran to Mr. Chabelo's store to buy material to make diapers for my sisters. Ana lectured me because it was not my responsibility. "It is Reyna's duty, she is the mother. Vani, listen to me, you need that money for your medicine. You know that I can't help you, don't you?" I hugged Ana but didn't say a word as to how I had won the money. I did tell her that I was going to help Mama Lucia. I changed clothes and took off. I fibbed a little. What I really wanted was to take the rest of my winnings to my hiding place. Afterward, I did go to the puesto, but she wasn't there. I ran to her house.

Mama Lucia was happy to see me. "Jovani, you look so pretty in those clothes and pigtails. Where have you been? You look like you've been running." I told her what I had been up to. She laughed when I told her about my winnings. "Mama Lucia, those boys didn't think that I could play because I'm a girl. Humph, I showed that I'm just as good as they are. Marcelo, the one that people say that is my brother, well, he even lost to me. He is the one that showed me how to spin the top." I didn't tell her that I had bought material for diapers, I didn't want another lecture. I did tell her that with that money I was going to buy the pictures of me from Javier, the photographer.

She was smiling and at the same time seemed puzzled. "What do you mean when you said that Marcelo is your brother?"

"Well, my aunt told us not to fight and told Marcelo to look after me because he is my brother."

"You mean that you and Marcelo have been fighting with each other?"

"Well, Marcelo took my bag full of marbles and took off. When he finally gave me back my bag, it was full of manure, my marbles were gone." Both of us laughed. "Yes, Mama Lucia, his mother told me that Jorge is his father and is my father also."

"Oh dear Lord! His mother told you that?"

"Yes, Mama Lucia, but she is not the only one, many others have told me the same thing. Except you, now that I've heard it from my aunt, will you find it in your heart to tell me what you know? Is he my brother? I know that his mother, Aunt Antelma, is not my mother, but she knows that Jorge Bustos is Marcelo's father. So why does she tell me that Marcelo is my brother?"

"Oh, Rosita." Mama Lucia took a deep breath, followed by a long sigh, and gave me a hug. After a long moment, she spoke, "Someday, mija, you will learn the truth." I broke away from the embrace; with tears in my eyes, I asked, "Why do I have to wait? Please tell me now."

"Rosita, I have to hurry and get ready for tomorrow. Go home before it gets too dark."

The sunlight was gone, the moon was not visible, and a few stars were starting to show. I waited a moment looking at the sky. "Diosito, why does Mama Lucia keep the truth about my father from me? Is she afraid of my mother?" I wanted to cry, but I didn't. I wanted to run, but something kept me from moving my feet.

Grandma Sinforosa Returns

I SAW THE LIGHTS TURN on inside my house. I had a feeling that maybe Reyna had come home. *Please, Diosito, forgive me, but I hope it's not my mother.* I made the sign of the cross praying that the visitor wasn't my mother. Ana met me at the door. "Vani," she said, "I have a surprise for you." I gave a sigh of relief; my heart told me that it wasn't Reyna. *Thank you, Diosito.* My sister grabbed my hand. "Close your eyes," she told me. Ana led me to the room, knocked on the door. "Who's there?" The voice that answered was none other than my mamacita Sinforosa. She opened the door, and I opened my eyes, and both of us opened our arms.

It was my grandmother! "Mamacita, you came back, you came back." We didn't say anything, but our tears spoke how we felt being together again. She pulled back to look at me. "Alma de Dios, you have grown so much, and so much more beautiful. Just look at how brilliant your eyes shine when you're happy. Mija, those eyes have always given us an insight of what's in your heart." She reached my forehead with her hands. "How do you feel, mija?"

"Oh, Mamacita, when I am at your side, I feel much more secure." I had just finished telling her how I felt when I felt weak, started to tremble, and feared the worst. I had a convulsion.

My grandmother held me in her arms until I woke up. My head was about to explode with a horrible pain. "You know, Mamacita, Diosito loves me."

"Yes, mija, I'm sure He does."

"Mamacita, you know why I say that, because when I get sick and believe that my life in this world is ending, I wake up from my nightmare."

"Alma, don't cry anymore, you got sick because you became too emotional in seeing me. Yes, I'm sure that's the reason you got sick." Still in Mamacita's arms, I thanked my Diosito for having mamacita at my side. "You came back, Mamacita. I prayed to God to keep you safe and bring you back to me."

"How do you feel now, my niña?" I got up before I said anything, just to show her that I was okay.

"Alma de Dios, have you gone to see the doctor?"

"No, Mamacita, Vani has not gone to see the doctor because we don't have the money."

"Alma de Dios, get ready, because you and I are going to see the doctor tomorrow. I want the doctors to give you an examination. I will see if he can change your medicine to one that is better." I could tell that my grandma was very disturbed by my condition.

Mamacita turned to face Ana. "Tell me, where is your mother?"

"Mamacita, I have no idea, she's been gone for some time now. She never tells us where she goes." Ana took her leave of us because Beni started to get restless. My grandmother looked at us and shook her head. "Reyna is such a jackass. I can't understand why she changed so much, and to think that Domingo loved her so much." I went to Mamacita's where I spent the night. I felt so comfortable being here with her. "Mija, tell me, by what name do your friends of the pueblo know you by?"

"Mamacita, some know me as *Alma de Dios*, some by *Jovani*, and Ana calls me *Vani*. My school knows me as *Rosita Jovani Reza Bustos*."

"You go by *Reza* in school, but why? *Reza* is not your real surname."

"Mamacita, that's the name Mother gave me when she baptized me."

"Reyna gave you that surname during your baptism? Reyna knows that Reza is not your father. Someday she must straighten this mess and tell you the truth."

"Mamacita, you know that Reza is not my father?"

"Yes, mija, he is not your father, Jorge Bustos is your father." That night I went to my grandma's bed with her. We recited prayers she had taught me and another that I didn't know. I slept with her feeling that nothing bad would happen to me. I felt protected being with her. With her last prayer, she thanked my Diosito and the Virgin Mary for taking care of me after every convulsion. After we finished, I still was full of questions for Mama Lucia. "Mamacita, what did you think of my little sisters?"

"They are so beautiful, the little one looks like a boy from Costa Chica. The other one the one with blond hair is a cutie also.

"I can't believe how your mother can have all these innocent children, and all from different men. Now I hear rumors that she is going out with one of the Figueroas from Pilcaya." I didn't realize what she had shared with until much later. That night I had trouble sleeping. I kept waking up hoping that my grandma was here and I was not dreaming. I'd give thanks to God that it wasn't a dream. I'd wake up thinking, *Where am I? What am I doing in my mamacita's house?* I turned toward the snoring sound. It was Grandma, sound asleep.

She was already up when I woke up. Again I couldn't believe that I was with my grandma; tears of joy flowed when I saw her. "Come here, hija, give me a hug." I gave her a big hug that made me feel happy. We cooked breakfast and cleaned up. After all was done, I took a quick bath. Mamacita combed my hair in pigtails; after she did that, she gave me a very pretty blouse and a skirt to match. "Alma de Dios, you look so pretty. I can't believe how much you look like me, your mamacita, *jua*."

We left for the bus station where we'd board the bus to the doctor's office. We waited along with lots of other people. I could hear people saying how far they were traveling to, some to nearby villages, some to Taxco. But regardless, I thought, eventually our passenger in life ends in the same destination. Just like this bus, the service has a final destination. Our lives travel the same path day after day until the moment, even though we are not ready, arrives. We all have a beginning and a finale.

Aboard the bus I think about my appointment with the doctor. *I hope he doesn't stick that needle in my behind like he did my sisters. Oh dear God, I hope he doesn't stick that big needle in me.* I was distracted by the different passengers; in fact, I was having a good time just watching them. A lady was taking several live chickens to market. She had secured them by tying their legs. Another had bags full of baked bread and homemade tortillas ready for the market. I saw ladies with long braids to match their long skirts.

Mamacita was being entertained as well; she pointed to the same ones that I was watching. "See, mija, I used to do the same before I met your grandpa Domingo."

"Really, Grandma, you used to sell your chickens and bread just like these ladies?"

"Yes, mija, I had to survive, but little by little, you will know more about my life. Mija, I know that I'm your grandma, but please don't call me *Grandma.*"

"Mamacita, you miss my grandpa Domingo, don't you?"

"Yes, mija, I miss him a lot. He gave me a life filled with happiness and love." She started to sob thinking of him. She looked at me. "Alma de Dios, don't pay attention to me, I cry every time I think of the beautiful time we had."

"Mamacita, I feel weak, I'm scared." I had another convulsion. I woke up in her arms, with a cloth that smelled of alcohol covering my nose. "Mija, tell me something that you like to do, I want you to relax."

"Mamacita, you know what I like to do when I get sick? I like to sing."

"Really, you like to sing? I have heard you sing, mija, but not in a bus. Do you want to sing to all these people?"

"Can I, Mamacita?" She stood up walked to the bus driver. After a short talk, she turned to face the passengers. "Attention, everyone." With stretched arms, she spoke loud for all to hear, even the chickens stopped to look. "My granddaughter is going to entertain us with a song." The bus driver signaled for me to go to the front of the bus.

I strode up to the front with pigtails bouncing back and forth. I turned to face them, smacked my lips, and sang, "¿Qué diran los de tu casa cuando…?" (What will your parents think when…?) A loud applause followed. The bus driver took off his hat. "Little girl, come here," he said. "Take this hat and collect your reward for singing with such a beautiful voice." I looked at Mamacita for approval. She gave me a positive nod. "Don't be ashamed, Alma, go ahead." I collected eighty-nine pesos. All of a sudden, I realized that I had a horrible headache; strange, but it hadn't bothered me until now, but I was happy with my money. I took my seat next to my beloved grandmother, placed my head on her lap, and fell asleep.

"Alma de Dios, wake, mija, we're here." I dreaded going to the doctor. "Mamacita, do I have to go? I'm afraid that he is going to stick that big needle in my body like he did to my sisters." She grabbed my hand. "Don't be afraid, this is a different doctor, and he is very nice. Mija, when the doctor sees you, tell him how you feel before and after you have a convulsion, okay? The information you give him will help him diagnose your problem." The odor of the inside of the hospital smelled very strange, I didn't like it. "Alma de Dios, wait for me here." She pointed to a chair. I sat, and curiously I checked all around while my grandma walked to the receptionist. There was a lot of people waiting.

Grandma came to the waiting room where I was. She had a bunch of papers in her hand. "Mija, the doctor will see you soon, now don't forget to tell him everything that happens to you."

"*Ujale*, Mamacita, it's going to be difficult to tell him everything that has happened to me. Better that I tell you. The worse feeling I have is that Reyna doesn't care about me, she doesn't love me, and I don't understand why she doesn't, because I do love her. But thank God that I have you, Mamacita."

Grandma smiled. "Okay, mija, just tell the doctor about the blows you receive on your head when you have a convulsion. Tell him that you suffer severe headaches after the convulsions." I heard my name mentioned over the speaker, "Rosa Bustos, come to window three." Mamacita quickly got up. "Okay, mija, come on, the doctor will see you."

"Mamacita, how do they know my name?" I felt happy to have heard my name mentioned over the speaker, and that it wasn't *Reza*. A nurse met us and told us to accompany her. She took us to the doctor's office. She was so nice with us. Sitting in my chair, I was intrigued with seeing the human body displayed in the charts in the office. The bed was odd-looking and looked cold, I wouldn't want to sleep in it; the smell inside was the same as the office where we took our sisters to have them vaccinated.

A short knock on the door gave me a warning that the doctor was coming in. I braced myself; my heart started to pound hard. Apparently Mamacita noticed my anxiety rising; she grabbed my hand. "Relax," she said. I remained in my seat, afraid to get up, afraid of the needles. "Señora, I take it that this lovely little girl is your granddaughter?"

"Yes, Doctor, she is. I'm here because her mother couldn't make it, but yes, I'm responsible for her."

"Señora, explain to me what is wrong with this child."

"Doctor, with your permission, it is better if she tells you."

The doctor turned to me. "Okay, little girl, I see that your name is *Rosa*."

"Yes, Doctor, but I prefer to be called *Rosita*."

"Okay, Rosita, tell me about your problem." I started by telling him about my sickness. I told him all that happens when I convulse, including the headaches that follow. When I finished telling him everything, he told us that he was going check my stomach. He led me to that strange-looking bed; the nurse followed. She pulled a cloth all the way around the bed so that I could have privacy. She told me to undress except for my panties, gave me a thing that looked like a dishcloth, told me to put it on. *What, why can't he just see my stomach?* "That's okay, Alma de Dios, don't worry, it's okay, I'm here. I'm glad that you know how to protect yourself."

"Come on, hija, take off your clothes." I did, and when I tried to put on the tableclothlike garment, I noticed that the back wouldn't cover my behind; it exposed everything but my panties.

The doctor entered the covered bed. He started to examine me. "My lord," he said, "just look at all the welts and bruises on your body. Señora, please tell me, are you aware of all these bruises? Has somebody been whipping this girl?" I spoke up, "Doctor, nobody has been beating me. See this bruise on my knee, that's where a dog bit me and tore up my dress. This one on my arm, I got when I fell from the church fountain, the other ones I get when I have a convulsion and I fall." I saw the look on his face. I felt as though he wanted to smile or maybe feel sorry for me, but he did neither, at least not out loud. "Little lady, allow me to ask you, *who are you?*" I just smiled. I had no words to express what was on my mind.

"Señora Bustos, I am going to change her medicine. From now on until she gets older, I want her to take Depakene. I am prescribing that she take 1,000 milligrams a day. The medicine comes in capsules of 250 milligrams, Rosita has to take two capsules in the morning and two at night.

"This medicine will control her convulsions. By controlling her convulsions, her falling and getting hurt also should be reduced."

"Doctor," I said, "it doesn't matter which medicine you prescribe, I will take it. They all taste horrible, but I want to live to be the same age as my grandma."

"Señora Bustos, you have a very intelligent granddaughter, and it could be because she asks a lot of questions."

"Doctor, I still have three containers of the other medicine. I would like to give it to you, and maybe you can give it to another person that doesn't have the money to buy it." With admiration, he tells me, "Rosita, I ask you the same question again, *who are you?*" I smiled, said nothing, just shrugged my shoulders.

"Señora," the doctor was now addressing my grandma, "I want to see this young lady in six months. I will analyze her condition then if everything is good, then I will see her once a year." I asked the doctor to pray for me. "If you pray for me, my Diosito will heal me more rapidly, and you, Doctor, will have many holy blessings."

"Rosita, you are so young and so pretty, let me tell you this: everything that you have experienced in this life appears to be very mysterious, yet in a secret kind of way.

"Señora Bustos, I congratulate you on having such a beautiful and intelligent granddaughter." The doctor asked me for a hug. "Doctor, you're a man of high society, you will give a hug to a sickly girl? I will give you a hug only if you don't think badly of me." The doctor laughed so hard tears ran down his cheeks. We hugged. The doctor left for a few moments. When he returned, he asked me, "Rosita, I have something for you." He had his hands behind him as though hiding something.

"Rosita, I'm going to give you a shot." I started to laugh. "Mamacita, did you hear that the doctor is going to give me a shot?"

"Yes, mija, but it's okay, I'm here, don't worry."

"I'm no drunk, why does he want to give me a shot?"

"Oh, Alma de Dios." Mamacita was laughing. "He is going to give you an injection, not a shot of tequila." With a frown, I looked at him. "I hope it isn't a needle that you want to inject in my butt, because it tightens up, and the needle bends, then you'll prick me with the needle again."

"No, it's not that kind, I need to draw blood from you so I can study it." The nurse took several vials of blood from me.

The doctor left the room during the time the nurse was drawing my blood. When he came back, he handed Mamacita the prescription for my new medicine. "Señora, take this paper to the pharmacy, it's the prescription for the medicine Rosita must take. I made it for a whole year, but I have already paid for the first six months. This I did with all my heart for Rosita." He handed my *abuelita* a business card with his name, address, and telephone number. "Señora, if this girl becomes homeless or for some reason you can't take care of her, I will adopt her as my own."

"Doctor, my husband was a blessing, my Alma de Dios is my second blessing in my life."

"Ma'am, does Rosita live with you and your husband?"

"No, Doctor, I am a widow."

"Señora, permit me to say a few words to Rosita."

"Of course, Doctor."

"Rosita, you are a special person, I sense that in my heart. My father used to give me advice, one of which I want to share with you. Always walk with your head held up high. Your epilepsy is no ordinary sickness, but always be strong and confront it." I didn't know exactly what he meant. But I remembered his words and wrote them in my diary. We thanked the doctor and the nurse and left them. We went for the medicine at the hospital pharmacy.

The bus wouldn't be boarding any passengers for some time. Mamacita and I went shopping; she bought me a pair of shoes and some clothes. I wanted to spend my earnings, but she didn't allow me, told me to save it. We boarded the bus—or the Arrow, as it is known in México. Mamacita and I were a couple of happy ladies, my grandma and myself. "Mamacita, that was so nice of the doctor to buy me medicine for six months."

"Yes, mija, he is a nice doctor. Mija, you look tired, come here." She put her arm around me and gently pulled me so that I could sleep on her lap. I don't remember much else. She woke me up when we arrived at the pueblo.

Walking home, I told Mamacita that I was going to the church to share my day with my Diosito. "Alma de Dios, I too want to thank God and the Virgin Mary for all their blessings." I was not alone this time going; my grandma is with me. "Mamacita, with the money I made singing, I want to buy candles for the saints that help my Diosito take care of me." On the way we stopped at my godfather's store to purchase candles. Entering the doors to the church, I feel God's love. Inside I thank my Diosito for watching over me day after day. He places persons of my pueblo on my path to help me, like my mamacita, the doctor, and many others. Before leaving, my grandma and I placed the candles on the saints that help me.

When we leave the church, she thinks I'm tired and need to rest. "I feel a little tired, but I have to take care of my sisters and help Mama Lucia."

"Alma de Dios, for being so young, you place too many responsibilities on yourself. I will take care of my granddaughters, you go help Lucia." I put on the clothes and shoes my grandma bought for me. I felt like showing them off. I pranced back and forth dancing like a lady in my shiny new clothes. Mama Lucia was happy to see me, but of course she always is happy to see me. But especially now with my new clothes. "My Jovani, you look so beautiful more now than ever. Now you look like your grandma Sinforosa."

"You think so, she will be happy that you say that. You can tell her that because she is here in the pueblo, she arrived yesterday. She bought me these clothes."

"Sinforosa is here in town?"

"Yes, Mama Lucia, she took me to the hospital in Taxco this morning, we just got back." I shared with her everything that my grandma and I had done. I also told her that the doctor wanted to adopt me, but only if I didn't have a family. I also told her about the eighty-five pesos I earned singing. I was so excited telling her about my day I pranced and danced around the puesto.

"Jovani, that photographer is taking your picture." I stopped dancing, looked at the person taking my picture. "I'm going to stop him from doing that," I told Mama Lucia. "Hey, muchacho, I don't like my picture being taken. You are always following me and taking my picture. Why? What do you get out of all these pictures?" Mama Lucia followed, "Jovani, maybe these pictures will help you in your book." I thought, *How can any picture help me with my book?* He snapped another one. I was angry. "Hey, muchacho, or, señor—

whatever, I told you that I don't like my picture taken." He didn't stop. I frowned, and *click*, he took another one.

"There, I won't take another one unless you give me permission. Tell me, little girl, what is your name?"

"Why do you want to know, and why do you continue to take my picture?"

"Okay, see, I ask around, and some people tell me that your name is *Jovani*, others say *Rosita*, and I just heard that it's *Alma de Dios*. Which name can I call you by?"

"I like *Rosita*, call me *Rosita*. Now tell my why you want to know?"

"Rosita, do you always ask so many questions?" He smiled. "I have been watching you for a long time. I have many pictures of you. I sell them, and that's how I make money to go to school.

"Rosita, I have seen you all over town, and I have seen when you faint and fall. Sometimes I take you to somebody's house and leave you on the steps. One time I saw you get sick at your kinder school, another time you were lying on the street.

"I thought that you were dead, you were cold, and your body was purple. I called the ambulance and the federal police. I didn't want to be accused of your demise. The federal police even started writing a death report on you, and look at you—alive talking to me."

"Ah, good, then you helped me? Thank you then, and accept my apology for being rude to you. Now tell me, where do you live?"

"You like to ask a lot of questions, don't you, Rosita? Well, I will tell you, I live in the federal district. I do have some distant relatives in this pueblo. I come here, I'm studying to be a photographer, and I do sell the pictures I take. The pictures I take of you are my best sellers."

"Really? My pictures sell that well, but why? I'm just a simple girl. Do you have any pictures of me now? If you do, sell to me, but don't charge me too much for them."

Mama Lucia told the photographer not to sell any more of my pictures; rather, he should bring them to her and trade for meals. He has taken pictures but need to be developed. He accepted her offer and indicated that the last meal he had was yesterday. The deal was sealed when he sat down to eat. I sat down with him only to know him better. I started the conversation by asking him where he was staying. He stayed all over, sometimes sleeping in the park. After he finished eating, he thanked us for the wonderful meal. I told Mama Lucia that he needed a place to stay. "Should I ask Mamacita if she has a room he can rent from her?"

"Jovani," she said, "always thinking of others." She nodded and told me, "I think that's a very good idea, go ask him."

I ran after him. When I saw him, I shouted for him to stop and wait for me. He heard me and waited until I met up with him. He waited for me. When I caught up with him, he asked, "What's up, little angel?"

"Don't call me *angel*, you know my name is *Rosita*."

"Okay, Rosita, don't worry, I will call you by that name from now on."

"When you told me that you didn't have a place to stay here, I thought of a place that you might be allowed to stay. That's if you want to live here."

"Why, yes, I want to live here for a while. That's good," he replied, "where is this place?"

"My grandma has a place, she'll rent it to you. An—" "Ah, Rosita, are you sure she will rent it to me?"

"Come with me. Only way to know is to talk to her. What is your name? All this time you haven't told me your name."

"Aha, I haven't, have I? Rafael." I waited for more, but that's all he said. I stopped in front of him. "That's it? *Rafael*, that's it? You don't have a surname or other names?" He smiled. "Oh, so you want to know my surname also, you sound like an investigator for the federals."

"Rafael, don't joke with me."

"Sorry little an—sorry, Rosita. My name is *Rafael J. Montes de Oca*, I was born in San Pedro."

"Okay, now I will ask my grandma if she will let you stay for free until you find a real job or until you make enough money to pay rent."

"See, Rosita, you are an angel. Can I give you a hug?" I looked up at him; I said, "I accept a hug only if it's a hug with respect." I smiled and allowed him to hug me. "Now, Rafael, let's have a race to my mamacita's house."

"Hey, angel, you believe that you're going to grow wings, that's the only way you can beat me."

"I told you not to call me *angel*." He smiled. "Okay, Rosita, a race you will have, I will give you a head start."

"No, that's not fair, we start even." We took off; I beat him by a small margin. "See," he says to me smiling, "your wings helped you."

"Hmm, I don't need wings to beat you.

"Rafael, we will go inside, I will introduce you to her as my friend. Otherwise, she'll kick you out and maybe even wield her gun at you. But you do all the talking."

"What? Are you serious, she will pull a gun at me?"

"Maybe."

"I don't want to live here."

"Ha, see, you hate it when I pull a joke on you, ha? Now don't ever call me *angel* again. My grandma is a very nice lady, just don't do anything to get her angry." I grabbed him by the hand so that Mamacita would see that we are friends. I led him inside her house. The smell of home cooking permeated throughout the room. She was surprised when we entered the kitchen where she was busy cooking.

She greeted me with a hug and a kiss to my forehead. "Who is this boy that you bring with you?"

"Mamacita, this is my friend Rafael, the photographer. He has taken several pictures of me and of the people of the pueblo." My grandma looked perturbed. "What's he doing here this coquet?"

"This boy, Mamacita, needs a place to sleep." She looked at me, put her hands on my shoulder, she said, "Oh, Alma de Dios, you are always helping others." I sensed that Rafael was very nervous. "Do you earn enough money to pay the rent? Now tell me where you are from, and what brings you to my pueblo?"

Rafael's knees were shaking, and Mamacita kept asking him question after question. Rafael kept his composure and answered to the satisfaction of my grandma. After some time, Mamacita asked him to sit and relax. She asked me to bring Rafael a glass of water. I gave him a glass of water. My grandma grabbed me and hugged me. She said, "Alma de Dios, for all that your Diosito has granted you, I will rent this boy a room." My response was a hug full of love. "Thank you, Mamacita. In time of need, somebody will help you like you helped him." Rafael, not nervous anymore, thanked Mamacita. Her reply was that he better treat me and the house with respect. "If you don't, I will kick you out. The one you should be thanking is my granddaughter, it is because of her that I welcome you into my place."

"Ma'am, I will respect your granddaughter, your rules, and this house. Señora, I'm thirty-two years old. I tell you even though I wasn't asked."

"That is okay, Rafael, the age of a person is not as important as the type of person one is. Now tell me more about yourself."

"I was born in the small town of San Pedro. Both of my parents died when I was very young, and my aunt took me in and raised me. She lives in the federal district where I grew up. My grandparents are the Guzmans from San Andrés.

"Señora, you asked what brought me to this pueblo. Currently I'm here in pursuit of my career and to study. I earn my living taking photos of people and selling them. The photos of your granddaughter are my best sellers. I've taken many photos of her even though she doesn't like it. I also get paid to take pictures of couples getting married, birthdays, and other functions, even funerals."

"You have taken many photos of my granddaughter?"

"Yes, ma'am, she is a very special person, and the people in the pueblo like to buy her photos."

"Well, Rafael, you say that you have pictures of me, so then when can I have the ones you promised?"

"Rosita," he smiled before he spoke, "I have many that are undeveloped." I said, "Another thing, Rafael, you lost the race, now you have to try harder to finish your studies. Now I ask you, what is the difference between living experience and learning in school?"

"Rosita, I guess that you learn in both."

"That is a good answer, but here is the way I see it. In life, first you encounter problems before you resolve them. In school, you first learn, and after, you are tested." Mamacita and Rafael laughed at my riddle. "Hmm," I got a little huffy, "don't laugh," I told them. "Mija, you are real witty, in spite of all that's happened to you." I didn't say a word; my ego was hurt because they laughed at me. Mamacita noticed that I was upset and changed the subject. 905603

"Rafael, have you seen here before? I seem to remember seeing you in the past."

"You are correct, señora, I have been here before. It was during the feast of Santa Cruz a few years ago. I took several pictures of the people of the pueblo. I also took pictures of the procession." I couldn't stay silent anymore. "Rafael, do you think that you might have taken pictures of my grandma? I hope you do, please check."

"Rosita, for you, I will look at all my past pictures. If I find any, I will give them to you." By this time Rafael was anxious to leave. He thanked Mamacita for everything, bade us farewell, and left.

"Mamacita, I too have to go, I don't want to, but I have to see my little sisters and help Mama Lucia." I gave Mamacita a long and teary hug, I hated to let go. I ran to the puesto; running makes me forget, and the wind feels good in my teary face. Mama Lucia became worried when she saw me. "Jovani, why is your face wet with tears, what troubles my little friend? Don't tell me that your grandma didn't rent a room to Rafael?" I took a deep breath accompanied by a sigh. "Yes, Mamacita rented a room to Rafael, but only because I know him. That's correct, but only for a few months. However, if he doesn't follow her rules, she'll kick him out." At that she laughed.

"Jovani, you have such a good heart, always helping others." We finished cooking and sat down to eat. I said grace thanking my

Diosito for the life He grants me and thanked Mama Lucia for all that she does for me. The food was really good, especially the mushrooms that were smothered in green chili. Thinking that I was eating meat, I asked her how she'd made the meat to taste so good. Mama Lucia told me, "Mija, they are mushrooms, not meat, aren't they good?"

"Yes, Mama, where did you buy them?"

"No, I didn't buy them, they grow wild. You know Doña Pancracia from San Andrés, don't you? Well, she goes to the field where they grow wild and picks them, and I buy them or trade for them. They only grow during this time of the year. To pick them, she goes real early because they don't like the sun."

"Mama Lucia, I thought that all the plants like the sun."

"Not mushrooms. Once the sun comes out, the mushrooms go back into the ground. There is another problem, bulls roam the field where Mrs. Pancracia gets these mushrooms, and they are mean. Those bulls belong to Mr. Hector, and they have hurt others trying to get mushrooms with their horns."

Bull and I Have an Encounter

My brain was thinking of mushrooms. Tomorrow I will get up early and go to the field for mushrooms. I know where Don Hector's field is, and I'm not afraid of his bulls. After helping Mama Lucia clean up, I took my sisters home and put them to bed. I got my basket ready, put a taco in it, I was set. That night all I could think of was the mushrooms. The rooster crowed; my alarm awakened me. I dressed as fast as I could, grabbed my basket, and took off for Mr. Hector's place. I passed by the corral full of his bulls below that I could see the beautiful pond referred as the Rump of So and So. The name is appropriate because of two huge rocks situated on the banks, which resemble buttocks.

Before I climbed the fence, I looked for bulls. I saw one among the cows, but it was far away from me and none other. I climbed the fence without fear of that single bull. I started filling my basket with mushrooms, humming one of my favorite songs. Suddenly I heard a strange sound that scared me. I turned in the direction of the sound. The bull was running toward me. "Oh my Diosito, help me," I screamed. I threw my basket at him and ran toward the fence. The fence was getting closer and closer to me, but so was the bull. I reached the fence, placed my foot on the barbed wire, and I slipped; my leg was caught. I couldn't move. The crazy bull was getting closer and closer, slobbering and making horrible snorting sounds. Instinctively I reached for a rock and screamed at the bull. He hesitated, or so it appeared that he had; that's when I flung the rock, hitting him between the eyes. My Diosito had come to my rescue once again; the bull left me strung on the fence.

I was real angry, first because I was not careful and because I was stuck on the barbwire fence and couldn't move. I did manage to free myself from the fence. I had a big gash on my right leg. I walked to the nearby stream where I washed my wound, took off my undergarment, and wrapped it around the wound. I took off for home without mushrooms. But my luck is no accident; walking home, the milkman caught up to me. "Niña," he shouted, "what happened to you?" I didn't hear him coming up behind; apparently I was too preoccupied thinking of what had just happened.

I waited for him. Again he repeated, "Niña, what happened to you?"

"Señor, don't worry, it's just a little cut."

"Niña, that is not a little cut, your leg is full of blood. Come here, let me help you." I hesitated a moment. I was too tired to move. "Come, little girl, allow me to put you on my burro, come on."

"But, sir, there isn't enough room for me with all those gallons of milk on your burro."

"Yes, there is enough room, you are not walking another step." It felt good not having to walk on my wounded knee. He gave me a cup of milk from one of his containers. The milk was warm and so good. He saw the look of pleasure on my face and smiled. "I just finished milking my cows. Good, huh?"

The nice milkman was so kind. We talked all the way to my grandma's house. When I told him about the episode with the bull, I could tell that he wanted to laugh, but he didn't.

Grandma was outside when we got to her house. She had a puzzled look on her face when she saw me atop the donkey. The milkman helped me off the burro. She saw my leg and skirt full of blood. "Alma de Dios, what happened to you? Oh, my holy saints, why does this happen to you?" She grabbed my hand, thanked the milkman for helping me, and led me to her kitchen. She sat me down in her favorite bench. "Alma de Dios, stay put, okay, mija, I'll be back with my medicine kit." In the meantime, I took off the bloody rag. Mamacita came into the kitchen with a bottle of vinegar, a large pan containing a yellow liquid, a clean cloth, and a thin layer of a pineapple.

She put my leg in the pan with yellow liquid and washed my wound. While she washed my leg, I told her how I had sustained the cut. It hurt a lot, but I didn't cry. She asked if it hurt. "Mamacita, looking at the bloody skirt you bought me hurts more." After she finished cleaning my leg, she wrapped it with the rag that smelled like pineapple. "This will prevent infection, so leave it on. I will change it every day, so don't take it off. Now, Alma de Dios, I want you to relax and rest. A lot has happened to you, and I don't want you to have a convulsion."

I hugged her and didn't want to let go. I felt the pain in my leg, but so long as I'm in her arms, I feel fine. "Mamacita, thank you for taking care of me and not giving a scolding for using the nice skirt you gave me to cover my wound. I have to go, Mamacita. I need to sell my candies."

"What? Alma de Dios, didn't I just now finish cleaning a wound, and you want to go sell candies for others?"

"Don't get angry with me, Mamacita, the candies I sell are mine, and I get good tips."

"Well, my Alma, if that's the case, I like what I hear. I much rather see people working than asking for money out on the streets. For the most part, some of those are just plain lazy and don't want to work. Now look at you, so young and injured, and you don't stay put. Tell me the truth, how do you feel?"

"Mamacita, I feel good, really, I feel good, thanks to you. I will feel better when I'm out there selling my candies. Yes, I do accept tips, because I treat my customers with respect, kindness, and with a big smile."

"Alma de Dios, you are so cute with a beautiful heart. You have the heart of your grandpa Domingo. He was always helping others. God bless you, mija.

"Alma de Dios, I want to tell you something, but before I do, promise me that you won't get sick." *Oh no,* I thought, *she is going to tell me something bad.* Reluctantly I said, "I promise. What are you going to tell me? Please don't tell me you are leaving."

"Mija, you are too clever, but yes, mija, I will be going back to my llano day after tomorrow."

"No, Mamacita, don't go, don't leave me alone, or take me with you."

"Mija, don't be sad. I promise I'll be back in June, then you can spend the summer with me."

"Mamacita, why can't I have a mother that gives me the love that you give me? You are the only one that truly loves me then you leave me. Remember, Mamacita, my mother has never given me her love, she has never given as much as a hug."

"I know, mija, that is sad, and my heart hurts leaving you alone. Reyna has the law on her side, so I can't take you with me. I know how you feel, I too lost the man that loved me dearly, but he won't return. I will return for you."

"Mamacita, what if something happens to you and I never see you again?"

"Mija, then I will be with Domingo, and wherever I'm at, you will always be with me. Mija, I think of you every day. Please understand that I must go to my ranch in Piedras Negras."

I didn't have any words to express my sadness; all I could do was to think of me being alone with my two little sisters. My tears flowed nonstop. I couldn't face my mamacita. I placed my hands over my eyes to stop me from screaming or to prevent me from bawling. *I have to be strong,* I thought, *stop this, I won't be alone, my Diosito is with me.* Mamacita grabbed with her gentle hands and hugged me. It was a hug so warm and tender, so full of love.

I forced myself from her gentle hug. "Bye, Grandma, I want to see my Chuchin. He never abandons me."

"Your Chuchin, who is that person?"

"He is my Diosito, my Señor that I talk that's above the main altar in the Santa Cruz Church."

"Alma de Dios, come here. I don't like to see you sad. Believe me, I love you very much." She grabbed my hand, placed several bills in them. I looked at the money and tried to return it. "Mamacita, thank you, but I don't want money, it isn't because I don't appreciate the money, but I would rather have you at my side. Take the money and hire some helpers, this way you can stay with me longer. Mamacita, I have to go, don't say goodbye because you plan to return. Say goodbye to those that die to never return." She grabbed my hand, insisting that I accept the money. I did.

I left her house, took a few steps in one direction, suddenly changed course not really knowing what I was doing or where I wanted to go. I found myself inside the church talking with my Diosito. On the way out to nowhere, I ran into a smart-aleck kid. He blocked my way. In no mood to play games, I told him to get out of my way. "Hey, Rosita, why are you crying? Did your ma or pa smack you around again?"

"Nobody does that to me, let me pass." The stubborn kid didn't want to move, so I shoved him out of my way; he stumbled and fell to the ground. *Why is this happening to me?* I ran and ran not sure where I was going. My heart was hurting. I stopped on the side of the street to rest.

The Secret of the Miraculous Child

I WAS CLOSE TO MY home, but going there wasn't an option. I continued running, past the cemetery where my godmother is buried. I ran past the pueblo dump site; somehow I arrived at the swamp where I rested. I sat under a tree; it was so peaceful. I closed my eyes hoping to fall asleep. I must have taken a short nap because I felt rested. I sat up, watched a calf wandering about near the swamp. Suddenly he slipped and fell in. I heard his cries as he was slowly sinking into the quicksand. I wondered if that was only temporary and that the calf would return to the surface after resting for a while.

My pain in my leg started to hurt. I started to cry feeling alone. *My Diosito has always helped me, He is always at my side, but I am a burden to Him.* I walked toward the swamp. *Maybe if I go in like that calf, I will forever be well guarded.* I made the sign of the cross and prayed, "Forgive me, Diosito, but I'm going to jump into the muddy swamp where I will be well guarded under all the mud, where I will rest for a few days." I started to climb the fence guarding the swamp.

Suddenly I heard somebody shouting at me. I came to my senses. I looked around, and I spotted a little boy. "Wait for me, little girl," he shouted. I moved away from the fence and waited for the boy. The boy was smaller than me; he was wearing really nice clothes, sandals, and a nice overcoat and a cane like Don Felipe's. Soon he was at my side. He offered me a drink of water. His water container was a pumpkin shell; he took it off his shoulder and gave me a drink. "I accept a drink because I am thirsty," I told him. "I don't know if I'm thirsty because I have been crying so much or because I have been running." He opened his pumpkin shell and handed it to me. I took a good drink of cool water that seemed to energize me.

174

"Little girl, do you want to play with me?"

"No." I lowered my head, stared at the ground for a moment. "I don't feel like playing with anybody." I cleaned the tears with the sleeve of my blouse. He came up to me and gave me a hug. I didn't make an effort to tear myself away from him. I thought, *Why am I allowing a hug from this boy? I never let anyone do that without my permission.* His hug felt good and warm; afterward, he put his warm and very delicate hands on my face and cleaned my tears. I was surprised at myself for allowing him to touch me, but he just felt so warm and caring.

"Okay, little girl, since you don't want to play, let's sit for a while, maybe you'll change your mind." We sat on the grass under a tree. He asked me, "Why are you here?" I answered, "I come here because of the natural surroundings, and I love nature. And since I don't have a father, I'm always alone. I come here to listen to birds sing, and it is so peaceful."

He said, "Sometimes little children are seen all alone because they are abandoned. Sometimes children feel unwanted, but adults also feel the same. Now tell me, why do you look so sad?" I wanted to answer, but his words reminded me of Don Felipe. I felt a change in me; instead of answering, I asked the question. "Niño, what are you doing here all alone? You appear to be younger than me, where are your parents, are they nearby?" The boy extended his arm out to me. Smiling he said, "Friends?" I smiled too. I also extended my arm. "Yes, for sure, friends." His hands were so warm and soft but surprisingly strong. "Don't be sad anymore, okay, my new friend?"

"Why do you want to be my friend? I don't even know you."

"But now that we are friends, I will tell you that you have a beautiful hat and your clothes are very fine. Another question, what is your name?"

He smiled at me. "Appears that you feel better, do you want to play now?" I thought, *Why won't he give me his name?* "Yes, I feel better, but before we play, let's have a little race." We raced and played like two little friends. "You look a lot happier now, you don't look sad anymore," he told me. "Your eyes say a lot right now, they are shining full of life. Do you feel better?"

"Yes, I feel better, but still sad because my mamacita, that's what I call my grandma Sinforosa, is going back to her ranch. That's why I wanted to go in there"—I pointed to the muddy swamp—"because I will be alone again. I have seen with my own eyes cows step on the water and never come out. I only wanted to go in there for a few days to rest."

We sat on the grass. I crossed my legs, placed my elbows on my knees, my hands on my chin to support my head, and turned to face him. "And you, where do you live? I've never seen you around here. Do you have a father and a mother?"

"I don't have a father, and my mother is always gone."

"Don't think like that, and don't feel sad," he told me. "My father and my mother are also your father and mother. Now, my little friend, it's getting late, time to go home."

"You go first, my friend. I will watch over you from here, like my father and mother always watch over you. In the future when you feel sad, don't come here, this place is dangerous, go to the church." I asked him, "How do you know that I like going to church?" He smiled but said nothing.

"Tell me, where do you live? I want to know, in case I want to play with you, I can go and visit you. I know that I am older than you, I'm six years old, and you look to be about three years old, but you are a good friend." He answered, "When you want to play with somebody, don't feel alone, call me. I warn you, don't come back here, this place is dangerous."

"My friend, tell me, where do you live? Why won't you tell me?" He didn't say a word; with his hand, he motioned for me to leave the area. I started to run, turned around to wave goodbye at my friend. He was gone! I ran to the cemetery, sat down to pray and to rest near my grandpa Domingo's tomb. For the first time, I was at the cemetery alone. I usually came with Mamacita to place flowers atop Grandpa's grave site. I sat thinking about my new friend. I wondered about him. *He didn't ask for my name nor did he want to tell me his name. He disappeared so quick, maybe his parents were close by.* I watched the sun slowly taking the sunlight with it. I got up, made my way to Mamacita's house.

I couldn't contain my tears; trying to be strong, I had to see if Mamacita had changed her mind. The house was empty; she left! She left early! I took a deep breath and cried and cried for a long time. I reached a point where I could no longer cry. I talked to myself, trying to gain strength. "Jovani," I told myself, "don't cry anymore. It's shameful for a young girl to cry." I arrived at my house. Ana and my two little sisters were home. Ana saw my teary eyes get more watery when I saw her. "Vani, come here." She gave me a hug reserved for a mother. "Vani, tell me, why are you crying? What happened?"

"Mamacita left. Ana, she left me."

"Come on, Vani, sit with us, you probably haven't eaten all day." We talked and ate supper. Blanquita was starting to talk and periodically said a few words to the delight of her older sisters. I didn't tell her all that had happened to me because I was tired. I went to bed soon after we cleaned up.

The following day, I was up before sunrise. I made Don Felipe his coffee and took it to him. He was happy to see me and his coffee. I shared with him all that had happened to me the days before. He was shocked when I told him what I had intended to do at the muddy swamp. He became happy when I told him about how the little boy had prevented me from jumping into it. Don Felipe wanted to accompany me to church. We were the first ones to arrive. Don Margarito Figueroa, the caretaker, had already opened the gates.

Don Felipe sat on the front row. I went to the steps of the main altar to speak with my Chuchin. I was praying to my Chuchin when I felt a hand on my shoulder. It was the priest. He startled me because I wasn't aware that he was inside the church. He greeted me before telling me that he was not going to perform Mass today. One of the parishioners was very ill and needed the last rites administered. He asked me to inform others. I notified all the people that there would be no Mass today.

Don Felipe and I walked back to the small diner that Mama Lucia owned. She was so happy to see me, and after talking with her, she was also relieved that I was okay. "Jovani, yesterday, I saw you running in the direction of the cemetery, and I hadn't seen you until now."

"Mamacita left for her ranch yesterday. I feel very sad and lonely when she's not here. When she left, I was really sad, I didn't know what to do, so I ran past the cemetery and ended at the muddy swamp. Mama Lucia, I don't remember too much, but I saw a calf jump into the mud and disappear. I wanted to do the same thing."

"Niña, what are you telling me?" Mama Lucia turned white and couldn't believe what I had just told her. "Wait, Mama Lucia, I haven't told you everything. Here is the best part, just when I was about to jump over the fence and into the muddy swamp, I heard somebody shout my name.

"'Did I just hear my name being called?' I thought. I turned around, and I saw a little boy. 'That's strange,' I thought, 'why is this little boy calling me, and what is he doing here all alone?'" Mama Lucia couldn't believe what I was telling her. I asked her if she wanted to hear more. "Yes, mija, please continue."

"The little boy was wearing sandals, a strange hat, a cane, and he was carrying water in a pumpkin shell."

"Jovani, don't scare me so much, I don't want to hear any more—no, no, I didn't mean that, please continue. You and the little boy were going to jump in the muddy swamp?"

"No, Señora Lucia, listen carefully and don't get scared, okay? He wanted to play, not to jump in the muddy swamp. I felt very happy playing with the little boy."

"Tell me more about the boy," said Mama Lucia. "Well, he is smaller than me and younger, but he was good company. He was dressed with very nice clothes."

"Jovani, did he tell you his name and where he lives?"

"No, Mama Lucia, he didn't want to tell me, and he didn't ask me for my name. When I told him that I don't have a father, he told me that his father and mother are also my father and mother." Upon hearing that, her mouth opened; quickly she put her hands over her mouth. I thought that she was suffocating. "Mama Lucia, are you okay? Talk to me." I ran to the faucet for water and quickly gave it to her before she fainted. "I'm okay, mija. Come with me, we must tell the priest what you just told me."

"Mama Lucia, I don't have anything to confess, I haven't done anything wrong, have I?"

"No, mija, you haven't done anything wrong. When we see the priest, tell him everything you remember about the little boy."

"But it isn't a sin to play with that little boy, we didn't commit any sins by playing. Besides, I haven't made my first communion. Another thing, the priest isn't here. This morning he didn't give Mass because he had to go administer the last rites to one of the parishioners."

"Jovani, I believe you, but when the priest comes back, you have to speak with him." She seemed to relax somewhat. "Mija, we are coming back in a couple of hours. The priest will tell you who the boy is that you played with."

"Oh, señora," I said smiling, "how can you believe that the priest knows the name of that boy?"

"Mija, when you see the priest, he will explain everything. For now, help me and don't ask any more questions, save them for the priest." I was busy getting my box of candies ready when Mama Lucia tells me, "Okay, Jovani, time to go see the priest." I thought, *That time already?*

Walking to church seemed different from the other times. Maybe my mind was thinking too much. I didn't know what to expect from the priest. Mama Lucia rang the bell to the parish house; that's when I realized that we had arrived. The priest answered the door. He invited us into his house and asked us to take a seat. His room smelled of incense. That was the first time that I recall of being inside his house. I looked around the room. He had many pictures, paintings, crucifixes, and statues of my Diosito, the Virgin Mary, and of many saints adorning his room.

"Jovani, thank you for informing the parishioners regarding today's Mass. Doña Lucia and Jovani, how can I help you today?"

"Father, I have something very special to tell you."

"Good, Doña Lucia, I'm always ready to hear good news, so tell me the good news."

"Father, remember yesterday afternoon when you rang the bells of the church after six o'clock? Do you remember what happened to one of the saints from our church?"

"Why, yes, I do recall, and very well too. Now tell me, did something special happen to this niña? Doña Lucia, what happened to Jovani? This child is forever encountering something of interest."

"Father, this is something more much more than special."

"Hmm," muttered the priest, "come, Doña Lucia, tell me about this special thing."

"Father, this child played with a young boy yesterday afternoon. I believe that the child was none other than el Santo Niño de Atocha."

"Doña Lucia, please don't come here with some absurd story like that. But, well, okay, continue, tell me why you think that it was the saint that she played with. No, better yet"—he turned to me—"Jovani, you think that it was Santo Niño de Atocha that you played with yesterday?"

"Oh, Father, I don't even know who this niño is you and Mama Lucia are talking about. I played with a boy yesterday, and I don't know his name, because he wouldn't give me his name."

"But you did play with a boy?"

"Yes, Father, but he never told me that he was a saint. I played with him, and nothing else. Father, I don't tell lies because it's a sin, and I don't want to sin."

"Jovani, that's fine, tell me everything that you and the little boy did yesterday."

"Father, like always, I go everywhere alone. Yesterday my grandma Sinforosa went back to her ranch in Piedras Negras, and I felt all alone and very sad. I walked to the swamp on the other side of the cemetery. I go there to see the flowers and listen to the birds. I thought of going into the muddy swamp where I would rest for a few days. When I got close and about to jump in, I heard a voice calling me. I turned around, then I saw this little boy.

"He said, 'Wait for me.' His voice was that of a small child. When he got close to where I was, he asked me to play with him. This boy, who was a little shorter than me, came up to me and wiped my tears away with a little cloth. He asked if I wanted a drink of water. I nodded my head. He opened the pumpkin shell and handed it to me, I took it and took a drink. The water was so good. Father, give me a second," I said. My legs were trembling; I thought that I was having a convulsion, but thank God, I didn't. "What else happened, my child? Tell me, niña, had you seen this child before yesterday?"

"No, Father, I had not seen him before yesterday. Father, like I mentioned before, he didn't give me his name nor did he tell me where he lives. I asked him a couple of times, but he didn't tell me.

"He did tell me that his mother and father love me a lot. He also told me that his father and his mother are my father and mother. But how can that be? I have a mother, but I don't have a father." The priest gasped and covered his mouth with his hands. "Oh, Holy God, how You love this child. Jovani, I can imagine who you played with yesterday."

"Father, why do you look alarmed when I told you that I played with a little boy? You sound just like Mama Lucia."

"I am alarmed, but I have to get to the bottom of this," said the priest.

The priest got me by my hand. "Come with me, we're going to church."

"Father, tell me, what are you up to?" I kept thinking of all my sins. *I haven't made my first confession yet.* "Jovani, I'm going to show you something, and I want you to tell me what you think."

"Father, are you taking me to confession?" He smiled. "No, niña, nothing like that, we are going to visit a saint." Now I was really puzzled. I asked myself, *Visit a saint, why? I see the saints every time I come into the church.* Well, nevertheless, I kept walking alongside the priest.

Entering the church, I made the sign of the cross with holy water. Suddenly I saw the statue of a saint that looked like my friend. I stopped and pointed at the statue of Santo Niño de Atocha. I was speechless; only "ah...ah," I uttered. The priest noticed my reaction when I saw the statue. "Jovani, do you see something of interest?"

"Father, that niño sitting in that chair is the same boy that played with me yesterday near the swamp. Why is he here in church today, and why does he look so stiff? Father, is he sick like me?" The priest was baffled but looked happy.

"Jovani, are you absolutely sure that he is the same boy from yesterday?"

"Yes, Father, he is the same one. I remember him well. Father, tell me why he is sitting way up there, so high. Help me pick up my friend, he is going to fall." I looked at my friend, and he smiled at me. In that moment, I felt like a thunderbolt hit my heart. I began to tremble. The priest noticed that something had happened to me. He bent over to speak with me. "Niña, talk to me, what just happened to you?" He took my hands in his sweaty hands. I thought, *What is wrong with the priest? I'm the one that is sick, not him.*

"Jovani my child, I ask you again, are you absolutely sure that he is the same boy that played with you yesterday?"

"Yes, Father, I don't lie because my Chuchin tells me that it is a sin to lie, also my friend Don Felipe tells me not to lie."

"Now then, Jovani, Alma de Dios, what did the boy tell you? That niño is Santo Niño de Atocha. He is the saint that protects all the children. Yesterday afternoon he disappeared from the altar. That was the same time he was playing with you. Everything that you have told us matches. It's very clear to me that you did in fact play with Santo Niño de Atocha yesterday afternoon.

"Jovani, Alma de Dios, God truly loves you, He illuminates you day after day." I thought, *My Diosito sent Santo Niño de Atocha to protect me.* "See, Father, He does listen to me. Thank You, Diosito, for looking after me when I get sick."

"Come with me, Jovani. We are going to sound the bells so that the people of the pueblo will know the miracle that happened to you yesterday." I helped the priest pull the rope to ring the bells. Soon the people gathered wondering why the church bells were ringing. I really didn't understand why the priest was making such a big fuss over my playing with that boy. I stood near the priest looking at the people as they made their way. The people were getting restless waiting; there was a buzz among them.

The priest raised his hands; the crowd that had gathered became quiet. "My brothers and sisters, I have something special to share with all gathered here today. What I'm about to reveal is not mere news, but it is that a great miracle was experienced by one of our young parishioners." At the mention of a miracle, the crowd began to speak among each other. "Yesterday afternoon, as most of you remember, the statue of Santo Niño de Atocha disappeared from the altar." Again the people started looking around asking each other if they knew what the priest had just said. Some shook their heads, some shrugged their shoulders. The priest said, "I first noticed that the statue was gone around four o'clock yesterday afternoon."

He paused for a few moments waiting for the noise of the crowd to subside. "This little girl most of you know as Rosita"—the priest but his hands on my shoulder—"was playing with a little boy near the *pantano*, the muddy swamp, at the same time I discovered the statue missing."

"It's a miracle, it's a miracle," the people started to shout. The priest raised his arms; the crowd quieted down. "Yes, it is a miracle," he said. People from the crowd started asking the priest questions. I wasn't feeling well, and besides, I didn't know what a miracle was. Slowly I walked away from the priest, made my way through the crowd, and went to Mama Lucia's.

She was still not home from church. When she came home, she asked me if I was okay. "Why did you leave the church so early? People wanted to ask you questions."

"I was not feeling well." I told her that I felt bad and didn't want to have a convulsion inside the church. "Mama Lucia, I don't even know what a miracle is."

"Well, mija, what happened to you when you played with Santo Niño de Atocha, that was a miracle!"

"But, señora, what is a miracle?"

"Jovani, next time you see a priest, ask him to explain to you what a miracle is." I thought, *She doesn't know what a miracle is, but Don Felipe does, he will tell me. He knows what a miracle is because he knows everything about faith.* "Mama Lucia, do I have your permission to go visit Don Felipe?"

"Yes, mija, just be careful."

The little old man was outside taking a siesta. I didn't want to wake him. He looked different; he was getting older. He didn't look healthy at all and very fragile. His pants were so old, full of stains, and what looked like a shirt was mended cloth. I got closer to cover him; that's when I knew that he also needed a good bath. Rafael was walking to his room. I left Don Felipe's room and ran to speak with Rafael. He'd gotten to his room before I could talk to him. I banged on his door until he opened it. I spoke before he could say anything. I asked him if he could spare a pair of pants. He told me that they wouldn't fit me. I laughed at his sense of humor. But I was able to persuade him to give a pair of pants and a shirt for Don Felipe.

I went back to my old friend's room. He was no longer taking a siesta; he was in his room. The door was wide open, so I walked in without knocking. I shouted a greeting to the deaf old man. I startled him.

"Rosita, my little friend, don't scare me like that. Want to give me a heart attack?"

"Forgive me, Don Felipe, but that's the only way you can hear me. Don Felipe, I was here when you were having your siesta, and I didn't want to wake you. I brought you some clothes, the ones you have on are old and dirty. Tell me, Don Felipe, where are the clothes that my uncle gave you awhile back?"

"Rosita, I gave those clothes to my friend, you know, the one I call Lazy José." I told my old friend that he could have these clothes, but he had to take a good bath before. He didn't argue or put up a fight; he went to the bathhouse. I went to Mama Lucia's while he took a bath.

Mama Lucia also looked different. I was astonished at her different appearance. I stared at her until she asked me if I was okay. I told her that she looked different. "Niña, are you going to have a convulsion? Come here, I want you to sit down and rest."

"No, Mama Lucia, I'm okay."

"Good, that's what I want to hear, Jovani. By the way, did you talk with Don Felipe?"

"No, Mama Lucia, but as soon as he finishes taking a bath, I will go back." She said, "What, Don Felipe is taking a bath?"

"Yes, Mama Lucia, I told him to, and he is getting good clothes also."

"Oh, poor Don Felipe, he is getting old. I have to take care of him. Jovani, you have such a good heart."

She placed her hand over her mouth and asked me, "Niña, who are you?" Smiling, I thought of the many things that have happened to me and my Diosito coming to my rescue, but I didn't say a word. I kept wondering what was different about Mama Lucia. "Mija," she said, "before you go, remember, this afternoon, we have to go to church to offer flowers to the Blessed Virgin Mary."

"Mama Lucia, I give her flowers all the time. Why today?"

"Mija, you are too young to remember, but once a year, it's customary for us Catholics to offer flowers to the Blessed Virgin Mary, and today is the day."

"Okay, Mama Lucia, thank you, I won't forget," I said as I was leaving to see Don Felipe.

I marched over to the old man's room. I was surprised at how much better he looked. "Don Felipe," I said, "you look so much younger. See, you should bathe more often." He just smiled. "Okay, mija. I hear rumors about some miracle that happened to you. Tell me everything." He took his handy pencil and paper ready to write down my notes. I told him everything, starting from when Mamacita left for her ranch leaving me all alone and sad. He almost fainted when I told him that I wanted to go into the muddy swamp to rest for a few days. But when I told him that I had played with the little boy, he stopped writing. He knew who I had played with. He asked me, "Niña, I've known you since you were born, I have written everything about you, but I honestly can say that I really don't know you." With teary eyes, he asked, "*Who are you?*"

"The rumors that I heard are true," he said. "That truly is a miracle, I've heard of stories and the miracles that Santo Niño de Atocha has performed, and because of our faith in God, we believe them to be true. But here you are in front of me, you are living proof that the miracles performed by Santo Niño de Atocha are real." I still didn't understand what was meant by the word *miracle*. Don Felipe explained it to me. I tried to fully understand what a miracle was, but it was difficult. I thought of some of the times people had used that word in explaining why I was still with life.

The sound of the church bells signaled that the procession to offer flowers to the Blessed Virgin Mary was about to begin. "Don Felipe, I have to go."

"Where are you going?" he asked. "I'm going to church."

"Again? You are always in that place. I go to church as do a lot of other people, but not as much as you do." I smiled. "Don Felipe, today is the day when we offer flowers to the Virgin. I want to see the little girls dressed in white when they march up to the Virgin and offer their flowers."

"Ah, yes," he said, "I remember when I was a little boy seeing the procession. That is a beautiful custom we celebrate in this pueblo." I arrived before the procession started. I stood near the bougainvillea and watched the procession.

I wonder why we offer flowers to the Virgin. I have to ask the priest, I thought. I got tired standing, turned around, and ran home.

My Godmother Socorro

As I was walking home, I met a lady coming out of Godmother Socorro's house. We exchanged greetings. I asked her if she was friends with my godmother. She was surprised that I called Socorro my godmother. She asked me, "Socorro Casteñada is your godmother?"

"Yes, señora, she is my godmother."

"Little girl, what is your name?"

"My name is *Rosita* to some, *Alma de Dios* to others, and *Jovani* too. I prefer *Rosita*."

"Well, Rosita, your godmother is not feeling well. In fact, she is pretty sick." I was asked to come over hoping that I could help her get well.

The news about my godmother was very upsetting, and I began to feel strange. The lady looked at me. "What is the matter, niña? You look tired."

"No, don't worry, señora, I feel okay, I was just thinking about my godmother, I hope she gets well soon."

"Rosita, do you know her son Alex? Well, her son Alex will be here tomorrow, he is coming to take her to the hospital in the federal district. Do you want to see your godmother? Now is a good time, she is awake in her bedroom." She didn't have to say more; I dashed into the house. Roseli and Bero, two of her daughters, were in the living room watching TV. Roseli asked me, "What are you doing here, snot nose?" Bero told her sister not to speak to me like that. "Don't be jealous Rosita is here to see her godmother." Roseli didn't pay attention to Bero; she kept anything—hurtful things—about me. "Get out of my house," she said, "we are not giving you anything."

"Roseli, relax and quit being cruel to Rosita." My godfather was coming down the stairs. "Rosita is like a daughter to us." He took me by my hand. "Come with me, Rosita." Before we entered her room, he told me that my godmother was very ill. "When you see her, don't go getting sick, because what am I going to do with the two of you sick?"

"Don't worry, Godfather, I will make myself strong, I won't cry." She was in bed with needles attached to her arms, some in her nose, and a bag full of a liquid hanging. She motioned for me to get close. She said, "Mija, you came to see me better than some of my own children."

We hugged. I felt her love for me when she held me with her fragile, warm, and gentle arms. I held back the tears. I sat up because I wanted to see her face. Looking at me, she said, "Alma de Dios, tell me in your own words everything that happened with Santo Niño de Atocha. Everybody in the pueblo is talking about you. Now, niña, tell me in your own words what happened." I saw the gleam in her eyes; she was anxiously waiting to hear from me the miracle that I had experienced. I started telling why I had gone to the *pantano*, the muddy swamp. All the while she listened with teary eyes. When I finished telling what I had experienced, she hugged me with all the love of a mother.

"Alma de Dios, when I heard the church bells ringing, I knew right away that something had happened to you. I told Martín, 'I know that something has happened to Rosita.' Mija, I couldn't get out of bed, but I sent my daughters to the church to learn why the bells were ringing. None of them said anything to me. But your godfather Martín heard what had happened, and he told me. Niña, tell me, *who are you?*"

"Oh, Madrina, I don't know. However, my Chuchin sent the Santo Niño de Atocha to help me.

"Godmother, I am going to pray to my Diosito so that you can get better and get out of bed. Madrina, I fall, and my body sustains hard blows wherever I have a convulsion and fall. People rescue me whenever they see me passed out, and look at you, Godmother, look at you, you are not alone. My Diosito keeps me with life so that I can help you, like He has put you in my path to help me."

with Santo Niño de Atocha was a very good memory, yet somehow unreal. The rats running around rummaging for food was entertaining for a while. Somewhat relaxed, I went back inside and fell asleep.

The crow of the rooster woke me up. It was still dark, but once my eyes open, I can't stay in bed. I started for the water hole. Time to wash up; at the same time I say the rosary. I repeated throwing water on my face until I couldn't feel my headache. Needing to take water into the house, I flung the pail attached to a rope into the hole. I was distracted by movement I saw with my peripheral vision. I looked on the direction; it was the lady in white. I was surprised to see her again. I always wonder who this lady is and why she walks so early in the morning. She saw that I was staring at her. She smiled at me and continued walking toward the bathrooms. I gathered the pail full of water, set it on the side of the hole, and went searching for the lady.

I searched for the lady in the grounds around the bathroom to no avail. I went inside the bathrooms—empty; she was nowhere to be seen. I prayed to my Diosito, saying, "Chuchin, this lady needs You to save her soul. Don Felipe has always told me that a person like the lady in white needs a lot of prayers because they are lost." I went home with the pail of water. I dumped it in the water basin. Ana was getting up.

"Vani, what are you doing up so early? You have to be resting. The convulsion you had last night was a bad one, and you have to recoup your strength."

"Good morning, Ana. I can't sleep. Once I wake up, I have to get up." We made a light breakfast and sat down to eat. "Vani, tell me what's been going with you, I haven't had time to talk with you." I started by telling her that I was very sad and lonely when Mamacita left for her ranch. I followed that up by telling her that I played with Santo Niño de Atocha. "Vani, you actually played with Santo Niño de Atocha?" I smiled and said, "But, Ana, I didn't know who he was. To me he was a little boy that wanted to play."

Ana got up; she couldn't stay seated. "Vani, and what were you thinking, don't you know that the muddy swamp is dangerous? Do you really believe that you played with Santo Niño de Atocha?" I told her about the priest being the one who realized that it was the saint that I had played with. I gave her the complete account of the events. At this point, Ana said, "Vani, you lead a life that's very interesting. Look at me. I lead a boring life. All I do is work, take care of our sisters, and come home." We laughed so much we couldn't stop; even our little sisters laughed when they heard us laughing. "But, Ana, that isn't all that happened."

"You mean there's more?"

"When the priest realized that I was telling him the truth, he made a big scandal. He rang the bells, and when the people gathered to hear the news, he told them that I had played with the Santo Niño de Atocha. The people shouted that is was a miracle, and I still don't know what a miracle is. Want to hear more?"

"Vani, you mean there's more?"

"Yes, Ana, permit me to tell you?"

"Vani, go ahead!" I continued, "My madrina Socorro is very sick. Her son is going to take her to the hospital tomorrow. I don't understand why Mamacita and my madrina Socorro are leaving me."

"Vani, believe me, they are not leaving you, that is part of life."

"Ana, that's what Mama Lucia tells me, but why does it happen to people I love?"

"Vani, I understand, and someday you too will understand."

"Ana, I have one more thing to tell you, I promise." Ana smiled and asked me, "Are you sure?"

"Yes, Ana, I'm sure, I saw the lady in white this morning, she is a lost soul, and I prayed for her."

"Vani, I hear many stories about you that are hard to believe, but I believe that you did play with the Santo Niño de Atocha. My little sister actually played with Him, how marvelous. I am happy for you. What more can possibly happen to you? I know that you are my sister, but I ask you, are you more than a sister of mine? Vani, the people of the pueblo love you. But it bothers me when they say that Rosita is a good girl, is very pretty, always alone, etc. I don't deny it, you are a pretty girl, even when you get angry and throw a few tantrums, but I love you more than the people of the pueblo.

"Vani, I hope that you have written in your diary in detail the day you played with Santo Niño de Atocha. That is going to help you tremendously in the future. You say that someday you are going to write a book. Can you imagine all the people that know you here in the pueblo when they read about the miracle? These notes will have the information that you might otherwise forget. Who knows, someday you might decide to go North like our sisters and many others. These notes will help you in the North also."

"Me, go North? I don't think so. First of all, I can't leave my two little sisters here. I can't leave Mamacita alone either. But what if you and I go to el Norte? We can unite with the other sisters. Ana, don't make that face, don't you want to unite with the others?"

"Well, Vani, maybe my father will come for me. If he does, I'll take you, and maybe Beni. Getting back to you, Vani, I hope the pictures and notes you have are in a safe place. But whatever you do, don't let Reyna know that you are writing notes, she will destroy them and maybe even punish you."

"Ana, I should go see Don Felipe. I have a lot of things I want to write down before I forget."

"Vani, before you go, tell me about the little boy you played with. Is he the same as the Santo Niño de Atocha that's in the church?"

"No, Ana, he was much bigger, the one in the church is much smaller. He had on the same type of sombrero, had on a cotton dress, a small jacket that covered his shoulders, sandals made of skin, a little bag hanging from his left side, and a dried-out pumpkin shell filled with water. I drank water from that pumpkin shell." I hesitated somewhat thinking of the time I had that drink; it was a very good, but somehow a different taste. "Come on, Vani, don't stop, tell me more."

"Ana, relax."

"Vani, what did the little boy say when you finished playing?"

"He told me that his father and mother are my father and mother also. Ana, how can that be? I have a mother and somewhere a father."

"Vani, he told you that? Vani, you're scaring me."

"Ana, don't say that, or I will stop. You can ask Father Ortega, he knows the truth. Others know part of the truth but not the whole thing. They all have different ways of explaining what happened to me and Santo Niño de Atocha."

"Vani, really you lead a very mysterious life. Your Diosito is always looking out after you, especially when you were a baby and Reyna wanted to take your life away."

"Ana, what did you say?"

"Nothing, nothing, Vani, don't pay attention to my foolishness." She was moving her hands back and forth. "But I will pray to Santo Niño de Atocha for protecting you and not allowing to do that crazy idea you had in mind. You would be dead, and you would never have been found, and all the people in the pueblo would have gone crazy looking for you.

"Go, Vani, talk to Don Felipe, that's a good idea. Be careful." I left the house thinking of el Norte. *What's in el Norte for me? I can't leave my mamacita, she will be very sad if I go. I can't leave my little sisters. What will happen to Don Felipe? No, I belong here.* I stopped thinking when I reached the old man's room. Don Felipe was sitting in his chair snoring away. I sat on the floor with arms on top of my crossed legs, hands on my chin. *I enjoy writing my notes,* I thought. *But how is it possible that these notes will become a book? Ana believes that many people will read it, but who will want to read about me? I will ask Don Felipe, he will know.*

"Wake up, mija, wake up." Don Felipe was gently shaking my shoulder. "Rosita, how long have you been here?" I stretched my arms. "Sorry, Don Felipe, I must've fallen asleep. I came a while ago, and you were asleep, and I didn't want to wake you, and then I fell asleep. Don Felipe, I have a lot of information that I want you to help me write. But before I do, I want to ask you something about my notes. You have told me that these notes will help others when they read my book. Ana also tells me the same thing. She tells me that I am a special person and that my Diosito is always taking care of me. Don Felipe, how is that going to help others? Will people cry when they read my book, will they become sad? I don't understand how that can be. Can you explain it to me and also explain how my notes will become a book?"

"Rosita, you are a very special person, I know what kind of life you have lived, and if it's an indication of what awaits in your future, your life will be an inspiration to others." He explained to me how

"Señora, I have an old friend, his name is Don Felipe. He tells me that a gift that comes from the heart, that's what matters."

"Rosita, you are a very bright and special girl, now I understand why my daughter talks about you all the time." I extended my arms and shrugged my shoulders and told her, "I guess it's because I'm always around grown-ups." She smiled. "Now, Rosita, will you sell me some of your candies?"

"No, ma'am, I cannot sell you candies, I will give them to you for being so kind to me."

"No, niña, don't give them away, you are a working girl." She gave me twenty pesos and told me to keep the change. I sighed, looked at her most generous face full of joy; all I could say was that I would pray for her. I said, "When I go to church, I will pray for you and your family."

I left the house with my new clothes and some dinero. *One more sale, and I'll go tend to my sisters,* I thought. I approached a gentleman sitting on a park bench. "Good morning, sir, can I interest you in buying some candy?" He didn't answer. I waited a few moments before asking him again if he wanted to buy candy. This time he looked up at me. He was a young man, not an old one as I had assumed. He had a well-trimmed beard and was well-dressed. I said, "Excuse me, sir, but I thought that you were an old man, but I was mistaken. Do you want to buy candy?" He smiled. "Good morning, little girl, how much do you want for your candy?" Still surprised that he wasn't an old man, I said, "One peso, but my candies are very good."

"Well, if they are that good, what if I buy them all."

"All of them?"

"Sure, I will buy them all, count them while I go inside this store for a bag."

When he came with a bag, I told him that I had thirteen in my cart but that I had another forty at Mama Lucia's. He bought the thirteen candies with a bill of one hundred pesos. He didn't want change and gave me a cold soda pop. "I have this soda pop for you but you have to sit and drink it with me, okay?" I thought, *I want to drink the soda pop, but I don't know this person.* But I talked myself into drinking and talking with this stranger. "Tell me what are you thinking, little girl."

"I'm thinking that I don't know you."

"That's okay, Jovani, but I know who you are."

"Wait, you know who I am?" I asked him. "Oh, Jovani, in this pueblo, even the walls talk, everybody knows you." I smiled and sat down with him; the soda pop was good.

"Well, then tell me who you are because I don't know you."

"Jovani, for sure you don't know who I am? I've known you since you were a baby. Rosita or Jovani, you don't remember me, huh? I know your whole family including your sisters that moved to el Norte. In fact, one of your sisters was my girlfriend. We attended the same school here in the pueblo. Rosita, you were just a baby, and now look at you. I was getting anxious to know who this guy is."

"Okay, young man, don't tease me anymore, tell me your name." He laughed before asking me if I knew Tino Rivera. "The only Tino Rivera I know is Ruben Rivera's brother." That's when it hit me. "You are Tino, right?"

"Yes, Rosita, I am Tino."

"Ruben told me about you. He says that you play marbles and other games. Your brother likes to tease me, and he's always joking around. Tell me, Tino, are you going to eat all those candies? I hope that you don't because you might get worms, and worse, you will have a big stomach."

"No, Rosita, I won't eat them because if I get a big stomach, the chicks won't like me."

"Ha ha ha." I laughed. "I can just picture you with a big stomach, ha ha. Tino, you're just like Ruben joking around." We talked a bit more. I learned that he'd just arrived from the Norté. It was time for me to go tend to my sisters. I told Tino that I had to leave. I mentioned that Mama Lucia was waiting for me.

"Mama Lucia? I thought that Reyna was your mother. I mistook you for Rosita because Reyna is her mother."

"No, you didn't, I am Rosita, and Reyna is my mother. Mama Lucia is a very dear friend, and she is like a mother to me. Right now she is helping me take care of my sisters, that's why I have to leave.

Maybe you know her. Her daughters are Estela, Cecelia, and Petra." Tino replied, "Yes, I seem to vaguely remember them. Doña Lucia has that small diner. She is a sweet lady, it is great that she is helping you with your sisters. But your mother, well, I can't say good things about her. She doesn't deserve having a daughter like you. You are something special. But she never gave problems when I was dating your sister."

Tino grabbed my hands. "Rosita, I wish that you were older, I'd marry you and take you away from here." I pulled my hands away from his grasp. "Quit joking around. I'm too young to get married. Tino, put your good looks to work and go find you a girl. Be careful around these parts. If you find a girl, make sure she doesn't have brothers because they can be very protective of their sister. Tino, I know a girl that is very pretty. She is the daughter of the butcher Mr. Rafa Arce."

"Come on, Rosita, that butcher will cut me to pieces with those sharp knives."

"Okay, Tino, you are on your own. I have to go."

"Jovani, did you sell all your candies?" I gave her a big hug. "Yes, Mama Lucia, I sold all of them." Mama Lucia was so happy after I told her about my sales and the tips the men gave me. I cleaned my little sisters then fed them. During nap time, I put them in their bed made out of a cardboard box. Once they fell asleep, I ran to my hiding place to hide my money. Once back, I helped Mama Lucia. When the little sisters woke up, I played with them. Later we took a walk around the neighborhood. I could hear the gossip as I walked with Beni strapped to my back and Blanquita trying to keep up with me.

One lady in particular mentioned, "Poor Rosita, always caring for little sisters. She doesn't have time to comb her own hair. Look at her, such pretty hair, but you would never know because it's never combed. Look at those three innocent children, what kind of mother would abandon them?" Another lady says, "Don't talk about Reyna like that. Weren't you and Reyna very good friends at one time? Remember the scripture that states, 'He who is without sin let him cast the first stone.'"

I was mad at myself for not taking better care. I promised myself that I would comb my hair every day. I bathe myself, so why not comb my hair. People are always ready to criticize others without first looking at themselves.

I was still angry when I started to wash the window of my first car. It was a very big and round that belonged to my uncle who had just returned from the United States. Uncle José and Bartolo Martínez didn't recognize me at first. After I introduced myself, they were surprised that I was the daughter of Reyna. Knowing that, they paid me good pesos.

The money didn't pacify me, I was still angry at the ladies who said that I always had matted hair, never combed. I was heading back to the diner when I ran into Bolita. "People say that this little ball of a man is my uncle. Why? I have no idea, but it doesn't matter to me. Uncle or not, he treats me nice. Bolita—drunk as usual, carrying his bottle of tequila—greeted me. He said, "Hey, niña, where you coming from so late?"

"Bolita, I'm washing cars to make money. But I'm giving that up, they are too big."

When he got closer to me, I could smell the liquor permeating from his body. I kept my distance to avoid the terrible smell. "Bolita, tell me the truth, when you see me, do I look like I haven't combed my hair and is all matted?"

"Oh, little niece, don't ask me that, a lot of people walk around with unruly hair, but not you. Niece, you want to make money without washing cars?"

"Of course, Bolita, what do you have in mind?"

"Rosita, I'm going to make you a game with bottle caps."

"Really, Bolita, you can make me one?"

"Yes, I can, I will bring it to you tomorrow." Some of the boys have that game; now I will be the only girl with one. I'll state now that Bolita did bring me the game he promised, but my conscience wouldn't allow me to use it to make money. Why? Because it requires a certain amount of cheating.

I arrived at Mama Lucia's to a warm greeting from my little sisters. Ana also came home unexpectedly. She made her way to Mama Lucia's because she knew that I would be there. She was tired and was happy when Mama Lucia invited Ana to eat with us. That night when all my sisters went to bed, I was uneasy and couldn't sleep. I kept thinking what those ladies were saying about my appearance. What bothered me also is the way they talked about my mother. I walked outside to the where the baths were. I took a bath with cold water, which was usually the case. I put on some clean clothes, sat on the steps to dry up. The moon was brilliant and the night ever so peaceful. Looking at the moon, I reflected back on my day. I had some sad and some happy recollections, I sobbed some and I laughed, then it was over.

The lady in white appeared. She stopped walking when she saw me. She stopped and signaled for me to approach her. Not having anything to fear, I got close to her. She opened her arms as though she wanted me to hug her. I saw her face close up; she was beautiful. I opened my arms and closed my eyes to hug her. I felt nothing. I opened my eyes, she was gone. I saw her standing in the middle of the patio. She smiled before waving goodbye. I waved back. I went back inside the house wondering who that lady was. *Why does she come to this neighborhood? Why does she always cry at the red rosebush? Somebody must know, I have to find out, my mamacita will know who the lady in white is.*

The following day was more of the usual. Ana went off to work, I fed my sisters and cleaned them. Don Felipe had his coffee on this beautiful Sunday. I had enough time to write Sister Sarita a letter. The three motherless sisters went to the house of our second mother.

Mama Lucia, as always, was happy to see us. I had taken extra time on fixing my hair; enough of this talk about my hair. All of us made our way to church. Don Felipe hobbling along, my two sisters walking holding my hand, and our adoptive mother caring for us all. After Mass we asked the priest for his benediction. Then I went to Sister Sarita's house to invite her to eat with us.

We had a very enjoyable lunch. Sister Sarita was most grateful for the invite and the company. After we ate, I handed her the note I had written to her. "Why did you write to me, Jovani?"

"You have been a very special person in my life, and I want to thank you. Someday I hope to be a nun and help other people just like you do." She read my letter. "Jovani, you are such a beautiful and grateful girl. Now I have something for you. But you are the only student that I am giving a present to, so keep it to yourself, okay?" It was a beautiful statue of an angel. Sister Sarita left, and we started to clean up.

Just as we finished cleaning up, Doña Lola Castillo showed up with a package. "I'm glad you are here, Rosita. I wasn't sure you'd be here." She saluted Mama Lucia and greeted my little sisters. "Rosita, I have something for you." Doña Castillo handed me the package. I looked very surprised. "But, señora, I haven't done anything for you nor do I have anything to give you in return."

"No, niña, you don't have to do anything for me, this is a gift from the heart, please accept it." The gift was a beautiful dress, a pair of shoes, and underwear. The dress reminded me of the dress that my godmother had given me. My eyes got teary-eyed. Doña Castillo asked me, "What's wrong, mija, don't you like it?"

"Yes, señora, I love it, it reminded of the one I had before, but a dog attacked me and tore it up."

We spent the rest of the day with Mama Lucia. Don Felipe also stayed; he was entertaining Tino and Javier with stories of old. Beni was asleep in her corner, and Blanquita was asleep on my lap. That afternoon I learned that persons lift their glasses and say, "Here's to your health," and take a sip. I thought that only drunks did that. When Don Felipe asked me to lift my glass of water and do the greeting, I was insulted. I told him that I wasn't a drunk. Everybody laughed. Tino said, "Rosita, you are so innocent." After some time the company left.

"Jovani, don't forget that you have been invited to a couple of fiestas, aren't you going? Go, I will take care of your sisters."

"I want to but, I didn't want to leave them here, you are always taking care of them."

"Go on, Jovani, you deserve to celebrate."

"Okay, I will go to the house of the Verdalles or Doña Guzman's." I didn't feel like running 'cause I started to feel weak. I looked up to the heavens. "Diosito, my life is in Your hands, enlighten me should I get sick." I saw nothing after that. I had a convulsion.

I came to not knowing where I was. I felt strange. I was lying on a sleeping mat. Ana was at my side. I could barely make out what Ana was telling me. But I did understand that Javier, the photographer, had found me on the street. Ana asked me how I felt. "Ana, I feel worse after I have a convulsion." I covered my eyes with my hands and pleaded, "Diosito, when are You going to send me my health? I feel that someday You will, but when?"

"Come, Vani, let's go home.

"Vani, you have to relax because you know what happens when you get excited."

"I know, Ana, but I want to have a life, I want to do so many things, I can't be somebody else. My mind gives me ideas, and I want to comply, but my heart doesn't cooperate. I feel when my blood isn't circulating, I am going to have a convulsion. That also happens when I'm sad or get too emotional."

"I know, Vani, it isn't easy being sick and having to take care of our sisters. It would be different if we had a responsible mother and a father, but we don't. I admire you, Vani, you do so many things for being so young. Diosito has you here for a good purpose, some day you will know what that is." We thanked Mrs. Montes de Oca for opening her doors for me.

My Godmother Socorrito Dies

WE WERE ALMOST HOME WHEN the church bells started ringing. It was the sound announcing that somebody from the parish had died. I immediately thought of my godmother. "Ana, I have to find out who died, I know that it's my madrina Socorrito."

"Vani, relax, I can't allow you to go, you need to rest. If it's your madrina, you can see her tomorrow."

"Ana, please don't try to hold me back, I have to find out who died."

"Vani, promise me that you won't run and don't get excited or emotional." I wanted to run, but I didn't; I held back. Near her house I could see many people entering, others leaving. In my mind there was no doubt, Madrina was gone.

I made my way toward her coffin where her body lay in peace. My padrino Martín stepped in front of me, picked me up in his arms. At that point I couldn't hold back my tears. Alex was close to his father. He told my padrino to leave me with him. "Alex," his father told him, "take good care of her." Alex led me outside by the hand. "Rosita, my mother told me to take care of you. I'm going to be here for you, Rosita. Whatever you need, please let me know." My mind was like in the clouds, nothing was making sense. I heard Alex telling me, "Mother, your madrina, went to heaven, she will no longer be here with us."

"Alex, when did she go? Why doesn't my Diosito take me? I want to go to heaven. Alex, is my madrina in that box?" I pointed to a white box at the end of the living room. "Yes, Rosita, do you want to go see her?" I nodded. I will take you, but promise not to get too emotional because I don't want you to get sick. "Alex, I don't like to be sick, but that is part of my life."

He led me by the hand. When we got close to the box, he picked me up in his arms. She looked so beautiful and so clean. "Madrina, take me with you," I said crying. Gavi, the other son, took me from Alex's arms and took me to the kitchen. He told me to relax and not to cry. He put me down in a corner of the kitchen on a small cot. That's all I remember. I was surrounded by strange ladies when I came to. For a moment, I didn't know where I was. One lady asked, "Where's your mother? Are you here alone? Listen to me, niña, are you here alone?" I got up without saying a word. I headed straight for the box. I wanted to see my madrina again. I pulled a chair and stood on top to get a better look at my godmother. I stood there crying until the priest came.

"Jovani, don't cry anymore. Doña Socorro went to heaven, let her rest in peace. She is watching you and always will." I said, "No, Padre, my godmother won't leave me like my grandfather left Mamacita. He went to the cemetery and left her alone." I jumped from the chair and ran out the house. The priest shouted for me to come back, but I couldn't stop. I kept running in the dark. "It's two in the morning, come back and talk to me." I ran to my corner of the world, which happened to be my grandmother Sinforosa's garden. I sat on the roots of my favorite tree. I attempted to clean my tears and running nose with the sleeve of my blouse, all the while looking at the stars in the heavens.

I talked to my madrina, telling her that her time had arrived. "Now you are going to be another star in the sky. I know that you will always be at my side and that you will illuminate my path in the darkness. I don't understand why you had to go before me. You are in better health than me, and I'm still here. We live our lives between birth and death. I believe death is our best friend because it doesn't see poor, riches, beauty, or ugliness, fat nor slim, health nor sickness. When *La Flaca* beckons, we go." My thoughts were interrupted when I heard someone shout my name. Somebody was looking for me.

I got up, not so much because they were looking for me, but because I had sat on an anthill. I saw the flashlight a distance away. I waited for the priest, Ana, and Mama Lucia. They escorted me home. But I decided to sleep at Mama Lucia's instead at my own house. Before we went to bed, Mama Lucia asked me if I wanted to see my madrina again. I couldn't resist. We went back to see my madrina. I felt that my madrina had given me a soul blessing. My madrina will always be alive in my mind. We stayed only for a short time, then we left.

The street was dark, but we knew the way home. "Mama Lucia, did you think that the box where my madrina is sleeping is pretty? I wonder if I could help my padrino pay for it. I have some pesos saved, and I would like to help pay for it."

"Mija, they have already paid for the coffin, you save your money." I didn't say anything after that. Mama Lucia showed me the room where I would spend the night. The bed was so pretty and clean. I couldn't sleep in it until I took a bath. After I cleaned up, I went straight to the room. The bed looked so inviting; out of curiosity, I punched the mattress a couple of times. "Are you hoping to find a scorpion?" A smiling Mama Lucia asked; she was behind me. "Oh, Mama, this mattress is so fine that it's probably better than the one the president of the pueblo has."

"Good night, Jovani, keep me in mind when you pray, okay?" I smiled and gave her a good night hug.

I walked toward the window. The moon was brilliant. I thought, *Someday I will find out why the moon shines only on some nights.* Since I couldn't sleep, I continued looking at the heavens. I was so intrigued when I saw a shooting star cross the heavens. I remembered my mamacita Sinforosa tell me that the stars are countless. *Diosito, there are so many things that I haven't learned yet, and I have a lot of questions, but You blessed me with good intelligence. Someday I will overcome my sickness, and I will write a book on my life and how much You have been at my side.* I felt tired and went to bed. But I still couldn't sleep.

I decided to go use the bathroom. The light of the moon guided me to the bathroom located in a public room. I sat on the steps close to the bathroom; still fascinated by the stars, I started to count them. I didn't notice a cat approaching. Both of us were startled when we saw each other. He did get close to me. At last I had a friend, I was not alone. I asked the cat if his mother had abandoned him also.

After I hugged him, he jumped out of my lap and disappeared. After trying to count the stars, I went to bed.

The next day was not going to be a pleasant one for me. The funeral was taking place, and I was not looking forward to it. Mama Lucia noticed my sad eyes. "Jovani, I know it's going to be difficult for you, but I will go with you so you won't be alone." I went home to change. I decided that I would write her a letter. I asked Don Felipe for his help. He knew that it was futile, but he helped me anyway.

The note:

> My beloved madrina, beautiful and lovely
> Like a reborn flower
> Your soul precious like a white flower
> Your life lives in me and for me
> In my destiny you will always be my angel.

My note wasn't long, but the words came from the heart. I covered my head with a long white shawl and went to her house. The box was still in place in the living room. Alex saw me; he came over to where I was standing. I asked him if he could put my note in her box. He took and placed it inside her coffin. I couldn't bear to see the box anymore. I wondered what death was like. If we go to heaven, why do they have to place a person in a box? Alex came back to see how I felt. "Rosita, I hope you feel better today, I want you to relax because I don't wish for you to have a convulsion like yesterday."

"No, Alex, don't worry, I feel good." Alex bent down to see me eye to eye. "Rosita, now I know why my mother always stated that you have a special gift, I believe her because I feel the same way."

"Thank you, Alex, but I try not to evaluate others, because it's far better to recognize who we are. When we prejudge others, we don't know what's on their minds."

I went into the kitchen. Some of the ladies that recognized me from the previous night were surprised that I was okay. I asked the ladies if I could help. They told me to empty the garbage. Some gentleman helped me take the trash out. His name was Rodolfo Martínez, a distant cousin of my madrina. He was dressed really nice.

I made a comment that he was dressed kind of like the president of the pueblo. I told him that I was glad he was not the president, because I don't like him. Rodolfo asked me why I didn't like the president. "Well, I'll tell you now. He goes around promising the voters that he will do everything. Once he was elected, he didn't do anything for the people, solely for his pocket."

"Rosita, you really have a way with words for being so young. Your words inspire me. Rosita, I can't believe how you look today. Just last night I helped carry you when you became ill."

"Thank you, sir, today I feel stronger."

"Enough, let's go empty the garbage." We gathered the dirty sacks and took them to his truck. On the way back to the kitchen for more bags, he told me that he was a teacher. "Rosita," he said, "you are pretty savvy, and I know that you haven't learned all of this in school. I can just imagine what kind of life you will have with education."

"I appreciate those kind words. Señor Rodolfo, I plan on writing a book on my life and the people of this pueblo, they have been very kind to me."

We put all the bags in his truck ready for the dump site. He told me to buckle the seat belt. "Oh, señor, how can I put on a belt since I'm not wearing pants?" He laughed and showed me how to buckle the seat belt. In the way, I was hanging on to the door handle for fear that I would fall out of the car. He noticed that I was nervous. "Rosita, you don't have to hang to the handle, the seat belt will keep you safe." We got back to the church. He asked me, "Did you like the ride?"

"Yes, but I like the ride on a burro better." He laughed. "But a burro doesn't go this fast," he said. "Señor Rodolfo, everything goes by so fast compared to a burro. When I walk, I see little rocks, birds, and all kinds of things, but not in this truck. But I like going fast," I told him. We laughed.

"Señor Rodolfo, can I tell you something?"

"Sure, go ahead, what's on your mind?"

"Sir, I value your friendship because I am learning from you. I learn from people with experience like yourself. My uncle Luis

Martínez gives me a ride on his burro and ties the belt around me, but I still have to hang with my hands so I won't fall." He laughed. "Now, Rosita, can I ask you a question: who are you?" I thought for a while, didn't answer him because I know that I am a little girl and not much else. What do people want me to say when they ask me, "Who are you?"

"Rosita, did I say something to upset you?"

"No, Mr. Rodolfo, I was just thinking that I have ridden a burro, a pig, a horse, a bus, and now a truck."

"Niña, all you need is to fly in an airplane, ride a train and a boat." Mr. Rodolfo gave me a $20 note. I tried to refuse, but he insisted. He took me to meet his family.

"I will take it with the intention of buying flowers for my madrina's tomb."

"No, Rosita, don't do that. We have plenty of flowers for her grave, and money for Padre Ortega. Use it on yourself." The procession to the church was starting. I covered my head with my shawl as was customary. The Mass was really nice; the son gave the eulogy. The priest blessed the coffin before it left the church. The last trip my madrina would take started to the cemetery. I felt nothing. I was numb. I didn't follow the procession; rather, I ran through a shorter path that I've used many times before.

I arrived at the cemetery ahead of everybody else. I sat for a while to relax so I won't have another convulsion. I climbed a tree from where I could see everything. I could see the procession approaching but still a distance away. I looked at the sky when I noticed a vapor cloud of an airplane going to places unknown. *What makes an airplane fly? I would like to know, maybe I could fly someday.* I lost my balance and almost fell. *Diosito, what is heaven like? Why can't we know before we die? Will we ever get out of the hole? Why then is the soul of the lady in white roaming as though she is looking for something?*

I hadn't noticed a drunk until I heard him urinating under the tree I had climbed. "Hey, what are you doing to my tree?" He looked up real surprised to see me atop of the tree. "Hey, little girl, what are you doing up there? Get down from there, you might fall and hurt yourself."

"Don't worry about me," I shouted, "you stand a better chance of falling for being a drunk." He and his friend walked away from the area. Maybe they left because they saw the funeral procession approaching. I stayed atop the tree from where I viewed the lowering of the box into the hole. Soon everybody left, leaving my madrina all alone. I climbed down and approached her tomb. I sat on the ground next to her new world, her new home.

Full of grief with tears flowing, I talked to her. I told her that she might be dead to the rest of the world, but in my heart, she will always be alive. "Madrina, your death has taught me that when your time comes, all the materials, the loved ones, and all that one values stay behind. What purpose does being an egotist or have all the richness in the world serve us? It's of no importance when we die. Look at me, I am sick, and at various times, I have been declared dead, yet here I am with life. Madrina, your health was better than mine, yet you are gone to heaven. Madrina, when you were in your last days, very few people came to visit you, but now that you died, a whole lot of people came to your funeral." I talked to her until I fell asleep atop her grave.

"Wake up, little girl, wake up." I felt the caretaker shaking me. I opened my eyes to the darkness of the night. "Niña, what are you doing this time of the night?" My head doesn't hurt, so I don't believe that I had a convulsion, I just fell asleep. The man introduced himself as Don Crispín, husband of some lady named Eva. Apparently he goes to care for the grounds on a volunteer basis hoping that he will get the job. He talked, but I didn't pay too much attention. I was too preoccupied with my own situation. I did understand when he told me that on nights like this, one of the lost souls wander about the cemetery. He gets pretty uneasy when he sees them. The priest told him that when he sees the lost souls to pray for the faithful souls. I told him about seeing the lady in white on several occasions. He took a piece of paper from his pocket and handed it to me. He said, "This is a prayer for the lost souls. When you see the lady in white, read it."

He said that he has never read it because he doesn't know how to read. "Mr. Crispín, I can teach you how to read."

"No, I'm too old to learn anything, much less how to read," he said. "Señor Crispín, it is never too late. Learn how to read, and you will find a new purpose to this life."

"Little girl, you better be on your way home." As I left the cemetery, I could hear the church bells ringing. I ran with my imaginary shadow to the edge of my aunt's garden. I sat for a while to rest. I threw five rocks just to see which one I could throw the farthest. Each rock represented something I desired, and that would be the one I accomplished first.

The night was clear, but the air had the smell of death. I talked to my madrina. I said, "Madrina, now you are a star among the stars. Enlighten my path in this darkness." I ran once again with my imaginary shadow toward my house. I made another rest stop near the house. At that moment, I saw the image of my madrina next to me with wings full of feathers. I wasn't scared or was surprised when I saw her fly toward the heavens. I shouted, "Goodbye, Madrina." I thought, *Was that my imagination, or was it an illusion?* I asked myself, *Why wings, why did she come to see me? Diosito, give me wings so that I can fly like my madrina.*

I walked by Don Felipe's room. He was outside in the dark wide awake. I stopped to talk with him. I told him everything I could remember, including the funeral. I told him about Don Rodolfo and the ride in his truck and the dollar bill that he gave me. I showed it to him; that's when I found out that Don Rodolfo had given me a $1,000 bill. I was surprised. I told Don Felipe to keep the $1,000 for himself. "I got it as a gift, now I give it to you, Don Felipe." I grabbed his hand and placed the money and closed it into a fist.

The old man, my mentor and friend, was speechless. All he could say was, "Rosita, where you coming from?" I told him again, but my old friend is getting older and not as mindful. I made him laugh when I repeated that the wings of my madrina reminded me of the wings of a big bird. "That was an angel watching over you," he told me. "Pray for your godmother so that she knows that you are okay, then she will rest in peace."

"You laugh at me now, but I promise to pray for you when you die. But don't even think of dying, you are my family, and I don't want to be alone. I give thanks to my Diosito for you and for Mama Lucia. I don't know what I would do without both of you."

"Rosita, thank God that I found you." I didn't see Don Rodolfo until he spoke. *Where did he come from?* I asked myself. "Rosita, come with me. My family is waiting for us, we are going to eat at your grandfather's house, they wait for us." That night before sitting at the dinner table, they wondered where I had been. I told them that everybody had left my madrina all alone. I shared with them that I was talking to her and how I had fallen asleep atop of her grave. They couldn't believe what I had just revealed. When I told them of the vision I had of her with wings, which was probably too unbelievable, they whispered among themselves, "*Who is this child?*"

My life didn't change much; the earthly days went by. It was difficult taking care of my sisters when Ana was working, selling candies, going to church—all the while Reyna was away. On this particular day I woke up with a strange feeling. I went to bathe with a prickly feeling. I took a cold water bath, walked back into the house. I saw Ana's suitcase near the door. I thought, *Oh no, she is leaving.* My tears ran down my cheeks before I reached Ana with open arms. I hugged her. "Why didn't you tell me that you were leaving?"

"Vani, I wanted to, but I wanted to spare you the grief." I slumped to the floor, unhappy feeling alone. "Why is everybody that I love leaving me? Why?" Ana didn't say much that would console me.

I rose from the floor. I stumped my foot and thought, *Be strong, don't give up, my sisters depend on me. I will not have a convulsion.* I walked past Ana toward my sisters. I dressed them before I combed my hair. My braids were tight; no more will people say that I have matted and unruly hair. I took my sisters outside, leaving Ana to finish getting ready. From a short distance we watched her leave for the federal district. Blanquita looked at me, "Vani, don't cry." I looked at her teary eyes, and I cried even more. I looked at the heavens saying, "Chuchin, here I am alone once again, but I give thanks that I have my two little sisters and Mama Lucia."

"Jovani, I see you are alone again, and I see that you dressed your sisters. They look nice, and you look prettier than ever, especially with those braids." Doña Lucia took me by my hand. "Come, follow me, I have prepared food for all of you." Afterward, my two siblings played together. Mama Lucia told me to be strong. She said, in time, Reyna will return; in the meantime, she will help me take care of my sisters. "Mama Lucia, do you have some information on my mother, do you think that she will come back soon?"

She looked at my sisters playing; she said, "Pretty soon, Blanquita will be three years old, and Beni will be two. I'm sure your mother is well aware of that. She will return." Those words gave me hope. I was ready to leave; Beni had fallen asleep. I asked Blanquita if she wanted to accompany me. She was thrilled. "I can help you sell candy?"

"Yes, Blanquita, I will show how to sell, I will even give you a tip for helping me." She asked, "What's a tip?"

"Oh, Blanquita, a tip is money." We left the diner hand in hand. For the first time, I had a selling companion.

"Blanquita, I'm going to show you some of the beautiful houses and places this pueblo has. Remember, this is where you and Beni were born, this is home." I showed her where different people lived. I showed her the park and other places of interest. People were intrigued with us, so much so that we sold all the candy. On the way home, I showed where Doña Tolita lived. I told Blanquita that Doña Tolita was the one who gave me the basket that I carried my candy in.

"Blanquita, I am going to show you what to do if I have a convulsion." She didn't say anything; she just smiled. I explained, "A convulsion is when I fall and pretend to be asleep. But, Blanquita, I am not asleep on purpose. It happens to me because I am sick. When I fall, don't be afraid, what you do is call for help. Shout, 'Help, help,' as loud as you can and jump up and down like this." I put my basket down and started waving my arms while jumping up and down. Blanquita thought it was fun, so she started jumping and laughing.

I felt tired, somewhat sad because the house was empty. That night and the days that followed, we stayed with Mama Lucia. The only reason I'd go home is to get clean clothes for us.

Reyna Returns with a
New Man, Figueroa

ONE DAY, A SAD-LOOKING DON Felipe came to the diner. I knew that he'd come with a message regarding Mother. I asked him why he looked so sad. "Rosita, my little friend, your mother has arrived, she is at your home."

"Really, Don Felipe, Reyna is home?"

"Yes, I think that she finally realizes that she has three daughters waiting for her." You know, when Reyna saw me, she didn't acknowledge me, no hello—nothing. I thought, *Aiii, Reyna is home.*

I was happy she was finally home yet sad and scared. I shed a few tears, but I talked myself into being strong. My heart started to *boom boom* very fast, I was confused. *What's the matter with me?* I thought, *Mother's home. I should go greet her. She might be happy to see me, she might give me the hug I've desired from her for a long time.* Don Felipe could sense my dilemma. "Rosita, she is your mother, you can't ignore that. I hope that she has changed her attitude toward you. You never know, maybe she has changed. You have to confront her, you must take her two daughters to see her." He took out his bottle of holy water, placed some on my forehead, and gave me his blessing.

I gathered Blanquita and Beni. I told them we were going home to see our mother. Blanquita asked me, "Is Ana here?" Poor innocent child, she thinks that Ana is her mother. "No, Blanquita, Ana is not your mother, Reyna is our mother. Ana is our sister." I didn't have the strength to confront her. "Blanquita, I have to run to the church for a while, when I come back, we'll go see Mother. Okay?" I ran inside the church, and that's all I remember. I had a convulsion. I was in front of the statue of Santo Niño de Atocha when I came to. How I got there, I'll never know, but that's where I woke up from my convulsion. I prayed before I left.

Doña Lucia was worried about me. My face was pale. I looked tired; she knew that I'd had a convulsion. She knew that Reyna was home. She had arrived yesterday and didn't bother to look for us. We don't matter to her, we are of no importance to her. Why then does she continue to bear children? "Mama Lucia, I should go see her. I hope that she gives a good reception like a proper mother would." Blanquita sensed that all was not right; she was teary-eyed. When I saw that, I started to shed tears as well. Beni just looked at Blanquita.

I kept telling myself to be strong as we walked hand in hand to the house. My knees were shaking, but I kept walking. *I hope she gives me a hug. My arms wait for the day that she allows me to give her a hug.* I didn't make sense. I was thinking like a mumbling child. Reyna heard when we entered the house. She was surprised to see us. With an angry voice, she asked, "What are you doing here snot-nose, dog-footed street loiterer?" Those are the words she greeted me with. They were hurtful; my heart wanted to explode. She hugged Blanquita with a hug a mother reserves for a daughter. She ignored Beni and I completely.

I was ready to dash out the door away from this woman. "Diosito, please give me strength." I held back my tears. I stretched my hand in greeting. "Good morning, Mother, I'm glad you're safe." Again she ignored my hand. "You have grown quite a bit, snot nose. I arrived yesterday, and none of you were home. Where were you, dog footed, were you loitering in the streets? What you need is a good whipping." I didn't want to face her because I know better; instead, I would glance her way. *This woman thinks of nothing but of herself. Doesn't she realize that I have cared for her daughters all this time? We feed her daughters, clean them, and take care of them. What a cruel woman. I can't stand it anymore,* I thought. I ran out of the house toward the unknown. *What am I to do now? This lady doesn't care for me, what mother calls her daughter dog footed! She knows nothing about me, she doesn't know who I am other that I have a sickness.*

"Jovani," I heard Reyna shouting, "jackass, snot nose, where are you? Don't you run away from me because I will give another whipping. Come back here, you dog-footed kid." I bowed my head and returned to face an angry so-called mother. "You jackass, when I'm talking to you, don't you run away from me." She grabbed me and whipped me with a leather belt. I slipped away from her mad because she had hit me. I dove under the table and quickly stood on the other side. She couldn't get to me. I was too quick for her. I shouted, "Are you really my mother? A true mother doesn't treat her daughter like you treat me. Why don't you treat me like a daughter, why don't you love me? I don't do anything to hurt you, all I do is take care of your daughters that you abandon all the time."

"Shut up, snot nose, I have an urge to—"

"To what? To kill me! I know that you have tried before, now is your chance, go ahead and kill me, what are you waiting for?"

"Shut up and get out of here, snot nose."

I waited until she dropped the leather belt before I ran out of the house. I ran to my refuge, the church, where I feel safe. "Diosito, what can I do about that woman? She is my mother, and I have to respect her. I beg of You give me the strength to cope with her. I want to leave, I desire to go to the convent and become a nun." I was concentrating so hard I didn't hear when Mama Lucia walked into the church. I didn't notice her until she touched my shoulder. "I knew you'd be here," she told me.

"Doña Mito told me that Reyna had given you a beating. You know that neighbor of yours is aware of everything that goes on in the pueblo. Niña, I feel so sorry for all the problems you have with Reyna. I wish that Reyna would allow you to go live with your grandma Sinforosa." She hugged and pulled me onto her lap. "Don't cry anymore. I don't want you getting sick. Come on, I'll take care of you at home."

Walking home, I asked my second mother, "Why doesn't Reyna like me? When Reyna saw us, she greeted Blanquita with a hug, and she ignored Beni and myself. The first time she sees me in months, she doesn't greet me with a hug but with a leather belt. She doesn't talk nice to me, instead she calls me some horrible names. I don't cause her any harm, I take care of her daughters, but that matters none to her."

"Jovani, you live a very difficult life with her, I have no answers why she treats you the way she does. She is the only person that can answer your questions."

"Mama Lucia, tell me everything you know about her."

We arrived at her home. "Jovani, if you think it's important to know about Reyna, then I will tell you what I know." She told me to sit at the table. She served me a warm bowl of atole. "Reyna moved to Texas a place in the United States, or el Norté. She lived there about three years, she returned to the pueblo in 1981. I saw her when she came back. She had gained weight, especially around her stomach. I was sure that she had been pregnant. She claimed that it was the good life she had in Texas. I have seen too many women after they have a baby, and I recognize the difference. Reyna always denied that she'd had a baby."

"Mama Lucia, Reyna denied that she had given birth to me? But why?"

"When I was born, do you know who helped my mother take me out of her stomach?" Mama Lucia looked at me. "Why do you want to know that, mjia?"

"Mama Lucia, I want to know because that person will know whether or not Reyna is my mother. I have to know the truth."

"Jovani, please, for your own good, don't ask anybody else that question. If Reyna finds out, you know what she will do to you. The only person that knows is Reyna, ask her."

"One time, I did ask her. Her response was not with words but with a beating with her leather belt. That's the way she answers my questions. It hurts to think back to that day." Tears flowed as I thought of that beating and others she's given me.

We didn't say much for a while, I believe that Mama Lucia was allowing me time to think. She took my hands and faced me. "Someday you will have answers to these questions that gnaw at your heart. Someday you are going to be a grand lady, and Reyna will have no control over you. On that day, ask her all the questions that are on your mind." I wiped my tears from my cheek. I made a noise in pain. "Let me see your cheek," Mama Lucia said. I had an imprint of Reyna's hand where she had slapped me. "How can anybody be so cruel? Jovani, you don't deserve to be treated in this manner. I should report her to the officials."

Mama Lucia went to her medicine cabinet. She brought a jar with some ointment that smelled horrible. She smiled. "Jovani, it smells bad but cures well."

"How can that smelly ointment ease my pain?"

"If you want to get well, allow me to put this ointment. If you don't, then I won't." She spread the ointment on my cheek and on my back where Reyna hit me with the belt. Doña Marta walked into the room at the same moment that Mama Lucia was putting the ointment on my back. When she saw my back, she said, "I see that Reyna is back, eh, Jovani. I just saw her getting into a white car driven by one of the Figueroas from Pilcaya. Seems that she's acting like a hungry dog with another man. She left your younger sister with Don Felipe. What an insolent woman, how can she be so uncaring about you girls. I feel for you, Rosita. I hope that you have a nice day." She left me thinking about the words she used to describe Reyna.

"Jovani, forget what that nosy lady told you about your mother, don't pay attention to what she says. To think that Doña Marta and your mother were once good friends." I asked Mama Lucia what Doña Marta meant when she called Reyna a hungry dog. "Jovani, please don't pay attention to what she said, she is very nosy. But if Reyna is gone, she can't hit you anymore. Jovani, get your basket, selling candies relaxes you."

She is right, selling candies does relax me; at least I don't have time to think about many things that bother me. I was in my little world selling candies and feeling good. A boy comes running up to me. "Rosita, I have a message from Don Felipe, he wants you to go and take care of your sister Beni. Your mother dropped Beni at the old man's house."

"Since you came to deliver the message from Don Felipe, I will give you a gum if you run back and tell Don Felipe that I will be there as soon as I can."

"Okay, give me the gum, and I will run back and give him the message." A man overheard the conversation I had with the kid. "Jovani, come here, get close to me." He handed me money. "Please accept it, don't say no." I took it and thanked him. "You don't want any candy?"

"No, I don't, not now, next time," he said.

Beni was thrilled when she saw me. Don Felipe was trying to feed her; her chin and cheeks were covered with food. I took her to the baths where I cleaned her. Poor baby, her butt was full of diaper rash. I went to the house, but Reyna had locked us out. But knowing her, I prepared for this. I had diapers and clothes stashed behind the house in a hiding place covered by a loose stone. We went back to Don Felipe to ask if Reyna had told him where she was going and for how long. The old gentleman knew nothing. All Reyna told was to hand Beni over to me. "She didn't leave any diapers, clothes, or food for us." I shrugged my shoulders and said, "Well, Don Felipe, at least she only left me with Beni." I took Beni and left.

"Where are we going to stay? The house is locked, and I don't want to bother Mama Lucia." I remembered that I had a key stashed. "Beni, give me your hand." She smiled and raised her hand to meet mine. We walked to the hiding place, but the key was gone. I searched other past hiding places, to no avail. "Beni, we are locked out, what are we going to do?" She hugged my leg smiling. *She is too young to panic,* I thought. "Beni, as long as my Diosito grants me life and watches over us, we will be okay. How sad to have a mother like Reyna. Beni, we must stay with Mama Lucia tonight." Beni repeated, "Yes, Mama."

We wandered about the pueblo. I even took Beni to a little park to pass the time. I didn't want to bother anybody because I felt alone and unwanted. I knew that many people had offered me refuge if I ever faced a situation like this one, but I decided that I couldn't impose on anybody. Mama Lucia was the only one I could ask for refuge. Beni and I ran into Javier. He took photos of us. "Rosita, I heard that your mother is back."

"Yes, Javier, you heard right, but she is gone again and locked us out of the house."

"Now I understand why you and your little sister are out here in the dark. I will walk you and Beni to check if your mother is back, okay?" We walked to the house. It was still locked, and nobody appeared to be home. "Are you going to Doña Lucia's?" He walked us to Doña Lucia's house. We knocked, but she didn't answer. Javier loaned us a small blanket. We went looking for a carton, a box, or anything I could convert into a box. We did and found a place to sleep. One of the daughters of Maria Castañeda saw us trying to make a bed. Whether she was concerned or just being nosy, she asked if we were hungry. Not trying to say anything negative about Reyna, I told her that Beni was a little hungry.

She was leaving when Javier arrived to see how we were doing. The girl came back with a bunch of tamales and some atole.

Javier took pictures before he left us again. In the middle of the night, Beni woke me up. She was freezing. I covered her in the blanket and carried her to the house of my second mother. This time she woke up and opened the door for us. "Niña, what are you doing here so late at night?" I told her everything. She was more concerned with Beni. She took Beni with her to bed where she kept Beni warm.

The banging on the gate woke me up early the next day. Mama Lucia was taking a shower. I went to the gate, asked, "Who is it?"

"Rosita, it's me, Andres Arce, I have a message for you from your mother." *Oh my, what did I do wrong this time?* I thought. I opened the door. "Rosita, your mother should arrive with two truck-loads of timber from her place. She wants you to make her and her workers something good to eat for this afternoon."

"She wants to feed her workers too?"

"Jovani, who was that man?"

"Oh, Mama Lucia, that was one of Reyna's workers. He gave me a message from Reyna."

"What does Reyna want from you this time?"

"Reyna wants me to have plenty of food for her workers by this afternoon."

"Well, at least now you know where she is. Mija, why don't you go pick mushrooms, we'll fix them with other goodies. I will take care of Beni, go on, mija, but be careful, you know what happened last time."

I was so happy that Mother asked a favor of me. *Maybe she does love me.* I ran to the field where I knew the mushrooms were waiting for me. *I am going to fix my mother a good meal,* I kept thinking.

I entered the property of my uncle Luis and my aunt Pina. They were outside doing their chores; they were happy to see me. After the usual greetings, they wanted to know why I was up so early. I told them that I had come for mushrooms. "Rosita, you came to the right place, our property is full of mushrooms."

"Then you give me permission to gather mushrooms in your property?" Uncle Luis said, "Of course, mija." He said, "The best place is right in the center of our property. You can't miss the place. Go straight until you come to a dry tree, it's the only dry tree that we have. There you will find *pitos de gallo* and *orejas de San Juan.* Be very careful, mija."

"Uncle, you don't have to worry, I'm an excellent tree climber."

Mushrooms and Fractured Arm

I CLIMBED THE TREE FULL of mushrooms. My basket was nearly full with *pitos de gallo* and *orejas de San Juan* mushrooms. Suddenly my world began to turn upside down. I made the sign of the cross and asked God to help me get down. I feared having a convulsion atop the tree. I stretched my arm to reach my last mushroom. The branch broke. I screamed as I was falling alongside the branch. I don't remember much else. When I came to, I had a horrible pain in my left arm and an equally bad headache. I couldn't move my left arm, and to top it all, I had fallen on a fresh cow chip. There was no way that I could clean the manure clinging to my back. "Why," I asked looking skyward, "does this happen to me, Diosito?" I gathered the mushrooms and started to walk with my basket of mushrooms. The pain on my left arm and the terrible smell of manure kept my senses busy.

I made a detour to the stream, and somehow I was able to clean the manure from my clothes. The cool water felt good on my broken arm. Didn't ease the pain, but the smell was gone. I dressed.

I could hear a cart slowly approaching me from behind. The driver of a pair of oxen with a yoke between them asked me to stop. He walked up to me; he saw my broken arm. "Niña, what happened to you? Are you all alone out here? Niña, I have to take you to a bone specialist, he lives close by." He didn't give me a chance to deny his help; he put me on his horse. The pain was unbearable, I couldn't think straight. I kept asking myself, *Why do these things happen to me?* I made a promise to my Diosito. I made Him the promise that on my knees, I would enter the church, and kneeling, I would make my way to the altar and place a bouquet of flowers and a candle in the main altar when my arm is healed.

Don Pascual, the bone specialist, asked the man who rescued me to place me on a chair. Don Pascual asked me how I'd gotten hurt and made other small talk. I didn't feel like talking. I looked down on my left calf because I felt something. It was a big caterpillar digging into my skin. I reached down and yanked it off. I left a mark on my calf. The bone doctor put some kind of liquid and covered up the wound. Don Pascual warned me that he was going to yank my arm, to brace myself for a lot of pain. My arm made a cracking sound when he pulled it. I screamed with pain. He couldn't do anything more. My arm was bent with a lot of pain and swollen.

He asked about my parents. I told him about that I had a mother but no father. I was in no mood to talk; I wanted to leave, I wanted to go and cook for my mother and her workers. He told me to return to him in five days. I agreed not knowing whether I'd be able to or not. I only wanted to get away. I did ask him if my swollen arm was going to rot. The boy that brought me to the bone doctor told Don Pascual that I was the daughter of Reyna Bustos. I didn't like him giving Don Pascual information about me. I thought, *Don't be so meddlesome.* I asked Don Pascual for the fee of fixing my arm. He looked at me. "Aha, so Reyna Bustos is your mother, eh. Well, you don't owe me anything." I turned to the boy. "So you know my mother?"

"Yes, Jovani, I work for your mother, and I have for some time."

"Well, then, if you know her, lend me money to pay Don Pascual, I will pay you back when I get home."

"I will pay him something, and you don't have to pay me back." He gave Don Pascual some money, and we left. "Jovani, I have to leave, but I will be at your house later to work."

"Señor, promise me that you will mention nothing to Reyna. She will be very angry with me if you tell her."

"Jovani, my lips are sealed. I will say nothing, I promise."

On the way home, I sat near the road to rest. I thought of Blanquita and Beni. I thought of the food Reyna wanted for her workers. I didn't feel like cooking, but at the same time, I couldn't let my mother down. I started to walk, and I prayed the rosary while I walked. I finished and began to sing. "Qué diran los de tu casa…" That song comes to mind mainly when I want to forget something or when I want to ignore something unpleasant or when I want to feel good. I walked to the church. I thanked God for having me with life. "I have a broken arm, but I'm here in front of You my faith stronger than ever. Diosito, I hope that You are keeping track of all the problems I have encountered. Diosito, my Almighty Father, don't forsake me, never."

I left the church full of energy that gave me the strength to continue my living. Singing, I headed to help Mama Lucia cook for Reyna. Walking along the street, I could hear people say that Reyna was back and that was the reason that I was all banged up, because Reyna has always given her beatings. Mama Lucia hadn't noticed my broken swollen arm until a gentleman asked me about it. When she saw my swollen and bent arm, she almost fainted. I told her all that I could in the short time that we had. After I had given her all the details, she heard my stomach growl. "Jovani, don't tell me that you haven't eaten all day."

One of the customers heard me refer to her as Mama Lucia. Señor Vicente asked her if I was her daughter. "No, Vicente, Jovani is not my daughter. She is a very good friend and assistant who I would be happy to be her mother. Why do you ask?"

"Well, this friend of yours is a very pretty girl." While the two talked, I took another customer his food, still with my stomach growling for food. The gentleman heard my stomach. "Niña, it appears as though your stomach needs food."

"Sorry, señor, for not being able to control the growling, but it's been a while since I ate."

The man called Doña Lucia to his table. "Señora, serve this a plate. I will pay for whatever she wants to eat."

"Don't worry, señor, I will serve her a plate, but you can give her the tip." The man called me over. He gave me a bill of five pesos. Mama Lucia sat and ate with me. "Now, niña, tell me the truth, how did you break your arm? I ask knowing that Reyna is back in the pueblo, and she is capable of doing this to you." I told her that I had really broken my arm when I fell off the tree. Beni woke up and approached me. "Mama, Mama." She lifted her arms to give me a hug. She had a sad look in her eyes the moment she saw my arm.

"Hurt?" she asked. "Yes, hurt. I broke it, and it hurts." She struggled but managed to get on the bench. She ate with us.

My thoughts wandered to what Reyna would do when she saw my arm. *How am I going to take care of my sisters with this broken arm?* I turned to Mama Lucia. "I apologize for all the problems we cause you." She gently took my arm and smiled. Beni sensed something, and she hugged me. I couldn't control my tears. "I understand how you feel, Jovani, but don't worry, I will take care of Beni. Go on home." I noticed a big car parked near the front of the house.

Several workers were busy unloading the lumber. I stopped walking. I sat on the edge of the sidewalk. I recognized the worker that had taken me to the bone man. When they finished, Reyna walked over with juice and glasses for the workers. My legs started to tremble when I saw her. She counted the pieces of lumber. As she walked back toward the house, she saw me. She saluted not like a mother: "Snot-nose jackass, now what the —— happened to you?" Trembling, expecting the worst, I answered, "I broke it, but I'm okay."

"I'll see what you can do tomorrow," Reyna answered. "We are leaving early for the ranch where you will take care of your sisters."

Mother is taking me to the ranch? She has never taken me to church or anywhere, now she is taking me to her ranch. I wanted to hug her. *She wants to show me her ranch, maybe she does love me. Maybe she wants to abandon me there and leave me alone. Diosito, please don't allow her to do anything bad to me.* I went to bed praying to my Diosito. "Get up, what are you doing in bed, you lazy girl?" Reyna shouted. "Make coffee and tortillas. I have to feed my workers supper." My arm was afire with pain, I was having trouble getting up. I expected a whipping. "Hey, jackass, I'm talking to you, get up before I give you another beating." She left without touching me. I managed to get up. I made the coffee and tortillas that the workers loved.

That night I woke up trembling, I felt cold. I touched my forehead. I was burning with fever. I went to the water tank to wash my face. I felt better. I decided to give myself a cold water bath. Somehow I managed to take off my clothes; the water felt good. After the bath, I didn't feel sleepy, I sat on the patio steps. Suddenly I felt as though someone was caressing my forehead. The hands felt smooth, full of energy and purity. *Diosito is taking care of me,* I thought. I remained outside with no desire of being in the same room as that lady.

The pain in my arm was horrible. I couldn't fall asleep. Again I felt a sensation on my forehead. *Is this a mirage I'm seeing, or is it real?* I cleared my eyes to make sure of what I was seeing. It's an angel! I cleared my eyes again; it was real. In front of me was one big angel. I couldn't believe what I was seeing. The angel smiled with me. Above in a distance, I saw the figure of my Diosito. With my good arm, I was able to lift my left arm. I lowered my head in reverence and asked, *Diosito, please cure my arm.* I looked up; the figure of my Diosito and the angel were gone. I asked myself, *Was that a mirage, or was it real what I just saw?*

I am wide awake, I thought, *that had to be the real thing. My Diosito loves me, He sent an angel to protect me.* I rose on my feet, still looking at the heavens, confused, happy, void of pain. I went to my corner. I was unable to have a comfortable sleep thinking of what lay ahead. I did sleep until the cock woke me up. I prayed one last prayer before getting up. "Eternal Sacred Father of souls, heal my arm. Diosito, I also ask for compassion for my health. Give me my health, if not now, then when You feel that I am starting a white page in my life." I felt that Diosito said, "Healed you will be." I sensed that he was up with the stars.

Eventually I got out of bed happy with a lot of energy, ready to confront the day. My sisters and Reyna were still asleep. I got dressed, quietly humming my song, "Que diran los de tu casa..." The church bells rang informing the pueblo that six o'clock Mass was about begin. I made my way to see Mama Lucia. I shared with her the events of last night. I could talk to her knowing that she would believe me. Unlike Reyna, I don't share anything with her for obvious reasons.

Then I visited Don Felipe with a cup of coffee I had prepared at the diner. He noticed my arm. "Did you break your arm during a convulsion?" he asked. I told him how I had broken it. "Niña, are you taking care of that arm? Do you have an ointment to reduce the swelling?" I told him not to worry, that I would be okay. I also told him that Reyna was taking me to her ranch. "I will feel much better at her place, so don't worry." I asked him to write what I was going to tell him. He got paper and pencil and wrote everything I told him about my Diosito and the angel. He laughed; he thought it was funny that I had seen an angel. "Don Felipe, you know that I don't like when someone laughs at me."

"No, Rosita, I was laughing because you see angels and the lady in white, and I'm happy for you." He stopped talking when he say Reyna coming out of the house. Don Felipe acknowledged Reyna and asked her how she felt. She looked at him with venom in her eyes. "Of what importance is it of yours, old man? Leave my daughter alone, nosy old man." The old man gave me his blessing before we parted company. "Hurry up, snot nose, it's time to leave. You have ten minutes to get ready before the workers arrive." She went back inside the house. I took off after Don Felipe. I caught up with him to apologize for the way Reyna had treated him. He said, "Niña, don't worry, I've known your mother for a long time, and she has always treated me like that." He told me to be very careful. I ran back home to got ready. I used a piece of rope as a sling for my arm.

The workers arrived on time. Reyna grabbed me by the sweater I had on and pulled me. "Hurry, snot nose." One of the workers helped me to the back of the big truck. Blanquita and Beni followed me atop the truck. Reyna threw a couple of blankets for them. I prepared a nice sitting place for them. Reyna sat in front. The morning was warming up with the brilliant rays of the sun. The dusty ride, the bumpy roads only added to the excitement I felt. For the first time, Mother was taking me to her ranch. I started to sing, "Que diran los de tu casa…"

The workers accompanied me in singing my favorite song. Beni crawled to where I was and sat on my lap. She put her hands over her smiling mouth; she was enjoying the moment. She applauded us when we finished singing. One of the workers complimented my voice; the others agreed with him. "Another one, sing another one," they pleaded. We sang a few other songs. The singing stopped; all I could hear was the sound of the motor of the truck. One of the workers told me that of all my sisters, I was the bravest. I was surprised. I asked him, "You know my sisters?"

"I knew them, Victoria was my girlfriend."

One of the workers said, "We are almost here," pointing in the direction of her territory. I dusted myself off. I could smell the scent of the pines and the cedars that I enjoy. The birds welcomed me with their singing and graceful wings. Reyna was the first to leave the truck. "Come on, all of you, get to work, we don't have all day," she shouted. Each knew what to do. She approached me. "And you, snot nose, get Blanquita and come with me." We followed her to where she showed us some loose barks. "I want you to pick the loose barks, but only the big ones." She showed us the size she wanted. "When you finish piling them up, call one of the boys so he can tie them in a bundle. Don't waste time, having a broken arm is no excuse. That's what you get for climbing trees. Use that arm—broken and swollen, hope you learned a lesson, burro."

"Doña Reyna, can I help your daughter?"

"Don't be ridiculous, nobody helps this snot nose. I hired you to do a job, concentrate on that and not on helping her. Let's go, let's go leave snot nose to do her job. Let her earn her keep the hard way like I have learned."

Blanquita and I piled the bark as directed. I was thinking of many things and didn't converse with Blanquita. I was thinking that Reyna has never bought me anything. No shoes, no dress, not even underwear, not even a taco. *Reyna lies when she says that I don't know how to work. But how would she know, she is never home. Now is my time to show her that I know how to work even with a broken arm.* Blanquita was tired, so I took her and sat her on a bag so she could rest. I went back to do my job. I started to sing my favorite song.

"Rosita, Rosita!" Somebody was calling my name. "Get out of there, the tree is going to fall on top of you." I saw Reyna's facial expression, as if she was thinking, "Who cares?" I saw the tree falling toward me. I took a few quick steps and jumped out of the way. One of the branches of the pine tree whacked me and fell on top of me. I was knocked out. I came to in the arms of one of the workers. "Put me down," I told him, "where are you taking me to?"

"Shh, don't say anything." We entered somebody's house where he laid me down on a bed. I asked him, "Why did you carry me?"

"You were trembling real bad right after the tree fell on you. Your mother gave you up for dead. But here you are, full of life. Your mother sent one of the workers to inform the president of the committee that investigates deaths that you had died. She was ready to have the funeral house, bury you right there. But one of your uncles told us that you suffer convulsions. Your mother knows that you suffer convulsions, so she knew that you weren't dead." I didn't say a word. *Reyna wants me dead, I know that now, and she intended to bury me alive.* My arm hurt more than ever, I wanted to move it, but I couldn't feel anything.

The bone healer, Don Pascual, arrived to check on my condition. He was informed how I had gotten hurt. He felt that I was lucky that I could have been hurt much worse. He checked my arm; it must have been hit by the tree. He told me that the arm would always be worthless. But if by some miracle my arm heals, it will always be bent. "Oh, niña, why does this happen to you? Just look at all the things that have happened to you, most people wouldn't have survived, but here you are with life. Really, niña, *who are you?*"

I turned to face him with my tears flowing. "Sir, my arm is a very important part of my body, but I value my brain, my heart, and the time that my Diosito continues to grant me. You wonder how I will cope with this broken arm, it doesn't matter. I value the rest of my body, like my intellect, and I continue living."

Reyna entered the place where I was being tended to. "See, you worthless snot nose, all you do is cause me problems. You are a good-for-nothing snot-nose brainless girl." She was snorting from the nose like my bull. "Get up, we got work to do." Don Pascual stood up to Reyna. "Have compassion with your daughter, she can barely move." He moved closer to Reyna. "Leave her here with us, we will take good care of her." Reyna, hands on her hips, stared at him for quite a while. "Okay, she can stay." She stared at me with a look that again reminded me of a raging bull.

A sigh of relief followed by a nice smile overcame me when she left. She does have a heart; otherwise, she would have taken me back home. "Why does she treat you so bad? She is your real mother, isn't she? A proper mother doesn't treat her children the way she treats you. Sure we scold our children once in a while and maybe a little spanking. She didn't give you a hug when you were out nor now when she left." The pain I felt from being ignored by Reyna was worse than the pain in my broken arm. I felt another convulsion coming; my heart started to beat faster, and my throat became dry, that's all I remember. When I woke up, I was in bed with all types of medicinal plants around the bed.

"How do you feel?" the wife asked me when I opened my eyes. I tried to get up, but I was too weak. The lady told me to rest. The husband walked into the room. "Ah, thank God that you are still with us. For sure we thought that you had gone with Diosito. He said there is no doubt that your living has been a miracle. There must be a reason Diosito keeps you among the living." I couldn't say anything because of the pain in my arm and the horrible headache that always seems to follow a convulsion.

"Rosita, you are a very strong young lady. You suffer a broken arm, not once but twice. The arm is painful and swollen, on top of that, a tree falls on top of you. You suffer convulsions and face a mother that mistreats you. In spite of all that, you talk to Diosito and pray with so much faith. It appears as though Diosito doesn't permit anything to hurt you. Niña, I have to ask you, who are you?"

"Sir, don't ask me, I don't know. What I know is that when I become of age, I want to be a nun. I pray that my Diosito will grant me that desire." I asked if I could take a bath. I said, "I promise not to use a lot of water." The lady helped me undress. She noticed the scars on my back made by Reyna when she takes the leather belt and whips me. She didn't say anything, but I'm sure she knew how I'd gotten them. I washed as best I could. The lady brought me some clothes. They were a little big but clean. We heard the dogs barking, and the family of the house wondered who could be visiting. The person knocking on the door was Mama Lucia.

"I'm looking for Rosita or Jovani, I understand that she is here." I recognized her voice, I shouted, "Mama Lucia!" I got up in a hurry and ran to meet my second mother. We hugged each with tears streaming from our eyes. "Thank You, Diosito, for giving Reyna enough courage to let Mama Lucia know where she had left me."

No, Jovani, she didn't want to tell me anything about you. I saw Reyna arrive at your house, but you weren't among them. I thought the worst, I gathered enough courage to ask her why you weren't with her and the others. I knocked her door, she answered with, 'What the ——— do you want, old lady?' I asked for you. 'None of your business, old lady.' She slammed the door in my face. One of the workers heard everything, he came over to tell me that you were staying here. He told me about the tree falling on top of you. Oh, mija, what more can happen to you?"

"Mama Lucia, I'm tired, I'm going to bed." She acknowledged me.

Don Pascual asked Mama Lucia, "Why do you cover up for that witch? Now tell us the truth, what did she really say to you when you asked for Rosita?" I heard Mama Lucia relate to Don Pascual how Reyna had talked to her. "Okay, Reyna told me, 'Hey, old hag, what the ——— do you care? Don't interfere with my family. You are lucky my mother owns the place you are renting because if it was mine, I would kick you out in the street where you belong.' Javier heard everything, he is my witness. He came with me, he is outside."

"Javier came to see me?"

"Yes, Jovani, he accompanied me."

Don Pascual invited Javier to join us. After introductions, the lady showed Javier to my bed. "Rosita, how does my grand friend feel?"

"Javier, I feel like running, like singing, like I want take a bath in the river. But as you can see, I'm in bed like a lazy girl with nothing to do." I made them laugh. Javier took some photos of me. "Javier," I said, "you know that I don't like my picture taken when my hair is a mess."

"Come on, Rosita, allow me to take a few more."

"Javier, you want to take my picture with my face all banged up? What are people going to say when they see my swollen lips and my face all banged up?"

"Rosita, if I don't take your photo, I won't make any money. In all sincerity, people like to buy your photo, that's when I make money. But if I'm not your friend, then you won't permit me to take photos of you."

"Javier, you know that I'm your friend, don't kid like that. But you have to give me a copy of all the photos you take of me."

"I will make a copy especially for you. These pictures serve as proof of what happened to you. You probably are too young to understand, but these photos will someday help you in whatever occupation you choose." *I guess that I'm too young to understand,* I thought. "But how are they going to help me? Javier, when you get the photos developed, give them to Mama Lucia." Everybody was in my room talking and enjoying the early evening.

The lady left us to prepare supper. I wanted to go help, but Don Pascual stopped me. "No, niña, you don't move from this bed."

"But, sir, I know how to make tortillas." I wanted to help, now I felt more helpless. Javier asked if I wanted to go outside for some fresh air. "Yes, let's go." Don Pascual accompanied us. I struggled to get out of bed, but I managed. Once outside, I started the conversation because I wanted both men to explain to me how it would be possible for me to write a book. Don Felipe had explained it to me a few times, but I wanted to know from other sources. Both men took turns explaining how a book was made. Javier told me that the photos would show a more complete picture of me. I thought, *I can put pictures of the beatings that Reyna gives me? I should allow Javier to take pictures of my back. But he better act like a gentleman, or he can take them when Mama Lucia is there. I could write about mamacita and Mama Lucia and Don Felipe.* I was beginning to get excited about my book. But I'm still so young, I want people to know now about me and my Diosito. "Looks like Rosita is thinking too much. Usually when she's quiet like this, she is up to something," said Javier. I smiled. "Javier, I was thinking about my book. You and Don Pascual are going to be in it. Javier, these pictures have to be good if I'm going to put them in my book."

"Look what has happened in just a few days. Rosita, you're an incredible girl."

"You want to hear something that happens to me but nothing that has hurt me?"

"Is it spooky, because I don't like ghost stories," said Javier. "Let me tell you, and you decide, okay? I call her the lady in white. The first time I saw her was around three or four in the morning." They looked at each other. Don Pascual asked, "What are you doing up at that hour in the morning?"

"Well, sometimes I can't sleep, so I get out of bed, I go outside to see the moon and the stars. Anyway, let me finish, I was sitting enjoying the moon and talking to my Diosito. Suddenly there's this lady dressed in a beautiful white dress. The slight breeze was moving her dress ever so gentle, she looked at me and smiled. She is a very beautiful lady. She doesn't walk normally, she kinda floats. She always goes toward the showers."

"Thanks for telling me," said Javier, "I don't want to use those baths again."

"Don't worry. That night, I followed her into the baths, and she was gone."

"Now for sure I'm not using those showers." Javier was getting scared. "I have seen her many other times since that first night. The second time I saw her, she waved at me and smiled. This time I watched her more closely. She went to that beautiful rosebush and appeared to cry before going to the baths. Another time that I saw her—"

"Rosita, stop, I don't want to hear more about that ghost of a woman."

"Come on, Javier, just this once and no more, okay? This one time she motioned me over to her. I walked close when she opened her arms to give me a hug. I closed my eyes and put my arms around her. I didn't feel anything. I opened my eyes, she was about ten feet away from me."

"Another one? No, no more, I want to sleep tonight," said Javier. We all laughed.

"Rosita, I believe you because I too have seen some strange things, but those stay with me."

"Tell us just one, come on, Javier." Just then they called us to eat. After dinner when all the kitchen was clean, Mama Lucia told me that if Reyna doesn't come for me tonight or tomorrow, that she will come for me. Don Pascual offered to drive me home. I couldn't, the pain was unbearable, and the thought that Reyna was not coming for me kept me awake. I woke up early, made my way to the bathroom. The sun was starting to shine its light. I love the mornings, but somehow this morning was different. The morning breeze seemed fresher than other mornings. I saluted my shadow, I smelled the flowers and talked to my Diosito, my faith always makes me feel stronger.

The lady saw me. "Niña, you appear to be much better than yesterday. After we eat breakfast, we'll take you home." I was getting ready when the dogs started barking. The lady opened the door; it was Javier. "Javier, don't tell me that you came for Rosita, how nice of you. You are in time for breakfast." I was really surprised to see Javier. "You came for me. Why? Didn't you take enough photos yesterday?" Of course I was kidding because I was happy that he came for me. But I made everybody laugh. "Now that you mention it, no, I didn't take enough, are you going to allow me to take more, this way I make more money? Rosita, you are a very rare person, with all that has happened to you, and you still have a sense of humor.

"The truth is yes, I came to take you home, but more important to let you know that your grandma Sinforosa is back in the pueblo."

"Aii!" I couldn't hold my yell back, I placed my hands over my mouth and yelled again. "My mamacita is back. I am no longer alone." The feeling I felt made me forget the pain, at least for a while. I couldn't stay another second as a guest of Don Pascual and his wife. "Let's go, Javier, I want to see mamacita." I thanked them for their generosity and kindness. "Señor Pascual, you don't have to take us, you have done enough. I can't ask any more of you."

"Be very careful, Alma de Dios, and God bless you."

I was happy to be on the road to see my mamacita. "Rosita, why didn't you allow Don Pascual to give us a ride to the pueblo?"

"Javier, I couldn't ask him to do that after all that he and his wife did for me. Understand, okay? Don't be mad at me. Mamacita says that it's good to entrust people but not to take advantage of that trust."

"Okay, Rosita, I understand."

"Javier, when you were at the pueblo, did you see my mother?"

"Yes, she was home, the wood is piled near the driveway next to that big gate."

"I guess that she just forgot to pick me up last night." He didn't say anything. I looked toward the heavens. "Diosito, someday Reyna will give me a mother's hug, I know she will." Tears started to fill my eyes. "Rosita, why are you crying?" Javier asked me. I told him a little fib, I told him the tears were from happiness thinking that my mamacita was home.

We walked a while before we heard a car driving up behind us going in the same direction. Javier told me to stop and to face the car. Javier stretched out his arm, raised his thumb; the car didn't stop. "What was that for, Javier?"

"Rosita, that is called thumbing for a ride." He showed me how to do it. So the next several cars that caught up with us, both of us thumbed unsuccessfully for a ride. "Rosita, your arm is going to swell up more and hurt even more, don't ask for a ride anymore, I'll do it."

"Javier, this is nothing. How many times did Diosito fall carrying the cross? I feel that the more I experience pain, the sooner my arm will be cured. Like I know that Reyna will someday give me a mother's hug." I don't know what Javier was thinking, he only shook his head and didn't say a word.

Thumbing for a ride got us nowhere. Close to the pueblo, I asked Javier if he could run ahead and inform mamacita that I was on my way. I wanted her to wait for me outside her home. He was just a good person; he didn't hesitate. He took off to inform mamacita that I was getting close to her home. I couldn't contain myself anymore, I took off. I ran until I saw mamacita waiting for me.

Warmth of Love from Mamacita

HER WARM AND LOVING EMBRACE feels like no other feeling in this world. She squeezed me and held me tight, both of us expressing the emotion with loud sobs. I didn't want to let go, and I wished that she didn't want to let go. We separated, she held me by my shoulders with stretched arms. "Alma de Dios, just look at your body, you are all banged up. That mother of yours, I hate her, I hate her. I know she did this to you. Why does she insist on punishing you? My Alma, you are still with me, I thank the Lord for having you with life. He surely has a reason for protecting you from Reyna. Never in my life will I forgive her for what she does to you. Enough talk about her. Mija, tell me what happened to your arm?" I told her the truth. I told her how I was looking for mushrooms and fell off of the tree.

"Now tell me, why are you all beaten up? Did Reyna do this?" I told mamacita that the night that Reyna arrived, we Blanquita, Beni, and I had stayed with Mama Lucia. The next day when I took my sisters to the house, Reyna greeted me with such foul language and called me by some horrible names. "She took the leather belt and hit me with it. In addition, she gave me a slap in my face that left her handprint and big bruise on my cheek."

Grandma Sinforosa started to tremble with anger; she tightened her mouth. "That no-good daughter of mine. It would give me great pleasure to take that leather belt and administer a beating to teach her to respect you. Forgive me, Diosito, forgive me, Domingo, for feeling this way about my own daughter. Mija, I am positive that Domingo would not forgive Reyna for treating you so bad. Enough. Alma de Dios. tell me, why were you at Don Pascual's house? I asked Reyna for you. She told me that you were at your madrina Socorro's house.

I knew she was covering up because your madrina is dead. Maybe what she meant is that she wished you were dead like your madrina."

"Mamacita, I was at the house of Don Pascual, the bone healer. Mother took me to her ranch to take care of my sisters. Mamacita, I was so happy because Reyna for the first time was taking me someplace. But when we got to her place, she told me and Blanquita to pick all of the loose bark from under the trees and place them in piles. Mamacita, she didn't treat me good at all. She doesn't address me by my name, but with some horrible names like *snot nose, dogged feet*. I had just finished placing Blanquita on a stump to rest. As I was going back to work, I heard my name being called. I turned in time to see a tree falling right where I was standing. How I was able to escape, I will never know, but I'm sure Diosito helped me. That's all I remember. No, that is not all, when I heard my name, I saw Reyna's face. She looked at me like 'so what if the tree hits you?' She had an 'I don't care' look on her face.

"I woke up in Don Pascual's house. My mother told everybody that I was dead. She wanted the officials to confirm my death because she wanted to bury me right away. My uncle happened by, he told Don Pascual that I had suffered a convulsion and that Reyna knows it too. Later, one of the workers told me that a branch from the tree had actually fallen on top of me. My broken arm was hit, and it hurts worse now. Reyna learned that I was awake. She stormed the house and ordered me back to work. Don Pascual stopped her. 'This child cannot work in this condition. Leave her here, we will take care of her.' Mamacita, you should have seen Reyna's face. She stared at Don Pascual, but he was not afraid of her. She turned and left the house. I waited all night for her, but she didn't come for me. Why doesn't she like me?"

"Alma de Dios, Reyna is not a good mother. That's the reason her husband took their daughters to el Norté, he didn't want them around Reyna."

"Mamacita, why didn't he take me to el Norté with him?"

"Aye, niña, that man is not your father, your real father is dead. Someday you will learn about your real father, then you will understand more about yourself."

"Mamacita, you are telling me that the father of my sisters in the North is not my father? Oh, Diosito, what else don't I know about my own life? Please, Mamacita, tell me more, I want to know the truth. You know who my real father is, don't you, Mamacita?"

"Alma de Dios, this I can tell you now, get along with Marcelo. You and Marcelo have the same father but different mothers. You two are related to the Bustos family from Huaztelica. Some day you will discover more. Mija, I want to take you to the city, the bus is about to leave."

"Mamacita, do I have time to go to church?"

"Yes, mija, but better hurry." I ran to the church, I talked with my Diosito. I ran to the house. Reyna was playing with Blanquita. When she saw me, her mood changed. I greeted her, and with the same breath, I asked her permission to go with Mamacita. She said, "You can go wherever the —— with that old witch, get out of my sight, snot nose." I got close enough to give Blanquita and Beni a hug, being careful to keep my distance from Reyna. We made it to the bus on time. The trip to Taxco, Guerrero, the city known for its fine silver, would take a while. The bus was loaded with people with one thing in common; they were all different. I was a little bored; to break the monotony of the long trip, I started to hum my favorite song. The gentleman in front turned around and told me that I had a beautiful voice. Others overheard what he told me. Soon it seemed that everybody in the bus was asking me to sing. "Please," they urged, "sing for all of us."

Mamacita nudged me with her elbow. "Come on, mija, I too want to hear you sing." I felt happy, and I sang my favorite song. The passengers loved it so much they asked for another. I gave it to them, and they loved that one also. A passenger took off his hat and collected 103 pesos for me. "Mamacita, I'm going to share this money with Mama Lucia and Don Felipe." She smiled. "Niña, you have the heart like your grandpa Domingo." We arrived, got off of the bus, and started walking. I love the city, but all I saw were busses and cars. No burros or horses pulling anything. "Why don't people use donkeys here?" Mamacita laughed. "Would you rather ride in a car, on a horse, or on a burro?"

I was happy not being alone and especially happy to be with Mamacita. I didn't realize that she was taking me to the hospital until we stepped on the grounds of the building. "Mamacita, what are we doing here? Are you taking me to the doctor?"

"Yes, mi Alma de Dios, I want the doctor to look at your arm and all those bruises."

"No, Grandma, I don't want to see the doctor. All he does is stick me with a needle full of some liquid, and it hurts. Let's go home."

"Come on, mija, don't be stubborn, you are going to see the doctor, and that's it, don't argue with me." I felt cold. Mamacita never talks like that to me. I told her that I was going to return to the pueblo. "Mija, I only want what's best for you, wait and see the doctor, he will help you get better."

I made the sign of the cross as we entered the hospital. The doctor wanted to file a report with the police when he saw my bruises. I pleaded with him not to. He cleaned them up and put my arm in a sling. He couldn't do much with the arm. We left the hospital. Both of us were hungry. I wanted to pay for the food, but Mamacita wouldn't allow me to spend my money. This is one restaurant somewhat busy with some Mexican ranchera music being played over the system.

"Now we are going to buy you some clothes because you are staying with me at my ranch."

"Mamacita, you are taking me to your ranch?"

"Yes, we better hurry with the shopping, or the bus will leave us here." She bought me clothes for the summer. We finished with plenty of time to catch the bus. My grandma noticed that I was really exhausted. She helped me lie on the seat with my head on her lap. Her caressing my head with her soft hand made me feel secure. I woke up when she gave me a gentle nudge and said, "Alma de Dios, we are here. Alma de Dios, I hope you feel good because we have to walk from here." We walked and sang all the way to her place.

Vacation in the Natural
Beauty of Her Place

IN THIS PLACE, THE PLACE Mamacita calls her ranch in the prairie, I spent the most joyful and happy days of my life. I had never enjoyed such bliss and happiness. At night we would sit outside and listen to the natural calls of the wild. Many nights we slept outside, falling asleep only when sleep overpowered me. I never wanted the night to end. Every night I tried to count the stars, every night she would tell me to learn from them. She taught where the moon got its light. To this day when I see the moon and the stars, I pray to my mamacita.

She would point to the brightest of stars and told me a story about that star. She would point to another and would tell me another story about it. I wish I could remember those stories. But at her place, I didn't have paper and pencil to take notes for my book. She mentioned that when the moon is full, my soul is illuminated. She would say, "When the moon is illuminated on the top half, it's going to rain."

The owls frightened me after she told me that many people thought that witches would turn into owls. The howl of the coyote also made me feel uncomfortable. Some nights I would sing with her, sometimes I'd sing her some of my favorite songs. Her two favorite songs that Domingo would sing to her were "El Adios del Soldado" (A Soldier's Goodbye) and "La de Porfirio Cadenas" (Balad of Porfirio Cadenas). But the one sang that made her cry was my very own song: "I'm Nobody's Daughter."

Another night after we had exhausted most of the topics of conversation, she asked me, "Niña, if we are attacked by a shark, wake me up, okay?" I smiled. "Ah, Mamacita, you know that sharks only live in the water."

"Okay, little smartie, what if we are attacked by a crocodile, will you wake me up?"

"Now that's possible because crocodiles live both in land and in the water, but don't worry, Mamacita, I don't think that we have any close by."

"My granddaughter has studied well, I am proud of you. When I was your age, I was real dumb, I didn't know anything. Your grandpa Domingo taught me how to count money and how to save." I was getting sleepy, I dropped my head on her lap. She sang a nice relaxing melody that was putting me to sleep.

A flash of lightning followed by a boom sound of thunder woke me up. "Mamacita, God is taking our picture." Another flash of lightning. "See, He took another one." During my sleep I had a convulsion. I woke up with a horrible headache. "Niña, how do you feel? You were talking in your sleep. You kept saying, 'Mother, don't whip me, don't whip me anymore.' You were delirious. Alma de Dios, you have a fever, and your arm is really hot." I drank the cold water that Mamacita gave me. "This should help calm your fever."

"Mamacita, can I take a shower with the rainwater? I don't like to be sick. I become sicker the more I think of being sick, cold water will help me."

"Well-spoken, my little child, I will fill the tub for you."

"Mamacita, I don't want a tub, I want the water that is falling from the sky."

"Well, then go give yourself a good cold shower." I got a towel and went out in the dark cool evening. I got under the "waterfall" beneath the eaves of the house. Mamacita wouldn't believe that I was actually taking a shower from the heavens. I enticed her to join me, and join me she did. My fever went away.

Next morning she told me to pick the fattest and oldest chicken. I went to the coop and wrestled the biggest and oldest chicken. I was horrified when I saw that she was going to wring the chicken's neck. I started to cry. "Niña, if you can't bear to see this, you better go inside."

"No," I told her, "I can handle this, the pull of ten mules couldn't make me go inside, I'm here to help you." My grandma killed the chicken, and I helped her to gut and defeather it. Mamacita enjoyed that I was not afraid to slay and then prepare a chicken.

That night was another learning experience for me. We were sitting outside enjoying the evening. "Listen," she said, "do you hear dogs barking?" At first I didn't, but their barking got louder. "Listen, mija, there are about five rustlers trying to steal some of my cows. Wait here, don't move." She left me and soon returned with a big rifle and some fireworks. She lit some fireworks one right after another. The explosion was loud enough to scare anybody. She held the rifle up high as though she was firing it. The sound of hoofbeats followed the sound of the fireworks. She shouted loud enough for the would-be rustlers to hear. "Next time, I won't miss!" she shouted. Now those rustlers know who Sinforosa Albarran, widow of Domingo Bustos, is.

She showed me the rifle. It was old and useless except to scare people. She had found it near a burned-out wagon in the prairie. She couldn't stop laughing, she had actually scared those rustlers. "Tonight we are going to say the rosary. You still remember how to say the rosary, don't you, Alma de Dios?"

"Yes, I remember because you taught me how to pray, Mamacita, I haven't forgotten. I also remember the mysteries, they are Glorious, Sorrowful, and Joyful." We prayed the rosary. At the end, Mamacita asked God to forgive Reyna for having a dirty and sinful soul. "I hope that Reyna will ask for forgiveness for the sins she has committed as a mother for having taken the souls she has buried in my property."

"Mamacita, what are you saying?"

"Don't pay attention to me, I'm thinking out loud."

"Mamacita, have I told you about the lady that I see near the rosebush near our house?"

"No, mija, you have not. Tell me, what do you see?" I see this beautiful lady dressed in white. She walks through the patio usually after midnight, she kneels near the rosebush and cries. She walks into the bathroom and disappears. I know because I have followed her."

My grandma cracked her knuckles. "Alma de Dios, that lady should appear to your mother. Your mother has to settle things with that lady. I hope that the lady and your mother meet." Mamacita got tears in her eyes and a running nose. "Don't cry, Mamacita."

"Mija, I hope that Don Felipe has written all of these things for you. Someday show the notes to your mother, I want to know what her response will be."

I didn't want to see her cry so I changed the subject. "Mamacita, you have a lot of statues of saints, but you don't have the Santo Niño de Atocha. Why?"

"Niña, for some mysterious reason, one day it fell and broke. I can't explain it. But I am looking for one to replace it."

"Mamacita, did you hear that I played with Santa Niño de Atocha?" She looked at me. "You did?" she asked.

She wasn't sure if I was playing with her or not. "Come, let's sit in our favorite place, I want to hear all about it." We sat at first very quiet. "Well," she said, "tell me about Santo Niño de Atocha."

"Mamacita, remember the last time you left to come here?"

"Yes, mija, I remember, is that when you played with him?"

"I was crying and very lonely. I ran and ran with no direction or purpose. I stopped near the mudhole where I saw a calf jump in and disappear."

"Niña, you mean where we call the quicksand swamp?"

"Yes, Mamacita, I wanted to jump in there so I could rest a few days."

"You what! Niña, you can't do that, you will die."

"Mamacita, I was so lonely. I started to climb the fence that surrounds the mudhole."

"Oh, mija, I am so sorry for leaving you."

"Don't worry, Mamacita. I was climbing the fence when I heard a little voice behind me. I turned around and saw this little boy calling me." She started to cry. "Mija, was it the Santo Niño de Atocha?"

"Yes, it was, but I didn't know at the time who he was."

"Tell me everything, Alma de Dios."

I told her everything. When I got to the part where the boy told me that his mother and father were my father and mother also, she hugged me and cried for some time. Finally she asked me when I had discovered that I had played with the Niño. "Mama Lucia wanted to know where I had spent the afternoon. I told her that I had played with the boy. She took me to the church to speak with the priest. The priest investigated me. I had to describe the boy to him. It happened that the Niño had disappeared from the altar the same time that I was playing with him. The priest took me inside the church, and that's when I saw the statue of Santo Niño de Atocha. Strange, Mamacita, but I had gone to the church many times, and I had never noticed the statue before."

"Mija, tomorrow we are going to town, and I will buy a statue of Santo Niño de Atocha. At the same time I am going to pay for a Mass in dedication of the Niño. Mija, one more time, I will tell you, you are truly an Alma de Dios. How many other things have you been up to that I don't know about?"

"Mamacita, I don't know too many things about you either. Are you willing to tell me about my grandpa Domingo?"

"Oh, mija, I will tell you because I want Domingo to be in your book. I had just lost my husband and was looking for work. I was hired by Domingo to do housework. I had your uncle Ruben with me, he was just a little boy."

"Mamacita, Uncle Ruben is not my grandpa's son?"

"No, mija, he is not, but your grandpa always loved him like his own sons."

"Oh, but tell, me when did you and Grandpa become friends?"

"Oh, niña, you ask too many questions. One day Ruben was really sick and couldn't stop crying. Domingo walked into my room and asked if he could help. After that, he would help me strap Ruben to my back so that I could do my chores. The rest of the workers had children, but they stayed home, they didn't accompany their moms to work.

"Domingo used to play with Ruben." When she mentioned that, I saw a glimmer in her eye. "One day when I was cooking, he walked into the kitchen, and we started talking. Before I knew what was happening, he grabbed my chin, and we kissed for the first time. My heart pounded so hard I thought that I was going to have a heart attack. My knees trembled. Oh, mija, I still remember that day. When he touched my chin, lifted my face, and planted a kiss on my lips." Just thinking back made her sigh as though she was experiencing that first kiss. "Mamacita, is that when you became engaged? Did you marry him right away?"

"No, mija, I wasn't sure if I wanted to marry him. My first husband abused me, and I didn't want to face that life again."

"Mamacita, what happened to Ruben's father?"

"Ruben's father died. One night he was coming home on horseback from the cantina. It was raining really hard, and the river overflowed. He tried to cross it, but the debris and the torrential water swept him away. He was found a few days later. That's how it came to be that I came to the pueblo looking for work.

"But in time I realized Domingo was a good man. We fell in love and got married. Your grandpa didn't care that I was so much younger than him. He didn't care what people said about me. We had a wonderful life together. Our love was as big as the stars are numerous and as hot as the sun."

"Oh, Mamacita, then you and my grandpa Domingo really lived it up, huh?" She smiled; her eyes looked upward toward the stars. She turned to me and grabbed my hand; she said, "I hope that you find a man, like Domingo, that loves you and takes care of you like he loved me."

"A man like that is my Diosito because I intend on being a nun."

"Really, mija, you want to be a nun? Blessed be God, I hope he grants you that desire, because you will be serving Jesus Christ, the most powerful man in the universe. You are a good girl, and I'm glad for you. Let me tell you a little more about Domingo. He taught me how to dance. I was so naïve that I didn't even know that. My first husband never took me anywhere."

"Mamacita, did you have a big feast on your wedding day?"

"Yes, we had one of the biggest feast the pueblo had ever seen. Domingo and I danced and danced all night long. Every time I had a baby, he threw a big feast.

"On Saturdays afternoons he would take me for a ride to Tetipac. It is a beautiful place. He took me to the top of Cerro de la Punta (Pointed Hill) and to Cerro de la Cruz (Hill of the Cross).

We would go swimming in the famous *las posas de agua* (bath holes). Your grandpa loved being outdoors enjoying the beauties of nature."

"Mamacita, do you know how to swim?"

"No, I am terrified of the rivers. I saw the raging waters that took Ruben's father. Since then, I will not go near the river. The posas de agua were different, and Domingo was there to protect me. Domingo taught me a lot about life. He educated me in many ways. Most important is that he taught me that as a woman, I had my rights. He taught me how to defend my property, how to value myself as a person and to have confidence in myself."

"Mamacita, did your parents accept Domingo?"

"Mija, for such a young girl, you really ask personal questions. But like I've told you before, you learn a lot by asking questions. My parents didn't like Domingo because he was much older than me. People like to gossip, and I heard that my parents resented that fact that I had married one of the richest men in the pueblo." I reached to her and hugged her. She held me with loving arms, I could sense the love that she had for me. But with each night, with every hug, I knew that my time to return home was closing in. I wondered about my little sisters, my school, and the promise I'd made to the teacher. I thought about Reyna, would she finally give me the hug I have longed for? I wondered why she didn't love me. Day after day these thoughts lingered. I didn't want to leave Mamacita. I had my happiest days here, but I had responsibilities reserved for adults. My Diosito was my guiding light, and I couldn't let Him down. My sisters needed me because Reyna was not a responsible mother. My grandma would ask me what I was thinking. My usual answer was that I prayed that my Diosito would have compassion with me and allow me to stay here in the ranch.

She knew that staying with her would be a problem. Reyna would not allow it. In the past, Reyna had taken Mamacita to court to prevent her from taking custody of me. Reyna had full control of me. Why? I never understood why she wants to keep me away from Mamacita, Reyna doesn't love me. I grew anxious day by day knowing that my stay was getting away from me. I dreaded the day, the day that my happy days would end. I asked Mamacita to go with me to church, I had to speak to Diosito. In church I knelt in front of my Diosito and prayed. "My dearest Diosito, I ask You to cure my ailing arm. On my knees, I will start at the end of the church and crawl to the altar with a bouquet of roses and place them in the main altar."

I was talking to my Diosito not realizing that Mamacita heard my prayer. I heard her cry, I turned to console her. "Mamacita, don't worry, my Diosito will fix my arm, and someday He will cure my illness."

"I believe you, mija, I believe because of the faith that you have in God."

"But you know what, Mamacita, I still have my arm. It might be crooked, but I still have it." We left the church on time to see lightning followed by thunder. We beat the impending storm.

"Niña, come with me." I followed her to her shed. "Help me with these barrels and these buckets, we must capture as much rain-water as we can."

"What do you use the water from the heavens for?"

"Oh, mija, I use it for cooking, for washing dishes and clothes, and I take a bath in it. Haven't you noticed that I don't have city water or my own well?"

"Mamacita, where does the rainwater go?"

"Alma de Dios," she said, looking at me with her hands on her hips, "you are full of questions."

"Oh, Mamacita, doesn't appear that you like my questions. Is it because we haven't filled the buckets with water?" I didn't talk anymore. We filled all the containers with rainwater. The rain subsided except for a drizzle. The birds were enjoying all the puddles, some even finding a worm.

I wanted to jump into one of those puddles. "Someday I am going to see the ocean," I said it out loud. Mamacita got close to me, put her hands on my shoulders. "Mija, someday you will. I have always dreamt of visiting Acapulco with the sole purpose of seeing the ocean. Your grandpa Domingo saw the ocean several times. He would tell me about the sharks and whales that he saw. He described the sharks with huge mouths. Can you imagine being eaten by one of those?" We smiled. "The news that a person was eaten by one of those sharks was scary. So, niña, as long as I don't go in the water, I'm safe." I never want to forget the wonderful time that I spent with Mamacita. I wrote my diary as well as I could.

I Return to the Pueblo, Mamacita Returns to Her Ranch

DON FELIPE WOULD HELP ME with the finished version. I wrote everything including the trips Mamacita and I would take to the lakes. She allowed me to swim in the cool clear waters. My arm always felt better in the cool water. Afterward we'd have us a picnic under the shade of the trees. I wrote how I was able to shuck corn with one broken arm. I wrote how I met some of my cousins, the sons of my uncle Manuel. They worked for Mamacita taking care of her livestock.

One day Mamacita wanted to know the content of my writings. She was sitting in her favorite chair, I knelt in front of her. "Mamacita, someday, when I write my book, I want people to know that I spent the most wonderful times here with you. I want people to know how much I learned from you. They will know that you showed me a life full of happiness. I want them to know that I learned that you don't need to be rich when there is love and respect in a home." The last night before I returned to my pueblo, we sat outside. We talked and sang some of our favorite songs and went to bed crying.

I returned to my pueblo with mixed feelings. I was happy to be back, but I knew it was short-lived because Mamacita was not staying. She stayed long enough to collect her rents before she left. That's when everything changed. I was lonely and sad to see her leave. Before she left, she gave me her benediction. "Be very careful, mija, you know that you can go with me anytime." Of course I knew that Reyna would not allow it. I stood watching her until she disappeared beyond the walls. I carried my bags as best as I could to the church. Crying in front of my Diosito, I prayed for Mamacita, and I asked

257

Him to heal my arm. I repeated the promise to go from the front of the church to the altar on my knees when He cured my arm.

When I left the church, struggling to carry my bags, I saw Marcelo. He was hiding near the church drinking a soft drink. I spoke to him asking him why he was hiding. "Jovani, I am not hiding, don't even say that. Jovani, where are you coming from with all those bags? Why don't you use a donkey instead?"

"Look, Marcelo, instead of making fun of me, why don't you help me?"

"Okay, Jovani, I will help only because it's you."

"Jovani, what happened to your arm? Don't tell me that Reyna beat you and broke your arm."

"Come on, Marcelo, that's not what happened. I broke my arm when I fell from a tree." He went as far as the gate and no farther. I thanked him and promised him gum or a candy for helping me. "Don't worry, Jovani, but since you are offering, why not make it two candies." He laughed, turned, and ran toward his home.

Am I to believe that Marcelo is my brother, really? I saw my old friend waiting for me. He was sitting all alone smiling because I was home. He rose slowly from his chair, motioned for me. "Come, give this old man a big hug. I missed you, Rosita," he said. "Now that you're home, I will not feel alone or sad seeing you every day."

"Don Felipe, I brought you a surprise." I handed him the package. "No, Rosita, let's go inside. I don't want to open it out here." Inside he cautioned me about taking care of my belongings. His room was very dark; it took my eyes awhile to see in the darkened room. I was surprised to see buckets full of rainwater and puddles all over the floor. "Rosita, it rained very hard yesterday, and this roof is very old, and it leaks, as you can see." I grabbed the broom to sweep the puddles from his room. He stopped me; he said, "Open my present, and then you must go home. It's been days that Reyna left the house and left one of your sisters with me. Thank your Diosito that Ana is home. If she hadn't come back from the city, I was going to turn your sister to the officials. By the way, Rosita, your mother has another friend."

I found a dry spot on his floor, got on my knees, put my hands on my bowed head. I cried, saying, "This is my destiny, this is my life. Mamacita, where are you, why didn't I stay with you?" From my kneeling position I asked Don Felipe to tell me about the man he saw with Reyna. "Rosita, you know that if Reyna notices that I am spying at them, she will chew me out. But he is a big man dressed like a *charro* (Mexican cowboy)." I told him, "Then he is not the father of neither of my little sisters."

"Rosita, how do you know?"

"I know because the father of Beni is Noel Pedrosa de Amatitlán, Guerrero. Don Felipe, you wrote all the information on her father, don't you remember? I have the documents."

"Rosita, I have written so much information that I don't remember half of it. But it's on paper, and someday you will have them neatly arranged in a book."

"I got all the information so that my sisters don't have to go through what I am going through. I don't know for sure that Jorge Bustos is my father. Because if it is true, why isn't he here with me? I asked Reyna if Jorge was my father. All I got was another beating from her and told me that Reza is my father, not Jorge. But my madrina Socorro and my *tia* told me that Jorge is my father."

"Rosita, I can't say for sure, but I don't think that Reyna likes Beni. I hear a lot, and I think that she wants to sell Beni."

"Don Felipe, please don't say that. I don't think my mother is capable of doing that."

"Rosita, I see many things, and I don't tell anybody. But from what I see, if it wasn't for Ana, I think that Beni would have died because your mother doesn't like her." My knees started to tremble. "Mija, I won't say any more, I've said enough."

I left his room discouraged, grabbed my bags, and dragged myself to the house. *Why does that woman make us suffer so much? Come on, Rosita, perk up like the other times. Think of the good time you had with Mamacita. Look, I'm here at home and alive.* I hesitated to enter the house, even with the knowledge that Diosito was at my side. But in reality, I knew that once again the responsibility for my sisters was on my shoulders. I sat on the step for a while. I thought of my uncles; surely they would help me. But if I approach them, for sure Reyna will give another beating.

Ana Warns Me about New Man in Reyna's Life

I FINALLY PUSHED THE DOOR and entered. Ana was ironing; when she saw me, she screamed. "Vani, you are home. Blessed be God you are here." We hugged, I said, "Ana, I am happy to be home."

"Vani, I hear you, but your eyes tell me something different. You look sad, my little sister. Tell me, why are you so sad?"

"Ana, I spent the most wonderful days with my mamacita, now I come home to learn that you will be leaving. I will be in charge of my sisters, what kind of life is that? I love my sisters, but they are not my responsibility."

"Vani, don't worry so much. Yes, I will be leaving, but our mother is coming home soon." Ana wanted to know about my stay with Mamacita. I was very animated when I told her.

I stood in front of the ironing board to face Ana. "And, you sister, how's Mother treating you, and do you know when she'll be back?"

"Vani, you know that she doesn't have a conscience or a heart. Who knows when she and that man will return? Speaking of that man, he is scary, he looks at me with evil in his mind. You have to be very careful with him. I tell you he is an evil person. Vani, I am grateful that you are back to help with Beni and Blanquita. Now that you are here, I can leave for my new job in the city knowing that you will take care of our sisters."

"Ana, don't worry. I will take care of them with Mama Lucia's help."

"Vani, Vani." Those were the last words I heard, I had a convulsion. I was on a blanket with a pillow under my head. Ana had wrapped a towel soaked in cold water on my head. I tried to get up, my head was pounding and pounding. I lay back to rest my head. "Ana, I heard you say something about the man that is seeing Reyna. Why did you tell me to be very careful when he is here?"

"Vani, he is very nosy and pries into our lives. The way he looks at me…well, I won't say more other than for you to be careful."

"Ana, are you sure? You know that Reyna needs somebody to help her with us and her land."

"Vani, listen to me, his intentions are not honorable, he means to take advantage of us. The first time I saw the look in his eyes told me a lot about his intentions."

"Ana, I don't understand what you are trying to tell me."

"Vani, do you know what it means when a man desires a woman? He looks at with lust in his eyes. Be careful, again I tell you. If he tries to do anything, go tell Don Felipe, and he will call the officials. Vani, you should talk to Don Felipe, he will explain to you what I've been trying to tell you."

Ana packed her recently ironed clothes. She was ready to leave for the city. "Vani, remember, tell Don Felipe or Doña Lucia, don't stay quiet. Be strong for all of us." We hugged before she left. I was left with a heavy heart, a face full of tears. "Please, Diosito, give me the strength to cope and please don't abandon me. My mother will protect me if that man tries anything. If not, I will fight him like I fight with others that try to harm me. Diosito, why do I want to marry, I am already a mother to my sisters? What if I marry a man that mistreats me? No, I will fight to become a nun and serve You, Diosito."

Blanquita was waking up; when she saw me, she shouted, "Vani," and ran to me. I couldn't pick her up because of my arm and because she was bigger. Beni started to make waking-up sounds. They were happy to see me. I was hungry, and I knew that they would be hungry also. I cleaned them up and dressed them. Blanquita helped me as much as she could in making breakfast. The three orphaned children ate together. We played some games before we went to Mama Lucia's eatery. We started to leave the house when I saw Ana entering the main gate. I was surprised but happy that she was back.

"Ana, what happened?"

"Oh, Vani, it's a big mess. When I got there, they told me that they had contracted another girl. I came back and talked with my ex-boss Doña Lucila and got my job back. I came home to leave my things and change." I was elated, I wanted to jump with joy. *Thank You, Diosito,* I thought. "I am sorry, Ana, but it's nice you still have a job." Ana didn't appear too happy; she said, "Yeah, thanks to God, I still have a job." She changed and left us. The three orphans walked to the diner of Mama Lucia. I sang all the way until we arrived at the diner. Beni was moving her arms to the song, and Blanquita tried to sing along.

"Look at my three happy little girls," said Mama Lucia when she saw us. I hadn't seen Mama Lucia since I got back to the pueblo. "Jovani, you look so grown-up." She gave me a big hug. "Welcome back, mija. I missed you, and seeing your sisters happy, I think they missed you also." I told her about the confusion with Ana and the job in the city so she had to come back to her old job. Mama Lucia said, "See how Diosito is watching out for you? That's another proof how He looks after you."

We spent the rest of the day talking. I told her of my happy stay with Mamacita. Beni needed a change of clothes. I told Mama Lucia that I would go home and get her a change of clothes. As always, I ran, but not straight home. I wanted to go this way and whichever path I desired, and yes, always thinking. *Why do I think so much?* I answered myself, *Well, maybe because I'm always alone.*

I entered the house then got Beni some clothes. I heard a knock on the window. I went to investigate; it was Doña Rebeca Hurtodo. I opened the window. "I am Rebeca."

"Yes, Rebeca, I know who you are, how can I help you?"

"I am looking for Ana, is she home?"

"One moment, Rebeca." I closed the window and went outside to speak with her. We exchanged greetings. Finally she told me that she wanted Ana to work for her, and she left. I was happy for Ana. I ran hoping to catch Ana before she reached Doña Lucila's house. But fate seems to interfere at the most critical of times.

I was stopped by Doña Carmela Fuentes. "Niña, where are you going to in such a hurry, what's the emergency?"

"No, Señora Fuentes, no emergency. I was trying to catch up with Ana."

"Ah, yes, I saw Ana, she is washing Doña Lilia's clothes. Niña, be careful, don't run so fast, especially with that arm."

Ana asked me, "Vani, did you come to help me?"

"No, Ana, I came to tell you that Doña Rebeca Hurtado wants you to work for her."

"Really, Vani, how do you know?"

"Because she came to the house looking for you. I told her that you were working for Doña Lilia, but that you would work for her if she paid you more than Doña Lilia. She said that she will pay you more.

"See, Ana, only God knows why things happen when they do. The best thing is that you have a job here, and I'm here to help with our two little sprouts. Now we must comply and give our offering to Diosito for giving us what our hearts desired. Sister, is it okay what I did?"

Ana couldn't stop laughing. "Where did you learn to talk like that?"

"Ana, you should laugh more often, you look very pretty when you laugh."

"Vani, go tell Rebeca that I will work for her. Tell her that I will stop at her house when I finish here. Vani, treat her good, you know that she is the wife of the president of the pueblo, don't you?"

"Yes, Ana, I know that." I asked Diosito to forgive me for telling Ana a little lie. I didn't know that Rebeca was the president's wife. I ran to her house. How else am I to get anywhere? I don't have a bike or a burro.

I was out of breath when I got to her house. It took me a short while to tell Rebeca that Ana would work for her. I also told her that Ana would come by after her work was done for the day. "Relax, niña, come inside, you need to drink some water." The cold water felt good. "Niña, when I went to your house, I saw two little girls with Doña Lucia. They were playing outside the diner. Are they your sisters?"

"Yes, the bigger one is Blanquita, the other one is Beni."

"We know that you and Ana have a big responsibility with that of a mother. Where does your mother live?"

"Ma'am, I have no answer."

"Well, it appears that your mother is not a very responsible person. Niña, if you ever need anything, you can depend on me and my husband." I was hurt with the words Doña Rebeca said about my mother. Of course I have heard that kind of talk from others. The people know that Reyna is gone a lot and we have to take care of ourselves and our two sisters. But it still hurts when they talk bad about my mother.

My little sisters were playing when I arrived at the diner. "Vani," Blanquita screamed when she saw me. She ran up to me and gave me a big hug. Baby Beni followed her older sister, and she also gave me a hug. Before long, Doña Rebeca arrived at the diner with bags full of food and other goodies. "Rosita, these things are for all of you." I was grateful because I knew that we were short of food. She stayed talking with Doña Lucia and myself. Ana arrived just as Doña Rebeca was leaving. Ana and Doña Rebeca talked about the job. I heard Doña Rebeca tell Ana that I should be her manager. They laughed. It didn't make sense to me, I didn't know what a manager is.

The four sisters from the same mother but different father sat down to eat. We ate, we sang, and Ana told us a story about a little country mouse going to the city. That night I had a nightmare. I dreamt that an earthquake and a tornado had destroyed our house. I woke up scared, my heart was beating very fast. I prayed to my Diosito and soon fell asleep.

The following morning, just about the time Ana was leaving for work, Reyna walked into the house. I was happy with reservations to see her, but I saluted her. She walked by completely ignoring me. Feeling that she hadn't heard, I saluted her again. This time she acknowledged me, she said, "I see that you are back, snot nose." She pushed me aside. "Why didn't you stay with your grandma forever? I don't want you here." Ana hadn't left for work. Ana began to argue with Reyna. "Vani doesn't go live with Grandma because of you. It's your fault, you know you won't let her. If you would have allowed Vani to go live with our grandma since she was born, she would be a lot happier. Vani wouldn't be suffering so much if she lived with our grandma."

"You ungrateful daughter, I provide you with a roof over your heads, and this is the way you talk to me defending this snot-nosed." Reyna slapped Ana. She grabbed me by the arm and shoved me out the door. "Get out of my house, snot nose, I'm having company, and I don't want you around." Ana grabbed me by the hand. "Vani, let's get away from here." Reyna is about to discover who the ungrateful person is. She is about to know how much you and I do for her two daughters. I feel sorry for Blanquita and Beni having to live in the plague that is Reyna.

I kept quiet. I was just surprised how Ana was speaking about Reyna. "I will never allow her to slap me again, never again." Ana was showing a lot of courage, confronting Reyna like she did.

"Ana, do you want to go to church with me? You will feel a lot better after you talk with Diosito." She agreed. "Maybe I can talk to a priest."

"Yes, Ana, he will make you feel better. You can also talk to Diosito, He will listen to you." The priest heard us sobbing. He asked if we were okay. Ana asked to talk with him. They went into the confessional, I spent the time praying to God.

"Vani, give me a big smile," she said when she left the confessional. "Ana, not only will I give you a smile, but two. The first is from my heart, the second is because Diosito always is with you even though you don't see Him. Have faith and confide in Him." The priest heard everything. "Rosita is right, your faith opens doors and always remain open." He looked at me and gave me a big smile. "Rosita, I can attest that you are truly a gift from God. I have seen with my own eyes many times how Diosito protects you." Before we left, the priest blessed us with holy water.

"Vani, I have never talked about Mother with any priest. When we entered the church, I didn't feel good. Now I feel much better after talking with the priest. Vani, I want to take Beni with me, Reyna doesn't pay attention to her."

"Ana, when I think like you are thinking now, I sing my song, 'I am the daughter of no one.'" Ana laughed. "Oh, Vani, talking to the priest and hearing you sing, I feel happier."

"I am happy being with you, Ana. I am always alone, Reyna denies me, she doesn't love me. But my Diosito is always at my side, so in that way, I am not alone. But he is in heaven, and I am here." I moved my arms and did a little dance step. "Ana, want me to sing you the whole song?"

"For sure, Vani, sing the song with all your heart and soul."

I sang my song. Ana applauded when I finished. "Vani, you use the words so beautifully, you can also be a poet the way you arrange the words."

"Ana, you like the way I use the words? I have a poem, you want to hear it?"

"Okay, my little sister poet, let me hear it."

> The faith and love in you
> Will open doors to success
> And attain miracles
>
> Living has an end
> But life, "no"
>
> Value and live your life
> Living is a love
> Enjoy your life's mystery, shielding in life
> Promise, achieve and conquer loneliness
> To treasure life is to love yourself

"You are really smart, little sister. I know you, but do I really know who you are, or should I ask, who are you?" Smiling, I said, "Ana, I am your sister. My own mother doesn't know who I am. She calls me *snot nose* or other names, and many times she hints that she wishes I was dead, but I don't die." I continued to do my dance steps; alone or not, I will find happiness. Ana looked at me. "Vani, the more I know you, the less I know who you are. Anyway, you are my sister, but I have to go work. I hate to leave you alone." I watched her walk away, but I was still happy. I danced to my steps all the way to the diner.

Mama Lucia was happy to see me prancing about. "Jovani, thank God you are here, I missed you." I told Mama Lucia, "I am happy being back at my pueblo and back with my second mother." She looked at me. "Jovani, your words say something, but those eyes say something else. You are hurting inside, your heart is in pain, tell me, what is the matter? I am here for you."

"It's my mother, she needs help. She is always angry. I try to help her, but she doesn't want my help. I wish that Reyna would go to church with me. I am sure that God is waiting for her."

"Jovani, what's behind all that talk about Reyna?"

"My mother kicked me out of the house. She told me that she doesn't want to see me. I don't want to talk anymore. I feel better when I'm selling my candy. I don't think about that woman when I'm busy talking to people."

"Good for you, mija." I packed my box of candy and took off. I continued my prancing because it made me feel good.

I was unaware that a well-dressed man was watching me. "Niña, come here. I want to buy some candy." I was startled because I wasn't paying attention. "Yes, sir." I walked over to where he was, sitting with four other men. "Do you want to buy only one? If you have children, I'm sure they would be happy if you brought them some candy."

"No, señorita, I only want one."

"But, sir, maybe your wife would like a gum or a candy. These men next to you are good customers, they buy candy from me all the time." He gave me ten pesos. He told me to keep the change.

One of the other men asked if Reyna had broken my arm. I told him the truth that I had fallen off a tree and broke my arm. I could tell that he didn't believe me because he told me, "Come on, niña, tell me the truth."

"Oh, señor, I am telling the truth because my Diosito won't permit me to tell lies."

"Okay, Jovani, I believe you." He bought fifty pesos' worth of candies for his sons. He told the others, "We must help this little girl." Hearing that, they all bought candy. It took me the rest of the afternoon, but I sold most of my candy and gum.

Based on instinct, I started to walk home. I suddenly remembered what Reyna told me. I was happy having sold most of my goodies. I pranced down to the church before going to Mama Lucia's diner. On the way, I ran into ladies, Doña Maria Castañeda and Doña Lola Arce. Doña Arce stopped me. They were making a big scandal asking me if Reyna had broken my arm. Before I could answer, Doña Arce makes a comment regarding how I could work with my broken arm. I told them not to worry, that Reyna had not broken my arm. I tried to tell them how it really happened, but they had already surmised that Reyna was the cause. I did sell them the last candies that I had. I saw them walk off talking. I thought I heard one them say that they should report Reyna to the authorities. *I don't tell lies, my Diosito doesn't permit me to lie. Oh well,* I thought, *I'm happy that I sold all my candy.* I took my earnings to my hideaway bank. I now had enough money to buy my medicine. I pranced all the way to Mama Lucia's diner.

That night I felt unhappy, full of sensation, and somewhat desperate. I wanted to make myself strong, to forget what Reyna had told me and how she treated me. *But how? My Diosito, my savior, guides me, but Reyna is another matter. She has to reconcile with Diosito. God can help me with my arm, but not with Reyna.* Morning arrived finally. I got up. Mama Lucia was already getting ready for the morning customers. I walked by one of the tables, I bumped into one of the chairs with the bad arm. I was so angry, I picked up my good arm and slammed it on top of the table.

Doña Lucia saw the frustration on my face. "Jovani, tell me you are up to something. Tell me, what are you planning?"

"Mama Lucia, I'm going to exercise so that my arm would get better."

"I'm going to help you." She warmed some water in a big pan; she added chamomile and salt. She told me to immerse my crooked arm in the water. I shouted, "The water's hot." I pulled my arm out as fast as I could. I talked myself into putting it back in; hot or not, this is a solution. She told me that we were going to do this every day. "Next time we go to the city, I will buy a sling for your arm." In the water, I exercised my arm little at a time. Mama Lucia wrapped it up after I finished.

I found myself in front my house. I shrugged my shoulders and walked in the house. Mother was sitting near the window, she ignored me. I greeted her, she looked at me with disdain. "You finally decided to come home, huh, little tramp." I flinched expecting a slap, but she didn't slap me. Instead she grabbed me by my hair. "Please, Mother, let me go, don't hurt me. If you don't love me, let me live in peace."

At that moment, Ana walked in. "Mother, let go of her, let her live in peace."

"Ana, you stay out of this. This snot-nosed girl's name is *Jovani*, not *Rosita*, and most of all, not *Alma de Dios*." She stood up; with hands on her hips, she repeated, "Her name is *Jovani*, daughter of Reza, not of Jorge Bustos like all you think." Ana grabbed my hand. "Come, let's get out of this house." Reyna stood in front of the door. "You two don't appreciate what I do for you. You don't realize how much I do for you." She pointed her finger at me. "You don't leave this house. Remember, you have two sisters." The next moments passed in silence. "What are you waiting for, snot-nosed, Beni needs clean diapers. Ana, helped me gather the dirty diapers." Blanquita and Beni enjoyed being close to us; they played while we washed diapers.

The Tension of a Man Living in the Same House

ANA DROPPED A SURPRISE ON me; she said, "Vani, I can't go on living like this. I am thinking of leaving and going to work at the federal district. I won't be making the same, but I can't live here anymore. Vani, I tell you this with a heavy heart because I don't want to leave you alone."

"Ana, I will be alone again. When do you think of leaving?" She talked, but I didn't hear anything for a while. I continued washing diapers among tears. I heard her say, "In a few days."

At night, Ana and I sat at the table talking. Our little sisters were playing with each other. Reyna sat without saying a word; she appeared to be worried. The knock on the door startled us. We looked at each other; nobody moved to open the door. Reyna always opened the door, but not this time; she just sat, didn't move. Ana answered the door. "Who is it?" she asked. "I am a friend of Reyna Bustos."

"Let him in," ordered Reyna. The man was wearing a big black cowboy hat, dressed like a Mexican cowboy. He walked in as though he owned the place. I noticed a big knife in a sheath hanging from his side. He took off his hat revealing his gray hair. He walked around the kitchen looking at Ana and at me. I noticed how much lighter his skin was than Reyna's when he reached down to kiss her.

Reyna stood up without saying a word. The man turned to face us. "You are Reyna's daughters?" I stood in front of him, his knife level with my eyes. "Yes, and who are you, and what brings you here?"

"Wow, look at this little virgin asking me that question."

270

"Well, señor, you enter our house, and we know nothing about you."

"You little virgins are right in asking a stranger that question. I come to see your mother, Reyna Bustos, the most beautiful lady in all of México." I had to move aside; he walked right by me toward Reyna. Ana pinched me. "Ouch, don't pinch me," I whispered.

Ana whispered back, "Vani, that's the same man that visited Reyna after Beni was born. I don't like that old man. I feel it in my blood that he is like a hideous thorn. Be wary of him."

"Hey, Reyna, I didn't know that you had such beautiful daughters like you." He took her hand, led Reyna toward us. "We don't have to tell them anything about us. We don't have to explain anything to them."

"I don't want to know, so don't include me," said Ana. "Jovani is the one interested, not me." I spoke up, "Yes, I want to know about any person that enters this house." The old man tried to hug me. I slapped his hand away. "Hey, niña, you need to learn some manners." He sat on a chair near the table, looked at me face-to-face. "My name is *Guadalupe Figueroa*, I'm from Pilcaya. Your mother and I have known each other since we were kids. I was good friends with all of your uncles since I was a kid. Now I come to visit your mother. Maybe she will allow me to help you with whatever I can." He turned to Reyna. "Right, my love? I see with my own eyes that this virgin is very tender and beautiful, we must take good care of her."

"Hmm." Mother, in a flirtatious mood, approached him. "Lupe, don't worry about my daughters, they know how to take care of themselves, and they are well educated. Except that snot-nosed one." She pointed at me. "She has a sickness, but she is still with life, as you can see." I couldn't stand any more of their ridiculous talk. I walked out of the house. I accompanied Ana; she was sitting on the stairs. "Vani, I told you about that man, you believe me now? Be careful, especially when I leave, okay? He might be related to one of our fathers. I mean Beni's, Blanquita's, and my father. I don't mean yours, Vani, that would be difficult. You are the only sister whose father has died, and you will never see him."

"Ana, then you know that my father is dead? In other words, your father is not my father, and I am not a Reza." Ana clamped up, didn't say any more. "Ana, please talk to me, I want to know."

"Vani, don't pay attention to me, and please don't ask me any more questions about your father."

"Everybody knows about my father but me. Why is everybody afraid to tell me?" She put her around me. "Vani, someday you will know the truth. I can't tell you anything, I don't want any more problems with Reyna.

"Come on, Vani, let's go inside, maybe we can learn more about that old man."

"Look at this girl," he said as we walked in the house. "Tender like a virgin. Come here, Jovani, let me look at your arm." I looked at Reyna, ignoring him, hoping that she would stop the dirty old man. Instead, she told me to allow Lupe to touch my arm. I didn't know how to avoid getting close to him; suddenly I asked Reyna if I could go visit Don Felipe. She moved her arm as though she was getting rid of a fly. "Leave." I know that Don Felipe goes to bed early, but that was the only thing that I could think of.

I sat on the stairs away from the house. My thoughts were not organized. I thought of Jorge Bustos. Is he or not my father? Why doesn't anybody tell me the truth? My thoughts were at the llano with my mamacita, then I could see myself on a horse with the man people say is my father, Jorge Bustos. That was too much, my tears wouldn't stop, and I let them cover my cheeks.

Ana left the house, she was looking for me. I called her over to where I was sitting. "Vani, I am surer now than ever. That man means to cause us harm, his intentions are not good. His leering eyes say a lot. When he looks at me, his intentions are not good. Vani, I am going to speak with our uncles Ruben and Matilde, they will tell me what sort of person he is." We saw the door open. "Vani, hide, the old man is coming out."

"Ana, I don't hide from death, neither will I hide from that old man."

He sensed where we were sitting. He approached us. "So this is where Reyna's daughters are hiding from me."

"No, sir, we don't hide from anybody, much less from you. We are enjoying the tranquility of the evening." With his hands on his belt buckle, he talked real macholike. "I'll say it again, you girls are beautiful and good like my mule. I bid you goodnight but not goodbye." He blew us a kiss and walked into the house. I had to laugh. "Ana, we are like his mule? Can't he tell the difference between us and a mule?"

"Jovani, I tell you that man is a bad person. I am going to show what I mean so you can protect yourself."

"What harm can he cause me? My mother beats me with a leather strap, I fought a bull, ha ha, I break my arm, I have convulsions, and here I am, alive."

"Jovani, listen to me, I am serious. When that man wants to touch, yell as loud as you can. Tell me, and I will report him to the officials."

"Ana, I don't understand."

"Jovani, he wants to sexually abuse us."

"Ana, I still don't understand you."

"Vani, you are really innocent." I thought, *What is my sister trying to tell me?*

"Some men, like that old man, want to take advantage of a young girl. Vani, do you understand?"

"I hear you, but how can a man take advantage of a little girl? Ana, don't worry because I won't permit that old man to do that with us." *Dirty old man,* I thought, *he should be ashamed of himself.* "Vani, promise me that you will protect yourself against that man."

"I promise, and if he wants to abuse me, I will tell Mother."

"Vani, don't confide on Reyna, she won't do anything. Especially if she has to protect you."

"Then I will go to Doña Lucia and tell her. Maybe our uncles will do something. I will have to talk to them."

That night I had a beautiful dream full of stars and a brilliant moon. I woke up in the middle of the night. Unable to sleep, I went outside. I looked at the time; it was 3:16. I thought of Diosito and of Virgin Mary. I fell asleep outside. I woke up when I heard Ana leaving for work. "Jovani, what are you doing out here so early? Did you sleep outside?"

"Ana, I was waiting for you." Tears started rolling down my cheeks. "Don't cry, little sister." She hugged me. "Ana, it's easy for you, but I stay here alone again. Mamacita leaves me, my madrina leaves me, now you leave me."

"Vani, I have to leave, you know that. But I will be back in a couple of months. Remember my words: be careful of that man." I watched Ana and her bag as she walked away. In tears I told myself to be strong. I sat down; my desire was nonexistent. Why am I always alone? Diosito is my companion, but I can't hug Him. Now I ask myself what others ask, *who am I?* I know that I have a sickness with a broken and crooked arm. I have a mother, but I don't want to think bad about, but I don't think badly about anybody anyway. I am with life, and people say that I am a pretty girl. I have a mamacita, two sisters, Mama Lucia, and Diosito.

Don Felipe came out of his room. I ran to greet the old man. "Why are you crying, Rosita?" I didn't know where to start. I just rambled on and on. "Okay, Rosita, calm down and start from the beginning. Before you do, I'm getting my pencil and paper. I want to write all of this down."

"Okay, señor, I will get your coffee." I ran to Mama Lucia and got his coffee. He wrote everything. I especially wanted to write about the lecherous man. When we were finished, Don Felipe told me that he overheard Lupe and Reyna talk. "Rosita, they mentioned your name many times. Ana is right, the man is not a good person."

The church bells rang indicating that church was about to start. The old man who could barely walk and the little girl with a crooked and broken arm made their way to Mass. The church is my refuge, Mass is my salvation. The sermon was about Padre Alfonso's cows, but the rest of the lectures were very refreshing. After Mass, the priest invited me to his room. Sister Sarita left some class information with him. I asked the priest if Sister Sarita was his sister. He laughed. "No, niña, but we both serve God. In His eyes, since both of us serve Him, we are considered, for religious purposes, brothers. Now, niña, do you understand?"

"It is clear to me now, very clear."

Don Felipe waited for me outside the church. "Rosita, your teacher came looking for you when you were away with your grandma. He wants to see you."

"Really? Did he tell you the reason he wants to see me?"

"Apparently the suggestion you had regarding using the auditorium for classes was approved by the president of the pueblo."

"That is great news." I placed my hands over my mouth. "Yes, yes, the president listened," I shouted. "Together the education services will prevail, and the children of the pueblo will benefit. The president of the pueblo finally is going to help the pueblo. Looks like the president appreciates us." Don Felipe laughed. "Rosita, I enjoy hearing you talk. Now if you were the president, this pueblo would really show progress. The people would love you."

"Oh, Don Felipe, don't kid with me. I am too young to be the president."

"Rosita, believe me, with your intelligence and the association you have with the people, I believe that you could be the president of the pueblo. Now go see your teacher David." I parted company with the old man. "Jovani, Jovani!" I recognized the voice of the person calling me. *Reyna! Oh, now what does she want?* I turned around. Reyna was standing near the stairs with hands on her hips. My knees wouldn't stop shaking, my heart wanted to jump out of my chest. "Where is Ana?" she shouted. I stayed where I was. I didn't want to get any closer to her.

"Didn't Ana tell you that she was going to the city, she got a new job there."

"No, she didn't tell me anything. She went without my authority. You and Ana don't give a damn about me. Come here, snot nose." I made my way fearing the worst. She grabbed me by my braid. "It's your fault that Ana left." She hit me over and over saying, "What a disgrace that I am your mother. Why haven't you died, snot nose? You are nothing but more than a thorn in my life." I stared at her, I grabbed my side where my heart was hurting. Her words hurt more than the beating.

My heart was hurting, but through tears, I asked why she didn't love me like a mother. "Shut up, snot nose, you don't make my life happy, you are nothing but a thorn in my life. I am tired of supporting you. You owe me more than your life. Now I want all the money that you have hidden away. I know that you make money selling for that old lady Lucia. Hand it over now, or you die."

Mother Threatens Me and
Takes My Savings

I NOTICED WHEN DON FELIPE closed his door. I was sure that he would write everything he heard. Reyna was insistent, "Tell me, snot nose, where do you keep it?" I answered, still crying, "Mother of mine, money doesn't give you complete happiness, but you can attain happiness without it."

"Shut your mouth, enough of your worthless words."

"Mother, don't hurt me anymore, quit living between being selfish and cruel."

"Look, snot nose, I told you to be quiet. Go get your money, you owe it to me."

"I don't have money."

"Don't lie to me, better to tell me that you don't want me to have it. Remember your sisters, do you want them to die of hunger? If you don't hand over the money and something happens them, I will tell the authorities that it was your fault, and they will put you in jail."

"No, no, I'm not bad. Only the sinners go to jail." I got up from the floor where she had thrown me. I wanted to run, but she must have read my mind. She grabbed my braid. "Where do you think you're going, snot nose? Don't even think that you can run away from me."

"Let me go, do you want my money or not?"

"Where do you have it?"

"Mother, that I will never tell you, so don't ask. Let me live in peace, and I will give you the money I have saved. I have earned that money with my sweat and honorably. But remember, my love I have for you as a daughter has more value than you have for me. I don't understand why, why you, being my mother, have no love for me, only hate. But I will never tire of waiting for a motherly hug from you."

"Shut your mouth, don't pretend to be stupid and hurry with the money."

I ran out the door, I jumped the trench where dirty water from the laundry dumps into. The gate to keep out the animals was not locked. I opened the garden gate, I held on to the railing guarding the garden. I ran past the trash dump to the location of my secret money hiding place. I took my money can from the secret hole. I spread the cloth on the ground. I placed the coins on the cloth. I left the $1,000 bills in the can and a few coins. I sealed my secret bank and neatly tied the cloth containing the coins. The coins were very heavy. I had difficulty carrying them, especially with a crooked and broken arm.

I struggled with my load, but living a life full of surprises, something was bound to happen. A gust of wind made it more difficult. I stumbled and fell on top of a bush; the cloth opened, and the coins scattered throughout the plant. My arm hurt more than ever. I didn't move because I was too frustrated, and the pain in my arm wouldn't stop. I cried trying to soothe my arm. Suddenly I noticed movement out of the corner of my eye. With my own eyes, I saw Jesus Christ, my Diosito, extend His arm to help me. He took my arm and soothed it. "Get up," He said, "continue on your way. I am here with you now and I always will be."

He left. I thought, *Was that an illusion?* I started to pick the coins, still wondering if it truly was Diosito who appeared to me. Walking with the coins, I looked to the heavens and asked Diosito to bless the coins. I prayed that this money would bring happiness to Reyna. I prayed for my sisters, and I prayed for Reyna, asking God not to allow her to hurt me. "Diosito, forgive me for not giving all my money to Reyna. But you know that I need the money for my medicine. My faith in You tells me that nothing is impossible." I finally arrived at home.

"You finally got back. Where's the money, snot nose?" She had just given Beni a bath. "Come here and dry your sister." Beni was happy to see me. I placed the money on top of the table. She went for the money and left Beni sitting on a towel. She told me not to leave the house. "When you finish dressing Beni, give Blanca a bath."

"Mother, please help me, my arm is hurting a lot, and I don't have any feeling in it."

"Don't be ridiculous, I am tired of your sickness, now you come with another one? Besides, I don't care. Look at you, snot nose, no matter what happens, you don't die."

"Mother, I help you with my sisters, I bathe them and feed them, that's the reason I ask you to free me of all the abuse and never hurt me again. Be compassionate so that your soul can rest in peace."

"Shut up." Enraged she grabbed me and pushed me toward the door. "Get out of here, go wherever you damn please. You want your liberty? You have it, now get out." I hesitated for a moment, I didn't know what to do. "I said leave. What are you waiting for! You are worthless." I left thinking, *Why is she so mean with me?* My heart was aching more than my crooked arm. *God, what more can I do to earn my mother's love?* I sat and prayed for Reyna. Don Felipe saw me and motioned me over.

I walked over crying full of sadness. My heart hurt more than my arm, my sadness stronger than ever. My old friend hugged me. He noticed that my arm was swollen and turning dark. "Alma de Dios, did Reyna hurt you again?" He kept talking, I was too emotional and didn't hear a word he was saying. I caught some words. I believe that he knew that Reyna had taken my money. He said something about Reyna. I told him not to talk badly about Mother. "Sometimes I think that she is not my mother." I asked Don Felipe if he knew for sure that Reyna was my mother.

I couldn't stop crying. He tried to console me, but only Reyna can make this pain in my heart disappear. My tears were flowing nonstop; they fell on my lips, eliminating the desire for food.

"Rosita, the true tear is not the one you shed from your eyes and slides down your face, but the one that pains your heart and slides down to your soul. You never forget the grief you experience. It's easy for one that has a memory, but to forget it is difficult for those with a good heart. You, Rosita, know how to love your life, and you value the time that Diosito lends you."

"Señor, you've told me before that the dawn and my age have dictated more of what my life has been. For that reason, I have valued my life full of faith in God. You have shared life experiences with me, thank you. I have to go now." I wish I could fly like when I saw my Diosito a while ago. I must have whispered my thoughts loud enough, Don Felipe heard my desire. "Rosita, what did you say?"

"Sorry, Don Felipe, I was thinking out loud."

"I heard you, tell me, did you see God?"

"Yes." I told him how Diosito had helped me. He took paper and pencil and wrote everything I shared with him. The abuse by Reyna, the money, and the way my Diosito helped me.

Jorge Bustos Came Looking for Me in 1982

"Don Felipe, I have to go, but first I want you to tell me if Jorge Bustos is my father. Please don't ignore me like everybody else has." I slowly made my way to the diner. "Oh, niña, I can't say for sure, only your mother can tell you if he is your father or not. But this I know for sure. When you were about a year old, a man from the North came looking for Reyna. You mother had left the pueblo. The man asked me if I knew Reyna Bustos. I was somewhat surprised that a man from the North would come looking for her."

I waited a while to answer. "Why?"

"If Reyna finds out that I snitched on her, she would kick me out of here. But I didn't lie to him. I said that I knew her." Don Felipe hesitated like he didn't want to continue. I felt that my old friend had information but was hesitant to continue. I sat on the floor close to him. I opened my eyes, smiled at him. "Please, Don Felipe, tell me more." He touched my head. "Yes, mija, that man told me he was Jorge Bustos, a friend of Reyna. He also told me that Reyna had borne him a child in Texas." I whimpered, wanting to shout with joy; tears filled my eyes.

"Rosita, I haven't told you this before because I'm afraid Reyna will kick me out of here."

"But, Don Felipe, please tell me more. Then you know that my father came looking for me."

"Well, yes, but maybe looking for Reyna."

"Don Felipe, please, please tell me more."

"Niña, relax, I don't want you to get sick. Your eyes tell me that you are enjoying the news, so relax. Okay, I will continue, but you have to relax. He asked me if I knew your grandma Sinforosa. I told him that yes, I knew her. He wanted to see her, but I told him that she was not in the pueblo but in her farm in Piedras Negras.

"Jorge was perspiring, he took of his hat to clean his brow with a handkerchief. 'Señor mailman, can you give Reyna a message that I am here looking for her.' I told Jorge, 'Write her a note, and I would see that she gets it.' He pulled a small photo of himself and wrote a message on the back. But then I thought, how can I give it to her, she can't stand the sight of me? So I never gave it to her."

"Don Felipe," I said, all excited to know that I might see a picture of my father, "do you still have the picture?" I jumped up. "Please show me the picture."

"Relax, Rosita, I don't want you to have a convulsion, in time, I will give it to you, it's yours.

"Rosita, do you want to hear more?" I was a little disappointed that I couldn't see the picture right away. Yes, I was desperate to hear more. "I didn't see Jorge after that day until your mother came home. He was waiting for her because when she came home, he showed up. When she opened the door, I got next to the window. I wanted to hear everything they talked about.

"She was surprised to see him at her doorstep. 'What are you doing here?' 'Oh my, Reyna,' he answered, I' came to see you because you don't answer my letters.' She lied to him. 'What are you talking about? I haven't received any letters from you, besides, you don't know how to write.' 'Reyna, you know that I know how to write. Reyna, don't you remember the little love notes I used to write you when we lived together up North?' Niña, I am not nosy, but I wanted to know more. Jorge asked your mother, 'Reyna, where is the baby that you carried in your stomach when we separated? I want to see her, to hold her in my arms, I want to love the child that I planted in your stomach.'

"She lied to him again. Reyna pretended to cry, she led him on. Jorge asked her why she was crying. 'Take it easy, I'm here with you, Reyna. Tell me, what's the matter?' 'Oh, my love, that little baby died

282

at childbirth.' She lied again. When she said that, I couldn't take her lies anymore, and I stopped listening."

"Diosito, then my father thinks that I am dead."

"Rosita, your father would have given you a better life than the one you're living with Reyna. After that, I heard that Jorge got in a fight with a man that was seeing Reyna. I understand that he spent some time in jail."

My vision went blank, I had a convulsion. I felt a cold wet cloth on my forehead, Mama Lucia was at my side. I was lying atop a blanket, a small pillow beneath my head. Don Felipe said that I was a divine gift. He urged me to go with Mama Lucia. Somehow I was able to get up. I went to the diner with my second mother. "Jovani, when we get home, I'm going to help you with your arm. It is all swollen. Did Reyna hit you again?" I told her what Reyna had done. In addition, I told her that Reyna had taken some of my money.

At the diner, she told me that she had a surprise for me. "I went to Taxco and bought you some more gum and candy. I went alone because I couldn't find you. Before I forget, your teacher David has been looking for you. He needs to see you. Jovani, let me do something about that arm. Tell me the truth, did Reyna hit you deliberately in your arm?" I couldn't talk, I remembered the words from Reyna wishing that I was dead. I thought of the lies that Reyna told my father. That I had died during childbirth. The beatings come and go, but the lie she told Jorge, that I was dead, will forever be carved into my heart. *My father thinks that I am dead. I will find him.* I cried and cried like the wounded girl that I am.

"Rosita, you don't have to cover for your mother, we know what kind of person she is. I heard her when she was shouting for you." I gathered enough energy to speak. "Ana left the pueblo because she can't stand to live with Reyna, especially now that Lupe is around. Reyna blames me for Ana leaving." I didn't want to talk about Reyna, I wanted to know more about Jorge.

I wanted to ask Mama Lucia whether she knew my father, Jorge, but I couldn't. The burning pain in my heart was very heavy, I needed to rest. Instead, I got on my feet and headed to the church. The tongue might be fragile, but it is the one that causes the most damage. There exists good and bad people, but even the bad people have heart. All depends on their dignity and faith in God. I didn't choose Reyna, but like it or not, she is my mother.

The church was so quiet and peaceful. I talked with my Diosito. I felt good after I talked to him. I sat in a park bench to think. *I have to put a stop to all the beatings that Reyna administers. I will not let it happen again. Diosito will give me strength. My smiles and good thoughts will help me overcome my loneliness.* I stood up and pranced toward the place I would find Teacher David. I was passing by the dried-up fountain; I jumped in. It was very enticing to see it dry, I danced around the base enjoying myself.

"Be careful, little girl, you might fall and break the other arm." I stopped and saluted Doña Conchita. "Oh, Rosita, you are always jumping and running like a little goat." I laughed, jumped out of the fountain, and ran toward the municipal auditorium.

I entered the gate, walked toward the door of the class. The teacher noticed the door when I opened it. "Jovani, come in." He walked to the center of the room to meet me. With his hand on my shoulder, he asked the students to stand up and greet me. They stood up to greet me. I felt happy to be among friends. I sat on the floor with the rest of the students. The first thing that I remember was one where the teacher drew three lines. The first line represented the students in the first grade. The second line represented the second grade, the third line the third graders. He told us to sit in the proper line according to grade.

While the students were sitting according to grade, three of them began whispering among themselves. The teacher reminded them that he did not permit that kind of behavior. "Now, Javier, tell me, what were you and Cesár whispering?"

"Señor, my friend Cesár says that Jovani is the daughter of the crazy woman of the pueblo."

"You believe that, Javier?" Cesar said, "Don't believe me, Teacher, because he is in love with Jovani."

"Cesár, I didn't know that you were a tattletale," Javier told him. "Señor David, I told Cesár that Jovani is very pretty, but she is too young to be my girlfriend." I was angry when I heard that, especially when the students laughed. *Crazy boys,* I thought. He lectured them on the etiquette he expected from all the students.

During recess, the teacher wanted to know about my arm. I told him, and I was glad he asked because it seems that everybody is blaming Reyna. He also wanted to know how I had spent the summer. I couldn't stop talking about the wonderful time I spent with my mamacita. I asked the teacher that if I became his assistant, would I be able to complete my first grade ahead of time? He told me that I could finish my first grade in eleven months. "Then I can become a nun much sooner," I told him. He laughed. "Oh, so you want to be a nun? The problem we have in this pueblo is that we need a new school. You are right, Jovani, I have but fifty students, whereas the other school, Nicolas Bravo, is overflowing with students."

My Birth Certificate Mystery
on My First Day in School

AFTER THE FIRST DAY, THE teacher asked me to stay behind. He asked me to bring my birth certificate. I didn't know what that was. He explained to me and told me that I needed it to continue attending school. That certificate contains information about when and where I was born. "Also contains who your father is and who your mother is and the name of your grandparents." My mind was thinking about my father; my heart was beating so hard I thought it was going to jump out of my chest. "Jovani, listen to me, it's important that you bring that document."

"Señor David, I can't ask my mother for that document."

"Jovani, why can't you?"

"Please don't ask me that. Can you ask my mother for it?"

"Jovani, that is not possible, unless she does not have one at her house."

"I don't know if Mother has a copy, but she won't lend it to me. Every time I ask her who my father is, she slaps me. The last time I asked her, she ordered me not to ask again. She said, 'Someday you will know, now get out of my sight.'"

"Rosita, many of the parents that I know have told me about your mother, now I believe what they told me.

"I never imagined that it was true. So in reality, you don't know who your father is?"

"No, Señor David, and neither am I sure that Reyna is my mother. She treats me real bad, always breaks my soul in pieces, and she answers with beatings." I began to sing with tears in my eyes, "I am nobody's daughter…" He allowed me to finish the song. He took my hand. "Rosita, today I will go speak with your mother, I don't want you to worry, okay?" I answered by nodding my head. "If your mother isn't cooperative, tell me who else knows about your life. The person has to be somebody that knows exactly where and when you were born and that knows for sure who your parents are."

"Three people have known about my life—my grandmother Sinforosa, Mama Lucia, and Don Felipe."

"If I can't get information from your mother, then I will talk to one of these persons. I've been a teacher for many years, and I know just how you feel. I know that you will continue learning and will get a good education. Jovani, your eyes say a lot about your desire to get an education, they also tell me that you're in great pain because of your arm. Knowing you, I have come to realize that you are a secret angel in this pueblo and someday for the whole world."

The recess ended, and the students filed into the auditorium. One of them raised his arm to speak. "Teacher, if my mother knows that I am in the same class as Jovani, she will pull me out of this school."

"Speak up, why will she pull you out of my class?"

"Because Jovani is the daughter of the Reyna Bustos, the crazy lady of the pueblo." Another boy stood up and told the student to shut up. "That is none of your business." Everybody was shouting; in the confusion, I ran out of the room clutching my head. The teacher came out, I could hear him calling me. I didn't stop. I ran all over the pueblo. I stopped at the edge of a ditch, I washed my face and soaked my arm. I lay down, looking at the empty sky. Alone again.

What did I gain by running away and not confronting those rumors about my mother? The whole pueblo talks about her. Even Mamacita doesn't get along with her own daughter. I will be strong, I will no longer run away from hurtful moments. At that moment, I saw a most beautiful bird singing. With each note, he seemed to sing, "Arise, be happy. Arise, be happy." He was perched atop a big rock in front of me. He made me laugh. "Oh, little bird, even you want to give me advice."

"Good morning, little girl." Somebody had seen me. *Can't be alone for a second,* I thought. It was my uncle Ángel Ortega. "What are you doing here all alone talking to the birds?" I smiled. "Oh, Uncle, you surprised me, to tell you the truth, I don't know what I'm doing here. But here I am talking to the birds." I walked toward him. His horse was loaded with two huge barrels full of fresh milk. "Niña, looks like you are a little thirsty, would you like some fresh milk?" I shook my head. He filled a metal cup with fresh warm milk and gave it me. I could feel the warm milk going down my stomach; it felt so good.

"Tell me, mija, what are you doing here?" I told him how the students had talked about Reyna and I had ran out of class. "Niña, go home, it's getting late, and the ghosts will start coming out. People have been spooked in this area by ghosts."

"Uncle, I've been through here many times, and I still haven't seen any ghosts, so don't worry about me."

"Come walk with me. I won't leave you alone out here."

"Uncle, how are you my uncle? Are you related to my mother?"

"Niña, with due respect, but thank God that I am not related to her. I am related to your father, Jorge Bustos."

"Uncle, you know that Jorge Bustos is my father?"

"Rosita, tell me the truth, in all of these years, Reyna has never told you that Jorge Bustos is your father?"

"No, Uncle, she has never told me."

"Hija, your Reyna is a wretched woman, I don't want any problems with her. Someday you will know the truth."

"I am the only person in the pueblo that doesn't know for sure that Jorge Bustos is my father. Why won't they tell me? What is the mystery?" I was upset that my uncle didn't want to tell me the truth. I didn't want to speak with him anymore. My pace was getting faster, I walked faster and faster, I turned back and shouted, "Uncle, thank you for the warm milk."

Mama Lucia was waiting for me. "Where were you, mija? I was worried about you, but I'm glad you are okay. Where did you spend the day?"

"Relax, Mama Lucia, I spent the day in the gorge near the ditch. Don't worry, Mama Lucia, I am okay."

"Jovani, next time you want to wander about, let me know. Once I know that you are okay, I stop worrying, but until then, I worry too much.

"Jovani, that so-and-so man from Pilcayo, you know your mother's new friend? Well, he is at your house. When I didn't know where you were, I thought that your mother and that man had done something terrible to you. See, that's why I want to know where you are. Otherwise, I worry."

"Oh no, I don't want to go home now, not with him there. What am I going to do? Now Reyna has an accomplice. Chuchin, help me, protect me against that man. I got shivers the first time I saw that man. If I go home, she will abuse me, slap me, and maybe worse. If I don't, she will be just as mad and beat me when I do go home. I'm between a wall and a rock. Why can't she treat me like a daughter? Why does she hate me? Now a dangerous man is at her side. Help me, Diosito, what am I to do?"

The Lecherous Man Abuses
Me for the First Time

MY SECOND MOTHER COULD SENSE my dilemma. "Niña, I wish you could stay here forever, but you know Reyna. She is capable of causing me harm and maybe kick me and possibly Don Felipe from our rooms. I am here for you, but we have to be careful."

"I understand, Mama Lucia, I should go." Don Felipe was waiting for me. "Old friend, what are you doing up so late, you are usually sleeping by this time."

"Mija, I was waiting for you. The man, your mother's latest friend, is inside your house. I want to warn you, and please be careful. I saw him unload lots of clothes. He plans on staying for some time." Now upon hearing what he told me, I really didn't want to enter the house.

I sat close to the old man. I said, "Don Felipe, I need my certificate of birth to continue going to school. The teacher tells me that either that or my baptismal certificate. Where can I get them without my mother finding out?"

"I will help you," he answered. "I believe that you were born the first part of '81 or '82, but I don't know where. Tomorrow you and I will go see the priest. He should have your certificate of baptism."

"Don Felipe, I will be at your doorstep before the rooster crows." I had no desire to go home. With trembling legs and minimal strength, I entered my house. I felt like a wounded bird entering the house of horror.

I was welcomed with a frown from Reyna. I greeted her, she ignored me. "Good evening, precious little virgin." The lecherous man was sitting near the table drinking from a bottle of tequila. "Broken or not, you have a beautiful body. The rest of you should be very good." I didn't know what he meant, but I was trembling even more. My heart wanted to jump out of my body. *Relax,* I told myself, *Mother will protect me.* I didn't respond. "Come sit here on my lap." He motioned me over and put his hand on his knee where he wanted me to sit. His ugly smile was nauseating, I looked at Reyna. She was smiling as well. *Oh, Diosito, she is not going to protect me,* I thought.

I didn't move; my legs were still trembling, and my heart was beating faster and faster. Again I looked at Reyna. Reyna, still smiling, said, "Come greet him, show your manners, don't be antisocial." The old man grabbed my hand and pulled me toward him. I could not get loose; he was too strong, but I resisted. "Don't be stubborn like a goat, snot nose, do what Lupe tells you. Don't embarrass me. Listen to me, snot nose, as of today, I order you, in front of Lupe, to obey him. You will do everything, and I mean everything, that Lupe tells you to do." She got up from her chair and pushed me onto his lap.

He smelled horrible, like a wet sheep. "Did you hear what your mother said? Obey me, and I will give you the education of your life. But you have to do what I tell you." I couldn't escape his grasp. Reyna sat in front of us. I was close to wetting my pants. The lecherous old man, looking at Reyna, smiling with eyes of an executioner, began to touch my back. He asked me, "How'd you do in school today?" All the while he was sliding his hand down my back. He continued talking, I couldn't listen to his meaningless talk. I kept asking my Diosito to help me. Somehow I was able to escape his grasp. I jumped out of his lap and gave him a slap. "Nobody touches me the way you are touching me. You are nothing to me but a dirty old man."

I was trapped and couldn't run from them. Reyna came after me with killer eyes, like the bull that wanted to injure me. She grabbed my collar. "You ungrateful snot nose." She slapped me. "Now, now, my love, what is wrong with your Indian mixture? This Indian is crazy. My love, it's better that I leave because your Indian daughter's accusations are very serious. Those are serious words, and I could wind up in jail."

"No, Lupe, don't leave. Forgive me for having this snot nose that doesn't know how to show respect to her elders. I would like to bury her, but she is well-known, and there's bound to be somebody that finds out. To tell you the truth, I don't even know who this girl is. With all that happens to her, she simply won't die." How many times have I heard Reyna say that she wishes me dead? Ana was right, Reyna will not protect me against the old man. I was angry because she had not protected me, but I was scared, and who wouldn't be? Now she has an accomplice.

The old man tells Reyna. "Let me have her. I will teach her about life, then we can finish her off."

"No, my love, she knows too many people, the officials will investigate. What I should do is take her to the city and sell her off. In the meantime, I will teach her to obey you." She dragged me outside by my hair. She took off her shoe, I saw her swing it at me. I dodged and didn't feel the blow. She repeated the words, "You little——, I'd like to kill you."

"Well, do it," I shot back, "what are you waiting for? That's what you have done to others. You are not even my mother because I am nobody's daughter. Don't hurt me anymore." That's all I remember. I woke up near the corridor outside the door on top of a carton.

I didn't have the strength to get up. I remembered what happened up to the time when I had my convulsion. The alley cat got close enough for me to hug him. I looked up to the heavens and cried. *Diosito, why don't You take me with You? I am tired of suffering. I find that I live between loneliness and darkness, sick without a father, and a mother that wishes me dead. Diosito, I am the daughter of no one, take me with You.* I had enough strength to get up. Everything was so quiet except for a few birds greeting the morning.

I dreaded going inside the house. But I had to because I have my medicine in there. I survived her last night; well, I will survive today. The door was locked, I looked through the window; they were gone. I felt relieved. I went to my hideaway where I keep some clothes. I took a bath before I went for my medicine I keep with Mama Lucia. On my way, I prayed that Diosito would not allow the old man to live in my house.

Mysterious Information on My Baptismal Certificate

DON FELIPE WAS WAITING TO go with me to church. We stopped at the diner for my medicine before proceeding to church. After Mass, Father Alfonso wanted to speak with me alone. Don Felipe stayed in the church. I asked the priest if I was going to confession. He laughed. "No, mija, I want to ask if you know when you were born."

"No, Father, I don't, my mother has never told me, and neither will she tell me who my father is. The times that I have asked her those questions, she gets mad and slaps me. She doesn't want to tell me anything about my birth or about my father. Father, in reality, I am the daughter of no one."

"Rosita, don't think like that, she is your mother, and you have to obey her."

"Father, a real mother doesn't treat her daughter the way she treats me." My tears wouldn't stop, and I couldn't stop telling the priest what those two had done to me. He couldn't believe what I was telling him. He stopped talking; the room got very quiet. Finally he said that he was going to help me. He told me to follow him.

We went for Don Felipe. He was sound asleep snoring in one of the pews. He woke up when the priest nudged him. "Don Felipe, come with Rosita and myself." We followed him to the room where they keep the church records. We looked under *Bustos* and under *Reza*, but we couldn't find my certificate. I wanted to ask Don Martín, my godfather, if he remembered under what name I was baptized. The priest told me not to. He didn't want anybody to know that we were looking for my document. He was afraid that if Reyna found out, she would put a stop to the search.

We were running out of documents to look at. Don Felipe rested, I continued not wanting to waste one moment. A rested Don Felipe continued to help. The priest left but came back when he thought that it was futile. Father Alfonso finally found the document. He gave a sigh of relief. He handed the document to Don Felipe to look it over. The old man was surprised. "Father, this document is not right."

"What are you saying, Señor Felipe?"

"Father, the surname is incorrect. The mother should know who the father is, why would she give us the wrong name?"

"I don't have an answer, but I know for a fact that *Reza* is not her surname. Reyna Bustos lied.

"For now, this document is the official, so relax, señor. If she put the wrong name, only she can change it now. Maybe in the future when Rosita is an adult and she finds proof of her real surname and father, she can change it." The priest wanted to know everything Don Felipe knew about my family. They wanted to be alone. I went in the church. I was tired from the search for my baptismal certificate. Everybody knows who my father is, but now even the document is showing that I am a Reza, not a Bustos. The scent of the burning candle alongside the statue of the Virgin Mary got my attention. I turned to see the Virgin, I don't know if it was an illusion or not, but I felt that she was moving her mouth. I pulled a chair and climbed on top so as to be closer to the statue of the Virgin Mary. She looked at me; her eyes spoke to me. I embraced her, and I spoke to her. I climbed down from the chair. I covered myself with my sweater and sat on the bench. I want to know who my father is now, not sometime in the future. I had a convulsion.

Father Alfonso and Don Felipe were at my side when I came to. The priest asked if I was okay to hear what he had to say. He told me that the baptismal document showed my name as *Rosita Maria Jovani Reza*. I grabbed my head with my good arm, disillusioned that the document didn't show that Jorge Bustos was my father. He told me that for now, I would be officially *Reza*. In time I would be able to correct my name.

This document is the official document until I could prove that Reyna lied. Father Alfonso had other commitments. We left the church, Don Felipe hobbling and me with my crooked arm. "Rosita, I should keep that document for you."

"Why? I want to keep it. At least it has other information when I was born and other information."

"Rosita, if your mother knows that you have it, she will take it away from you and probably give you another beating for having it. Also, you shouldn't have it because you are underage. The priest allowed us to have it in confidence."

At his room he showed where he was going to save it for me. I grabbed my broken arm and skipped unto the street. I wished that I could speak with my late grandpa Domingo and my late godmother Socorro. I wanted to share the news that I had the document. I ran to the cemetery to tell them the news. From there I ran to the water hole surrounded by huge stones that resemble a person's butt. I didn't resist; my temptation to jump wasn't a factor. I jumped into the cool waters.

The cool waters felt good; my broken arm felt even better. I lifted my arm and slammed it on top of the water, I didn't feel any pain. I slapped the water with both arms screaming with joy. My noise excited the birds. The startled birds flew from tree to tree chirping. I didn't want to have a convulsion in the water. I got out, lay on top of a boulder enjoying the warm sun. I noticed a few animals playing. I knew they were not alone like me. I thought even though my journey through life is slow, I continue with my Chuchin at my side. The sun semidried my clothes, time to go home.

Reyna was talking with Don Felipe. I noticed that she was well dressed. I greeted her and told her that she looked very nice. She didn't say anything derogative when she saw me. "Take care of your sisters, I'll be back whenever."

"God be with you, Mother, have a nice trip." She took off. Poor Don Felipe; he looked pale after talking with Mother. "Hi, Don Felipe, did Mother say how long she is going to be away?" Your mother has very few words for me, and one of them isn't *friend*. She left her daughters, and that is all, no food and no diapers." Beni ran to meet me with open arms. Blanquita also ran. "Vani, Vani," she shouted with open arms wanting a hug. *Well, I'm not alone, but again, I'm in charge of two babies, one nearly three years younger than me, the other four years younger.*

We walked home; we sat on the steps. I played the part of a music teacher. I sang hoping that they would join; they didn't, but just smiled. I taught Blanquita to say "Mama." I taught her how to make eyes while smiling. Blanquita is a very lively, very happy little girl. She can be stubborn but not often. For a pretty girl, she likes to run after the chickens. I like to take her to play with the chickens of Doña Mito. She likes other animals, especially if they aren't mean. Beni is a bit younger than Blanquita and also much more reserved. But she is aware of everything about her. She too is a very pretty girl. Both my sisters are growing very fast. Beni eats almost as much as Blanquita but doesn't gain weight. Whereas Blanquita is gaining weight. Her weight is more noticeable in her thighs. Her godmother Doña Tolita calls Blanquita Olga Big Thighs. Don't know why, but it must be somebody with big thighs.

We three orphans spent the night at the house Reyna provides. Early the next morning, I heard Don Felipe cough. I glanced out the window, there was my old friend basking in the sun. I made him a cup of coffee. He smiled when he saw his coffee being served. "Rosita, do you know that coffee in the morning to me is like blood is to a vampire at night?" After a bit conversation, I reminded him that I had to go to the president's office for my birth certificate. "Rosita, it's best that you go early. I will take care of your sisters."

"No, señor, they are too much trouble for you. I will get them ready and leave them with Mama Lucia."

I was getting ready to leave the house when a young man came looking to buy lumber. I sold it to him. He, in a return favor, helped me carry Beni and some clothes to the diner of Mama Lucia. I took off in search of my birth certificate. The president saw me enter the main office, he wanted to help me. I refused at the same time thanking him for what he'd done for the pueblo children. He remembered that it was I who had requested the use of the auditorium. He told me that if I wasn't so young, I could be the president. Several people heard him, they agreed that I could be a good president. Whether they were kidding or not, I'll never know. His secretary, Gavi, laughed agreeing with her boss.

The president opened the door and asked me to enter the office of Señora Paz. She was real happy to see me. She met me at the middle of the room. She lowered herself so that we were seeing each other eye to eye. "Tell me how you feel?" I had never seen her this close, and I was surprised she was a pretty lady. "How can I help you, Jovani?"

"Señora Paz, I am here to see if I can get my birth certificate. By any chance can you remember whether she registered me or not? I need my birth certificate because I'm in school, and the school needs it also."

"Rosita, have a seat and wait here, I'm going to check on your birth certificate."

I waited for the paper, the paper that would show the information I have longed for: who is my father? The anticipation grew when they called my name. "Jovani," Mrs. Paz looked disturbed when I approached her, "you are not registered. Your mother hasn't been here to register you." I was stunned, I didn't say a word. I turned and ran out of her office. I didn't have a direction, I just ran and ran. *I am nobody's daughter.*

Not having the strength to run anymore, I found myself under one of the biggest trees in the pueblo. Somehow I climbed that tree and immediately climbed down. I spoke to the tree. "For many years you have been dry, now look at how pretty you have blossomed. Someday you will be chopped down. But you continue to grow and blossom. I also will continue to be strong and brave and will come out of this misery." Disappointed with the actions of Reyna, I kept walking toward my responsibility, my sisters. My will to live is strong, my Chuchin will guide me.

Bitten by Doña Rebequita's Dog

Not having been registered at birth was not going to prevent me from getting an education. I stopped by the shop of Doña Rebequita, the dressmaker. I was going to ask her if she would make a couple of school clothes for me. She was outside her house when she saw me approaching. "How is my little Jovani?"

"I'm okay, but my clothes aren't. I came to see if you can make me some clothes for school."

"Ah, that is right, you are about to start school. Come, let me take your measurements." Her dog was looking at me like I was a piece of meat. I ignored him because most animals are friendly with me. She measured me, and I noted down my measurements. I was on my way out when her dog attacked me. I wasn't expecting anything like this from the dog, he bit me on my leg. I screamed with fear accompanied with pain. Doña Rebequita was frightened. She grabbed the broom and whipped him with it. Her son grabbed the dog and threw him out the door.

He tore through the dress I was wearing. Doña Rebequita cleaned my wound and put some antiseptic on it. She gave me a couple of dresses. I changed my torn clothes into one she gave me. I had a convulsion. I don't know how long I was out. Mrs. Rebequita was worried, she was not aware of my convulsions. I told her not to worry, "I have these convulsions all the time, and I usually have one after something excites me." I scanned the room for the dog; when I didn't see him, I asked Doña Rebequita for him. She told me that her husband had taken the naughty dog far away where he will put a bullet in his head. The dog has bitten many others, I was the last one he would ever bite.

She asked me how I felt. "Ma'am, my tears are more from fear than from pain. Sometimes I cry from being ignored by my mother and not from fear."

"You are a valiant young lady," she said. "Tell me, how did you know that I make clothes for kids, uh, young girls?"

"Mama Lucia, the lady that owns the diner, she told me about you."

"Doña Lucia is your mother, I thought Reyna is."

"Yes, señora, you are right, Reyna is my mother. Mama Lucia gives me shelter, love, and affection, and I love her like a mom."

"Well, when you see Doña Lucia, give her thanks that you don't have to pay for these clothes.

"Rosita, it hurts when I think of what the dog did to you."

"Don't worry, señora, I now have a scar on this leg to match the one I have on my other leg."

"Ha, ha, ha, niña, how I marvel that you still have a sense of humor after all that has happened to you. Jovani, who are you? Jovani, listen, I want you to come by my store every Sunday because I want to help you with some pesos. Don't ignore what I want to do for you, I want to help you. Come by the store every Sunday, promise?" I thought what I could do with that money. First buy flowers for the altar to be in front of my Diosito and the Virgin Mary. "Thank you, Doña Rebecca, I won't forget. I must go, but can you give me your blessing before I go?" She did saying that Reyna doesn't know what a wonderful child she has for a daughter.

I was leaving her house. I felt like vomiting. I had a convulsion. Mama Lucia was at my side when I came to. She told me that Doña Rebequita had sent for me when I had my second convulsion. She asked me how I felt. I answered, "I feel good because Diosito is watching over me. My grand faith I have in Him keeps me among the living. The moment that I open my eyes after a convulsion is like He hands me more courage to continue forward with my life. I have a sickness, but I am not a drunk nor do I have negative vices. Those with negative vices think like machos, but they are cowards, nothing more."

"Where did you learn to speak in those terms?"

She turned to her son who was listening to my words. "Son, did you hear what she said? I hope that you learn from her words."

"Cheez," he said, "I better leave. Listening to her brings fear to my conscience." He left the room. The daughter invited us to eat with them. Mama Lucia had to leave, but I stayed. After we ate, the daughter said that she would accompany me to the diner. Doña Rebequita told me that it had been a pleasure to have met me and was very glad that I was leaving the same way I arrived.

My sisters were happy to see me. I cleaned them up before I fed them. We played to the enjoyment of Mama Lucia. I told her that Doña Rebequita wasn't going to charge me for the clothes. Mama Lucia jokingly said, "I guess the bite was worth it after all." I didn't think that was funny at all. "Don't say that. I prefer my health, my body, and my soul much more than any material." I could tell that Mama Lucia was hurt with my response. "Jovani, I was just joking, please relax, okay?"

She wanted to know if I had gotten my birth certificate when I went to the president. I told her, "Reyna had never registered my birth. But I have my baptismal certificate."

"Really?" She was surprised; she asked, "When did you get it?" I went over in detail how Don Felipe had looked at my documents, and finally Father had found it. I was disappointed that my surname on the baptismal certificate was not *Bustos*. I know that most of the people in the pueblo know that I am the daughter of Jorge Bustos, so why do they deny me? What is everybody afraid of? I promise to find the truth, and someday I will.

The sun was slowly disappearing. I was going home to see if Reyna had come back. I wondered where the sun goes when it hides beyond the city. I walked past Don Felipe's room, I glanced over, but I didn't see him inside. I saw my old friend lying on the steps near the gate. The worst thought came to mind. I rushed over to see whether he was okay or not. He must have heard my thoughts because he woke up. "Don Felipe, are you okay?" He smiled. "Looks like the sleep got the best of me. I have been waiting for you to let you know that your mother left you a bag of clothes for your sisters."

"Don Felipe, did she say anything else?"

"Only that she would be gone for a few days."

"That is all she said?"

"Rosita, you know that the only time your mother talks to me is when she threatens me. She locked the house and took off."

I placed my arms on my hips, stretched my legs; I thought, *That's customary, she does this all the time.* "You want to know something? I prefer to take care of my sisters to the beatings she gives me whenever she feels. Señor, do you think that she will let me live in peace when she comes back?"

"Ha, ha, Rosita, surely you are a comedian." I laughed as well. I sang, "A smile is inexpensive, but the smile is productive. I don't need to be rich to smile." My old friend asked me not to sing because he didn't want to cry. I stopped with a smile and stretched my arms. I was relaxed knowing that my body was free from beatings for a few days.

The bag of clothes Reyna left was heavy. I tried to run with it, but I couldn't. I dropped it on the street to rest. My other godmother Rosalba was walking by, stopped to look at me. "Rosita, is that you?" She looked at my load and asked me why I was carrying such a big load. I greeted her saying that the load wasn't heavy. She tried to lift the bag. "Niña, this bag is very heavy, how can you carry such a load, especially with a broken arm? Niña, tell me, where are you taking it to?"

"It's difficult to explain. Mother left the pueblo and left me in charge of my sisters, and these are their clothes."

My godmother pulled some pesos from her purse. "Don't refuse this money, please. Take it with my blessing."

"Thank you, Godmother, for helping me and my sisters."

"Rosita, I'm your confirmation godmother, and I am here for you. Remember, my house is always open to you. Your mother has no compassion whatsoever, I must have a talk with her." She gave me a hug and kissed my forehead before she left.

Mama Lucia looks so tired. Who wouldn't be? She works in her diner and takes care of us three sisters. When she saw the load I was carrying, she made a comment. "Don't tell me that Reyna left you and your sisters alone again?"

"Yes, she came only for an instant, then left."

"I see that she was responsible enough to leave some clothes for your sisters. Well, niña, what can we do? Help me clean up, and we will all go home." A late customer, Carlos, a cousin, son of my uncle Jose and aunt Rosa, walked into the diner after closing. We took advantage of his strength. He helped carry the bag full of clothes and one of my sisters.

Arriving at her place I started to feel weak, I asked Diosito for strength. My arm was hurting, my head was aching, but I fought the pains. I promised my cousin some candies for helping us. The pain continued. I didn't let on that I was hurting. I pleaded with Diosito to place a good doctor in my path of life that would cure my epilepsy. I suffered another convulsion. Like most other times when I awaken from my convulsion, I was nauseas with a horrible headache and Mama Lucia at my side. My sisters were sound asleep, so I must have been out for quite a while. Mama Lucia is a godsend, always at my side when I need a mother the most.

Blanquita woke up crying, she was probably having a nightmare. We sat on the floor, her head on my lap. I sang her favorite song, "For ruchi, ruchi…" She fell asleep in my arms. I set her down in her carton, covered her up. I went outside to admire the brilliance of the moon. The surroundings reflected different colors inspired by the moon. I felt a surge of energy permeate my body caused by the natural beauty around. I will cherish these days that Reyna is gone, no one to abuse me, no one to scold or hit me. I smiled as I looked at the moon. *Temporary freedom,* I thought.

Tonight I didn't feel alone. Always thinking and planning ahead or thinking of my real father. Interesting that I know who the father is of all my sisters but mine. Tomorrow I must visit with Don Felipe. I have much to write. The sound of the rooster woke me up. I had fallen asleep outside. I shuffled my feet to the baths. The cold water felt so refreshing. I put on some clean clothes. Don Felipe knew that I would be bringing his coffee. I shared the activity that I wanted my mentor to include in my diary. After Don Felipe and I finished, I woke my sisters and helped them clean up.

On the way to the diner we ran into my uncle Juan. He took us out to eat breakfast. He carried Beni in his arms to the diner. He likes to come into the pueblo every Sunday, his day of rest. Sometimes he brings his goods to the market to sell, like lots of other ranchers. During breakfast he told me that his daughter Sonia was studying with the nuns at their academy. He gave me money before he and his family set out to the outdoor market. I wondered how Mother could be so mean and her brother so nice. Why couldn't she be more like him? I watched my uncle and family walk away from the diner. "Good morning, señora." The sound of a man's voice startled me. I turned around to face a man dressed in the style of a cowboy from the Norte. "What's on the menu this morning that is especially delicious?" Mama Lucia's response: "Señor, whatever you desire."

I continued listening to the Norteño and feeding my sisters. "How wonderful to see you taking care of your sisters." His voice seemed closer to me, but I still didn't pay attention to him. Mama Lucia gave me a look. I knew it meant that I should offer him some coffee. I stood up and talked to him. I served him coffee. He mentioned that he'd been in the pueblo a few days. He came to comply with a promise he'd made, not to drink any alcoholic beverage for a year. He was staying with Sofia Rivera, his aunt.

His food was served. He ate quietly not saying a word. As soon as he finished eating, he didn't say much. He paid his bill; he said, "I will be back, pretty little girl." We looked at each other wondering what he meant. "Who was that man, Mama Lucia?" She shrugged her shoulders indicating that she didn't know anything about him. Before long he came back with several bags full of goods. "I bought these goods for the little girls," he told Mama Lucia. "I would like to take them with me to the United States. What beautiful girls and so well-mannered." He sat near the table, motioned me to get close. He took his hat off. "Why do you take medicine?" I was surprised. *How does this stranger know that I take medicine?*

Mama Lucia looked at me. "Jovani, tell him why you take medicine."

"Tio," I said, "I am an epileptic, so I have to take medicine. I have several daily convulsions."

"You have convulsions? How can you take care of your sisters being sick?"

"Señor, Mama Lucia helps me, or I couldn't do it alone." The Norteño became very emotional. He took his handkerchief to clean the tears. "Señor, please don't cry because I will start crying, and then Mama Lucia and then my sisters will cry. Señor, I will sing you a song if you don't cry anymore."

"Don't tell me that you know how to sing."

"Not only sing but I will sing a song that I put my own words to an old song."

"Jovani, who are your parents?"

"Mister, if I knew who they are, I wouldn't be singing this song." He gave me with a puzzled look. "Come on then sing, but don't make me cry. What is the name of your song?"

"I call it 'Hija de Nadie' (Daughter of Nobody). Okay, señor, here it comes."

> I am the daughter of nobody
> I answer but to one surname
> Although it belongs to my mother
> In my daily notes I write
> The truth I will someday know
> My surname my real father amigo
> I am the daughter of nobody
> Everybody knows the truth
> That I am not a Reza
> That my father was killed
> The pain when Reyna denied
> My living and my beauty to my father
> I am the daughter of nobody
> Although this woman is my mother
> Her hugs and love she denies
> My heart broken into pieces
> I fight to find my answer
> That the blood of my father
> Jorge Bustos flows through my veins

The Tejano's wife arrived in time to hear the last of my song. "Bravo, young lady, you have a wonderful voice. It sounded sad, tell me, did you write the song?"

"Señora, I live that life. What I sang is true." She said to her husband, "This little girl is Rosita, the daughter of Reyna Bustos."

"Oh, then you do have a mother." He looked at me. His wife smiled. "Then soon you should know who your father is," she said. "Come on, dear, don't tell her that." She asked, "Why not? You know very well who her father is. We should take her with us to her grandmother Maria and her uncles."

"My dear wife, don't say that, let's go."

"Señora, do you know my grandmother Sinforosa?"

"Oh, niña, I know Sinforosa, but I am talking about your other grandmother, Maria, that lives in Tejas in the United States."

"I have another grandma? How can I have another grandma?"

"Yes, Rosita, you do. I will give you my telephone number, call me whenever you get the courage to leave here, and I will come for you. If I can't come for you, I will inform your uncles, Jorge's brothers. They will surely come for you."

"Come on, wife, you have loosened your tongue enough, let's go."

I was numb, another person knows who my father is, and I have another grandma, in the Norté? I wanted to run after them, but I couldn't. What held me back? Suddenly I got the courage to go after them. Mama Lucia sensed it and held me back. "Jovani, now is not the time. The lady left her telephone number and some money for you." The one person that had the information and the courage to tell me more of my father was disappearing in the horizon. My second mother held me in her arms. "Are you okay, mija?" What could I say, I have always listened to Mama Lucia, I'm sure she had a good reason for holding me back. But did she or did I hold myself back? I'm free-spirited, and I could have run after the lady.

I sat on a chair outside the diner, sad, a still confused. Mama Lucia handed me the money the lady had left for me. Green money from the Norte, I knew because I had some of those in my hideaway bank. Two $20 bills. I now had four hundred pesos more enough to buy a box and a half of my medicine. With a few more pesos coupled with the money I have saved, I can pay the doctor to x-ray my head. Here I am alone thinking of my health. *Well,* I thought, *I have to think for myself. I can't get emotional, or my sickness will tumble me.* I couldn't see my shadow to speak with; my companion in loneliness wasn't available.

My sisters! Thinking of them brought me out of my trance. I looked into the diner; they were very quiet, which was unusual. Blanquita looked uncomfortable, Beni at her side trying to console her sister. Blanquita coughed and coughed; little Beni looked concerned. I walked over to console Blanquita. I touched her forehead, she was burning up with fever. "Mama Lucia, Blanquita is sick." Our second mother came over; she also touched her forehead. "Oh, mija, she is burning up. Jovani, go for the doctor." I ran to the office of Dr. Genaro. I was out of breath when I arrived at his office. The doctor looked at me and waited until I could speak. I was able to finally tell him why I was at his office.

Dr. Genaro slipped his white doctor's clothing to accompany me to the diner. He asked Mama Lucia whether she was the mother. She told him that Blanquita's mother was away. The doctor wanted to know if she was responsible for Blanquita, to which the reply was that she was. He picked Blanquita up and placed her on the table I had cleaned. He checked a crying Blanquita. The doctor concluded that Blanquita had pneumonia and something in her blood. "I have to admit her to the hospital immediately." Doctor, what is wrong with my sister?"

"She has an infection, and her lungs aren't well. Also, she has these blotches on her skin. It is critical for her mother to contact me immediately."

"Doctor, how much are you going to charge me for getting my sister well?"

"Niña, you have the pesos to pay for my services? You act like the mother that isn't here. What is your name?"

"Doctor, you can call me *Jovani,* I prefer the name *Rosita,* but my mother doesn't like it, she prefers *Jovani.*"

"Hmm, listen, Jovani, I will help you, besides, your mother is the one responsible. I should go to the president's office and report that your mother abandoned you and your sister."

The doctor took us to the Adolfo Prieto Hospital. I wasn't allowed to go into the room with Blanquita, I waited in a waiting room for her. How long did I wait, don't know because I fell asleep. Dr. Genaro woke me up. "Jovani, your sister is going to be okay. She needs medicine to help her get well. Your mother has to come and buy the medicine."

"Doctor, my mother will be very angry with me and will give me a beating like always." I held my tears back. "Besides, she is gone, and we don't know how long she's going to be away. I have some savings, I will buy her medicine."

I showed him the two green dollar bills and handed them to him. He was surprised that I had that kind of money with me. Smiling, the doctor told me that I had enough to buy the medicine. "Follow me, Jovani." He took me to see Blanquita. He and the nurse spoke briefly. After signing some papers, he took us back to the diner. The doctors gave the medicine to Mama Lucia with instructions. In time, Blanquita felt much better. That whole night I thought of how Reyna was going to react. For sure, though, Blanquita was her favorite, and I was almost sure that she would take Blanquita for a follow-up exam.

Don Felipe had finished with my diary for the day. The booming voice of a huge heavy man startled me. He was the same man that I have seen visit when Don Felipe gets money. I stared at the man that resembled a large earthen pot with a small head and huge midsection. He ignored me because this man's mission was to get drunk at the expense of my old friend. I have witnessed the Earthen Pot from Ahualulco wait for Don Felipe to get drunk with cheap tequila that he brings. Then Don Felipe gives him money to buy more tequila. Well, the Earthen Pot buys the good tequila for himself with Don Felipe's money. Of course Don Felipe is always happy to see his friend. I wanted to confront him, but I held back. I went to the diner.

During the time Reyna was gone, I was pleasantly void of beatings. I felt sorry for my sisters; they really didn't know our mother.

But unlike myself, I knew who their father was. Every day I would help Mama Lucia with the diner in the morning and sell my candies in the afternoon. Sometimes I would take Blanquita with me; she enjoyed that. The presidential council had decided to fix the street in our neighborhood. The workers needed a place to eat. Mama Lucia's place was chosen to feed the twelve hungry workers. Noontime the workers showed up at the diner. I helped, my sisters played, and the hungry men ate.

I was really happy that Mama Lucia was serving a large crowd. I served the water, salsa with tortillas. One of the men flirted with me; he said, "Hey, little girl, you are quite a worker. That broken arm doesn't slow you at all. How'd you break it?" I replied, "Hey, señor, eat your food before it gets cold, and don't ask so many questions. A person shouldn't speak when he eats with a mouthful." Everybody laughed. One of his fellow workers shouted, "Be careful with her, she will control you." All of them said something; I didn't pay attention. I continued being their waitress. The same man asked me to marry him. Another shot back, "Niña, you don't want to marry that man."

I pointed my finger at the one proposing marriage, I told him, "Señor, make every effort to value yourself before you make that decision." Another tells me, "If marriage is your destiny, I myself will wait until you become of age." Another worker told me that he would buy me a plate of food and that he would wait for me to become of age then marry me. "Looks like all of you want to marry me. If you are serious, show me by letting me shine your shoes." I made forty dollars and three plates of food shining shoes. I gave one to my old friend Don Felipe, another to my aunt Eulalia.

I Learn How to Use a Telephone

MIDAFTERNOON I WAS GETTING READY to sell my candy and gum. Chemito came to the diner to deliver a message. "Rosita, you are wanted on the telephone, come with me." Mama Lucia smiled and jokingly said, "Hmm, you are going to use a telephone before I do." Chemito told me that Ana was on the phone. I looked at the thing they call a phone. "How can Ana be in there?" Chemito showed me how to talk on the phone. I became annoyed because he kept telling me to talk, "Come on, talk."

"Don't bother me so much, Chemito, you know that I want to speak with my sister."

"Don't get mad and start running away, come talk into the phone."

"Oh, I have to talk?"

"Yes, your sister is on the phone in the city where she is calling from." I was so happy to speak with Ana. The minutes went by too fast. I handed the phone back to Chemito. I started to feel weak, I don't remember anything else. I had another convulsion.

I opened my eyes, I was dizzy with a horrible headache; the cold wet towel on my forehead didn't seem to help. Gaining consciousness I looked around the room. Doña Silvia Ortega was at my side; next to her was Mama Lucia. I attempted to get up, but Doña Ortega asked me not to. "Just rest, you had a bad convulsion."

"Lucia, does Rosita tremble this way every time she has a convulsion?"

"Yes, comadre, the worse are the blows to the head every time she falls. Many times she is alone when she has a convulsion, she lays where she falls."

"Ana called, she is coming home pretty soon—that is all I remember."

"Thank God, now maybe you can rest. Jovani, I have to leave. When you feel better, come to the diner." Mama Lucia left me in her comadre's care; she left. Doña Silvia treated me with kindness. She gave me a warm glass of milk with a homemade cookie. She wanted to give me a painkiller for my headache. I told her that I didn't take any kind of medication except the one for my sickness. I gave thanks to my Diosito for the milk and cookies. "I know why God takes care of you, your faith is incredible." Doña Silvia was being sincere. I told her, "Diosito loves us all, it is us that are not always with him. Each one forms our own life. I am alive because of the faith that I have in my Diosito. He has always placed somebody in my path of life to help me."

"Permit me to ask you a question. What is your name? I hear some people refer to you as Rosita, others Jovani, so which one is it?" I smiled. "Both, I answer to both. Mother doesn't like the name *Rosita*, she likes *Jovani*, I prefer *Rosita*."

"Do you know who your father is? I don't mean to be nosy, but I want to know, so I guess that yes, I am nosy."

"Ma'am, most of the people in the pueblo believe that Jorge Bustos is my father, Mother denies that, she tells me that Reza is my father."

"What I can tell you, Rosita, is that the mother knows who the father of each child is. Whether she wants to tell the truth or deny, that's on her conscience.

"This much I know, Jorge Bustos visited the pueblo many times from the Norte. I know that he loved your mother. He was a good-looking man, always dressed like a charro. When I think of him, I see a rather tall and thin man. Close up he revealed bright eyes always alert. You have the same look in your brilliant dark eyes. You look a lot like Jorge. I can't believe your mother, giving you that name. There isn't a drop of Reza blood in your veins. Your mother has never admitted that Jorge is your father?"

"Never, and I stopped asking because she whips me every time I ask information about my father."

"Señora, I have to go, I have a convulsion when I get excited. What I am learning about Jorge might trigger one again." Doña Silvia couldn't hold back her tears as she hugged me. "Please, señora, don't cry, I don't like it when people cry on my account."

"Rosita from heaven, I cry for another reason, no fault of your own. My problem is that my sons don't live with me, they live in the Norté. Your mother doesn't know what a wonderful daughter she has. If I had a daughter as pretty and hardworking as you, I would value her very being. Plus, you are a very intelligent little girl for your age. Rosita, I don't have much to offer, but poor as I am, please know that my house is always open to you, and I will welcome you with open arms. I am your aunt on the side of Jorge Bustos, your father."

I was getting closer to knowing that Jorge Bustos is my father. Why, I asked myself, didn't I question Doña Silvia? She knows Jorge, she knows that he is my father. I went to the church to speak with my Chuchin. I knelt in front of the statue of my Chuchin. *When are you going to cure me of this sickness?* I got closer and asked Diosito to look at my forehead. "See this knot? How much longer before you grant me a miracle? Diosito, I love You, and I know that You love me. Otherwise, I wouldn't be alive today. I am not angry with You. On the contrary, I have more faith in You than ever before. I am sure that someday You are going to put in my path of life a professional doctor who can cure me.

"Diosito, when are You going to answer my questions that I have? When I come to visit, You don't say anything, please don't do that. I will never abandon my dreams. Better that I abandon the barriers that prohibit my cure." I looked away to speak with the Blessed Virgin in time to see a tear in her eye. "Oh no, please don't cry, I do not intend to reproach you. You will see that I intend on keeping my promise. My arm is still crooked and broken, but I still have it, but I will keep my promise."

I left for the diner. When she saw me, Mama Lucia asked if I had had another convulsion. She said, "You poor child." I smiled. "No, Mama Lucia, on the contrary, so don't look so sad. I am happy to be alive and happy to be here at your side." My stomach growled loud enough for her to hear. "Mija, come here, sit, and feed your growling stomach." Doña Tolita entered the diner just when I was about to start eating. "Niña," she said looking at me, "you are all beaten up, look at the bump on your forehead, smiling like nothing happened." Smiling, I answered, "Remember, Ms. Tolita, the sun returns its brilliance from a cloud cover as strong as ever. I also treasure the time my Diosito lends me." Doña Tolita addressed Mama Lucia, "I am convinced that this child is blessed by our Lord."

My lunch was going to be a busy one today, I thought when I saw Señor David, the teacher, walk into the diner. He came and sat next to me. "Jovani, tell me now what happened to you, just look at those welts on your forehead and arm."

"These are nothing, Señor David. The hurt I feel in my heart are the denials and avoidance of telling me the truth of who my father is."

"Rosita, don't tell me that your mother didn't register your birth?"

"Well, no, she hasn't, I went to the presidency to see if she had registered me, they couldn't find the birth certificate. Mother has to go and register my birth. However, I do have my certificate of baptism. The certificate shows the information needed for me to continue in school."

David, my teacher, was happy for me. He advised me to copy the information for future references. "Rosita, I have to advice you not to miss any more school. If you don't attend school, I will not advance you to the next grade, understand?" I nodded my head. "I will be in class tomorrow."

"That's what I want to hear, Rosita. Bring your certificate of baptism, the one the priest gave you. Again, don't miss class, I know that you have your sisters to watch over. I must talk to your mother. Let me know when she comes back. Another thing, I need your assistance with the class. If you don't show up, I will have to replace you."

I continued with my responsibilities. I cleaned and fed my sisters before going to school. My convulsions came periodically, never stopping. I helped in the diner, and Reyna away only she knows where. Nothing out of the ordinary happened to me. Except one day when two men and a woman came into the diner. One of the strangers asked me about the welts. I told him that I was epileptic and the bruise was the result of my falling when I have a convulsion. Mama Lucia asked me to tend to my sisters.

I heard one of the gentlemen ask Mama Lucia if she was the mother of us three orphaned sisters. She smiled. "I wish I was, but I am not." *I am nobody's daughter,* I thought when I heard the man's question. I had to say something; with my back to the man, I said, "My mother isn't here. Señor, don't worry about us." The other man told me that they were not concerned. They had come into the diner because their son has the same sickness that I have. "We are visiting your church to tell Diosito about my nephew's epileptic condition. Our friend that lives here in the pueblo told us about you."

The lady came over to where I was, she bent over where she could see me eye to eye. "Niña, where are your parents?"

"Please, señora, don't ask me because it breaks my heart when people ask me that." She hugged me. "I'm sorry I asked," she said. "But as a mother of a son that has the same sickness as you, I just wanted to know." She held my broken and twisted arm, asked me if I had seen the doctor. I told her that I didn't have money to see the doctor in Taxco. "I work selling candies and gum to pay for my medicine. Someday I will have enough to go see him."

"Your parents haven't taken you, how can that be?" I started to cry. "Please don't ask about my parents."

The lady straightened up to speak with Mama Lucia. A short time later, Mama Lucia went to where I was. I wiped my tears. "Jovani, these people want to take you to the doctor in Taxco. They will pay for you to see the doctor and bring you back. Do you accept their offer? I wish you would, they seem to be nice people. The doctor will clean your arm." She winked at me. "Go, mija."

A young man with a well-trimmed beard identified himself as the doctor that would see me. He didn't look old enough to have gray hair, but apparently he was. I looked at his hands looking for evidence of a needle. I don't like being poked with those—ugh!—needles. I sat on the designated chair still leery of a needle. I watched his every move hoping that he wouldn't pick up a needle.

The posters of a person's body hanging on the wall fascinated me. "Jovani, tell me, how did you get all of these bruises on your body?"

"Doctor, if I account for every one of the bruises, you will be so bored you will probably fall asleep. I can tell you that I am an epileptic and suffer convulsions all the time."

"As a doctor of neurology, I understand you. So these welts and bruises are the result of your convulsions? Are you taking any medication for epilepsy?"

"Yes, Doctor, I take medicine, and now I feel like a drunk, weak and dizzy without taking a drink of tequila or a beer." He laughed, including the nurse, who was cleaning my arm. The same nurse took out a small container and retrieved a needle that she handed to the doctor. "Oh, Diosito, help me." My knees were trembling.

"Don't worry, I'm giving you a shot, don't you want to feel better?"

"Doctor, I'm not sick, why do you want to give me a shot?" Smiling, he thought for a moment. "Oh, I see, you think that I'm giving you a shot of mescal."

"Yes, because that's what they give the kids when they have diarrhea."

"No, I'm giving you a shot of medicine with this needle to make you feel better." The shot made my pain go away.

"Doctor, being that you are very good, how much are you going to charge me?"

"Hmm"—he looked at me with a funny look on his face, crossed his arms—"hmm."

"Listen, Doctor, I hope not too much because I'm poor."

"Tell you what, pray for me. And listen to me carefully. Promise me that you will be very careful. Money you don't owe me anything. Something else, some little bird told me that you are very good at writing poems. If someday you happen to write a book of poems, promise me that you will give me one of your books."

"Doctor, with all my heart, I will pray for you. The little birds don't know how to tell lies. My intention is to write a book of my living.

"I have many notes that Don Felipe writes for me. He writes everything I tell him that happens to me. I write about the beautiful and generous people of my pueblo, how they help me when I have a convulsion. Doctor, I will give you two books because your name is going to be in my book. Also, if you desire, I can come to wash and iron your clothes, and you don't have to pay me. Don't worry about transportation. The bus driver is my friend, he will give me a ride. I will sing to the passengers, they tip me, and with that money, I will invite you for an ice cream."

The doctor and everybody else laughed. "Don't laugh, I can iron and do everything with this broken arm." I was angry. The doctor held my hand. "We don't laugh at you, on the contrary, we laugh because we are noticing what a grand little girl you are. I'm grateful that you want to pay by doing work for me, but really, think of your health first." He gave me three pills to control my vomits. Leaving the hospital, I apologized for my bad manners in not knowing their names. I was so preoccupied with the needle that I forgot to ask their names. "Don't worry, Rosita, you have so much on your mind. My name is *Margarita Ocampos*, and my husband is Armando Ocampos. Rosita, how is your headache? I prefer to call you *Rosita*, it has more life than *Jovani*. We have a home here in Taxco, if you like, you can stay with us tonight, and we'll take you home tomorrow."

"No, I have to take care of my sisters. I can take the bus."

"No, we'll take you home as we promised."

During the trip, I entertained them with my singing. I sang, "Que diran los de tu casa…" (What will those in your house say…). They wanted to know how I handled my convulsions. I told them about the faith I have in Diosito and the support I receive from the people from the pueblo. I decided to tell them about the miracle of the Santo Niño de Atocha. Silence followed, Mrs. Ocampos sighed followed by a deep breath. "Rosita, truly you are an angel of God."

Arriving at the pueblo, Mrs. Ocampos asked me, "Rosita, really, who are you?" I shook my arms in the air indicating ignorance. "Señora, I don't even know because I am the daughter of no one."

"I would be blessed to have a daughter like you. Our house is always open to you." She handed me a piece of paper with her address. "We will now consider you part of the family. Whenever we come into the pueblo, I will come to see you, I will find you no matter where you might be." They left me in front of Mama Lucia's house. She wanted to come in and visit, but her husband was tired, so they left.

Mama Lucia was waiting for us. She was so happy when she saw me. "Jovani, you look really good."

"Thanks to the doctor, he gave me a shot, and I don't feel any pain in my arm."

"The doctor gave you a shot of mescal? What kind of doctor gives a child a shot of mescal?" I laughed and laughed; after a long day, I was ready to release tension, and I laughed some more. I showed her my arm where the doctor had given me a shot of a painkiller.

The following day, I readied my sisters for Mass. Toward the end, the priest, Father Ortega, called me to the altar. I was caught by surprise, I didn't have prior notice that I was going to be called up to the altar. I walked up as fast as I could. The priest asked me to stand next to him. He raised his hand to silence the parishioners. "Brothers, many of you know this young girl as Rosita Jovani. This girl suffers from epilepsy. I ask all of you to offer prayers for a cure of her sickness so that she is able to take care of her sisters."

The people were so helpful and complimentary. One lady carried Beni, others talked nice about me, others said bad things about Reyna. I don't appreciate when people talk bad about her. I took my sisters to the sacristy where I asked the priest to give us his blessing with holy oil. He also gave me the unction of the sick. The three forgotten orphans made our way to the diner. I was able to carry Beni. Blanquita didn't want to walk, but with my broken arm, I couldn't carry her. She was pouting to the delight of Beni.

The diner was always busy on Sundays. That day was also good for me, I made good tips helping Mama Lucia. I generally received about sixty-five pesos in tips on Sunday. After she closed the booth, all four of us sat down to eat. We were going to spend the night again with Mama Lucia. However, Israel, a friend of Ana, came to tell me that Ana was home. It took Israel longer to tell me that Ana was home than it took me to go see her. I ran as fast as I could to the house. My tears flowed freely as we hugged. She leaned them with her hand noticing the bump in my head. "Vani, you are banged up, how do you feel?"

"Ana, now that you are here, I feel better than ever." We talked for a long time. I gave her all the latest happenings since the day she left.

"Vani, I am here now, I will take care of you. Beni and Blanquita, are they with Doña Lucia?"

"Yes, they are sound asleep."

"I will go for them tomorrow. But now, Vani, I want you to open a present I got here for you." I held the package in my hands wanting to open it but held back. "Ana, I want to wait and open it for my birthday."

"Okay, Vani, if that's what you want, it's fine with me."

"Ana, I dream of celebrating my birthday. Someday I will."

"Vani, someday is this year. I promise to give you a big party for your birthday." I was so happy that Ana was home, I felt safe. I slept well that night.

The Miracle of My Broken and Crooked Arm

I GOT UP EARLY, I felt as though my Chuchin was calling me. I took a cold bath, put on some clean clothes. I took the candle from my corner, one that I had been saving for today. I purchased this candle with pesos I had saved. I cut a bunch of flowers from the rosebush to take with me. I made my way to speak with my Chuchin. The lady taking care of the garden was the only person I saw. The church was empty, I was the only one there.

I stood in front of my Chuchin. "Good morning, my Chuchin. I am here to honor my promise." I knelt. "Diosito, I'm here to honor the promise I made to you. The day that I fell from the tree and broke my arm, this crooked arm." I raised my crooked arm so that He could see it. "I promised that if my arm was cured, I would crawl on my knees from the entrance of the church to the main altar to give You thanks.

"My arm is crooked and stiff. Although it doesn't hurt, I am ready to offer this bouquet of roses. I will now complete my promise." I walked back to the entrance of the church. I took my skirt off, revealing shorts. My shorts were not going to interfere with my bare knees. I knelt on the cement floor. I struck the match and lit the candle. I crawled praying the Magnificat. I crawled until my knees bled, but I didn't feel any pain. I kept moving until I reached the altar. Reaching the altar, I felt happy and full of hope.

I looked at the image of my Chuchin hanging in the main altar. I felt that He said, "You are getting close. Advance, advance." I turned to see a happy Virgin Mary; her eyes were shining bright. I went to the candle that when lit signifies that the Holy Sacrament is present. I lifted my candle and the flowers, stretched my arms above the altar. I felt a sensation, a surge of energy through my body. The sensation made me lift my head up; my eyes fixed on my Diosito. At that moment, I lifted my arms offering him the flowers. I heard a crack and felt energy passing through my arm. My arm straightened out! My arm was very hot for a few moments. I didn't know what to think, just stared at my Chuchin. I turned my attention to the Virgin Mary; her eyes were more brilliant than ever.

I touched my arm. It was no longer crooked, it was no longer broken, nor was it stiff or swollen. "Diosito, You cured my arm." My tears broke from happiness. I knelt on my bloody knees but felt no pain. Kneeling I put my hands on my face and bent over until my forehead touched the base of the altar. Crying and praying I thanked Diosito and the Blessed Virgin. I didn't move for quite a while. I looked at Diosito again to thank Him for curing my arm. "Thank You, Diosito, of the main altar in the church of Santa Cruz. I know that You love me, You do exist." I got up got put my skirt on. I walked to the Santo de Atocha, I climbed on top of the bench to reach him. "Thank you, my little friend, for also helping me. I will never forget the day you stopped me from entering the quicksand, you saved my life." I hugged the image of my lifesaving saint.

The priest entered the church, walked to the main altar; he saw the flowers. "Who brought these beautiful flowers?" He spoke loud enough for me to hear him. He looked around until he saw me. Whispering he wanted to know what brought me to church so early. "You brought these beautiful flowers, didn't you?" He kept looking at me unsure of what he was seeing.

In a low voice I told him that I cut them from the rosebush I see the lady in white visit at night. I'm sure he didn't know what I was talking about. Suddenly his eyes lit up. "Your arm," he said pointing at it. "Niña, your arm has healed!"

"Father, my Diosito, or Chuchin, the name I use lovingly, cured my arm." The priest didn't say a word during the whole time that I told him about my arm—how I broke it, the promise I made to Chuchin. He was shocked when I showed him my bloodied knees. He said, "Rosita, the prayers the parishioners said on your behalf helped God cure your arm.

"Come with me, I want to give a blessing." We went to the front, and with holy water, he gave me his blessing. "Rosita," he paused for a short while, partly folding his arms, grabbed his chin with his hand, "I ask, who are you?" He replaced his hand on my shoulder, bent over to talk eye to eye. "I do know that you are somebody special. I will do something special for you. I am going to exercise my duty as a priest and permit you to make your first Holy Communion. Why wait any longer? God has already accepted you. Now you can receive the host body of Christ when you receive Holy Communion."

"Really?" I covered my mouth and cried. My tears flowed uncontrolled.

The priest reached out to me, with his hands on my head. "Yes, Rosita, I will permit you to make your first Holy Communion." I asked if he would be my godfather. He smiled. "Niña, I would be very proud to be your godfather, but the church does not permit it. You will make your first Holy Communion on the feast day of the Santa Cruz. That should give you time to choose a godfather." I thanked the priest and left the church. I was anxious to show people my arm. I ran home anxious to show Ana.

Don Felipe's little room was the first place I reached. Ana was coming out of the house onto the patio. "Ana, come here, I want to show you something," I shouted. "Vani, is this going to take long?"

"No, hurry, please." I told Don Felipe to come out but not look at me just yet. Ana arrived; she hadn't seen my broken arm. I asked them to close their eyes. I extended my arm. "Okay, open your eyes." Ana was amazed. Pointing at my arm, she said, "Your arm is healed.

But last night I saw your arm, and it was still broken." Don Felipe looked astonished. "A miracle," he mumbled.

"Ana, I complied with the promise I made to my Chuchin." Lifting up my skirt to reveal my bloodied knees, I told Ana about the promise and how I had crawled from the entrance of the church to the main altar with a candle and a bouquet of flowers. Don Felipe kept mumbling, "Miracle, miracle, it's a miracle." Ana heard the whole series of events starting when I broke my arm and culminating today. "Vani, do you really believe that God cured your arm and not the doctor?"

"My Chuchin cured my arm, of that I'm sure. You saw my arm crooked and broken and swollen. Look at it now. Ana, I felt the surge of energy going through my body, and I heard the sound of the arm when it cracked and straightened out. I was unsure of what happened until I saw my arm, it wasn't crooked or broken anymore. See, Ana, Diosito cured my arm."

"Vani, I see your arm is healed, and how you believe it happened, continue believing it. The important thing is that your arm is healed." Ana gave me a big loving hug. Don Felipe motioned me over; he wanted to give me his benediction. "It's a miracle," he kept mumbling.

"Ana, I have to show my arm to Mama Lucia then I have to go to school. The teacher came over yesterday to tell me that if I don't attend school, I won't pass to the next grade. I don't want to be dumb like a burro."

"Vani, be careful, although you hardly pay attention to me, stay out of the trees."

"I promise," I answered smiling.

Mama Lucia could not believe when she saw my arm. "Jovani, you're going to give me a heart attack. The healing of your arm has to be a miracle." She was surprised to a point that she was speechless; all she could say was "It's a miracle." I made my way to school, happy, running like the wind. I was in the clouds, skipping and jumping toward the school. I realized that school wouldn't start for some time. I was too early. My mind was guiding my every step, I passed the cemetery where many loved ones were resting. I continued to my favorite of water holes. I swam for some time. My arms were completely healed, no ailments. I splashed the water as hard as I dared, no pain. I have learned to enjoy myself in my solitude. The ducks were my company.

I arrived at school a little late. My excuse for being late was in the form of a little lie, which the teacher accepted. In school, neither the teacher nor the students noticed my arm. That was just fine with me, because I didn't have to explain, especially little boys and girls that wouldn't understand anyway. The people did notice as I walked to the diner. Strange but everybody that saw my healed arm made a comment regarding how it had been healed. Many did believe that it was a result of a miracle Diosito had performed because of my faith in Him. Another made a comment that almost made me laugh. Her comment was, "I am diabetic, my sons are mean and drunks. I pray to God, and I still don't get well."

Ana being home, I have more liberty to play with my friends or just go about the pueblo enjoying myself. I happened near my padrino Martin's place; my cousins Lolis and Jisela were outside playing. They invited me to play a game of *conicas*. They invited me to their house. They were having a party. El Quique, a friend of the family, son of Doña Mito, was the first to greet me. Others greeted me as I entered. The whole place was jumping. On one side was a wrestling contest, a band, and dancing on the other end. "Rosita, do you want to play marbles or other games? We are looking for someone that will wrestle against Jisela."

"I don't want to wrestle, I'd rather play marbles," I told her. "Rosita, the winner of the fight wins five pesos."

"Five pesos! I can win five pesos if I win? What do I get if I lose?"

"Nothing, the loser wins zero. No rules nothing, you down your opponent, and you win." The kids used old pans to make noise; others beat spoons to make noise, some sang. Jisela was no match for me. She was not quick enough. The fight was over real quick. Jisela was not quick like me. She did not offer any competition at all. I stayed at the fiesta until the sun was about to hide beyond the earth. Ana was home taking care of our sisters. "Vani, where have you been all day?" I told her that I had gone to a fiesta at my godfather's house. She was interested in hearing all about the fiesta. But when I told her about the match, Ana didn't like that I played wrestling against Jisela. In fact, she was angry. "Ana, I made five pesos, and I didn't come close to losing."

"Not the point, Vani, don't you have enough already?"

During the following days, I started to sell enchiladas and Jell-O in addition to my candies and gum after school. The Jell-O I prepared at night. We didn't have a refrigerator, so the way it jelled was to leave the small jars filled with the mixture atop the roof overnight. I alternated days selling the Jell-O and enchiladas with the candy and gum. I attended school every day, I didn't want to be a dumb burro. I passed to the second grade. The teacher would ask me every day if Mother had come back home. He was concerned that my birth hadn't been registered. I was going to complete my seventh birthday, and I still wasn't registered.

My First Ever Birthday Celebration

"LAS MAÑANITAS," THE HAPPY BIRTHDAY song, woke me up. I usually wake up early but never to somebody singing. It's my birthday, I thought, but who can be singing so early? Maybe I'm dreaming. The sun hadn't risen yet; I was still sleepy. I stretched and went back to sleep. "Vani, wake up." Ana was shaking me. "Happy birthday. Vani, were are serenading you. Get up!" Ana opened the door for me. I stood at the doorway where they serenaded me. Don Jose, known as El Tres Pelos (Three Hairs), was at the guitar, Mama Lucia, Don Felipe, the sons of my aunt Rosa and Ana sang to me "Las Mañanitas."

My hands covered my opened mouth. Diosito, never before has anybody serenaded me on my birthday. I wasn't about to cry, no tears, today I don't permit tears. Instead I joined in the singing. I received hugs from everyone. Ana reminded them about the party later today. After the people left, I asked, "Ana, you are giving me a party?"

"You bet I'm giving you, remember that surprise I told you about? Well, you are having a party to celebrate your birthday."

All day we prepared food for the party. We prepared tamales, atole, tacos, and lots of other goodies. Doña Tere prepared my birthday cake, it was beautiful and delicious. La Bolita helped Ana get the patio all cleaned up. La Bolita arranged the flowers and swept. All day was a true celebration of my birthday. We were busy preparing something that was going to be totally mine. When it was almost time, I told Ana that I needed to take a bath. "Vani, before you do come here, I want to show your present." The dress was gorgeous. "I love it, Ana." She smiled and showed me the shoes to go along with the dress. I couldn't believe that I actually was going to wear a dress of my own for my own birthday. I wanted to cry, Ana stopped me. "Vani, relax, you know what happens when you get too excited, don't you?" After my bath I went into the house to try on my gifts. The dress reminded me of the one my madrina Socorro gave me for my graduation.

The dress and shoes fit perfectly. I looked in the mirror, my eyes sparkled like never before. Ana fixed my hair really nice. My newly discovered face stayed with me. I was so happy, felt full of love. For the first time in my life, my convulsions did not surface, thanks to my Diosito. I invited my Chuchin to the party. "Vani, are you ready to accompany the guests, they wait for you outside." Ana was very excited also.

"Vani, when we start serenading you, relax, okay, because I know you don't want to get sick on this day." She got in front of me. "Promise me." I smiled. "I promise to relax."

"Okay then, ah, Vani, you are quite a girl, let's go." She grabbed my hand. We faced the people together. The guests were ready and waiting, "Estas son las mañanitas" (Happy birthday to you). I gathered my hands as though I was praying, looked up to the heavens, and cried. I will never forget my seventh birthday party. I will forever be grateful to Ana and all the people who celebrated that day with me. I opened my presents. Ana gave me a doll that I had forever desired to have.

Bullfighter Gives Me Gold Medals

WEEKS LATER THE CELEBRATION OF Santa Cruz day arrived. May 3, the day of the celebration, the pueblo streets are completely clean, tents are set up, food booths abound. The street where the procession of the Blessed Virgin Mary will pass through is packed with the faithful. The lead of the procession is a famous band playing religious hymns. Later a witchlike figure is burned in the castle to the delight of the spectators.

Before the day of the Santa Cruz festivities, I discovered that a famous bullfighter, a matador, was coming to perform in our own arena. On that day I went to where I believed the matador would be coming into the pueblo. I waited on the side of the street—why, I have no idea other than I wanted to see the famous bullfighter. The big car followed by a trailer full of bulls was what I was waiting for. I dashed to the middle of the road, I waved my arms so as to be noticed and not be trampled. The big car stopped a few steps away from me. A gentleman got out of the car. "Hey, little girl, why are you stopping us, aren't you afraid of being hit by the car?"

"I am selling candies, do you want to but any?" I lifted my carton of candies to show them. "I also clean windows." The man stood tall, hands on his hips. "Little girl, aren't you afraid of being run over?"

"No, sir, see, you didn't run over me. Sir, I will not ask if I can clean your car windows because your car is too big, and I can't reach the windows." Another gypsy-looking man, with a hat big enough to handle all my candies, got out of the car. The leather pants fit him like a glove, the pistol with ivory handles hung by his side encased in a matching leather sheath. He walked close to me. "Pretty little girl, what are you selling, and why are you alone?"

"Señor, I sell very special candies."

"Niña, what you sell has to be very delicious. A pretty little girl like you isn't going to stop traffic to sell just any candy."

"Like I told the other gentleman, I also wash car windows."

"Niña, for that you risk your life? What's your name, little girl?"

"My name is *Rosa Jovani*, and I live in this pueblo, Tetipac. Señor, you look like the bullfighter that has his picture plastered all over the pueblo." I lifted my box of goodies. "Come on, señor, buy some candy."

He stooped over to be able to see me face-to-face. With his finger he touched the bruised bump on my forehead. "What happened, who did this to you?"

"Señor, please don't ask me that. But I will tell you if you buy candies."

"Oh, Rosa, I will buy some candy.

"Now tell me."

"Señor, I get hurt all the time because I am epileptic and suffer convulsions."

"So you get hurt when you have convulsions?"

"Yes, señor, I fall wherever I have a convulsion. People in my pueblo help me when they see me passed out. Sometimes I don't know how I get to a friend's house, I believe my Diosito places somebody in my path of life to help me."

"Then, Rosa, tell me, how are the people of this pueblo? I want to know before I make myself comfortable."

"Señor, now I ask you, how are the people where you come from?"

"Rosa, for such a little girl you ask a very interesting question. But I will tell you. Rosa, the people in my pueblo are nice and generous. I give thanks that I come from a very fine family, and with their help, I have my own business."

"Okay, señor amigo, well, here where you are standing, we are also fine families. Even though our pueblo is poor, the families are good families. By the way, señor, do you have a place to spend the night? My grandmother has rooms for rent, and she would be happy to be of your service."

"Rosa," the matador spoke while taking the chains from around his neck, "sometimes the person that has, wants more because he is an egotistic individual, and the one who doesn't have, shares more than others. I give you these chains with all my heart." He put them around my neck, he took a roll of money and gave them to me. Everything happened so fast; when I started to refuse, he said in a very firm voice, "Rosa, don't reject these gifts. These chains are made of pure white gold and are worth a lot of money. If you are going to sell them, ask for a lot of money for them. Do you understand?"

"Señor, the money is necessary, you can pay for some Masses."

The bullfighter stooped over, looked me eye to eye; he asked, "Niña, who are you?" He stayed eyeing me for a while. "Rosa, will you give me your blessing?" I started to take the chains off, but he stopped me. "Please don't, accept them as a gift. Rosa, when I first saw you, I felt as though I was looking at someone special. Now I ask, who are you?" He was being sincere. His eyes reflected that of an admirable person. I grabbed his hands in mine and gave him my blessing. The blessing seemed to relax him.

"Rosa, let me give you a ride to your pueblo. I don't want you wandering out here alone." I accepted but only because he seemed like a very honorable man. He helped me get into his car. I couldn't believe how beautiful the inside of this big car was on the inside. I was his guide through the pueblo, showing him the main attractions. He dropped me off in front of the corral at my request, I still had candies and gum to sell. The area was busy with people, vendors, and entertainers, the festive mood exciting. Sales were very good, soon I would have to replenish my basket.

The roar from the bullfighting area changed to screams. "He's going to be killed…the bull is killing him," they were shouting. I ran to the corral, I crawled under the stands to see why the people were screaming. What little I could see was the bull dragging the bullfighter. It was one of the men that had befriended me, it was *la* Rubia. He appeared to be unconscious, one of his eyes protruding from his head. I dropped my basket and tried to enter the arena. Somebody held me; fighting and kicking, I screamed, "Let me go, I need to help him," but he held me. "Don't go in," the man holding me told me, "it's dangerous in there. Looks like the bull has already killed the boy."

I screamed, "Pull *el* Rubia away from the bull." I broke loose, crawled on my belly into the corral, I grabbed the shirt of *la* Rubia and pulled him; others ran to help. Men with ropes lassoed the bull and contained him. I got close to my friend, his eye hanging close to the socket. His friends picked him up in a stretcher and took him away. I returned to retrieve my basket. It had been trampled; what was left of my candies and gum supply was scattered full of dust.

"Let me help you get up." One of the matador's friends I had met was there lending me a hand. He said, "Niña, don't blame my bull, that is part of the profession we chose." He grabbed my hand and placed another roll of money in it and closed it. "With this money you can buy the candy and the basket that you lost. Thank you, Rosa, for coming to the rescue of la Rubia. Now I must go. I have another bullfight planned."

"Señor, please take your gold chains back, sell them and give it to the bullfighters so that they won't have to fight anymore."

"Rosa, please don't take them off. Some day you will use them for something good, I know." He got in his car and drove away.

No, I didn't run home, I walked. I was too dazed with what had happened, that I was in no mood to run. I prayed the rosary for the boy la Rubia. I prayed for him often, even though I never heard of him again. But I will never forget the third of May 1988. It was on this day that the priest asked people again to pray for my health, on this day the bullfighter gave me the gold chains, on this day the bullfighter was gored. On this day I foolishly stopped a car in the middle of the road, why? I kept walking, praying, and thinking.

The church, my sanctuary, I will go there and think. The bench outside the church was inviting. I lay down trying to rest. I closed my eyes thinking of what happened the past few hours. A lady's voice brought me out of my trance. "See, that's why I don't believe in God. You, Rosita, you have so much faith in Him, and look at you, always sick, you don't get well. I've seen you with my own eyes how sick you become, almost dying." That's all I heard, I had a convulsion. When I woke up, I remembered the lady. I thought, *Did that lady help me? I believe she did.* I looked all around, and I saw her walking away. I shouted, "Señora, wait for me." She stopped, turned around, put her hands above her eyes to shield the sun's rays; she waited for me. "Señora, see how you helped me now that I got sick? God put you there at that particular time so that you could help me. Didn't you just tell me that I nearly die when I get sick? Well, look at me. I'm very much alive. I got sick at the moment you were going into the church. Why? Because God wants you to be a witness to what it is to have faith in Him and the Catholic faith." The lady started to cry. "Little girl," she asked me, "who are you?" She made the sign of the cross, turned around, and walked back into the church.

Mother Returns with Knife Wounds on Her Hands

How long had Mother been gone? I couldn't really say, but it was months. But the day arrived when she came back. I came home, Ana met me at the door, she was crying. "Don't go inside, let's go where we can talk. Vani, Mother is home."

"Really? Mother is home?" I started to walk in to greet Mother. "Vani, wait, she is taking a shower. Vani, Mother has a nasty cut that looks like a knife wound on her hand and several bruises on her arms. I asked her what happened, but she wouldn't tell me. When I insisted, she told me to stop asking questions. When I persisted, she slapped me. Vani, she did not come alone, that creepy man came with her. Ana, I want to help Mother, I want to know if she is okay.

"Be very careful of that lustful old man. He isn't here, but when he returns from Taxco, everything is going to change around here." I walked in as Mother was coming out of the shower room. I ran and gave her a hug. "Mother, how are you? You look so pretty." She pushed me away. "Now what the —— happened? Look at your arm, not broken or crooked. You look okay, your arm is healed. The more —— you get into, the more you are rescued. Let me see, come closer. Where in blazes did you get these gold chains?" She touched them. "Look at you, snot nose, now you are even wearing gold chains. Come on, give them to me." She jerked me toward her.

"I will not give these chains to anybody, especially you. Forgive me, but these chains are mine. The bullfighter gave them to me. If you take them from me, I will tell the matador because he is coming to visit me."

"You ungrateful girl, give them to me." She pulled at me. Just then the lecherous old man entered the room. "Good afternoon, my beautiful little girl." I was so angry, I wanted to scream when I saw him enter. Mother pushed me toward him. "Give Lupe a hug," she ordered me. I was angry, but I felt a sense of fear when I saw him. He advanced toward me, picked me up in his arms, and planted a kiss on my cheek. He had aimed his kiss at me mouth, but I turned away. He smelled like old cigar. Worse, he smelled like wet dog.

He had a disgusting smile when he finally set me down. I wanted to vomit, but Reyna broke in, told us to help lecherous Lupe with the groceries he had bought for us. We did, then Ana and I left the house leaving them alone. Later we entered the house just as the old man had finished eating. Reyna called us over. "Lupe wants to talk to both of you." He stood up acting real macho. "Reyna, tell your two oldest daughters to come and eat." I walked over to where Blanquita and Beni were playing. I was going to take them to the table so that they could eat with us. The old man blocked my way. "Where are you going, gorgeous one?"

"Señor, I am going for my sisters, they want to eat also."

"Not those two, they aren't going to do me any good." I was so angry, I wanted to tell him to leave the house and much more. Reyna grabbed me by my arm and sat me at the table next to him. "Jovani, don't be afraid of me, I won't bite you."

Ana was frightened. Reyna grabbed me from the arm. "Don't be a jerk," she said as she pulled me toward where the lecherous old man was sitting. "Listen to Lupe, now sit here." Her pinch hurt, she made me sit next to him. Mother turned to Ana. "And, you, sit here," pointing to a chair next to the old man. When Mother turned to see Ana, the lecherous visitor reached under my dress and grabbed my thigh. I jumped up. "You mean old man, you are nothing to me. Why did you grab my thigh? You have no shame." He pretended as though nothing had happened. "Now what is wrong with you? Hey, Reyna, your daughter is hallucinating. Listen to her words and what she accuses me of doing. You have to teach your Indian daughter some manners."

He stood up looking real serious. "Reyna, I'm not about to support your half-breed Indian daughter from another man, especially this ungrateful bad-mannered one. But I tell you what, one of these two or maybe both are going to be mine, believe me, they will be." He grabbed his sombrero and left. Reyna ran after him, shouting, "Don't leave, my love, please don't leave. Don't forget that I'm carrying your baby." He drove off in his car.

I knew that I was in trouble. She entered the house, her eyes red with anger. I tried to run before she grabbed me by my hair. "You little bastard, you have never liked Lupe. Now you accuse him of committing a serious act. That loose tongue of yours has the whole pueblo talking bad about me, now you make false accusations against my Lupe." She beat me and beat me, saying, "You have chased him away. Your false accusations have driven Lupe from me, now you will pay. Never will you know about Jorge nor about his family." Hearing that gave me courage; wiping my tears, I said, "Repeat what you just said. Then you have no idea that I am your daughter or of anybody else." She gave me another slap. "Daughter of mine, you are, which I regret, but your father is not Ruben Reza, and you will never know anything from me about your father, Jorge.

"You are an ungrateful girl, you don't appreciate anything. Lupe bought you food and other necessities, and you pay him by making up some serious accusations against him. From now on you will obey Lupe whether you like it or not. You understand, snot-nosed?" I didn't respond soon enough, she slapped me again. Ana got between us. "That is enough, don't hit Jovani anymore."

"Mother," I told her, "you have never loved us all, and you have given us nothing but a miserable life. I'm beginning to understand why Ruben took his daughters to the Norte. What I have now will hurt you more even though you know it to be true. I suffer my epilepsy because of you. Another thing, I will uncover the truth about Jorge, I know that he is my father, and someday I will have the truth. One thing I will never understand is why you have never loved me like a mother loves her children. The whole pueblo knows how you treat me."

Reyna grabbed the broom and whipped me with the handle. Ana tried to defend me, but Reyna slapped her and knocked her to the floor. In reality, I don't know what possessed Mother. After that day I doubted more and more that she was my mother. Every time she saw me, she wanted to hit me, to beat me. I dreaded going home. But if I didn't, she would hit me; if I did, she found a reason to hit me. I would take Beni with me, but she wouldn't allow Blanquita to go. But that nightmare got worse when the lecherous old man returned. The more I saw him, the more repulsive he appeared. I hated living under the same roof with those two demons.

When he returned, Reyna ordered me to greet him. To avoid another beating, I said, "Hello, señor." He smiled. "Hey, little girl, you look more gorgeous now than ever. Come, let me show the gift I have for you." He handed me a backpack. I couldn't look him in the face; with my eyesight set on the floor, I thanked him and told him that I didn't need anything from him. He threw the backpack on the floor. "Reyna, look at her, she doesn't know how to respect her elders."

"Listen, snot nose, I'm going to teach you some manners and how to respect me, Lupe Figueroa," hitting his chest like a real macho. "I am not a snot nose nor am I badly educated." I felt my head spinning. I had a convulsion. Mother was beside me when I woke up; she appeared shaken. "How do you feel? You got sick." Ana was on the other side of my bed. I hugged Mother. "Thank you, Mother, for helping me, I love you very much."

"How does your daughter feel?" It was the voice of the old man standing near my bed. "I thought I don't want to see that man around here, he should leave." Maybe I wasn't thinking, maybe I did say what I meant.

"Jovani, don't be so rude with your elders. That is one reason you don't get well. Imagine the scare that Lupe had when he saw you get sick. He carried you to bed, and this is how you pay him? Get up and give him a hug."

"Mother, Vani is too weak, let her rest." I grabbed the pillow hoping to hug it; that's when I noticed that I was in the bed that the old man had purchased for Reyna. Weak as I was, there was no way that I was going to remain in that bed. I rose with Ana's help. I walked to the table and sat on a chair.

The intruder wanted a beef steak for dinner. To please him, Reyna sent Ana to the store. Mother left momentarily, Blanquita broke the silence with her crying and woke Beni from her nap. I was cleaning both my sisters when Reyna entered the kitchen. They hugged and kissed in front of me. "My love," (yuck!) Lupe addressed Reyna, "I am not happy taking care of those two young daughters, we have to do something with them. My love, I don't want you to get angry, but I can't stand those two little girls. If Ana and Jovani weren't taking care of them, I wouldn't be here. I can't stand those two pests. You have to do something with them, especially now that you are going to have my baby.

"These two little pests will not be permitted to play with my son. Soon we should take them to Toluca and sell them. You have to help me as the mother that you are. This sickly snot-nosed one, I will help with her medicine only if she obeys me. She is going to be of some service to me." I was feeling angry and afraid. I was angry because of what they intended to do with my sisters. He pointed a finger at Reyna. "You have to be very careful. I don't want you to lose this baby. I want this baby to be born in good health. If he isn't, Reyna, I will blame you."

I stopped listening to them, quietly I snuck out of the room to where my baby sisters were. I cleaned and changed them and put them to bed. I was about to leave the house because I couldn't stand to be in the same house with those two. Their conversation held me back.

Lupe was telling Reyna that he wasn't wasting his time with her for nothing. He told her, "I'm helping you with your snot-nosed daughters now, but that is going to change when my son is born. He is going to be the heir to your property. I tell you, Reyna, we have to do something with Doña Sinforosa. Somehow we must have her fingerprints on the deed to her properties that you have. I want my son to have all her properties that her husband, Don Domingo, left her. Your brothers will have nothing."

"Lupe, listen to me, I have daughters that are heirs to my property."

"Reyna, I cannot accept that. You will sign everything over to our son. Do you understand me? Reyna, there will be severe consequences, you know me." I had no desire to hear any more, I went outside to wait for Ana. Soon after he finished his steak, they left the house without saying a word to Ana or to me. My house is my own prison.

My Diosito and the Blessed Virgin Mary are my companions, the church is my refuge. This particular day I don't feel like going to school, but I forced myself. The school keeps me busy and entertained. I struggle at times to be the person I want to be. I see children my age healthy and happy, not having to work to buy medicine, food, or clothes. Sometimes I want to get lost in the world of goodness, but I never find it. My faith in Chuchin is my strength. He picks my spirits when I need to be me, to be the person that I am. But who am I?

My thoughts are interrupted by the squeaky voice of Sergio Guadarrama, the dumb airhead of the class. "Wait for me, Jovani." To my regret, I waited. "Jovani, is it true that your mother is going to have Lupe's baby? No wonder they say that she is like a dog." I thought, *Why did I wait for this dumb kid?* "What business is it of yours, you dumb airhead blabbermouth?"

"Jovani, don't call me that, or you won't be my friend."

"Sergio, that is fine with me."

"Good, I am no longer a friend with the daughter of the crazy lady of the pueblo."

"Sergio, you airhead, get out of my sight."

"Jovani, like it or not, you are the daughter of the bitch, the crazy lady of the pueblo."

I saw the face of the lecherous old man in that boy. I picked up a rock and threw it at him. "Say all you want, it means nothing but nuts to me, but you continue to be a dumb airhead. I will not help you with your homework anymore, now you will be dumber than ever. I am going straight to the teacher, he will know how gross you are in school. Your parents will be summoned to school." Sergio was speechless; he stood as though paralyzed, his face turned pale.

"Forgive me, Jovani, please don't tell the teacher. If my father finds out, he will punish me, and it will be your fault."

"If you don't want me to tell the teacher, come with me."

"Where are you taking me to?"

He followed me quietly to the teacher's room. Both of us agreed that he had treated me badly. The teacher found out that I had been helping Sergio with his homework. From then on, Sergio would get help with his studies. From that day forward, Sergio treated me differently.

The old man Lupe was like the wind. Home one day, gone the next, which was fine with me. The days he was home were always tension-filled. One day he tried to grab Ana when she was taking a shower, but she fought him off. She told me how he had tried to grab her. She had just finished taking a shower and thankfully had the towel wrapped around her body. "Vani, be careful of that wretched person. You are smaller and can't fight him off like I did, so be careful of that demon.

"Vani, stay with Doña Lucia, don't stay around here, Lupe is a very dangerous person. Mother will not help you, she will not stop him, believe me, stay away as much as you can. Vani, I have to go work again, be careful." Ana was leaving, but Reyna stopped her. Her eyes were afire ready to leap from her head. "Ana, tell me, what is the matter with you? Why are you provoking Lupe?" Ana, with a surprised look, told Reyna, "Your man is the one causing all the problems. Ask him. If he is man enough, he will tell you."

"Ana, you are wrong, you are the one causing all the problems. Why did you choose to take a shower when you knew that he was going to be there? You are the one provoking him."

"Mother, that is ridiculous, don't say any more stupid things, that man is playing with your mind. Your man is the one that grabbed me this morning. Vani nor I are not safe so long as he is here, I hate your wretched Lupe."

Eyes burning with anger, Reyna intended to slap Ana. My sister held her ground; she stood tall, hands on her hips, and told Reyna, "I will not permit you to ever slap me again." Reyna stood looking at her defiant daughter kind of surprised. "Also, I will not permit you to sell Beni. Not you nor that old man will sell her. I will take her and take care of her." Reyna looked straight at me. "I suppose this snot-nosed nosy Jovani told you, huh? Now she will pay for this." Ana walked passed Reyna out the door. Mother approached me. "What happened between Ana and I remains in this house, do you understand? Now go finish the salsa."

I Was Violated Again by That Man

MOTHER LEFT ME ALONE MAKING the salsa; she went outside to make tortillas. I was too deep in thought making the salsa. I felt a presence behind me. I heard his venomous words, "My precious, I want you to feel me like your mother feels me when we are in bed. I have it in my hand, turn around, look at it, it's ready for you. I'm talking to you, remember your mother told you to do whatever I want." I turned to run away; he grabbed me and covered my mouth with a handkerchief. He showed me his man part. "This is going to be yours, and you mine, like your mother."

I couldn't scream, I was terrified; he held me tight. He said, "With Ana, I couldn't do anything, but you will be mine." He grabbed my underwear. I was so scared; I kicked hard and somehow hit him where it hurt him the most. He grabbed between his legs screaming in pain, "Reyna, Reyna, come!" Mother entered. The old man took off his belt and, with his knife, cut off the buckle. He handed the belt to Reyna. "Here, screw your snot-nosed daughter. If you like, kill her right away, she tried to kill me." Reyna believed him. The two took turns in giving me a beating. He kicked me various times while Reyna hit me with the belt. My whole body was bleeding. "Yes," I told them, "kill me. You señora, may God forgive you because I will always wait for the love of a mother."

"Kill your Indian half breed. Kill her, or I will." I tried to run away, but the two had me cornered. My own mother kept hitting me. "Kill this snot-nosed because if she opens her mouth to the law, I'll go to jail. If I go to jail, it will be your fault. Do you hear me, you will be responsible."

Rosita after the Beating by Both Reyna and Lupe

MY BIRTH MOTHER, WHO BROUGHT me into the world, wants to kill me. How I was able to grab the belt with my hand, I will never know, but I did. Crying with tears flowing down my face, I told her, "I know that you don't love me like a mother loves her child. Go ahead, kill me, come on, do it and spare me from more suffering."

She stopped hitting me. I felt alone more than ever before. My body ached all over. My clothes full of blood stuck to my skin. I faced her. "It's true, I am the daughter of nobody. A mother doesn't beat her daughter like you and that man just did. You will pay for this, someday you will, I promise you that. God is my witness, He knows what you and that man did to me."

"Leave, get out of here, and I warn you to be careful what you say that happened here." I tried to run toward the cemetery, but I was in too much pain. I went to my madrina Socorro's tomb. The ladies that make a living selling tamales were heading home. They saw me but did nothing. Crying looking at the heavens asking Diosito to spare me from those two. "Take me with You, please take me with You. Madrina, please help me. Grandfather Domingo, help me." I spent the night under the guayaba tree in the corner of the cemetery. The ground is solid clay, no place to find a comfortable area to sleep. The pain didn't allow me to sleep anyway. I spent the night looking at the stars in the heavens. Not even the moon was my companion tonight. I was alone. My body was bloody, some of it dry, some still dripping from my wounds.

My tears were flowing more from loneliness than from the pain. Pray I did for my mother's neglect. I asked my Chuchin to heal me, I fell asleep talking to the brightest star I believed to be Venus. Dawn arrived; the roosters crowing woke me up. Last night's nightmare with that lecherous old man and Mother is etched in my heart, I could feel the hurt. "Come on, let's get up," I urged myself. I cheered when I saw the sun rising, it gave me the will to live. *Diosito is with me.*

My body was in pain, I felt it more when I tried to get up. I stretched little by little; the pain was a nuisance, but I was going to beat this. My hands were bloody from touching my wounded body. I was close to the river where I have often washed my body. Now would be a day that I would bathe for necessity and not for pleasure. I tried to make it a fun bath, but to no avail, my body didn't respond. In time I reached the riverbank.

I remembered the story of the *llorana*, the weeping woman. My mamacita told me the story of the llorana. In a fit of jealousy, feeling that her husband had betrayed her, the llorana took her two children and threw them in the river. Later realizing what she had done, crying she ran down river trying to find her children. The lore is that people hear the llorana crying at night along the river.

Standing on the riverbank I talked to the mythical llorana. "Let me hear you cry now, llorona. Is this where you threw your kids into the river when they drowned? Here I am not to cry, that I did all night last night. I have a mother like you, but she doesn't cry for me, like you cry for your sons." The water was refreshing, I washed my face and body as best as I could. The church bells sounded, I started my walk with a painful body because I couldn't run like I usually do.

Doña Chela Rivera Treated My Wounds

THE PAIN WAS UNBEARABLE, I couldn't walk without wincing in pain. Doña Chelita Rivera's house was close by. She always told me that her house was open to me anytime. She answered my knock on her door. "Good morning, Jovani, what brings you here so early? This is Saturday, and you don't have to wash diapers today." I greeted the señora of the house. I didn't have time to say anything else. "Niña, what is the matter, you look weak." I followed her to the kitchen. She served me a glass of milk. I took the glass full of milk. I felt a pain in my back when I tried to take a drink. She heard me yell. "What is wrong, are you in pain?" She touched my back. I don't remember much else; I had a convulsion.

She was at my side and very worried when I came to. "You were trembling really bad," she told me. "Niña, what happened to you? I noticed your back is all bruised. The marks appear to be made by a leather belt. Does your mother know about this?" I lifted my blouse so that she could see the front of my body. "My Lord, look at all the bruises on your body. Who did this to you? I ask you again, does your mother know?" My tears flowed. I couldn't control them, nor could I deny that Reyna and the old man had beaten me. Dona Chela realized that it was my mother who had done the beating. "Please, Doña Chela, don't tell anybody. If Mother knows that I told you, she will for sure kill me the next time.

"My mother is not a bad person, it's that bad man Lupe Figueroa, he wants to kill me. He threatens to take the child that Mother is carrying away from her. If he does that, she will never see her son again."

"Jovani, look at me and answer me honestly, did your mother whip you like this?"

"Yes, she did, she whipped me with the man's leather belt. Please don't tell anybody, I don't want Mother to go to jail." Doña Chela cleaned my wounds with warm salted water. Rede, her husband, walked in when she was cleaning me. "Rede, look what they did to Jovani." He was shocked with what he saw. "Who the —— did this to you? Tell me, niña, don't be afraid, you are safe here. Tell me because this very moment I will take my gun along with my brother Mario, and we will make them pay."

Between sobs with tears, I told them about the lecherous old man. I told them how he had tried to grab Ana and that he tried that on me also. "When I resisted, the man tried to kill me and forced Mother to beat me. Reyna loves him, but she is afraid of him. She is pregnant with that miserable man's child." Don Rede left the room momentarily; when he came back, he was armed with his pistol. His wife stood in front of him. "Rede, think what you are doing. You will only make matters worse for this girl."

"Somebody has to teach them a lesson. I'm going over to beat the life out of that son of a dog or kill him."

"Rede, if you go over to her house, you will cause a commotion. The policemen will be called. They will investigate and learn the truth. Reyna will go to prison. If that happens, Jovani will suffer the most. We can do nothing."

Don Rede relaxed; he got next to me. "Niña, don't feel unwanted, think that you are part of this family. My wife is related to your father, Jorge Bustos's side of the family. From now on you can look at me as a father and Chela as a mother." Don Rede grabbed a beer and downed it in one huge drink. "Señor Rede, I appreciate those words, but please don't do anything to those two demons." She was almost finished cleaning and fixing my wounds when their son Javier walked in. He saw my body all beat up; wondering, he asked, "Who did this to you?"

"Javi, she is not dressed, please leave the room."

Doña Chela took me into a room. She dressed me in one of her son's clothes. Once dressed we went to where Don Rede and Javi were waiting for us. Javi couldn't believe that a mother was capable of doing this to her own flesh and blood. I spent the rest of the day in the comfort of their home. For some time I held back asking Doña Chela if she really knew that Jorge Bustos was my father. She'd been so nice to me, and I didn't want to think that I was ungrateful. Before I knew it, I was asking her, "Doña Chela, is it true that Jorge Bustos is my father?" Her reply was, "What does your mother tell you?"

"Mother slaps me or, worse, beats me the times I've asked her about my real father. She says that Reza is my father."

She couldn't believe that Reyna would do such a horrible thing and, worse, that she had not registered my birth. She was also shocked when I mentioned that my baptism certificate shows my surname as *Reza*. After she had heard enough, she hugged me. "Rosita, I have to do something about this, I must report her. If she goes to jail, nobody will be around to beat you up."

"No, señora, please don't, she is not a bad person, he is the one that was telling her to kill me." Chan, her other son, walked into the room where his mother and I were talking. After the introduction, Doña Chela asked Chan to inform Ana, and only Ana, that I was at their house.

Ana went to the house where I was staying. "Vani, why are you here and not at home?" I didn't say anything, just ran up to her and hugged her. Her return hug made me wince with pain. "Vani, what's the matter?"

"Tell your sister what your mother did to you, go on, don't be afraid." Ana asked, "Mother did what to you?" Doña Chela told Ana to raise the boy's shirt I was wearing so that Ana could see what Reyna had done to an innocent child. Ana lifted the T-shirt, she couldn't believe that Reyna had done such a horrible thing. "I don't understand why Reyna treats my little sister with so much hatred."

"Rosita, tell Ana the reason she beat you so bad."

"Doña Chela, I don't have the strength to repeat what that old man did to me."

"Well, I will," shot back Doña Chela. She did almost word for word tell of the way the man grabbed me and the subsequent beating by both of them. Ana repeated to Doña Chela and to Don Rede what that lecherous old man had tried to assault her earlier that morning. The family offered us a place in their home if we desired to stay with them. The señora assured us that we would be safe at their home. "Señora, we thank you for that offer. We would be putting our lives in danger if we did that, you don't know what Reyna is capable of doing. Your family would be in danger also." Ana told the señora that we should be going home. "Remember of our offer, both of you are welcome to come live here with us."

I didn't want to go home. I prayed to Diosito all the way home. My body ached, my legs were trembling with fear. I walked half-heartedly to the prison I call home. Ana entered first, I followed. I greeted her. Her reaction was expected. "Where the —— have you been, snot nose?" I greeted her again. "Answer me, snot nose, I asked you a question."

"Answer your mother, precious, tell her where you have been." Hearing that repulsive voice sent shivers up my spine, I almost vomited. "Now apologize to Lupe for the way you acted yesterday." I didn't say a word, and neither did I move from the door. I was wary of both as they looked at each other. I thought, *I don't want to live in this house with this wretched old man.* Reyna grabbed my arm and pulled me to where he was sitting.

"Sit here next to Lupe, he isn't going to eat you." The moment he got close to me, I vomited. I ran outside. Ana had cleaned the mess by the time I came back. He looked at me, and with a lecherous smile, he said, "See, that's what happened because you wouldn't let me touch you. Your mother told you to obey me, you have to do as you're told. If you don't, Reyna will give you another beating." Ana couldn't take it anymore, she left the house.

Reyna went to take a shower leaving us alone. My heart was beating fast from fear of what the lecherous old man was thinking of doing to me. He approached me. "Hear me, Jovani, do as I tell you." He tried to touch my thigh. "Leave me in peace, señor, don't hurt me." He laughed. "Me, leave you in peace? That will be very difficult. Do you know why? Because you belong to me." He touched my face, then he tried to touch my behind. I kicked him and ran toward the door. Just my luck, Reyna was entering as I was trying to leave.

"Where do you think you are going at this time of the night?" She turned to Lupe. "Did she disrespect you again?"

"No, Reyna, she was a good girl. But remind her that what happens in this house stays within these walls. Jovani has quite an imagination, she is capable of telling lies about me." Reyna looked at me. "Go take care of your sisters and all of you go to bed."

I was asleep, but the sound of their squeaky bed woke me up. They were making some horrible noises. The noise didn't last long. The place got real quiet. I could hear them whispering. He asked her what she was going to do with me because I wasn't being obedient with him. "Reyna, I will not pay for her medicine nor will continue to support your snot-nosed daughter. Talk to her because if she doesn't obey me, I will take that child you are carrying away from you, and you will never see him again."

"Lupe, my love, don't worry, I will punish her. As of this moment, I will not allow her food nor will I permit her to leave the house until she gives the respect you deserve."

Nightmares are dreams, mine was a living nightmare, it was real. The following day Reyna ordered me to follow her. I knew that she was up to something because the first time she took me anywhere was to her ranch for lumber, and nothing good resulted from it. But I was happy to accompany her. "Where are we going, Mother?" Reyna replied that she needed help within the storage shed. The shed was located underneath the railing near the garden. She unlocked the door and told me to go in first. I trusted her. The open door allowed some light to the otherwise darkened room. I walked in, and everything went dark when she closed the door behind me.

"Mother, open the door, I can't see anything." She had not followed me, I was alone in the dark shed, she had locked me in. "Mother, Mother, open the door," I screamed. No answer. "Why do you punish me like this?" After a while, the cracks in the walls allowed some light. I tried the door; it was locked. I prayed to my Chuchin. I couldn't go to school, I couldn't help Mama Lucia. Now I was a prisoner in my living nightmare. La Bolita, I remembered, walks past the garden every day about this time. Where he goes, nobody probably knows or cares.

"Bolita, Bolita," I screamed for a long time until my throat started to hurt. I screamed again, "Bolita, help me!" Bolita heard my desperate call for help. He opened the door, but my prison was only expanded to include my house. I could hear Beni crying, I ran to the house. Reyna was asleep. I changed Beni's diaper and fed her and Blanquita some atole. Reyna didn't say anything to me when she saw me, didn't even seem surprised that I had escaped her jail. She did prohibit me from eating the food that Lupe had bought. She also didn't allow me to leave the house. I had to be obedient and do whatever Lupe, the lecherous Lupe, wanted from me.

I looked at Mother; my thoughts must have been registered in my face. I was thinking, *How can Reyna be so blind? That man is a monster, a bad lecherous person, why can't she see that?* She stared at me. "Listen, you snot nose, don't even think whatever you're thinking, or I will give you the worst beating ever." I spent the days feeding and taking care of my younger sisters. I would share their food when Reyna wasn't around. On one of the days of my imprisonment, she left the house not saying anything to me. I was taking care of my sisters unaware that the lecherous monster was next to me.

He grabbed me from behind, turned me around to face him with such force, I couldn't fight him. He showed me his man thing. "Look at this, and look at it good because soon this is going to be inside of you. Keep quiet, understand? What happens in the house stays here. Don't even tell that old man Felipe nor Lucia, your sister, or anybody from the pueblo. I promise that if you tell anybody, your mother and I will kill them. I might even take care of your mother. The Figueroas will not allow the Bustos to step over us. My sons know about vengeance. Between them and their friends, we can take vengeance on all of you.

"Niña, I tell you this, I'm not here because of your mother, no, I am here because you and your sister will be mine. You are clean, you are virgins, and you are so pretty. I am anxious to show you what it is to be a woman so tender. Your mother has been around, not a virgin like you. But soon you will not be a virgin anymore." I was so scared trembling with fear. I couldn't free myself; he was too strong for me. He let me go when he heard Reyna enter the house. I dropped to the floor, trembling; I crawled to where my sisters were playing.

"My love, is everything okay between you and this snot nose?"

"Yes, my Reyna, we had a nice conversation. I think that we came to an understanding. I told your daughter that if she lies about what we do here, I will go to jail. But you know me, Reyna, I will not allow that to happen. Jovani understands, she seems intelligent enough not to tell anybody what goes on in this house. My love, I understand everything will be okay." He ate and left the house. My imprisonment days were over. She allowed me to leave.

Don Felipe was the first person I visited. He was angry with my two prison guards. He wanted me to see Lucia because she was worried about me. He said, "Talk to Lucia and then come back. I want to write everything that happened these past days." I too was anxious to write my diary. "What they did to me must be written." Mama Lucia was so happy to see me. I stayed for a short while. I told her that I couldn't stay because I wanted to see Don Felipe, we had writing to do.

Don Felipe was waiting for me. "Niña, are you mentally prepared to tell me everything?"

"Yes, señor, I am mentally prepared to tell you everything. But for now, you are the only that will know. But we can't write anything here, we must go someplace else to write. If Reyna sees us writing, she will beat the life out of me, and she will kick you out of here. The place near the church is perfect, nobody will be there today, it's Saturday." We decided to meet there. I went home for Beni and Blanquita; this way, Mother wouldn't suspect anything.

We met at the place near the church. He was ready with paper and pencil. I told him, "Don Felipe, señor, here in front of Diosito, only you will know what happens at my house. You cannot tell anybody because if word gets out, he is liable to kill all of us. That horrible man told me that he will kill everybody if he goes to jail. Please write for me, I am too emotional to write. For me to write will be painful, and I will cry."

"Rosita, I will keep these notes for you, and I will guard them with my life."

He wrote every word, every bit of what happened last night. I couldn't stop crying. When we finished, he gave me some information about the lecherous old man. Apparently he was married;

his wife lives in Pilcaya Guerrero. "The knife wound in her hand, I understand that his wife is the one that cut her. Guadalupe, or should I say Lupe, had your mother living close to his home. His wife found out, the two had a fight, and that is when your mother was knifed. A brother of Lupe is married to the daughter of your uncle Matilde. You should talk to Matilde, he might help you."

"No, señor, if I blab, my mother will give me another beating, and he has threatened to kill anybody that betrays him."

Reyna was not a comfort being pregnant. She had me running all over the place doing her favors. But I wouldn't miss school. The living nightmares continued especially when the lecherous visitor was visiting. Her shouts woke me up when I was sound asleep. "Jovani, answer the door, are you deaf, don't you hear the knocking on the door?" Sleepy eyed I walked and opened the door, only to see the old man standing in the doorway with a smile in his face. "Hello, my little precious girl, here I am just for you." He reeked of perfume, I ignored him.

"Lupe, come quick, I think your son wants to come out. Take me to the hospital."

"Oh, Reyna, you are not due for another month, stay in bed and wait for me." He hung a sheet over the bed so that I couldn't see anything. My bed was close by. "Hey, snot nose, go to sleep. Don't want you to see what I'm going to do to your mother, and what I'm going to do to you soon."

"Lupe, leave my daughter alone."

"Oh, Reyna, since when are you concerned about your snot-nosed daughter?"

"Be quiet, Lupe my love, I'm waiting for you."

Old Man Wants to Sell My Sisters

I WAS FALLING ASLEEP WHEN I heard them whispering. He told Reyna that he was tired of supporting her daughters. He told her that he had found a childless couple and were interested in buying Beni and Blanquita. Mother didn't want to sell Blanquita, her favorite daughter. "Lupe, offer them Jovani and Beni."

"No, Reyna, I will not offer Jovani, she is to be of service to me. Besides, she will be difficult to sell because of her medicine, it's too expensive. Besides, Jovani will give me pleasure like a man that I am."

"Don't talk like that. If her grandmother Sinforosa finds out, she will press charges against you."

They didn't speak for a short time. Reyna whispered, "Be careful, don't hurt the baby." I didn't know what she meant. After a few minutes, I heard mother snoring. I was sleeping on my back. I felt his hand on my mouth. I tried to scream, but I couldn't; he stuck his handkerchief in my mouth. I was helpless against his strength. He touched my body with his manly part. "Look at it, Jovani, you are going to feel it like your mother did. I can hardly wait for you to be mine, and mine you will be now." I was trembling with fear, he was on top of me. He was able to separate my legs. He moved awkwardly; somehow I was able to bite his hand. He let go for a second, enough time to remove the handkerchief from my mouth. "MOTHER, MOTHER," I screamed, "Lupe wants to grab me." The lecherous old man ran out of the house. Reyna woke up; she asked, "What is the matter with you? Why are you screaming like crazy?"

I was traumatized, shaking so much that I wasn't able to speak. "Now what is wrong with you? Can't you speak? Say something, don't just stand there." I couldn't tell how her how bad it was for me living under the same roof with her and the lecherous old man. Finally I was able to speak with a breaking voice. "Mother, please make that man go away."

"What are you saying, snot nose? He's not even in the house. Now what are you accusing Lupe of?"

"My love, I'm here, what's going on?" He looked at me. "And you, Indian half breed, what's the matter?"

"Apparently she was dreaming because she is acting crazy. Notice how crazy the knocks on her head are making her. Maybe that's the reason she is telling lies, all those lies."

I was between a rock and a wall; if I tell her what that man did, she won't believe me, and she will probably beat me again. However, if I don't, he will continue abusing me. He was laughing saying, "Yeah, my love, your snot-nosed…" I walked quietly out of the house.

I was crying unable to control my tears. The night was dark, moonless. "What's the matter, my little friend?" The voice of Don Felipe startled me. I ran toward him and hugged him. I cried until I couldn't cry anymore. "Cry, don't hold any sentiments back, let every emotion out of your heart."

"I can't live in the same house with those two horrible persons."

"Rosita, what did he do this time?"

"That lecherous man wants to do to me what he does to Mother in bed. That wretched old man wanted to do that with me and when Mother was in her bed."

"Your mother was there and did nothing? What kind of mother is she? You didn't tell your mother?"

"Now, señor, I'm just as afraid of her as I am of him. They accuse me telling lies. They say that all the hits I've taken on my head are making me crazy.

"He told me again that I'm his and that soon I will feel what Mother feels in bed. I also heard them talk about selling Blanquita and Beni to some people away from here. Mother doesn't want to sell Blanquita because she is her favorite. She wants to sell me and Beni. Lupe told Reyna that not me because I was good and I would be his."

"Your mother said nothing to him?"

"Señor, I can't talk anymore."

"Rosita, we are going to write this down in your notes." He took paper and pencil and wrote everything down. "I will keep these notes safe for you. If that man does anything to you, I will take these notes to the officials or the government in Chilpancingo." We were writing when Ana came home. He saw us and came over. "Vani, it's ten thirty, what are you doing out so late?" I was so happy to see Ana. I ran up to her and hugged her.

"Ana, let's leave the pueblo, I can't live with those two. Again he tried to grab me like he grabs Mother in bed. That's what he told me he was going to do. Mother doesn't do anything, she thinks that I am telling lies. Ana, I also heard them saying that they are going to sell Blanquita and Beni. Believe me, I heard. He doesn't want to sell me because I'm going to be his."

"I knew it, dear god, I knew it. That's the reason he got together with Reyna. Vani, I will not permit them to sell Beni. I will take care of Beni. But I can't understand Mother, why Blanquita, she's her favorite."

"Ana, let's leave the house and take our sisters with us. I can't stand to live here another day. The old man wants to open a business where she can sell sweets. He wants me to help Mother sell. His reason is that this way I won't be selling candies out on the street. I don't believe him, he wants me close by because he has bad intentions."

"Vani, it's not that easy. Besides, Reyna and Lupe will pursue us, you know them. They will never—and I mean never—allow us to leave, especially with our sisters whom they intend on selling. No, Vani, we can't leave, we just have to be careful when the old man is around. Be strong, Vani." That night I slept with Ana. Lupe left the house early the following day. Later that same day, Reyna started to feel real bad. Ana knew what to do, and I was ready to assist her. Lupe arrived a short time later.

Mother had prepared a bag of necessities to take with her to the hospital. He looked at her. "Are you ready, is it time for my son to come into the world?"

"Yes, Lupe, my love, it's time." Reyna asked me to give my bag to Lupe. I grabbed the bag, took it to him, I dropped the bag at his feet. He looked at me saying nothing. Mother got into the car. I told

Ana that I was going to the hospital with her. I ran to the car and jumped in the back. "Where do you think you are going, snot nose?"

"I'm going with Mother to help her, she needs me." He didn't argue. Mother was in a lot of pain.

The Secret of the Medallion

SHE WAS RUSHED INTO A room as soon as we got there. Soon afterward a nurse emerged from her room. She asked me, "Are you the daughter of Reyna Bustos?"

"Yes, I am, how is she?" If she said something, I don't remember. "If you are the daughter, come with me, she wants to speak with you." Boy, was I happy because she wants to talk to me! The nurse told me that they had to operate on Mother. "This kind of operation is very dangerous, and she runs a big risk. That's the reason she wants to see you."

She looked real sick and in real pain. I had never seen my mother sick before, not like this. I gave her a hug. "Mother," I said, "I know you don't love me, but please don't die. Mamá, now is the moment that you should ask God for forgiveness for all of your errors."

"Shut up and listen to me, I have something for you. Go to my bag, search in one of my pockets for a medallion." The medallion was a beautiful one of the Sacred Heart of Jesus. I handed it to Mother.

"Come closer to me," she said. Mother placed the sacred necklace around my neck. I was in shock, Mother does love me, she does, I was so happy. "Your father gave me this medallion for you before he died in the Norte. I'm giving it to you now because I'm very sick. I might not recover from this operation. Take good care of it. Now leave, leave me alone."

"Mother, give me a hug, please give me a hug."

"Nurse, nurse," she shouted, "take this child away, I want to be alone." How life changes for me from a moment of sheer joy to one of reality. *Why doesn't she love me?*

The medallion! My hand reached to touch the medallion. My father is Jorge Bustos! He gave this to me. Mixed with emotions of learning that Jorge is my father but he is not alive. Reyna doesn't love me, and Jorge, my father, is dead; Reza is alive, but he is not my father. In reality I am the daughter of nobody. Teary-eyed I hummed my song, "I am the daughter of no one..." The nurse interrupted my thoughts. "Niña, is that man your father?" What a jolt. *Heaven forbid, and I thank my Diosito that he isn't,* I thought. "No," I answered, "he is a very bad man, I loathe being around him." Even in print, I don't like to see him.

Lupe showed up while I was talking to the nurse. He took my hand. "Let's go rest," he told me. The nurse left us alone. The aged man grabbed my chin so that I could see him face-to-face. "Listen, open your snout to say something bad about me," he touched his big menacing knife. He moved his opened hand across his throat. "I will kill you like this, *swish*. I will kill you right here in the hospital."

Terrified, I didn't know what to do. My Diosito is watching me, I know that He is. The nurse approached me. "Niña, are you okay?"

"No, señora, I don't feel good being here, do you have a safe place that I can wait?" She took me to another room where I felt safer. Mother came out of the operation; she was going to be okay. I went to an altar in the hospital and placed a bouquet of flowers in front of the statue of the Virgencita. "Thank you, Virgencita, for helping Mother." I wanted to see my new baby brother, but Lupe was in the room, I'd wait until he left. When he left the room, I hid out of his sight. He was leaving the hospital.

I walked into the room, Mother acknowledged me. I saw my little brother for the first time. He was so tiny and so beautiful. I asked her if I could hold him. She handed him to me, I held him in my arms. My little brother let out a loud cry, I held him closer and rocked him in my arms. He opened his eyes, and I saw them for the first time. I stayed in the hospital two days with Mother and my little brother. On the second day, I saw Lupe arrive at the hospital. I hid from his sight. I left the hospital, got on the bus to the pueblo.

The bus trip seemed longer than other times, I guess I was too anxious to share the news with Ana. Soon after I arrived home, I shared with Ana everything about our baby brother. She asked me about Mother. "The doctors had to perform a very dangerous operation on our mother because she was very sick. She is okay now, the operation went well. You should see Mother, she is really involved in being a mother to Rafael." Ana asked, "Who is Rafael?"

"That's what they named the baby."

"Vani, really? Rafael was the name of a man that our mother used to date.

The medallion was not forgotten, I was saving that story until I had told Ana about the baby. I pulled it through the top of my blouse, still hanging from my neck. "Look, Ana, what Mother gave me." Ana was so surprised; eyes wide open, she asked, "Mother gave you that medallion? Come on, Vani, now you have to go to confession for fibbing, Mother would never give anything like that especially to you."

"Isn't it pretty? Before she was operated, I told you she was very sick. She called me into the room and gave it to me. Jorge Bustos had bought it for me when she was going to give birth to me. She had it all this time, but she was sick and probably felt guilty or something, that's why she gave it to me. She said in so many words that my father bought this for me. But Jorge Bustos is dead."

"She actually told you your real father bought it for you?"

"Yes, Ana, she told me that and told me to take good care of it."

"Vani, you are correct, someday you will know the truth."

"Ana, what truth are you talking about? I know that you know that Jorge is my father, but you are afraid of telling me, why? Dead or alive I am going to get proof that Jorge is my father."

"You probably will, but please don't ask me, you know what I have to face here if I tell you what I know. Speaking of that, hide that medallion because Mother will ask you for it. When she asks you for it, tell her a little lie that you lost it on that bus or wherever, because she'll want it back. This is a keepsake from your father, treasure it." *Oh,* I thought, but didn't react, "keepsake from my father," she does know.

We had the house clean. Mother's bed were with clean sheets ready for her arrival from the hospital with the newborn brother. Their arrival was a happy one, Ana carried the baby inside the house, I carried her bag. We helped Mother settle into her comfortable bed. We took her food that we had prepared. Moments after she had eaten,

Lupe walked in with a groceries. The lecherous old man showed the groceries. "This food is for Reyna and the baby." He made it clear that the food he bought was strictly for his son and Reyna. Under no circumstances were we, "moochers," going to partake in the food. He looked at Reyna. "Now you hear me, I don't want my son to share anything with your dirty snot-nose daughters. I'm not going to support all of your daughters. I take responsibility for my son and Reyna, that is all." Never before had we separated anything before. Now we separated our food from his son's.

My Diosito is forever watching over me. We have never depended on anybody for our support, and certainly we were not depending on that old evil man for our support. Doña Graciela Castillo offered us employment. Her daughter-in-law had also given birth. My duties were to prepare the baby food—the mother fed him most of the time—and keep the house clean. Ana was the cook and would help me clean house. The husband, Don Felipe Castillo, was a very nice man.

Working away from my mother was difficult for me, I kept thinking of my two sisters and Mother with her new baby. Ana helped me in not thinking too much about them. "Vani," she would say, "don't worry about Mother, that old man Lupe should pay a servant to help her."

"Ana, I worry about Blanquita and Beni. Reyna is their mother, not you or I, she is responsible for them. Before we know it, she will leave the pueblo like the many other times. You know that she will not take her daughters with her."

Doña Graciela and her husband were really good people, they treated us extremely good. They would pay us weekly and always gave us food for our sisters. They were in charge of a store that catered to the farmers. Getting to their house from ours was not easy, but I was not alone. Ana and I would wake up as early as five in the morning. We walked to their house; on a normal day, it took us about forty minutes. On an abnormal day, longer; that's when I had a convulsion or two. But like I said, I was not alone, Ana would take care of me when I had a convulsion.

Rubicet Castillo, the niece of Doña Graciela, became my best friend. She and I attended the same Union and Progreso School. The memories of Ana and I working at the same place will forever be etched in my memory. Ana reminded me to relax, because I always wanted to run. Señora Castillo knew that if we were late, we had a good reason; otherwise, we were on time. The time we spent walking, we got to know each other. But my mother and my little sisters were always on my mind.

Mother realized how much we did for our little sisters. She resented not having us helping her with Blanquita and Beni. She wanted to concentrate solely on Rafael. Her favorite saying was that we were ungrateful daughters and don't appreciate all she does for us. "You don't realize how difficult it is to care for your sisters and Rafael. Your sisters are a load, one of these days you are going to find me dead, and it's going to be your fault."

Those words resonated in my head constantly. "Ana, is she right? If she dies, will it be our fault?" Ana stopped walking, put her hands on my shoulders. *Uh-oh, Ana is going to say something important,* I thought. "Vani, that old man has money, he got her pregnant, let him pay for a maid to help Mother. If he hires a maid, she better be ugly—and I mean real ugly—or he will grab her." She made me laugh, then she couldn't help it, she also laughed. "Don't worry about those two. You know what happens when you worry too much." *She is right,* I thought, *sometimes I have more than one convulsion.* But on these occasions, I haven't been alone. That was the summer of 1987. By the end of summer, Liliana, the daughter-in-law, had fully recovered and didn't need my services anymore. I had become attached to Liliana's baby, and I missed him a lot. Ana continued working every day but Saturdays. Beni accompanied her most of the time. I worked on Saturdays with Doña Chelita and on Sundays with Doña Arce selling tacos, and during the week, I continued selling my candies and gum.

The building of the new school was looking almost completed. I'd walk by it every chance I was selling my basket of candy. One of the days I ran into the teacher, David. I greeted him with the question, "Señor David, are you here to buy my candy?"

"But of course, only if you give me a good price."

"Señor, if you buy me ten, I will charge you for nine."

"Niña, that is a good price. However, I only need one."

"The school looks really nice, will it be ready for the start of the school?"

"No, Jovani, the construction of the school is taking longer than we expected. The longer it takes, the more money we will need, and we are running out of funds. The new president has imposed new regulations, and it's costing us more money to finish."

The school won't be finished; I was a little sad because I had been looking forward on attending a new school. *My medals,* I thought of the ones given to me by the bullfighter. He told me that they were worth a lot of money. "Señor David, I have some very valuable chains. I will be happy to donate them."

"Jovani, how does it happen that you have such valuable jewelry? Does your mother know that you own these chains? Also, what will she do when she knows that you are willing to give them up to finish the school?"

"Señor, the bullfighter gave them to me. He told me that if I ever sold them, to ask for a lot of money because they are very valuable. My mother knows that I have them, and they are mine to do what I want with them. Señor, if you permit, I will tell you how I became the owner of these chains." He listened to me. I gave him the complete story of how I became the recipient of the chains.

Cuando Termine La Primaria
Yeni, Cristina, Minerva, Ruby, Rosita (kneeling),
Maria Elena, Rafa, Oscar, Ruben

Word spread rather quickly that Rosita/Jovani, the sickly little girl, had donated some rather valuable jewelry for the purpose of finishing the school. Apparently my gift stirred the pueblo's conscience because donations from the people, including the president, were enough to finish the school. The names *union* and *progress* were given to the school for a pueblo united and progressing forward.

The year went by pretty fast. The old man would visit but didn't stay long. His primary reason for visiting was to see his son. The name was changed to *Sergio* when he was baptized. The old man found out that Reyna dated a man by the name of Rafael, thereby the name change.

Sergio's godfather was a business associate of Lupe; his wife, the godmother, was Reyna's niece. We met two of the old man's sons, Oscar and Chester. They made the trip from the Norte to visit and meet their new brother, Sergio. They presented themselves like Northerners. They stayed in the pueblo about a week before returning to the Norte.

Blanquita enjoyed playing with Sergio, but only when Lupe wasn't around. Lupe would get angry if we played with him. He didn't allow us near his son. Not only would he get angry with us but he would scold Reyna for allowing Sergio near us. He told her, "I don't want him playing with your shabby and filthy daughters, he is a Figueroa." He was always pushing Mother for the birth certificates or the baptism document of my sisters. He wanted to sell them, because he was tired of supporting them. That was not true. Ana and I provided all their food and clothing; he just didn't want them around.

The Old Man Sold My Two Sisters

A FEW DAYS LATER, HE walked into the house in a hurry. "Reyna, get your daughters ready, I have a family that is interested in having one or both of them. We'll take both to see which they prefer. But I don't want them around here, I will be forced to give them a good price for both of them." I approached them and pleaded with them not to sell my sisters. I asked Reyna, "What kind of mother are you? I don't know of any other mother that sells her own children." Lupe stood right in front of me, Mother said not a word. "Shut up, you snout snot nose. You don't support them, so you don't have a say in this matter."

"Don't sell Beni, leave her with Ana, she will take care of her. Sell me and Blanquita."

"That is not possible, Lupe has already made the arrangements to sell them. We have to sell them, I can't care for them, they are a lot of trouble."

Mother grabbed me by the collar, looked at me with venom in her eyes. "Don't you dare say anything to anybody. Not to Don Felipe, not to Doña Busybody Lucia nor anybody else." The old man threatened to kill me and anybody else who knew that Lupe and Reyna were selling my two sisters. "Remember what I told you, Reyna, don't pay attention to your screwball daughter." They were taking my two sisters like an owner of livestock takes his cattle to market. Blanquita and Beni were happy to be going with Reyna. The poor little girls had no idea what was in store for them.

He got out of the car, came to the doorway where I stood crying for my sisters. "Now you are more ready than ever. Soon you will dis-cover what it is to be with a man," the lecherous man told me. They left with my two siblings, I couldn't stop crying for them. Once again I have lost the persons that I love, alone again.

Don Felipe realized something was wrong when he saw the two of them put my two sisters in the car and left me crying. I walked over to him. "What's the matter, niña?" I had to tell him what those two were up to. "What can we do, Don Felipe?"

"Niña, there is nothing we can do, your mother has all the right to sell them. Jovani, look at it this way, if they stay here, they will suffer the same life that you're going through. That man is going to abuse them, you know that."

"That lecherous old man is trying to abuse me, but I won't let him." I repeated to Don Felipe words that Lupe had said to me before they left to sell my sisters.

"I avoid him as much as possible when he is around. Reyna too is a big problem, she doesn't believe that he wants to harm me." Don Felipe wanted to say something, but I stopped him because I'm so tired of talking about the lecherous man. I left for the church where I can converse with my Chuchin. Inside I felt faint, I fell. I don't know how long I was out. My head was exploding with much pain. I was able to get on my feet by holding on to the bench. How was I going to break the bad news to Ana? I went to the ditch, washed my face, and wet my head hoping that the cold water would help ease my headache. I sat on the bank of the ditch waiting for Ana. The sound of the water flowing relaxed me.

People passing would greet me with a friendly smile, others would make comments about me always being alone. My headache was not as bad; my ache was going away, but I still felt a little faint. I vomited. "Niña, what are you doing out here by yourself?" she asked when she saw me vomit. "You look sick." She helped me to my feet. "Thank you, Señora Maria, I'm waiting for my sister. She comes this way from work."

"Niña, you are coming with me, you can't be here by yourself. You can wait for your sister at my house." Doña Maria Castañeda walked me to her house. She took me to a bedroom where I was to rest. She fixed me a cup of tea, told her daughter to stay with me. Before closing the bedroom door, she told her daughter not to leave me alone. I noticed the bedroom door opening very slow; in came Rede, her son. "You shouldn't be here Rede," his sister told him. "I came to see Jovani." He got on his knees close to the bed where I was resting. He said, "Jovani, you have to get well. Please make every effort to get well because I like you a lot, I always have. Every time I see you alone, I want to take you with me. But you don't pay attention to me like you pay attention to Ruben Rivera. Now you know that I like you a lot, so don't die."

"Oh, Ruben, I like you too, but for a best friend…" I wanted to say more, before he was chased out of the room by his sister. Running out of the room, a smiling Rede blew me a kiss.

Doña Maria fed me. She had prepared a meal composed of goat with garbanzos and an iguana. She told me that iguana was a good remedy for my attacks. Loverboy Rede waited for Ana. He led Ana to his house where I was being taken care of. Ana turned down the same food I had enjoyed because her boyfriend had invited her out to dinner. "Oh, you have a boyfriend?" asked Doña Maria. "Well, a good-looking girl like you probably has many boys that would like to date you."

"Señora, I don't pay attention to them. Besides, I have two little sisters that occupy most of my time." Ana thanked the señora and her family for taking care of me.

On the way home, I thought of numerous ways on how to break the bad news to my sister. "Vani, why are you so quiet, are you feeling sick?"

"No, Ana, I'm feeling better, I'm searching for the best way to tell you something very important."

"Well, Vani, tell me now, what's so important that you can't tell me now?"

"Ana, go with me to the church, I will tell you inside."

"Jovani, what can be so dramatic that you want to tell me inside the church? Diosito is everywhere. Besides, I'm tired, and I have to get ready for my dinner date." I grabbed my sister by her hand, we entered the church. We made the sign of the cross and sat on a bench. "Ana, Mother and Lupe have sold our sisters and have taken them to the state of Mexico."

Ana went numb, just stared at me. "What? No, no, no, that is not possible," she cried, lowered her head to pray. "No, no, how can Mother do that? Tell me, dear God, that it's not true." She cried for a long time. "That malicious lecherous old man forced her to sell them, I know it. Mother wouldn't do such a thing. He threatened her, I'm sure of it, like he has threatened me." We left the church without saying a word. Ana went directly to where she kept Beni's clothes. "It's empty," she cried, "Vani, it's empty, she has taken Beni." I wanted to comfort Ana, but she told me to leave her alone.

Now more than ever I felt alone. Ana doesn't want me around, my sisters are gone. I felt lonely and sad. Without a father, without my sisters; and now with Beni gone, Ana will be leaving, of that I'm sure. This house will be a cold place to be with all my sisters gone, and I will be the prisoner of those two. My Diosito and my Virgencita will always be with me.

My second mother, Doña Lucia, was happy to see me when I arrived at her diner. "Niña, come here." She gave me a hug. "Jovani, I haven't seen you in quite a while. Your eyes look sad, tell me, what's the matter?" I couldn't stop talking; meanwhile, Mama Lucia continued preparing the food for the midday crowd. I told her everything, in spite of the warning not to say anything from the terrible two I was living with. "Mama Lucia, I am sure that Ana will be moving away soon because she can't stand to live in the house with that mean man, especially now that Beni is gone. If I didn't have you, I would be all alone, thank you for being so good to me."

"Rosita, you may think that you are alone, but the people of the pueblo know what you are going through. Most of these people would take you into their family as one of their own. Speaking about the people of the pueblo, Señora Belen and her husband, Rodolfo, want to see you. She has asked me several times for you. She says that you are like the elusive cat, she can't catch your tail."

"Ha, ha," I had to laugh. "Tomorrow I will go see her, it's too late to go now."

"Good, go tomorrow, now come and eat, your stomach is growling." *She can hear my stomach growling?* We sat and ate together for the first time in quite a while. I ate, helped clean the kitchen, and went home.

Ana was leaving to go meet her boyfriend. She invited me to go with her. I declined. "Vani, you will be all alone in the house."

"Don't worry, Ana, I'm used to being alone." I walked into the empty house—no Beni, no Blanquita, my companions for the past three years. I walked into their bedding area; it was so lonely I started to cry. The lights cast my shadow. "Oh, shadow, if you could talk and disclose what goes on in this house, Lupe would be in jail." I couldn't stay inside, it was too lonely and lifeless. I walked outside into the darkness; tonight, even the moon was not going to keep me company. The only noise was made by the neighborhood dogs' constant bark. I fell asleep, until Ana came home; she carried me to bed.

The following morning I made coffee for my old friend and told him to get ready for Mass. I went home, got dressed for Mass. The old man and I walked to the church. After the church services, we went our separate ways, him to his room, myself to see what Doña Belen wanted. She was watering her flowers while her husband, Don Rodolfo, was outside drinking coffee. We warmly greeted each other. "I suppose that Señora Lucia gave you my message?"

"Yes, ma'am, she did, and here I am to assist you." She invited me to sit with her in the garden bench her husband had just vacated.

"Rosita, I want to hire you for some light work, but first I must ask if you are well enough to work. I have to ask you because I don't want you to get hurt while working here."

"Señora, you mean my sickness? I have always had it, and believe me, I can work, so please don't worry about me."

"But you still have convulsions?"

"Yes, I still have the sickness, and I don't get any better. Like I said before, don't worry about me, I can still work." She hired me. I was hired to work three days a week, four hours each day on Mondays, Wednesdays, and Fridays. I started to work immediately that day. She treated me really nice, as did the older lady who did the laundry. On Saturdays I helped Doña Chelita to make tortillas. On Sundays I sold tacos and fresh water with Don Rafa and his wife. The other days I helped Mama Lucia and sold my goodies.

The house was cold and lifeless, it was sad. My little sisters were always around playing or crying or sleeping—whatever they gave life to the house. Now they were gone, taking the warmth with them. I was not comfortable inside. I would visit my old friend or go to church to make me forget them. Ana felt uneasy as well, she would cry when she was alone. I was aware of her crying, but I'm sure she didn't realize that I knew. But I have learned that change is inevitable, especially when you least expect it.

After leaving the house of Doña Belen, I decided to sell candies. It usually kept my mind occupied. Leaving all my work behind, I headed for my house. For a few moments I thought I was dreaming, but I wasn't, Ana was actually walking toward me with Beni in her arms. I ran and embraced my little sister. Ana whispered, "Blanquita didn't come back with them. Mother appears very sad but isn't talking."

We walked into the house, the first person I saw was Mother. She was sitting down looking very sad. I didn't greet the baby seller, but I did ask Mother for Blanquita. "Where is Blanquita, whom did you sell her to?" Her reply was expected. "Shut up, snot nose, it's none of your business. She is my daughter, not yours. I can do what I damn please with her. Stop asking questions and keep this to yourself, don't go blabbing to anybody." She grabbed me by my collar. I could see the anger in her eyes; she pointed her finger at my face. "If somebody asks for Blanca, you tell them she's with Alejo, her father, you understand?" I nodded and walked away.

Ana left with her boyfriend, Gordo. I kept Beni by my side playing with her. Mother and Sergio were in bed. The old mad arrived later that night. The two baby sellers whispered, so I wasn't able to hear what they were talking about except that the people had accepted Beni also. I woke up early the next morning, Ana was already up and ready to leave for work. "Ana, I want to walk with you for a bit, is that okay with you?" Outside I told Ana what I had heard the old man tell Mom, that the people had accepted Beni as well as Blanquita. "Vani, are you sure?"

"I heard him even though he was whispering."

"Okay, Vani, I hope that you heard right because I will talk to Mother after work."

They didn't notice when I snuck back into the house. I did hear Mother tell Lupe to stop treating us so bad. "You know that the couple wants to buy Blanquita. Ana will take care of Beni, not you." At the point, Lupe grabbed Mother by her shoulders and slammed her on top of the bed. I held back, but I wanted to hit him. "You prefer your snot-nose, dirty, and filthy daughters to my son? Tell me now if that is the way you feel. If that's the case, I will make Jovani mine now and take Sergio away from here."

"Leave Jovani alone, don't do anything to her. You know very well that she is sick."

"I desire that snot nose, and you know it, don't deny it."

"Lupe, I want no part of that."

"Reyna, you know that I have never liked Blanquita or Beni."

"Okay, Lupe, offer them Beni so that Blanquita won't be alone. Do that, but don't take Sergio away from me. While you are selling my daughters, offer Jovani to somebody also."

"No, Reyna, not Jovani, you know she is going to be mine." I didn't make a sound, I went to bed with Beni.

The baby sellers left with Sergio early the next day. I was so relieved when they left. Beni, with my help, and I got ready; we ate breakfast and left the house. I thought, *Did Mother actually try to stand up for us against that wicked old man? Diosito, I hope Mother doesn't allow the lecherous old man to harm me.* The words the lecherous old man repeats is imbedded in my mind: "She is going to be mine when she is a little older. If I show her what it is to be with me, she is liable to die. Who knows when, but she will be mine." My legs tremble every time I see that mean old man.

That night Ana spoke to Mother about Beni. She got the same answer, "I am the mother," etc. etc. The day arrived the day Beni would be taken away and sold. Ana was getting ready for work, I had just gotten up. Reyna grabbed Beni from our bed. The old man carried Beni's bag with her clothes. "Come on, Reyna, hurry up, let's go." I shouted to Ana, "Mother and the old man are taking Beni." Ana ran and confronted the baby sellers. The lecherous coward pulled his big knife and told Ana, "Don't even try to take this child if you value your life." Ana of course backed off. He got in his car and drove away with Mother, Sergio, and Beni. I felt so sad, I suffered a convulsion.

We didn't hear from them for months. That time was a very sad one for me. My sisters were on my mind constantly. My companion was my Diosito, my faith in Him never faltered; in fact, it grew stronger.

Examined by Dr. Cuevas, a Specialist

I SPENT MOST OF MY time with Mamacita Sinforosa when she came to the pueblo. She was the person I loved the most in this world. However, she was always concerned with my sickness. We inquired in Taxco about the possibility that my sickness would someday go away. The doctors in Taxco were not knowledgeable nor did they have the facility to help me. However, one of the doctors recommended a Dr. Cuevas. The problem was that Dr. Cuevas's practice was in Acapulco.

Mamacita was determined to see the doctor, she wanted me to be cured. The doctor in Taxco made an appointment for me to see Dr. Cuevas in Acapulco. Mamacita, Mama Lucia, and I prepared for the trip to Acapulco. Before the cock had crowed the following day, the three of us were on the bus to Acapulco to see Dr. Cuevas. He was a very kind man, treated all of us with respect.

I remember my head being full of cables. On my skull, the nurse shaved a small part where she placed a cable. We waited for the results, I was full of hope that I could be cured. I couldn't read the minds of Mamacita or of Mama Lucia, but they appeared relaxed. Dr. Cuevas called us into his office. "Señoras, I want to explain to Rosita the results in front of you, this way you will understand the situation of her illness. Rosita, your illness is caused by the fracture in your skull. Every time you fall and you hit your head only makes your skull weaker. That fracture has created many cysts in your brain." He paused for a few moments. "You also have an inflammation in your respiratory system because of your asthma. All of these ailments are the result of the hits to your head when you have a convulsion. I am sorry to say this, but at this moment, there is no cure for your epilepsy. The only solution now is that with medicine, your epilepsy can be controlled.

"Señoras, let me show you the neurological results of Rosita's head." The picture of my head reminded me of a dead person's skull I'd seen in pictures. He pointed to the area where my skull was fractured. "Niña, you have to be very careful." The trip back to the pueblo was not as cheerful. I didn't feel like singing to the passengers like I had on other times. The summer ended, Mamacita left for her ranch.

Before I realized it, I had completed my fifth grade. I along with Rafa and Ruby was at the top of the class academically. We celebrated the end of the school year by going swimming in the river. That day there was another fight between Ruben and Rede—ha ha—for me. I felt somewhat honored that they were fighting for me, at the same time I thought it to be silly fighting for a girl. I knew that both boys liked me. Ruben used to leave me half of his lunch in my backpack and would blow me kisses when nobody else was looking. I kinda liked Ruben, but don't know why.

I played conicas with Ruben and sometimes with Rede. One day out of curiosity I asked Rede why he and Ruben fought over me. The embarrassed Rede looked at me. "Why do you say that we fight over you?"

"Come on, Rede, everybody knows why you two fight."

"Well, then, don't you know why we fight?"

"No, Rede, I don't, you tell me."

"Really, Rosita, you don't know? You don't know the things he and Israel say about your mother? They are always laughing about her. Have you noticed he doesn't talk to you in front of others like I do? I tell him that he is a traitor to you because he doesn't come to your defense like I do. That's why we tangle."

Mother's Day is on the tenth of May. One of the teachers asked me to write a poem and to recite it to the class. Although Mother wasn't present, I don't hate her. I dedicated the poem to her. The written poem I placed in her purse. *When she reads my poem I dedicated to her, she will embrace me like I have always dreamed.* To Ana I gave a rose for being my sister mother. The store that Mother had opened to sell candy and other sweets was closed for lack of business.

In its place she opened a shoe store. My sisters were gone, so on occasion when his father was gone, I would play with a growing Sergio.

One of the anticipated dreaded days arrived. Lupe, Reyna, and Sergio left the house. Ana immediately started to pack her clothes. "What are you doing, Ana?"

"Vani, I have to leave this house. The lecherous bastard tried to grab me again and do what he does with Reyna in bed. I scratched his neck, and he let me go. He smiled, 'you are really nice, and you will be mine,' he told me. 'I haven't succeeded in making you mine, but soon I will.' Vani, I'm leaving with Gordo."

"Ana, don't leave me alone with those two, take me with you, please take me with you."

"Vani, I'm going to be staying with his parents, and there is no room for you. We will take you with us when we build our house.

"Vani, we'll be seeing each other, I promise. Will you give me your blessing? But hurry, Gordo is waiting for me." I couldn't stop crying, I paced the floor. *I can't stay here either,* I thought. I grabbed my bag. I started to fill my bag. *I will not permit those two to hurt me anymore.* My heart started to beat faster when the door was opening. Mother entered; immediately she saw the bag I was packing. "What are you doing with that bag, snot nose? Where are you going with those clothes?"

"I'm going to wash them" was my answer. "Jovani, you are not a good liar, so don't try to fool me now. You are planning something, show me the clothes." *Oh, Diosito, she is going to give me another beating.*

She dumped my clean clothes on the floor and stepped all over them. "Now your clothes are dirty, snot-nosed liar." I tried to flee, but she grabbed my long hair and flung me to the floor. Lupe watched as she beat me and beat me. "Reyna, don't hit her anymore, let me finish her. I believe that she is ready for my kind of punishment." She stopped hitting me then walked over to the closet where Ana kept her clothes. Empty, her closet was empty! "Son of a ——," Reyna screamed.

"What's the matter, my love?"

"Lupe, her clothes and suitcase are gone, Ana is gone." Reyna came close to me. "Stop your damn crying and tell me, where has Ana gone to? Don't lie to me this time." Lupe embraced Mother. "Don't worry about Ana. She is mature and old enough, let her leave. Look at your other two daughters, they are enjoying a good life. I'm here for you, and we have Sergio and your pretty and maturing daughter Jovani. I will be responsible for her. From now on, I have my two Reynas, mother and daughter."

The lecherous bastard of a man tried to hug me. I bit his hand. "You are nothing to me, and I will never allow you to touch me. You are nothing but a lecherous bastard, a venomous mean man. I hate you, I hate you." *Please, Diosito, forgive me for my language,* I thought. He flung his sombrero, with the same motion, he slapped me so hard he knocked me to the floor. He kicked me several times. He took his knife. "I'm going to kill you, nobody offends Guadalupe Figueroa like you did. All those times, you have rejected me. Well, no more! Your hour has come, then I will kill you."

"No, Lupe, don't kill my daughter, the people will think that I killed her, and I will go to prison. What is going to happen with Sergio?"

"Reyna, I don't give a damn, whatever happens to you happens. I will take Sergio. Now shut up, I'm going to take your daughter, she will be mine. Have you forgotten the night when she got sick? Yeah, you wanted to take her where she would get lost and die. You wish this snot-nosed girl gone because she is a nuisance in your life."

"Enough, shut up, and do what you want with her." I could barely move; my ribs hurt from the kicks he gave me with his pointed boots. He took off his clothes, then when he started to undress me, I kicked him in the part where it hurts the most. He doubled over in pain, I gave him another kick. He fell to the floor, I grabbed a chair and wacked him in the head. I had knocked him out. I ran out the house, my heart pounding so hard I believed it was going to explode out through my chest. Mother caught up to me in the patio, grabbed me by my hair. "You killed him. I'm holding you until the police come and take you to jail. My son is going to be an orphan like you." She led me by my hair back into the house. "Look, snot nose, Lupe is dead." She knelt crying next to Lupe. I touched the veins on his throat, I felt the pulse. "He is not dead, you take care of him because I will not help."

Crying I ran into the darkness without a destination. I just ran away from my jail house. I knew that I had to go far away from those two. My mother, my own flesh and blood, gave me up to that lecherous man. I repeated the words, because in reality, "I AM THE DAUGHTER OF NO ONE."

My unplanned destination ended on top of the hill overlooking my beautiful pueblo. I felt a pain on my foot. It was full of blood caused by a piece of glass I had stepped on. In my haste to escape my jail of a house, I had run out barefooted. *Ouch, how can all of these problems be happening to me?* I took my blouse off, cut the sleeve into pieces. I spit on a piece to clean my wound. I was afraid, not of the moonless dark night or the distance from my pueblo, no, I feared those two bastards, Mother and the lecherous old man.

My tears started to flow, once again my heart was palpitating. I felt a sensation, I could see everything around me very clear. Everything became calm and so peaceful. The whole atmosphere put me at ease, my heart stopped palpitating. An apparition of an image of a person was becoming clearer and clearer the closer it got to where I was. My Diosito, the Sacred Heart of Jesus, appeared accompanied with a grand angel behind. Diosito placed his hand on my head. "You are not alone." I hugged him with all my strength. His hug felt different than all the others I've felt. It is impossible for me to explain the feeling like no other. I also can't explain the feeling I felt at the moment, but I felt loved and blessed, which gave the strength and tremendous hope in my living.

My sickness took over, I had a convulsion. The first thought when I came to was, *Did Diosito appear to me, or was that a dream?* I looked around. Where am I? The voice of a lady said, "Niña, you are awake, thanks to God."

"Señora, where am I?"

"Niña, relax," she said, sitting next to the bed. "Who are you, señora, and what am I doing in your bed?"

"Niña, those questions I should be asking you. Last night I heard a knock on my door, when I opened, you were the only one on my doorstep. You were cold and trembling real bad, so we brought you into our house and put you in this bed.

"Now you tell me who you are and who your parents are so I can tell them where you are." Hearing that she wanted to inform my parents, I panicked. "No, no, señora, don't tell my mother and the man she lives with, they are really mean with me." I wanted to tell the lady my name, but the fear of those two prevented me from doing so. I got up without a headache that I normally have after a convulsion. "No, niña, don't get up, you are weak, tell me who you are."

"Thank you, señora, a thousand thanks for helping me, may God bless you." I felt great, no headache and no vomiting feeling.

I felt good, and being curious, I ran to where I had had my convulsion. The place was close to the road. Someday I will come back here and tell the kind lady my name and explain why I couldn't tell her my name or my mother's name. I stopped running because a car stopped alongside me. It was my uncle Juan. "Jovani, is that you?"

"Yes, Uncle, it is me. Don't you recognize me anymore?"

"Well, Jovani, I wasn't sure especially with those knots and bruises on your face. Niña, get in, I'll take you home." Uncle Juan kept staring at me. "Hija, tell me the truth, who did this to you? Was it Reyna? Tell me the truth, was it her?" I didn't say anything, my tears spoke for me. "Come and tell me that bastard sister of mine did this to you, didn't she?"

"Uncle, I fell, I had a convulsion and fell on my face. A nice lady that lives close to where I had my convulsion helped me."

"A lady from here in Ahualulco?"

"Yes, Uncle, she helped me."

"Okay, I will take you home, Reyna is probably worried about you."

"No, Uncle, nobody is home. Take me to the diner of Mama Lucia." He didn't ask me any more questions.

I sang until we arrived at the diner. I gave uncle a hug and thanked him for the lift. But nothing was subtle when Mama Lucia saw me. Her mouth agape when she saw me, I thought that she was going to faint. She sat with knees shaking. "Niña, what happened to you?" I spilled everything, I didn't omit anything. "Mother gave me up to be his to do what he has always wanted to do. My own mother did that to me. He wanted to take me and do what he does with

Reyna in bed, and then he was going to kill me." Mama Lucia finally spoke, "That vicious man of the Figueroas is a very violent person. The bastard deserves to be in jail." Doña Lucia was exhausted after hearing all they had done to me. She moved slowly to the refrigerator to get me a glass of milk.

Fear overcame me when I saw Reyna storming into the diner. It reminded me of the raging bull once again, trying to gore me when I was stuck in the barbed-wire fence. I had no defense against her, I wasn't going to hit Mother with anything, much less a rock. She was so angry muttering her words. I understood enough though. "Here you are, you little telltales, making up lies about Lupe and me. You snot-nosed bastard, what a disgrace to call you my daughter. I dread ever denying Jorge to take you with him. Lucia, you old woman, stop paying attention to my daughter. I remind you, this property is going to be mine soon, and don't say a word to me." The owner of the prison I call home grabbed my arm and led me away.

"Don't take me into that evil house, let me go." My knees were trembling, and crying, I tried to get loose of her grip, but I couldn't. "Why don't you love me? Why did you give me up to the lecherous old man? Tell me the truth, are you my birth mother? I ask you because a mother doesn't treat a daughter like you treat me. What kind of mother sells her daughters? What is the reason you have me around me, you don't love me. You want that lecherous man to do what he does to you in bed, don't you? You have no heart, no conscience."

"Shut up, enough out of you, snot nose. Tell me, where have you been?" I was about to tell her the truth. But she doesn't believe me nor does she care, so why bother telling her the truth? I didn't say a word. "Answer. Don't play dumb. Where have you been?" I answered, "With Mama Lucia." All she said, "It's best for you not to say anything. Lupe is at the hospital, that's the second time you have done something to him. I warn you, if you do that again, I will kill you myself. I will not defend you for being an ungracious brat."

Days later the old man arrived; upon seeing the bastard, my knees trembled with fear. I know that Mother will not protect me from him. I'm on my own in the prison I call home. "Jovani, come here, Lupe brought you a present." Her words surprised me, did I hear right? These two are up to no good. I made the sign of the cross. I don't believe this lecherous person has changed since the last time he was here.

He had a backpack in his hand. "This bag is full of school supplies just for you." I didn't move nor did I say a word. I waited to see what vicious trick he had in his mind. "I will give you this bag full of school supplies on the condition that you don't reject me any longer. I very much want you. Hear me, from now on, you are obliged to obey me. Your mother knows what I do for you, and you also must obey her. Understand this, of all the daughters that Reyna has, you are the fortunate one to be living here with your mother.

"Living here however doesn't give you the right to tell lies about what happens here. I have told you before what happens here in this house is nobody else's business. What you did the other days, I forgot about it. Why did I forget it? Because if I tell the police that you hit me while I was in bed, who do you think the officials are going to believe, you or me? They will put you in jail along with your mother because she is responsible for you." Mother interrupted, "For your own good, do what Lupe tells you."

I just stared at them. What else could I do? Mother will not protect me; she does what he wants. No matter what, I don't trust them. I took the bag to avoid another beating at their hands. I planned to sell it, because there is no way that I was going to use anything coming from him. I had a very restless night. I couldn't sleep. I thought of ways to protect myself from him. The following morning I got up real early. I put on extra underwear and two pairs of pants. I had thought of this the night before, believing that it would be difficult for him to do anything. I was tired, and instead of leaving the house, I fell asleep.

"Hija, wake up." Mother was at my bed. "Come with me," she said, "Lupe wants to see you." My heart started to pound, my mind blocked with fear. She led me to their bed. I made the sign of the cross. "Hey, mija, you look pretty this morning, but why are you wearing so many pants? Take them off and wear a skirt. I don't like a girl who wears pants. Your mother and I are going to buy some nice clothes later on today." I didn't trust him. *He is up to something bad, I know it.* "Go change, wear one of those pretty dresses your grandmother Sinforosa bought you."

I left the room without saying a word. I went outside where I sat traumatized on the stairs. Mother came looking for me. "What the —— are you doing here?" She grabbed my hand. "Come with me." She dragged me to the bed where the lecherous old man was waiting. He sat up completely nude. He grabbed my arm. "Come sit here at my side close to your mother. I love both of you. Now I will care for you like I care for my son. Isn't that right, Reyna?"

"Yes, my love, just look at what you do for us." Mother looked real happy. "Come on, Jovani, hug Lupe, show him how much you appreciate what he does for you."

"Come on, pretty girl, do what your mother tells you."

I wanted to escape, but how could I? They had me surrounded. "Reyna, my love, go into the kitchen and warm me some of that soup you made last night. Jovani can stay here taking care of Sergio while I take a nap." I spoke out of fear, "Mother, I will go warm the soup." She turned her back to me and walked out of the bed area. I tried to follow her, but he grabbed me and covered my mouth with his huge hand. He touched my leg and placed it between his naked ones. He replaced his hand with a handkerchief, which he stuffed into my mouth.

He held my hands so I couldn't move, nor could I scream for help. He tried to take my underwear with his teeth; he licked my stomach. I don't know how, but he managed to touch my private part with his finger. I tried to separate my legs from his, and thank God I was able to. In the process I gave him a kick in his man part so hard that he let me go. I ran out to the kitchen crying. "That bastard grabbed me, Mother, he grabbed me, kick him out of this house. Lupe took my clothes off, kick him out."

"Shut up and go change and do it quickly." Mother went into the room and questioned Lupe. "What did you do to Jovani? You told me that you were going to treat her good."

"Reyna, what are you talking about? I was asleep, you woke me up. Where is your daughter? I thought she was going to watch

Sergio? She disobeyed you, she is making a fool out of you. I think that your snot-nose daughter wants something with me."

Mother believed him, she took the wicked man's word. She went outside where I sat crying. She yanked me by the hair and dragged me to where the lecherous man pretended to be innocent of violating me. "Kneel in front of Lupe and ask to be pardoned. The next time you accuse him of any wrongdoing, I will hang you from a tree until you die. Come on, ask him to forgive you." She let go of my hair. When she let go, I screamed, "Never will I ask this vicious man for forgiveness. He is the one that should be asking Diosito to forgive him so that God can shed light in this hell he lives here and in the other life. I do not forgive him nor you, Mother. When Mamacita comes here, she will know what you two are planning on doing to her."

I got hold of my school bag and threw it in his face. "Take this filthy bag, I will never use it. You lecherous old man, I will never allow you to touch me, never. I hate both of you, and I will tell Mamacita, and she will kick both of you out of this property." I ran out of the house.

It was early in the morning, nowhere to go. School didn't start until much later, and I didn't want to visit Mama Lucia. I passed by the pigsty, and finding a stool, I sat down to think. All alone again, but even more so this time. Ana was gone, Mamacita was at her ranch, my two little sisters were gone, and worse, my father is dead. Where can I go? Better, who can I confide in? I kept thinking of all possibilities; finally I stopped myself. Diosito is with me. I stopped crying, I got angry with myself. I smiled halfheartedly, got up, went to the school bathrooms since they were open. I noticed blood when I cleaned myself. *Why am I bleeding?* Being innocent, I didn't realize the significance of my bleeding. At first I thought that I wasn't going to have a stomach.

I ran to the river. *Now what? Diosito, I have another sickness, why do these things happen to me?* I walked into the river and washed and washed until the bleeding stopped. I left for school. I hated living with those two, but where could I go? Anywhere I went, she would bring me back. Mama Lucia? No, she would get in trouble with Mother...same with Don Felipe or anybody who took me in.

Reyna would make trouble for anybody who took me in, I was stuck with them. I noticed that my convulsions were becoming more frequent since that old man started to live with Reyna. The convulsions were more frequent at night. The nights that he was in the house, I couldn't sleep out of fear that he would grab me.

The times he was there I would leave the house very early and sleep near the cemetery or near the river. That's how I was able to rest. School became very different. The students would talk negative about Reyna and the old man. The pueblo was much more critical of Reyna. I was like an outcast, I had some friends, but not like in times past. Maria Elena was one of my few friends who I could talk with. What comes to mind when I think of her is the plastic camera she had. She took the first photos, with difficulty, but she did. They came out very nice.

Living was very complicated, my life was complicated. The vicious dirty old man that Mother appeared to fear but also appeared to enjoy being with was my worst nightmare. He promised to buy Mother a house away from the pueblo but not until I finished my school. I knew that he was planning to take us away from the pueblo where people knew me to a place where I wasn't. He was controlling my life through Mother. He forced her to take me out of the school I was attending. I had attended the Union and Progreso since it was built. Now I didn't have a choice. I was forced into the other school. Once every so often I would sneak over to attend class at my old school. However, the public schoolteacher was a friend of Mother. Naturally every time I was absent from his class, Reyna was notified. Soon she and the old man would force me back.

My life didn't change much, I was a prisoner in my own house, and because of my age, I could go nowhere. Ana was able to escape because she was older, but me, where can I escape to? No matter where I was given refuge, Reyna would force me back. The house that the old man promised, it never happened. Did he comply with a promise? He promised to protect and take care of Mother and myself. The cowardly bastard of a man verbally abused me instead. He told me what he wanted to do with me. He tried, but I never allowed him to sexually assault me.

I accepted nothing from him, I worked to buy my medicine and usually ate at Mama Lucia's or by myself, hardly ever at home with those two. Doña Chelita Rivera employed me on Saturdays. The other days I sold my goodies and helped Mama Lucia. While I worked with Doña Chelita, I met her mother, Conchita, and in-laws. The brothers of her husband, Rede, were Rodolfo and Mario, the sisters Cotita and Chela. The whole family knew Reyna, they thought of her as being a grand lady. When they learned from me the injustices she and Lupe were causing in my life, they were puzzled. "How," they wondered, "can she be so cruel with you?" When I told them that she had sold my two smaller sisters, they defended Reyna. Rodolfo said, "I've known her all my life, so I'm sure that man threatened her. That damned and wicked man should be in jail or, worse, dead."

Mother visited Rede and Doña Chelita, asked them to represent me as my godparents during my graduation from the sixth grade. Don't know why, but Lena, the sister of Doña Chelita, accepted to be my madrina. Reyna stayed for a few minutes before she left. Rodolfo was waiting for Reyna to leave to speak with me. "Rosita, we have to be careful and nice to Reyna because we want to help you. If you are really interested in leaving, we will take you to Mexico City with us. You will be treated like our daughter. We will take you with us as soon as your graduation is over." I didn't have to think about going with them, not for a moment. My reply was a quick and decisive affirmative response: "I will go with you. I will work to pay for my medicine like I am doing now. Thank you. I can't live with those two another moment. Reyna doesn't love me, doesn't care about me, and Lupe wants me for one reason only, to abuse me." Rodolfo looked at me with an assuring smile. "Relax," he said, "we will help you."

Graduation day was a few days away, and Reyna had not selected my graduation outfit. Mr. Toño was not going to allow me to graduate unless she—and not I—selected the outfit. Against my objection because I feared the worst, he spoke to her. He assured me that all would be fine, because he knew how to deal with parents. She agreed! I paid for the pistachio-colored outfit, which she chose with my savings. She also assisted with the celebration. Both Reyna and her old man companion paid the food for the godparents.

I was ten years old when my sixth-grade graduation day arrived. I was happy because I would finally be leaving the prison those two had created. Lena, my graduation godmother, presented me with a beautiful bouquet of flowers. The program was wonderful, lots of people were in attendance. After the certificate presentation, we released the swallows. They flew away like I believed I would be flying away from here. Then we danced the waltz and other dances. I had mixed feelings seeing Mother at the dinner table with the rest of us. Now that I had intentions of leaving her, she attends my graduation? Is she changing, is she starting to care about me?

Walking home with Reyna also felt strange. I walked behind her thinking about my future. My desire in getting educated was never a doubt. I would continue that quest. I also imagined myself in a nun's attire. I would become an educated nun in order to serve my Chuchin. Reyna walked into the house, I stayed outside. Nobody is going to prevent me achieving my dreams. In the federal district I will continue to achieve my dreams.

The days of waiting for Rodolfo and his family passed. The promise of taking me to live with them in Mexico City was a hoax. It filled my aspirations with hope only to vanish. Why did they deceive me? Had Reyna known about the deception, was she involved? I needed to know the truth. I visited Lena. She told me, "Relax. In time, they will come for you." Several days later after I visited Lena, she came to visit. In confidence she told me that Elena had been in a bad auto accident and was hurt very bad and would not be able to come for me.

How many times have I asked myself this question? Why me, why does this happen to me? I cried and cried, my dreams are not happening like I have envisioned, why? I cannot live here anymore, I wished Mamacita Sinforosa would come and take me away. The days passed with me doing my best to avoid being in the house. I worked for Doña Chela and Mama Lucia and visited my Chuchin daily, sometimes more than once.

The avoidance came to a sudden stop. Mother was having one of her moody days, this one worse than others. She looked at me with anger; she asked, "Snot nose, where are you living these days?" The lecherous old man chimed in, "You are never home, you don't bathe here, you don't eat here. I now ask you, where do you live? You have changed, like the night changes to day." Upon hearing Lupe's voice, I froze. "Now, Jovani, look at you, your boobs are growing into very pretty ones. You are turning to be quite a pretty young woman. I see that your legs are quite hairy, I can imagine how hairy your little piece is. Reyna, prepare yourself because one of these days, your daughter is ready for her punishment. If I don't, somebody else will beat me to her virginity.

"Reyna, should I go rent a house somewhere away from here? We really should move away from here, what do you think?" Reyna gave him a big hug. "I go where you go, my love. You are so good to us." She looked at me. "Come, Jovani, give my Lupe a hug. Give a hug to show how much you appreciate what he does for us. Look what he did for your graduation, and you haven't thanked him." I wasn't about to give that bastard a hug. Not even the pull of a thousand mules can make me change my mind, nor move me toward him. Those two demons have planned something. That scheming lecherous old man wants to take me away from the pueblo where people know me and my situation. He doesn't dare touch me here because he will go to jail.

"Mother, I have to use the bathroom." I said nothing else. He followed me into the bathroom. He tried to grab me, but somehow he slipped on the wet floor and fell hard. I ran out of there as fast as I could. Without thinking I found myself in front of the church, my refuge; I escaped the jail. I entered the church where I will be safe at least for the moment. When those two come looking for me, I will not be alone, I will have my Diosito.

Sister Adoracion Hears My Cry for Help

DIOSITO, PLEASE HEAR ME. My tears continued to flow, I could hardly speak, but I felt safe inside the church. I was finally able to speak, "Diosito, soon Mother and her friend Lupe will be coming for me. If You're with me, please don't allow that mean man to harm me again." I felt a presence at my side, I turned to see my teary-eyed Chuchin. "Please, Diosito," I pleaded, "help me, You know what kind of life I live with those two. Mother has given me up to that man so he can take pleasure with me. He tries to sexually assault me, but with Your help, he hasn't been successful. Take me with You, or take me where I will be safe from them." My Diosito heard more of what they have done to me, including the whippings and the beatings because I won't allow the old man to have his way with me. I had a convulsion.

The room was unlike any other I'd been inside before. It smelled different, like incense, but clean and in order. *Maybe I'm in heaven with Diosito. No, that is not possible.* I looked all the way around the room. *I've never seen a room like this before.* Getting out of bed was not a problem. I checked around the room, there were a lot of statues of saints, of the Blessed Virgin Mary, a statue of my Chuchin. I started my walk toward the kitchen where the two nuns were having a conversion.

"Don't get up, Jovani." Sister Adoracíon was watching out for me. Any move I made, she would notice. "Sit down, you are still sick, you are safe here at our home. Sister Sarita wants to speak with you. Wait here, Jovani, I will get Sister Sarita." Sister Sarita came rather quickly. "How do you feel, my Jovani?"

"Sister, I have a bad headache, and I feel like I want to vomit." She handed me a cold glass of water. "Jovani, nobody is going to touch you anymore. You are safe here." Sister Adoracíon left the room allowing Sister Sarita and myself alone to talk.

"Jovani, you know that what happens here in the pueblo, word gets around very rapidly. I've known since you were a baby. I have followed your life all these years. Do you remember what you were telling our dear Lord before you got sick?"

"Yes, Sister Sarita, I remember every word I told my Chuchin inside the church."

"Let me tell you, my child, I listened to every word you said to your Chuchin. I was sitting on the bench behind you. I listened to what that man has done to you. I hid from you so you couldn't see me. It hurts to hear all that you have endured. Niña, I am going to help you." She grabbed my hand. "However, it all depends on you. We are going to confront your mother. We are going to confront her in good faith. Whether she wants to or not, we are going to talk to her."

I didn't have any words to express how I felt, I cried and cried. I was afraid of confronting Reyna because I didn't have an idea how she would respond to Sister Sarita. How can she help me? How is it

384

possible that the wicked man will allow Reyna to protect me? I didn't understand. Sister Sarita told me, "Jovani, from this day forward, you are not going to be alone nor will you be alone. You will no longer continue living with those two." Sister made the sign of the cross while saying, "May the Lord Jesus Christ forgive us, but we will take you away from that hell." I had to cry and cry. I knew that she meant what she said. A burst of sensation overwhelmed my body. *My Diosito is watching over me.* Sister Sarita meant every word, she was coming to my rescue.

"Rosita, we belong to an organization called Slaves of the Divine Infancy. We have two orphanages up the mountains. We have been waiting to see if you would be interested in going away form here. You won't know anybody, but you will be safe. The place is quite a bit far from here. It is far from this pueblo, it takes us eighteen hours to get there." I was crying the whole time she was talking to me. "Sister, please help me get away from those two, I can't live like this anymore. That man is evil, and Mother believes all the lies that he tells her. I will go to the orphanage no matter how far it is from here."

"We are going to help you. In the meantime, nobody knows that you are here. We do have a small problem. The students in the orphanage are from the indigenous people living in the villages nearby. I will speak with Mother Superior, she will understand your situation, she will open the doors for you.

"Rosita, I want you to wait while I go for your mother."

"Sister Sarita, please don't tell her anything. That man is liable to kill me. He threatened to kill me if I told anybody."

"Relax, nobody is going to hurt you anymore, drink your tea, I will be back soon. Niña, you have an opportunity to enter another chapter in your life, and it's strictly up to you. Those two aren't going to hurt you anymore.

"In the event your mother doesn't allow you to leave, we will do battle with her. I will send Sister Adoración to speak with your uncle. We will make trouble for both your mother and Lupe Figueroa. We'll put them in jail for the injustices they have caused you. We are prepared to defend you. In reality, we don't want that for your mother, what we want is her authorization to let you go." Unbeknown to me, Sister Sarita sent Sister Adoración for Reyna.

The loud knock on the door startled me. I looked at Sister Sarita, thinking, *Who could that be?* Sister asked, "Is that you, Sister Adoración, with Reyna Bustos?" I was terrified. "Reyna is here? Sister, please don't let her take me away, she doesn't love me."

"Relax, mija, she won't take you away, don't worry. Stay here while I talk to her." I prayed the rosary asking Diosito to enlighten me with the Holy Spirit. I was still praying when Sister Adoración walked in the room. "Your mother has allowed you to go with us. Come here, give me a hug." The hug Sister Adoración gave me was one of the most wonderful hugs that I can remember and one that I will never forget.

"Come with me, she is waiting for you. Be as it may, she is still your mother, give her a hug." Rather than a hug, she gave me a warning. She whispered in my ear, "Remember, snot nose, I am still your mother." Her voice felt like a hot arrow going through my heart, I was so scared. She started to leave, but Sister Sarita stopped her. "Reyna, before you leave, we have to talk." A belligerent Reyna answered, "Go ahead, you talk, I have nothing to say to you. Both of you have already listened to this little liar. But one thing I will tell you, should I go to jail because of this snot nose, I will sue you." Reyna and the two nuns stared at each other, I was surprised with the standoff.

I asked, "Did she let me go with you?"

"Yes, yes, she let you go far away from here."

"REALLY? I am free!" I gleefully shouted, "I am free." I hugged them both, happiness permeated the room. "Now we should thank the Lord." We knelt and said thankful prayers to our Lord. Sister Sarita accompanied me for my clothes. Reyna allowed us in the house. I went straight to where I kept my clothes. The wicked old man came near to where I was. I was no longer afraid of him, but my knees couldn't stop shaking. He whispered, "Don't think for a second that you are going to escape from me, I won't permit that to happen. You will be mine, like it or not, you will be mine, snot nose."

"Sister Sarita, will you come and help me please," I asked in a loud voice. She moved quickly to where I was packing my clothes. She realized why I had called her as soon as she saw him standing near me. We packed my clothes and got into the car driven by Sister Adoración waiting for me. Once in the car, I felt safe. "Sister Adoración, I need to make one more stop." She looked at me with a puzzled look on her face. "Is it that important?"

"Yes, Sister Adoración, I have money stashed away, I need it."

"Really, mija, you have money hidden away? Okay, but I will go with for your money."

Filled with Fear, I Flew Away
from My Dreadful Home

WE TRAVELED TO THE CITY of Taxco in the car. A friend of the nuns would drive it back to the pueblo. We boarded the bus to Tlapa. I was excited to be leaving the house of dread. I'd traveled with Mamacita to her llano, and I was used to a long bus trip. This bus trip was different. This trip, which I didn't realize at the time, was one where I was entering a new chapter in my life.

The beautiful landscape, the mountains, and the prairies were entertaining. The first small village was exciting to visit; afterward they were all the same to me, just a village. I'd fall asleep unexpectedly, cry when I thought of Mamacita, knowing that I had not notified her of my escape to the orphanage; she would be worried. I thought of my sister Ana, Mama Lucia, Don Felipe—they would all be worried, wondering what had happened to me. Sister Adoración saw that I was rather quiet. "Jovani, why so quiet, mija? You shouldn't be thinking so much, I don't want you to get sick."

"Sister Adoración, nobody knows that I left the pueblo. The only ones that know are you, Sister Sarita, and Mother."

"Oh, mija, don't worry so much, Sister Sarita probably has informed your friends that you are safe with us. Jovani, tell me all the people you want to inform of where you will be, and I will make sure they know."

Her promise made me feel more relaxed; I could rely on Sister Adoración. I hummed my song of being motherless, because now I really didn't have a mother. The man sitting in front of me turned around. "Niña, you have a pretty voice. Niña, what is your name?"

"Señor, some people call me *Rosita*, some know me as *Jovani*. I like the name my mamacita gave me, *Alma de Dios*." The man answered, "I like all your names, but can I call you *Rosita*, because it reminds me of my mother. Now, Rosita, can I ask you to sing so that all the people in the bus can hear." I glanced at Sister Adoración; she smiled and gave a positive nod with her head.

The man went to the bus driver, I saw the bus driver nod his head. The señor standing in front of the bus shouted, "Ladies and gentlemen, there is a young girl riding with us with the voice of an angel. Do you want to hear her sing?"

"Canta, canta, canta" (sing, sing sing), they shouted. The initiator walked over to my seat, told me, "The bus driver wants to speak with you." The bus driver wanted to know my name. I simply answered, "*Rosita Jovani Bustos*." The driver made the announcement. "Rosita will sing for our entertainment. Please don't forget to tip her." They started applauding until I raised my hands.

I sang one of my all-time favorite songs, "Paloma Blanca" (White Dove). Sister Adoración didn't seem pleased at first. I was wrong; she was very happy, based on the big applause she gave me. I started to walk back to my seat. "Another song," they shouted, "sing another song." The passengers wanted more. I sang another of my favorite songs. "Que dirán los de tu casa…" I finished, and another applause followed with shouts for another one. I obliged them, took a drink of water. I raised my hand to silence the passengers. "The title of this song is 'I Am the Daughter of No One.'"

I Am the Daughter of No One

I am the daughter of no one
I answer but to one surname
Although it belongs to my mother
In my daily notes I write
The truth I will someday know
My surname, my real father, amigo
I am the daughter of no one
Everybody knows the truth

That I am not a Reza
That my father was killed
The pain when Reyna denied
My living and my beauty to my father
I am the daughter of no one
Although this woman is my mother
Her hugs and love she denies
My heart broken into pieces
I fight to find my answer
That the blood of my father,
Jorge Bustos, flows through my veins

I gained strength with every word I sang. I was free of those two, the words were flowing stronger, full of freedom that I felt. My heart and soul felt stronger, the song had heart and feeling like never before, I ended the song with my face covered in tears. The shouting for more songs ended. The whole of the passengers were in tears. Ladies came with very generous tips, which I tried to refuse, to no avail. The men, also in tears, contributed their blessings along with tips.

We were starving by the time we reached the beautiful depot of Chilapa. I treated us to a nice lunch with the tips. Once we continued the trip, one by one the passengers were starting to chant, "Rosita, Rosita, another song." Being that I was not tired and since we didn't have any other kind of entertainment, I obliged them.

I repeated the song "Que dirán los de tu casa…" They asked for another one. I sang a song that made Sister Adoración blush. "Estoy en el rincón de una cantina, sirviendo una copa y nada mas," (I'm in the counter of a bar, drinking a glass of liquor and nothing else." The passengers loved to hear the song, especially from me being so young. I made enough pesos to pay for lunch and the whole trip for both.

Being on a long trip with strangers arouses their curiosity. A lady asked me if I was on my way to a convent to become a nun. Others wanted to know if I was an orphan. I wasn't prepared to respond, so I hesitated. Sister Adoración spoke to her, saying, "Señora, everything is in God's hands. This girl would be a wonderful nun, but the calling must come from the Lord, only He knows. I believe that when the Lord calls, she will be an excellent emissary for the Lord." I was tired of sitting and not being able to run to stretch my legs. My thoughts wandered back to the pueblo. I had left my beautiful pueblo without saying goodbye to my sister, to my friends. I was beginning to miss Don Felipe and Mama Lucia. Mamacita would be worried. I hoped that Sister Adoración would get in touch with her. I fell asleep hoping that my Chuchin would summon me to be a nun. "Mija, wake up, we are here, we are here in Tlapa." The nun was sitting next to me waiting for me to wake up.

The Start of Another Page
in My Life, 1991

THE ORPHANAGE WAS NOTHING LIKE I anticipated. The place was surrounded by solid walls guarded by a big gate locked from the inside. "Rosita, this is where you will call home from now on. Well, for how long, I can't say, but you will be safe here for as long as you stay. Once you step inside these walls, you will enter a blank white page in your life, a new beginning for you." She rang the bell that was hanging on the huge door. The dogs inside the compound barked when they heard the bell. *Oh my,* I thought, *the dogs are going to be my friends.*

The door was opened by a very nice attractive nun. "Come in," she said with a very caring and happy look. Her whole face seemed to be smiling, her voice kind and friendly. She appeared to be very young, probably younger than my mother. I felt like I knew this sister, like we had met someplace before. Inside the walls, I saw a place filled with flowers and a place very clean and well taken care of. The lack of other orphans or students was surprising to me.

"Sister Adoración, is this the young lady that is going to accompany us?" Her voice was peaceful and soft yet full of authority. "Yes, Sister, this is Rosita," answered Sister Adoración. "Welcome, Rosita, your eyes tell me a lot about you. You appear to be a very bright girl. But you are wondering why there are no other students here, aren't you?"

"Please forgive me, but I am surprised that I don't see any students, I was expecting to see many students being that this is an orphanage."

"I like that you are observant and speak up. Rosita, here, you are free to ask questions without fear of reprisals. Whatever you want to know, the best way to learn is by asking questions. You don't see students here because we are on vacation for the summer. Don't worry, you won't be alone. As the Mother Superior, I am here all the time. I am Sister Maria del Mar Rivera Medina."

"Ah, you are Mother Superior?"

"Yes, that is true, I am in charge of this place."

She opened her arms and gave me a hug full of love. I cried with joy. *Diosito, thank You for placing me under the care of this wonderful person.* "Come, my child, you must be hungry." The table was ready. Sister María informed me that only the nuns eat at this table. She pointed at another much bigger table, which is where I will normally eat with all the students. "But now you will eat with us here until the students return. Rosita, in reality, you have a very pretty yet secretive face, and I can sense a certain God-given gift within you. My respects as the Mother Superior, but of all the generations of children that I have educated, you have that certain gift within you." I thanked the Mother Superior for the kind words, which at the time I didn't quite understand what she meant.

I volunteered to say grace before we ate. I thanked my Chuchin for the meal and the company. After eating, Sister Mar asked me to step outside because she wanted to speak with Sister Adoración. "Rosita, don't worry, nobody will cause you harm here, especially those two." I walked into the garden. *What a difference from my house to here. I have escaped from those two and gained my freedom.* The place was so peaceful, surrounded by the tranquility of the place.

I entered the chapel; the first statue I saw was the Infant Divine. The aura about the statue was most beautiful. His eyes wanted to send me a message. Just then the nuns entered the chapel. "Here you are, I thought you might be in here," said Sister Adoración. Madre Mar was impressed, very few students come in here.

"Rosita, do you like what you have seen so far?"

"Yes, Madre Mar, I like it very much."

"Rosita, my name is *Mariá del Mar*." I grabbed my head and asked for a thousand pardons. "Sister Mariá, the chapel is most beautiful. My Chuchin is very beautiful, very beautiful."

Sister Mar smiled. "Who is this Chuchin?"

"He, Sister Mariá, is the great person who gave up His life for us by being crucified. He is always with us, but we are not always with Him. I am forever grateful to Him because He has performed several miracles to keep me among the living."

"Now I understand who Chuchin is. Be assured that those two will not harm you anymore. You have experienced a terrible life and are mentally scarred by actions of those two. By the way, Sister Adoración tells me that you are known by several names. Here in the orphanage, you will be known as Yovanita or Yovani. Of the forty-three students, I have four Rositas, and to have another one would complicate things somewhat."

The first night I prayed the rosary with the nuns. After the prayer session, I went to my room. My own room. The following morning I helped prepare breakfast. During the meal, I asked the question, "Sister María Mar, how many years must I wait before I can start my preparation to be a nun like you and Sister Adoración? I want to be married to Diosito and to serve the pilgrims that are lost for lack of faith in God."

"Blessed be God," was the response from a very happy Sister Mariá, "that you want to be one of us and to serve our Catholic faith. I will do all I can to secure the approval when you finish the preparatory school and must confront your illness. Yovani, I am so happy to have a niña like you in the path of my life."

Sister Adoración left for the pueblo. We stayed alone, but I wasn't alone like before. Sister gave me a tour of the entire orphanage. The dogs were caged, but they didn't bark at me. Sister Mar was surprised because as she told me, the dogs bark at anybody that gets close to their fenced compound. She said, "Look at these dogs, they seem to like you. They don't like anybody else but me, and that's because I feed them. Yovani, who are you, I mean it, who are you?" I just smiled, walked closer to the pen where the dogs were waiting for me to open the gate. I told the dogs to be patient, that soon I would be feeding and playing with them.

She took me around the neighborhood. I met several of the neighbors. I met Doña Rafa, Don Ezequiel, Don Chalpa y a Doña Ninfa. Doña Ninfa was pretty talented; besides being a barber, she had a small mill run by electricity, where she had the capability to grind the corn into flour. When I was introduced to Doña Rafa, she wanted to know from where I had come from. "Sister, I was wondering," she asked, "where did this niña come from? I ask because the moment I saw her, I got chills all over my body. This girl gives off a good vibration, she is someone special."

"You are correct, Doña Rafa, one of these days, I will tell you what this Alma de Dios has gone through. She has suffered a lot. She has nobody, and she is not from here. She comes to us from the state of Guerrero, a pueblo near Taxco." Doña Rafa said, "Sister Mar, I don't know the place where she comes from, but I do know that I would like to have her come to live with us. Will you consider allowing us to keep her?" She shouted to her husband, "Ezequiel, come in here, I need your opinion." Her husband came out of the house. "Oh my, who is this young girl? Pardon me, Sister Mar, for acting like an idiot, but when I saw this girl, my dizziness went away. Where is the girl from?"

"Oh, Ezequiel, she comes from Taxco or someplace close to there.

"Ezequiel, what is your opinion? I asked Sister Mar if we could keep this girl."

"Yes, I agree with you, I would like to keep this girl, she is a person that lit my life when I first saw her." I was really surprised at how easy it was to be given away. I thought of my two little sisters. Sister Mar told them that she would think about the proposition then they would talk. She did ask them if they would take care of me for a few days while she went to a seminar. She couldn't take me and neither could she leave me alone. In a few days I would stay with the family.

We walked back to the orphanage. She led me to one of her favorite places in the garden. We sat on a bench next to several cages full of canaries. The peaceful afternoon was interrupted by thunder. The dark clouds opened up drenching the dried land. "Jovani, we must take the birds inside before they get wet." We replaced the papers full of droppings and replaced them with clean ones, we cleaned the cages. That afternoon I learned a new lesson: how to take care of her canaries. At the beginning of my stay, I learned that Sister Mar never scolded me when I didn't know how to perform some of the tasks. Patiently she showed me how to feed the dogs and many other tasks. I always wanted to thank her for teaching me without getting angry when I did the task not to her liking. She answered, "I do it to help you polish your personality. I don't scold you or any of the girls, I just want to show you. Jovani, you are going to be a great example to the other students. None of the students has lived the life that you have lived. Neither of them has the kind of sickness that prevents you from living a normal life. I know that learning about your life, these students are going to value their lives more.

"The students that come here to learn stay until they reach their eighteenth birthday. When they graduate from here, they must choose their profession. The profession they choose depends on the individual—some choose marriage, others the religious life like myself, others remain single. If they accept the religious life, we send them to Mexico City where they start the initiation process at the convent. Should they choose the other professions, they must leave the orphanage. Jovani, you will remain here as long as I am alive.

"Jovani, one of these days I want you to meet Bishop Alejo Zabala Castro. He is the shining light that keeps the orphanage going. His desire is to see the students get an education. He has friends from Canada that visit our orphanage. They bring lots of necessities for all of the students. Another thing that you must know, the girls that I have speak their own indigenous dialect. They speak mixteco, tlapaneco, nahual, chuchimeco, and tolteco. Many come from the pueblo named Martinez, a pueblo where they speak mixteco. I only speak to them in Spanish."

"Sister Mar, on that you don't have to worry about me. We all have the special gifts of being born and dying. How we live our lives is important, but of most importance is our faith, our heart, and our level of intelligence. It's like a car, if it's in good condition, it will run." Sister Mar commended me on my level of intelligence, but told me that I am afraid to show it. "Jovani, learn from me, and you will overcome that fear. Jovani, with time and education along with your strong faith, you will be a very successful person.

"I believe that the Lord has you here for a certain reason. There is no doubt in my mind that your life is a mysterious one. Remember that I was given a stack of papers to save for you by Sister Adoración along with some pictures. Jovani, write about the life that you have lived and what you expect your future will be like."

"Sister, the stack of papers that Sister Adoración gave you are my notes that I have been writing for a long time. My friend Don Felipe helped me write them." I didn't mention to Sister Mar that included in my notes is the time I met the Santo Niño de Atocha, the bullfighter and the gold chains he gave me, how my Diosito cured my broken arm, among other things. "Sister Mar," I asked, "can you save the other treasures that I have?"

"Am I to believe that you have more valuable treasures?"

"Yes, Sister Mar, these are in addition to my photos and notes that Sister Adoración brought with her and you are saving for me. The notes have been in the possession of Don Felipe. He is the person that wrote them for me when I didn't know how to write. He is the one that taught me how to write. Someday I will write a book on my life, the pueblo, and this orphanage.

"I have the medal that my father bought for me. He gave the medal to Reyna when I was a baby. Reyna kept it until she was about to give birth to Rafael. She gave it to me because she thought she was going to die giving birth to Rafael."

"Jovani, I will save all your valuables for you. I truly believe that you will write a book. Niña, I know because I feel that you are a special person that you will write a book, and I will teach you all I can to help you achieve that goal.

"Jovani, I get up very early, but I don't want you getting up when I do. I want you to stay in bed and sleep."

"Sister Mar, I am used to getting up early also. I get up early to make coffee for Don Felipe. He and I go to church. From Mass I go to school or to Mama Lucia's to help her. I had sold my candies and gum. With the money I made, including the tips, I earned enough money to buy my medicine. When Mother was gone, and if Ana wasn't home, I took care of my sisters." Sister Mar reached out to hug me. I don't remember anything else, I had a convulsion.

Convulsion Brings Fear
Followed by Support

I WOKE UP IN A strange room, but the smell of a hospital I couldn't forget. I tried to move, but the nurse stopped me. I had needles stuck to my arms connected to bags hanging from my bed full of liquid. I looked around the white room. I prayed to Diosito to cure me. Now Sister Mar will surely tell me to leave the orphanage because I cost them too much money if I stay. My body started to tremble from the fear of believing that I was going to be told to leave the orphanage. I don't have any money to pay for the hospital. *My dear Diosito, please help me, I don't want to leave the orphanage.*

The nurse said, "My, your pouting tells me that you want to be breastfed." She made me laugh. "Good morning, Yovani, how do you feel today?"

"Where is Sister Mar?"

"Mija, don't worry, you are in the hospital, and we are taking good care of you." The nurse took my temperature and pulse. "Sister Mar will be coming for you pretty soon. Do you remember that you had a convulsion?" I told the nurse that I remember talking to Sister Mar and nothing else. "I am used to having convulsions and waking up in different places."

"Yovani, Sister Mar brought you here. You have gastritis and very low on energy. The tubes attached to your body are feeding you with energy."

The nurse was very nice, she was sorry that I don't have an immediately family but was happy that I was staying at the orphanage. The nurse left the room. I must have fallen asleep. I woke up to a familiar voice; Sister Mar had come back for me, she was standing next to my bed. I opened my eyes. After a while she asked me if I was all right. "Your eyes tell me that you are tired. I thank God that you are back among the living."

"I'm afraid that you will kick me out of the orphanage. Sister Mar, please don't kick me out of the orphanage, I will make money to pay for my medicine. I will work to pay the hospital, even if I have to wash clothes."

"Relax, niña"—Sister Mar caressed my head—"you don't have to pay anything. Lucky for you, I ran into the Barrera family. The family helps us in many ways, they have agreed to pay some of the cost." The knock on the door interrupted what she was telling me. Sister Mar told whoever was knocking to enter. A few elderly men entered the room. They greeted Sister Mar; the visitors included Don Jose Luis, Don Victor and his family. Sister Mar had informed them of my dilemma. They had agreed to pay for the rest of the cost. Upon hearing of my situation and the life I had left behind, they had to come and see me. The Abel Barrera family and Doña Amparito donated the medicine from their pharmacy. They signed a contract with Sister Mar indicating that would be responsible for the costs. I was overwhelmed with their generosity. I thanked them all.

Sister Mar and I returned to the orphanage. She taught me how to say the prayers the students were required to learn. Morning prayers were recited when the students woke up. The prayers included three Hail Mary's, followed by a response of love to the infant child. The rosary followed. Sister Mar selected the few that were instructed to say the rosary, the rest were sent off to make the beds. One thing I was prohibited from doing was the usage of my camera except on special occasions.

The Miracle Prayer

Lord Jesus, I come before you, just as I am.
I am sorry for my sins, I repent my sins, please
forgive me. In your Name, I forgive all others
for what they have done against me. I renounce

Satan, the evil spirits, and all their works. I give you my entire self, Lord Jesus, now and forever. I invite you into my life, Jesus. I accept you as my Lord, God, and Saviour. Heal me, change me, strengthen me in body, soul, and spirit.

Come, Lord Jesus, cover me with your precious blood, and fill me with the Holy Spirit. I love you, Lord Jesus. I praise you, Jesus. I thank you, Jesus. I shall follow you every day of my life. Amen.

Mary of God, Queen of Peace, St. Peregrine, the cancer saint, all the angels and saints, please help me. Amen.

Another set of prayers were said before lunch, after lunch thanking the Lord for the meal, and before starting off to school.

The daily routine: Get up at 5:30, Mass at 6:15, breakfast at 6:55, and be in line ready for school at 7:20. All the students left the school with their parents every Friday, except me. They returned back on Monday mornings. The girls received, besides an education, personal items like clothes, toilet paper, and some money. The parents collected some personal items as well. Since I didn't have any parents, I shared some with the nuns. I told Sister Mar that when I started selling candies, I would share pesos I earned to buy necessities for the nuns and even tortillas to be used as needed. She liked the idea, but was concerned primarily with my health. That was the most important: "take care of myself and my health," she told me. I was beginning to feel more and more at home.

I had been living at the orphanage about two weeks; some of the students were arriving for orientation, and one of them approached me. She was a little shy, hands held behind her back; twisting her head, she said, "Sister Maria wants to see you in her office." She delivered the message and ran off.

Sister Mar was waiting for me. I remember that day, it was a Saturday morning when I walked into her office. Sister was always happy to see me, and that day was no exception. The news that she had for me was a little troubling. She told me that the nuns back at the pueblo, Sisters Adoración and Sarita, were going to visit Mother. "Yovani," she said, "Sister Sarita and Adoración are visiting your mother to see how she is coping with you gone." I didn't see any reason they would do that. I certainly didn't want to go back to live in that prison she calls home. I guess my face was talking for me because Sister Mar told me to relax and to quit thinking the worst. "The sisters are taking an affidavit for your mother to sign. We need her to sign to avoid any litigation with her."

"Sister Mar, I thought the worst. I thought that you were going to send me back to live with her." She stood up, approached me, and grabbed my hand. "Yovani," she said, "the strongest forces in your pueblo couldn't force me to give you up to her." I thanked her from the bottom of my heart. "Don't worry so much, Yovanita. Now while I go freshen the flowers in the chapel, why don't you make something to eat for the two of us?"

Reyna and That Man Appear at the Orphanage

I WAS BUSY PREPARING BREAKFAST when I heard the visitor's bell. The dogs started to bark.

I ran to the front gate, looked through the peek hole. The visitors were none other than REYNA and LUPE standing at the gate. I slammed the little peek hole door and ran back panting with fear. "Who was at the gate?" Sister asked me. I couldn't answer, my voice had abandoned me. "Yovani, you look scared, tell me, what's wrong? Somebody at the door scare you? Aha," she said, "somebody is at the door, is it your mother?" she asked. I could only shake my head. I hugged her. "Please," I pleaded with her, "don't let her take me. She and the wicked old man are at the gate. He wants to kill me, send them away please, send them away."

"So they are at the gate, huh? Yovani, stay here, don't go out for any reason. Stay here, understand? I will speak with your mother only because he doesn't have any legal right being here." Sister told me not to worry. She went to our neighbors Don Ezequiel and Doña Rafa, brought them to act as witnesses and to show the wicked man that we were not alone." I was nervous but curious. I left the room and peeked through the window. I saw when she arrived with the two neighbors.

Feeling much safer but still with a touch of fear, I ran to the chapel. The words that Sister Mar said to me, "The strongest forces in your pueblo couldn't force me to give you up to her."

"Yovani, look who came to visit you." I turned to see Mother standing next to the nun. "Yovani, this lovely lady came to see you. She tells me that she misses you a lot." Sister Mar stood behind me, put her hands on my shoulders. My mother approached me crying, with open arms. "Mija, hug me, I love you very much."

"Mother, don't come near me and tell the truth. Your words are meaningless filled with venom."

"Don't say that, mija, I do love you, come back with me, I need you."

"Mother," I said, "look at the altar, we are in front of Jesus Christ, please tell the truth. Don't play the honesty and sincerity part because I don't like you anymore. You and that wicked man have hurt me so much that I have lost all the confidence in you. You have hurt me, Mother, you know that. Maybe you are not my real mother." She continued to get closer to me. I stopped her; with a firm voice, I told her not to get any closer.

I asked Sister Mar to show the lady out before she hurts me. I give thanks to my Diosito that He has kept me alive and continues to protect me. Sister Mar stood in front of her. I took the opportunity to say my piece. I said this in front of Sister Mar, "Mother, you have wished that I was dead, yes, that is true, she has stated over and over that she wished me dead. Now you can't hurt me anymore. Mother, you will always be in my prayers. No use crying, Mother, you will not take me away. Mother, it is never too late to ask for forgiveness. That day will come, believe me, it will come. Please save your tears of pretense because I will not go with you." Mother let out a loud cry close to being a scream. "Mother, I prefer to die here than to go with you and that man."

"Niña, let me talk with your mother, wait here in this room." As soon as they left the room, I walked over to the statue of my Diosito. I thanked Him for giving me the courage to speak to my mother like I did. The tears that flowed were for a different reason than those of past ones; these tears tasted of joy, not of pain inflicted by Reyna. I was talking to my Chuchin when Sister Mar walked in. "It is good to see you cry like this and not for other reasons," she told me. "Come with me, your mother is waiting for you, go say good bye to her." She said that in front my Chuchin. "Your mother is suffering because she has lost you. She feels responsible for your sickness. Come, let's go, and relax, you're safe with me."

Mother was standing in the middle of the room. I couldn't contain myself, I ran over and hugged her. I look at her saying, "Please, Mother, allow me my freedom, I am happy here. I feel free like the birds, I feel that I can breathe in freedom, nobody tries to hurt me here. Mother, I will ask you to do something that might be difficult for you, please pray for yourself. I have always prayed for you and will continue to pray for you." She hugged me. "Jovani, someday you will know the truth. You will discover what I have not been able to tell you. Others have told you many things that are true, but I cannot." She blessed me and left.

Sister Mar escorted Mother out the main gate. I walked to the statue of the Blessed Virgin Mary. "Virgencita, please forgive me for speaking to Mother in the manner that I did." The words that Mother spoke before she went left me confused. "Virgencita, I know that you are with your son Jesus when He helps me every time I fall. I know that you're present along with the angels when I express my doubts, now I ask for forgiveness for speaking to my mother like I did." Just then Sister Mar entered the room. "Your mother has left along with the man. Now they can't take you from here, and they can't hurt you anymore.

"Come, Jovani, let's go into the garden where I find it very peaceful. I want to be honest with you." Walking through the garden, I felt as though I was walking in the presence of Mamacita, my grandmother Sinforosa. We sat in what she called her favorite place, on a bench beautifully situated under a mesquite tree. From there I could hear the canaries singing from the four bird cages that housed them. The area was surrounded with beautiful plants, many of which grew in huge burgundy-colored flowerpots. Close by was another tree full of oranges that provided shade when the sun moved about.

Sister Mar began to speak, "Yovani, the first time I saw you, I felt something in my heart that touched my soul. Now that I have seen the hurt that your mother has caused you, I realize that she needs a lot of prayers. Indeed you are a very special person. I feel it even more now here," she said and touched her chest, "and in my heart. Mother Adoración told me of your desire to become a nun. Because of your illness, I don't believe that you becoming a nun is possible. I am being honest with you now. I want you to pursue another vocation. Niña, if you didn't have the illness, we would accept you into our vocation. Don't feel rejected because we'd love for you to be one of us. But we are a very poor order and don't have the money to take care of your illness. Yovani, I cannot predict the future, but anything is possible. Also there are other vocations in which you can serve the Lord. As long as I am in charge of this place, I will help you reach that goal.

"The strong faith you have in God will help you control your emotions. I too will teach you ways to confront your illness, I will teach you to have confidence in yourself. Niña, don't take this as a rejection. Rather, I want to prepare you for the future. It's very possible that someday you will overcome your illness. I never thought that I would be married to God and serve Him in this vocation. Yovani, again I say to you, don't take this as a rejection. As long as I am here, I will teach you how to attain another vocation.

"Yovani, I have an appointment with the president of the city. We will continue talking when I come back. During the meeting, I will submit a request to the president asking for assistance in meeting the cost of your medicine."

I found myself alone again in the confines of the orphanage, but not for long. Ruby and Perla, the daughters of Doña Rafa, came to play with me. They also wanted to play with the dogs. Since I felt that that I could control the dogs, I let them out of their enclosure.

We ate fruits right off the trees and played with the dogs until Sister Mar returned.

She was so happy I could see the glow in her eyes, and her whole face was aglow. "Girls, come help me." Apparently the towns-people or the merchants had donated sacks of food for the orphan-age. We helped her carry all the provisions to the house. After the girls left, Sister Mar told me she had good news to share with me. We sat in what was becoming my favorite bench as well. "Yovani, I have good news for you. I talked to the president of the pueblo. I caught her at a good time, she was campaigning, I told her about your situation. She was shocked when I told her. Immediately she called her assistant and gave her instructions. Soon she came back with some official papers.

"The president told us to fill the papers. These papers will authorize the government to pay for your doctor expenses. An assis-tant of the president will pick them up from the orphanage. For sure Diosito is watching out for you. The Barrera family is paying for your medicine, and now the president will pay for the doctor expenses. Come, niña, we have to give thanks to the Lord. We will pray the rosary and thank our Lord and the Divine Infant for watch-ing over you." On the way to the chapel I told the sister that I was not comfortable accepting charity from others. I have paid for all my expenses. However, I am grateful for her effort and will reluctantly accept their generosity.

"Very well then, show me your gratitude by taking care of your health and by studying hard. Also, I will ask you to periodically help in the kitchen in preparing the food. That is not all I will keep you busy. I will ask you to help in keeping the beds made." She grabbed my hand, she confronted me face-to-face, she was smiling. "Yovani, I am playing with you. Your priorities are your health and your studies. However, if your grades are more than satisfactory, you can help us."

Next morning after breakfast and cleaning the kitchen and morning prayers, I was given the green light by Sister Mar to enjoy the day. I cut the old tortillas into pieces and added rice plus some scrambled eggs to feed the dogs.

The dogs were as follows:

Sultán was my favorite, he protected me. He reminded me of a big black bear. His bark is that of a wolf except when I was sick. If he sensed that I was sick, his howl is a whimper.

Rumbo was the leader, reminded me of a giraffe—with a long neck, light-brown coat, with blue eyes. He would not eat until I ate with him. He saw me kneeling to pray, and from that day on, he would kneel and pray with me.

Capitán reminded me of a foxhound—long ears and even longer body, light-brown. He would notify the nuns when I had a convulsion. He'd run to the nuns and bark at them. Once or twice when they didn't pay attention to him, he grabbed their dress and dragged them until they willingly went along with him. Other times if the nuns didn't pay attention, he'd run to the neighbors.

Férulays—white haired but for a few black lines—was the wanderer. He would jump over the fence to join us on the way to Sunday Mass. The last time he jumped the fence and didn't come back for a few days proved fatal. Rumbo and Sultán were very incensed with him and injured him severely, costing his life.

I was feeding them when the threat of rains came. Sultán grabbed my skirt and barked and barked. "Oh, you want me to eat with you, huh?" The sunlight gave way to the clouds, and the clouds unleashed its reservoir of water on the land. I felt free, and the temptation to run overcame me. I ran throughout the garden followed by the dogs. We splashed, we jumped with joy. The dogs jumped on me, they jumped on each other until I was exhausted. Sister Mar was in the kitchen when I walked in soaking wet. She looked at me and smiled. "Yovani," she said, "since you are all wet, why don't you go feed the dogs."

"Sister, I have fed them already." I told her what I did when Sultán had invited me to eat with him. "I pretended to eat some of his food and how I pretended that it was delicious." She laughed again. "Yovani, you are going to make things around here very interesting. Just remember when school starts and the girls come back to school, I don't want you to do everything. I expect you to help the students with their responsibilities. Yovani, go change out of those wet clothes, I will be at the chapel waiting for you."

Praying the rosary was so different because now I was not alone. But I couldn't take my eyes off the crystal windows; it was a rare sight. The moon was shining at the same time the rains were pounding the chapel and the surroundings. I felt safe and completely comfortable. The doorbell atop the huge door sounded, we had company. The dogs barked and ran toward the main gate. Capitán nudged me toward the gate. Sisters Veronica and Pati were waiting for us to open the gate. They were soaking wet.

I was introduced to both of the nuns. I helped Sister Pati with her suitcase. She appeared to be real nice and easygoing. She wanted to know if I was the young girl that Sister Adoración had brought to the orphanage from Tetipac. I acknowledged that I was the one. I said, "Sister Mar has accepted me with open arms." Sister Pati knew about me and most of my life story. "Yovani, I understand that you go by the name of *Rosita* as well. How should I address you?"

"Well, Sister Pati, I like *Rosita*, but I understand that the orphanage has many other girls with the name of *Rosita*. Sister Mar prefers to call me *Yovani*. So *Yovani* is the name I prefer here." She smiled and said, "Can I give you a hug? Yovani, for me, you are an Alma de Dios." I couldn't say anything; we embraced.

"Yovani, you and I are going to be good friends. The short time that I have known you, I feel lots of energy around you. I don't understand why, but it has me thinking, who is this girl? Yovani, who are you?" I managed a smile, I just shrugged my shoulders. Sister Mar called for us. I walked with Sister Veronica to the chapel. Personalitywise she was very different from Sister Pati. She appeared to be friendly but stricter and not as outgoing as Sister Pati. After prayer, Sister Mar talked to me. "Yovani, as of today, you will follow this routine. Take your medicine and go to bed. Sleep in the bed I showed you when you first came. I will bring you additional bedding later on."

The students began to arrive. Their parents dropped them and left. I was at the porch meeting them. They came from different parts of the mountains. Some spoke different languages; they were mixteco, tlapaneco, nuhual, and chichimeco. I spoke to them in Spanish, and for the most part, they ignored me, not even paying attention to me. The girls brought chicks, corn, beans, and cans of beehives. What was left of the hives when the honey was squeezed, we used to make candles. The leftover hives were mixed with a shredded cotton cloth to make like a torch. We used the torches to make fires on the cooking area where we cooked for all forty-three girls plus the nuns.

My first friend was from Metlatonoc, Ofelia Martínez. Yes, it was difficult to make friends, I was an outsider. An older girl Maria was the culprit. At fourteen she was one of the older girls and demanded the others' respect. It became apparent that most of them were related. When Maria found out that Ofelia was being friendly with me, she tried to stop her from talking to me. But Ofelia knew enough Spanish that we were able to communicate. She told me that Maria was the favorite of Sister Mar. "Be very careful with her, she will try to hurt you," Ofelia told me several times.

From left to right: Sister Pati, Sister Maria del Mar, and Sister Veronica.

"Ofelia, does María know how to speak Spanish?" I asked. "She knows a few words, but she prefers to speak her own language."

"Ofelia, do you think that she will treat me nice if I teach her Spanish?"

"Jovani, you are not from here, you are from the city. She has forbidden me to speak with you because you are an outsider. We are all indigenous and related one way or another. There are other older girls you must be aware of."

"Really, Ofelia, can you tell me their names?"

"Yes, those girls are Martina, Marisol, Chuchita, Delfa, Marquita, and Felicitas."

"Ofelia, if María is mean with you, why don't you tell Sister Mar?"

"Whatever María is, she is still my cousin, and she is the favorite student of Sister Mar. We are related yes, but our families are more enemies than friends. If I tell Sister Mar, María's mother will know, and she'll go to my house and have a fight with my mother. Don't want that to happen, that's why I don't tell Sister Mar."

The day before the start of the school year, Sister Mar gathered all the students in the courtyard. She presented me to the other students. She had some nice words to say about me. Apparently that didn't sit too well with María because she would seek me out and harass me along with her cousin Lupita Martinéz. I avoided them as much as I could, or ignored the insults they flung at me. I didn't want to incite trouble with María, it wasn't my personality. I would much rather be friends with her and anybody else. But it became known to me that María used to accompany Sister Mar to the market on Sundays before I came to the orphanage. However, I was now accompanying Sister Mar to go shopping with her on Sundays. That didn't sit too well with María. She started treating me even worse.

The news of the bad treatment I was receiving from María spread throughout. The nuns were not aware of the treatment. One day the social workers that checked on the condition of the orphanage paid us a visit. They had heard through the grapevine of the situation. They checked with some of the students; that's how they realized that the allegations were true. I didn't realize until later that the social workers had contacted Sister Mar. After hearing from the social workers, Sister Mar conducted her own investigation. Most of the students she investigated told her that María in fact was making life miserable for me. Sister Mar confronted María. The bad treatment from her stopped. Soon after that day, María dropped out of school.

My Second-Generation Studies Begin, Tech #132

THE SECONDARY SCHOOL WAS LOCATED about thirty minutes away from the orphanage. I walked alone and sometimes with other students. The dangerous part, although we didn't realize at the time, was crossing the river. The Tlalpan River where we crossed didn't have a bridge. The only way to cross was the way we did, and that was to jump from rock to rock until we crossed. After a heavy rainfall, we had to wade across. Some of the students would take an extra set of clothes to change at the school.

My second year of school started. No longer was I the only outsider, now the students from the orphanage were the outsiders. But I was the exception, now I was among other students that spoke Spanish, and I could relate to them. On the first day of class, all the students had to choose a profession. I stated in the written report that I desired to be a high-fashion dress designer. I don't know if that is what I really wanted to do or if I chose that profession because of the teacher. The orphanage kept track of our progress. Sister Veronica would periodically check on our progress. I imagined that she had the same trouble crossing the river. Sister Veronica was stern and appeared to be in a foul mood most of the time. She demanded complete attention from her students. Anyone she admonished was scolded and forced to perform additional homework. She never spanked or hit anybody with a ruler, like we hear others doing.

The school had a student organization. The older students were in charge of the election. Students from each class were selected to run for election to represent them in the educational system of the school. I was selected to represent my class. Day of the election, I got sick, I had a convulsion. I woke up in the school's infirmary. Catita, the social worker of the school, was taking care of me. I felt a patch on my forehead, it was covering a big lump on head. Catita followed me to the mirror. She introduced herself and asked me how I felt. I told her I felt fine; at that moment, somebody knocked on the door of her office.

Catita opened the door; several students—mostly ones that I had seen before—walked in. One of them, a girl named Cheli, introduced herself as the president of the school's alumni association. She added, "We came here to meet you because it appears that you are going to be a runaway winner of the election. Most of your compatriots voted for you." Each student introduced themselves to me. Cheli wanted my opinion on some task they were working on, but Catita stopped her. Catita said to them, "Listen, what I hear about the election is really good news. I myself would vote for her, but now she is sick and a little weak. I will explain everything later. I along with the other teachers are happy that she will represent the association. Now she has to rest." The students left.

Catita congratulated me on being elected to the association. Of course I didn't know specifically what my job was. I asked Catita to explain what my duties were now that I was part of the association. "The association members meet with the representatives of the secretary and the director of the school to talk about scholarships. They grant scholarships to the best students that we have. I have been informed that you are on that list. If you feel good, I suggest that you get dressed because they are waiting for us."

My head was throbbing with a horrible headache, but I didn't want to miss out. "Really, Catita, you think that I will get a scholarship even though I live in the orphanage? That being the case, I will work hard for our school, the students, and the teachers. I will accept." That day, I was elected to the association and I was selected as one of the recipients of a scholarship. I returned to my history class. The students were waiting for me. When I entered the room, two students, Tlaloc and Doroteo, were standing atop the teacher's desk giving me an applause. They shouted, "For our future representative and the most beautiful girl present. The door is open to those that don't like our representative."

Some of the other students grabbed me and lifted me as they marched me around the room. Doroteo told me that they were really concerned when I had my convulsion. "Now that we see you again with life, we are happier that we elected you to represent us. You give us reason to continue with our quest. Yovani, I tell you this as a friend, not as a boy that likes you. If Sister Mar finds out, she will ban you from the orphanage, and the dogs will bite me to death. Aside from that, you have a big influence on the other students. Yovani, I have to share with you something, most of us that have seen you and talked to you notice that you are so different than the other girls. I don't mean the girls from the orphanage, I am talking about the girls from here."

Apparently Doroteo's views and feelings weren't shared by all. One of the female students approached me in front of the class; she said, "I didn't vote for you and never will vote for you. These bastards voted for you, why, I don't know. How can a girl from the orphanage with a sickness help us?" Tlaloc stood in front of her. "You do not talk to Yovani in that manner. Where she lives with the nuns is none of your business. Besides, the nuns have given her a good education, she has morals that apparently you lack. Yovani is an honorable person. If you are against what we are prepared to accomplish, I suggest that you stay calm. Otherwise, I suggest that you change classes." Everyone shouted, "Leave, leave, leave."

I stood up on the desk, raised my arms; the room went silent. "Let's be at peace with this girl, let's give our friend another opportunity. All of us are here for a reason to learn and to meet our goal in life." The students looked at her; she stood up and apologized. She turned to me and said, "Yovani, I misunderstood you, I thought you were here because you were an opportunist, but I find out that you are truly honorable." From that day forward, Angelíca became one of my best friends.

Walking back and forth to school every day was an adventure. The river was the interesting part of the thirty-minute walk. I walked alone sometimes but never alone with a boy; Sister Mar forbade that. It was completely different from the schools in my pueblo. My Spanish teacher's favorite subjects were operas and the study of poets, especially Enrique Gonzalez Martínez. I was selected to recite "Cuando Sepas Ayar Una Sonriza" (When You Know How to Find a Smile), a poem by Martínez. I presented the poem during an assembly of the whole school.

Sister Mar was very happy with my presence at the orphanage. Every afternoon after class, I helped her with the catechism class. I was still selling candies to buy my medicine. Even though my medicine was being taken care of, I needed to pay my own. The monthly 120 pesos of scholarship money I received was used to help the orphanage and to pay the school tuition. My convulsions didn't stop. Sometimes I was taken to the clinic after a bad convulsion, and I used the money to pay the costs.

The student association was very interesting. I made several suggestions on how we could improve the school. Some were accepted, and some weren't mainly because of the cost. One of my suggestions was a big hit. We didn't have an eating place other than under the trees. During recess and during lunch, that is where we sat. However when the rains came, we had to scramble and eat indoors. I recommended that we construct an eating place equipped with a nice roof and benches. Money was the problem.

We needed money for that kind of project; in addition, we had to have the director of the school approve such a venture. To raise money, I suggested that one day a week, the seven elected members of the association cook the meals and sell them to the students. On that day, the regular lady that sold us her food would be given the day off. Once we had some money, we would buy different popular products and raffle them off. We presented the plan to the school director. He approved it on the condition that the teachers and the association members approve the project. They voted and approved it.

The seven members gathered others to help with the cooking and cleanups. Within a few months, we had money to buy merchandise to raffle off. We purchased tools, phones, silverware, and other various items. We sold raffle tickets; needless to say, I sold the most raffle tickets. Within eight months after my suggestion was approved, the eating area was constructed. Well, it wasn't totally a student effort. The carpenters, electricians, and professionals helped us by donating their services.

My days at the orphanage were happy ones. The fears I had living with those two monsters were nonexistent. I was no longer alone, and I didn't have my two sisters to take care of. That was a big worry because I didn't know where they were living. I prayed that Mother had sold them to a good family. I worried about the day that I had to leave the orphanage. That day would be when I reached my eighteenth birthday and had graduated from school. I still hoped that I would be accepted into the convent.

A Canadian Couple
Desired to Adopt Me

My worries would in all probability end if I would accept to be adopted by the Canadian couple. A Canadian couple interested in adopting me paid us a visit. They were accompanied by the Reverend Archbishop Alejo Zabala Castro. I remember that day. I was sitting in the kitchen talking with Sister Mar when the doorbell rang. It was the archbishop along with several people from Canada. The archbishop greeted us and gave me a big hug and his blessing. The archbishop introduced the people from Canada and some from the United States. They were doctors on vacation with their families. Sister Mar led them to our favorite spot where I served some pastry and lemonade.

The doctors from Canada were very interesting. The archbishop had told them about my sickness. The archbishop and the Canadian couple would speak in English and some Spanish. The archbishop asked me if I would be interested in being adopted. The catch, he told me, was that I had to move to Canada with them. "They are prepared to help you with medical expenses, and there is a good chance that the doctors in Canada can operate on you, and maybe your sickness will go away. My thoughts ran wild. I imagined being cured and what that could mean. *Could I be a nun after all? Would I be accepted into being a nun? Can these people help me find my real father and his family?* But I was not prepared to answer.

I knew nothing about Canada, I knew even less about the doctors. I knew that I couldn't leave the orphanage nor could I leave Mexico. I talked to Sister Mar in a low voice; I said, "Sister Mar, I appreciate what these people and the archbishop are doing for me, but I can't leave. I am very happy here, I enjoy helping you with the students. I believe that someday my Diosito will place me in the path of a doctor that will cure me of my sickness. God will guide the doctor, and I will be cured. More important why I want to stay here is that I want to meet my father. People say that he is dead, but I have to find out for myself."

Sister Mar told them what I desired. One of the touring doctors understood why I couldn't leave; he gave me a hug and some green dollar bills. I didn't want to accept them, but the archbishop told me it was okay. After a few moments, Sister Mar rang a bell; it was the signal we were waiting for. The girls walked in, in an orderly fashion; I joined them. We sang a few songs for the tourists. Afterward Sister Mar excused the students except me. She asked me to stay. Another doctor handed me some money; again the archbishop told me it was okay to accept the money. Another handed me a beautiful necklace. It was a heart with several brilliant stones; again the archbishop nodded his approval. Later I asked Sister Mar if she would keep it for me. She told me that she would save it aside the other one my mother had given to me. It was the one my father bought for me.

The doctors were getting ready to leave on their journey. They made a yearly pilgrimage to the mountains to help the poor and sick. Sister Mar was delighted when the archbishop allowed me to join them. I was overcome by their poverty, their lack of doctors and medicine. Little children thin from lack of nutrition, blind, and some hard of hearing. Others with their mouth deformed, others with various physical handicaps. Many adults in need of some type of medical help. We worked day and night. I heard that the doctors had performed 150 operations. When we left the mountains for the lowland that was the city, we left with lots of love and a goat, turkeys, a pig, and several chickens. The president had his employees take the animals to the orphanage.

The orphanage was short of pens for the chickens and the turkeys. We also didn't have a pigsty because we had not had a pig before. Thanks to the archbishop, the chicken coop was enlarged, and I built the sty. Most of the students would ask me when I was going to slay the pig, they wanted to make tamales. I didn't give any-one a date. Some of the chickens provided us daily with eggs, and the ones that didn't were cooked. We untied the legs of the chickens and the turkeys to shoo them into their coops. That was a big mis-take. The turkeys were spooked by Firulays; they started running all over the garden with us running after the turkeys trying to capture them. One of the turkeys escaped the compound of the garden. We never saw that turkey again. In all the commotion, we left the gate to the chicken coop wide open. The chickens got out, and they ran all over the yard.

Firulays, the wanderer and free-spirited dog, slew three of the chickens. But apparently didn't like the taste of chicken because he didn't eat any of them. Poor Firulays, he got a beating for his mis-takes. We were eventually going to eat the chickens anyway, he just expedited their demise. For some time after the beating, he didn't follow us to chapel. I missed not seeing him waiting for us under the altar.

My Thirteenth Birthday and
First Holy Communion

MARCH 29, I CELEBRATED MY thirteenth birthday. That morning I thought of my tenth birthday celebration, I thought of Ana and the feast she had provided for me that day. This year's celebration would be much quieter, or so I thought. I gathered my dirty clothes and went to the laundry. I started to feel sick, but I continued to wash. Next thing that I remember is when I opened my eyes, I was coughing. Am I dreaming? The archbishop was sitting next to me, then I saw Sister Mar and some of the girls from the orphanage. I took the cottonball from my nose, but not the wetcloth atop my forehead. "You're a miracle," whispered the archbishop, "we thought you were dying, and here you are among us full of life." He took some holy water and gave me his blessing. "Niña, surely the Lord has blessed you with life for whatever reason I can't explain."

The archbishop said to Sister Mar, "I want you to be the witness and godparent to this child because I am giving her the holy sacrament of communion."

"Señor Archbishop, I have to make a confession before receiving communion."

"No, my child, I don't believe that you have committed any mortal or even a venial sin. I being able to forgive your sins, I have forgiven them." With tears of joy I received my first Holy Communion. I received Diosito in the host. I felt a surge of energy throughout my body. I started to pray the rosary. The nun and the girls accompanied me. After the rosary, the archbishop gave me another blessing saying, "May God bless you, and please don't change, continue being who you are," and left. Soon everybody left except the nun. "Yovani, you had a very bad convulsion, you lost a lot of blood." I began to talk, but she stopped me. "Niña, don't say anything, let me talk." I fell asleep, on my thirteenth birthday, from the fall I sustained. I slept for three days.

Sister Mar told me that the doctor that came to check on me had declared me dead. "You were cold, stiff, and no color at all. We all assumed the worst. We called the archbishop, but he couldn't make it because he was up in the mountains administering to the sick. He came back two days later. When he heard about your condition, he came over immediately. When he gave you his blessing and sprinkled the holy water on you, you coughed. The moment we heard that cough, we stopped praying. All of us were amazed, I jumped up and ran up to you. The archbishop declared your awakening a miracle."

Word of my awakening spread quickly. The ladies that help around the orphanage brought me a bouquet of flowers. Another lady brought me a pan full of atole (blue corn porridge) with fresh homemade bread. Señor Luis and his wife came to visit me. They gave me the gift of some money. Señor Victor and his daughter Rumy also visited me. My thirteenth birthday will be another one that I will never forget.

After a short visit, Don Victor went to speak with Sister Mar. Rumy stayed with me. Rumy asked me a very personal question. "Yovani," she said, "can I ask you a very personal question?"

"Of course, come sit by me," I answered at the same time patting the edge of the bed for her sit. "Yovani, I enjoy being your friend, but I would like to be more than a friend. I want you to be more like a sister to me. I realize that I am a little older than you, but you are a person I can trust and talk girl talk. I have three brothers, but I can't talk to them, besides, they know nothing about girls." We laughed. "Yeah, boys don't know anything about girls. Rumy, I will be happy to be your sister.

"Rumy, in return, I ask a favor, and that is that you call me *Rosita.*"

"*Rosita? Rosita* is your name? Okay, from now on, I will call you Rosita. When I heard about you and all that you have been through,

I cried. Ever since then I've wanted to meet you. My father saw me crying and asked me why. I told him that I didn't have a sister or a mother that I could talk with. Mother died a while back. I told him about you and my desire to meet you. He told me that he was going to speak with Sister Mar to see if we could adopt you." A very happy Sister Mar walked into my room. It was rather odd that she walked in at that moment.

"Yovani," she said, "the archbishop is going to celebrate a Mass in our chapel to thank the Lord for giving you back to us." Rumy accompanied me to Mass. The chapel was decorated with beautiful flowers and linen reserved for special occasions. It was a day replete with benedictions, donations, faith, and love.

I didn't go to school the following day. Close to midday the teacher Catita along with other teachers came with several of the students to visit me. They brought some bread for the orphanage. Sister Mar entertained them by telling them what had happened to me. The townspeople came visiting bringing breads, meat, and other prepared foods enough to feed all forty-three of us students. The owners of El Torito, a meat market, donated always about twenty kilos of meat and bones that we used to make soup. Señora Coral, also a regular, contributed fifty pieces of chicken. Another big donor was Doña Teresita. Every week she sent over five kilos of chicharones with chelitos. Other times in addition she would send us sugar and other goodies.

I recognized several people that I had come in contact with when I went to buy groceries with Sister Mar. Other times I was accompanied by Ofelia, and she also introduced me to many of the people. October was a very interesting and delightful time for all of us at the orphanage. We started preparing gifts for Christmas. We made several types of cookies, powdered cookies topped with anise. We also made for Christmas. One of the more rewarding things that we made were detailed hearts for those people that helped us. I always felt good when I gave from that heart, regardless of the quantity.

The years that I had spent at the orphanage were very happy ones. On weekends I stayed inside the confines of the orphanage. My family didn't visit. I thought often of Mamacita, Don Felipe, my sister Ana, and Mama Lucia and my two little sisters. I wished that I could go visit, but the fear of running into Mother and that man kept me from visiting home. Such thoughts brought tears to my eyes. I thought of writing, but that too scared me. I was sure that they knew that I was here at the orphanage where I was safe. Sister Mar knew that I was longing to visit with them. She thought that I would be happy to speak with my sister Ana. She made arrangements with the Rivera family, making it possible to speak with Ana via the telephone whenever I wanted to.

Summer Vacation

Sister Mar called me into her office. She told me that she and the other nuns had to refresh their educational vocation. She also told me that she prepared a report detailing another visit of people from Canada. I wondered why she was telling me about the Canadians. She added that these people come—like in the years past—to help us. But I was shocked when she told me that the people from Canada knew about my sickness and would most likely try to help. I misunderstood her. I thought she was trying to get rid of me. I started to cry. "Niña, that's not a reason to cry, they are here to help us, that is all."

"Sister Mar, I thought that you were trying to get rid of me."

"No, Yovani, I am not saying that I want you to leave and send you back to your pueblo. I am only telling you what my plans are this summer. You will stay here or with the Rivera family. This way you don't stay alone here. You might also decide to visit your sister. Yovani, these doors are always open to you.

"Yovani, I was thinking of going to the gardener to buy some flowers. Tomorrow you and I are going to the garden place, and I will buy fifty rose plants. I will instruct Toño, the gardener, to fix the areas where you will plant them. Those roses will forever bear your print."

"Sister, I will take care of the roses with lots of care. Like you say, the roses will grow more beautiful day after day, and they will bear my print forever."

"I cry for other reasons. When I think of my friends and my people of the pueblo, I become sad. I don't have a father or a mother, you are my only family I have. Mamacita Sinforosa doesn't know that I am here. She is getting old, and I know she is worried about me. Mama Lucia and Don Felipe also are probably worried sick not knowing that I am okay. My sister Ana doesn't know where I am, and I think about my little sisters. Sister Mar, this is the only home I have, and I thank you from the bottom of my heart for taking care of me.

"I will be okay alone here. The dogs will protect and keep me company. If I get too lonely, I will visit the Rivera family. I will work in the garden and clean the altar."

"Yovani, I don't want you to stay here alone. What if you have a convulsion, who will take care of you? The Rivera family will take good care of you, please consider staying with them. Yovani, you still look sad, what else is troubling you?"

"Nothing, other than that I desire to visit my pueblo, but I am afraid of Mother and that man. I miss my grandmother Sinforosa."

"Yovani, maybe it's time that you write to them, they should know that you are okay. Who knows, maybe someday they can come visit you here." *Finally,* I thought as my heart pounded inside my chest, *I am allowed to write to them.* The fear of retaliation from Reyna is far removed. "Sister Mar, I will start writing those letters today."

I wrote letters to Mamacita Sinforosa, my sister Ana, Mama Lucia, and Don Felipe. I basically told them that I was safe and getting my education. I told them about Sister Mar, the families that I had met, and of course the dogs. I took money from my hiding place to buy the stamps. When I mailed the letters, I could picture Don Felipe when he got the letters, especially his. In all the years that he had been the postman, he'd never received a letter from anyone.

The last day of school was a sad one, but it also was a day to enjoy. Sadly I saw the families come for their children. They would be going back home into the mountains until next school year. I was accompanied by Firulays to my favorite spot in the garden. I went and sat, from there I could see the students being picked up by their families. That day I discovered who my true friends at the orphanage were. Many of my friends took their families to where I was sitting to bid me farewell. That gesture on their part made me feel good. My heart pounded with delight with each presentation, and my tears of joy were held in check.

That afternoon the Rivera family came for me. I was sitting at my favorite place in the garden. They sat with me for a while. I had a few personal things packed knowing that I could come back into the grounds anytime I needed anything. Besides, I had to care for the roses we had planted. I spent the days talking with the mother of Mrs. Rivera, who lived with them. She was a very nice lady. The stories she would tell me were very interesting. I played with the baby, helped Mrs. Rivera clean house, and occasionally helped her cook.

I had been staying with the Rivera family for a few days when I got a telephone call from my sister Ana. Señora Rivera told me to speak as long as I wanted. Ana told me that she had gotten my letter. We talked for a long time. Ana told me that Reyna was saying that the lecherous old man was paying for my education someplace in Mexico. Ana also told me that many people had asked her about me. She asked me if I had any intentions of returning to the pueblo. My answer was, "Never as long as Mother lives with that man."

"Vani," she said, "you can come and stay with us. I got married and have a daughter, her name is Claudia."

"Ana, really, I am an aunt?" I was never so happy to be an aunt. "Ana, maybe I will change my mind and go visit you next July 1993." Before we hung up, we promised to write or call each to other.

My stay with the Rivera family was a very rewarding one. They took me with them wherever they went. I visited a city for the first time. I learned what to be on vacation meant, I saw the love that families share with one another. The grandparents were there for the children to enjoy. I never had seen this kind of affection in other families but rarely in mine. At the end of my stay, I wrote a letter to the Rivera family. When Mrs. Rivera read the letter, she told me, "This letter is full of beautiful words of love and affection. The tears I shed when I read it are tears of joy. This note tells me that you were welcomed by our family, and I see that you appreciated what you saw in our family. I will save this letter forever in a place where the pages remain fresh and will never disappear. Whenever you feel lonely, you know that the doors to this house will always be open to you."

In time, the vacation ended, and I found myself back at the orphanage. The young girls started to arrive from summer vacation. That year I learned what totopos were. Totopos was a large, thin tortilla made from red ground corn. I received many gifts from my indigenous friends. Ofelia, one of my best friends, presented me with a rooster. "This rooster," she said, "will make your chickens have many chicks." I in turn presented handmade rosaries to all the girls.

The beginning of the school year was different from the previous year. I saw many new students, and the older ones had changed; we were all so much bigger. The student association was involved in making the school a better place. Even the other students noticed the change and became involved. The teachers were involved more than in the past year. The plan to build an eating place became a reality. We finished the dining area in October 1995. The director of the school along with other school faculty thought that I should be recognized for my effort. First because it was my idea, second because I had presented the idea to the school board, and I was involved with raising the funds to build the eating place. My reward: I have my name etched in stone that is situated near the dining area. During the ceremony when I was honored, the director presented me with a certificate of appreciation.

Later, the president of the pueblo, along with some of her personnel, visited the orphanage. She had learned how the dining place was constructed. She made a special trip to check out the dining area. She was impressed, and when she learned that I was the young girl living at the orphanage that had come up with the idea, she went to the house to thank me and really to meet me. We talked for some time in the presence of Sister Mar. The president of the pueblo asked me if there was anything she could do for me. I looked at Sister Mar and asked her if I could speak freely. She didn't see a problem and told me to feel free and speak to the president.

"Señora Presidenta," I said, "we need blankets and sheets for our beds and backpacks for the girls. Sometimes we run short of food." Sister Mar was surprised that I had the courage to ask for the beddings and the food. The president wasn't surprised; she told me that I should do well with a good education. The bedding, the backpacks, and food arrived within a few days. The president had promised me that she would send us the supplies along with food, and she complied with her promise. She sent us blankets, sheets, and backpacks for each one of us. She sent us beans, rice, corn flour, and powdered milk.

Once the girls chose their individual blanket and backpack, the orphanage was quiet once again. The school was having a social event to honor one of the teachers. My teacher asked if anyone was interested in participating either as a performer, singer, or just share an unusual story with the student body. I volunteered to recite a poem I had written. It was about the orphanage and what living there had meant to me. The teacher gladly accepted my participation. I recited the poem in front of the whole assembly of students. It was a big hit; all my friends commended me on the poem. My teacher asked me if he could have a copy. I gladly gave him one. The following day, I saw it posted on the bulletin board.

> For a friend
> Desirous to hold in our hands
> All the roses from the garden
> To possess a tender fine voice
> To harmonize a song most cheerful
> A song that translates a sentiment
> Of praise, gratitude, and affection
> A song that becomes a moment
> For him that fills us with hope
> Desirous to open our hearts
> To allow our happiness to escape
> For he that gives us illusions and daily bread
> God knows to award good deeds
> From heaven to our benefactors
> And with his goodness relieve a pleasing console

My days at the orphanage, my home, was never boring; I was busy with the dogs, the garden, and cleaning the chapel. I never forgot to write my notes. I treasured and safeguarded them always. At times I cried, other times I laughed when I wrote them. But it was a relief, it was something that I was doing for myself. Sister Mar was an inspiration. She always thanked me for all I did for the orphanage, helping with the other girls that stayed at the home. I never forget what she told me one day. She said, "Yovani, I have been the mother superior many years, I have met various generations of students, but I have never had one like you. You are not afraid to confront the president of the pueblo or anybody. You have a fascinating aura that draws people to you.

"The note that you wrote to the president of the pueblo made her realize that we needed help. Nobody had done that before. Now we are receiving assistance from the presidency. I am glad, Yovani, that you are part of the orphanage and are receiving an education. I do regret that you were not accepted into the monastery to become a nun. What you have done for the orphanage and others is more than any of us could have done."

"Sister Mar, I value your words, but it pains me that I cannot be a nun. My first dream was to be a nun. Since I was a little girl, I dreamt of serving my Diosito. But now that dream is gone, but Diosito will guide me, I believe He has me with life for a reason. I will always serve Him in another capacity."

"Listen to me, Yovani, the most difficult sacrifice you have to make is to make peace with your mother. Forgive her, someday she will give you that motherly hug, she is your mother, forgive her. Say prayers for her, believe me, someday she will tell you the truth about your life."

"Sister Mar, your words are engraved in my heart. I think of her, and I pray for her. Yes, I hope someday she will tell me who my real father is."

My Fourteenth Birthday

I CELEBRATED MY FOURTEENTH BIRTHDAY. One of my fellow students gave me a stuffed bear. The stuffed animal was my companion. I hugged him when I woke up in the morning or after a convulsion. My daily routine didn't change, I taught catechism to fifteen of the neighbor's children and twelve from the orphanage. In time they made their first Holy Communion. The bishop celebrated the Mass. Afterward the families celebrated with a huge barbeque for everybody.

My sickness required periodic examinations. I had to travel to Acapulco. My companion to Acapulco was Tere, my social worker. The arduous trip to Acapulco took several hours by bus. We became acquainted and got to be good friends. Her husband had died very young. She shared with me other personal things. Her daughter Lupita was in a college in Chilpancingo studying to become either a doctor or an engineer. I met Lupita, she was a wonderful girl. We became instant friends. She told me about her boyfriend and other personal girl things. I shared with Lupita my troubles with my mother and the lecherous old man. Lupita had heard of my convulsions. I added more detail about my sickness and how it had affected my relationship with others, mainly in a positive way.

I told Lupita to value her mother. "Notice all she does for you day after day, with the love of a mother's sweat. I have never felt a mother's hug. I have never had a boyfriend, so I can't tell you anything about relationships, but I can tell you, take care of yourself. Complete your studies before you take on added responsibilities." Lupita laughed. "Look at you giving me, an older girl than you, advice. Don't worry, Yovani, my studies are very important to me. I am aware of the sacrifices that my mother has made so that I can get an education." We exchanged addresses; she added her phone number in case I needed to talk to somebody.

I met with the neurologist at the general hospital in Acapulco where they examined my head. They determined that the convulsions I was having were advancing at a pace faster than expected. They believed that I could experience leakage in my brain. The examination also showed that I had thirteen cysts reproducing in my brain. Not the kind of news I expected; naturally I became very sad. I asked the doctor if there was the slightest of possibilities that I could be cured. The doctor told me that it was a possibility, but they didn't have the capability in the hospital. The doctor believed that the cure for epilepsy didn't exist, at least not in México. "I hope that the cysts cease to reproduce because in that part of the brain, we can't do more."

"Doctor, is there a medicine or an operation that you can perform on me that will help me attack my sickness? Doctor, can you take the animals inside my head before they multiply?"

"Yes, Yovani, there is, but not at this hospital. We don't have the capability because we don't have any neurosurgeons. Besides, an operation would be very expensive."

"Doctor," I asked, "can you give a rough estimate as to how much an operation like that would cost? Doctor, I earn money selling things, and eventually I can save for my operation. I want to rid myself of this sickness."

Dr. Cuevas got close to me; he said, "We would love to be able to help you. An operation like that is also very risky. What I can do is to increase the dosage of depakene. The cysts remain, but your convulsions can be controlled. The medicine will also control your emotions, allowing your brain to function better. Confront your emotions, learn to live with them until we find a cure. Now I want to speak with your mother."

I looked around the room. "Doctor, is my mother here?" He was confused, thinking that Tere was my mother. "Doctor," Tere interrupted, "I'm not her mother, I'm a social worker from DIF, and Rosita lives in the orphanage." The doctor was really surprised. Nonetheless, he still wanted to speak with Tere. I was told to leave the room while they talked. I was given an EEG on my head and three additional x-rays. When the examinations were completed, Tere took me to a restaurant. For three years Tere took me for an examination every three months. After the three years, every six to eight months, we made the trip to that hospital.

Holy Week 1996 was welcomed by the nuns and equally by the girls in the orphanage. The sisters enjoyed the time by going to Mass, Stations of the Cross, and meeting with the sick. The girls went home with their families. Me, well, I stayed at the orphanage but continued teaching catechism to the neighborhood children. When I wasn't teaching the class, I would spend some time in church. I spent my excess time talking with Don Toño, the gardener. He and his wife lived close to the orphanage.

My convulsions didn't occur at a given time, they happened whenever. I had a very bad one—I mean all were bad, but this one occurred when I was on my way to visit Don Toño and his wife when I had it. Don Toño saw when I fell. He rushed over, and I remember him saying the word *Chalma*. Later I learned that Chalma is the Virgin Mary and is revered in the city because they believe that she has performed many miracles within the city. The aged couple kept praying to Chalma to grant them a child. Their prayers were answered when at their advanced age she got pregnant and had a child. At the time, that was the biggest miracle that had occurred.

They carried me into their house and took care of me. The whole family prayed to Chalma and offered their prayers for me. When his wife saw that my eyes were starting to open, she carried out, "Another miracle."

My fifteenth birthday fell on the Sunday of Holy Week. I went to the chapel to give thanks to Diosito for granting me life and asking Him to please grant me more. Sister Paty Galindo invited me to have breakfast with the nuns. That invitation made my day, I was very happy to join the nuns for breakfast. As I entered the eating place, I noticed a birthday cake on the table. Immediately when I entered, the nuns sang the birthday song to me. Apparently they knew that my favorite plate was chilaquiles with red chili because that is what they served me. They also presented me with a pair of tennis shoes, which I couldn't afford but dearly needed for gym class.

Sister Mar told me that she had another surprise for me. She handed me a little box in the presence of Sisters Veronica and Paty. She told me, "Sister Adoración brought this with her when she came with you the day you came to stay with us. Sister Adoración told me how significant this is for you." It was the medal that Reyna had placed on my hand the day in the hospital when she thought that she was dying. It was the eighteen-carat gold medal with the Sacred Heart of Jesus on one side and the Blessed Virgin Mary on the other side. Sister Mar put the chain with the medal around my neck. She told me, "This is your day, I don't want you to do anything." I tried to hold back my tears of joy with somewhat success. I left the eatery very happy not knowing what my day would be like. I heard the dogs bark. In an instant I let them out of their cage to play with them.

We ran and ran. Sultan enjoyed playing with me. He wrestled with me, he hugged me and kissed me. I could sense that he really liked me. I began to tire and didn't want to have a convulsion, so I lay down on the bench to rest. I held the medal in my hand and kissed it, I looked up to the cloudless sky, the canaries were singing, and the doorbell broke the silence and the tranquil moment I was enjoying.

Sister Mar came out to see who was at the gate. On her way to the gate, she asked me to feed the chickens. The preprepared food for the chickens was nothing more than wet tortillas. I started feeding and singing to the chickens. According to some of the neighbors, a happy chicken lays more eggs than an unhappy one. My singing probably didn't entice them to lay more, but I sure enjoyed singing to them. Sister Mar interrupted my singing, "Yovani." She told me to wash my hands, that I had company.

Tere Barrera and her friend had come to wish me a happy birthday. They sang to me and handed me a couple of presents. They gave me a ring made of white gold and a huge stuffed teddy bear. In addition they gave some clothes and a backpack and a cake. Later in the day, the rest of the Barrera Family came by, and so did Don Victor and his wife, Hugo, the Porras family, Don José Luis and his wife, Doña Pilar, and Don Rito. Each of the families brought with them food and a present for me. I received gold earrings, perfume, a hand-woven cape with my initials on it, some money, and many other gifts.

That day on my birthday, I became friends with the son of Señor Porras. That boy gave me his own personal ring and put it on my finger. He said, "Jovani, I know that I'm younger than you, but when I get married, I want to marry a girl like you." By 10:30, people were beginning to disperse. After everybody left, I went to my room, but I was full of energy and couldn't sleep. I opened the window to glance at the moon. Madre Mar must have heard that I was restless. "Jovani, I see that you are still awake, that's good because I didn't want to wake you up. Jovani, the dinero your friends gave you amounts to two thousand pesos." I asked her to save it for me along with the other money I had saved.

However, it seems that when something good happens to me, a setback follows. The following day, I was sitting on my favorite bench under the tree. I was reading a book, admiring the sky all the while kissing my medal, the one my father gave me. The main gate doorbell rang, which was like a signal for the dogs to start barking. "Yovani," Sister Mar shouted, "put the dogs in their cage, then come for the key to open the door." The young novice nuns and twelve students from the academy led by Sister Corazon had come to celebrate my birthday.

They had come unannounced, but we had enough food for everybody. After the celebration, I reached for my medal. It was gone. I didn't have it around my neck! I panicked. Sister Mar noticed the shock displayed on my face. I shared with everybody when the last time I had touched my medal. We looked everywhere, but we didn't find it. Even Sultán was looking. I had lost the only reminder of my father. I cried for a moment, then I said, "Diosito, I might have lost the medal, but I have not lost the desire to meet my father, Jorge Bustos."

The school was back in session, the short-lived March vacation was a memory. I was selected by my classmates to be the flag bearer for the school. Again as many times in the past, my illness kept me from complying with such a big honor. The school was one of the best in the whole district and was invited to participate in numerous events. Another opportunity was lost, my convulsions made it impossible to participate.

Living in the orphanage was an experience I will treasure forever. Besides being in a secure place, I witnessed abused children mainly from the mountain indigenous people being taken care of by the people of the pueblo. I was walking to my room after teaching one of my catechism classes; I heard the sound of a child crying. I opened the gate. I was surprised to see three little kids huddled together in front of the door. I asked them for their parents, they didn't answer, they just looked at me with sad eyes. The baby was a cute little boy. He had a note attached to his crib made of cardboard.

I ran to inform Sister Mar. The mother had left her three girls and a boy on the doorstep of the orphanage. Sister Mar read the note. The note didn't say much that made sense. One of the little girls spoke, but I didn't understand much either. What she said was that she didn't know the baby boy. We took them in, gave them a bath, and checked them for lice. I saw the two little girls and thought of my two sisters. Sister Mar informed the president of the pueblo. Within three days, the investigators brought the mother over to the orphanage.

The mother declared that her husband had been abusive and actually had killed their other children. The three children stayed in the orphanage. Sister Mar asked the president of the pueblo if she could help the mother secure a job. Through the effort of Sister

Mar, the mother was given a government job. I never learned what happened to the father.

The three-year-old girl was baptized and given the name Petrita. The other two Nohemi and Sinahi. They were also baptized with their given names. Petrita knew how to pray the rosary, including the mysteries. The church allowed them to make their first communion along with the other children that were ready. The mother of the abandoned children would visit them every week, and each visit she would bring me fresh fruits.

The people that I met, the acquaintances that I made proved to be beneficial to the orphanage. When the people came to visit, occasionally they would ask me if I needed anything. I would always tell them that we needed clothes and shoes for the girls. We needed powdered milk and toys for the children. I never asked anything for me, only for the orphanage. Sister Mar was very grateful for all the things that I did for orphanage. I was more grateful to her for giving me a secure home and education.

She made us a big meal when we finished the school year. I had three more years before I would be cast out into the real world. To prepare myself, I started taking college classes at CBTIS. At the college I earned the premier place in education and in geometry nationwide. I was elected as the representative for CBTIS in education. I was awarded 3,500 pesos for being the top student of the class. I was befriended by Cristi, a girl who worked at the school. Upon receipt of my qualifications and having passed all the exams, I shared the news with Cristi. In time I met her husband, a professional photographer. Both of them treated me with love and friendship. They wanted to adopt me, but Sister Mar resisted. Cristi was from Costa Chica. Many times when I had a convulsion, Cristi was at my side.

Graduation: Myself in the Garden

THE WORST CONVULSION I CAN remember having was during a history class. I was about to give my presentation, I walked to the front of the class, suddenly I started to feel sick. I fell and hit my head on the same spot where I had sustained a bad cut before. I lost a lot of blood. The only person that came to help me was Cristi. I don't know why none of the other students came to assist me. Maybe because I was from the orphanage, and they didn't know how to help me. For whatever reason, they didn't, and thank my Diosito for Cristi. Doña Conchita was another person from the school who helped me, besides Cristi. Doña Conchita used to sell her food to the students from CBTIS, and she supplied me with the lunch, which I shared with another girl.

When I turned sixteen, I knew that my stay at the orphanage was coming to an end. I prepared myself to continue my life away from the security of the orphanage I called home. I had no idea where I was going afterward, but I had to be ready. Many of the students that called the orphanage home, even if it was only during school year, would leave the orphanage before their eighteenth birthday. They survived, and so would I. Yes, I was alone, and no, I would never return to my pueblo, not as long as Mother and the lecherous old man lived there.

My First Boyfriend: A Sweet Indecisive Love

I WAS SIXTEEN, AND SOON I would be facing the world alone. It was also an age when I met my first serious boyfriend. He was different than most others who had asked me to be their girlfriend. He was very quiet and respectful. He was in the same class with me. On the first day of class, we were paired to do our studies together. We introduced ourselves; his name was Rafael Reyes Cantoran. I used the name *Rosita Jovani Reza*. We became friends because I allowed him to copy the homework. He gave me the excuse that he didn't have time to study. I never asked why, feeling that eventually he would tell me, but I felt that he had to work because he missed a lot of classes.

On the day of the first exam, we had a problem. He wanted my help during the exam, but I couldn't help him because mine was an oral exam. Ever since I was a little girl, I was given oral exams. I usually become very nervous during an examination. The doctors claimed that it was caused by my epilepsy, and they believed that it was also a result of feeling alone most of the time. The results were better when given an oral exam than when I took written exams, and it showed during examination time.

I was eating just outside the classroom thinking that my nickname should have been *Sola*, meaning alone. Funny thing, Rafael approached and asked, "Why are you sitting alone?" My mouth was full as I had just taken a big bite of my taco. I smiled. "Rafa, you startled me."

"Rafa?" he asked, "Is that what you are calling me?"

"I'm going to call you Rafa, is that okay?"

"That's okay, many people call me *Rafa*. Well then, I will call the most beautiful girl Rosi. I ask you, why is the most beautiful, intelligent, and studious girl in the school eating alone?"

He sat next to me, took out his lunch. "Rosi, am I permitted to sit next to you?" I wanted to respond, but he wouldn't let me. He sat next to me anyway. "Rosi, continue being who you are, please don't change. You are a very sincere and responsible girl. I would like to talk to you, but the bell is going to ring any moment. I can't meet you after class either. Can I come to your house, I want to talk about the assignment. Tell me where you live, and I will go to your house. This way I can meet your family."

"Rafa," I said with teary eyes, "I don't have a family."

"What? Come on, don't kid with me, how can that be?" He noticed the tears, he grabbed my hand. "Then where do you live?"

"Rafael, don't ask any more questions." I pulled my hand away, and nervously I ran a little late into my class. I felt relieved when I sat at my chair because the teacher wasn't in class yet. A few moments the school administrator came to our class and announced that the teacher was not holding class due to personal reasons.

All the students left the room except me. Rafael came into the classroom. I thought, *Why don't you leave me alone?* But my heart was pounding very hard hoping that he would stay. "Rosita, please permit me to speak, I am not a bad person. I really want to be your friend."

"Rafael, I am trying to do my homework."

"Rosi, I prefer that you call me by the name *Rafa*, most of my friends know me by that name. Can I talk to you, please?" I felt as though I was about to hear a sermon from the priest, but I was ready to listen. He told me where he lived. He lived with his mother and Toño, a younger brother. They have a clothing business. He told me more of his life story. When he finished, he wanted to know where I lived.

I wasn't ashamed that I lived in the orphanage; in fact, I was very proud to say that I lived there. However, I couldn't understand why he wanted to know. So I asked him. He wanted to know where I lived because he would be very happy to give me a ride home. He told me that he had a car and knew how to drive. I was surprised. I asked, "You have a car? You also want to be my friend, but why? Rafa, I walk alone to the orphanage because I am the only one from there that comes to school here."

"You live in the orphanage, you really live there?" I nodded my head. "Yes, that is where I live." Again he grabbed my hands, his were warm, and they felt very nice. "Aye, Rafa, you sure like to hold my hand, don't you?" I smiled. "Then, Rosi, you are going to be a nun? No, you can't, please tell me that you are not going to be a nun."

"Rafa, my dream has always been to become a nun." He squeezed my hands. "Please tell me that you are not going into the convent."

He let go of my hands, moved them to his forehead. He moved his head back with his hands. "Oh, God," he said, something else I didn't quite understand. He talked to the ceiling, loud enough for me to hear. "Rosita, you are the only girl that I have felt something in my heart for, and you tell me that you are going to become a nun." *Hmm, I'm going to let him talk some more before I tell him the truth,* I thought. He let go of my hands. "When will you be leaving to wherever girls go to become nuns? Rosi, I told Mother all about you and how I felt every time I saw you. She wants to meet you, but now I'm not sure." I was smiling. I made sure that he saw. "Rosita, your smile tells me that you are very happy with your decision in becoming a nun."

"Rafa, now you listen to me. Yes, I told you that my desire always was to become a nun. You didn't let me finish. I was not accepted, I can't be a nun because of my epilepsy." He gave me a hug, which took me completely by surprise. I pushed him back. "Rafa, nobody hugs me, especially a man. Don't ever do that again." I grabbed my backpack and ran out of the classroom. I didn't know what I was thinking, I had reacted like a child. My heart was pounding. I thought, *Why did I act like that? He is a nice guy, he means no harm.*

The next day, I went early, I needed to talk to Cristi. She would give me advice on how to act; after all, Rafa was a nice person. I surprised her when I walked into her office. "Rosita, what are you up to so early this morning?"

"Cristi, I need some advice, and you are the only person I can confide in."

"Okay, Rosita, which boy is making your heart beat faster?"

"Oh, Cristi, how do you know?"

"Aha, some boy has made an impression on you. Tell me, what do you want to know about boys? Come on, tell me and get that thorn out of your chest, you can confide in me." I told her about Rafa. "I have trouble talking nice to him, I want to, but I don't. Instead of talking nice to him, I reject him, why? I really want him to be my friend."

"Rosita, there's a difference between being a friend and a boyfriend. Which do you want? Remember, you are seventeen years old, and soon you must leave the orphanage. You don't have family here, so I suggest that you make some friends you can rely on for when you leave the orphanage. Tell me, are you going to be able to go on your own?"

"Cristi, I don't know what is going to happen to me after I leave the orphanage, it had been my home for almost eight years. I will not return to my pueblo, so I really don't have any idea, but my Chuchin will guide me."

"Rosita, I know Rafael. He seems like a nice person. Talk to him, tell him what you just told me."

"Cristi, I will talk to him after the class is over." I walked out of her office feeling unsure how to approach Rafa.

I sought Rafa after class, hoping to speak to him. I got cold feet, and instead I went into Cristi's office. She wasn't in her office, so I went over to my favorite place, my little corner of the world. I started to unpack my lunch, but I stopped when I saw Rafa approaching. My heart pounded with excitement. For a moment neither of us spoke, we just looked at each other. "Rosita, forgive me for pestering you." I gestured him to stop with a raised my hand. "Sit down, Rafa, I need to talk." He didn't listen; rather, he grabbed my hand. "Rosita, I can't keep this inside of me any longer, I am in love with you." My heart beat even faster. *What am I supposed to do now?* I thought. Instead, these words came out of my mouth, "Rafa, why did you tell me that? I am the daughter of no one, I have this sickness. Rafa, there is no room in my heart for you or in my feelings. My health and my form of living do not permit me to accept your love."

I cried, my tears were flowing from the bottom of my heart, I was shaking for fear of losing him, but I couldn't tell him how I felt about him. I cried because I didn't want to say what I did, and I couldn't take those words back. I didn't want to reject him, but I did. "Rosita, I love you, and I am prepared to help you in any way that I can. Don't reject me using your sickness as an excuse, let me help you. Look at me, and tell me that you will accept me as your boyfriend."

"Rafa, please understand, I still desire to become a nun, so please do me a favor, don't interfere by trying to become my boyfriend."

Rafa left without saying a word, with head downcast. My heart continued to pound even faster, and my tears flowed more freely when he left me sitting in the little corner of my world. I thought, *I can't chain anyone to me with this sickness, I just can't. I want to be married to my Diosito.*

I couldn't stop thinking of Rafa. Late that night I made up my mind to speak to Rafa. I don't know what I would say, but I wanted to see him. Next day I sought him out, but he was not in school. I talked to Sister Mar once again about my desire to become a nun. I was hoping that she would change her mind. No, she was of the same mind-set; I was rejected once again because of my health. Sadness overcame me, my heart needed someone to speak with. Where was Rafa? I needed to see him. I wandered toward the pigsty, it stunk really bad. Strange, but the stench had never bothered me before. I felt faint, I thought I was going to faint.

"Yovani, Yovani," I heard Sister Mar calling me. I was too weak with emotion, I tried to answer her call. I had a convulsion. I kept thinking about my future away from the orphanage, that problem was always on my mind. I had no future as a nun. Now Rafa was nowhere to be seen. Am I to wander the world alone forever? My future is in the hands of my Diosito, I have faith that He will show me the way. Sister Pati was dedicated to the Lord, she tried to console me. She didn't have the same worries that plagued me. Another nun, Sister Veronica, was transferred to another convent. Sister Edith was sent to replace Sister Veronica.

Sister Edith, being the new nun in the orphanage, was given the laundry duty. I helped whoever was on duty. Sister Edith and I met at the laundry for the first time. We became friends, she was the youngest nun in the orphanage. I told her that she was the youngest nun that had been assigned to the orphanage. I wanted to know how long she had been a nun, so I asked her. She didn't respond, she smiled, and I could tell that she was thinking. She stretched her arms toward the sky. "Rosita Jovani, why do you ask me that?"

I looked at her. "You know who I am? Nobody calls me Rosita or Jovani."

"Sure, Rosita. When I arrived here, I saw you. You are different than all the other girls, so I asked around. Another sister told me who you were and gave me your name. She didn't tell me where you came from though. So, Rosita, where did you live before coming to the orphanage?"

"Sister, I come from Tetipac, Guerrero."

"What!" She dropped her basket half full of clothes. "Rosita, you come from Tetipac?" I thought it strange that she would be surprised that I was from Tetipac.

"Yes, Sister Edith, I come from Tetipac, why are you surprised?"

"I got nervous when I heard where you are from because I come from Chonta."

"Sister Edith, you come from Chonta?"

"Yes, I come from Chonta, and so does my boyfriend."

"Sister Edith, you have a boyfriend, and you are a nun, how can that be?" She wanted to cry; instead, she forced a smile. She placed her hands in front of her mouth and semiwhispered, "My father doesn't like my boyfriend. My father and my boyfriend's father don't like each other. I told my father that I loved my boyfriend and that we intended to get married to each other, he got very angry."

"Your father got angry because you wanted to get married?"

"Yes, Rosita, he was so mad he took me to the convent against my will. He forced me to become a nun, I didn't want to be a nun, I wanted to get married and become a mother. I became a nun just two months ago."

"Sister Edith," I asked her, "are you happy being a nun?"

"No, Rosita, I am not, but each day I pray to God for his help."

"Oh, Sister Edith, life is really complicated, here I am with the desire to become a nun, but they won't accept me. Now you are a nun and desires to be a wife and a mother. I would love to trade places with you and be a nun. Sister Edith, you are of legal age, aren't you? Nobody—not your father or mother or anybody else—can force you to be something that you don't want to be. Your father can't force you to be a nun." She told me that she and her boyfriend write to each other all the time.

Several days later, I ran into a very excited Sister Edith. "Rosita, come with me, I want to speak to you in private." She grabbed me by my hand and hurried to her room. "Rosita, Sister Mar has given me permission to visit my pueblo. Rosita, you are right, I'm of legal age, and my father cannot legally force me to do what he wants. Nobody can force me to do things that I don't accept. I'm going to my pueblo and speak with the love of my life. I will make the decision whether I remain a nun or get married and become a mother."

"Sister Edith, God will accompany you in my prayers. Sister, if you are not happy being a nun, you will not be able to serve Diosito in the manner He deserves. God be with you, I'll pray that you make the right decision."

I left her room, my tears waited until I left her room. I went into the chapel. I said, "Chuchin, he that can doesn't, he that can't is left wanting." I never saw Sister Edith again; apparently she made the right decision for her. Sister Amparito, a little old nun, replaced the young Sister Edith. Sister Amparito was a sweet sixty-six-year-old lady who was very nearsighted. When I spoke freely with her, she told me that she had been a nun for most of her life.

Soon after she arrived, she had an experience that I will never forget. She knew her music and wanted to teach music lessons to the students. She was told that the orphanage had an old piano that nobody had played in quite some time. She made it known that she would play the piano for us. The date was set, and we all walked into the library where the piano was located.

Some of us stood while others sat in the available chairs. Sister Amparito started to warm up hitting the piano keys. Some of the keys were not sounding right. Sister Amparito tried to open the piano. At first she couldn't, then after a while, she pushed the top of the piano really hard. The moment the top of the piano flew open, dozens of rats busted out of the piano. "Rats! Oh my, rats!" She screamed again and fell to the floor. The girls shouted "Rats!" and ran out of the library as fast as they could. I checked on her, she had fainted. I ran to the kitchen and grabbed an onion. I ran back and placed a piece of the onion near her nose. Sister Mar entered the library and saw Sister Amparito on the floor with me administering the onion on her nose.

"Yovani, what happened to Sister Amparito?" I answered, "She fainted. When she opened the top of the piano, a bunch of rats jumped out, they were living inside the piano. They scared Sister Amparito, and she fainted." Sister Mar left the library in a hurry. She returned with camphor oil, applied the oil to her nose. Sister Amparito opened her eyes looking a little shaky. "Oh dear Lord, those rats scared me. I have never liked rats, and when I saw them jump from inside the piano, I must have fainted."

"Sister Amparito, I am so sorry, but nobody plays the piano, so we had no idea that rats were living inside it. But now I will have the janitor get rid of the rats, and he will clean the piano."

Arrival of Sister Carmela

SISTER MAR HAD TO LAUGH. She asked, "Are your bones okay, nothing broken?" Sister Amparito also laughed. She said, "I know those rats meant no harm, but I still don't like them." I didn't dare laugh, but inwardly I was smiling just thinking how Sister Amparito reacted when she saw the rats. Soon after the rat incident, Sister Amparito asked for a transfer and was granted. Before she left, she confided in me that she was leaving because of the rats and no other reason. She gave me her blessing before she departed for Monterey.

Sister Carmela was different, personalitywise, than all the other nuns that I knew. Not only was she different, she turned out to be one of my worst nightmares. She replaced Sister Amparito. A few days after her arrival, I noticed that she was treating me different than she did the other girls. Late one afternoon she approached the chicken coop where I was feeding the chickens. I was thinking of my future and busy feeding the chickens, I didn't hear her approach.

I was startled when I heard her say, "Hear me, Yovani." I turned to face her, I greeted her. She didn't return my greeting. Instead I was greeted with, "Who do you think you are?" I was surprised with that question, and kiddingly I answered, "I am Rosita Yovani Reza, and I come from Tangamandapio."

"Don't make fun of me," she said, "I am not like the rest of the nuns. I come to ask you something that appears rather strange. Why does Sister Marcito favor you? You are not from here, nor are you an indigenous native like all the other girls. I've noticed that you are always number one on her list, why?"

I was puzzled by her attitude, so I didn't know how to respond. I did ask her why she was asking me questions that I couldn't answer. I suggested that she ask Sister Mar. Sister Carmela said, "I can't accept that. Tell me, what is your motive for being here? You are not from the mountains." Before I could say anything, she raised her hand to stop me. "Yovani, don't say anything. Listen to me and listen carefully, I am not going to permit your help with the girls that help me. I am warning you that things are going to be different for you from now on. Remember what I'm about to tell you. There are other girls here besides you, and they deserve the same opportunity besides you. Are you listening?"

"Yes, Sister Carmela, I heard you, and may I say that you need to go for a blessing? I can't believe that you are a nun after talking to me with that attitude. Are you really a nun?" She made a turn and left me standing with a puzzled look on my face. I thought back at all the other nuns who have helped me during my lifetime. Sister Sarita, Adoracion, Mar, and others. *This one wants to destroy me.* With a heavy heart, I sang, "I am the daughter of no one..."

The following Sunday, Sister Carmela approached me. She didn't greet me with the usual but rather with a pinch on my arm. "Follow me and don't say anything." I followed her to Sister Mar's office. "Sister Marcita, Yovani doesn't feel well. I know that she goes with you on Sundays for groceries and do other errands. But I don't want her to get sick while she's with you. I recommend that she stay here. Why don't you take Lupita or Aida? I will stay behind and take care of Yovani and the other girls."

I was stunned, but what could I say? I was saddened by Sister Carmela's actions. Sister Mar gave me a hug. She said, "Yovani, go to your room and rest, Sister Carmela will take care of you." She and one of the girls left for the market without me. "Come, Alma de Dios," Sister Carmela said laughing, "isn't that what others call you?" Still laughing she said, "I beat you, didn't I? This won't be the last time, so prepare yourself because you are just beginning to know me. I am going to make life miserable for you until they kick you out of here. Where will you go, think about it. Do you think that your people will take you in? Oh, I forget, you don't have a family, you can't be a nun, so where will you go?" I couldn't understand why she was treating me this way. She truly was a living nightmare.

I felt a change in the way Sister Mar was treating me also. Apparently Sister Carmela was spreading lies about me. Sister Carmela told Sister Mar that some of the girls were missing their hygiene supplies and that I had them in my locker. Without investigating, Sister Mar took her word, and she punished me for the first time since I'd been at the orphanage. The bad nightmare continued spreading lies about me. This time she went around the neighbors and told them lies about me. The ones that hurt the most is what she told the Pilar and the Porras families. They had been some of my strongest supporters.

My convulsions became more frequent, I couldn't sleep at night, only cried. Nobody could help me. Her poisonous lies eventually forced Sister Pati, once my friend, to stay away from me. That wasn't enough, Sister Carmela eventually drove Sister Pati away from the orphanage. Apparently as I found out later, it was because Sister Pati stood up for me. My nightmare nun told me, "See now, Sister Marcita is on my side, soon I will have you kicked out of here. Yovani, now I ask you, *who are you?* Now you know who I am, I am your nightmare.

"I told you that Sister Marcita believes everything I tell her. Well, I just told her that you have a boyfriend. She in turn had told the families that help you with your medicine that you are not the nice person you appear to be, that you have a boyfriend. I am not finished. In time I will let everybody know that you make fun of the girls and all of the nuns in the orphanage. When they hear that about you, we'll see who will accept you."

I stared at my nightmare. "You call yourself a nun? You dress like one, but you don't deserve to use it, you have a rosary for what, to deceive the people? How can you pray to my Diosito? You cannot deceive Him, the one that is being deceived is you." I cleaned my tears, I was angry. "Your poisonous words have hurt my clean reputation. You say that Sister Mar is on your side and that she will run me out of here. I am going to speak with the Bishop Alejo Zabala Castro. He will discover the type of nun that you are. He will help me send a letter to Sister Corazon. We will see whether you remain a nun or not." She grabbed me by my hair. "Don't try to make trouble for me. If you do that, it will be a war, and I will beat the life out of you."

I struggled to understand how a person like her had ever become a nun. I think to myself and wonder why she is a nun and I can't become one. The night was long, daylight would never arrive; somehow I fell asleep. When I woke up the following morning, I didn't feel like going to school. The noise of rain descending on the orphanage changed my mind. I loved walking in the rain. I felt that somehow the rain cleared all the dark moments of my recent past. I dressed looking forward to walking in the rain. My Diosito sent this rain to clear my mind, I thought. I walked to the edge of the swollen river, took the first leap to the nearest rock, then another and another. I sat there on top of that rock, soaking wet, crying the tears mixing with the rain.

"Rosita!" I heard someone call my name. I turned to see the lady that sells food to the students. "Rosita, what are you doing in the middle of the river in this downpour? Mija, can I help you get to the riverbank?"

"No, señora, I'm okay, don't worry about me. I needed to speak with Cristi, I trust her, she will guide me." I told the lady that I wouldn't be able to work with her today. She understood, didn't ask me for a reason, that's the way she was. I jumped two more rocks, and with added energy, I set off to see Cristi.

I entered Cristi's office, my hair soaking wet, and the rain gear hadn't kept the rest of me dry. "Rosita, look at you, you are going to get sick." My smile told her that I was okay, I took off my trench coat. She took it from me and hung it out of my sight. That morning, I spilled the whole truth about Sister Carmela. Cristi was so angry, she told me that she was going to charge Sister Carmela with child abuse. Just then a certain so-called classmate by the name of Rafa was passing by. He saw Cristi hugging me, entered the room thinking that something was wrong.

"Cristi," he asked, "is something wrong with Rosi? Can I help?"

"Rafael, let her be, all I can tell you is that this girl is a special person. If you want to help, treat her like the grand person that she is. Help her like you would help a special classmate." She turned to me. "Rosita," she said, "talk with Rafa, he doesn't mean to harm you, he is a good person, you can trust him. Don't be afraid, he will always respect you and who you are." I must've looked like a wet and nervous little girl when he took my hand.

"What is the matter, can I help you with anything? Rosi, you are all wet, let me go to our store and bring you some clothes. If you would rather go to your house, I'll take you." I stood still, dumb as could be, not saying a word. He took his jacket off and wrapped it around my shoulders. "Rosita, it really hurts to see you like this. You aren't going to tell me what happened to you?"

"Rafa, I am in a situation where I can't accept you as a friend nor can I accept your jacket. Thank you for being a good friend." Rafa looked very unhappy and somewhat sad; he turned and walked away.

That day, Cristi spoke with the director of the school. She told him how I was being treated by Sister Carmela. The director called me into his office. In front of Cristi, he told me that he was not going to allow that treatment to continue any further. He let me know that they felt very bad for the treatment I was receiving from that nun. "Cristi and I are setting off for the orphanage now to speak with Sister Marcita. If she tells you to leave, we are ready to adopt you immediately."

Sister Mar met us at the front of the orphanage. "Yovani, look at you, my, you are all wet." The director and Cristi greeted Sister Mar rather warmly, I would say. She returned a warm greeting herself. "Sister Marcita, we wish to speak with you."

"Yes, of course, what's this about?"

"Sister, it's about the bad treatment that Rosita, or Yovani as you know her, has been receiving from Sister Carmela." Sister Mar started to get nervous. "Yovani, why don't you go change while we talk." Cristi spoke up, "Sister, we would rather have Yovani present during this conversation." Sister Mar showed her irritation but relented to have me in on the conversation.

After the conversation, we all felt relieved. Cristi and the director left satisfied with the action that Sister Mar was going to take to quell the problem with Sister Carmela. I in turn felt that I still had a home at the orphanage and Sister Carmela would no longer bother me. "Yovani," Sister Mar said, "I cannot mistrust Sister Carmela—

after all, she is a nun. I feel really bad that I have listened to her and the way she has treated you. Yovani, you still have a home here, I have always told you that, and I mean it. But you are well aware that your days here at the orphanage are coming to a close."

"Yes, Sister Mar, I think about that every day. But I thank you from the bottom of my heart for giving me a home for all of these years. I also have been thinking about my future away from here. Am I allowed to have a boyfriend?" The words just blurted out of my mouth. She looked at me. "Yovani, are you thinking of having a boyfriend? You don't have to answer, that depends on you and you alone. I will pray that you find a nice young man to share your life with. Your vocation that of a married woman will become a reality." She finished talking, turned around, and went into the chapel. I was left alone, but my thoughts were far away from the orphanage and closer to Rafa.

A Visit to My Pueblo

THE SPRING BREAK WAS NEARING, and I had made plans to visit my sister. I would be returning to the place where I grew up until the age of ten, when I left for the orphanage. I hadn't seen Rafa since the day he loaned me his jacket. But I was preoccupied getting ready for my visit. Don Toño, my friend and gardener, gave me a box for my clothes. I didn't own a suitcase, so the box would serve me well. I packed my clothes and some toys and clothes for my niece. I had saved enough money to pay for my bus fare. Going home after all these years was like riding an emotional roller coaster. I thought of all my friends and how glad I would be to see them. Then the two that made life miserable would pop up in my brain.

I was so happy when I got to my pueblo. The changes that I saw were to some extent acceptable to me, while others were not. Everything seemed so different, so many people that I didn't recognize. But when I saw the steeple of my church, I dropped my box, covered my mouth with both my hands, and cried. I carried my stuff to my church where I prayed to my Chuchin and to the Blessed Virgin Mary. I thanked them for my living and for always being with me. After I finished my prayers, I left for Ana's house.

She was waiting for me inside her house. She opened the door the very moment I rang the doorbell. I felt the love when we hugged each other that I hadn't felt in a long time. Claudia, my niece, gave me a loving hug as well. Ana had a meal prepared, and I was glad because I was really hungry. We were eating when Ana told me that she had a surprise for me. "Really," I asked, "what kind of surprise?" Ana said, "I will tell you as soon as you finish eating."

"Why wait, tell me now."

"Vani, if I tell you now, you won't eat." I looked at her. "Ana, don't tell me that Mamacita is here."

She laughed. "Vani, is that what you think? I will tell you after we eat, okay?" I agreed not to pester her. We talked and talked. She brought me up to date on all of the people that I knew. I in turn told her about life in the orphanage, some information about Rafa, and Cristi, my friend. When we finished eating, she said, "Vani, our grandmother Sinforosa is going to be very happy to see you."

"Mamacita is here? I knew it, I knew that she was here."

"Yes, Vani, she is here, and she wants to see you. She asks for you all the time, she waits for you, go see her. Claudia will go with you so you won't go alone."

The moment we saw each other at her doorstep, we embraced, we cried and held on to each other for a long time. My cries were loud and full of meaning. "I love you, Mamacita, I love you with all my heart." I feel that Mamacita is the one person who loves me with all her heart. "My baby mija, let me see you." She held me at arm's length. "Mija, you have grown so beautiful, you are a grown woman. You are more beautiful than ever." My crying wouldn't allow me to speak. She kept looking at me. "Niña, you look so much like Jorge, your father." Upon hearing those words, I cried even harder. I had to embrace her, I couldn't let go, I wanted to be in her arms.

"Jovani, come sit with me. I don't want you to get sick."

"Claudia, I forgot that you were here, forgive me." Mamacita took some money from her purse, gave it to Claudia. "Hija, I want to speak with Jovani alone, take this money go buy something for yourself." Claudia left us alone. "Mamacita, you know that Jorge is my father. For the first time I have been told who my father is. Mamacita, tell me about my father, I want to know everything about him." That day she told me that she knew him. She also told me that she always intended on telling me, but was waiting until I was older. She was waiting because Reyna had threatened to harm her if she did.

"Jovani, I wanted to tell you when I heard you singing in the bus. Your voice reminded me so much of him. He had a beautiful voice. His favorite song was 'Que diran los de tu casa cuando…'" Inspired with the information, with tears streaming down my cheeks,

I sang her the song. She had heard me sing that song almost eight years ago in the bus, and we had sung that song in her llano. "Jovani, your voice is more beautiful now than the last time I heard you sing. Jovani, you are truly my granddaughter. Your father, Jorge, and your grandfather Domingo would be so proud of you. Jovani, you are a very gifted person."

"Mamacita, what else can you tell me about my father?"

"Hija, I have a surprise for you. I will tell you about Jorge while I show you something I have for you." She asked me to move the dish cabinet away from the wall. Behind the cabinet was a brick wall. I removed one of the bricks as instructed. "There are some keys behind that brick, give them to me," she instructed. "These keys will open my trunk that I have hidden between the ceiling and the roof." She opened the ladder, climbed up the attic, and took the trunk. From the trunk she took a large bag full of money, mostly coins. "Jovani, half is for you, and the other half is for the sisters from the orphanage that take care of you."

"Mamacita, why do you give me so much? I came to see you and not for you to give me money."

"*Hay caramba*, Jovani, you haven't changed that much, you still argue with me.

"Jovani, now you get up and bring down the other trunk." I tried to pick it up, but it was too heavy. "Mamacita, it's too heavy, I can't lift it."

"Okay, mija, underneath the money, there are some very valuable papers, try to get them." I was able to get all the papers. I handed them to Mamacita. "Mija, I want you to see these papers." She opened a large envelope and took out some papers. "These papers name you as the heir to my properties. It's a testament declaring you as the owner of my property upon my death. This other document is the bank statement where I have money saved." She showed me a small bankbook with a photo of her fingerprint. Mamacita didn't know how to write, and the bank regarded her fingerprints as legitimate. "Alma de Dios, if the bastards from the bank don't want to release my money to you, show them this card with my fingerprints.

"The treasure that I have hidden, you know where that is because I have taken you there many times. That money is to stay there until some fortunate individual finds it. Your uncles have plenty of property because Domingo gave them their share of his properties. Rosita, I don't want you to climb up here anymore, I don't want you to get hurt."

"Mamacita, I don't want any of the money in the attic. I want your prayers and your love above any money you give me."

"Mija, my Alma de Dios, my prayers always are for you, and my love you will have forever. Even when I kick the bucket, I will be dead to the rest of the people, but I will always be with you. My body will die, but my soul will be with life always at your side. You have suffered much, but you have remained strong, and I want you to continue your strong faith in God." Mamacita placed the papers under my blouse. I asked, "Mamacita, explain again the paper that states that it is a testimony."

"Okay, mija, listen carefully, that paper states that you will be the owner of all my properties. I am the legitimate owner of the property that your grandfather Domingo Bustos left me. That same property I am giving it to you and to the orphanage.

"Nobody can take this property away from you. Not Reyna and that miserable man that lives with her can take it away from you." Mamacita pounded her chest, she was angry. "Domingo worked these properties with sweat and hard work and took good care of them. This is the reason that I am giving them to you. I know that you will take care of them. When you go back to the orphanage, show these papers to the nun in charge. Tell her to read them. I am giving them a portion of the property for taking care of you. When I die, you will be the heir to the property your grandpa Domingo left me." I understood some of what she told me. But one thing for sure, I knew that these papers were valuable. Claudia arrived happy with the things she bought for herself.

She had prepared a meal for us. The three of us ate and talked and talked. Mamacita wanted to know more of my life with the nuns. She was unhappy for me when I told her that I couldn't become a nun and the reason being my health. I helped clean after we ate, then it was time to leave. Again we hugged and cried not knowing when we would see each other again. Mamacita made sure the title to the property was secure under my blouse. "Take good care of them, mija, these papers are very valuable."

We had just left her house when I heard my name being called. *Oh dear Lord,* I thought. I recognized Reyna's voice. I turned around, my legs started to shake, it was Reyna with the lecherous old man and their son. My mother started to walk closer to me, I grabbed Claudia by the hand and ran. Claudia asked, "Why are we running away from Grandma?"

"Claudia, run and don't ask, just run." We entered the house seemingly out of breath. "Vani, why are you in such a hurry? You are going to get sick." Ana was right. I started to feel weak. She gave me a glass of water, I had a convulsion.

When I came to, for a moment I didn't remember where I was. Then as I gained my senses, it came to me, *I'm with Ana,* I thought. Ana got close to me. "Vani, what happened? Claudia told me that you ran away from Mother, but she didn't understand why."

"Yes, Claudia is right, I ran into Reyna and that man."

"Did they harm you?"

"No, Ana, Reyna saw me coming out of Mamacita's house and shouted my name. I recognized her voice, turned around to face them. I couldn't bear to talk to them, I grabbed Claudia by her hand, and I ran away from them.

"Ana, I can't stay here as long as those two are in the pueblo, I have to go back to the orphanage."

"Oh, Vani, what a shame, you just arrived, and now you have to leave. But you're right, that man hasn't forgotten you. He wants you and to cause you harm. I know because I heard him say that he would love to take you away from the orphanage. He has tried, but the nuns won't allow him to take you out. That bastard isn't going to let you live in peace. I agree with you, Vani, it's best that you return to your orphanage where you are more secure.

"Vani, relax, and when the time comes, Claudia and I will take to the bus station. You must rest, because you have a big bruise on the back of your head. Those two can't force you to do anything."

Claudia brought me a glass of water. She hugged me. "Aunt," she said, "I love you, take care of yourself. Can't you stay a few more days with us? I will take care of you."

The knock on the door froze me. *It's Reyna*, I thought. "Who is it?" Ana asked. I recognized Reyna's voice. "Ana, don't let her in, please don't let her."

"Vani, don't worry, I will take care of Mother, go into Claudia's room." I hadn't felt this type of fear since I had left the pueblo. I prayed to my Diosito for strength. I took the papers from under my blouse and secured them in my suitcase. Ana opened the door and walked in smiling. "It wasn't Reyna, it's my mother-in-law. Vani, you have to decide whether to stay a few days with us. Reyna won't bother you. We want you to stay."

"Please, Auntie, stay with us, I want to know you better." Claudia was near tears.

I hugged her. "Claudia, as long as those two are here, I won't be safe." My bags were packed. Ana and my niece walked with me to the bus station. They stayed with me until I boarded the last bus out of the pueblo. The fear of staying in the pueblo was stronger than the desire to arrive at the orphanage. I had no other choice. I feared the freedom that awaited me after I left the orphanage, what kind of future awaited me? The trip back home, a place that had given me shelter, was coming to an end. Where will I go, how will I live? The trip appeared long, yet not long enough.

The sound of the doorbell alerted the dogs, my voice aroused them. They jumped the fence and greeted me at the front door. They jumped all over me, licked my face, and they hugged me. Sister Mar opened the gate. She was surprised to see me back. "Yovani," she said, "what happened? I thought you were going home to visit your sister? Tell me, how did these dogs get out of the yard?"

"Sister Mar, they jumped the fence when they heard my voice," I said smiling. "Sister, those two were in the pueblo, and I was afraid to stay. I hope you don't mind, but I had to come back, I couldn't stay there.

"Sister Mar, I beg you to let me stay here until the end of the school year. I have nowhere to go." She answered, "What can I do?

You are here. Yovani, I've been told many negative things about you. Many of your supporters are asking questions, asking if the rumors are true."

"What kind of rumors are you hearing? Sister Mar, you have known me for a long time. I am not a bad person. But tell me, what are you hearing about me?" The nun didn't answer. "Sister Mar," I asked, "if you don't tell me what people are saying about me, how can I defend myself? Sister Mar, you know that these rumors started when Sister Carmela came to the orphanage. What you hear about me are lies. But when lies spread, you can't undo the lies. But you know the truth about me, and someday you will recognize the lies being spread about me."

The lies that Sister Carmela has spread about me are so absurd, how can anybody who knows me believe her? "Yovani, I can't believe that you mistreat people when I send you to the market. I hear that you insult the people in town and that you mistreat the other girls living here."

"Sister Mar, please tell me exactly, how do I insult people?" She started to go into detail when Sister Carmela approached us. Sister Mar spoke, "People have seen you kiss your boyfriend around the school. The girls tell me that you are mean to them, always pulling their hair just to be mean. Sister Carmela has to come to their aid." The pretend nun nodded her head in an affirmative manner. I couldn't hold back the tears any longer; the lies were too difficult to take.

I stared at Sister Carmela. I told her, "Sister Mar taught me that once a lie spreads, you can never recall it. Sister Mar, allow me to speak to the bishop. He will ask Sister Carmela to prove that the rumors are real. She has to tell the truth in front of him." I turned and confronted Carmela. "You have a loose tongue. I can't understand how you can call yourself a nun and wear the robe of a nun." She stood her ground; the look in her eyes reminded me of Reyna. She said, "Yovani, what are you doing here? I thought you had gone away. But being here, don't think that you're going to prevent Sister Mar from going to the seminar. Leave, there's nobody here, all of the girls are gone. Go wherever you want, just leave."

She came close to me as though she wanted to push me out of the door. I could tell that she was very angry. The dogs sensed it too. They growled at her and got between us, prohibiting her from getting close to me. I was surprised but with admiration because someone had come to my defense. Angrily she turned to Sister Mar. "See what this girls is capable of? She has turned the dogs against me. I can only guess what she did to her family. It must have been pretty severe for them to abandon her because none of her family wants her."

"My, Sister Carmela, respect your vocation, don't talk to Yovani like that. Sister, leave us alone, I want to speak with Yovani." She gave an angry stare when she left us, reminded me of the angry bull that tried to gore me. "Yovani, today I will speak with Mother Superior, and I will ask her to transfer Sister Carmela to another convent."

"Thank you, Sister Mar, and I will try not to have any contact with Sister Carmela."

We were walking away when I remembered the papers. "Sister, can I ask a big favor from you?"

"Yes, mija," she answered, both of us walking as we spoke. "Sister," I said, "Mamacita gave me some important papers, can you keep them for me?" She answered, "Of course. Why are the papers so important?"

"Sister Mar, my mamacita said that I am to be the heir to all of her property and that this orphanage is also to be part heir as well." She stopped walking, softly grabbed my shoulder. "What did you say?"

"Sister Mar, I don't know exactly what all this means, but Mamacita told me to have you read the papers. She told me that the papers were important because when she dies, it is a testament, whatever that means."

"Hmm," Sister Mar was surprised, "okay, mija, I will read these papers, and I will guard them for you."

"Oh, another thing, Mamacita said that when you read them, you will be a witness of her testament." I opened my suitcase and handed her the papers. "Your grandmother did this for us, but why?"

"Yes, Mamacita wanted to thank you for what you have done for me."

We continued our walk to the house. "Yovani, I almost forgot, the dogs refuse to eat. Since you left on your trip to the pueblo, they haven't eaten. They will probably eat if you feed them. Go feed them, I'll take your suitcase to your room." The dogs followed me, they were so excited, they knew that I was going to feed them. They ate, they hugged me, and they licked my face; they were real happy with me. I didn't notice Sister Carmela standing behind me. "Hey, Yovani, what are you going to do should these dogs die? Then you will have nobody to defend you." Rambo also noticed her; he growled showing her his fangs. "See, did you see that mean dog? I will buy me one that will defend me against your horrible dogs." Sister Mar returned. "I see my little dogs have eaten," she said. "Yes, Sister, they were real hungry." Sister Carmela wanted to get close to Sister Mar and myself; Sultan growled at her, him too showing her his fangs. Sister Carmela looked at her superior, wanting to say something. Sister Mar stopped her. "Sister Carmela, why don't you leave, not even the dogs like you." She turned and left us alone with the dogs. I smiled within, not wanting to offend anyone.

The people of the pueblo were preparing a surprise birthday for the bishop. The Barrera family was in charge of coordinating the festival. I was invited along with all the nuns and lots of the people from the pueblo. The surprise celebration was a few days away. Every day I thought that I had to speak to the bishop regarding the situation with Sister Carmela. I wanted to free myself of my nightmare. The problem was that I would probably place Sister Mar in an awkward situation.

During the celebration, I had many opportunities to speak with him, but I held back. Each time I got close to the bishop, Sister Carmela would give me the evil eye. That was incentive enough to speak with the bishop, then I would see Sister Mar speaking with the people. I just couldn't do it. After the party was over, Sister Mar, Sister Carmela, and I walked back to the orphanage together. "Yovani, I thought that you were going to speak with the bishop." I gave a big sigh. "Ah, Sister Mar, you have been a savior, you have been my family since I was ten years old. In my heart I could not talk to the bishop and make trouble for you.

"Sister Mar, I have told you that Sister Carmela has made it very difficult for me the last few weeks. If the bishop hears that, he will make trouble for you also. I don't want that for you."

Sister Mar didn't say a word, she grabbed my hand. It was a beautiful moonlit night. I didn't know the time of night, but I figured that it was past eleven o'clock because that's when the birthday celebration ended. I caught a glimpse of the son of Doña Rafa and his girlfriend sitting near the main gate of the orphanage.

For several days after we celebrated the bishop's birthday, I began to notice a change in attitude that Sister Mar had toward me. I didn't know what to think. I was unhappy but didn't know how to approach her. Maybe it was only my imagination. I couldn't turn to anyone for advice, I was alone. But my will to survive was too great. I gave myself pep talks all the time, I prayed to my Chuchin. I would think, *These things will pass, but my Diosito will always be with me.* But some things are more difficult to get rid of. My nightmare was around and not about to make life easy for me.

I tried to stay busy during the weekends to avoid meeting my nightmare. But she wouldn't leave me alone. She approached me when I was cleaning the pigsty. She was showing a wicked smile. "You think that Sister Mar will favor you over me? Think again, she and I have the same vocation, the one you so desire. We are related in that respect, and you, you only wish to be one of us. That will never happen. Don't mess around with me. The people that have helped you are learning that you are a fake. When they hear what I have to say about you, they will stop helping you. Without their help, you will wind up in the street." She left taking her wicked smile with her. I was so angry, I wanted to toss the tortillas at her; instead, I flung them at the pigs.

"That witch has no heart," he said, walking from behind the bushes. He surprised me. The gardener heard everything the make-believe nun said to me. "Yovani, what kind of nun is she? That is not the first time I hear her talking bad to you. Why does she want to cause you harm? I can't believe that she is a nun. I wish I could tell Sister Mar what I just heard, but I might lose my job," he said. "Señor Toño, don't worry, I don't want you to lose your job. Thank you anyway, Señor Toño."

"Yovani, if that wicked nun wants to kick you out of the orphanage, then I will talk to Sister Mar. If she doesn't listen, then I will go to the president of the pueblo."

"Thank you, Señor Toño, and may God bless you."

My little corner of the world was waiting, I walked to my favorite place. There under the tree, I sat to think crying, like so many other times. This time I was worried about my future, my place in the orphanage. I thought of Mamacita and if I would ever see her again. Nobody to turn to, I was alone. *No, I have myself,* I thought, *I will survive because of who I am, I will fight. Diosito is in my corner, and with His guidance, I will prevail.* I wiped my tears and relaxed as I listened to the sound of the canaries singing. The atmosphere became more tranquil, my thoughts drifted back in time to my pueblo.

The barking of the dogs broke the silence. Sultan ran up to my corner barking and wagging his tail. He wanted me to follow him. I really wasn't in the mood to open the main gate. *Let the wicked nun open it,* I thought. "Yovani! Yovani!" I heard my name being called. "Yovani, come quickly." Sultan accompanied me to the front gate. Joy overcame me when I saw the bishop walking in the garden. He was not alone. Foreigners from the United States and Canada were with him. I recognized one of the lady doctors from Canada.

"Alma de Dios, come my child," the bishop opened his arms as he greeted me. I ran to him. "Tell me, my child, how are you feeling these days? Any improvement in your condition?"

"Oh, Señor Bishop, I wish that I could say yes, but my sickness continues, but my Diosito is going to cure me."

"Come with me, I want you to meet some people from Canada. These people make it possible for me to keep the orphanage open. Their donations allow us to pay the bills. Because of their generosity, I will be able to finish the seminary." I didn't know anything about the seminary until much later.

The attractive lady I saw was younger than most of the nuns, with blond hair, neatly combed her dress; she was not from Mexico. "Dr. Letty," the bishop said, "this is Jovani, the young girl I have told you about." I thought, *This young and pretty lady is a doctor? If she can be a doctor, why then can't I be a nun?* For a few moments we just looked at each other. I don't know what she was thinking during those first moments; as for me, I was in admiration to see such a young and pretty doctor. We greeted with extended hands; her Spanish was good enough for me to understand what she was saying.

"Yovani, the bishop has told me a lot about you. He really likes you, I can tell by the way he talks about you. He also tells me that you are epileptic." I understood enough of her Spanish. I asked her if she was a doctor who specialized in my type of sickness. She was a dentist and knew very little about my sickness. "Jovani, Dr. Letty is interested in helping you," said Bishop Alejo. "She might not be a specialist, but she knows several doctors in Canada that will help you." I was very much interested in hearing more. "How is that possible?" I asked. "I live here, and I don't know where Canada is."

"Jovani, Dr. Letty will help get you to Canada. She wants to adopt you and take you with her to live in her country of Canada."

Canada? But I don't know anybody in there, I thought. *What happens if I don't like that country, will I be able to get back to my pueblo?* So many other thoughts entered my mind. My heart started to beat really fast. "Jovani, these people will give you the love that you lack here. You will never be alone again."

"Oh, Señor Obispo, I don't know what to say, can I have a few days to think about it?"

"Jovani, the doctor and the others will be here for a couple more weeks. You can give me your response anytime before then." Bishop

Alejo gave me his blessing. Before leaving, he told me not to worry about him, that the decision was mine entirely.

The bishop left, the doctor and I stayed behind to talk. I asked her if she would like a tour of the grounds. The next several days were spent in each other's company. We became good friends. She took me shopping, bought me some clothes and shoes. I tried not to accept them, but she insisted. I thought of Canada but also about my pueblo and my mamacita. My desire to leave for Canada was especially true when I had a convulsion. I was so tired of them, tired of being sick. But now I had the opportunity to start a life without threat of being ousted from the school. Dr. Letty never pushed for me to accompany her to Canada. The only time she mentioned anything was when she told me that the decision was mine entirely.

I made my decision on the last day the doctor and all the others were leaving. I gave her my decision before I told Sister Mar. Dr. Letty accepted my decision to stay in Mexico. She was hurt that I wasn't going with her, but she understood. I made a remark about the money she would be saving by not taking me to Canada. She smiled. "Yes, Jovani, my organization has money to spend on orphans and adoptions, but we weren't as successful this year as in other years."

"Doctor, then you saved money when I decided not to leave with you?"

"Yes, Jovani, we did."

"Doctor, the orphanage needs many things, you could donate that money to the orphanage." The amazed doctor looked at me. "Jovani, you are really concerned about others, aren't you? I ask myself over and over, who is this girl?"

Her organization donated ten thousand dollars. The funds were enough to finish the seminary and fix the surrounding fence. The seminary would serve the students from the nearby churches of San Antonio and Nicho. I continue my quest to be a nun. I pray that I be granted the religious vocation of a nun. I have not given up, I will continue to pray as long as my Diosito gives me life.

My life at the orphanage was slowly ending, but not the nightmares, the perpetrator saw to that. Sister Mar was summoned on some official business. Before she left, she told not to antagonize Sister Carmela while she was gone. I was sure that Sister Carmela would seek me out. I got my clothes and headed to the outside laundry. It was very quiet, I could hear the birds chirping and a few dogs barking, but I could also hear the footsteps of my nightmare. She was following me. I wanted to run and let the dogs out of their kennel. But I wasn't fast enough, she caught up with me.

"You can't hide from me, you little s——." I started to sing trying to ignore her. She shouted, "Who do you think you are? I hate you," she said, "you think that you are better than all the other girls here." I didn't stop singing and continued to walk, she got in front of me. "I hope that my Sister Mar stays away long enough to give me time to kick you out of here. I will send you out on the street like a stray dog. When sister Mar returns, I will tell her that you left on your own. I will tell her that you can't stand it here anymore." I walked around her to laundry. I threw the clothes on the ground, reached over to the water, and soaked my head. "I am talking to you," she said, "you act like a deaf, snot nose." I'd had enough of her insults. I stood up, looked at her, and was going to return her insults. That's all I remember, I had a convulsion.

A lady was applying a cold cloth on my head, I recognized her; she was Don Toño's wife. El Chalpa, as Don Toño was known, was at her side. He told me that he had heard every word that "the bad nun Carmela" had spoken to me. "She left you on the ground where you fell," he said. That nun has no heart, she shouldn't be a nun. His wife spoke to me, but I couldn't understand her dialect, but I'd heard it before in the orphanage from one of the mountain girls. Don Toño talked to me in a low voice, "Yovani, you are her in the house of Don Rafa. I brought you here when you fainted. I went for the doctor, he sewed some stitches in your head where you fell.

"Sister Mar just arrived at her house, I will inform her that you are here," said Don Toño. The Rafa family was really upset at my nightmare nun. One of the sons wanted to get his gun and do away with her. His mother scolded him. "No," she said, "we don't do that, God will take care of her." Mrs. Rafa was really angry with the nun, but she didn't want any harm to come to the nun. She turned to me, I could tell that she was really angry. "Yovani, you are being dumbheaded for not telling Sister Mar about that no-good nun. Don Toño has told us of the maltreatment she gives you."

Sister Mar arrived at the house where I'd been treated after I had my convulsion. "Yovani, Sister Carmela didn't tell me that you were gone from the house. If it wasn't for Don Rafa that came to tell me that you were at his house, I would never have known. I will speak to Sister Carmela." I was very tired, I went to the chapel to pray. Afterward I went to my room to sleep. The pain in my head was horrible, I couldn't go to sleep. But I finally did. However, Sister Mar woke me up. I don't know what Sister Carmela told her about me, but Sister Mar was very upset with me.

"Yovani, you should be ashamed at yourself. All the lies that you spread about Sister Carmela. I don't want you to ever go out on the street alone. If you insist on doing that, I will ask you to leave this place. I can't be responsible for you if you leave this house without informing me, Sister Carmela, or one of the other nuns, do you understand?" I couldn't respond, my head hurt, and I couldn't go back to sleep, it was a long night.

Next day I left early for school. I went to speak with Cristi. We had a friendly conversation, she always made me feel good. She advised me to write my memoirs because, she said, "someday they will help you. Someday you will read these notes and reflect on the life you have been living. I believe matrimony is more likely to come your way, now that you were denied being a nun. I can't give you advice regarding being a nun, but I hope that the man that is lucky to marry you will listen to what your life has been like. You can even read him some of your notes.

"Speaking of marriage as a vocation, let me tell you. My husband and I didn't date until we had known each other for some time. You and Rafa have known each other for a short time, he seems like a nice person. He likes you, but he tells me that you reject him. Before I married my husband, we treated each other like friends, with respect. That's what you and Rafa should do, you can be friends to see if you and he are compatible. Rafa talks to me all the time. I understand that he is not a good student, but he is a good person and a good worker and appears to be very loving."

Rafa walked into her room. I looked at Cristi. The smirk on her face told me a lot. *She set this whole thing up*, I thought. He politely greeted us. "Listen, I have to finish something very important, you two stay here if you want, I will be back shortly." She touched my shoulder and left. *I've been had*, I thought. We looked at each other. I smiled. "Rafa! What are you doing here? I'm surprised to see you here so early." He smiled, scratched his head. "Yeah, I'm here because I wanted to see you." I don't deny it, but my heart was pounding seeing Rafa standing in front of me. "Rosita, I want to talk to you, but not here, can we go someplace else?" We left the building.

He opened the door to his car so that I could get in. The car was comfortable, and this time I did buckle myself. I thought back to the time I first used the seat belts. I smiled at myself. He drove on a dirt road to a secluded place near a stream. He stopped the car, got out of the car; I figured that this is where he wanted to talk, so I got out. This part I don't remember too well, so I consulted my notes. I wrote from memory and with the aid of my notes.

I stated in my notes:

> We walked to the edge of the river bank. Rafa was very quiet, I glanced at him also not saying a word. He looked very serious. My knees were shaking worse than my heart was beating. I had

an idea what he was going to ask. He grabbed my hand, we faced each other. He placed his hands on my shoulders, heart pounding I instinctively placed my hands on his waist. Rosi, hmm ah, do you want to be my girlfriend? This time without hesitation I answered, yes. I was ready to have a boyfriend one that I could trust.

I don't have to consult my notes for what happened next. I remember the kiss, my first ever kiss. I will never forget the first time I kissed a boy. At the age of eighteen years, I felt the lips of a boy with mine. For the first time, I hugged a person of the opposite sex. I felt his body pressed against mine, and I became very nervous, it just felt strange. My heart beat faster than ever. I put my head on his shoulder, he gave me a strong hug full of affection.

We pulled apart, his hands on my shoulders, mine on his waist. "Rosi, I promise that I will always respect you, I will never take advantage of you."

"Rafa, I have consented to be your girlfriend because I also have confidence in you, and I believe you will always respect me. But you have to be patient with me, Rafa, because I don't know much about being a girlfriend. If I become a burden to you, tell me. You know about my sickness, and I don't want to be a problem. Also, I can see you in school, but I can't be seen with you near the orphanage. As you know, it is forbidden by Sister Mar for any of the girls to have boyfriends."

I didn't want to leave the scene, but school was calling. He drove me back to my class. We talked about meeting after school. Cristi was waiting for me. "Jovani, you look different, your eyes look happier than earlier." She smiled. "Tell me what happened." I smiled. "Cristi, I accepted to be his girlfriend. Cristi, we kissed. I had never kissed a boy before."

"Your teacher is late, come into my office, tell me everything."

"Cristi, we kissed. It was scary, but it was nice—not nice, I just can't explain it. Cristi, thank you for teaching me to value my life. I have been afraid to be around men because of that evil man that lives with my mother. Rafa is nothing like that, he is very caring and very affectionate. Cristi, I thought that kissing a boy was like when people kiss the bishop's ring." We laughed. "I remember the first time I saw a boy kissing a girl, that the stork was going to deliver a baby." Cristi couldn't stop laughing. "Well, don't worry, Jovani, the stork will not deliver you a baby because you kissed Rafa."

"Oh, Cristi, I am learning that I know very little about being a girlfriend."

"Yes, Jovani, you have much to learn. You did the right in accepting Rafa as your boyfriend. He is a respectable person, he won't do anything to hurt you, believe me, I know him and his mother. They're good people."

Class could not end soon enough. I wanted to see Rafa, I wanted to be with him. For the first time ever, I had a friend I could share my life with. After a long day in school, Rafa picked me up. "Where do you want to go?" he asked me. I pointed to the highest hill. "There, I want to see the whole village from up there." The crooked dirt road led us to the very top of the hill. I got out of the car, stood in front of it. He stood next to me. "You like it up here, eh, Rosi."

"Yes, Rafa, this is beautiful. I always wondered what is was like up here, now I know. Thank you for bringing me here." I pointed out the orphanage. He pointed to the school. We kept pointing all the areas of interest and laughing. The faraway mountains presented a beautiful sight.

He touched my hand, I turned toward him, we embraced. I tilted my face to meet his, and we kissed. We didn't want the kiss to end, I was falling in love with him. We stopped the kissing to catch our breath. "Rosi, my mother wants to meet you. I have told her about you, she knows how I feel about you."

"Really? Your mother wants to meet me? I would like to meet her also."

"Rosi, Mother has always told us—well, my sister and I—to pray for a good person to share our lives with. Rosi, you are that person." I smiled. "What kind of person am I?" I gave him a little nudge. "Come on, Rafa, tell me, what kind of person am I? Why have you wanted me to be your girlfriend?"

He didn't know how to answer, he became a little nervous. "Well, because," he said. "Come on, Rafa, tell me." I gave him another playful nudge. "Rosi, because you are very pretty."

"Is that the only reason, because you think that I am pretty? Rafa, there's lots of girls that are pretty, I'm sure many would like to be your girlfriend." He lowered his head to the side, lowered his voice. "None of them are intelligent or honest like you. Rosi, you are a very determined person." He faced me; smiling, he said, "Now, Rosi, you tell me why you finally agreed to be my girlfriend." I shrugged my shoulders and smiled. "Rafa, give me time, and I will answer you, but not now."

"Can I give you another kiss?" I was glad he asked, because I wanted to kiss him again. He drove me home.

Last year of high school. In a few months, I would have to leave my refuge, my home for the past eight years. I thought about it every day. One thing I was sure of, that I would not return to my pueblo to live. Every year the school elected a student to carry the school banner. The student elected had to meet certain requirements. I was one of three students selected to run for election. I was elected by the students to be the flag carrier. I was overjoyed to have been elected to such an honorable post. However, Sister Mar didn't allow me to be the flag carrier. She mentioned that I couldn't do it because of my sickness. That was another honor that was denied me because of my sickness, both denials by Sister Mar.

Rafa and I saw each other more often, I was beginning to fall in love with him. Our relationship was forbidden by the nuns, so I considered it as a forbidden love. It was exciting because I had never disobeyed Sister Mar. Rafa and I exchanged notes; he left his in my backpack, where he knew I would leave one for him. On occasion he'd leave me a rose with a special note. The time went by real fast, and I had no idea where I would be living after my graduation. I ignored Sister Carmela, she tried to confront me, but I slipped away from her.

The last week was especially busy. The graduation dress was not to my liking, but I had no choice, I had to wear it. I was very happy that my education at this level was over; now I could concentrate on the next level. I choose the field of law. I would not be denied by anyone this time. My main goal was to defend the rights of mothers and their children. The graduates were visited by several universities, I talked to the representatives of the universities I was interested in.

Cristi kept me in formed of the graduation activities. The president of the pueblo and her husband were selected to represent us the night of the graduation. After the ceremony, we were going to have a grand dance in the most famous ballroom in the pueblo. Cristi shared with me that three of the most gifted students would receive scholarships. The big one to be granted was worth five thousand pesos, the other two would receive lesser amounts. I got real excited when she told me about the dance. "I want to go to the dance, but I don't know if Sister Mar will allow me to go."

"Rosita, don't worry about that, I will talk to Sister Mar. This very day after work, I will talk to her.

"Yovani, have you thought about where you will live after you graduate? I don't know how much time Sister Mar will give you after you graduate, do you have any idea?"

"Cristi, the president of the pueblo told me that she has many friends and that she will help me find a suitable family. This way I can continue my education. She is trying to find a home where I can help with the children and clean house."

"Jovani, I wish you would agree to live in Costa Chica with my parents."

"Cristi, I have thought a lot about Rafa, maybe he and I can get together. His mother wants to meet me."

"Oh, Yovani, if that happens, I will be very happy for both of you."

Rafa didn't show up to take me to my house, the orphanage. The river that I had crossed so many other times looked more menacing this time. The Huajuapan River was overflowing because of the heavy rainfalls that the area had experienced the past few days. Rock after rock I jumped until I came to my favorite one. It was the biggest one nestled at the riverbank's end. I thought, *This rock is waiting for me.* I sat where I could feel the warmth of the sun. I feel that the sun gives me energy. I sat listening to the birds singing and the water flowing downstream.

I was startled when Rafa unexpectedly hugged me from behind. My heart jumped before I realized that it was Rafa. I didn't move. I remained in his arms because it felt good. "Rafa, can you hear the birds? They are singing a love song just for us." We laughed, I turned my head, and we kissed. He sat next to me, I put my head on his lap and made myself comfortable. "Rosi, I've seen you on top of this rock many times before. Every time I come this way, I say, 'There's Rosi's rock.'" I smiled. "I like this rock," I told him. "Well," he said, "I christen this rock, Rosi.

"Rosi, are you ready for your graduation?"

"Yes, Rafa, I am ready and very happy also." I asked him, "Are you ready?"

"Yes, I am ready, but I'm not expecting to get my certificate because I didn't complete many of my classes. Rosi, I'm happy for you, you have worked very hard and gone through a lot, especially since Sister Carmela arrived." He looked at me. "I'm also happy to be the boyfriend of such a beautiful lady. I say *lady* because you have grown up."

He kept looking at me. "Rosita, can I call you Jova?"

"What? Rafa, you want to call me *Jova*? Why? Don't you like the names that I already have? People know me by *Alma de Dios*, *Rosita, Vani, Jovani, Yovani*, and you call me *Rosi*, now you want to call me *Jova*."

"Rosi, I want to call you by a name that belongs to the two of us only, it would be very special." I smiled, placed my head on my hands. I repeated, "Jova? Well, Rafa, if that's the way you feel, then I also like it." He was happy with my decision. Again he hugged me, and we kissed. He pulled away. "Jova, is the nun going to allow you to go to the graduation dance?"

"Yes, I think she is, Cristi is going over this afternoon to ask her. She won't turn Cristi down."

"I am so glad, can I give you a ride to your home?"

"No, Rafa, I want to be alone for a while longer."

"Okay then, I will see you at the dance." He left.

I stayed at my boulder receiving more energy from the sun. *Hmm, he didn't give me a kiss when he left.* I felt somewhat empty, my emotions had taken a lover's hit. The lover's emotional roller coaster was having an impact on me.

Graduated from CBTIS,
I Was Eighteen Years Old

THE DAY ARRIVED, I WOULD be graduating from high school. I was up early, anxious to start on a good note. I put on a skirt that I had made. The shoes were old but shined to perfection. I tried to speak with Sister Mar, but she appeared as though my graduation was not important to her. When Cristi went for me, Sister Mar opened the main gate. She greeted Cristi but wasn't cordial at all with her. I met Cristi at the front door, I also greeted Sister Mar. She forced a half smile and wished me a good night.

Cristi took me to the house of my friend Cheli. On the way over, she asked me, "Is that the dress you are wearing to the graduation?" I told her that I didn't have any other. "I made it myself, don't you like it?" Cristi laughed. "Yes, I like it very much, but this is your graduation followed by a dance, and your dress isn't the appropriate dress for this occasion." I was a little hurt because I had worked really hard making this dress. Cheli's mother, Doña Conchita, greeted us at the door. I used to assist Mrs. Conchita when she sold food to the students.

"Jovani, we're going to fix you up so that the people can see what a beautiful young lady you are." They fixed my hair really nice, I was surprised how nice I looked. Next they showed me the skirt they wanted me to wear. I looked at it. "I can't wear that skirt, it's too short," I told them. They laughed. "Yovani, you are a young girl, not a nun, and you are not going to dress like one. This skirt is below the knee, it is the style, and you will look real nice in it." I put on some nylon stockings before I tried on the skirt. Next they provided me with a blouse that matched and some beautiful shoes that also matched.

When they were through dressing me, Cristi told me to look at my new me; she led me to a full-length mirror. I took a few steps toward the mirror. "Ahh"—I placed my hands over my mouth—"I didn't expect anything like this." My eyes were full of life, shining like never before. I looked like a different person. I have to admit, I really looked beautiful! That had to be one of the happiest days of my life. Cristi and Cheli led me to the church where the bishop was presiding over the ceremonial Mass. I was a little apprehensive yet hoping that some of my family members would show up for my graduation. No one showed up, not even Sister Mar. I would graduate alone.

After the Mass, my friends and fellow graduates took my picture with their families. Every moment was full of gladness; the townspeople who knew me gave me gifts and wished me well. I caught a glimpse of Rafa with his mother. He also saw me but kept on walking with his mother, didn't stop to introduce us. He was right about not getting his graduation certificate. He had missed too many classes and missed too many assignments.

The graduation ceremony continued inside the auditorium of the school. The place was full of flowers, balloons, and other decorations. I was thrilled to be inside; it was just beautiful. The mariachis were singing one of my favorite songs. People were congratulating me; everywhere I turned, people talked to me. Some were surprised to see that Sister Mar wasn't at the graduation ceremony. I made the excuse that she was busy with the other girls. I did tell them that Sister Mar always prayed for them, and that seemed to pacify them.

The juryman started the ceremony. He mentioned that the first order of business was to award the certificates to the graduating students. I was really nervous, I don't know why, but I was. I heard my name. I have worked hard for this moment, I would be graduating. My tears didn't prevent me from walking up to the front. No obstacles existed that would stop me now. It was my courage that guided me to get my certificate.

The lady president of Tlapa de Comonfort, Guerrero, gave me a beautiful bouquet of flowers and a gem in the form of a flower. Some of my teachers and their families presented me with gifts. Cristi and her friends showered me with gifts, shoes, and clothes. Cristi helped me with all my gifts. She and I put them in the car and took them to the orphanage. Sister Mar was really surprised to see me dressed so pretty. She told me that she had never seen me look so pretty. She hugged me and gave me her blessing before we returned to the ceremony. The dance was just getting started.

Sister Mar had told me that I had to be home by midnight. I remember thinking of Cinderella and how she lost her shoe. I prayed that it wouldn't happen to me. I pepped myself up; tonight was my night, and nothing was going to spoil it. Cristi gave me another beautiful dress. We arrived at the dance. She asked me if I was okay, she didn't want me to have a convulsion. We entered the dance hall. "I feel really happy," I told her. "This is the first dance like this one that I attend." I told Christi that I felt like Cinderella. "Cristi, I will be very careful not to lose any of my slippers." We laughed. "Rosita, this is your night, enjoy it."

I ran into three of my fellow students—Karina, Carol, and Cintia. At first they didn't recognize me. It was when I spoke to them that they recognized my voice. One by one they asked, "Rosita, is that really you? You look so different and pretty." They hugged me. "Cristi, are you the one responsible for dressing this pretty girl?"

Cristi said, "I helped her some, she did the rest." Karina and the other two wished me the best, I in turn wished them the same. I mingled among the people, talking and receiving compliments from them. I saw when Rafa walked in. He looked really nice, he'd gotten a haircut. The wardrobe he was wearing made him look like a young gentleman. I informed Cristi that Rafa had just walked in. "Good, go to him," she told me. "I should mingle with other students," she said.

My knees started to shake as I walked up to him. Rafa was looking all over the place, hopefully looking for me. I stood right in front of him; he didn't pay me any attention. I waited a while. "Hi, Rafa, don't you recognize your girlfriend?"

"Ah, Jova?" His eyes got real big. "Aye, Rafa"—I gave him a little shove—"it's me." He stared at me. "Jova, I didn't recognize you. My god, you look so pretty. I thought I knew you, but I really don't. I have to ask, is it really you?"

"Rafa, it's only me, nobody else."

"No, you are not the Jova that I know, who are you? You're not the same girl from the orphanage. You are prettier than ever."

"Well, then, Rafa, let's go where we can enjoy the full moon, the heavens are full of stars, and I want to enjoy this particular night with you."

We left the dance. "Where do you want to go?"

"Rafa, take me to the top of the hill of Axoxuca. I want to see the moon and the stars with you from up there. Rafa, I have confidence that you won't try anything."

"Ay, Jova, don't be afraid of me, I won't try anything, okay?" He drove us to the top of the hill. He opened the door for me. I jumped out, and we hugged; in the process, he touched part of my upper body I considered off-limits. That touch surprised me, I pulled back. He was surprised too. "Jova, sorry, I didn't intend that to happen."

I didn't know how to react, I walked away from him looking at the moon. He followed me. "Jova, please forgive me, it was an accident, I didn't do that on purpose."

I was confused; the past would not go away. I believe that he didn't try to touch me, so why can't I accept that? I heard him say, "Jova, I never thought that I would love a girl as much as I love you."

"Rafa, why do you love me? I am the girl that lives in the orphanage, I am the girl with no family. I'm always alone, but not tonight. No, not tonight, because the night belongs to me." I slapped my thigh and forced a laugh.

I looked at the heavens; inspired by my mood and the moon, I sang, "No soy la hija de nadie…" (I am the daughter of no one). Tears started to fill my eyes. He interrupted my singing, "Jova, what's the reason you wanted to come up here?"

"Oh, Rafa, look at the stars and the moon. Now look down at the city, so peaceful. Rafa, let's count the stars."

"Jova, it's getting cold, let's go to my house, Mother wants to meet you." We left the hill and the beautiful sights for other lovers.

I didn't want to leave the hill and its beauty, and I sensed that Rafa was hurt because of what happened. Nothing was going to spoil my night; I sang another of my favorite songs. He didn't say much; maybe he muttered a couple of words. I was too busy with my own thoughts. Doña Toñita, his mother, was a very pleasant lady. She was almost as tall as me, a little heavier with a pleasant smile. I also met his seven-year-old sister, cute little girl, her jet-black hair pulled back and braided.

"Rosita, my son speaks very highly of you. I want you to know that this house is your house, visit anytime you want. I would be very fortunate to be your mother-in-law." Rafa and I looked at each other. "Mother, don't say that." His mother looked at me. "Rafael, don't pay attention to me." She reminded Rafa to give me the present he had for me. "Yes, Mother, I was waiting for a proper moment, and I guess now is a good time." He gave me white pajamas.

His mother apologized because she couldn't stay and talk with us. She and her daughter had a prior engagement. They left us alone in her house. I thought it strange, I thought she wanted to meet me.

Well, I was happy that Rafa and I were alone. We sat on the sofa where I hugged Rafa. We were kissing when one of my earrings fell off and landed on the floor. He reached down to retrieve it; my dress was above my knee revealing part of my leg. He saw that part of my body, and that made me very uncomfortable. But I wanted to be brave, I wanted to overcome my fear of being with a man.

I reached over and kissed him. "Rafa," I whispered, "I want to be with you." He stopped embracing me. "What are you saying?"

"Rafa, show me what a relationship is like between a boy and a girl."

"Jova, don't ask that. I love you very much and respect you even more. I noticed how upset you became when I accidently touched your breast. You are not ready to have a relationship. We will have that kind of relationship when we get married. I don't want to dishonor your innocence. Jova, you know that I don't have a lot to offer you. You need a man that will give you a life that you deserve. I will work to be that man. I love you, and I will not lose you.

"I don't earn enough working for Mother to give you a life you deserve. You have suffered too much, and I don't want you to suffer any longer. Jova, if you only knew how much I desire to be with you, but I can't. Tonight up on the hill, I realized how much you have pained living as a child. I meant what I said before, I love you, and I respect you. I don't want to hurt you emotionally. Besides, I feel that you will never give up on being a nun." I was disappointed that I didn't learn what I asked for; at the same time, I was relieved. *Rafa means well,* I thought. "Okay, Rafa, we better go. Cristi must be looking for me."

Cristi was looking for me. She'd learned that I had taken off with Rafa, so she was waiting patiently for me at the front door. She smiled a frantic smile when she saw us. "Rosita, come with me, I have a surprise for you." She led me to the front of the auditorium, told me to stand next to her. She took the microphone and spoke, "Ladies and gentlemen, I have found our lost recipient." Everyone applauded. Gently Cristi raised her arms to silence the crowd. "Please welcome Rosita Jovani, the recipient of our first prize scholarship award of five thousand pesos." The director of the school presented me a check for five thousand pesos of scholarship money. I had never heard such a strong applause and whistles for anyone. Maybe because it was for me, and of course, I was biased. I took the microphone, waited for the applause to finish. I thanked the people responsible for the grant—Cristi, Sister Mar, and all the people who were in attendance.

After the awards ceremony, the music again picked up, and the dancing started. There was a commotion near the entrance of the auditorium. I saw Rafa pulling his cousin Carlos away from the commotion and out the door. That was the last time I saw Rafa that night. I joined my friends on the table. That night I danced with my girlfriends; we had a wonderful time. It was my night, and nothing was going to spoil it. Cristi gave me a ride to the orphanage, my home. I couldn't sleep thinking about the dance, the graduation, the hilltop called Axoxuca. I was thinking about my future, I had to move out into the world with no clue where I would be living or how I would support myself. I had reached another goal, my education, now what? I woke up early the next morning. Ha, I must have fallen asleep thinking about my future.

I Left the Orphanage for Another Life: Adoption Awaits

I WROTE THIS LETTER:

Tlapa de Guerrero
20 June 1999

Diosito and divine Mother bless me full of blessings so that the president of the city and the nuns have a family in mind that will take me and help me. My sickness will not prevent me from earning my keep. I am not a burden and You know how much it has hurt that I was denied being a nun. I have dreamt of going to the convent but I was denied by Sister Mar. Sister Mar listened to Sister Carmela stating that the medicine and hospital costs would be prohibitive and besides that I worthless.

I don't have problems with any of the people from the pueblo. I get along with everybody. Realistically Diosito the twisted lies from Sister Carmela split my soul with sadness. I question how she can be married you pretend to serve the people without showing you the respect required of a nun. I ask you Diosito to guide me in the other two vocations, remain single or to marry and bear children.

482

Give me your blessing and give me the strength because I believe that due to my sickness I will not be able to become a mother. I want my suffering to cease. I confide in you my Diosito and I always will have faith in You. Others don't know that you exist but you never abandon them. I know that you will never abandon me, illuminate my path, protect and guide me. Never permit anyone to separate us and above all free me of my illness.

Diosito please protect me and place a family in my path of life that will adopt me. I have nowhere to go so please do this before Sister Mar kicks me out on the street. I will not return to my pueblo for fear of being taken by Reyna and her that old man. Besides I never want to see them again. Virgin Mother help your son and understand me being your daughter also that I wait for the day when Reyna will give me a motherly hug.

Diosito, Virgin Mary, I Implore You

IT DIDN'T MATTER. I WOULD survive. I survived as a young girl, now I am grown and educated, there is a place in this world. Diosito is at my side, He will guide me.

The day that I must vacate the orphanage arrived. Personnel from the government arrived at the orphanage. The government personnel showed up at year end to hire girls as maids. Sister Mar led them to the classroom where all the graduating girls were to be introduced to them. We were led into the room as a group. Sister Mar had told me to prepare myself because she wanted me to sing a song to them. She also asked me to write a poem and to recite it during the introduction.

Sister Mar introduced each one of us. During the introduction, she shared personal information about each girl. I was the last one introduced. "Yovani," Sister Mar told them, "has written a poem especially for this occasion, but first she will entertain us with a couple of her favorite songs. After the songs, she will recite her poem." I loved being in center stage. I sang my songs, then followed that with my poem. I received warm applauses after each song and especially after I recited the poem I had written.

Afterward we were asked to mingle with our guests. Several of the families expressed a desire to adopt me. Diosito was watching out for me. I was elated to hear that I would be going with one of these families. Sister Mar introduced me to a lawyer, Fernando Hinterjoker. Sister Mar told me that Mr. Hinterjoker was very much interested in me. He wanted me to go live with his wife, himself, and two daughters. I told him that I wasn't prepared to give him an answer, I wanted to talk with other families.

He went directly to Sister Mar. I could see that he was trying to convince the nun that his offer was better than any other. Some of the dialogue I heard included politics and the poor people that lived in the mountains. The thought of going with him when he mentioned politics was repulsive. The politicians talk a lot but do very little for the people. I wanted no part of him nor his house. I approached them. "Sister Mar, I don't desire to go with this lawyer. I want to meet others that are interested in taking me with them." She gave me a slight pinch; smiling, she said, "Mr. Hinterjoker, this girl accepts your help, and she is ready to go with you now."

Everything happened so fast. Mr. Hinterjoker's chauffer took my cartons full of my personal stuff, and Sister Mar pushed me into the car. The gardener, Mr. Toño, saw the whole thing. He rushed over to the car and gave me a quick blessing. Sister Mar became very angry with him and ordered him away from the car. I was very upset with the way Sister Mar had treated me. I had no words for Mr. Hinterjoker on the way to his house. Why did she push me onto these people? I wanted to pick the family; instead, she chose this lawyer, but why? I still trusted the nun; after all, she has helped me since I was ten years old. In all probability, she knew best.

When we arrived at his house, I asked, "Señor, what is the name of this place?"

"Yovani, that is your name, isn't it?"

"Yes, sir, that is my name."

"Well, Yovani, forgive me for not telling you about your future home. This is Chilpancingo, Guerrero, this is where you will be living. I will introduce to my spouse. You will also meet my two daughters. The oldest is thirteen years old, her name is America. The youngest is three years old, her name is Amparo." The gate guarded the property full of flowers and a beautiful garden. Behind all that, I was surprised to see their house. It was simply the most gorgeous house that I had seen in that whole area.

I am going to live here, I thought. *This can't be happening. Now I know why Sister Mar pushed me in their direction.* The car kept moving closer and closer to the house I would be living in, I kept admiring it more with each second we got closer to the front door. I saw an elegant lady walking down the steps to greet us. We got out of the car, I walked next to the lawyer. He introduced me to his wife. Happily I extended my arm to greet her. "Señora, I am so glad to meet you." She didn't acknowledge; she completely ignored me. *Oh, wow,* I thought, *what is going on here?*

"You dared to bring me another filthy girl. I hope this one can do the work, if she can't, I will send her out on the street like all the others." *Uh-oh, this is doesn't look good for me,* I thought. She turned to me asking, "What housework are you capable of doing?"

"Well, ma'am, I know how to cook, I can wash and iron clothes. I am capable of doing other things, whatever you want, I can do it." She asked me, "What have you studied?"

"I just completed my high school studies. I got several certificates. But I want to continue with my studies to become a lawyer."

"You want to become a lawyer, and you want to continue going to school while you live here? You are crazy to you think that I will allow that."

The señora was angry. "You are going to be a servant and nothing else. Don't even think that I will pay for you to go to school to become a lawyer. Now start working, go inside and change into the servant's clothes and clean the kitchen."

"Señora," I asked, "can you show me where I can put my belongings?" She stared at my carton full with my belongings. "You have your things in that filthy carton? I don't want that filthy thing in my house, looks like it's full of fleas. Leave it outside, I will find a place for it." I couldn't contain my emotions any longer, I had a convulsion.

When I came to, she was sitting reading something. She did nothing to help me. I woke up with a bad headache. "Oh good, you are finally waking up," she said. "I have never seen a person faint like you did a few minutes ago. Yovani, I don't think that I can keep you here, I believe that you can't do anything."

"Señora, I guess that your husband and the nun didn't explain to you that I have epilepsy, and I have these convulsions all the time. In spite of all that, I know how to work, and I can do all the things that I told you I could do. I want you to know that I am very intelligent. I received a $5,000 scholarship for being the top student in my school. I intend on using this money to pay for law school."

"Okay, Yovani, you can relax. Go into the kitchen and prepare the chicken breasts. I want them breaded and juicy, not dry. I will leave you alone, my sister is coming over. When you hear the doorbell, it's going to be her and her family, let them in."

I wasn't happy anymore, I questioned why Sister Mar had sent me here. It's a nightmare; although unlike the one I experienced with Sister Carmela, it was still a nightmare. I continued to think while I prepared the chicken, *This lady doesn't like me. For that matter, I don't think she likes herself. I will not stay here, I intend on pursuing my studies, and nobody is going to hold me back.* I prepared a good meal for the señora, her sister, and their children. They ate in the formal dining room, I ate alone in the kitchen.

America came into the kitchen; she talked while I finished cleaning up. "Yovani, my father told me a little bit about you. He told me that you were a very intelligent girl. When he told me that, I wondered why you had come to work for my mother."

"Really, America, why do you ask that?"

"Because he knows very well how Mother treats all the girls that come to work for her. She has mistreated all the other girls and eventually fires them. She is always angry and scolds the workers. My father and mother are in the process of getting divorced. Father stays away, he hardly comes around anymore. When the divorce is final, I am going to live with him.

"Yovani, Father also told me that you don't have a family."

"America, I do have a family, but it's somewhat complicated. I have a sister and a niece, I also have my grandmother Sinforosa. But I don't like to talk about the others because, like I said, it's complicated."

"Yovani, can I be your sister and friend? You can sleep in my room with me."

"America, I would love to be your sister friend." We hugged, sealing the friendship. "My father also told me that you have convulsions because you are sick." I shook my head, thinking that if I didn't have this sickness, I would have become a nun.

America helped me with my carton full with my belongings. She asked me about my studies. She had overheard the conversion that her mother and I had earlier. I said, "America, nobody—and I mean nobody—is going to keep me from my studies."

"Yovani, tell me more about what you want to study."

"America, my name is *Rosita*. When I went to the orphanage, Sister Mar changed my name to *Yovani* because there were too many other girls named *Rosita*. So now that I'm no longer there, I prefer to be called by my real name, *Rosita*." America smiled. "I like that name much more than *Yovani*."

"Now to answer your question, I want to be a lawyer. However, your mother told me that as long as I am here, she won't permit me to attend school."

"Rosita, that's the way Mother is, she wants to control everybody."

Living with Reyna was my first nightmare; Sister Carmela was another one, although somewhat different. Why must I face another one? That's exactly what I was facing with that lady. Three weeks was more than what I was willing to endure in that place. I thought of other places that I could go to, of people who had offered me a place to stay. *Diosito would lead me out of here, He will guide me.* I waited for her lawyer husband to visit, but he stayed away.

I had to confront her. I wasn't going to live this nightmare any longer. She was sitting in the living room when I approached her. She looked at me with venom in her eyes. "What are you doing here?" she asked. "Señora, I need to speak with you about the living condition. First of all, I need my medicine, and I have no way of going to the pharmacy nor do I know where it is." I started to say, "Next I—" She stopped me, stood up to face me. "Listen, the arrangement you made was with my husband, not with me. He is responsible for you, not me. When the divorce is final, you are gone from here. Where you go is not my concern, he brought you here, he can help you, not me. I will then give you three days to pack your carton and leave.

"Tomorrow morning, you go to the government office to see if they will help you with your medicine. I will show you how to get there. I do feel sorry for you. You are sick and poor with no family and was raised in that orphanage. But until my divorce becomes final, you will do as I say, or I will kick you out of here. You will walk the streets like an abandoned dog." I couldn't stand her conversation anymore, I ran out of the room with tears rolling down my cheeks. That night I had a convulsion.

I woke up with a horrible headache. The water felt good; the morning shower helped calm my nerves. I hummed my favorite song. I started to dress for work, but I changed. I wasn't going to wear that silly maid's dress today. I looked inside my closet. All my clothes were gone except for a single dress. I put it on, put my shoes on, and walked out of my room. My latest nightmare was waiting for me near the front door, my carton next to her.

"I changed my mind, I don't want you in my house a minute longer." She picked my carton up and flung it out the door. *This lady has no heart,* I thought. I walked past her without saying a word. She followed me outside, probably to make sure that I would leave. I picked up my belongings then turned to face her. "Señora, I am going to pray for you, because you need more love in your life. How sad you don't even love yourself. Thank you, señora, for giving me my freedom back." I placed my carton down, raised my arms, and happily shouted, "Free, I'm free!" She looked sad and depressed, all alone in her big and cold lifeless house. I made the sign of the cross and left.

My world doesn't end; no, on the contrary, my life is just beginning. I remembered Lupita, one of my dear friends. Her mother, Tere, works in Tlapa as a social worker. I called Lupita from a pay phone. She was really happy to hear from me. I told her why I was calling. Before long, she picked me up. On the way to her house, I told her about my latest nightmare and the heartless señora. I made Lupita laugh the way I described the señora and the way she talked. I had to laugh because I really did a good job in describing the heartless lady. "Lupita, I feel free, I have nobody to tell me how to lead my life except myself and my faith in my Diosito."

We spent the rest of the day and night talking and singing. I sang, "Yo soy hija de nadie…" But this time it had a different meaning. This time I was free, I was on my way to secure my life. I sang other songs that I loved, and they also rang a different meaning than before. I was no longer that little girl singing in the bus to strangers. I sang with a happy heart, unlike other times when sadness overwhelmed me.

Lupita told me that I should look for a job with the government. I was not ready to look any place simply because I didn't know where to start. Lupita told me that I should have no trouble finding a job there. I asked her why she thought that. "Rosita," she said, "everybody that works there knows who you are. I am sure they will help you." Free of my latest nightmare, I had a good sleep at Doña Tere's house. The next morning, Lupita dropped me off at the government office where I would seek a job. Lupita continued on to the university.

I recognized several people walking hurriedly to their jobs. They didn't see me, but seeing them made me feel more comfortable. I talked to the receptionist, told her that I wanted to see the director. She gave me the register book, told me to put my name and that I would be called when he was available. I was about to sit and wait for my name to be called. "Good morning, Yovani." Huh, I was surprised to hear somebody addressing me. I turned around; it was Señor DeVargas. "Good morning, Señor DeVargas." We extended our hands to complete the greeting. "Yovani, what a surprise to see you here. Tell me, how is Sister Marcita? I haven't been to the orphanage in a while, and I haven't heard from her. Yovani, come into my office, we can talk in there." The sign on his door indicated that he was head of Human Resources.

"Tell me, Yovani, what brings you here, why aren't you at the orphanage?"

"Señor DeVargas, I graduated from high school. The orphanage could keep me there until I graduated, then I had to leave. Sister Mar was well when I left."

"But, Yovani, that was about a month ago. Where are you staying now?"

"Well, Señor DeVargas, I was working for this lady, but she fired me. Now I'm looking for a job, that's why I came here."

"Yovani, how can anybody fire a sweet and intelligent girl like you?" Just before I started to answer, his receptionist came in with a glass of water for me and coffee for him. I told Mr. DeVargas everything—starting from my graduation, including the $5,000 I was granted. How I was forced to take the job with that nightmare of a lady.

Mr. DeVargas playfully touched his chin with his fingers. "Yovani, I will never forget that beautiful poem you recited for us. You dedicated that poem to us and to our campaign efforts to help the orphanage. I also recall the conversation I had with Sister Mar about you. She told me that she had never had a more intelligent student like you. She told me that you are very religious and not afraid of work. She told me about your sickness. I not only remember that particular poem, but others as well and the songs you sang to us. I think about that all the time."

He placed his hands on the desk. "Yovani, a girl like you is very rare. You are a strong person, that sick or not, you are determined to seek your place in this world. The nun told me that you are always helping others. Those are the types of individuals that our government is seeking, especially in this organization. We are known as EL DIF." He opened his desk, took out some papers. *Is he going to hire me?* I thought. I was mesmerized happily waiting for the director's next move.

"Yovani, you are looking for a job, and we are looking for people like you." He called his secretary into his office and instructed her to take me to another office. He gave me what he called an authorization for hire. "Give this authorization to the lady there. She will tell you where we are going to give you shelter. This other one I am personally going to send to the doctor for your medicine. We are going to pay for your medicine. This one will show where you will be working. Take this application with you, fill it out, and bring it tomorrow with you. Tomorrow, Yovani, you will be working here."

I have been surprised many times in my lifetime, but nothing like this time. I was so surprised that I had trouble responding, I just sat looking at Señor DeVargas. I finally had the strength to stand up, I thanked him more than once. I probably felt a tear or two. I followed his secretary to another office. The whole process was like a dream.

Started My Job and Enrolled at the University

THE JOB WAS NOT IN the field that I desired, but it was a paying job! I cleaned offices from six in the morning until two in the afternoon. Each one of the cleaning crew was assigned offices. When one of us missed a day, we helped clean the ones assigned to that person. It happened often, but this day in particular, I was sent to clean one of them. I was sent to clean the administration office. The office was empty. I started to mop the floor when a man walked in. We stared at each other. "Yovani, is that you?" He got close to me. "Yes, señor, I am Jovani, and you are Mr. Colin, right?"

"Jovani, you were hired to clean offices?

"Jovani, you have grown up. I understand that you graduated from high school. I also heard that you intend on going to the university."

"Yes, Mr. Colin, that's correct. But I am not your regular cleaning lady, I was sent here because the regular one was sick."

"No, Jovani, not what I meant. I mean you are too talented to be cleaning offices. Sister Mar always told me that you were a very intelligent girl."

Mr. Colins called Norma, his secretary, into his office. Norma was a sweet girl with her dark hair combed tight and pulled back, revealing a small bun in the back of her head. He introduced us. "Norma, I want you to prepare the paperwork for Jovani. She is going to work as the assistant in the administration department of the chauffeurs. She is going to be in charge of tracking the costs." He instructed her to go to the office of employment for my current paperwork. We waited for a while in his office. He told me to sit and not to clean anymore. When Norma arrived with the paperwork, Mr. Colins took it and made several changes.

The title was changed to Administration Assistant. My salary—*mother of god,* I thought—it was much more. Nothing else was changed, they were still going to pay for my medicine and shelter. "Jovani, if you agree, sign your name next to the changes." I gladly signed the document. He handed the papers to Norma. He instructed her to take the paperwork to Mr. Bustamante, the accountant, and nobody else. Norma took the papers, she gave me a strange stare before she left the room. Mr. Colins noticed and gave me a smile. "Norma has never seen me hire somebody so fast," he said, smiling.

"Jovani, tomorrow you come here to my office, and my assistant will show you where you will be working. If you have any questions, ask him, he is a good person and knows everything that goes on around here."

"Señor Colins, I can't believe this is happening. I thank you from the bottom of my heart."

"Jovani, I think of you all the time. I remember the way you treated the people and the little girls in the orphanage. You were so caring with them and so gentle with the girls. I always remember the beautiful poems you recited. Another one that I remember all the time is the song you sang: 'Yo no soy hija de nadie…' I have to be honest with you, when I heard you sing that song, I got tears in my eyes.

"Jovani, I am so glad that you are going to be working here. I will see you tomorrow at eight, okay?" I thanked him again, I started to take the cleaning stuff away. "No, Jovani, leave it, I'll call someone, and they will take it. You go home and rest."

"Thank you again, Mr. Colins, now I have time to check out the university."

"You intend on registering at the university?"

"Today I want to check the required courses I want to take and just get acquainted with the area."

"What vocation do you want to pursue?"

"I really want to study to be a lawyer, and I want to take computer classes."

"When you are ready and know what courses that you are going to take, we, DIF, will pay for them.

"To help you with your computer classes, we have computer classes on Saturdays. The class lasts three months. Are you interested?"

"Oh, Mr. Colins, yes. I can't believe this is happening to me."

"Good, I'm glad for you." He reached in his desk and pulled out an official-looking paper. "Jovani, this is an authorization enabling you to start taking the computer class starting this Saturday. Taking this class will open the door for you to work in other areas. One of them will be the Human Rights. Once you start working here, you will also be able to work computers in that area."

"Mr. Colins, I don't know how to thank you."

"Jovani, you deserve this. A young girl like you is very rare. Look at your life, you were raised in an orphanage, you were given a job under false guise, you've been abandoned, and in spite of your sickness, you are a wonderful young lady. I truly believe that your faith in God keeps you going. I ask myself this question about you, now I will ask you directly: who are you? Really, who are you? There is a wonderful personality surrounding your being that attracts people to you."

Leaving the office of Mr. Colins, I ran into Estrellita Bello Hernandez. We became friends the first few days after I started to work. I was eating alone, and she accompanied me in the lunchroom. "Rosita, where are you going, aren't you working today?" I smiled. "No," I replied, "I don't clean offices nor sweep floors anymore."

"What? Did you quit your job?"

"Well, sort of," I said, "toying with her."

"Rosita, what are you up to?" I told her how I happened to get myself another job. She was surprised that I had made these contacts while I was at the orphanage. She was headed back to her job; we parted.

I sat on a bench outside the university thinking about my good fortune. But I knew that I was fortunate to have met these people at the time that I did and under the circumstances. I have a very important reason for being nice to others. My Diosito is my mentor; I can't treat people any different. Nor did I treat Mr. Colins any different than others. I wasn't nice to him hoping that someday he would repay my kindness by giving me a job. Sister Mar spoke to them about me. I recited and sang for all in attendance because that's who I am. They happened to be there and liked what I did. I got up and went inside the university.

Studying at the university was a girl by the name of Trinidad Valdovinos from Zihuatanejo. Another was Paloma Adaliz; the three of us became friends. Both of them knew how to dress really nice. Me, well, they hadn't learned that I had been raised by the nuns in the orphanage, and they said I dressed like a nun. Paloma loved to wear high heels and the dress. The dresses she wore were beautiful. In time they helped me to dress more like a girl. Others like Estrellita and her friend José gave me advice on how to act away from the orphanage.

After some time, Trinidad indicated that she wanted to rent a room and live away from her parents. Another friend, Lupita, heard us talking about renting a place. Her uncle had two rooms he'd like to rent us. The rooms were in a settlement called San Mateo. We liked the rooms and rented them. I was enjoying living in San Mateo and meeting with my friends. At first only a couple of my friends knew where I grew up. Eventually all of them knew that I was reared by the nuns. When they learned that I wanted to be a nun, comments followed such as "Now I know why you dress like a nun" or "Now we know why you never shave your legs" or "Now we know why you never use facial makeup." I knew they meant no harm, they were just having fun. I didn't appreciate them having fun at my expense, but it was all done in fun.

Trini was serious about how I looked. She said, "Rosita, you have a beautiful body, dress like the girl that you are, not like a nun." Forcing a half smile, I told her not to make fun of me. The other girls were in agreement with Trini. "We are going to help you dress in style, and we are going to comb your hair and even show you how to shave your legs."

"Oh no, nobody is going to shave my legs."

"Don't get mad, Rosita, but your legs are vary hairy. Rosita, do you even know that you have pretty legs, but nobody can tell because they are so hairy."

"Nope, nobody is going to force me to shave my legs." In time, all my friends contributed clothes, including shoes. I began to look and dress better at work, except I refused to shave my legs.

In time, my friends accepted that Mr. Colins in fact had employed me with the speed I mentioned. But little mattered because we were friendly with each other. Secretary's Day was approaching. We all decided that we would celebrate Secretary's Day. I was hesitant because I felt as though I was within the grasp of Sister Mar. That feeling was soon overcome. I went to the celebration with Estrellita. Why not, I was young, and why not? It was all very different to me. This was unlike the graduation party. I felt alive and free. Near the entrance close to the ticket booth, I spotted another where they were selling raffle tickets. They were raffling several prizes; the main one was a car. I bought one! During the course of the night, the various prizes were raffled off. I didn't win a single one. The last raffle was for the car. I WON THE CAR. I couldn't believe it. I don't know how to drive, so what good does it do me?

I went up to where the governor was going to present the car. He congratulated me. After all the fanfare, the noise had died down, I asked the governor if he could do me a favor. I asked him if he could sell the car and, with the money, buy computers for the school in my pueblo, Tetipac. I asked him to buy blankets, clothes, and food for the orphanage. I further requested that he give any money left over to the school in the pueblo I went to. I kept on talking; he stopped me. "Listen, Rosita, come to my office, and we will talk there, okay?"

The governor announced to everybody in attendance what I had requested. He told the audience that I requested that he sell the car and donate the proceeds to the orphanage and to the school in my pueblo. When he was through and the applause died down, he looked at me and said, "Young lady, I have heard many good things about you. I can't believe that you are so sincere. In reality, who are you, really, who are you? Rosita, come to my office tomorrow morning, and we will talk. You are not alone on this matter. My office will help you. We will do everything to make this happen."

My friends were happy that I had won the car and surprised at what I done. I felt happy that I was able to pay back for what Sister

Mar had done for me. Estrellita and I walked together to our rooms. I had a convulsion. Next thing I remember was seeing Estrellita, Trini, and the other girls in my room. *What happened? Why are all my friends here?* I thought. "Good morning, sleeping beauty," said Trini, holding my hand. "Rosita, we have a surprise for you." I didn't say a word, just thought, *A surprise?* "Rosita, get up, go take a shower, before we give you your surprise." I asked, "Are you giving me more new clothes?"

My energy level was low, but I managed to enter the shower. The surprise I got was when I started to soap my legs. They felt strange; my legs were shaved! *I couldn't believe they would do this to me. So this is the surprise they have for me.* I was mad. They shaved my legs when I was asleep. Lupita knocked on the door. "Come on, Rosita, hurry up and get dressed."

"Why did you shave my legs?" I asked angrily when I left the restroom. "We don't have time to discuss that right now." Lupita grabbed my hand; she said, "Come with me to my room. Close your eyes, and don't open them until I tell you." I thought, *Why am I falling for this after what they did to me?*

"Okay, Rosita, open your eyes." Inside her room standing in front of me was Rafa. "Ah, Rafa!" We hugged in front of all my friends. My friends had set me up to my delight. They applauded and closed the door behind them. We were alone, a moment to taste each other's lips, we kissed. "Jova, I can't be without you. I love you too much. I am not going to lose you again." We looked at each other; our eyes said it all, we wanted to be alone. We went to a park nearby. He had a small blanket in his car, took it, and placed it under a tree where we sat.

I asked him, "Rafa, you say that you can't be without me, well, I feel the same way. So what are we going to do?"

"Jova, you know that I work for my mother. I don't get paid much working for her. What I'm trying to say is that I have to find a job that pays me enough to support both of us. Jova, I'm planning on leaving Mexico to find work up North."

"Rafa, you are leaving? When?"

"Probably before the year is over. My plan is to work, and when I have saved enough money, I will come for you."

"But, Rafa, if you can't be without me, why not take me with you now?"

"Jova, I can't take that risk because of your health. I've heard that it is very difficult going across the border for a single person, and worse if we try to cross together."

"You should try to get a visa and cross. Getting a visa should be easy for you being that you work for the government." We spent the rest of the day enjoying each other's company. For the first time in my life, I felt alive, I felt someone's love for me. Well, besides the love of Mamacita, but that is different. I enjoyed our relationship. I didn't want the day to end, but it did; the moon started to end it. The rain that showered on us ended it. He took me home. Before he left, I took of the jacket he'd loaned me during the rain and gave it back. We saw each other two more times before he left.

To my knowledge, he'd gone North to the United States, but I wasn't sure because I didn't hear from him anymore. My life has been a roller-coaster ride full of emotions. Just recently Rafa made me feel alive; he treated me with love and respect. I felt like our time together would never end. Now I feel lonely. I don't have him around anymore. I am sad most of the time; all I want to do is immerse myself within myself. I'm not happy around anybody. Yeah, I pretend, but nobody can see inside my heart. I talk myself out of my misery, I try to ease my feelings by crying when I'm alone. My inner strength kept me going. My faith in my Diosito, my conversations with Him gave me more and more strength.

The university kept me busy, my job made me forget, and my friends showed me how to smile again. My convulsions reminded me—not that I needed reminding—of my sickness. My convulsions also taught me the importance of keeping a bank account. I lost my money when I experienced one of my convulsions. I kept my money in a special purse that I carried with me wherever I went. I had a convulsion on the steps of the university. When I came to, my purse and all my savings were gone; somebody absconded with my money. After that, I went to the local bank and opened an account.

However, money doesn't control my life. In time I had accumulated some more money. It's very interesting how I was able to survive on my earnings. I earned $1,500 a month. My rent was $450, my medicine was $2,400; of course, my employer paid for most of it. I had to eat, pay utilities, but I managed. Making and selling tamales helped. My tuition at the university was paid, but not the books; I had to pay for them.

I've heard people say that time heals all wounds. I have to agree, but not entirely. I still thought of Rafa and wondered if he would ever send for me. My life is not controlled by money nor is it going to be controlled by emotions. Yes, I experience it all, but I will not be controlled. My face started to look livelier because I came out of my emotional shell. Guys noticed me more than before. Maybe because I was being more attentive or maybe because I looked happier. Whatever the reason, I was getting marriage proposals from the students at the university.

My prospective was to finish my education. Nothing else was important. Dancing or parting with my friends was not of interest. Yeah, they made fun of me stating that I was not a nun anymore, to go out and have fun. Statements like "Rafa has forgotten you, he probably found himself a girlfriend in el Norte." One guy that had an interest in me told me, "Rosita, you can't be a nun, so why don't you marry me?" As time went on, my barrier started to wane.

Trini was always after me to join her and friends at a dance. One day she told with a firm voice, "Rosita, you are not a young girl anymore, you are a very attractive young lady. I am going to take you to a dance, even if I have to carry you." She made me laugh; by now I was ready to party. I was ready to go to a dance but not drink any beverage with alcohol. I agreed, but when she said that I would meet a guy there and forget Rafa, I became nervous and almost backed out. But I didn't. "Trini," I said, "I will go, but I don't want to meet a guy." *I don't have time for boyfriends,* I thought. I kept telling myself that Trini was right. I pushed myself out of my shell. *I am young, I should get out of my little corner and meet someone.* My friends were well-off, and they had the support of their families; I was alone like always.

"Rosita, you are not going to change your mind, are you?" I came out of my trance. "No, Trini, I haven't changed my mind." I was preparing myself mentally to go dancing. The night of the dance, my friends came over and helped me get dressed. My favorite dress was displaced by one that didn't make me look like a nun. I was dressed like a young lady. Trini and Paloma gave me instructions on how to act in the dance hall. Paloma told me, "The dance hall doesn't allow little girls," and smiled. "No one but adults are allowed to enter. Some guy will ask you to dance, don't be afraid. Another will want you to go outside to talk. Don't leave the dance hall with anybody. Also, some guy will want to buy you a drink, don't turn him down. Tell him that you want a bottle of whiskey or scotch. Rosita, believe me, you will have to shed your angel wings little by little."

The smell of smoke and other awful odors didn't sit too well in my system. Nothing but adults, loud music, noise, and laughter. The noise drowned our conversation; we practically had to shout. Paloma and Lupita were taken out to dance as soon as we sat down. The waiter came over with a bouquet of roses for me. I was surprised. "Are you sure they are for me?" I asked the waiter. He smiled and said nothing. "Young lady, a gentleman is buying you a drink. What is your preference?" Trini answered, "Whiskey." The waiter told her it wasn't her choice because the man was buying me a bottle, not her. I said, "Whiskey."

My mischievous friends got a little dizzy with the whiskey. I didn't drink any of the whiskey, but I sang along with them. We were a happy bunch, laughing and singing. We arrived home with no problems. For the first time since Rafa left, I enjoyed myself. I went out with my friends and had a good time.

The university was one of my favorite places to go. Most of the time I packed a lunch for work and one for the university. I made many new acquaintances that had attended other high schools. Those students plus the ones I knew from my own high school made the university a pleasant place to be. I didn't realize that I was that well-known until I was elected by the student body to be the University Queen. It was a great honor, but I had to turn it down. When the director told me that I had to march in a bikini in front of everybody, I told her that I couldn't do that. I could not imagine walking in front of a multitude of people modeling a bikini. I don't even allow my friends to shave my legs nor do I walk around them in my underwear. Walk in a bikini onstage in an arena full of people, not me.

Rafa was still on my mind, but not as much. I started to be more aware of other guys—not interested, only aware. One day Trini and I were walking toward the university library. I noticed a familiar guy walking toward us. He made an impression on me, don't know what it was, but we sort of stared at each other. It was a strong stare apparently because Trini took note. "Hey, Rosita, do you know that person? He gave you the eye, or did you notice?" I smiled and turned around to catch another glimpse of him; he had turned to see me at the same time.

Trini was witness to the whole incident. "Oh, the nun is learning to be a woman. Rosita, do you know who that guy is? He is Uriel Loeza." I smiled. "Trini, this nun has to go to class."

"Rosita, remember his name is Uriel." After class I walked out with another student not realizing that Uriel was walking in my direction. "Hi, señorita, where are you going so fast?" I was surprised that he was addressing me. "You are Rosi, aren't you?"

"Yes, I am Rosi, and you are Uriel, right?"

"That's right, I am Uriel from Chilpancingo, and where are you from, Rosi?"

"I am from Tangamandapio." He smiled. "Can I walk with you?" I don't remember how I answered, but we wound up inside the cafeteria. We talked until I had to leave for my other class.

Uriel turned out to be a very interesting individual and intelligent. We kept seeing each other, and we talked about many things except personal matters. That was until he asked me to be his girlfriend. I was hesitant to answer; with my sickness, I could not be anybody's girlfriend. With much trepidation and with tears filling my eyes, I told him that I already had a boyfriend. He apologized. "I'm sorry," he said, "I didn't know. I never see you walking with another guy, and I thought that you weren't promised to anyone."

"Uriel, my boyfriend is in the United States."

"He went to the North and left you here? If I was him, I wouldn't have left you here, you would be with me." He wanted to know more about Rafa, but I had told him enough. I stood up.

"Uriel, let me think about it. I will give you an answer next time we see each other."

I wanted my friends to help me with my decision, so I told them about Uriel. Trini wasn't surprised because she'd seen the glances Uriel and I had exchanged. The others were surprised. "Uriel doesn't give me a second look," one of the girls said; the others mentioned that I was getting more attention than they were. Paloma chimed in with, "Rosita, how many more boyfriends would you have if you dressed like us and not like a nun?" We laughed and laughed, making light of my situation with boys and my manner of dress. Trini stepped up to speak, "Listen, I know who Uriel is. He is good-looking, very intelligent, and is studying to be a lawyer."

"Rosita, if you don't want to be his girlfriend, I will," one of them volunteered. More laughter; another said, "Rosi, you are not a little girl, and he is going to be a lawyer. Forget Rafa, tell him yes."

"Yeah, Rafa doesn't call or write, forget him," another of my friends offered her feeling. "Give Rafa the boot from your heart, he probably has an Americana girlfriend."

"You girls are wrong, Rafa will come for me. Besides, I don't have time for a boyfriend."

I turned to my Diosito, I prayed the rosary before going to bed. *Diosito, my new family is my friends, I can't continue being alone.* I fell asleep speaking with my Savior. The following day, I met Uriel on the university grounds. He had a rose for me. "Rosita, this rose is for the most beautiful girl I know. Did you think about my proposal?" I looked at him for a few moments. *He is very good-looking,* I thought. "Yes, Uriel, I decided to be your girlfriend." The words left my mouth before my brain could stop me. My answer made him smile, seemingly happy. He wanted to hug me. I lifted my hand. "Wait, you have to agree to my conditions." Again, these words came out without giving the conditions much thought.

My mention of *conditions* caught both of us by surprise. I thought, *Rosita, what are you doing? What's wrong with you?* "Uriel, never deceive me, treat me with respect, never make fun of me." He was speechless. "Huh," was all that he said. "Rosita, are you for real? Who are you?"

"Uriel, ignore me, don't pay attention to me."

"Rosita, I will accept your conditions."

"Okay then, I will agree to be your girlfriend."

"Rosita, can I now give you a hug?" I felt strange walking beside him to my class because I usually walked with my female friends or alone.

Uriel was waiting for me when class ended. He invited me for coffee to celebrate our first day as sweethearts. He also wanted to take me to a dance or to eat someplace. I accepted but on a certain condition. He laughed. "Oh, Rosita, do you have a condition for everything?" I shrugged my shoulders and smiled at him. "Okay, I accept, what is the condition?"

"Let's go eat tamales and a bowl of atole."

"That's how you want to celebrate our first day being sweethearts?"

"Uriel, these aren't just any tamales, they are great tamales, and the atole is really good."

"Okay, Rosita, where is this place?"

"My neighbor, she is the one that makes these good tamales." We had a good time.

I was starting to know Uriel. He is very intelligent and lots of fun to be with. He was a complete gentleman, never tried to abuse any of my conditions. Rafa? He was on my mind. But I had to make a decision if Rafa returned for me because I was now committed to Uriel. Being with Uriel served two purposes: I was not alone, and it silenced my friends. I was no longer the little nun but a grown-up female.

On the third day of being committed to Uriel, the roller coaster of my life surfaced. My supervisor had given me the day off. That afternoon I left early for the university to make a few pesos before class. I usually helped in the university cafeteria making tortillas. On the way to the cafeteria, I ran into some of my friends. I talked and talked; they in turn were somewhat subdued. I asked, "Okay, what's going on?" Trini said, "Rosita my friend, I'm glad that we ran into you. Let me tell you it's time that you leave the attitude of an angel and get rid of your wings."

"Trini, what's gotten into you, why are you telling me that?"

"Come with us to the edge of the stairs." I didn't know what they were up to, but I followed them anyway. At the bottom of the stairs, Trini told me to walk to the very top. These girls are acting very mysterious. I followed their orders and started to climb the stairs. They followed me at a distance. I continued to climb halfheartedly, not knowing what to expect. Trini pointed to the top.

Uriel, my boyfriend of three days, was kissing another girl. WHAT! I stopped to make sure that indeed it was Uriel. It was! He was embracing and kissing another girl. Shoot, nobody makes a fool out of me. I ran up the stairs so fast as though wings were helping me. The two were completely unaware that I was nearby and approaching fast. My friends followed me to the top of the stairs and witnessed the whole affair. I stood next to them, I tapped Uriel on his shoulder. "Sweetheart?" Uriel heard my voice and immediately let go of his latest girlfriend.

Caught completely off guard, Uriel could only say, "Good afternoon, señorita." His latest girlfriend asked, "Who are you, and why did you disturb us? Uriel, do you know this girl?"

"Yes, she is just a friend. Rosita, why don't you go to class, and we'll talk later." He tried to hold my hand. "Uriel, don't touch me. Uriel, tell this girl who I am. It's been what—oh yes, three days that we became sweethearts, isn't it, Uriel? Come on, tell this girl how you promised to be my boyfriend. Tell her that you promised to follow certain conditions before I would consent to be your sweetheart. They were all lies, weren't they, Uriel?"

"Rosita, let me explain." He came close to me. I slapped him hard.

"Uriel, don't try to cross my path of life again. Nobody—not you nor anyone else—toys with my emotions. From this moment on, you and I are nothing to each other. Uriel, did you plan to be with this girl and have me on the side? I didn't believe that you were capable of deception until this moment." The latest girlfriend said, "Uriel, you bastard, are you also deceiving me?" She also slapped him. I turned and walked away from them.

My friends surrounded me trying to console my battered ego. We sat on benches to discuss what had just happened to me. The girls were talking and talking. I was occupied in my thoughts. I was somewhat upset and angry—not at anybody in particular other than myself—for believing Uriel. I was inexperienced in this matter, but dumb I'm not. I thought of Rafa, was he also deceiving me? I opened up, "Listen, I love all of you, but please, from now on, let me decide my own personal business." I told them that I appreciate all they do for me and not to take it personally, "but right now, I'm having an emotional breakdown." Trini hugged me; then one by one they hugged and whispered words of encouragement.

I walked to the cafeteria to help, then off to class. Uriel was waiting for me. He asked for forgiveness and tried to give me three red roses and a note. I told him that I forgave him. But the roses, I told him to give them to another of his girlfriends. I turned around and left him standing like a rock. Every day I thought of Rafa, I don't know why, but I felt as though I was liking him more and more. He did respect me and didn't try to abuse me. Maybe that is the reason I wait for him. But months without hearing from him also gave me reason to feel that he might not be coming for me.

I wasn't waiting in my little corner, I still went to an occasional dance with my friends. I talked to other male students, some that kept asking me for a date. One of my classmates, Agustín in particular, kept asking me for a date. He was one intelligent person. We'd discuss class and even had lunch with him. He kept asking me why I didn't want to have him as my boyfriend. I didn't want to chain some guy to me. My sickness didn't allow me to have a boyfriend. I felt that in time if I accepted, he would get tired of me due to my being epileptic. Agustín knew about my sickness, and it didn't seem to bother him, but to me it didn't seem right. At times I wanted to tell the handsome Agustín that I would be his girlfriend, but I never did.

I had a favorite bench that I used when I was between classes or when I just wanted to be in my own corner of the world. I left my books for a few seconds; when I returned, there was stuffed teddy bear on top of my books with a note:

> Rosita, what a beautiful person you are. Not only physically but you have such a wonderful personality.
>
> —Agustín

That day in class, he kept glancing at me and smiling. I knew that he was interested in me, but he also knew that I wasn't ready for a boyfriend. After class he came over and asked if he could talk to me. Before I answered, I thanked him for the teddy bear. "Rosita, I gave you the teddy bear with lots of my love." We started to walk. "Rosita, can we talk on the way to your house?"

"Yes, that is okay, but do you mind stopping for some atole?" We got some atole and sat under a tree. We settled down.

"Rosita, I fell in love with you the first day I saw you. You are a beautiful girl. Will you be my girlfriend? Please don't say no, you will break my heart."

"Agustín, please don't ask me that. I don't feel pretty, only happy in life. Please don't tell me that you are in love with me."

"Rosita, if that's what you want, it's okay with me. Tell me face-to-face if there is a chance that someday you will be my girlfriend. I want to know because you have been on my mind like, forever. I will not betray you like Uriel did." I was surprised when he said that. "How did you know about Uriel, who told you?"

"Rosita, there are no secrets in this place, nothing goes unnoticed.

"Rosita, you have inspired me to be more attentive in class, to be smarter, because I want you to accept me. I hope that you will give a chance, if not now, maybe in the future. I want my future to be with you, to be part of you." I was really tempted to say yes, but again my sickness places my own future in doubt. I can't tie anybody to something they will regret later. Rafa was an exception, but then he isn't here to see me struggle with my epilepsy. "Agustín, I wish that I could, but I can't. Believe me, there are reasons that I can't be anybody's girlfriend." My thoughts drifted back to the beginning of this sickness. That woman that left me for dead as a baby is the cause of my sickness. My sickness has prevented me from being a nun. My sickness has stood in the way on so many other occasions, and now this. I didn't want to break his heart, but I had to say something. "Agustín, I have a boyfriend, I gave him my word, and I can't break that promise."

He gave me a questioning look. I felt that he was thinking that if that was true, then why had I agreed to be Uriel's girlfriend? I added, "My boyfriend is in el Norte. With all sincerity, I am not looking for a boyfriend. The fact that Uriel betrayed has nothing to do with my decision. Believe me, Agustín, if my situation was different, I would love to be your girlfriend, but now I am not ready." His tears enforced his feelings for me; he grabbed my hands, we stood up, and I allowed him to hug me. He left without saying a word.

Once again I felt alone, I was sad and heartbroken. First, I hadn't heard from Rafa, next because my sickness again prevented me from being a normal being. Agustín was a very sincere person and would have been a great partner for me. But I am not a normal person. I took my journal and wrote. I thought back to the time Don Felipe wrote my first diary because I didn't know how to write. I thought about the times when I learned from him how to write and how much I miss those times.

My computer classes were coming to a close. My desire to get an education was not impacted by my sickness. Probably it is more instrumental in my drive to finish my education. Knowledge in computing was already paying rewards for me. I was thrilled when I along with Trini finished the classes. Our other friends were equally happy that we had finished the classes.

Trini and I getting our Computing certificates.

My friend María and I.

After Trini finished with the computing class, she informed me that she was moving. I couldn't believe that she was leaving; after all, I had moved to that place only because of her. The day she moved out was one of the saddest days in my life. I wasn't the same anymore. I was learning who I was. I kept thinking about my sickness wondering if I would ever be cured. My faith in Chuchin never wavered. I knew that He would put me in the path of a doctor who would cure me. But was that path in Mexico or in the United States?

August 16, 1999, is a day that I will always remember. I along with my immediate supervisor were requested to attend a meeting in the Human Resources room. The head of the Human Resources department and Divina, the supervisor of the Accounting department, were waiting for us. Divina gave me a big hug. That was a sign for me that I wasn't in trouble. Divina asked me, "Rosita, do you have any idea why we sent for you?"

"Señora Divina, I have no idea."

"Rosita, every year we reward the best employee with special bonus. The department heads get together, and we evaluate all of our employees. You, young lady, have been recognized as the best of all employees. Your proposals to better the workplace and how we can better serve the community have been very useful. For these reasons, we found you to be the best employee, and you earned this bonus."

She presented me with a check for 1,500 pesos. I accepted the check and thanked Divina. I said, "I am very happy that my ideas have served the people."

One day Mirna, the governess, and René Juarez, the governor, paid me a visit to thank me for all I was doing for the needy. They told me that I was on the right path and soon I would be elevated.

My emotional roller coaster was on the high rail. I seemed that nothing but positive things were happening to me. But having experienced this before, I was apprehensive. My being was to be friendly with all that I encountered. I helped raise funds for the needy as a volunteer for the worthy causes. I met many people, and as a result, I became well-known.

Dinner, wedding, and baptismal invitations were always extended to me. When I had time, I would accept their invitations. Estrellita, one of my dear friends, invited me for breakfast to celebrate the baptism of her baby. Estrellita prepared a wonderful meal. However, I was unable to enjoy it, I had a convulsion.

When I woke up, I looked around to see another strange room. I never get used to waking up in somebody else's room. Estrellita was at my bedside. "Rosita, I am so happy that you are conscious. I don't know why you fainted, all I could do was take you to the emergency room at the hospital. Now you are in my house. Rosita, I want you to stay as long as you like, this is your house."

"Estrellita, I appreciate what you have done. Tell me, how much do I owe you for the hospital?"

"Rosita, you owe nothing, everything is paid. The whole DIF department got together and took care of the cost. Rosita, tell me, what happened?"

"Oh, señora, forgive me for not telling you before. I am an epileptic, and I suffer these convulsions periodically. I've had these convulsions all my life because of my sickness."

"Well, Rosita, I have to admire you. You have a lot of courage for going through life with this sickness and alone.

"You didn't have time to eat, but we have enough. Please join us in the kitchen so that you can eat." Martín Zuñiga, Estrellita's husband, and their daughters sat with me. One of her lovely daughters said to me, "*Manita* (little sister), being in this house, you will never eat alone." The whole Zuñiga family made me feel at home. Such a wonderful family; I wished that mine was different.

They took me to my little home. Esrellita walked up to my room. She was shocked when she saw the inside. "Manita, this is where you live?" My shabby furniture, my cardboard bed, candles for light were apparently too much for her to bear. She couldn't hold back her tears. "Rosita, this is too much, I am going to make sure that these living conditions improve." I didn't know what to say, I was content in living a life void of problems, free of a cruel and dominating mother and a lecherous old man. I smiled at Estrellita. "Don't worry, señora, I'm happy, and someday I will have a better place."

The doctor had recommended that I shouldn't work the next day, but I felt fine. I dressed and left for work all the while talking with my Diosito. I walked into my office; first thing I noticed was a bouquet of flowers on top of my desk, next to it was a card with my name on it. I thought, *This card is for me? Why? It's not my birthday.* I picked up the card, and before I could read it, the door opened, and several of my coworkers walked in, led by Mr. Colins, the manager. He saluted me, and one by one the others also greeted me. "Rosita, don't look surprised, we are here to share some good news with you."

Señor Colins said, "Rosita, you are a great example for the rest of us of what a good employee is. In spite of your illness, you are the most punctual employee of the department. In spite of wrestling with a life without family, you manage to help others."

"Olé, olé," accompanied by an applause, ignited my tears. He continued, "Rosita, we want you to know that our homes are always open to you. Rosita, why don't you open your card." I opened the card and read it. My salary was increased considerably, and I was given a week's paid vacation to start immediately.

"Eey!" I covered my mouth when I made that joyful scream. "Thank you, Señor Colins. I thank all of you for making this possible." He continued, "Rosita, the accounting office has agreed to pay for more computing classes." My coworkers applauded, Mr. Colins raised his arms to silence the applause. "In addition, the department is going to provide the orphanage where you grew up with blankets, food, and other necessities." That was incredible; why they were doing this had to be the work of my Diosito. Murmurs permeated throughout the room when they heard that I was raised in an orphanage. Mr. Colins told them, "That's where I met Rosita. She was raised in that orphanage."

Mr. Colins stated, "The fact that she was raised in an orphanage further explains the type of person Rosita is. She has not given up on life, no, rather, she has embraced who she is. Now you know a little more of this person whom you work with. I must leave, you all can stay for a while with Rosita then off to work." With that message, Mr. Colins left the room. My coworkers wanted to know more about my life in the orphanage. One by one they gave me a hug before they left me alone.

Vacation Spent at the Orphanage

MR. COLINS, HIS CREW, AND myself packed all the goods purchased by the department. My vacation was all arranged, I would go to the orphanage and deliver the goods. Sister Mar had no idea that I would be coming to visit. She was surprised when we arrived with blankets and shoes for all forty of the girls. Equally surprised when we started to unload sacks of beans, corn, and corn flour. She could not begin to understand how I had managed to deliver so many goods to the orphanage. After the goods were stored and the workers left, she invited me to sit with her under our favorite tree.

We walked to our place; before we sat, she grabbed my hand and hugged me. I felt a hug only a mother would give, full of feeling and love. Sister Mar was crying, we sat in silence on the bench where I had spent many times all alone. She grabbed my hand, faced me, and spoke in a low voice. "Yovani, I will be not be able to rest in peace when I leave this world knowing that I have done you wrong and you have not forgiven me. Yovani, forgive me, my child, for treating you bad, forgive me for not allowing you to pursue your desire to become a nun. Forgive me for not believing in you and allowing another nun to mistreat you."

"Sister Mar, please don't cry anymore," I implored. "You gave me refuge when I needed it the most, you took me in even though I'm not from here. I never would have survived if you didn't take me out of that horrible situation I was in. Only my Diosito knows what I'd be like if you hadn't given me refuge. I will never forget what you did for me. In addition, I don't think that you did anything deserving forgiveness. However, Sister Mar, if you believe that I need to forgive you, I forgive you."

"God bless you, Yovani." She wanted to know how I had managed to get all the goods for the orphanage. I told her, and I also told her how I had been treated by the lady that I worked for after I left the home. We concluded our talk with a good hug.

After Sister Mar and I parted, I went looking for one of my friends still at the home. I met up with Ofelia, the girl I was looking for. I gave her a box of chocolates. We played in the garden with the other little girls. We walked the grounds to the pigsty and the chicken coop. Each place brought memories, some of which I shared with Ofelia.

I visited all the families who had helped me during my stay at the home. I visited the Barrera family, the Porras family, and Don José Luis and family. I spent a very happy time at my prior home. I was somewhat sad when I left. But I was glad to be home and ready to face my future. The house was different. I no longer had Cristi to hang around with. I wanted to move, but I wasn't sure where. One of the neighbors had a small room. She'd heard that I wanted to move and offered it to me. I made the move because the rent was less than what I was paying. The room wasn't anything to brag about. The place was put together with boards; the roof appeared to be made out of cardboard boxes. I moved because I wanted to make ends meet. I figured to rent for a few weeks then move out to a better place. I got some plastic and covered the walls and the ceiling hoping to keep the wind and rain out.

We celebrated Secretary's Day with a big party. Estrellita gave me a lift to the party. The food was really good; the speech by the managers were too long. The best part was when the goods being raffled started. I have always been lucky with these raffles. Tonight was no exception. I won a real nice bed and a refrigerator. The bed I kept, and the refrigerator I sold for 3,000 pesos. In time I bought a small refrigerator, a mattress, a small stove, a small table, and a closet for my clothes. Now I had enough to furnish my little place.

I had enough money left over, I thought of my sister. Maybe I would go visit her. I was walking through the front office when I thought I saw my uncle, Matilde Bustos, in the building. I got a closer look; it was him. He and the president of the pueblo were inside the DIF office. I asked the secretary to call me when the meeting was over so that I could talk with my uncle. It happened, and we had a nice conversation. We met after work, and he took me to eat. In the process of speaking, I asked him if he would take a washer to my sister Ana. That is how my sister got a washer.

I was on my way to the university, and the clouds were getting darker and heavier. The rains came, something that I had dreaded. The plastic did nothing to prevent the rains from coming into my shabby room. When I entered my room, I saw my furniture floating, my clothes were soaked. The box with my important papers, my diaries, the papers Mamacita left me—all were in a waterproof box, so I knew they were safe. Alone in my ill-constructed room, I made the sign of the cross, I prayed with tears in my eyes. "Diosito, why do these things happen to me? Isn't my sickness enough? I worked for what I have, now this? What am I supposed to do now?" I closed the door and left the shabby hut.

The taxi dropped me off at Trini's house. I was crying when she opened the door. She hugged me before she led me to the kitchen. She prepared some tea, and we talked. I told her how I had lost everything that I had worked so hard for. She offered me shelter for the night. The following day, she and I went to my shabby shack to retrieve what was salvageable. With my valuable papers and some clothes, I moved into an apartment where Trini and my other friends lived. I was paying 550 pesos a month. I figured that my income would cover the rent and other expenses; as for food, well, that was another thing. Somehow I would manage that necessity. Now I was happier being closer to my friends and a more livable place.

My life was spent between the university and work. I had no nightlife, although on occasion I would accompany my friends to a dance. I never danced, but I did accept the whiskey from the guys. Naturally my friends enjoyed it, and I enjoyed watching them get a little tipsy. Work was another place I enjoyed; something was always going in that involved me. Mr. Colins was always interested in helping the less-fortunate people from the area. He needed ideas on how best to serve the poor. With that purpose in mind, he formed a committee to come up with ideas. I was on that committee.

My idea was to prepare an event for Christmas where we would raise money for the needy. My idea was to make decorations for Christmas and sell them. I selected a group of people to make the decorations. Estrellita Bello Hernández and many of her friends were very eager to help. We made big signs and posted them all over the area. The signs read, "WE SHALL PLANT BEFORE WE RECEIVE." We made the decorations in time for feast of the event entitled the Nativity. On the day of the event, we sold everything we made.

The governor of the pueblo presented me with a Major Donor Certificate. In the audience were several of the wealthy men of the pueblo. I heard a great applause after the presentation. I felt happy that I was able to help my people. After the event, all the volunteers and the department employees were rewarded with a nice dinner.

I was beginning to enjoy getting dressed for these events. Trini gave me a very nice dress and shoes; besides that, she helped me get ready. Trini told me that I looked like a young woman and not a nun-child like before. She made me laugh with the way she said that. Nun-child? Hmm, that was in the past. I was emerging into the world of womanhood, and I was looking like a young lady. I enjoyed my life, I was happy with my life.

After the dinner, the accountant took the microphone. My friends and I were laughing having a good time. I thought I heard my name being called. Trini looked at me. "Rosita, I think that he just called your name." He called out to me, "Come on, Jovani, come up here." I didn't know what to expect or why he had called my name. I walked up to the front where the accounting manager was waiting. "Jovani, we are glad to present you with this Christmas bonus for 2,500 pesos. Your idea to hold this event is reason number one, second is you are the most punctual of all the employees in the department. Good job," he said, handing me the money. I walked back to my table accompanied by a great applause.

The little girls in the orphanage would be happy with the shoes I bought for all forty of them. Sister Mar also would enjoy the 1,000 pesos I was going to send her. I invited Trini and the other friends to dinner. With some of the money, I planned to buy me some clothes and take a trip to my pueblo to visit my sister Ana for Christmas.

Christmas vacation arrived. I was getting ready to make the trip to visit my sister. All my friends had gone or were planning on visiting their families as well. I had mixed emotions about going. The problem with visiting was the presence of Reyna and her lecherous friend in the pueblo. But I wanted to be with my sister and my niece. I really wanted to visit Mama Lucia and the aging Don Felipe. Mostly I would visit my church, I would again be with my Chuchin. I had another convulsion. Estrellita worried when I didn't show up at her house. She had offered to take me to the bus depot. She found me lying on the floor, and she took me to the hospital. I had a big gash on the left side of my head. The doctor sewed five stitches to close the gash. I spent both 1999 Christmas and New Year 2000 in the hospital.

The days in the hospital gave me time to reflect on my past. I thought back to my days in my pueblo playing with my childhood friends. I thought of Mother. Would she ever give me a mother's hug? Don Felipe was getting old, I wondered if I would ever see him again. Although I heard that he would not leave this life before he saw me again. Mama Lucia, my third mom, was constantly on my mind. But nobody occupied my thoughts like Mamacita Sinforosa. I have spent the happiest days with her, especially at her ranch in el llano. I pray to my Diosito, my Chuchin, constantly.

I hear rain, I walk to the window. The moon is trying to peek through the clouds. The rain doesn't stop, yet the moon tries to sneak through. I smile. "Diosito, You are listening to me." The moon is no longer visible, the clouds are hiding her but only for a moment. The moon appears again brighter than ever. I saw enough to know that my Diosito is listening to me.

My stay finally ends. I still have a few days' vacation, and I decided that no matter what, I am going to my pueblo.

After Nine Years, I Return to My Pueblo

JANUARY 5, 2000, I ARRIVE at the bus station. My niece Claudia was waiting for me. She is such a pretty girl, and I tell her so. I also tell her that I want to see the Santa Cruz Church before anything else. I wanted to thank my Chuchin and the Blessed Virgin for the safe trip. Ana and I were so happy to see each other, we both cried. It had been a long time since we'd seen each other. We talked, ate, cried, and laughed for hours. She brought me up to date on Don Felipe, Mama Lucia, and Mamacita and others. I asked if she had seen Ruben. "Vani, that bum is still in love with you. Every time he sees me, he asks for you. I hear rumors that he has a girlfriend. He has girlfriends all over town, but he waits for you." Ana wanted to know about my life, especially if I had a boyfriend. I told her about Agustín, Uriel, Rafa, and others who wanted to marry me. Her response was, "Well, Vani, you are a very attractive young lady. Look at your body, you are not a little girl anymore, you are a woman."

The next day I put on a dress that Trini had selected because it was in style. It was a beautiful dress, a little short, which made me feel somewhat uncomfortable. Claudia went with me; I was going to visit some friends. The boys from the pueblo liked what they saw because they started whistling at me. That was it. I turned back to Ana's house to change into something more comfortable. I felt more at ease walking to see Mama Lucia with my change of clothes.

Mama Lucia was busy cooking and didn't notice when we entered. Quietly I walked behind her, placed my hands over her eyes. She cried out, "My *bebé*, my *bebé*, it is you!" She hugged me.

"My bebé," she cried out, "you are alive, thanks be to God you are alive."

"Yes, Mama Lucia, I'm alive, look at me, I'm here."

"Mija, your mother is telling everyone that you are dead!" We talked for a long time. Between preparing the food, we talked and talked. Mama Lucia told me that the people in the pueblo have different stories about me. Some say that indeed I am dead, others say that I'm in a convent. "Mija, whatever the rumors say, you are here with me again.

"Oh, mija Rosita, you have grown into a beautiful young woman. I am so glad that you grew up with the nuns. I always knew where you were because the priest told me. I let the people think whatever they wanted, I knew that you were off and that I would see you again. Mija, Don Felipe is growing old. You should go see him. He tells everybody that wants to hear that he will not die until he sets his eyes on you again."

Don Felipe looked old! I stood at the doorway for a few seconds looking at my half-asleep mentor. I looked around at his darkened room thinking of all the times I would run to him when I needed a friend to talk to. So long ago, yet it seemed like a moment that I was the little girl giving him his coffee. I spoke softly so as not to startle him. My greeting surprised him. "Alma de Dios, you are here." He recognized my voice. "Diosito sent you here before I die." I knelt and hugged him.

He stared at me, touched my cheek. His feeble and cold hand sent a message of love. I grabbed my old friend's hands, his teary eyes locked on me. Not wanting to say anything, I held back my tears.

"Mija," he said, "you have changed so much, you are so beautiful! For sure now you look like an Alma de Dios.

"Alma de Dios, you know that I'm getting old, so before I forget, I have some notes and pictures that I have been saving for you." He told me where he'd hidden them. In the corner of his little room, he'd dug a hole in the ground. I followed his directions. Inside the hole was a metal box. I retrieved it; inside was another box full of my old notes. I gave him the taco plate that I'd brought him. He ate while I told him what he wanted to know about me since I left the pueblo. I gave him a hug before I left. He gave me his blessing. Claudia and I left and went for a walk aoound the pueblo.

My pueblo had changed in so many ways. But mainly it was the way I felt being home. I really didn't have a home there anymore; no, my home was someplace else. However, some customs don't change. That night we'd just finished cleaning the dishes. Somebody was whistling outside. Ana looked at me. "Aye, Vani, I'll bet some guy knows that you are back, and he's come calling for you." I said, "How do you know?"

"Vani, don't you remember, when the boys come calling, they don't knock on the door, no, they whistle outside. I'll bet you it's Ruben, he's always asking for you."

"Ruben? You mean Ruben the playboy?"

"Yes, Vani, the same one. He has several girlfriends, but he likes you the best, you know that." We heard more whistles; this time Claudia went outside to investigate. She came back in with a smile on her face. "Auntie, it's Rubén, he wants to see you." Ana said, "I knew it, I knew that as soon that he heard that you were back in the pueblo, he'd come to see you. Vani, he'll want to hug and to kiss you, be careful."

"Ana, you worry too much. If Rubén wants to kiss me, I'll let him. I will give him a kiss he'll never forget, he will discover that I'm not a little girl anymore."

"Vani, what are you saying?" I laughed. "Ana, don't worry, I'm not little girl, I can handle him."

I changed to the dress that I was wearing earlier, the same one that elicited the whistles before. His eyes lit up when I stepped out the door, he moved toward me. He grabbed my hand but continued to stare. "What's the matter, Rubén, I thought you wanted to talk?"

"Ah, gee, you're more beautiful now, I don't know what to say." He guided my hand toward his chest. His heart was beating very fast. "Rubén, you better relax," I told him as I pulled my hand back. "Jovani, man, I can't believe how much you have changed."

"No, Rubén, I'm the same girl that you used to ignore my friendship when we were younger.

"Come, Rubén, let's sit on the bench under the tree. Now," I said smiling, sorta teasing him, "your not ignoring me, huh, why?"

"Forgive me, Jovani. Look, I was what, seven or eight years old, I didn't know anything about girls, much less about love. Honostly, Jovani, as God is my witness, I was in love with you then, and I still love you very much." Smiling, I said, "Well, you sure had a way of showing it with all your rejections, and many times you ignored me completely."

"Jovani, you have changed, but not in that respect, you still like to throw digs at me. You are still a sincere person and very attractive. Jovani, when my friends told me that you were here, I went home, cleaned up, and came to see you."

"Rubén, I noticed that you too have changed. You are more serious and not as mishievious, I like that.

"Rubén, what have you been up to since I left the pueblo?"

"Well, I didn't realize that you had left the pueblo. Somebody mentioned that you had gone away. Nobody knew where you were. Talk was that you were sent away to an orphanage, others thought that you were sent to the convent. Eventually I left for el Norte, like so many others from here. But I always thought of you."

"Aye, Rubén, you probably use that line on all your girlfriends. Don't try that line on me, I know you."

"Okay, Jovani, I won't lie to you, I do have a girlfriend, but I don't love her like I love you. Your love is engraved in my heart and always will be."

"Rubén, I have to go, and you too should go—but to confession."

"Huh, Jovani, why do you say that?"

"Oh, Rubén, just think of all the things you have been telling me. But if they are true, then you don't need to confess anything." I smiled.

"Jovani, seeing you in front of me, I can't help it, but can I have a kiss? Please don't say no."

"Rubén, were you in love with me like I was in love with you?" Rubén hugged me. I allowed him to kiss my cheek. I could feel his tears. "Jovani, come with me. I will leave my girlfriend. I will do anything to be with you."

"No, Rubén, I can't do that to anybody. Besides, I have a boyfriend. I'm in love with him. He is also in el Norte, and he promised to come for me." I watched as he walked away from me. He stopped and came back. "Jovani, I am going up North alone. I am not taking my girlfriend. If your boyfriend doesn't come for you, let me know, I will come for you. Think about my offer, I will come for you." He started to walk away. I stopped him.

"Rubén, I appreciate those words, I believe that you will come for me." It came to me that I can't leave my job, my friends, and my country. I belong here, not in some strange country. For some reason, I couldn't let him leave without a word of encouragement. I spoke, "Rubén, remember that I always said that I was going to write a book about my life? That is more than a dream. I have notes, diaries, and many pictures, and someday I will write that book. You are going to be in my book." Rubén shed more tears. "Why, Jovani, do you torture me?"

He walked away—probably from my life—forever. But who knows, maybe not, the future dictates such things. If I have to leave my country, then I shall. My Diosito will continue to guide me. After all, health is my priority. My heart felt sad seeing him walk away from my life. The image of Rubén and Rede Casteñada fighting over me came to mind. I thought how Rede Casteñada used to defend me. He would bring me flowers and some candy. Rafa was not on my mind as often.

Vacationing in my pueblo brought many memories, both happy ones and sad ones. I didn't fit there anymore. My mentor, Don Felipe, was aged. I probably saw him for the last time. Mama

Lucia will always be my third mother, and Ana and Claudia will always be family. I returned to Chilpancingo with distant memories of Mamacita and others. I continued to work and to finish my studies at the university. A constant reminder was my health. I was getting to a point in my life where I had to do something. My convulsions continued, I was prevented from becoming a nun, I couldn't be a lawyer, and maybe not even a mother. Which occupation was the right one for me? I continued my search for that one occupation.

Trini and I received our computer certification on the twenty-seventh of January from the university. One more step in search of my future. One more birthday, I turned nineteen that year. I was given a really wonderful party. My friends and coworkers made it all possible. Singers Orlando and Norma Martinez sang "Las Mañanitas," a Mexican birthday song. Estrellita gave me a bouquet of flowers and a beautiful blouse; the lady university cook gave me a blanket and a rosary. Being nineteen years of age means that I am a preadult, as per some customs. I feel the same age doesn't dictate anything different, except now I can go into a bar legitimately.

My male classmates invited me to a dance and wouldn't let me say no. Trini stepped in, told them, "Rosita will never go to a dance, especially with a bunch of guys. But invite her friends including me, Adaliz, Magda, Paloma—we are always ready to go dancing, and Rosita will come with us. However," Trini continued, "we will order the drinks, and you guys pay for them, agree?" Agustín was at the dance. He said to me, "Rosita, with all my heart and my love, I wish you the best of birthdays. Remember, I love you very much." He presented me with a red rose and a note. I read it; it was so touching, full of feeling for me. I thought, *Here I am thinking that Rafa will come for me, when in reality, he never will, and I feel that.* I danced with Agustín and had a great time.

We left the dance very late in the night. Trini asked if she could help open my birthday presents. One of the gifts was a golden chain with Jesus on the cross and a Blessed Virgin medal. Another was a gift of 1,793 pesos from my fellow employees.

My health kept reminding how fragile I was. I started to feel weak during the first days in April. I was at the university when I became ill. The three teachers who witnessed how I ill I became very concerned. They had a conference with me stating their concern. They asked me not to attend any more law classes; their reasoning was that I needed to rest. They also told me that they didn't want to be responsible if something happened to me during class. I had to withdraw from the law classes. Worse was that I would not be able to be a lawyer. I had to take care of my health; somewhere there has to be a cure. My sickness was preventing me from pursuing another profession.

Working for the government was good, but it was not a solution. The government wasn't in a position to help me with any kind of operation. I had been to Acapulco, and they currently didn't have the expertise to help me. I was alone, yes, I have very good friends, but they have their own lives. I became very sad, my friends tried to console me, and that helped me a lot. Esmeralda, one of my older friends, told me her story. She had become a mom and had to withdraw from the university. In time when her child was older, she returned to the university and got her degree. I was older when I finally finished my studies. Trini and Paloma laughed at the mention that she was old. She got a little perturbed. "Laugh all you want, but I may be old but, I'm not an old lady. Rosita, take a semester off, come back and get your education."

My education was now less important than my health. "I will take time off from my studies, and I will seek the right doctors who can help me." Trini was truly worried about me, she didn't want to see me sad. She would accompany me to Acapulco to have further studies; maybe now they could help me. My other friends were also concerned. I was tired of everything. I told my friends to leave me alone. They told me not to act so brave, and they didn't leave me alone. Trini told me, "Suppose we leave alone, and you have a convulsion, some idiot might take advantage of you. No, we won't leave alone. Try to go to Acapulco, you have the money." I spent the night at Trini's place.

I had indeed made an appointment months prior with a doctor in Acapulco, but I had forgotten. I told Trini about my appointment. I learned that the company actually had a program to help the workers that needed medical assistance. With Trini assisting me, I applied to the program Integral Development of a Family. Within three days, the application was approved. The government accepted my petition to pay for my expenses to see my doctor in Acapulco. Friday morning, Magda and I were on our way to Acapulco. We arrived at her home in Acapulco the same day at seven that evening. I stayed with her family for the time I was in the city or Acapulco. Magda's mother and I became very good friends. That Saturday morning, I helped her sell tamales. On the weekend, Magda introduced me to many of her family and relatives.

Magda and her mother wanted me to meet another of her cousins who had just arrived from el Norte. Both Magda and her mother claimed the cousin was a very hardworking and very responsible individual. Magda said, "Rosita, my cousin lives in a place called Kansas City. He can tell you a lot about los Estados Unidos (the United States)." Magda and her mother were getting all excited talking about this cousin who could help me somehow. Unbeknown to me, Magada's mother had sent for the recently arrived cousin. They were still talking about this person when we heard a commotion. A couple of kids were leading an unwilling young man by the hands unto the yard. We walked outside to investigate the commotion.

The young man took off his hat when he saw me. Believing that this was the cousin they were telling me about, I stood in front of him. I saluted him, surprised to see that he was taller than what I had imagined. He appeared to be surprised to see me as well because he just stood looking at me. Magda said, "Come on, Melchor, say something to Rosita." *Well, what's going on, why was I asked to come here?* Magda told Melchor who I was and that I wanted to ask him about the United States. They went into the house and left Melchor and I alone.

"Señorita, I don't know why I was asked to come here, but seeing a beautiful dove in front of me, I'm happy that I came. I can't imagine why such a beautiful dove wants to see me." Smiling at his words, I thought, *Don't tell me that you're like all the others?* "We'll talk about that later," I said. "I came here because I have an appointment on Monday with a doctor in Acapulco."

"Really? I know the city, if you let me, I can go with you." I didn't respond because Magda's mother came out to keep us company. "Rosita, I'm happy that you met Melchor. He is prepared to help you in any way possible. Excuse me for interrupting, I will leave you alone again."

"Rosi, ah, can I call you Rosi?"

"Sure, why not, I've been called by other names, one more won't bother me." I smiled. "Well, Magda told me that you live in the United States. She believes that you can help me find my sisters that live in a place called California."

"Aha, now I understand your motive. In reality, I know how, but are you sure you want to go to the el Norte? If you are sure, I will do what I can, yes, I'm ready to help you. I can help you locate your sisters."

"Melchor, I'm not sure yet that I want to leave Mexico, I'll let you know."

"Okay, Rosi, now, can I accompany you to Acapulco?"

"Yes, Melchor, but be here early on Monday, don't be late, or I'll leave without you. Rosi, I can't believe that you are so pretty."

The rooster's crow woke me up, I rushed to the shower. I dressed and got the rest of me ready for the trip to see the doctor. Magda and her mother were getting up as I was leaving. We greeted each other, they saw me off with a hug and their blessing. Melchor was already outside waiting for me. He greeted me with these words: "Good morning, and how is the most precious girl I know?" I was slightly upset. "Melchor, please don't talk to me like that. I appreciate your company, but if you are going to talk like that, I would prefer to go alone." He place his hand over his heart. "Forgive me, I want to gain your confidence in me and mean no harm. Though truly I liked you from the first moment I saw you, actually, I think I'm in love with you."

I was beginning to regret allowing him to accompany me to Acapulco. I'm not interested in having a boyfriend anyhow, not now. He talked about the United States and how he would help me find my sisters. I thought all along that he just wanted to let me know how much he knew about el Norte, a place I knew nothing about. Melchor admitted that he didn't know anything about California, where my sisters lived. He mentioned that he was sure that the United States had the doctors and facilities that would cure my epilepsy. I wasn't too talkative, my mind was occupied thinking about my pending date with the specialist doctor. He did mention one positive thing that stuck in my mind more than anything else. He told me that he would help me—whether or not we got into a relationship. However, the rest of the conversation was offensive because he kept mentioning how much he wanted to have a relationship with me.

Entering the hospital, he mentioned that I should make up my mind pretty soon because he was leaving for el Norte in a week. "However, if you accept me as your boyfriend, I am willing to wait as long as it takes you to get ready."

"What? Melchor, I don't know you. I do appreciate your help, but I can't. You know that because I am an epileptic, I was denied going into the convent, I can't be a lawyer, and I certainly can't be a mother. Let me be truthful with you, I already have a boyfriend that I fell in love with. He understands me and has accepted me." He grabbed my hand. "Rosi," he said, "I am in love with you, and I don't care if you are in love with another guy. Give me an opportunity, and with time, you will forget him." I was at the reception and didn't have time to respond.

My examination showed that I was getting worse. I had a tumor inside the left side of my head. They didn't have the knowledge or the capability to help me. Besides, if they were to bring a specialist from someplace else, it would be extremely expensive, and I had no means to pay for the operation. I became extremely despondent with the medical capability, I didn't know what to do. Melchor noticed how sad I became. He invited me to breakfast. After breakfast, we walked to the ocean and sat for a while and talked. He tried to kiss me, but I shoved him away. Later, Magda and I boarded the bus to Chilpancingo. We arrived at our destination. Trini was waiting for me. She was anxious to know, first, about the results of my examination and, second, if I had met Magda's cousin. She was not happy with the results either. "Rosita, you should try to go to the United States with what's his name?" I smiled. "His name is Melchor. But,

Trini, all he wants is to be with me, he wants me to have a relationship with him."

"Rosita, forget that Rafa guy, he doesn't even so much as write to you. Look, he probably already forgot you. Otherwise, he would write. If he was in love with you, he would, at the very least, call you."

Magda said, "Isn't one of your dreams to locate your sisters who live in the United States? Aren't you always saying that you want to know your father's side of the family? Well, this is an opportunity to find them. Aside from all that, you want to be cured, well, el Norte is the place to go. Melchor will take you, he knows how to get you across." Esme, another of my friends, said, "She is not capable to cross, what Rosita should do is get a visa and go that route."

"Okay, Esme, then what? She arrives, and who does she know there? Where will she go? With Melchor, she has a place to stay, and he can take her to locate her sisters, that's what he promised to do."

I told them, "I don't trust Melchor because all he talks about is to be with me. I am not ready. He believes that women are here to do as he likes, and he is very aggressive."

"Rosita, what makes you say that about him?"

"You know why, Trini, because he wants me to be his girlfriend, and he has me up in a pedestal among the stars. I don't like that. He tried to kiss me without my permission."

"Rosita, that's called love, he has fallen for you. But I can't blame him, you are a very attractive girl. Rosita, you should take advantage of this opportunity. Think real careful before you make your decision. What you should do is report with your manager. He just might be able to help you with your visa or a passport before you go up North."

"I have no idea what a visa or a passport is."

"Rosita, did you get Melchor's telephone number?"

"Yes, Trini, I have it." I took it out of my pocketbook and gave it her. "Okay, little sister, tomorrow you call him, because we all want to meet him. We will scrutinize him and tell you what we think of him. I know men, and, Rosita, I will know if he is sincere or not." He was beside himself when I called him. I asked him to come and visit me and my friends. He came over; he was very polite with my friends and especially with me. "Rosita," they told me later, "he is not good-looking, not like the other ones that want to marry you. You are right, he thinks that he is a lady's man, and he does like you. Rosita, he seems capable of helping you find your sisters, but it's your decision. If you decide to go, don't tell Melchor how you feel about Rafa."

"Why? I don't hide anything, I already told him about Rafa. That's one thing I told him when he asked me to be his girlfriend."

"Rosita, that's what I mean when I say that you have a lot to learn. Rosita, remember, you are no longer that little girl that was raised by the nuns, you are a young lady."

Before he left, Melchor went looking for me. I was with my friends when Trini spotted him. "Guess who is coming, Rosita? It's your ride to the United States." After he greeted all my friends, he asked if he could talk to all of us. He focused his attention on me. "Rosi, I want to say this in front of your friends." He appeared sincere when said, "Rosi, I have fallen in love with you, and I am ready to help you." My friends were touched by his sincerity and his love for me. Trini pinched me. I was too choked up to say anything, but I thought, *Why is he saying this?*

"Okay, Melchor, if I go with you, there's something that you must promise in front of my friends. First, that you don't cross the boundary and take advantage of me. I'm having some confidence issues with you, but I will confide in you. I appreciate your help, but that does not give you the right to abuse my confidence in you."

"No, Rosi, I will do nothing to lose your confidence in me." He tried to grab my hand. "No, Melchor, listen to me, second thing I want you to promise. Second, promise me that you will go with me to speak with my sister Ana. I want you to tell her how you are prepared to accomplish everything you have promised me. Precisely tell her that you will help find my sisters and you will help me find a cure for my illness."

"Melchor, now in front of all of us, promise that will you take care of her and that you will not abuse her. She is still very innocent and doesn't know much about the opposite sex. She may still be in the dark when it comes to men, but she is not a weakling, no, she is very tough, but take good care of her." Trini told Melchor to give me a hug and nothing else. "Don't try to steal a kiss from her, understand?" I heard her words to Melchor, I said not a word, I was thinking about what it would be like for me to live in another country. I don't know the language; if I wasn't sick, I would not leave my friends, my beautiful pueblo, or my mamacita.

I kept thinking many of my friends and relatives are in the United States, so why not me? My sickness must be cured, el Norte has the expertise, they will cure me, then I can come back. My Diosito! He will take care of me, He will put an expert in my path of life to cure me of this sickness. I have some family here, Ana and Claudia, my niece, and my mamacita, and that is all. Reyna, my absentee mother, is here, but she is the reason that I must flee my country. Ay, Diosito, give me the strength, please continue to give me the guidance now more than ever.

I Agreed to Go North with Melchor

WE MET AT THE BUS station. It felt strange to meet someone other than my mamacita at the station. We left for my pueblo. I was heading home for probably the last time, but who knows what lies ahead in the future? I was quiet for the longest time, not speaking to Melchor. I finally snapped out of my shell, I told myself that this a life that I chose. I started to hum my song, "I'm the daughter of no one," but I stopped and smiled. He looked at me. "Are you okay?" he asked. "It's not easy leaving this place, especially to a country that I know nothing of." Melchor didn't respond to my concern, but rather, he wanted to know about Ana and my pueblo. I tried to humor myself by telling him that my pueblo was far away and that if he'd had a car, we would have gotten there faster. That didn't work, he didn't say anything. He probably was thinking, "What did I get myself into?"

"Melchor," I asked, "do you regret your decision to take me to el Norte?" He just looked at me and smiled. "Well," he said, "it is different for me because I have always crossed alone." He talked about some of the difficulties one faces once an individual crosses the border. I listened, but I really didn't realize that it would be that difficult since many cross it every day. Instead, I felt strange riding the bus with someone other than my mamacita. My thoughts wandered back to the times I rode with Mamacita and sang for the travelers. I wanted to sing again. *No, no,* I thought, *not this time.* I smiled. "Rosi, you keep smiling, must be good thoughts."

"Yes, Melchor, I have many good memories riding the bus, especially with Mamacita."

The church steeples greeted me, they were the first thing I noticed. Other areas brought memories, but not like my church. I wanted to run and talk to my Chuchin. "Melchor, will you go with me to my beautiful church?" He stared at me. "I don't believe in going to church." I felt the cold truth coming from him. I thought, *He doesn't go to church?* I didn't continue the conversation, only because I wanted to be happy when we got to my sister's house.

Claudia answered the door. My little niece was soo happy to see me. Ana came out of her room when she heard the commotion caused by Claudia and me. "Vani, what are you doing here?" She was doubly surprised to see Melchor. She was not too happy to see him. I introduced them. I said, "Ana, don't be too surprised, but I decided to move to el Norte. Melchor is going to help me get across, and he will help me find our sisters."

"Vani, are you sure? Have you thought how hard it will be for you in the United States?" She sat down, placed her elbows on the table and her hands on her head; she was crying. I sat next to my sister trying to console her. "Ana, you know how much I've suffered with my illness, the United States will help me. I went to Acapulco last week for an examination, and they told me that they don't have the capability to help me."

"Gordo, Ana's husband, arrived home from work. He too was happy to see me but puzzled to know why Melchor was there. Gordo initially stared at him, didn't say anything when I introduced Melchor. Moments later, he said, looking at Melchor, "And you, what are you doing with my sister-in-law?"

"Well, sir," answered Melchor, "we came here to speak with Ana and you. I am taking Rosi to el Norté."

"You are taking Vani to the United States?"

"Well, yes, sir, I live there, and I will help her."

"Melchor, how long have you known my sister-in-law?"

"Well, señor, we met a few days ago."

"What? Dang, how did you convince Vani to go with you?"

"Gordo, it's not what you think. This person is going to help Vani find our sisters, they will help Vani. Vani wants to be cured, and the United States has the capability to do that, Mexico does not." Gordo walked near where Melchor was standing, pointed a finger in his face. "Take care of this girl." Gordo took a deep breath; he said,

"You mistreat her, and you will answer to me." Melchor assured them that he would take care of me. The tension lasted until we turned in. He slept in an extra room, I slept with Claudia.

Ana made breakfast for all of us. I didn't feel like eating; my stomach was very upset, probably with the thought of leaving the only family, besides Mamacita, behind. I wanted to vomit, but I held back. *I have to be strong, I must do this,* I kept telling myself. *The North awaits me, my Chuchin will guide me.* Ana gave me a phone number I could call in case I needed help. She didn't have our sisters' address in California, but the people whose phone number she gave me did. "Vani, I don't think that Gordo likes Melchor."

"I know. I saw the way Gordo treated Melchor, but, Ana, I have to do this, you know that." Ana gave me her blessing.

We left for the city to get my belongings. When I went to visit Ana, I hadn't convinced myself that I wanted to leave my home for a strange land I'd heard of, the land where many of my paisanos had found the American dream. My dream to be rid of my sickness was in the North. I was more convinced now than before. I packed my belongings. My last night in the city was spent with Trini where I slept. Trini allowed Melchor to sleep in the room I had been renting.

Next day we set off for Juarez, the border city. Melchor continued his attempt to be intimate with me. He tried hugs and kisses, but I rejected him every time. He didn't force himself on me, so I believed he wasn't capable of taking advantage of me. Juarez amazed me; it was unlike any city I had been to in Mexico. Melchor explained to me that we had to meet a coyote to help us cross the border. Another term that I couldn't comprehend, because to me, a coyote had always been a wild animal roaming the hills. We met the coyote out in the open—nothing clandestine, like I originally thought.

The coyote was not interested in taking me across. "Melchor, you know that I don't like to cross women."

"Amigo, don't worry, I will take care of her." The coyote agreed as long as he was not responsible. The coyote instructed us when and where to meet. The first night that we tried to cross was much more like I had anticipated, more covert. We tried, but for some reason, we couldn't. The following night was even worse for me. I hadn't eaten in days. The lack of food caused me to have a convulsion.

I woke up in very strange surroundings. I saw Melchor next to me. The other faces were all strangers; the walls full of holes appeared to be falling. "Where am I, and who are all these men?" I asked. "Don't worry, Rosi, I'm here with you, these are all paisanos trying to cross." I didn't feel comfortable in that dump of a place, it was dirty and smelly. I felt dirty myself, I hadn't taken a bath or a shower since we left Trini's place.

My American Dream among Promises

I GOT UP WITH A horrible headache, but taking a shower was more of a concern. I told Melchor to find me a place to bathe. The water felt so good hitting my head, washing all the days' filth from my body. Melchor stood outside the door guarding the entrance.

"Rosi, we need to cross tonight, these guys are anxious, but they are waiting for me."

"Melchor, I am not strong enough to cross tonight."

"Rosi"—he hugged me—"the coyote will not cross you because of your sickness." *Oh, my Diosito,* I thought, *now my very sickness prevents me from going to the place where I can be cured.*

I found myself in a strange place, seemingly alone. I wanted to cry, wanted to run, to hide, I felt helpless. "Rosi, I will take you back to your sister's house." I looked at him, I had no energy to spare, too weak to fight life anymore. "Melchor, don't worry about me, you go on. What you can do is take me to the bus station, and I will go to Chilpancingo."

"Come, you panders, let's go," shouted the coyote. We were getting ready to leave for the station when we heard the cry. The coyote came close to us still shouting, "We cross now, let's go. Señorita, I cannot cross you, not this time, maybe later. I will cross Melchor tonight, and he can wait for you in Arizona, and I will take you to him."

"Melchor, go, don't worry about me, go on! Pray that I can cross later, but you go now, don't wait for me." He hugged me. "Rosi, are you absolutely sure?"

"Yes, I'm sure, my Diosito will take care of me and guide me."

"Come on, you son of a gun, let's go."

I was left alone like so many other times. I saw him walk into the darkness, and that's all I remember, I had a convulsion. The paramedics were around me when I came to. They were asking me questions, but I wasn't ready to respond; my head was pounding with pain. They wanted to take me with them probably to a hospital, but I resisted. They left me when I told them that I was okay.

A man and a woman approached me where I lay atop a baseboard near the crossing area. I looked around to see many other hopefuls waiting to cross. They had their belongings ready to reach the land where dreams are fulfilled. Coyotes walked the area hoping to cross others, each one claiming that he was not expensive. I saw couples, single girls, and young boys just waiting for the right coyote to help them cross. A couple days I waited to cross. On the second day, I was more desperate and afraid of being alone among all these strangers. I reached out to a lady that was dressed different than the ones ready to cross.

I asked her what part of the United States she was planning on going to. She didn't respond to my specific question. Instead, she asked me where my destination was. I told her that I had family in California and a boyfriend someplace in el Norte, but I wasn't sure where. She asked me if Melchor was my boyfriend. "No, he is a friend only, trying to help me cross the border." She told me that her husband was the coyote that helped Melchor cross. I was surprised; that's all I remember.

When I came to, I was in another strange room, but this one was more modern. The señora I was speaking to when I had a convulsion was sitting next to me. "Ay, señorita, you got very sick, you were trembling a lot. Tell me, why do you faint like that, is this normal with you?"

"Señora, I'm sorry that you had to see me like this. But can you tell me where I am?"

"Yes, my niña, you are in my house. Now tell me, why do you faint so strong?"

"Señora, I'm an epileptic, and what you saw was a convulsion. I suffer these all the time, I have always had them. I hope that someday

I can be cured. That is the main reason that I am going to the United States."

"Mija, my husband and I are going to get you across the border." Suddenly my headache was gone, or I didn't feel it.

The news that I would be going to the land where dreams are fulfilled made all the pain go away. My eyes lit up, I could feel my whole being transform into a different feeling. "Tell me, what is your name?"

"I am Rosita Jovani Reza, I lived in Tetipac, a pueblo in the state of Guerrero."

"Rosita, why did you decide to stay here in Juarez all alone when Melchor crossed?"

"Ay, señora, I asked myself that question over and over, but in reality, I must be cured of my illness, and I know I will. My Chuchin will guide me and guide an expert doctor to cure me."

"Rosita, I told you that we will get you across. Listen to me, this is how we will do it." She gave me specific instructions, and I learned my first English words, which I will never forget: *good morning*. "We will take you to where Melchor happens to be." The lady was so nice and her husband, the coyote, who helped Melchor cross was also very nice. She fed me, and then she took me to a doctor in the Juarez. I slept in their house somewhat uncomfortable, but I slept. The next morning, the lady gave me a new backpack, which I used, and I dumped my old one. She gave me a school uniform and told me to put it on. "Rosita, remember, now you are in Juarez, México. In a few minutes, you will be in the United States. This is my daughter's uniform, she is scheduled to have an off-camp day in Arizona, but she isn't going. You will board a yellow school bus, follow my niece and do what she does. When you board the bus, remember what to say."

"Is that when I say 'good morning'?"

"Yes, you say those words just like an Americana." She smiled.

"Remember, when you board the bus, keep your head down, don't look up for nothing when you say 'good morning.' When you reach the school, go into the bathrooms. Again, my niece will show you. Stay inside the bathroom until you hear the school bell. After the bell rings, count to thirty, walk to the back of the bathrooms, we will be waiting for you in the car."

My heart was pounding like a runaway train when I boarded the bus. I didn't look up as I climbed the first step, I continued walking until I sat next to the niece. It seemed like an eternity before the bus took off. We stopped at the border; the border patrol looked briefly inside and waved us through. The niece said, "We are in the United States."

"What?" I whispered mostly to myself, "I'm in the United States." The rest was fairly simple. I waited in the bathroom as instructed before I walked out. They were waiting for me. I got into the car; the señora told me that I was blessed.

"Oí," the señora let out a yell, "Rosita, open your window, we are in Arizona. This is part of the United States. We have never had this easy of a crossing, Rosita, somebody is watching over you." I smiled with her thinking that this where my sisters live.

Arrived in Kansas

I LOOKED AT THE WHOLE landscape, but the roads and the traffic was most impressive. The people drive fast but follow the rules. We'd driven quite a while before the señora asked for Melchor's telephone number. During the six-day drive to Kansas, the señora got in touch with Melchor. He agreed to pay my coyotes the amount of $1,300 for taking me across the border and into Kansas. If he hadn't agreed, the couple would adopt me and take me back to México.

The drive to Kansas gave me lots of time to think. Many of my thoughts focused on life in the new country. Always though I knew that my Diosito would guide me. Maybe I was depending too much on my Chuchin. I have to step up on my own. I have arrived at this country that will help me with my illness, now it's up to me. My thoughts filled with anticipation of a life without epilepsy; it was all that occupied my mind.

Melchor was outside a small camper with some other guys when we arrived. They opened the doors of the car for us. Melchor gave me a hug, and I allowed him to kiss me. They were very polite with me and my traveling couple. The coyote remembered Melchor. They had a conversation before they left. I thanked them for being so kind to me and for bringing me across the border and into Kansas. I was surprised that I was in the United States, but all I saw were paisanos. Am I really in the United States or someplace in México? Melchor grabbed my bag and my hand. He took me inside a small mobile home. He gave me another hug, but I wouldn't allow him to kiss me again. I didn't feel comfortable being inside that little mobile home, and I didn't feel comfortable being with him. The inside was a total mess—clothes scattered all over the place and dirty dishes in the sink. "My friends live here, me, and now you will live here also."

"Melchor, you told me that you lived with your aunt, not here in this dump with all these guys. How can that be? Did you lie to me about living with your aunt?"

"Rosi, I don't know what happened between my aunt and myself. I found my belongings in the street the day I arrived from México. She didn't tell me why she dumped my belongings unto the street. That's why I came here." I didn't believe him. How can that be true? He gave me this address when we were in México so that I could send my belongings here, not his aunt's. He lied to me. I began to feel more insecure around him. I needed to get away, I needed to make contact with my sisters.

I asked him if he could take me to California and meet my sisters. He told me that his truck was not in a good enough condition to make the trip. I didn't know that California was that far away. "Why are you so anxious to meet them?" he asked me. I told him that he'd promised to take me to them. "Rosi, you and I can start a new life here, you know how I feel about you. Give me a chance, and I will prove it to you."

"Melchor, I came here with a purpose, and that was to find a doctor to cure my illness and not to have a life with you, and you know that."

A week in Kansas City living in a small motor home was not what I envisioned. My convulsions were occurring more frequently. I asked Melchor if he could take me to see a doctor. Hopefully a doctor that knew something about my illness and willing to cure me. I saw a female doctor, but unfortunately she was not an expert. She did say that besides having convulsions, I was also having asthma attacks. She prescribed some medicine. I did not purchase the medicine, Lamictal and Depakene, here because it was far more expensive than in México. I was able to get it through a friend in México.

The daily routine consisted of cooking for the men, and I kept the small place clean. Melchor treated me with respect; he would hint that he wanted to be intimate with me. I tried to ignore him. Sundays was a time the guys gathered at a local park to play *fut-*

ból (soccer). The respect and little confidence I was starting to have for Melchor was shattered. I was sound asleep. I felt a tug on my shoulder. I woke up; the blankets had been pulled away. Melchor was naked sitting atop my legs. "I want to have sex with you, you are my woman, and I need to be with you."

"Melchor, please, you know that I don't want to be intimate with you or anybody. Love can't be demonstrated through forced sex, it must be a mutual feeling, and I don't feel like having sex."

"Shut up, just take your clothes off. Understand that I'm a man, and I want you now." I saw him; he was ready. I was in shock, I heard him say, "You are a woman, my woman, my partner."

"Melchor, let's talk, put your clothes on. Yes, I'm a twenty-year-old woman, but I can't give you sex now. I don't love you." I saw the anger in his eyes, flashback to the time Reyna's lecherous lover wanted to do the same thing to me. He tore my clothes off and took advantage of me. That moment lasted forever; when he finished, I walked to the kitchen. I sat under the sink, stayed there for hours, traumatized in pain and crying. My body was trembling in fear. Melchor was watching television, I had a convulsion. I don't know how long I was out. I opened my eyes; the others were sitting close to me drinking tequila. "Rosi, you gave us a fright, but we are glad you are awake." They got to their feet, walked out, and left Melchor alone with me.

"Melchor, you are worse than an animal. Everything you promised, you violated. I'm going back to México because I can't be around you another second. I confided in you, and look what happened. I told you that I was an epileptic when I first met you, that I could not have sex with anybody. Remember?" Melchor shed tears; he knelt in front of me. "Rosi, forgive me for being a stupid bastard. I love you very much, and I don't want to lose you."

"Melchor, your tears are gone with the wind. Melchor, I take the blame for the way you treated me. I don't know how to respond like a woman responds. I will fight and learn to accept you and to be happy. But now, leave me be. You are free to find enjoyment someplace else." I went to bed tired mentally and physically hurting.

He tried helping me to the bed, pulled back the cover. Melchor was terrified when he saw blood on the sheet. "Rosi, why…oh no…" I saw the blood on the sheet too. *I don't have my period, why…* I looked at my underwear; it too was covered in blood. I went to the bathroom unable to hold back my tears. I slid under the sink crying. *He deceived me, Diosito, he deceived me.* I couldn't stop crying. *Diosito, please help me out of this inferno. Melchor is worse than Figueroa, Reyna's man. Diosito, I can't be intimate like a normal woman, I can't live this kind of life. Diosito, why was I not allowed to be a nun and serve you?*

Melchor knocked on the door. "Rosi, are you okay?" I didn't have the desire to speak with him. "Rosi, I'm off to work." I heard the outside door close, I waited until I heard the car leave. I spent the day alone, ashamed to leave, full of guilt, full of questions, and doubtful of the life in the United States. I sought solace in the rosary, I prayed it and repeated it over and over. I thought of packing and leaving for México. No! That is not the answer, I came to this country to rid myself of another nemesis, my illness. Diosito will guide me.

I was living an emotional life complete of trauma, I lost confidence in being here and with him. I fought the desire to return to Chilpancingo, I had to find a way out of here. Being alone gave me time to think. I thought of returning to México. I thought that his friends might want to take advantage of me also. *This place is a jail, not a house, I have to leave,* I thought over and over. I looked in the mirror, I saw a girl with swollen eyes, I had a colorless skin. My face looked like a zombie. I forced a smile, I pointed at the image in the mirror. "You are not Rosita! You are an impostor! I took the towel and cleaned the image off the mirror. "Use your faith in Diosito and become strong. Become the woman that you once were." I forced another smile and walked away. I took out my diary and wrote. It was good therapy to write what I was going through.

His friends knew what I was going through and what he'd done to me but did nothing to stop him. Alex, the *chilango* from México City, was the exception. I was alone the day Alex knocked on the door to the camper. "Rosi, can I come in? I want to speak with you." I let him in; he sat on the stool near the small table in the kitchen. I remained on my feet, close to a pan full of hot water.

"Rosi, your eyes say a lot, your eyes show that you are tormented by what that bastard did to you. I have known him, that stupid bastard, for a long time, and I never thought that he was capable of raping you. The moment I saw you all curled up under the sink, I knew what he'd done to you. I wanted to beat the crap out of him. I'm sorry now that I didn't. Rosi, let me help you. I'm ready to help you in any way that I can. Melchor does not deserve to be with a person like you."

"Señor Alex, I appreciate that, but I ask, don't try to hurt me like Melchor has."

"No, Rosi, I'm not like that. I only want to help you. Rosi, give me a list of your relatives and friends and their phone numbers. I will get you a prepaid telephone card so that you can call them."

My diary contained all the phone numbers. Alex bought the card, which I used to call out of this jail. I communicated with Sister Paty, Ana, Trini, and my old job. I apologized for leaving at the spur of the moment and tried to explain the situation. Mr. Colins understood and told me that he would have helped me get a student visa and a passport. Too late now. I spent part of the day on the phone; boy, it felt good. I was among the living once again. I thanked Alex again and again for the phone card.

A week or so after I had communicated with my Méxican contacts, I received a couple of letters. Alex presented them to me in front of Melchor. Surprised to see me receive mail, he asked, "Who is writing to you?"

"Relax, my friend," Alex told him, "she is entitled to receive mail, isn't she?" He looked perturbed, told Alex to stay out of our conversation. "You have been in touch with your friends in México, haven't you?"

Before I had time to show him the letters, one from Sister Paty and the other from one of my friends, he stood up from the sofa and flung the remote control. "You are going to leave me and go back to México, aren't you? Why? I haven't been intimate with you again, I've respected you. Forgive me for the way I treated you that night, I don't want to lose you. But as long as we are living together, you have to give me pleasure. I lost my family for helping you, and now I'm fighting to keep you. Don't you realize that I love you?"

I sat on a chair, not wanting to antagonize him any further; I waited a while to respond. "Melchor, you are a good worker, you don't have any vices, find yourself a woman that will appreciate and love you and give you the pleasure you desire. I cannot be that person. I appreciate what you have done for me that I will never forget, but let me be."

"Rosi, show me your appreciation, give me sex like I desire and give me a son."

"See, Melchor, that's all you think about. I never imagined that you were a sexual maniac. I will be truthful with you, I will always have doubts as to why you have helped me."

Melchor didn't like what I told him; he slammed the door on his way out of the camper. I felt guilty for being the woman he desires, and I can't be that woman. For the next few days, he didn't bother me. I started to move about the grounds where other of my *paisones* lived. I met Silvia, a very nice lady who sold tamales. In the course of the conversation, she told me that she made some money selling tamales. The same time, I told her that I also had made and sold tamales. Several days later she came to the house. She offered me a job making and selling tamales.

The *tamalera* was leaving when Melchor and the others arrived. They were happy to see the tamalera; they bought their dinner from her. When we were alone, Melchor was not too happy that I had met the tamalera. "What did you tell her about us?" I was not too happy with the way he'd asked the question. I answered, "Nothing, what's wrong with you? She came to offer me a job. I can make money to pay for my medicine, do I have your permission to work?" Why I asked his permission is beyond me, the words just came out. "Sure, it might be good for you. Maybe then you will give me pleasure."

I grabbed his hand. "Melchor, listen to me, there are too many reasons that prevent me from having sex with you. I am willing to go see a counselor, maybe they can help us. It's possible that they can give us advice on how we can be intimate the way you desire."

"Rosi, you think that I'm stupid or crazy? Nobody is going to tell me how to be intimate with a woman. You need to see one, not me. Those ideas are for a weakling, not for me." No more conversation; he sat on the small sofa and turned the TV on. I took out my diary. I wrote, "I am a weakling." I smiled.

Silvia was a really nice person to be around. The money I made gave a good feeling. I had told Silvia about my convulsions and told her not to worry because I had them all the time. I mentioned that the reason I came North was because I wanted to be cured of my illness and that the United States had the capability to cure me. Ironically I had a convulsion that afternoon. Silvia helped me. She asked me if I was happy being with Melchor. I was curious why she was asking. "Rosi, I'm not a nosy person, but when you had your convulsion, you kept moving your head saying, 'Melchor, leave me alone, leave me alone.'"

"No, Silvia, I am not happy." I sobbed. Silvia hugged me trying to console me. "Rosi, tell me, how can I help you?"

"I am not happy with him, and I am not happy living in that camper. I need to get away from here."

That afternoon after we had finished selling the tamales, Silvia helped communicate with my sister Oli. It was a relief complete with happiness to hear my sisters on the telephone. Victoria and Oli agreed to help me get to California. I gave my address where they could contact me. They promised to do that by sending me money and their address. Oli is a couple of years older than myself, Victoria is one of the oldest sisters. I don't remember too much about them, but I did recognize their voices. I asked Oli to send me pictures of them, which she agreed to do. Oli wanted to come for me in Kansas City. The problem was that she was busy for a while, but I wanted to get away from this place, now!

I couldn't thank Silvia enough. I mentioned that I hadn't spoken to my sisters in several years. I was grateful to have made contact with them, I would have a family in California. Dinner was ready when Melchor and the others arrived from work. He looked at me throughout dinner; the look in his eye put me in alert mode. "Rosi," he said, "being outside agrees with you. Every time you are outdoors selling with the tamalera, it appears to make you happy." I wanted to tell him that I had communicated with my sisters, but held back. Later that evening, the others left us alone. Melchor tried to hug me, I shrugged him off. "Rosi"—his eyes full of tears—"please don't leave me." I didn't respond, I felt bad, my conscience was grabbing at me. But I kept quiet, but my tears gave me away. "Rosi, I want to help you, tell me how, and I will, but please talk to me. You don't say much, but your eyes tell me that you are holding something back."

"Melchor, it's better this way. Besides, your words say one thing, and your actions are completely the opposite." I excused myself and went to bed. I felt bad for holding back. I didn't want to deceive him because that is not me. I anticipated the worst when I went to bed, but I slept with no interruption from him.

Silvia went to the post office on a daily basis, so she volunteered to get my mail. The mail that I was waiting for arrived. My sister Oli sent me plenty of dollars and photos of my sisters. Oh, Diosito, I was so emotional seeing pictures of my family, I had a convulsion. When I fell, I hit the very same spot on my head that I had hit so many other times before. But next day, I went with Silvia to sell tamales, I wasn't about to stay in that camper. I showed her the pictures of my sisters. In exchange, she mentioned that her son was coming from San Francisco, where he is attending college, to visit her.

"Rosi, if you are really serious and want to leave, my son can take you all the way to California." At that moment, I couldn't answer her, all this was happening fast. "Really? Yes, yes, please tell him yes, I accept. How—I mean how can I get away from Melchor without his knowledge?"

"Rosi, pack your clothes little at a time so that he won't suspect anything." I met Helder, her twenty-seven-year-old son. He could give me a ride as far as Arizona. I called Oli and told her the news. Her in-laws lived in Arizona, and I would meet her there. I was entering another chapter in my young life, with Diosito's guidance.

Melchor was always analyzing my emotions. He asked me if I was holding something from him. "I cannot deceive you, Melchor, I've made contact with my sisters in California. They await me."

"What? You actually have talked to them. Who is helping you, da——— it."

"Melchor, my world doesn't stop nor does it end. You see me alone, but I fight for my life. I don't depend on anybody but myself. I got here, didn't I? I will get to California the same way, with the help of friends. I'm advising you so that you won't be surprised to find me gone." He was hurt, I could tell. This time he didn't throw anything; he simply walked outside without saying a word.

Due to the circumstance with Melchor, I was afraid to stay in the room. Another night passed without incident. Alex, the chilango from México City, wondered why I looked much happier lately. He said, "What's up in that brain of yours?"

"Señor Alex, I am happy because I'm going to California with my sisters."

"Really, Rosi? I am so glad for you. But when, because I haven't seen you pack your clothes."

"Señor, I don't have a suitcase, but I have my boxes already packed."

"You packed in boxes, but why? Don't you have a suitcase?"

"Yes, but Melchor has it stored away. He knows that I'm leaving, but I don't want him to know when."

"Rosi, come with me, I'll buy you a suitcase."

The luggage was perfect, I packed my belongings. Alex took it to his room and stored it for me. "Rosi, if I'm not here when you leave, you'll find it under the bed." I informed Silvia that I was packed and ready to leave anytime.

The following morning, I was on my way to Arizona. Helder was very gracious and funny. We talked all the way to Arizona. We went through New Mexico. I remembered traveling these roads a few months ago. Some of the terrain reminded of my own pueblo. I wondered why it was called New Mexico. I saw nothing new about it. The cliffs where the Indians lived appeared older than life itself. I wanted to ask Helder, but I wanted to find out on my own. I thought of being cured and attending college. I would study everything about these *united states*. The whole trip was a wonderment for me.

California Arrival

I WAS WARMLY WELCOMED BY Oli's in-laws, they were friendly. Helder didn't stay long; he was in a hurry to reach his destination. I stayed with them for a few days. The time spent there was so free of problems and stress. Oli's sister-in-law and I became acquainted, got to know a lot about each other. We parted good friends when I left for California. Oli went for me.

The trip to California with my sister was most enjoyable. We learned more about each other in the few hours than ever before. She kept me informed about every little Arizona town we passed. Before we reached the California state line, she told me to be ready, we were about to cross into the grand state. I couldn't contain my excitement when we started to cross the great Colorado River. My excitement didn't wane when we crossed the desert. I was trying to read the names of the places we passed. Some were in Spanish, which made me think, *Why are so many places given Spanish names? There is so much to learn about this country.*

The palm trees were similar to the ones we had in my pueblo; what we didn't have was the heat. It was hot in a place called Indio. The heat was bothering me, but the wonders I saw driving down into a place called Palm Springs made up for the discomfort. I pointed to the apparatus, white columns of machines with propellers turning with the wind. "What are those things?" I asked Oli. She smiled. "Little sister, those are called so and so." *I can't understand the words, but in time, I will find out,* I thought. She told me that they produce electricity. Again, I didn't really understand how that was possible, but I will learn. The roads were getting wider and wider and the cars nicer and more beautiful and faster. *This country is so different than mine.* I took notes when I wasn't looking at the scenery. I didn't ask more questions, but I wrote them down. *I will learn about these things. My Chuchin has led me to this country to be cured, and I will write a book. Yes, someday soon, I will write a book.*

"Rosita, we are close to home," she said. I was amazed at how clean the streets were and the crowded apartments rising high into the sky. Oli was my guide. She showed me where they shopped, the park where they have picnics, and so much more. I was amazed, simply amazed. We drove around some of the apartments until she found a place to park. "Rosita, we are here. This is where Victoria (Viki) lives. The other sisters are waiting for us, come on." I noted the address on my small diary, took out my camera, and took a picture of the place.

Victoria, her husband, Gilberto, and children—Anagil, seven-year-old daughter, and Wilien, the older son—were waiting to meet me. My other sisters met me for the first time since I was about two years old. We spent the whole evening knowing each other. I told them about my epilepsy. I mentioned that I experience convulsions and not to be surprised when they happen. Ana had mentioned that I was sick, but they didn't realize the problems that I encountered because of it.

My temporary home was with Viki. She was probably the one where I would best fit in. The others, for various reasons, weren't able to accommodate me living with them. The first few days, we got to know each other pretty good. Her daughter Anagil was so sweet, she was my partner. In time the situation of my living with them was getting more intense. The problems were more about relationships than money. Granted the cost of my medicine and food was a burden, and I had no means of paying for it. I did what I could; I cleaned the apartment, cooked for them, and watched the children when Viki and Gilberto went out.

But it was the change in relationship between Viki and me. This changed occurred because of misunderstandings. She was at a point where she started accusing Gilberto of paying more attention to me than to herself and their children. Viki started treating me like any stranger and not like a sister. I didn't realize it at the time, but when

Gilberto came home from work, he'd greet me and ask how I felt or something. Another time when he came home, he asked Viki if she had taken me to apply for assistance from Medicaid for my medicine. That day, Viki scolded Gilberto in front me and their children. Viki asked him why he was concerned about me first, why not ask about her or their children. "Gilberto, since that snot-nosed girl came to live with us, you are more concerned with her than your own family."

"Viki, if something happens to Rosita while she is living with us, we are going to have problems." I felt very uncomfortable, and even Anagil felt bad. Over the years, I've learned from experience that jealousy among people is harmful. I wanted no part of the conversation, I escaped into Anagil's room, followed by my niece.

I had a convulsion. Anagil was at my side when I came to. "Auntie, you fainted, I was so scared because you were trembling so much, I thought that you were dying. I remembered what you told me, and I didn't call anyone. I made you some tea with cinnamon and some food."

"Anagil, thank you so much for doing this, but I don't want to create any problems between you and your mother."

"Auntie, don't worry, my parents aren't here." I felt uneasy being in their house, I had to do something.

The following morning, Viki was more cheerful. "Rosita, today you and I are going to social services to apply for assistance."

"Forgive me, Viki, I don't understand."

"Look, Rosita, you don't have to understand, just follow my instructions, and I will do all the talking." We entered into a nice building, I couldn't read the lettering on the doors, but I assumed that this was where I was to apply for assistance. Not being one to accept any kind of charity, I didn't feel comfortable at all. Viki told me to wait while she went up to the receptionist. After a short time, she pulled me aside, she whispered instructions.

These were her instructions: "Rosita, tell them that the reason you are here is because you are sick. Explain to them about your convulsions, this is very important. Tell them that you have no relatives, that you are alone. Don't tell them that you and I are sisters. Tell them that we just met and that you rent a room from me. I know how the system works, so if you want them to help you, you must follow my instructions. I can't be responsible for your medicine, it's too expensive. Rosita, I don't know why you came here, why didn't you stay in México? You have no idea how much of a burden you have become, I regret having met you."

I was in shock! I thought, *Why does Viki say such hurtful things? I have done nothing to hurt her.* My tears flowed gently down my cheeks, I wiped them with my trembling hands, unable to speak. My name was called. We entered the office of what I assumed was a social worker. Viki tried to answer the first question the worker asked me. The lady interrupted Viki, "These questions are not for you to answer." She told Viki to leave the room. At that instant, Viki grabbed my arm, turned to the social worker. "Excuse us, señora, but Rosita is not feeling well. She needs some air. Can I have your permission to take the application and fill it at home?" The lady agreed and told Viki to mail it. She gave Viki a card with the mailing address. "Thank you for your time, I must help Rosita. I take care of her when she gets sick because I really love her." The worker was impressed with how Viki cared for me.

What was her motive for saying those hurtful things? Walking out of the office, I asked her, "Why did you deny being my sister? Don't you know anything about our family?"

"Shut up, Rosita, I know more than you think. For one thing, you are not a Reza. According to Ruben, my father, a certain Jorge Bustos is your father. Do you hear me? My father is not your father. I don't know why Reyna gave you that surname. I repeat what I said a while ago, I regret allowing you to stay at my house. Since the day you arrived and I let you stay with us, my husband has paid more attention to you than to me and his children."

Her attitude was very clear, I didn't want to live with her anymore. I had no idea that I would be such a burden to my sister. I had no intentions of hurting her or her family. When I decided to come to California, I wanted to meet my sisters, but I never realized the burden I would place on Viki. *Where can I go? The only people I know are my sisters. Maybe I can return to México? No, that is not an option, I will not leave this country. I will stay here, and by the guiding light of my*

Diosito, I will succeed. I began to cry. Viki told me to quit crying, that I wasn't a little girl anymore. The conversation between us ceased, we didn't say a word to each other until we got to her place.

I filled the papers and sent them back. A few days later, Viki handed me a letter from the Social Services. "Open it and tell me what they want." Viki was acting like Sister Carmela. "They want to speak to me in person."

"That's good. I'll take you," answered my sister. She instructed me what to say. One instruction was to ask for assistance with the rent. I only wanted to ask for help with my medicine. But I thought it only fair to ask for rental assistance; after all, I'm not paying rent, and furthermore, I can't since I don't have a job.

I wrote in my diary: FRIENDLY CENTER OF ORANGE COUNTY. This is the place in Orange where Viki took me to seek assistance. Amy was the name on the badge of the girl who led Viki and me into the office. I had high hopes that I would receive assistance with the cost of my medicine. I filled several additional papers with Viki smiling and watching everything. The worker presented me with a green card with the name Rosa Bustos. "Check the name on the card," the lady instructed.

I saw the surname *Bustos*. I thought, only in my dreams is it Bustos. Viki had helped me fill out the papers, but why had she done this? She knows that my official name is *Rosita Jovani Reza*. That moment, everything got dark, I had a convulsion.

"Señorita, are you okay? Señorita," I barely heard my name, I was waking up. "Señorita, I'm going to call the paramedics."

"No, please don't call them, I'm okay. I don't have any money to pay for the hospital. I'm fine, just a horrible headache. Don't worry, I get these convulsions all the time." Viki took this as an opportunity.

"Now you see how sick this girl gets. That's the reason that I take care of her like she was family." Amy commended Viki for taking care of me. "We are going to approve temporary compensation for the care you provide this young lady. We are also going to give you a month's rent and will pay your gas and light bill." Amy led us to a room full of food. She gave us a bag full of food, clothes, and personal items. She handed me a card that allowed me to pick a bag full of food every month. Amy took my hand. "Rosa, I'm here to help you."

"Here is my card, call me anytime you need help." I thanked Amy. She hugged me before we left; it felt so good I wanted to cry.

Viki couldn't wait to leave the office to start her preaching. "Jovani, I really don't know who you are. Who are you?"

"Viki, you know very well that I'm your sister." I was getting annoyed with her attitude. "No, Jovani, you are nothing to me, you are a sickly girl making trouble for me. Yet I wonder, why are these Americanos always willing to help you? Why do they open their doors to you and so willingly? I was sure they were going to call the Migra and deport you back to México. Instead, look what they do for you. When we came to el Norte, the government gave us nothing, not even a taco."

"Enough, Viki. Enough." I placed my bags on the sidewalk. "I'm grateful for what you've done for me." I stood face-to-face with her. "Go ahead and call the police or Immigration. Come on, do it, but before they take me, they will know all about you. They will know how you treat me and the lies you put on the application. Go ahead, Viki, do it. I prefer to be with the police than to continue living with you. I hate receiving this food and clothes and the money under ignorance and lies that you put on the application. I need it yes, I don't deny it, but I'm not comfortable receiving it under dishonorable lies. Another thing, quit being so ignorant, your husband means nothing to me. He is my brother-in-law, your husband, that is all."

Her face turned to fear. I turned to see a police car approaching. A terrified Viki said, "Shut up, let's go, we'll finish this conversation at home." On the way home, Viki veered off to pick up the children she babysits. I didn't feel comfortable going into the apartment. I was too tired and fell asleep in the room my niece and I shared. My niece and Viki came home. I heard my nephew Wilien tell his mother that he was going to take a shower and didn't want anybody bothering him. Viki told her son to wait. He didn't, but Viki went in after him.

Anagil and I heard Wilien pleading with Viki not to hurt him. He cried in pain saying, "Don't hit me," yet we could hear the beating. Anagil was crying, I was in shock. She pushed Wilien out of the bathroom. "Anagil, call the police, look what Jovani did to Wilien."

"Mama, why are you doing this to my aunt? She didn't do anything to Wilien."

"Shut up, Anagil, and do as I say. I am getting rid of this plague that has infested my house. The police will ship her back to México in boxes. Look at his back, Jovani, look what you did."

"Why are you doing this, what is wrong with you? I didn't touch him, and you know it."

"Since you entered my house, my husband has ignored me and has ignored his children. I am not your sister, and I don't want you, so stop saying that I'm your sister. Also, I don't want to hear another word about that woman Reyna, your mother."

"Viki, you offered me a place to stay in front of your sisters. Why did you agree? Viki, call the police. If I'm kicked out of here, you will also be kicked out. I will see to that."

"Shut up, I may not have papers, but my children were born here. They won't kick me out."

"Viki, like I said, call the police, go ahead, see who gets kicked out." She slapped me in front of her children. Anagil cried out, "Mama, don't hit my aunt, she isn't doing anything wrong. I will help her." Viki was raging mad, she told Anagil to go into the kitchen and wait for the police. "If the police come, don't say anything, and don't tell them that she is your aunt."

Viki grabbed the bag with all my documents; she took out a paper with Melchor's phone number. She said, "Call him, or I will call the police. You will arrive in México in pieces in a box." Viki gave me the phone. "Call the boy in Kansas." I looked at her thinking, *Is she crazy? I don't want to call him.* On second thought, I'd rather be with him than this crazy woman. I took the phone, started to walk into my room; she stopped me. "No, señorita, you call him from here, I want to hear you talk to him. Whatever he has done to you is not my concern, call him." She grabbed the phone from me. "I'll call him!"

I heard Melchor answer the phone. "Melchor," she said, "this is Viki, Rosi's sister." Viki changed her voice completely, trying to be sweet. "I'm calling for Rosi to tell you that she is very sad without you. She has been remorseful for leaving you. Yes, ah, really, she is willing to give you another opportunity... Don't worry, I will rent you a room, uh-huh... You will be here in a few days? That's good, she will be very happy. Yes, she is here, she wants to speak with you." I got the phone, he sounded happy. He promised that he'd changed and that things would be different between us. I hung up. Viki had my medical card in her hand. "I will keep this card in a safe place," she told me. I was too traumatized to fight her.

The bathroom was my refuge. I slid down to the floor and cried. *Diosito, I can't continue without your help, not in this condition. Give me strength to continue.* What a disillusion meeting my sisters was, what a disaster. What a disaster living with Viki. Now I await Melchor, another nightmare. *Diosito, be compassionate.* I got up on my feet. I noticed a bottle with crossbones on it. *This is poison to kill rats, what if I take it?* At the instant I opened it, I felt someone grab it from me. I picked it up again. This time the lid was tight, I couldn't open it. I looked at myself in the mirror. At the back of me, I saw very clearly my Diosito. He shook his head saying, "No." He disappeared.

I felt a rush of heat throughout my body. With my hands, I covered my face, my mouth wide open, my tears stopped. *Forgive me, Diosito.* My whole disposition changed; no longer was I sad, no longer did I feel alone and helpless. I felt peaceful. I took a shower to cleanse the negativity away.

Viki waited until I entered the living room to send Anagil to the grocery store. She wanted me to hear everything. She told Anagil to buy certain food for them because a "certain overly hungry rat is eating all of our food." I thought of the image of Diosito I had just seen. I thought as I calmly shook my head, *Diosito, forgive her.* I was grateful to Amy, the social worker, for giving me the food and the monthly food card.

"Jovani, sit, I want to talk." She pointed to the chair next to the dining table. She threw money on the table. I found this money among your belongings. *What is she doing going through my things,* I thought, *she has no business with?* Although I was fuming, I didn't say a thing. "Jovani, I have a suggestion for you. Jovani, you have enough money to buy the ingredients to make empanadas, tamales, and bread to sell. Go to the store and buy everything you need. On the way to the store, go to the school on Highland Street. The director will give you more groceries. They do that to needy persons. As soon as you have enough money, you move someplace else away from me."

I took my money and asked Viki if I could take Anagil with me. "Why? Are you afraid to walk alone?" She smirked at me. "You're not a child anymore, go on, she can't go with you." I left not knowing where the school was or the store. But leaving that dreaded environment was a welcome relief. I have been alone in the woods in the hills and all over my pueblo, and I survived. Going to a store with directions was simple; going to that school would not be a problem either. Simple, first lady I saw on the street, I asked for directions to the store. Not a problem getting there—no, the problem was not having a convulsion, which I did inside the store.

I woke up in the hospital. The nurse was at my side asking me questions in English. I smiled at her and indicated that I didn't understand English. In Spanish, I asked if she knew Spanish. She spoke enough broken Spanish for me to understand. She told me that I had fainted inside the store. I answered that I didn't faint; rather, I had a convulsion caused by my epilepsy. I gave her my name and the address where I was staying with Viki. The nurse told me that the police were waiting to speak with me. She told me that I was in a very delicate condition and wanted me to relax. She told me that I had suffered a bad fall and had injured my dentures.

A policewoman and a policemen walked into the room. The policewoman asked me in Spanish my name, my address, and if I had any family she could contact. I gave them all the information they asked for. They continued their investigation by going to Viki's apartment. Viki told them that she rented me a room, and that is all she knew about me. They returned to ask more questions. I asked them if they could help me go back to México. The law lady was surprised. "Señorita, why do you want to return to México?" I answered, "Señora Policia, the American dream is not possible for me."

I saw her face; she seemed to care. "Tell me about your life here. I want to know everything." I told her about my epilepsy and that I was in the hospital because I had a convulsion because of my illness. I proceeded to tell her about how I had met my sisters and the way they had treated me, especially Viki. I told her about Reyna and the nightmare of a life I had lived with her. I gave her my whole life story including that I didn't know who my real father was. I talked about being raised in the orphanage. The policewoman couldn't believe my story. She wanted to know more. I couldn't stop. I mentioned Mamacita, Don Felipe, Mama Lucia, and Ana. The more I talked about my life, the bigger the audience got. Soon the room was full of nurses and even doctors. Various persons took pictures with me. A doctor identified himself, except I don't remember his name. I told them about my diaries and that someday I was going to write my life story.

The lady cop had seen my address in the application I had filled for assistance. She told me they talked to Victoria. I was surprised. "You talked to Victoria? Please don't charge her the cost of the hospital."

The policewoman assured me, "It doesn't work that way here in the States." She was going to help me get some temporary housing. She gave me several phone numbers where I could find refuge. The doctor came into the room to release me. The policewoman and her partner waited for my release to give me a ride home.

Viki was waiting inside the apartment for me. She was furious thinking that she would have to pay for the hospital. She continued giving me grief. "I hope the hospital doesn't find out that I'm your sister, I'm not responsible for you" etc., etc. "How could you do this? You know, Jovani, you are going to wind up in jail, you don't have the money to pay." She kept sounding off. "I hope they don't find out that we're sisters," she repeated. Anagil was really upset with her mom, but that didn't stop Viki. I went outside and left my denying sister talking to herself. As I closed the door behind me, Viki shouted words that I can't repeat.

The charges for the hospital and paramedics was $45,000. One way or another, I would pay the bill. I started selling rice pudding, cinnamon-banana bread, and tamales. I wrote in my diary the amount of money that I was earning and the ordeal I was living with my sister. I met a lot of nice people, even made a few friends. My convulsions continued, one happened while I was doing my laundry. I don't know how long I was unconscious; when I came to, I was inside the house of a lady I'd met during one of my days selling my goodies.

The lady knew that Viki was mistreating me and couldn't believe that we were related. I met her husband and her sister-in-law. I mentioned that I had applied for Medicaid and had been approved, but I couldn't get my card from Viki. Her sister-in-law offered to take me to the Social Services office to see if I could get a copy. She dropped me off at the office with instructions on which bus to take back home.

The social worker checked her computer for *Rosita Jovani Reza*. She didn't find that name but did find a Rosa Bustos with the same address and other information. The worker was curious; after questioning me, I told her that I was the same person. She thought that I was committing fraud. The social worker wanted to know why I was using two different names. I explained that Viki had filled out the application because I didn't understand English. I didn't realize the ramification when Viki filled my name as *Rosa Bustos* until the worker questioned me.

I can prove that I'm innocent. I mentioned that Viki had taken charge, and she did. I wasn't about to commit fraud because that is not who I am. I asked her if she would kindly talk to the other lady that helped me on my first visit to the office. She asked me to accompany her to see the supervisor. We were joined by other individuals wearing ties and white shirts. I repeated to them what Viki had done. One of them asked me, "Who's the one with epilepsy, you or Viki?" I showed them my banged-up head.

The social worker said, "This is not right. Don't worry, we will straighten this out." She instructed me to bring her all the paperwork that I—or rather Viki had filled out. She also wanted to see all the paperwork concerning my treatment for epilepsy, she wanted photos, receipts of my medical costs, addresses of past residences, and even the phone number of the orphanage. "Bring these records so that I can do my job and help you."

How I felt wasn't happiness alone, it was also a feeling of relief knowing that I would get help here in the United States. I took out a loaf of my cinnamon-banana bread and gave it to her. "Señora, please accept this for helping me, and thank you, thank you."

"Rosita, where did you get this bread?" She was totally surprised to hear that I had baked it. "Good heavens," she said, "with all you're going through, and you still have time to bake?"

"Oh, señora, I also make tamales and enchiladas to sell. How else could I pay for my medicine?" She smiled. "Ay, Rosita, in reality, who are you?"

"Rosita, are you hungry?" The social worker apparently heard my stomach growling. "You don't have to answer, come with me, you and I are going out to lunch, my treat." I waited for her in the waiting room, feeling sorta embarrassed because the growling in my stomach had betrayed me. She insisted on taking me to the grocery store first, bought me some groceries. We had a nice lunch hour. The bus system was becoming my mode of transportation. I arrived at the apartment around six. The door was locked; nobody was home. The lady that lived next door heard my knocking. She asked me to step into her apartment. The elder lady brewed me a cup of tea. She asked me to stay the night. I was exhausted and welcomed the chance to be away from my false sister.

The following morning, I waited for Viki to leave the apartment. I met her at the door to the apartment. My greeting was returned by Anagil; Viki greeted me with a frown, no words. Soon after I entered my new jail, I heard the knock on the door. It was Maritza, the mother of the two children that Viki takes care of after school. After the usual greetings, she asked if she could talk to me. She mentioned that she waited for Viki to leave to speak with me. "Rosi, I see you selling tamales and other goodies, is there anything I can help you with?" I smiled. *What a thoughtful lady,* I thought. I told her that I have prepared and sold enchiladas and cinnamon-banana bread.

"Rosi, that's not the only reason I want to speak with you. I hear gossip, as you know, everybody knows everybody's business around the apartments. They are saying that Viki mistreats you badly. My daughter Daisy also knows this to be true because she has seen how she treats you." We talked some more. Maritza learned that I had applied for the medical card with Viki's help and the problems with that. She was surprised that I didn't have any other identification from here. Maritza told me to get ready, she would take me to the Méxican Consulate to get an identification card. "The card will give you some type of protection." She told me to take all the papers that proved who I was.

The workers at the consulate were very kind and helpful. I got my first identification card in the United States, I was ecstatic. Soon I would have a new Medicaid card, also with my very own name. I looked up to the sky and quietly talked with my Chuchin. I knew that I had made the right decision to come to this country. Maritza left me at the apartment. It was locked, so I had no choice but to wait on the stairs for my grand sister Viki. No greetings; she ignored me completely. Opening the door to the apartment, she spoke. She didn't let me go inside. She did instruct me to go seek assistance at the nearby school. I thought she was being ludicrous. Help for my need is not going to be found in a school. To keep the peace, if that is possible to achieve with my grand sister, I agreed. I asked around the apartments; my newly found friends were helpful. I found my way to the school.

The director of the school was Corni. I was relieved to hear her speak Spanish. Apparently she felt that I didn't speak English because when she first saw me, she asked me a question in Spanish. I mentioned that the only reason I'd gone to that school was to keep the peace at home. Corni agreed that she couldn't assist me with my medical costs. "Why do you need assistance," she asked, "is this for you?" I told her that I was epileptic and periodically suffer convulsions. I was starting to leave; she asked, "What is your name?" We had not introduced each other. I told her that I go by several names but that I prefer *Rosita*. She then told me her name, *Corni*. "Rosita, we do have some very nice retired people involved with this center. They volunteer their time here at the center. I've known several of them that take in children to help them. Maybe one of these kind people is willing to help you. My husband and I have adopted five Méxican kids."

Meet My Grandpa Casey

Corni told me, "Wait, don't go away. I'm going to see if someone wants to help you." She returned accompanied by an older Americano. "Rosita, I want you to meet Mr. Francis Casey."

The gentleman reached his hand out to me; he said, "Glad to meet you." He introduced himself as Francis Casey. He even asked, "May I call you Rosi?" However, at the time, I didn't quite understand. Corni translated what he'd said.

I smiled and said, "Yes, *Rosi* is okay," as I extended my hand to meet his. Thank my Chuchin that Corni was there to translate. She translated everything he said; the most important was that he was willing to help me with the cost of my medicine.

Mr. Casey asked Corni if a student could accompany us to the pharmacy. The cost was too much for Mr. Casey to absorb, $1,050 for thirty pills. I understood that Mr. Casey thought the cost to be too expensive and didn't buy them. I tried to make the Americano understand that it was okay. I believe that he knew what I was trying to say. He drove us back to the school. He and Corni talked for a while. "Rosita, Mr. Casey wants to treat us to lunch, are you interested?" I accepted. During lunch he wanted to hear more about me. I talked, and Corni translated. He learned all that I was willing to share at the time. Mainly I wanted him to know about my sickness. I made sure that he knew that I had left my country because I could not be cured there. I wanted to talk about Viki and the way she was treating me, but I didn't. Some of the memories that I was sharing brought tears to my eyes. I stopped talking because I was getting too emotional. Corni and Mr. Casey spoke. At some point of their conversation, I saw a surprised expression on her face. They stopped talking. "Rosita, do you know what Mr. Casey is willing to do?"

Based on what has happened to me in this country, I was apprehensive. "He wants to adopt you and help you in any way that he can." That was a total surprise. I looked at him then at Corni. I asked, "Is that possible?"

"Yes, Rosita, it's possible. He wants to know if you accept." I looked back at him. I nodded my head in the affirmative, saying, "Sí, sí, acepto." He spoke to Corni. Her translation was that he was going to take me to apply for Medicaid. I will never forget the day I met Mr. Casey Francis.

Melchor arrived at the apartment. Another day I won't forget is April 2, 2002, the day he arrived. I was confused and did not know how to greet him. He hugged me asking me to forgive him. I found it difficult to express myself, especially when he expressed his love for me. All I could do was thank him for coming. Viki had no difficulty in telling Melchor how much I had missed him. She offered to rent him a room while we found another place. I needed to speak with Melchor in private.

I grabbed his arm. "Melchor, let's go eat someplace where we can talk." Viki interrupted, "You can talk here." I pulled him by his arm and walked away. I turned around to see Viki fuming with eyes bulging red from her eyelids. I smiled; she reminded me of the bull that tried to horn me long ago. We rented a room from Viki for a few days. Believe me, living with Viki and Melchor in the same apartment was too much for me. I talked to Maritza; she rented us a room.

Preparing my goodies to sell was one way to forget the negative issues in my life. Selling and meeting others was a blessing. I was able to get Melchor a job. A husband of one of the ladies who bought tamales from me gave him a job. His words meant nothing; his promises were meaningless. He forced himself on me. I left him behind in Kansas because of the same problem. He kept promising that he would change, but he didn't. I realize that we were living together and the temptation was too great for him, but I wasn't ready.

Mr. Casey and I kept in touch. He helped me clear some things with Medicaid. We communicated with the orphanage regarding some of the documents that I had left behind. These documents were going to help me get medical assistance here. We met with a judge to have Mr. Casey adopt me. I was twenty-one years old, which made me too old to be adopted. However, the judge put me under his custody. This meant that I could apply for my residency card after I had lived here ten years and eventually become a citizen. Melchor couldn't understand why an Americano came to my aid. Viki felt the same way. I had only one response, which I kept to myself. Americanos are a giving people, and my Diosito placed Mr. Casey in my path of life.

Mr. Casey asked me if I went to church. My response was probably a lame one. But I didn't have transportation, and I didn't have a car, and the bus was not an option for me. Melchor didn't believe in going to Mass, and he refused to take me. Mr. Casey agreed to pick me up and take me to his church, the Holy Family in Orange.

I met and made more friends at the church. I tried to persuade Melchor to accompany me, but he refused. He and most of his family belong to another denomination and won't change. I can't say that I blame him because I won't change my being a Catholic. I tried to convince him to join me. The discussion usually ended in an argument. He didn't want to be part of who I was. I wanted to share my past with him, but he ignored me. I needed an audience to share what I had gone through, but he was not interested. But yes, his interest was to have a sexual relationship with me. The Melchor that I ran away from in Kansas continued to take advantage of me.

Maritza knocked on the door to the room we rented from her. She wanted to know if I was okay. I wasn't surprised, I realized that she'd heard the commotion coming from our room the night before. "Rosi, I wanted to call the police and report what Melchor was doing to you. Rosi, I'm very happy renting a room to you because you are a good person. However, these walls are too thin. I can hear everything that goes on in your room. That man doesn't have the right to force himself on you. I can't stop him from how he's treating you, but I can't continue hearing what he does to you. I had to stop my boyfriend from going into your room last night. One of these days, I won't be able to stop him, and he will hurt Melchor. I'm sorry, but I have to ask you to move."

Melchor was very apologetic, but we had to move. The place we moved to was very noisy. I could hear noises from the apartment above us; they were similar to the ones I was experiencing with Melchor. My life had to change. I made it out of México, I survived Reyna and her lecherous old man, I most certainly will change my situation.

I enrolled at Santiago College. I had my high school certificate from the school in México, but it had little value in this country. Receiving a certificate from here had, and my intention was to study English and whatever other classes I needed. During my lifetime, I learned that when I was under stress or became emotional, I would suffer a convulsion. Attending college could be stressful. I tried to control my emotions and avoid stressful situations. I laughed, I sang, and I told myself silly jokes I made up. My Chuchin was a constant on my mind, and I was always talking to Him. I hid my feelings from my classmates and the teachers. None of them knew nor did they realize the unhappy life I was living. However, my attacks continued. Some weeks I would suffer up to three in a given week.

I visited the counselor every time I had a question or needed advice. I was offered an English language tutor, marriage counselor, and other services. Melchor was trying to make amends for the way he was treating me. I believe it was for this reason he agreed to attend a counseling session with me. He didn't realize that we were seeing a person that might help us with the sexual problem we were having. He attended the first session only. He didn't attend again. His reason was that I was the one needing counseling, not him. He thought that maybe with some advice from the counselor, I would be more willing to have sex with him.

I continued with my classes regardless of the uneventful experience I was having at home and with my convulsions. One day, during my computer class, I felt that I was about to have a convulsion. The teacher summoned her supervisor. They led me to a lounge where I could rest. While I was resting, the supervisor wanted to know me. We chatted for a while until I got better. In the meantime, she shared some good news with me. The news made me feel really good, even my headache went away.

The supervisor told me that she would grant me a high school certificate provided that I could provide her with (a) my high school records from México, (b) take intermediate English, (c) study the history of the United States, and (d) be punctual and receive good grades. If I complied with all of her requirements, I would be awarded my high school certificate within two years. I left the campus toward the bus stop, I looked up to the sky and released a yell that I was holding back. My eyes released a tearful of sheer happiness. Still looking up I knew that my Chuchin was watching, I made the sign of the cross. My education was on track, this was a good start. My dream of being a lawyer here in America was no longer a dream, it was becoming a reality.

I hated to move because Maritza was such a good friend, but we had to. We lived for six months in a room we rented from Doña Dalila. During that time, Melchor bought a car. He actually enjoyed taking me to the beach. I felt free walking along the ocean water with the sand covering my feet. However, I never felt free enough to wear a bathing suit, much less a bikini. My sister Oli even paid me a surprise visit. We talked for a while inside my apartment until we decided to go where it wasn't so hot.

For the first time, I rode on the 55 Freeway up to the Main Place mall. Naturally I didn't know that Main Place existed. From Oli I learned what a mall was. I loved the stores and the beautiful dresses on display in the windows. I wanted to try on the shoes, touch the purses, but I was too reserved. I didn't know how to act, I was afraid to enter any of the stores, and I didn't want to ask my sister anything that went through my mind. We sat on a bench. From my vantage point, I saw many types of people, many different races. Oli wanted to gossip; she asked me about Viki, about Melchor, and Mr. Casey. I answered as little as possible because I didn't want to say anything about Viki for fear that it would backfire. But Oli assured me that she was not in good terms with Viki. She also mentioned that Viki had alienated the sisters.

I continued baking and selling my goodies and making new friends. Mr. Casey was always ready to help, but my health didn't improve; rather, I felt that it was getting worse. I suffered another convulsion inside the classroom. I wound up in the UC Irvine hospital. I was assigned a neurologist to check my illness. He told me that it was possible to cure me. However, the cost was prohibitive; I couldn't afford the cost. There was no way that I could come up with that kind of money. Disillusioned with the cost and the fact that I couldn't come up with that amount, I went home. I prayed to my Chuchin for strength. I didn't give up hope; within a week, I was back at the hospital.

The security at the hospital remembered me from prior visits. He spoke Spanish, and I was grateful because he helped me. He led me to the office of a neurologist. I had no idea how to get around the maze of buildings and offices, but the security did. I walked in and registered with the secretary. I waited for a call and waited. People entered, people left, and I waited. It was closing time; the secretary was getting ready to go home. The secretary kept looking at me and smiled but didn't call my name. She did ask me something once, but I didn't understand.

Around closing time, a janitor walked in, I assumed, to clean the offices. He greeted the secretary and then turned to me and greeted me in Spanish. *My lucky day,* I thought. I asked him if he could speak English. He spoke some but not fluent. I asked him if he could interpret for me. He followed me to where the secretary was getting ready to leave. I wanted to know when I could see the doctor that I had been waiting all day. She wanted to know whether I had an appointment because all the doctors had gone home for the day. "Oh no, how can that be?" I asked her in Spanish. I was so disappointed I started to cry. The janitor stopped me. "Señorita, the secretary wants to know if you have insurance."

"Ay, señor, tell her that I have no insurance, but that I have thirty-one dollars to pay for a visit."

"Oh, señorita, I don't think that is enough," the janitor told me. "Señor, just tell her, please tell her what I said." He did, and she looked at me in amazement, I got closer to where she was sitting. I pleaded in Spanish asking if she could give me the name of a doctor that could help me. The secretary looked at the janitor. He started to translate when the door labeled PRIVATE opened.

I Meet Dr. Kim

AT THAT PRECISE MOMENT, I saw a doctor and a nurse walk into the area. The secretary called out to him. The secretary talked to him at the same time looking at me. The doctor and the nurse approached me; she spoke in Spanish to me. "The doctor wants to know about your illness." She asked, "You don't speak English, and you have been here all day waiting for a doctor?" I started to answer; all I could do was shake my head in the affirmative, I had a convulsion.

I regained consciousness in a strange room; the nurse I met earlier was taking my pulse. The doctor was standing next to the bed. "Señorita, Dr. Kim is going to help you." I looked at the doctor and thanked him. Dr. Kim spoke to me. The nurse told me that he wanted to know my name. "He is interested to know about your illness." I spoke, and the nurse translated. I shared everything about my epilepsy. The nurse told me that they had performed tests on me while I was unconscious. The doctor had looked at the results and concluded that my epilepsy was very high. The falls I experienced had caused a lot of damage, especially on the left side of my head. The damage to my head is causing the continuous convulsions.

I asked Dr. Kim if my life was in peril. I saw the doctor's reaction. I realized that my life was in danger before the nurse translated the answer. I asked, "Can Dr. Kim cure me?" Through the nurse I learned that the doctor had to perform several tests on my skull and brain before he could perform an emergency operation.

Oh my God! I thought, *Diosito, you put a professional in my path to cure me.* Tears poured. I started to sob. Dr. Kim gave me a handful of tissue. He took my hand. "Don't be afraid." I told him that I wasn't afraid, that I was happy that I would be rid of my illness. "Dr. Kim, is there really a cure for my epilepsy?" I waited for the question to reach his ears and the translation by the nurse. He was going to be assisted in the operation by experts in the field from throughout the country. Still holding my hand, he said that he would help me; and in the process, I would be helping the medical world. The information gathered during my treatment and the eventual operation was going to help them understand the illness much better. He assured me that he and the other top neurologists would do their best to make the operation a successful one. He said that anything above 80 percent cure was good.

I told the nurse that for years I have prayed to my Diosito to send a doctor to cure me. I couldn't stop the tears. When the doctor heard the translation, he smiled. He said, "It starts now. I have to perform some studies to see which medicine is best for you." I informed the doctor that I didn't have any money and that I was already in debt and owed the hospital for past services. "Now I will be further in debt to you." By this time, several other doctors had joined Dr. Kim in the room. They assured me that I would be helping them understand what caused my illness. I would not incur any costs and that past debts would be taken off the books. I was given literature on the subject before I was sent home.

I waited outside the hospital for Mr. Casey. I looked beyond the tall buildings up to the sky above the clouds and saw an angel. I lifted my arms in adoration of my Diosito. I thanked Him for always being with me. I felt that I had entered a new chapter in my life. I shared the news with Mr. Casey. He didn't understand how I was able to get the doctors to help me. He reasoned that because my faith in my Diosito was very strong, God had led them to me. He was a religious person and didn't question it anymore.

October 2003, the judge approved to place me in the custody of Mr. Casey. He helped me a lot. He accompanied me to most of my appointments at the hospital. He was also my interpreter. The doctors gave him the results; he in turn relayed them to me. My Diosito was always at my side. I knew because I would see the angel high above the clouds. I knew that Diosito was watching over me. I continue my faith in Him, I have never denied Him in my soul or in my lips, especially now.

The pending operation put a stop to my education. I was still very much interested in getting my education. But I was changing my mind about being a lawyer. I thought of studying to be a counselor or psychiatrist. I tried to share with Melchor all that was happening with the doctors and with my educational plans. His typical answer was, "What can I do about it?" or "If you need money, let me know, and I'll see how we can manage. Maybe I can get another job," is all he'd say. "Melchor, the money is not as important as a good relationship. I need compassion, I need love, I need affection."

"Okay, Rosi," he would say, "give me what I want, and you will have all of that."

"See," I told him, "that's all you think that I'm here for. When there is love between two, it's demonstrated in other ways, not only by having sex. I told you what I need, the doctors say the same thing. The way you respond shows that I am not the companion that you desire. You are a man that doesn't get drunk, smokes, or takes drugs. You can find yourself a lady that will give the pleasure I cannot."

He stood up. "Rosi, forget the doctors for a few moments and give me what is mine." I endured the trauma, which seemed like an eternity. What else could I do? I saw blood on the sheet, he noticed it also. I got up from the bed. He tried to apologize, I ignored him and went to the bathroom to clean up. The daughter of Doña Dalila walked into the bathroom after I let her in. I went into the room. The daughter noticed the blood inside the bathroom. She ran and told her mother. Doña Dalila called the police.

Soon after he had his pleasure, Doña Dalila knocked on my door. "Rosi, the police are outside, they want to speak with you." I was surprised. I asked her, "They want to speak with me? Why, I haven't done anything wrong." I was scared. "Yes, Rosi, I know, go speak with them." The policewoman was very nice but firm. She asked if I lived at this address and if I lived with Melchor. I was very cooperative and answered all her questions. "Why are you investigating me? I haven't done anything wrong."

"Señora, we received a report of domestic violence. We understand that you were shedding blood, and we are here to determine the cause of it. Don't be afraid, we are not here to arrest you." The other policeman came out with handcuffs on Melchor. She asked, "Is this the man you live with?"

"Yes, but he hasn't done anything wrong," I said. "My boyfriend is a good person, we had an intimate moment, and I started to bleed. He didn't do anything wrong." After further questioning, the policeman took the handcuffs off Melchor. "We are going to release him this time. However, any more calls like this one, and both of you are going to jail." She gave me her card.

Every so often, Oli would come to visit. I always asked if we could visit away from the apartment because I hardly left my jail of a room. Melchor seemed upset every time I left with Oli. I continued to visit the doctor with Mr. Casey's help. I also kept busy baking and selling my cinnamon-banana bread, tamales, and enchiladas. My convulsions didn't stop, but I knew that the doctors my Chuchin placed in the middle of my path would solve my illness.

We moved again; this time we rented a room from Chela and Alex. They were a nice couple, always together and having a good time. They loved the beach, attended movies and parties. I was in another jail hardly going out. Melchor worked six days a week, and on Sundays, he felt tired, so he refused to take me out on his day of rest. Chela asked me to go with them on several occasions, but to avoid a conflict with Melchor, I didn't. Chela knew that he and I didn't have anything in common. "Rosi," she would say, "you are a beautiful girl, why doesn't he take you out?" I would smile and say, "I don't know why."

"But look, Chela, we can see the face, but we don't know anything about that person's heart." Chela would say, "Rosi, that man doesn't know that you are a classy woman. Someday he will recognize the type of woman you really are, and it's going to be too late."

"Chela, Melchor may not be the perfect match for me, but he does help me a lot."

"Rosi, I don't know what to say other than, it's your life."

"I endure a lot, that I don't deny, but it's my cross to bear."

Most of the people we knew were worried by the way he treated me. Mr. Casey knew, and he offered to rent me a room whenever I decided to get away from him. I needed to get away from him. I told him that Mr. Casey had offered me a room and I was considering moving. He didn't seem to care. For some unknown reason, I wanted to save what little relationship we had. On Sunday I asked if he'd go to Mass with me. Again he declined. "Rosi, you know that I don't believe in your religion, just like you don't believe in mine. Besides, you know that Sunday is the day I rest. Yeah, you sell bread and I don't know what else during the week, but that doesn't compare with the work I do. Call Mr. Casey, he will take you to your church." He gave me $20. "Now go wherever, just leave me alone."

I waited to hear news from the hospital and waited. I knew the day would come, I knew because my Chuchin was looking out for me. The day finally arrived, I was asked to come to the hospital for a conference with Dr. Kim and his associates. Chela was so happy when I gave her the news; she volunteered to take me.

Dr. Kim gave me the good news first. My cost of my operation and my medicine would be covered. The other news he shared was that I had to be operated as soon as possible. My condition was getting very critical. I was having up to ten convulsions daily; the left side of my head was shattered, and I had cysts growing inside. The cysts were reproducing and, if not removed, could prove fatal. "We have the equipment, and the other neurologists are ready to perform an emergency operation." There was no question in my mind that I wanted to have this operation. This is what I have waited for all my life. But everything had happened so quickly.

I was still in a state of amazement when the social worker at the hospital asked me several questions. She had a file on me with most of my personal information in front of her. She advised me that Melchor would not be given any of my information. The hospital preferred to have Mr. Casey be the intermediary because of his command of the English language.

Dr. Kim assembled a team of neurologists from around the country and even some from foreign countries. Most of them were full-time employees at the UCI Hospital. The preparation for my operation was to commence in May 2004. This included performing studies on me before I would be medically fit to be operated on. I guess I have to sacrifice something if I want to get well. The date of my intended operation was in conflict with the day of getting my certificate from college. I could attend school later, my health had priority.

Word of my impending operation spread throughout the church. The congregation held prayer meetings, and the bishop held a Mass in my honor and gave me a Holy Cross medal. The orphanage was informed of my operation, and I understand that they also held prayer meetings. My letter with my name was taken to the Vatican by a congregation of persons from my church and given to Pope John Paul II. How I felt about all the preparations and prayer meetings is hard to describe. I knew that somehow my Chuchin was involved. I talked with Him daily, and I also said my prayers. I was not concerned with the operation, I knew that My Diosito had placed my life in Dr. Kim's capable hands.

In spite of all the attention I was receiving, I needed to speak with somebody that understood what I was going through. I tried to communicate with Melchor, but he didn't seem to care. I wanted to share with him the risk I was taking. His typical answer was, "Why tell me, what can I do?" He really didn't understand that all I needed was someone to share those moments with. I was alone; if not for my Diosito, I would be completely alone. I was getting desperate to leave the environment; my jail was without bars or locks, but I was in isolation.

I called Mr. Casey. He picked me up and took me to lunch. He figured what I was going to ask. When I asked him if the offer to rent me a room was still open, he smiled and asked me when I wanted to move. He did mention that he would be going to South Korea with members of the Diocese of Orange. If I was able to live alone for about a week, I could move in right away. I sorta smiled before answering; I said, "Mr. Casey, I have lived alone most of my life, I can handle the short time that you're gone."

Melchor was saddened when I told him that I was leaving him. I repeated what I'd told him many times before. I told him to find another girl, one that would please him. I mentioned that I was sorry that I couldn't be that person. I have too many past memories that prevent me from being a person that he would be happy with. His sad eyes spoke for him. He left the apartment without saying a word. Next day I packed my belongings and left.

I Moved to Mr. Francis Casey's House

MR. CASEY WAS VERY HAPPY when I arrived at his house. He led me to the room that would be my new home. It was a very nice home in a very well and wealthy part of Orange. What struck me strange was that he lived alone. Since the first day I met Mr. Casey, I had assumed that he was married and had children living at home. The fact that I would be living alone in a house with a man was awkward. I wasn't scared because Mr. Casey had always treated me with respect. I was speaking and understanding English. Being enrolled in English class and the association with other Americanos like Mr. Casey helped me a lot.

He felt my uneasiness. "Rosi, don't worry, okay? You will be safe here. I've told you that I live alone, but you didn't understand me. Your lack of English and my lack of the Spanish language, my message was lost." Now that I understood some English, I understood him telling me that his wife had died and his two daughters lived close by. His daughters were aware that he was helping me and that I was under his custody. I still felt uneasy. Moving back with Melchor was not an option. If things didn't work out living here, I would move out. I knew that I had to learn English.

Living away from Melchor was much more pleasant. My room was small, but it was my room. The window faced the side street. Living there was so quiet, especially more quiet than the apartments. Mr. Casey would drive me to my appointments at UCI Hospital and translated the orders from the doctors. In time I was being more open with him. I told him more and more about my life. Once he asked me if I wanted to call him *Dad* or *Daddy*; after all, he had custody of me. I settled in calling him *Grandpa*. I thought, *Jorge Bustos is my dad and nobody else.*

Grandpa Casey liked to go shopping. His favorite destination was Costco and/or Home Depot. Staying home was boring unless he was working in the yard. I helped him, and since I knew something about flowers, I would take care of his flowers. I had several convulsions when I was in a store with him. He didn't take me to the hospitals nor did he liked calling the paramedics. However, he was always at my side when I came to.

The time was approaching soon he would leave for South Korea. He asked Mary, a lady I had been introduced to at church, to check on me. He instructed Mary not to allow me to leave the house alone because I didn't know the area. There was plenty of food, and she had an ample supply of medicine. Mary had the telephone number to the house, and I had her phone number. Meanwhile, Melchor started coming around to see me. I welcomed him provided that he meet a few of my conditions. One was no talk of intimacy, another being that we meet outside in the patio. He was very prompt with his visits; he arrived at seven and left at eight thirty. Mr. Casey was always peering through the window.

Mr. Casey Leaves for South Korea

Secrets among men hardly remain unrevealed; it is probably a weakness or simply the chance to make conversation. I have no clue. Melchor started coming around because Mr. Casey asked him to. Grandpa was concerned that I was going to be alone while he went to Korea. Melchor never mentioned that Grandpa had asked him to come and visit me. I thought if you want a secret to cease being that, tell a man. I learned of the request from Mr. Casey himself. He asked for my forgiveness. He wanted me to have another contact besides Mary. He tried to assure me that Melchor would act like a gentleman and not bother me. "Rosi," he said, "Melchor promised me that he won't kidnap you. Besides, you never know, you might decide to be with him again." I sobbed some, thinking of the past and what the future would be with Melchor. Grandpa told me to pray for Melchor. I just smiled knowing that I always have.

Two days of being cooped up all by myself was too much. I was used to being outside, and even though I was warned not to venture outside by myself, I did just that. I walked outside; the streets were empty and so quiet and so peaceful. I started to feel a convulsion coming, I tried to get back inside the house. I woke up in the hospital. I was not alone, I could see some policemen and a nurse in my room. The nurse summoned the policemen waiting to question me. They asked me several questions. I answered as best as I could. I informed them of my sickness and shared that I was waiting to be operated to cure me. The police went about the neighborhood getting information on myself and the owner of the house, Mr. Casey.

After the questioning, one of the lawmen poked his head outside the door and summoned Melchor. They discovered that Melchor and I had lived together. Under no circumstance were the police allowing me to stay alone, not in my condition. They hoped that I would go live with Melchor until Grandpa returned. What could I do? A person that is between a rock and a hard place has to make a spur-of-the-moment decision. The hospital would release me to him if I accepted; otherwise, I would have to stay.

The emptiness I felt entering the apartment building got worse as I ascended into his apartment. The tears, fed by the loss of my confidence in him and the fear that he would grab me again, wouldn't stop. He offered me a drink of water or a cup of tea. I grabbed a glass of water. He assured me that I would be safe and that he would not make advances toward me. "Rosi, you look tired, you need to go to bed. I won't bother you. I really am sorry for the way I have treated you. Give me another chance, and I promise to take good care of you."

I had a difficult time falling asleep. I realized that I had fallen asleep when Melchor woke me up. "Rosi, you were having a nightmare saying my name telling me to leave you alone. Relax, I'm not going to hurt you. Rosi, I know why you don't love me, but believe me, I love you very much. I will prove myself to you, and maybe you will learn to love me. I don't care that you are sick, I love you. I'm a man, and when I see your beautiful face, I want to be with you. Every time I hear your voice and I see the way you walk makes me fall in love with you more and more. Give me another opportunity."

My response was stuck inside my throat, I swallowed my tears before I could answer. I told him that I had no confidence in him. "Both of us suffer living together—you because I can't give you what you desire. I suffer because I am nothing but a sex object to you. Right now, and I mean this moment, I have my mind on my operation. You know that I have dreamt of this operation since I was a child. I can't have any turmoil in my mind, I need to have peace." Melchor promised to be at my side when I had my operation and take care of me. Melchor seemed sincere, I wanted to believe him. "We'll talk tomorrow," he said. I fell asleep.

Mr. Casey went looking for me at the apartment. He'd gotten home from his trip, and not finding me there, he figured where I was. He and Melchor had a long talk. Afterward, Grandpa talked to me. He relayed the words of Melchor. Simply stated, he believed that Melchor loved me deeply. So much so that he was willing to go with me to my church and talk to a counselor. I couldn't believe it, Melchor go with me to my church and speak to a counselor? Nonsense, I thought. I asked him if what Mr. Casey had told me was true. "Ha, you know the answer, I won't step inside your church, and neither will I see a counselor."

Why would Mr. Casey say that what was his motive? Maybe he wanted to make sure that Melchor wasn't going to persuade me to go back to him. However, the response I got from Melchor was reason enough not to stay with him. My foster dad took me home. I waited and waited for word from Dr. Kim. Seven months passed, and no word. Melchor visited me during that time. Señor Casey's attitude toward me appeared to change. Maybe it was me that was changing; with all the wait, I was getting a little cranky. He would make statements that didn't make sense to me since I didn't fully understand English.

The curiosity was too much. I wrote the statement as best I could and took it to my counselor at school. "If I was your boyfriend, I would not treat you like he does. The nights would be different, I would treat you like a lady, not like him. He doesn't appreciate you." She interpreted what I wrote down. She asked me if I had written everything that he said, no mistakes. I thought that I had written everything. She wanted to make sure. I wondered if that was the reason he took custody of me. I was upset with him, but I wanted to make sure. I asked Mr. Casey to take me to the church group. The group met once in a while. I wanted a friend that spoke both English and Spanish to interpret his words. After the two spoke, she didn't share with me what Mr. Casey meant. She did tell me that she wished that I marry him so I could get my resident card.

Marriage Proposal Refusal

GRANDPA WAS VERY JOVIAL MORE so than other times when he picked me up from the college. He spoke, but the words were still foreign to me. I understood a few words something about papers. He stopped in Santa Ana, motioned for me to follow him into an office. *Abogada* was written on the door, I knew the word. Lawyer? Why was he bringing me to a lawyer's office? We entered the office. A señora lawyer walked around her desk to meet us. She was a very physically attractive lady, except for her eyes. They sent a strong vibe when she looked at me. Beware, I thought.

I recognized a few words they spoke, but enough to put me on alert. Sitting in that office made me feel uncomfortable, I believe that my Chuchin was somehow present. The señora lawyer handed Grandpa some papers; he glanced at them and asked me to sign them. I stared at the lawyer and asked, "Are you a licensed lawyer?" She kinda smirked. "Of course I am."

"Okay then, señora lawyer, why are you asking me to sign papers that I know nothing about?" Mr. Casey didn't understand what I had asked in Spanish. "Señorita Rosi, Mr. Casey wants to marry you so that you can get your United States resident card. All you have to do is sign these papers. I then will take them to the immigration office. Now you, señorita, being married to a US citizen will be able to get your resident card. But I have to tell you this, before you can become a resident, you have to return to México for a time between six months to a year."

"Stay calm, stay calm," I said to myself. "Señora, I may not be a citizen of this country, but I have rights. I don't have to sign anything. Not you or Mr. Casey can force me." I took the papers and tore them up into pieces. My memory took me back to the time Reyna and the lecherous old man tried to use me to steal Mamacita's property. I didn't sign anything then and I won't now. "Señora, I have permission to be in this country. I have rights and justification to be in this country. Believe me, I will talk to my counselor in college, she's also a lawyer." Grandpa, raising his voice, said, "Rosi, are you stupid?"

I rushed out of that office so fast that not even the fastest animal in the world could catch me. Grandpa ran after me. "Rosi, why did you do that?" I stopped. "Señor, why don't you ask your lawyer what she wants me to do?" He didn't understand what I was saying. We drove home without talking. It wouldn't do us any good because we didn't understand each other.

Next day I arrived early and went straight to my counselor's office. I recounted all that had transpired in the lawyer's office. The counselor told me not to worry, she would help. We were waiting for Grandpa to pick me up. She spoke to Grandpa. She realized that the so-called immigration lawyer we'd talked to the day before was telling Mr. Casey something entirely different from what she was telling me. She was a fraud. My counselor and other volunteer lawyers paid the false lawyer a visit. A few weeks later, I decided to check on the so-called immigration lawyer. The office had a sign on the window, FOR RENT. I smiled for a second. I was glad, I wondered where she'd moved to. Maybe to another locale where she could fraud other immigrants.

Mr. Casey and I didn't talk much at home. We did understand each other better. We communicated in our own interpretation of sign language and my English that was getting better. I didn't want any confrontations with him because where would I go if he kicked me out? Melchor was being very friendly, but for now, he was not an option. Presently I had too much on my mind to worry about trivial matters. My pending operation, the one I've waited for all my life, was constantly on my mind. I worried about my school and my medicine then my convulsions. I didn't need to be saddled with worries about where I was going to live, I had a place to live. In a moment of silence, I would glance at the sky, I knew my Diosito was watching. I felt His spirit all around, I relaxed. I felt safe.

Living in the same house with Mr. Casey was rather difficult. I especially felt uncomfortable when he drank his wine. He never gave me a reason to fear him. He took me shopping, we attended Mass and church group meetings together. Maybe my past was too much to forget what men are capable of.

Melchor continued his visits. He wanted to prove to me that he'd changed. The problem was that we had gone this route before. His promises were like the tumbleweeds blowing in the wind. They stick to a fence until another gust blows them away. I realize that living with me is difficult for a man like Melchor. I can control my desires because my priorities are different than his, he can't. He comes home from work, tired. He doesn't accept a refusal because he feels that it's his right and it's my duty to comply.

Operation and Rehab

THE MOMENT I'VE WAITED FOR my entire life became a reality. The months of waiting since I met Dr. Kim ceased. The American dream, my reason for coming to America, was no longer in waiting. The phone call from Dr. Kim's office was eagerly received by Francis Casey. The call was followed by a letter of confirmation stating the date of my appointment and other information. My foster father handed me the unopened letter. To say that I was trembling trying to open the letter would be an understatement. Tears flowing from my eyes blocked my view. *Rosita, relax,* I thought. I smiled at Mr. Casey, he was anxious to read the letter as well. I had to undergo another examination required before the operation. Not what I wanted to hear. But I realized the precautions that Dr. Kim was taking, and I appreciated that.

Another setback! My American dream would not be realized until later. I had a urinary infection. My operation was moved to August 26, 2004. More waiting, more convulsions, and more drama in my life. In my mind, everything was a drama. I was alone facing my future, my Diosito was my healer, my security, and my everything. Without Him, I'd be lost. Meanwhile, the school informed me that I had completed the requirements necessary to get my high school diploma. My diploma would be sent to me at a later date.

The operation was set—no postponements, no more delays. The night before, I prayed the rosary over and over. I'd walk into and out of my room restless. I couldn't sleep, I couldn't think, only pray. Mr. Casey was sitting in the living room, Melchor stayed away. Somehow I survived the night. My date with…destiny? Arrived. Mr. Casey and Melchor drove me to the hospital. I filled papers giving my consent that would allow medical students and some observers inside the operating room. With the registration complete, Mr. Casey and Melchor left. The nurse prepared me for the operation. I was placed in the operating table and given an injection. I saw the Sacred Heart beside me. I smiled thinking, *Thank You, Diosito, for placing these doctors in my path of life.* That's the last thing I remember.

The first of the operations, the doctors probed inside my head to determine the cause of my convulsions. My skull was going to be cleaned of all the small broken pieces caused by the numerous falls I sustained every time I fell. I was in a coma for a few days. I don't remember much except for the nurses: Rosario, Marcela, Ofelia, Reyna; and assistant nurses took care of me day and night. The probes inserted in me showed that I was still having convulsions. The tests revealed that some bone fragments were not removed during the first operation. The doctors determined that these fragments might be the cause of my convulsions. To be sure, they didn't give me medicine for a few days. After analyzing the results, they determined that the small pieces of bone had to be removed. A second operation was performed to remove them.

The most critical of the operations was the third one. This operation was performed to remove the cysts that were reproducing in my skull. The operations were very critical. But I survived all because of my faith in God. I truly believe that Diosito placed these doctors in the path of my life to cure me.

After the last operation, I stayed in the hospital a few days. Grandpa Casey provided me with the following information. He told me that Melchor signed papers taking full responsibility for me. When I was released from the hospital, Melchor took care of me because Mr. Casey insisted that he didn't want any nurses coming to the house. Grandpa rented him a room so that he could be close to me. Melchor bathed me three times a day, changed the gauze on my head, and gave me my medicine. I don't remember much during that time. Sometimes I would see light, and other times I could feel movement. I knew that somebody was feeding me. Later, Mr. Casey told me that he would feed me during the day, and Melchor the other times.

I was provided with services to a counselor and psychologist, which helped me gain my memories and health. I was placed in the care of a neurologist who helped Dr. Kim with my operation. Whatever information the doctors and nurses shared with me went directly into my diary. Mr. Casey also provided much more information.

Grandpa gave me most of the information, which I wrote in my diary. Melchor also gave information but never knew that I was writing everything he told me. The psychologist I saw provided some information by the questions he asked. Eventually I was able to see, but I couldn't walk. Mr. Casey wheeled me around the house and to my appointments.

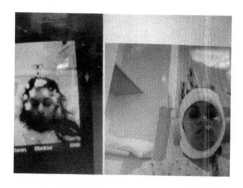

Of significance was one of the tests performed on me. The neurologists wanted to determine whether I could reason or if I could remember any of my past. They asked for my diaries and notes. My foster father knew where I kept them. He presented them to the doctors. The doctors connected cables from a computer to my brain. They asked me if I could write anything.

I understood much of what they were telling me to do. Slowly I wrote as much as I could. Then the nurse showed me my diaries and notes. Memories lost were slowly coming back. My body was not responding fast enough for me. I was wheeled around mainly by Mr. Casey. I wanted to walk on my own, but my foster parent didn't allow it. He was instructed by the doctors to not allow me to walk on my own. Any moment that I was alone, I tried to walk, only to have

Mr. Casey pick me up from where I'd fallen. Eventually I started to crawl before Mr. Casey picked me up and placed me back on the, ugh, chair. In time I was be able to get on my knees and move before he came to my rescue. The physical therapists were great, they helped me a lot. When I wasn't in therapy, I would read any periodical, and Grandpa Casey had plenty of reading material. My neurologist was surprised how much I had progressed each time I saw her.

My Diosito placed experts in my path of life to cure me. Now the rest was up to me. Now why am I not able to walk on my own two feet? This challenge is nothing compared to what I have overcome in my past. I was a little girl, tangled on the barbed-wire fence when I defeated the raging bull. Santo Niño de Atocha stopped me from going into the quicksand, I survived the tree that fell atop of me; and most of all, I survived that lecherous old man and my mother. My Chuchin watches over me, I am safe under His care, my faith in Him never ceases. In time I began to dress myself. Yes, I will admit it wasn't easy. I struggled, but it was nothing to the struggle that my Diosito faced carrying the cross to save me and mankind.

Each day, I felt better and better. My convulsions were almost nonexistent. My headaches at times were excruciating, but in time, they stopped. I started to walk. Little by little I got rid of the wheelchair. My little steps became longer and faster, but no stamina, I had to rest. Mr. Casey, Melchor, and my doctors were amazed at my progress. But I knew that my Diosito was watching and smiling at my progress.

Physically I was progressing, but mentally I wasn't progressing to my satisfaction. There were times when I couldn't think, I felt strange. I would see the figure of a man, not realizing that it was Mr. Casey. I recognized voices, but I failed to place the voice with the person. What I learned from my doctor was that I had lost part of my memory. My determination to recover memory led me to my diaries and notes. Originally, when the doctors were asking me to read them, I wasn't aware why they were asking me to read them. In time I knew that memory recovery depended on my past writings about my life. I truly believe that my Diosito was guiding me even as a child. How else would I be able to recall all that has happened to me?

Melchor stood by my side; at times we would have a decent conversation. I wanted to walk the beach to feel the sand under my feet, feel the cool ocean water, I wanted to feel alive. Melchor asked me if I wanted to go for a ride. First place I wanted was the ocean. We went to Newport Beach. I stepped on the sand, I felt vibrant and alive. I wanted to run and wet my feet. The ocean waves were beckoning me; I took my time, held under control my desire to run. The water washed the sand from my feet; I looked up into expanse of the heavens, blew a kiss to my Diosito; tears welled in my eyes. I don't recall ever when I felt as happy as I did that moment.

We sat on a beach towel, he wanted to talk to me. He took the opportunity to ask me if I'd consider moving in with him again. Melchor said, "Rosi, I love you very much, you know that. But I need you by my side, please come back to me." I wasn't surprised because I had felt that the time was coming when he would want me back. We faced each other, held hands. I answered, "Melchor, I appreciate what you have done for me, especially the past months when you stood by me. You took good care of me, you fed me, gave me my medicine, you in your bed and I in mine. But to be with you like in the past, no! You want us to be together? Then marry me in the Catholic Church. I will give you ten sons, married like husband and wife. I want my privacy with you."

"Never," he said standing up. "I won't marry you or anyone else in the church. Rosi, you know how I feel. We don't have to get married to have children. I would be happy to be with you and have children, but I can't marry you in the church." At that moment, I didn't feel comfortable being with him. I thought, *Well, I can ask the stork to bring me a child or two.* We didn't talk about marriage the rest of the day.

That night, Melchor knocked on my door, asked if he could talk to me. He said, "I won't do anything." I knew that Mr. Casey was in the house and Melchor wouldn't try anything. I told him that I'd rather go to his room. I took him a box of chocolates, but since I'm allergic to caffeine, I didn't have any. He asked if I would have an intimate moment with him. I said, "Melchor, I can't do that with you because I have lost my confidence in you. Show me that I can confide in you, then I will, but until then, I can't."

He was furious. "You, Rosi, are ungrateful. I watched over you and took care of you all the time you were sick. I even lost my job to care for you, and this is how you show your gratitude. Recall also that I lost my family in Kansas when I took you in. Just remember all that I have done for you, but all you think is that I can't be with you. Why?"

I sat, quietly not muttering a word. I thought back on all that he had done for me. He was right, maybe I wasn't being fair with him. I was going to allow him to be with me, but I got a horrible headache. The pain was so bad that there was no way that I could have sex with him. "Melchor, understand that I appreciate everything that you have done for me. When I was a little girl, my grandma Sinforosa taught me that when someone voluntarily does something for another, you should never reproach that person. I didn't ask you to take care of me. You did that voluntarily, didn't you? Now, Melchor, tell me how much I owe you. I will pay you for all the time you took care of me.

"Melchor, if I consent to be with you to satisfy your desire or to show my gratitude, without being lawfully married, I will be committing an error in judgment." His facial expression showed a disappointed person. "Rosi, you are very clear, you don't care for me. You believe that I'm a good-for-nothing bastard. I've been an idiot for all I have done for you. Rosi," he said, pointing to the door, "leave my room."

"Melchor," I said, "you are the one that hurt me. What do you want from me?"

"Rosi, I want justification for what I have done for you. Give me a son that will be justification enough. I don't care if we are married or not, give me a son."

"Melchor, how can that be?" The word *son* stuck in my brain. I suddenly thought that I could be a mother. I stared at him; the words rang out of my mouth, "You want a son? I will give you a son. Give me time to ask my doctors if I'm strong to have a baby. If they give the okay, I will give you a son."

Desire to Be a Mother Puts
My Life at Risk

I LEFT THINKING THAT I could actually be a mother. I spoke, through prayers to my Virgin Mother, asking her if it was possible for me to have a baby. My emotions were starting to give me the energy and desire to become a mother, to have a baby of my own. Could it be? Can I experience another miracle? "Blessed Virgin, my request to be a mother is in your hands, please heed my desire."

The following morning, my foster father asked me if I had been with Melchor. He lectured me, stating that I was too weak to be with him. Furthermore, that if I got pregnant, we would have to leave his house. I understood, he knew that I was too weak to bear any children and was looking out for my best interests. Now I was in a situation where Grandpa Casey didn't want a child running around his house and Melchor wanting a child. What I wanted was not to be between a rock and a hard place, that's the way I felt.

My escape from them was necessary. The daily visits to the physical therapist kept me away from them. I joined the church choir and became a volunteer at the senior community center of Orange County. Another temporary setback occurred with the school. I went to obtain a copy of my high school diploma. However, during the time that I was sick, the school had changed computers, and my records were lost in the process. As a result, I couldn't prove that I had attended school. All the work and the time I spent to earn my diploma was lost. Was I upset? Yes, I had worked very hard to get that diploma. I talked to supervisor after supervisor, and neither could help me. I was not going to give this up, but I had another problem I had to solve.

I was indebted to Melchor for all he'd done for me. However, being indebted to him was no reason to get pregnant. I was willing to be a mother; my child would be of great company for me. My Chuchin would understand. I would baptize the child in the Catholic Church.

I went to church, where I feel at peace more than any other place, with Mr. Casey. I knelt down and prayed, "Diosito, don't forsake me, please help me with Melchor so that he can believe in You. Yes, Diosito, the man that attended to me, the one that helped me during my recovery does not believe in You. Diosito, do it please for the grand faith I have in You." I looked to Diosito on the cross. "Diosito," I prayed, "I don't like to ask for anything free because I don't like to be indebted to anyone." At that moment looking at the cross, I felt a sensation going through my body.

I met with Dr. Kim. I wanted to know if I was strong enough to have a child. He set me up with a gynecologist. The doctor was a specialist with first-time mothers. Before I met with the specialist, I made a list of all the medicines that I was taking. I presented them to the gynecologist. I also made a list of all the questions I wanted to ask the doctor. I had a conversation with Melchor to make sure that he was prepared to be a father. I also consulted with the bishop. He was not happy with the arrangement because we were not married through the Catholic Church. Melchor refused to marry, especially in the Catholic Church. But at this time in my life, I was determined to become a mother.

He felt comfortable enough to go see a consultant. We agreed to accept the child regardless the condition of the birth. I had taken medicine all my life, and this might affect the life of a newborn child.

The desire to become a mother was continuously on my mind. The volunteer work I was doing with the senior citizens helped relieve the pressure I felt. This is where I met a white dove, an older Italian lady. Mrs. Paloma loved to hear me sing, especially Mexican rancheras. One of the days she asked me if I knew the song titled "Virgen del Carmen." I'd heard the song, but I didn't know the lyrics.

She pulled out the song from one of her folders. "I want you to sing it with me," she said. We sang.

Virgen Del Carmen

> With love, white dove,
> I come to salute you
> I salute your beauty
> In your celestial reign
> The mother of the creator
> You captivate my heart
> With love I give you thanks
> White dove, with love

I couldn't hold back my tears. When we finished singing, Mrs. Paloma asked me, "My child, why do you cry? Don't look so sad. Is everything okay with you?"

"Señora Paloma, you are like a white dove to me. I want to be a mother so bad, and this song reminds me of my desire."

"Rosita, don't tell me that a young and beautiful girl like you isn't a mother."

"No, señora, I want to be a mother, but I can't."

"Rosita, what's on your mind? Talk to me."

"Señora, can I talk to you woman to woman?" She looked at me with a concerned look that I always remember. "Yes, Rosita, you can confide in me, tell me what is bothering you."

"Señora, I'm not married, but I live with my friend, and someday we will be married. But now we have tried to have a baby, and nothing seems to work. I can't get pregnant, maybe I can't."

"Rosita, tell me how do you feel during intimacy?" I tried to tell her, but I couldn't divulge everything. "Come close," she said. She held my hands. "Soon we will be in the full moon cycle. How do you feel about a full moon?" she asked. "Señora, I love the full moon. Many times since I was a little girl, I would talk to the moon, and I still do."

"Good," she said, "next time when we have a full moon, you have to do your part. You have to relax during intimacy. Imagine that you are someplace where you have experienced the best time of your life. The moon will give you energy, forget the past and don't think of anything negative." She continued to tell me what to do afterward. She said, "Follow these instructions, and you will get pregnant."

"The moon—the same one that I've talked to, sang to, and cried—to will do that for me?" No reason not to believe my friend; after all, she was a mother herself. I waited for the full moon, my companion during many long and lonely nights. Melchor was aware of the full moon; the waiting was over. I prayed to Chuchin to give me strength and explained why I was willing to be intimate without being married.

October 2007, I went to see a gynecologist. After an examination, she told me that I wasn't pregnant. However, she told me what to do that night. She asked me to have intimacy that night. To return in the morning. She didn't want me to use the bathroom, walk fast, and gave me other instructions. I followed her advice. I returned the next morning as instructed. A few weeks later, I returned for an examination. I was pregnant! Miracle? Who knows other than my Diosito? As a precautionary measure, she kept me in the hospital for three days. My foster father learned that I was pregnant. He didn't miss a day without visiting me. Melchor, was he happy? I believe he was ecstatic.

Grandpa Casey also appeared to be happy. He took me home from the hospital. When we arrived at his house, he wanted to know what had gotten into me. Why had I decided to get pregnant, especially with my medical history? He seemed rather upset. He felt that I was endangering my life. I explained to him that I wanted to be a mother. I wanted to feel like a woman. Since I couldn't be a nun, and that I had other limitations, at least I could become a mother, regardless of the danger to my life. I relaxed, I didn't want to spoil the moment. I said, "Grandpa, now you will be a grandpa for real." He was concerned for my health; every day he'd ask me how I felt. I believe that he was accepting the pregnancy.

Mrs. Paloma, my aged white dove, continued to be under my care. She was happy for me knowing that I was going to be a mother. The bad news was that she was being moved to an assistance living place. Both of us prayed that she wouldn't fly away before I had my baby.

Being pregnant was new to me, I experienced symptoms unlike any before. I was constantly at the doctor's office checking on my unborn baby. An ultrasound revealed that my baby had complications. The news was something that I was not prepared for. *Why me?* I thought. Haven't I faced enough problems in this life? I tried to be strong, and I would accept the baby no matter what. The medication that I'd taken for my epilepsy was impacting the health of my unborn baby. The doctors consulted with Melchor and myself. An option was to abort the baby and later try again. I refused; under no circumstances would I commit to an abortion. My faith in Diosito would have been a lie, I would not only be betraying Him but myself.

My foster father was worried with the health of my baby. He wanted me to have the baby at his house and not at the hospital. I wanted to have the baby no matter what, I was going to live for my baby. I wanted to share the news with my sister Ana. I placed a call to her home in Mexico. A lady from the past answered, I recognized the voice. It was Reyna! Without thinking, I asked, "Reyna—ah, Mother, is that you?" She answered, "Yes, this is Reyna. Which of my daughters are you?" I was in shock; hearing her voice was so unexpected. I accidently dropped the telephone. I couldn't believe that I was talking with her after all these years.

I stumbled into the kitchen with tears running down my cheeks. Grandpa saw me. "What's with the tears?" he asked. I told him that Reyna had answered Ana's telephone and that I was shocked to hear her voice and hung up on her. Grandpa told me to call her back. He said, "Regardless of the past problems you've had with her, she's still your mother." He gave me a hug to relax me. "Go on, call her back," he said. "If you feel like forgiving her for what she has done, do so. Tell her that you are pregnant. Come, Rosi, talk to her."

I called back, she answered. I held my head high and told her that I was Jovani. I must've shocked her because it took her a while to answer. She said, "Don't tell me, are you still alive?" That voice, her attitude, and the words that came out of her mouth gave me the urge to scream. I wanted to fling the telephone against the wall. But I held back, I thought of so many times that she had wronged me. The bad memories I experienced with her and that lecherous old man came to mind. She kept talking; most of her words kept bouncing, not penetrating my mind. The ones that made it through were, "Jovani, if you are in the United States, blah, help me."

"Mother, I can't help you. I called to speak with Ana." She didn't pay attention, just kept talking asking for help. She reminded me that she was still my mother and that she always cared for me. She also mentioned that because of her, I was alive and living in el Norte. I stood listening, unable to say anything like when I was a little girl.

I thought, *How can she tell those lies, does she really believe that she was a good mother?* She wanted to know where I lived and if I knew anything about her other daughters. She kept talking, until I got the nerve to stop her. I said, "Mother, let me talk. I called Ana to tell her that I am pregnant, not to speak with you."

"What? Jovani, how is it possible, especially in your condition? I don't believe you," she said. "Reyna, you can believe it or not, I don't care. But I'm telling you that I will become a mother, and you will be a grandma."

"Jovani, so now you are going to have a baby? That being true, you always did some crazy things.

"Listen to me, Jovani, why did you give the will and testament to your uncle Matilde that Sinforosa, your grandmother, gave to you? Your uncles refuse to give me my part because they hate me, yet they adore you." I didn't want to be on the phone with her anymore. I can't answer why I didn't hang up on her. "Jovani, say something, answer me. Have you forgotten that I'm your mother and how much I cared for you?"

"Señora, I have never denied that you're my mother. What you claim to be true are nothing but lies. You never took care of me. Reyna, you have denied me many times. I know that you tell people that I am dead, yet here I am talking with you and very much alive and pregnant.

"If you cared for me so much, why didn't you ever visit me when I was in the orphanage? Señora, I don't mean to reproach you, but I will never forget the horrible things you did to me. I have nightmares thinking what you and that lecherous Figueroa did to me. Another thing I will never forget is that you sold my sisters Beni and Blanquita. I could have taken care of them."

"Jovani, please don't talk like that, remember that I'm your mother. Jovani, help me, I need your help. Send me money, and I will go help you with your baby. Tell your gringo doctors to help me also." I felt like boulders were choking my throat. I couldn't believe what she was asking of me. "Jovani, before I go up North to help you, tell your uncles to give me the will and testament your mamacita left you."

"Mother, I will write a letter to Uncle Matilde. In the note, I will ask him to respect the wishes of my mamacita Sinforosa and divide the property according to her will. The property that is mine, I plan to give half to the orphanage and the other half my pueblo. I will instruct the pueblo to build a home for the aged people of my pueblo." Reyna started to speak very loud and animated. I hung up on her without speaking with Ana. After I hung up on her, Mr. Casey tried to speak to me, but I wasn't in the mood. He looked at me and probably realized that I wasn't in the mood to talk.

My pregnancy was not void of complications. I went to the emergency room eleven times during my twenty-eight weeks of pregnancy. One particular night, I felt very uncomfortable; the clock read 12:34 a.m. Melchor was sleeping in his room, I yelled out to him. He took me to the hospital's emergency room. The studies conducted indicated that my child was deformed. I asked the doctor, "How can that be?" I didn't believe him. "Miss, listen to me, your child's mouth, her hand, and her head are deformed. At this time, it's also possible that her heart is weak." The doctor told me that he could abort the baby, but I had to approve the abortion.

I touched my stomach. "I will not abort you, my baby, I will not abort you." I talked to her all the time. I told her, "My Diosito is with me, my baby." I talked to the Blessed Virgin Mary, asking her to save my baby. Before they released me, the doctor told me that my baby was okay. I stopped taking my medicine at the risk of losing my life. My baby's life was more important.

My complications weren't limited to my pregnancy, no, I had to deal with Mr. Casey's religious belief, and Melchor never took my side. The problem with Mr. Casey was that he didn't trust the doctors or the hospitals and refused to take me when I felt sick.

My neighbor Joanna would call the paramedics for me, or if necessary, she'd call 9-1-1. Other neighbors were aware of my dilemma and became close friends, always willing to help me. Neighbors Michael and his wife would check on me on a regular basis.

My friends and neighbors held baby showers for me. Mr. Casey was very agreeable to hold them at his house. Other neighbors offered the use of their homes.

My pregnancy was nearing its time. I started to feel small pains that turn into heavier and more intense pains. I told Melchor to take me to the hospital. He wanted to know what I felt. I told him about the pains and that I had noticed traces of blood. At that instant, I felt a very sharp pain that doubled me over.

We left for the hospital. Melchor was very calm and told me to relax. At the hospital, the receiving nurse questioned why I had made the trip to the hospital. "You are not due yet." She seemed somewhat perturbed. I could not answer I was doubling over with pain. She told me to get up from the wheelchair and walk around the corridor three times. I did as instructed. Afterward she took my pulse and blood pressure.

The Birth of My Daughter

THE NURSE LOOKED AT THE results. She stared at me. "Señorita, you are not ready to give birth, go home."

"Señora, I feel bad, I'm in pain. Listen to me, call the doctor." She ignored me. "Go home and rest." Since she wouldn't accept me, we went home. I got out of the car, took three steps, when I felt a warm stream of liquid down my legs. We turned around and rushed to the hospital. The same nurse met us at the front desk. She was irritated. "Señorita, don't you understand that you are not ready to give birth?"

"Listen," I said, "call your supervisor now, or I will hold you responsible if something happens to my baby." Another nurse was close by; she attended to me. I was rushed to a room.

The supervisor came into my room and apologized for the treatment in which I was received by that nurse. I was in labor for eighteen hours. The doctors didn't want to wait anymore. They were considering birth by caesarean method. The machine started to beep. I felt sharp pains near my heart and in my back. The pain in my heart was, according to the doctors, placing my baby in peril. They must perform a caesarean. My prayers to my Chuchin were answered. I had a natural birth.

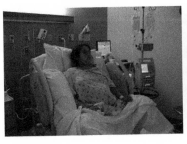
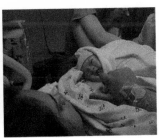

Never had I experienced a moment of happiness like the one when I held my baby in my arms. I kept thanking my Diosito for this miracle.

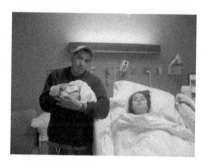

Melchor, with tears rolling down his cheeks, thanked me for giving him such a beautiful child. The doctor allowed us to hold the baby for a short while. He met with Melchor and me in the room. He wanted to inform us that the baby had been born with complications, and he had to perform some studies on her. Melchor accompanied the doctor to another room where they would conduct tests on the baby. I was left alone to pray. I started to pray the rosary and to the Blessed Virgin and fell asleep.

I woke up not knowing how long I had slept, Melchor was at my side. I asked for the baby. He told me that the doctors were still performing tests on her. He shared with me the complications our baby had. *Regardless,* I thought, *I am a mother, and Melchor is a father.* A nurse walked into my room. She gave me additional information on my baby. She felt sure that the complications would be controllable with time.

Babies have a power over people, I guess because they are little, helpless, and pretty. Grandpa came to visit us. He looked like a changed man when he saw the little baby. He asked if he could hold her. He was so happy, I couldn't believe the change in him. Melchor also went through a temporary change of heart. When we were released from the hospital, he went to the church with me. To me it didn't matter that he didn't have the faith I have in God, but he entered the church with us.

Being a mother changed my life. Mainly I would no longer be alone. My whole body had weakened, I couldn't rest on my feet. But I had my baby at my side. Mrs. Marina, a sweet lady, would cook various soups for me. She would remind Melchor to stop on his way home for the soup's ingredients she planned to cook for me. The chicken soups and the beef soups are my all-time favorites. The soups she sent with Melchor, but the advice was always delivered in person. The one she would repeat was that Melchor and I should get married. She used to say, "Look at the beautiful child you two have. And you, Rosi, you are such a pretty girl. You two should really get married. Melchor appears to be a good worker, and I have never seen him take a drink of alcohol."

Another lady friend who cooked food for me and helped me in many other ways was Carmen. Her specialty was the preparing of juices. The ones I enjoyed were the carrot and the fruit juices. She was good company as well. She drove me and the baby to many of the recommended visits to see Dr. Coba Brown.

In spite of the changes I've seen in my foster father and Melchor and in myself since I gave birth, some don't change. My daughter turned one month of age; it was time to have her vaccinated. I asked Melchor to take me to the doctor. He couldn't because he had a lot of work. "Besides," he said, "you are the one that knows about these things, I don't." Of course I didn't want to ask Mr. Casey because I knew how he felt about shots and vaccinations. I readied my daughter and myself and walked to the nearest bus stop. To my surprise, my grandpa drove up at the same time as the bus arrived. He told me to get in the car, that I shouldn't be walking alone with the baby. The bus driver asked me if I knew him. I told him everything was okay, that the man was my grandpa.

I told Grandpa to take us to the hospital. Naturally he wanted to know the reason that I was going there. When I told him that my baby needed to be vaccinated, he blew up. He was so angry that he refused to take us to the hospital. I threatened to call 9-1-1 if he didn't drop us off immediately. He drove us to the nearest bus stop where my baby and I got off.

I had registered and was waiting for the nurse to call me when I saw my foster father walking into the waiting room. I didn't make a scene, I did warmly greet him. When my name was called, he walked in with us. Inside the room, Mr. Casey spoke rudely to the nurse, saying, "This baby doesn't need to be vaccinated, do you hear me?" A surprised nurse looked at him, then at me. She said, "Pardon me, Rosi I'll be right back." When we were alone, I told Grandpa not to cause problems. I wanted my baby to be vaccinated, and it was my decision, not his. The nurse returned with a doctor. The doctor asked Grandpa to leave the room. I respect my grandpa's beliefs. I know that he doesn't trust medicines or drugs of any type.

The doctor asked me questions about Mr. Casey. I answered that he was my foster father. I told the doctor that he didn't believe in vaccinations and other medicines. He then asked me about the baby's father. The doctor was concerned with the relationship I had with Melchor because he never showed up for any of the appointments. The reason she was asking was that it was her responsibility to protect the baby. She told me that I wasn't alone, that what Grandpa was wrong in his belief. The pediatrician left the room and told Grandpa to go home, that she was not going to allow me to go with him. He was not too happy; when he started to complain, the doctor threatened to call the police. The doctor asked me to call Melchor. He started to refuse because he had a lot of work and couldn't leave. The doctor took the telephone and let him know that it was his responsibility as a parent to come for us.

He couldn't say no to the doctor. When he arrived at the hospital to pick us up, the doctor had a few words with him. Again the doctor lectured him on his responsibility as a parent. Melchor was getting advice and lectures not only from the doctor but also from the social worker assigned to look after the baby. She also told him to be a more responsible parent. It was easier for me than for him. I had taken care of my two little sisters, so I had some experience, but he never had that type of experience.

My Baby Was Declared Dead

SIX MONTHS, MY BABY WAS feeling very sick. The diagnosis was a bad case of anemia, and her head was bigger than normal, and the weakness she felt in her knees was also abnormal. She had other problems, especially with her gallbladder. The worst day as a mother happened on the eighteenth day in November 2008. I had finished feeding her when she started to tremble, and her body was turning purplish. She became stiff. I thought that she had died. I ran to the neighbors and called 9-1-1.

The first policeman to arrive took my baby's pulse; he turned to me and told me that she was dead. I was devastated. I grabbed my baby and held her in my arms. I shouted, "My baby is not dead! Diosito, help me, please don't take my baby." The paramedics grabbed the baby from my arms, another held my arm. "Señorita, relax, your daughter is not dead, she is breathing." They put us in the ambulance and drove us to the hospital.

After the doctors had examined my baby, they told me that she'd had a very bad convulsion. The baby would have to remain in the hospital for several days to conduct more tests to determine why she had experienced a convulsion. Apparently the stress was too much for me, I had a convulsion, and I too was kept in the hospital. During the three days that my daughter and I were in the hospital, Melchor visited us daily. He asked me not to die, that he needed me to care for our daughter. My baby was released after three days. I was kept another two days. The social worker assigned to see after my baby assured me that she would be taken care while I was in the hospital. The days I spent in the hospital, I was told by the doctors

604

that I had temporary facial paralysis. My foster father, Señor Casey, visited me frequently.

My baby continued to experience problems with her health. She was eleven months old when the doctor told me that my baby had liquid in her brain. The cause of her head being bigger than normal was because of the liquid. The liquid was of some concern, at present; however, in time, she would have to be operated on. My poor baby, she doesn't know anything about being in the hospital like I do. But at this young age, I was really concerned for her. Again I reached out to my most holy mother, Virgin Mary, and asked for her blessing.

The doctor suggested that I get a second opinion. I was given the name of another doctor. The problem was that her practice was in Garden Grove, which was some distance from my house. However, since my daughter was my priority, I took the bus—or rather several buses—to her office. After the doctor finished conducting tests on my baby, we left the office. It was raining hard. I couldn't walk to the bus stop under those conditions with the baby. I dialed Melchor. He was too tired and busy to pick us up. He told me to take the bus back and hung up.

The nearest bus stop was in front of a Korean market. We waited inside until my first bus arrived. I don't recall how many buses I had to take to get home. However, I still had to walk several blocks to the house. Was I angry? I don't believe that there was a word in my vocabulary to describe how I felt, but it was beyond angry. Señor Casey was very upset that I had been allowed to take the buses in the type of weather. He asked me why I hadn't asked him to take me to the appointment. I simply wanted to avoid any confrontation between those two.

Melchor was in the room, nice and cozy and dry. I gave him the baby. "Here," I said, "take care of your child." I walked into the bathroom and took a good shower. When I came out, Melchor and the baby were asleep and Grandpa was gone. I felt so good being alone and not having to put up with anyone. I gathered my diary, the rosary, and my knitting material, took them with me to my little corner where I felt comfortable, inside the garage. There in my little corner, I wrote my daily notes, knitted some baby clothes, and talked to my Chuchin and prayed the rosary.

I finally got tired and went to bed; it was 2:00 a.m. The following day, I got up early, fed the baby, dressed her and myself, and accompanied Mr. Casey to Mass at the Holy Family Church. I talked with the bishop and shared with him the medical problems my baby was facing. He insisted that I baptize the baby before any operation. He instructed me to take her the following day to the Purisma Catholic Church, and he would perform the baptism. He didn't want to wait any longer. I knew that I had to have her baptized in the Catholic Church. I had waited too long; my baby should have been baptized by now. I didn't want to have a confrontation with Melchor was the reason she hadn't received her first sacrament.

Immediately I thought that Mr. Casey would be the perfect godfather, and a good friend, Salian Moa, the godmother. Melchor had others in mind—his boss, Fernando Martinez, and his wife, Berta. He would consent to have the baby baptized in the Catholic faith only if I agreed to his choice of godparents. Mr. Casey wasn't upset with the choice of godparents; he was happy that the baby was being baptized.

I asked Mr. Casey for forgiveness. But he understood the situation. I didn't know the godparents, but I had no choice but to accept them. The important thing was to have my baby baptized by respectable people. I truly believe that a parent is responsible of raising a child, and that responsibility is followed by the godparents. Fernando Martinez and his wife, Berta, agreed to be the godparents. I wasn't too happy, but in order to avoid a confrontation, I reluctantly agreed with Melchor.

My child was baptized in the Purisma Catholic Church. I told the bishop that my child was to be named *Kimberly*. In this issue, I was the sole person to decide the name, and nobody was going to change my mind. *Kimberly* it was.

The godparent Berta offered to hold the celebration in her house. It was a nice gesture on their part. Kim being baptized was the important thing; anything else was secondary and really not too important.

Grandpa was happy; he enjoyed holding Kim and feeding her. He called her his little sweetheart. He didn't like the idea of Kim and I taking the bus, so he took us shopping and to my appointments. By the very fact that my foster father was taking us everywhere, I stopped taking the bus. Sometimes the escape to my little corner wasn't enough to relieve me of the feeling that I was trapped. I needed to be active to be productive, to experience being a mother away from my current environment; the four corners and the walls were suffocating me. For this reason I became a volunteer at the Friendly Center. I also offered my services to Saint Vincent de Paul. For all the work I did, I was awarded certificates, which meant a lot to me.

I received the call from the doctor; he had the test results from the ones taken of Kim's head. He wanted us to come to the office the next day. My daughter was going to be a year old, and I was planning a birthday party for her. The call came at a very inopportune time. Another sleepless night, another trip to the doctor. I didn't say anything to Melchor or to Señor Casey. I got up real early, fed and dressed both of us.

I took the bus to my church before my appointment. I took flowers to my Chuchin. I prayed to God, saying, "My daughter's life is in your hands, please, dear God, give her Your blessings." In the meantime, Kim crawled toward the Lady of Guadalupe statue.

I picked Kim up. "Come, don't get close to the Lady of Guadalupe. I've prayed and prayed to her, and she ignores me."

I looked at the statue of the Lady of Guadalupe, and I honestly saw a tear in her right eye. I became stiff; surprised, I said, "If I hurt your feelings, grant me a miracle. Heal her damaged head, and I promise on this twelfth day of December, I will dress her like an indigenous child, and I will bring her and stand her at your side."

We left for my appointment. The doctor didn't attend to us right away; we waited some minutes. I took my rosary from my bag and began to pray. When she called us into her office, she said, "Señora, I am waiting to receive the latest test results from the hospital in Magnolia Street. That's why I want to speak with you in person." She looked at Kim then at me.

"If your daughter has liquid in her head, an operation is necessary, and we are prepared to operate on her today. Another problem is that your daughter is anemic. Anemia is not a problem. I will prescribe medication to cure it."

She asked me to sign a bunch of papers while we waited for the results. I was left alone with Kim. Soon after, the assistant summoned me to Doctor Brown's office. She was reading the results; her face said a lot, she looked happy. She asked me to sit. Kim was sound asleep in her little basket. The doctor said, "Señora, I can't believe the results." I waited patiently to hear the news; she seemed to take forever.

Virgin De Guadalupe's Miracle

HER FACE WAS GLOWING WHEN she said, "Señora, your daughter doesn't have any liquid in her head. I have not seen this before, but it's true. When I got the results, I had to call the hospital that conducted the tests, and they assured me that the results are true. Another thing is that the legs are much better." She asked me to look at the tests results; the doctor spread the papers on top of her desks and showed me the results. The doctor couldn't medically explain how Kim's health had changed. I smiled thinking of the Lady of Guadalupe and my Diosito.

The doctor gave me a hug; that hug released a bunch of tears that washed away so many fears I had. My faith in the Lady of Guadalupe grew, I was no longer angry with her. We left her office, but when we tried to leave the hospital, we couldn't; it was raining really hard. I waited until the rain subsided to take the bus. The first bus would take us part of the way home; the second would take us close to home. The bus dropped us close to the Main Place mall. My daughter needed a diaper change, so I took her to the bathroom in the mall.

Kim felt a lot better with a clean diaper. We were passing a few candy machines. Kim pointed to one of them. *Oh well,* I thought, *why not?* I put a quarter in the candy machine. To my surprise, what came out of the machine was not a candy but a large transparent ring with the image of the LADY OF GUADALUPE!

Kim wanted a piece of candy, so I dropped another coin in the machine. This time I got a candy. Interesting! The more I saw the ring, the more I began to believe how strange that I got the ring out of that machine. Could this be a message? Did the Lady of Guadalupe do this? Not possible, I thought, not possible especially since I talked to the Lady the way I did. I checked the time; my watch read 2:33 p.m. "Kim, let's go to the church." My head was spinning. I had to clear something in my mind, and the church would provide the answer.

The bishop saw me walking into the church. He came over, his voice and his presence put me at ease. He read my face and knew that I needed to talk to him. "My child, tell me, what's on your mind?" I told the bishop the way I had disrespected the Lady of Guadalupe. Then I said, "A ring with her image imprinted on it comes out of a candy machine. How is that possible?" I showed him the ring. He smiled. "Señorita, she loves you dearly, and I believe that she is apologizing to you."

"Tell me, to whom does she send such messages?"

"That message was sent to you because of the strong faith that you have in God and the Virgin." He took the ring and blessed it.

"Rosi, what happened today is a testimony of the Catholic faith." Those words coming from the bishop rang true. My heart was pounding, my chest held it back. I walked to the statue of the Lady de Guadalupe. My approach was so different from the previous one. This time I prayed to her, this time I was more relaxed and sorry for the way I acted before. I knew that she was hurt with my words and my behavior. I walked away and went to where the bishop was praying. We talked for a while before I left.

The cell phone rang as I was leaving the church. The doctor's office was calling. The doctor wanted me to sign more papers. Another trip to the doctor, another bus or two, but it had to be done. I was reading and signing the papers when Dr. Brown walked into the room. She asked me if I had time to speak with her. I followed her to her office. "Rosi, I didn't read all of the report when you were here. Since you left, I read them, and I noticed that your daughter's head is normal, there is nothing wrong with her. What did you do?" She took Kim's hat off. She saw a normal head. The nurse assisted the doctor in measuring Kim's head. "It's normal," she said, "but I can't believe it. I can't believe that one day her head is not normal, and now it is." I half smiled when she asked if I had done anything different.

"Doctor, I believe in miracles, and this is a miracle. The Lady of has granted me a miracle."

"Rosi, you are very religious, I can see that, but I am a doctor, and I need to study her one more time to learn how this happened." Before we left, she made an appointment for Kim and me to come back.

I pushed the baby-loaded carriage with my baby, diapers, and some snacks to the nearest bus stop. The waiting bench was partially occupied by an elderly lady. I sat next to her; she looked at me with a half smile and very sad eyes. I took the snacks from my bag and shared them with the lady. "Señora, are you okay? Forgive me for asking, but you look so disconsolate, so unhappy, do you feel like talking?" Speaking in Spanish, she told me that she was coming from the hospital. She looked down at the pavement, stayed mum for a few seconds. "I have cancer," she said. I barely heard her answer. "The doctor told me that I have cancer, and yes, I'm unhappy. The doctor talked to my sons, but none of them seem to care. All of them have ignored me, I'm alone." I tried my best to console her.

The elderly lady told me that she had seen me before. She asked, "Are you the young girl that used to sell tamales and other food near the Highland apartments? It's been a while, but I remember because you used to have convulsions, and sometimes I would help you."

"Yes, señora, that girl was me. You remember me?"

"I remember you, and now you are trying to help me." Isn't that something my mamacita used to say? We all reap now or later what we sow. I started to eat some of the snacks while we talked. We'd run into each other pretty often after that day.

One day she was waiting for me near the bus stop. She wanted to talk, but not in the street. We went to a nearby Mexican restaurant. Her cancer had advanced and didn't know how much time she had. We cried for a while. She looked at me, took hold of my hand. "Rosa, I have a house in Riverside. I want you to have it." She was serious. "Señora, why? I don't think that I can accept such a large gift." She insisted, saying that I was a wonderful person and that I was the only friend that she had. I suggested that she give the house to her sons. She shook her head. "Rosa, you don't have any idea how badly they treat me." Before she left the restaurant, she said, "I love the manner you live your life." That was the last time I saw her.

Another day, I was leaving the Friendly Center, where I did volunteer work. I noticed an elderly lady lying on the side of the street. The African American lady was unconscious. I immediately dialed 9-1-1. I stayed with her on Lemon Lane until the paramedics arrived. A few days later, I got a call from the same lady. We had a conversation on the phone. She asked for my address and directions to Mr. Casey's house. She went to the house to personally thank me. I was the only one who had helped her and was glad that I did. She was a widow, just recently losing her husband of many years. They didn't have any children. She had thought of leaving everything to her dog. However, after she met me, she wanted to get my information because she was going to name me in her will and leave everything to me.

Again I rejected the material rewards for helping a person in need. Under no circumstances could I accept such a reward for such a small favor. She offered me a gold chain with a medal of the Blessed Virgin Mary. That gift I did accept, not because I felt worthy but because she was genuinely offering it. She gave me other gifts for Kim. After that, Grandpa would take Kim and myself to visit her at her apartment. That lady knew how to prepare some delicious meals. The chicken she fixed was great, and the fish dishes were the best that I have ever tasted. The last time I went to visit, she was gone; her house was up for sale.

My confidence in the Lady de Guadalupe was improving. My baby was healthier because she had listened to my prayers, I truly believe that. But more tests had to be performed on her. I took the bus to one of her appointments; one glaring difference was that I was not alone, I had Kim. From the doctor's office, I decided to go to church. The daily Mass was conducted by Bishop Tod Brown. After the Mass was over, I spoke to him briefly. He gave us his blessing before Kim and I left. Actually we tried to leave; it was pouring, and we could not go back into the church. We stood outside the church sheltered from the rain. But luck sometimes is on my side; this time it was a neighbor. Johana was driving by when she noticed us. She veered away from the traffic, came back for us, and offered us a ride home. Johana was always a good neighbor. When I needed help, she was always ready to help me. In time she moved away, but she is always in my prayers.

Grandpa Casey was annoyed that I had left early in the morning without telling him where I was going to. But he doesn't appreciate it when I take Kim to see the doctor, so why tell him? He kept asking me where I'd gone to. I finally told him that Kim had an appointment. I could tell that he was upset. He left the house, and I saw him drive away.

Kim indicated that she was hungry. I started to prepare a meal for us. I looked at my daughter and thought, *Is it possible that we are in October 2010? Soon Christmas will be here.* Don't know why, but I felt dizzy and grabbed the back of a chair. I blacked out. When I came to, I was on the floor, couldn't move, and worse, I couldn't talk. Thanks to Grandpa, he found me on the floor and tried to move me. When I didn't respond, he called 9-1-1. All I remember is waking up in the hospital. The doctor informed me that I had suffered a stroke along with a convulsion. He advised me that I was in danger of being paralyzed and should be careful.

Quiet Wedding

I WAS KEPT IN THE hospital three days. During the first day, I couldn't feel anything; my whole body was numb. But my mind was alert, my praying gave me wings of courage. Legally Grandpa couldn't take care of me, and since I wasn't married, Melchor couldn't take care of me; I was alone. The social worker told me that if I was sent to a rehab place, the State would take Kim and care for her. However, if I was married to Melchor, the state would place Kim under his care. I wasn't going to let that happen. I couldn't and I wouldn't. I thought, people get married for various reasons other than love. My need to marry was for the love of my daughter, which would bring me happiness. I realized that my health was weak, and I needed someone to care for Kim. Who better than her father? Now more than ever before, I wanted to be legally married. But would Melchor consent? He has refused to marry in the Catholic Church before.

I was in rehab for many weeks after I was released from the hospital. The persons selected by the social services would come to the house. It was tiring, and I wasn't responding. I felt that I was a prisoner in my own little corner. When I had an appointment with the doctor, they would drive me and take care of Kim.

The gardener by the name of Don Panchito, and his wife, Marina, would visit me often. They knew that I needed to get married and the reason. One of the times that they were visiting, Don Panchito asked me if it was okay to speak with Melchor. I wondered why he was asking me because they talked all the time. He wanted to speak about our situation with regard to Kim and if something happened to me. Don Panchito and Marina waited until Melchor came home from work. Don Panchito waited a while allowing Melchor to relax. The older man whispered something to Melchor, and they got up and left the room. Doña Marina looked at me with a smile.

After some time, they entered the room where Doña Marina and I were talking. He approached me asking, "Rosi, how do you feel?"

"He has been worried about your health," Don Panchito chimed in. It's rare that Melchor asked me about my health or how I felt. Continuing, he asked if he could hug me. Another rarity, why is he asking me now? He hugged me, and I felt tears coming from his eyes, not mine. I was puzzled with his change of heart. He looked at me, not saying anything but my name, *Rosi*, I waited while he contemplated what he was about to say.

"I am proposing marriage, would you marry me?" Now I understood what Don Panchito and Marina were up to. It all made sense. I thought, *This is what I want, isn't it?* Melchor said, "Rosi, I love you. I know that I will never meet another girl like you." I accepted his proposal.

Therapy day seemed to be forever, but I was determined to recover. After my session, Mr. Casey went to JCPenny and took me along. He told me not to worry, that he'd take care of me. I didn't argue, I was happy to get out of the house. He was wheeling me around the store. Near the jewelry, I noticed a person that reminded me of someone I knew. The person was my sister Lucy! "Grandpa, Grandpa, that is my sister." I pointed her out. "What? Your sister is here?"

Grandpa walked over and spoke to my sister. She turned around to see me in the wheelchair. "Oh, you youngster, what happened to you this time?" We hugged and smiled before I told her why I was in the wheelchair. I told her that it was only temporary. Lucy, motioning her head toward Grandpa, asked me in Spanish, "Is this the old Americano that you're married to?"

"What, where did you hear that? Lucy, whoever told you that is a liar." Then I smiled. "Rosita, it was Viki, she told me that you had married an old man." Grandpa saw that I was smiling looking at him. That's when he asked me what was said that made me smile. As best as I could, I told him in English what Lucy had said to me. He smiled and shook his head. "No, Lucy, Rosi and I aren't married. Rosi is my adopted daughter." Grandpa and Lucy talked for a while.

Before Lucy left, she gave me a hug and invited me to her house. I in turn invited Lucy to my upcoming marriage to Melchor.

My rehab continued, but I didn't keep any of the data, I left that up to the male nurse and Grandpa. My life revolved around my daughter. I was anxious to be free of this condition. I prayed to my Chuchin daily, not asking for anything for myself, only that my daughter be taken care of in case I wasn't around. Getting around in the wheelchair was tiring and boring. I was unable to get around by myself. One night I was so exhausted from wheeling myself around the house, I went to bed earlier than usual. I fell asleep like a rock. That night I woke up. Everything was quiet, so peaceful. I was curious as to why everything appeared so different, so I sat up on the bed. At that instant, I clearly saw my Chuchin enter the house through the crystal doors.

He was dressed in white, stood next to my bed. He looked at me. His appearance was a brilliant glow with a loving smile. The instant that He raised His right arm, stars poured from His hand and streaked into my brain. The stars spread throughout, filling my body with energy. He looked upward and said, "Raise yourself and continue on your journey." Instantly looking at my Chuchin, I attempted to stand up. I stood up, and I could move my feet. I tried to embrace my Chuchin, but He disappeared.

I questioned myself hoping that it wasn't a dream. Had I actually seen Him? There was no question in my mind that it was the real thing and not a dream. I walked as fast as my feet would allow me to. Grandpa and the nurse were talking. The nurse looked puzzled when he saw me walking toward them. Finally it occurred to him that I shouldn't be walking; he took hold of me and sat me down. He called the paramedics, and off I go to the hospital. I didn't understand why I was taken to the hospital especially since I was walking again. True my left leg was weaker than my right one, but I was speeding about on both legs.

The doctors were curious, so they decided to perform tests on me. Again I questioned why they had to perform more tests. I told them how it happened, and I mentioned that I felt much better. The doctors didn't believe that God had cured me; they needed to know the medical and earthly reason why I was walking. After the tests were completed, the doctor told me that I was okay. "Clearly," the doctor told me, "your faith is your medicine, not mine."

Melchor and I were married by the judge in a civil ceremony. True to my Catholic religion, I didn't feel comfortable. But be as it was, my daughter was protected in case something happened to either one of us. Six months later, we were married by the Catholic Church. Married life didn't change my lifestyle. Melchor continued doing what he generally did and so did Grandpa Casey. What changed was that now I was the wife of Melchor. The problem was my health. I seemed that one illness followed another. I was always in need of medical attention. My cross to bear was getting heavier.

My husband wanted to have more children. I talked to the doctors, and I was told that I was incapable of bearing any without the risk of dying. I couldn't reason with Melchor, so I tried talking to Grandpa Casey. He didn't want to get involved. That issue was to be resolved between husband and wife and of course the doctors. I was looking for someone that would advise me besides the doctors. I was looking for a way of explaining to Melchor that I couldn't bear any more children. Mr. Casey was the only one I trusted, so I continued to talk to him about my situation.

He probably had had enough of my insistence for a sound word of advice; he said, "You are just like my ex-wife, Ruby. You women are stupid," and left the house. I prayed for a sign, I prayed to my Chuchin, my only companion. The most relaxing times was when Kim and I were left alone in the house.

Sister Mar Dies

For various reasons, I was never to answer the telephone. Mr. Casey had his reasons, so I never did. That is until one day the phone rang. Kim and I were alone, and something overcame me, and I answered. The caller was Sister Juanita calling from the orphanage. Sister Juanita, speaking in Spanish, asked for the little girl that Sister Mar had accepted into the orphanage. I was really happy to hear that voice, a voice from the past. I told Sister Juanita that I was that girl. "Oh, I'm so glad to reach you, Jovani."

I asked her, "Sister Juanita, what is wrong? You seem sad."

"Jovani, Sister Mar is very ill. She is in the hospital. Niña, Sister Mar insists that she needs to speak 'with her niña angel.' That's what she calls you, before she leaves this life. She regrets denying you the vocation of being a nun."

I asked Sister Juanita if I could speak with Madre Mar. Sister Juanita told me that it was not possible because the room didn't have a telephone and she was too weak to walk to the nearest phone. I said, "Sister Juanita, can you please send me a photo of Sister Mar? I believe that you can send the photo electronically, can't you? Also, please tell her that I forgive her and that I pray for her every day. Tell her that I want to thank her for everything that she did for me."

"Yes, my niña angel, I will do it right away." I heard the click of the phone, with tears in my eyes. I cried for Madre Mar and started to say the rosary. I received the photo of Madre Mar.

I showed the photo of Madre Mar to Grandpa Casey. In the past, I had shared with him everything I knew about Sister Mar. He was aware of how much she had helped me, and he knew how I felt about her. Mr. Casey and I thought that we should talk to our religious group about Sister Mar.

Soon after, I got the dreaded call. Sister Juanita called to tell me the bad news. "Jovani, when I told Madre Mar that I had contacted you, she became really happy. She reached for pictures of you from under her pillow. She held your pictures in her hand, crossed her arms over her chest. She looked at me and said, 'Thank you, Sister, for contacting my niña angel and letting me know that she has forgiven me.' She closed her eyes in this life forever."

My heart beat furiously. "No, Madre Juanita, tell me it's not true. She is too young to die." My tears flooded my eyes. "Jovani, I wish I could, none of us believe that she left this life upon hearing from you." Madre Juanita continued speaking, but her words were muted by the sadness I felt. I thanked her for giving me the sad news and hung up. I didn't know what to do except to call my good friend Carmen. She came over to console me. Grandpa Casey arrived at the same time. I was sitting outside when they arrived. I told them that Madre Mar had died. We went inside the house. I talked and talked about Sister Mar. I mentioned all the good she'd done for me. Finally when I had exhausted all that I remembered, Grandpa Casey led us in prayer. We knelt and prayed the rosary.

That weekend I had a garage sale. All the proceeds from the sale went to the orphanage. I made calls to all the families who lived near the orphanage and who I remembered. The families rallied, and they too helped with the cost of the funeral. The knowledge that Sister Mar was gone and all the sadness I felt in all probably contributed to the small electric shocks I felt in my heart. I sat down to rest not knowing why I was experiencing heart palpitations. I felt that my tongue was swollen. Another trip to the hospital. Why was all this happening to me, I couldn't understand why my health didn't improve?

The doctor kept me in the hospital several days. He told me to control my emotions. Apparently my emotions had been aroused with the loss of Sister Mar. He also mentioned that I should quit smoking, not consume liquor, and stay away from coffee. We both laughed because he knew my record and knew that I had none of those habits. "Seriously," he said, "you have to control your emotions and start relaxing more." The doctor made a follow-up appointment for me. Several months I went back as scheduled. The test results showed that my heart was okay. The doctor again emphasized the importance of controlling my emotions.

I'm alone no longer. I have my Kim, but do I have anyone that I can rely on? Grandpa is around and is a lot of help, but he has his faults, especially when it comes to doctors and hospitals. I'm alone in that respect. My belief in Diosito and the Virgin Mother tells me that I'm not alone.

Melchor comes home from work tired most of the time. I usually have dinner ready, and Kim is always ready for her father. He's at the table, and Kim is around him seeking his attention. She says, "Papa, money, Papa, money," and raises her arms wanting to be picked up. He gave Kim a dollar bill and told her to go with me. "Melchor," I said as I was serving him his food, "Kim wants your attention, not money. Hug her, pay some attention to her."

"Rosi, I am tired, I just got home, give me time to rest, okay?"

Kim came to me, showed me the money. Melchor, after eating, went into the room. He started his computer. Kim followed him into the room. She dragged a small blanket with several coins that she had placed on the blanket. I thought, *Poor baby, all she wants is a hug from her father.* Kim went up to him again like before. "Money, Papa, money, Papa." He looked at her, put his computer aside, and reached down and picked his daughter up and hugged her. Kim was so happy. For a long time, he held her and talked to her. When he put her back on her feet, she ran off to see Grandpa Casey.

Grandpa hugged his sweetheart, as he called her. I wanted to be alone, I walked outside to the moonlight accompanied with my shadow. I thought, *Money doesn't buy love. Communication is the foundation of a good relationship at home. My life lacks that. I'm living in a vacuum not being able to share my thoughts with others.* I was preparing a salad when Grandpa came up to see what I was doing. We started a small talk. But I committed an error in telling him that I was taking Kim to the doctor. It just slipped out, I knew how he felt about doctors.

He looked at me with anger in his eyes. He was so angry that I would dare take Kim to the doctor that he kicked me out of his house. Really, he opened the door and asked me to leave. My heart shattered. I stood shell-shocked in the middle of the kitchen. He left me standing there. I felt sick and weak. I felt like vomiting, my body felt a chill followed by coldness. I thought, *What is wrong with me? Be strong, Rosi, come on, relax.* I heard Grandpa's car take off.

I drank a glass of water, but the knot in my stomach wouldn't go away. I was having a hard time breathing. I continued to prepare the salad. With knife in hand, I started to slice the tomato. I felt a stronger chill, and my eyesight left me. I didn't know where I was when I came to. My eyesight was cloudy; all I could see were balls of fire. I was lying facedown on the floor with the knife stuck on my left side. I looked toward the phone, I crawled until I reached the phone and was able to dial 9-1-1 and passed out.

The nurse was the first person I saw when I opened my eyes. I thought, *What happened?* The nurse asked me, "Do you know what happened, do you know where you're at?" I shook my head indicating that I didn't. I knew that I must be in a hospital but didn't know which one. I began to feel much better. The nurse told me that I was the luckiest person that she had ever seen. She asked, "Who are you?" Trying hard to crack a smile, I answered, "Well, none other than Rosi. But what happened to me? I have no idea why I wound up in the hospital."

"Rosi, all I can tell you is that you had a convulsion. *You had a knife in your hand when you fell, and the knife got stuck in your left chest, near your heart.*"

I said, "What? I had the knife stuck in my chest?" At that moment I remembered that I was slicing the tomato when I started feeling bad. "You still had the knife stuck on your chest when the paramedics brought you here. The doctors studied your situation very carefully before they took the knife out. The strange thing, though, was that when the knife was removed, you didn't shed one drop of blood." It took me a moment to realize what the nurse had just told me. I touched my left side, but all I felt was the gauze, but just a slight pain. The nurse asked me if I wanted to see my small incision. Being the curious person that I am, I told her that I did. The small incision was small compared to the ones I received when I was chased by the bull and other accidents I'd experienced. I looked upward and smiled. *My Diosito,* I thought.

The nurse told me that the doctors couldn't believe that I wasn't bleeding. Neither could they believe the x-rays that showed the knife stuck inside my chest close to my heart, and I survived. I remained in the hospital a few days until the investigation was completed. During my stay, the lead investigator and a female partner for Orange County investigated my case. The female investigator asked many questions, some rather personal. I had to ask why the line of questioning. She told me that the investigation was necessary to determine the cause of my injury. She told me that they had determined that my injury was accidental and not suicide or foul play.

I signed the report and asked the investigation officer for a copy. She asked, "Why do you want a copy?"

"Señora police, I keep a diary of my life, this information will be included in a book that I plan on writing about my life." The lead investigator and the policewoman looked at each other then at me. She asked, "Señorita, who are you?"

"Ma'am, I'm a person that is being watched and that is well protected by my Diosito." I smiled with them. She gave me her business card. "Call me when you write your book. I want a copy." Upon my release from the hospital, I was given a copy of the report along with the papers from the hospital. Before my release, the doctor made an appointment with the psychiatrist at the Hospital Mental Center. Grandpa Casey gave me a ride home when I was released. Melchor was too busy working and couldn't take time off to go for me.

My appointment at the Hospital Mental Center was another trip to the hospital. I was not too happy, but I felt obligated to go. The doctor determined something that I already knew, that I had problems with those two men. He told me that my mind was constantly mindful of those two. He did show me to value my life; he told me that I have rights and should defend myself. He emphasized the importance of taking care of me, not only for myself but also for my daughter, Kim.

My days were occupied taking care of Kim. I became a volunteer at the school for infants and preschoolers. I was really involved because I enjoyed being around the children. I was elected to be the president of the board by the other parents. At the end I was presented a certification of appreciation.

The social service organization approved Kim to receive therapy sessions at home. The first day of therapy, the social worker met Grandpa. When the worker arrived to give Kim her therapy session, Mr. Casey went out to meet her. At that moment, Mr. Casey knew that Kim was going to have daily therapy at his house. He was not happy. The social worker explained that Kim was autistic and anemic. She stated that overall her health was below standards and needed therapy. Grandpa didn't allow her to enter the house and told her to leave. He told the worker that Kim didn't need the government interfering in her life. The worker left without helping Kim.

Naturally the social workers were displeased with his attitude. The system was concerned with Kim, and so was Grandpa Casey. I was in the middle, and it was difficult for me. But I had to care for my baby, she was my responsibility. I discussed the problem to Melchor, and we decided to move.

Move to Our Own Place

WE MOVED INTO A ONE-BEDROOM apartment. It was a big change from living in Grandpa's house, but it was home. Melchor showed me how to use Facebook and opened my own page. Using Facebook, I was able to contact some of my friends back in Mexico. I even met Rafa on Facebook. He was living in one of the Carolines in the United States. I made the mistake of telling Melchor that I had contacted Rafa. I mentioned that Rafa had respected me and never attempted to abuse me. His answer was, "What do I care? If he likes you so much, where is he now?" I only smiled. I also contacted Rede Castañeda, another boy that had a crush on me when were young. I also found out that Reyna, my mother, was telling people that she was paying for my studies in Rome. Others she would tell that I was dead.

Melchor and I had difficulty understanding each other. I wanted to make our marriage work. So when I saw a recipe in Facebook that I thought he might like, I tried it. That evening, Kim and I prepared the meal. He entered the apartment, looked around, saw the table all set. He greeted us, got himself ready to eat. He didn't say anything about the meal, ate, and took his computer with him to the couch.

His attitude didn't change for the next couple of days. It was difficult trying to read his mind. I finally decided to confront him. I put our daughter to bed. He was using his computer when I approached. "Melchor, what is bothering you?" He didn't face me; rather, he looked at the floor when he talked. "My fellow workers tell me that I'm an idiot." I said, "What?" I started to talk, but he stopped me. "No, Rosi, let me talk. You do as you please, they are right when they say that I'm stupid for being with you. You are always sick, but you manage to look good all the time. Besides, they ask me why I allow you to be friends with gringos. I won't say any more, but you, Rosi, from now on, you do as I say, or else the rest is up to you."

"I'm surprised at your words, those words are venomous. You allow those guys to say those stupid things to you? How long have you known those guys? Now tell me, how long have you known me? Whatever, if I allow you to treat me so you can please them, what then? Have I forced you to stay with me? Melchor, do you think your coworkers will stand beside you when I take you to divorce court? I don't force you to stay, but say the word, and I will grant you a divorce."

"Rosi, I didn't mean to offend you. I'm sorry for listening to them." He tried to hug me, but I shrugged him off. "Melchor," I said, "people like that are like the plague that ruins the fruit. When the fruit is ripe, the plague attacks and doesn't stop until it has ruined a perfectly good fruit. It releases its venomous worm until the fruit is ruined. You have to learn and choose your friends more carefully. The more you listen to their venomous words, the more they will feed you bad advice."

I excused myself, left the room. I didn't feel like staying in the house. I changed clothes and went for a walk around the neighborhood. Later I wrote in my diary. Writing, I felt as though I was between a spade and a brick wall. Entering my activities in my diary was a salvation of the reality I encountered in my life.

Kim woke up with a cough. I called Melchor when I saw that her vomit had traces of blood. He dropped us at the emergency room. The doctors kept Kim in the hospital all day and into the night, I stayed with her all that time. I called Melchor to come and get us. He was not happy that he had to go for us; after all, he was tired. I didn't want to hear any of his excuses, so I hung up on him. He did go for us. He was still angry for having to go for us. He was driving faster than ever before. I told him to slow down. His reply was that if I wasn't happy with his driving to jump off the truck. *What an ignorant thing to say*, I thought. He slowed down. He said, "I'm doing it for my daughter, not for you."

I carried Kim up the apartment stairs to our place. He opened the door. What a mess! The floor was littered with my books, cassette tapes, my pictures, and the furniture. I stumbled about the room with Kim in my arms and made my way to her bed. After I placed her in her bed, I entered the kitchen. I was close to the refrigerator. I heard Melchor say, "Aren't you going to ask me why I did this? My coworkers have a good reason for telling me that you have always ordered me about. I'm stupid for living with a sickly woman like you."

"Melchor, please leave me be, I need peace. I don't give a darn about the loose fiery tongues you call friends. Right now my only concern is the health of our baby." He raised his voice, "You still like that Rafa fellow, don't you? I read the exchange you two had in Facebook. Why? You are married to me now, so why do you talk to Rafa like that and not to me?" Now I understood why he was so angry.

"Look, Melchor, I never denied that I liked Rafa. I never talked to Rafa about what you are accusing me of, especially in Facebook. You should be happy that he respected me. He never forced me to have sex with him. You know very well that you were the first one. I have not been unfaithful to you."

"Rosi, shut up!" He raised his hand up as if to hit me. I ran to the phone, but he grabbed it before I could dial 9-1-1. Through tears I told him, "Hit me, go ahead and hit me." He stopped his advance and told me to leave. I ran out of the apartment alone because he denied me taking Kim with me. I borrowed a phone from the neighborhood kid and called my friend Carmen. I didn't have to wait long; before I realized it, we were at her home.

I was traumatized trembling with fear. Carmen fixed me a cup of tea, which helped alleviate the cold feeling I had. My other friend Lilia came over. Her advice was for me to go back home. She reasoned that my daughter was my priority. She was sure that Melchor had acted the way he did because he was emotionally hurt. She advised me not to talk about Rafa anymore. "Rosi, what if something happens to Kim and he calls 9-1-1? What do you suppose that Melchor will say when the police ask them about the mother? He can say anything, and they will believe him. Where does that leave you?" She made sense. I finished my tea before I asked Carmen to take me back to my prison.

I entered the place where I was living a life I didn't deserve to live. The first words that exited Melchor's mouth were, "Did you tell the police? Are they coming for me?" I ignored him, I was trembling with fear. I walked into the room where Kim was fast asleep. I closed the door, walked to the window, and opened it. I reasoned that if Melchor walks in trying to hurt me, I will scream so loud that the whole complex will hear me. I prayed the rosary; afterward, I spoke with the moon. "Diosito," I prayed, "you were able to forgive Judas the night of his betrayal, help me find the strength to continue living. I have faith in You and in the Blessed Virgin and the saints that I will find peace and happiness in my life."

I was staring at the moon; suddenly a ray of light flashed before me. A sudden burst of air rushed through the open window. I got chills all over my skin, and my body burned with the heat. *My Chuchin was beside me.* I saw His image clearly, it was Him. I started to pray the Magnificat prayer. He hugged me. He asked, "Niña, why do you want Me to take you?" I answered, "Diosito, nobody loves me, I don't want to suffer any longer. You love me, that's why I want to go with You."

He extended his arms revealing a roll of paper in each hand. He said, "You have somebody in this world that loves you. If you didn't, you would be with Me. In this list are names of those that love you, including the Virgin Mary, My Beloved Mother.

"In this other list are the names of those three that are driving you away from this life." I didn't want to see the list because I knew the persons that He was talking about. Diosito told me that He was leaving, He gave me a hug before He left. I saw a white shadow flying high beyond the darkness. An enormous angel appeared in the sky. I checked the time; it was 3:24 a.m. I had to use the bathroom. Melchor was still awake using his computer.

I received a notice from the doctor's office indicating that I needed to have a breast exam. I was very uneasy the night before one of my exams. The tension brought about just thinking of my examination, and the attitude of Melchor was too much for a single person like me. Carmen was my salvation, she took me to my examination. The results showed that I had cysts in my breast. The doctor informed me that it was important for my husband or a family member to be present during my exams. The reason being was that the exams were going to be critical, and my epileptic condition made the situation more critical. My health, the well-being of Kim, and the life I was experiencing with Melchor continued to fill my life with drama. I talked to Melchor. His answer was the typical one. "Why do I have to be there, what can I do? I'm no doctor." Or he would say, "What, another sickness?"

The doctors got to know Kim and myself pretty good. Maybe not on a first-name basis, but they certainly knew our illness. Kim started her home therapy. The therapist visited us three times a week. The therapist recommended that both parents should be present. The reason being was that we should know how autism affects a child. Because Melchor had to work, it was difficult for him to be available. I was the lone parent, but then I was an experienced person in being alone. When the therapist was with Kim, I found time to relax by knitting baby clothes.

One of the times the therapist was helping Kim, I took my computer, but it wouldn't start. In turn I opened Melchor's. He had forgotten to turn it off. What I saw in the pages he'd left open shocked me. The social worker also saw them. She was startled at what she saw. "Oh my god," she said, "is that your computer?" I said, "No, it belongs to my husband, why?"

"Rosi, I need to speak to you about this, but not today. I will come back tomorrow, tomorrow because I'm not prepared to discuss a very serious problem I see with this computer."

As promised, the social worker, accompanied by a colleague, came back the next day. They showed me the data that Melchor had in his computer. She told me that I could not continue living in the same place with him. She continued to tell me that I was in danger of losing Kim if I stayed with Melchor. They gave me two weeks to decide what to do.

I had more pressing problems at the time. My health was an issue. The therapist also was concerned about my health. She was curious and asked me if I had made plans if something happened to me. I hadn't seriously thought about making plans until she brought it up.

Determined to make plans, I visited several funeral homes in the Orange County area. The first ones didn't treat me with the respect I believed I deserved. However, that was not the case when I paid a visit to Family Funeral Home in Santa Ana. I'd made an appointment with the place. Ana, the secretary, was very friendly; she made me feel comfortable. She asked me to wait for a few minutes. She explained that the rain was causing traffic problems and the agent was running a little late but was on his way.

Kim and I waited in the waiting room watching the downpour. Soon afterward, I saw this man walk into the funeral home. He startled me! He reminded me of the horrible man from my pueblo, Mother's boyfriend. I had a flashback, which was interrupted by Ana. She came into the waiting room, greeted Mr. Martinez. I heard when Ana told the agent that I was waiting for him. I rose from the coach before Ana introduced us. He extended his hand to greet me. "Very glad to meet you, Rosita," he said. I still wasn't sure that he wasn't the horrible man from my pueblo.

His hand was firm but gentle, his voice more a peaceful one and very professional. His Spanish was good but had a different accent than other Mexicans. He asked me to follow him into his office. He left the door open, explaining that he didn't want to cause any complications. Kim was sleepy. I asked Mr. Martinez if I could put her to sleep on the sofa. "Certainly," he answered. He asked me what type of coverage I wanted. I wasn't sure, so he went over some plans he felt were good for me. The more he talked, the more confident I felt that he was honest.

During all the questioning required to make a contract, Mr. Martinez learned a lot about my life. I disclosed my past that few knew about. I paid cash for the plan. Mr. Martinez asked Tony, the manager, to come into the office so that both could count the money. More confidence was gained in him. Kim was still asleep, Mr. Martinez and I stayed alone waiting for the copies of my contract. "Rosita, you have had an incredible past, you should write a book." I thought for a while before I answered, "You are right, Mr. Martinez, but it's difficult finding someone that I can trust. I have had some of my poems stolen, and now they appear on TV." Ana made all the copies for me, and they kept the originals. She took them into the office where I was waiting for them.

Mr. Martinez stood up from his desk and told me to wait a few seconds; he left the room. I thought of the statement he made. Lots of people have told me the same thing, but where do I start? I want someone that I can trust. The señor came back into the office. He placed two books in front of me. "Look at these," he said. I picked up one, the first one, and glanced it over, turned the book around to view the back. A picture of the author appeared on the back. He looked like Mr. Martinez. I picked up the second book, which was a little thicker than the first one. I turned the book to view the back cover; again the author looked like Mr. Martinez. I looked at him. I asked, "Is this you?" He smiled. "Yes, that is me, I wrote those two," he said.

"Aha, señor, you are a writer?" I asked. "You wrote these two books? My desire to write my own story has been a dream of mine forever. I have kept notes and a diary since I was a little girl." He interrupted me and told me to look the papers over one more time just to make sure they were okay. I looked at them and approved them. I looked at him and asked again, "You wrote these books?" He just smiled. He said, "I like to write, and now that I'm retired, I work at this place part-time and to pass the time."

"Señor, I've wanted to have somebody write a book on the story of my life, but I don't know who to trust." He just looked at me. He said, "Yes, you need someone you can trust."

"Señor, will you help me write my book?"

"I don't know whether I can. You see, I'm making plans to move back to the state of my birth, my roots, so to speak, which is New Mexico." I thought, *Now I know why his Spanish is somewhat different than mine.* "Rosita, think it over, and we'll talk later. The contract papers contain my phone number, call me when you are sure that you trust me enough with your life story." Kim was waking up. Before we left, Mr. Martinez signed his book and gave it to me.

Leaving the office, I felt more comfortable knowing that I could trust Mr. Martinez. Was my book going to be a reality, finally? My thoughts wandered throughout my past and what the book would look like. I had little time to pursue the book, Kim was my immediate concern. When she was asleep, I would make hats, scarfs, and sweaters to sell. One place that was always a success was the fair at the Holy Family Catholic Church. The time came, I took all my inventory to the church. Being that I was a volunteer at the church, I had an assigned spot to set up to sell my homemade clothes. After selling some of my clothes, I wandered about the fair. I wanted to see if there was any interesting activities. I walked about the grounds talking to people I knew.

The director of the fair asked me if I wanted to take charge of one of the stands. I was glad to take charge. The stand was one where the contestant tries to knock six bottles that resemble a bowling pin off the stand with three softball-size balls. It was different, and being that I'm not a sports fan, I kind of liked it. However, it seems that bad luck follows me. I had just handed the third of three balls to the contestant. He threw it so hard and so off line that it hit the edge of the stand, bounced up toward me. I wasn't fast enough to dodge the ball that caromed off the stand and slammed unto my nose. The force was too much, I was knocked unconscious.

I woke up in the middle of a crowd of people, my nose was bleeding. Somebody wanted to call 9-1-1, but I stopped him. I didn't want to cause any problems for the fair. In reality, I didn't want to incur another cost for the paramedics. I called Melchor; he would take me to the emergency. Several of the people standing around heard when I called him. They began to whisper among each other. Many were surprised that I was married because they had never seen my husband and I together. He showed up, and I could tell that many of my friends and others that knew me were upset with him. He dropped me at the emergency room and left taking Kim with him.

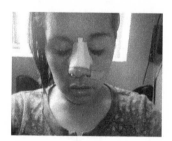

Into the hospital again and alone. I didn't have to wait long before I was called to see the doctor. The examination revealed a broken nose. The left nostril was damaged, and the doctor had to install a permanent plastic type tube to keep the nostril secure; otherwise, I would not be able to breathe.

After the operation, they wanted to release me, but not until I had a ride home. Melchor went for me. I had another restless night, my nose was hurting so bad that I couldn't sleep. Painkillers are not something I like to take, I'd much rather endure the pain. I urged myself to be strong. *I am alive and in the care of my Diosito. Relax, in time, I will be well again. My Chuchin is with me.* I smiled and started to say the rosary. I walked to the window praying.

The sight of the moon made me smile some more. For some reason, the moon has always lifted my emotions. The moon was bright; for a moment, I thought I saw a small image of a cross. The more I looked, the bigger and brighter the image of the cross got. Perched on top of the cross was a white dove moving its wings. I called Melchor, he walked into the room where I was standing near the window. He was surprised when he saw the cross. "It's very beautiful," he said. I stayed looking at the moon until the cross and dove disappeared. I got into bed, fell asleep praying the rosary.

I felt a hand touching my forehead. The touch surprised me so much that I felt shivers all over my body. My heart started beating fast because I thought of the worst. The time was 1:43 a.m. A tunnellike hole appeared near my bed. Inside the tunnel was my Chuchin surrounded by four angels. I made the sign of the cross. "Diosito, You and Your angels are here with me, a thousand thanks." Diosito extended His arms, and in His hands, I saw several persons I knew.

He told me to look at the faces of the people. He said, "These souls help Me take care of you in this world where they and I lived at one time." I saw the face of my mamacita Sinforosa, Don Felipe, my madrina Socorro, and the face of a man I couldn't place. Tears flowing from my eyes hampered my sight. I couldn't see anything, but I was so happy with what had transpired I had to tell Melchor. He listened. Thinking of Diosito aroused my emotions so much so that I slept through the night.

The following morning, I was feeling the pain in my nose. I took Kim to catch the bus. Climbing the stairs into the apartment was a chore. I had to climb slowly and with a lot of caution because my headache did not let up. My face was aflame, I started to tremble. My only friend available was Carmen, I called her. She noticed my swollen and inflamed face as soon as she arrived at my house. She called the paramedics and the priest. I wanted the priest to go see me at the hospital. However, the priest arrived at my home before the paramedics took me to the hospital and heard my confession and host. I was kept in the hospital for two days. Carmen took care of Kim. During my stay, I made the decision to entrust Mr. Martinez with my notes, my diaries, and my life story.

By August 2013, I had my notes in order; it was time to take them to Mr. Martinez. I packed the papers; Kim and I took a few buses to his house. In front of his house were two huge bins called pods. He answered the door when I rang the doorbell. He was surprised to see us but appeared happy. He invited us in. I asked if I was intruding. He smiled. "No," he answered, "in fact, we are celebrating my birthday."

"Señor, I can't stay, I just came to bring you my notes and diaries. You are still interested in writing my book, aren't you?"

He informed me that he was moving to New Mexico. The two big pods contained his belongings. He couldn't take my papers with him because he didn't want to be responsible should something happen to them. He introduced me to his family and some friends. I met one of his sons, a very special person to Mr. Martinez. His son is a federal agent. He wanted to hear more of my life and go over some of my papers. He glanced over the papers and gave me advice on how to arrange them. Also he wanted to know if I could type them because he had trouble reading my writing.

Time passed before I was ready to send him my notes in typewritten form. We decided that I should take them to him; at the same time, we could plan how it was going to be formed. In 2014, I made the trip to New Mexico with the sole purpose of working on my book and making my dream become a reality. I flew into Albuquerque, where Mr. Martinez picked me up. We drove through a place that I fell in love with, Santa Fe. In a way it reminded me of some of the pueblos in Mexico but so much more different.

I had confidence that Mr. Martinez was going to be a gentleman and not bother me. That was the case. He was interested in the book. The first day after I had unpacked, I handed him my rough manuscript. We sat outside his backyard. He asked me to read one part that he was particularly interested in. I read, or rather attempted to read, with a stream of tears running down both sides of my face. He smiled, told me to relax and to try not to cry. He realized that I've lived a very difficult life and is one of the reasons he's willing to write my book. He told me, "You are not alone, what you have written is in the past, and look, you're still among us."

Lifelong Dream Becomes a Reality

DURING OUR DISCUSSIONS, HE LEARNED that I wanted to meet my father's side of the family. Most of them lived in Texas; the other passion was the writing of my life story. We were in the backyard talking about my life. As a writer he wanted to know as much about my life as possible. He asked me if I wanted to meet my family in Texas or work on the book in the short time I was visiting. I must have misunderstood his question, which was not unusual. "Really, you will take me to Texas to meet my family?"

"I will pay for the trip! Rosita, answer me the question."

"Señor, I want to meet my family and know the truth about my father. I want to meet my brother Marcelo." We planned the trip, another dream would become a reality.

Maria Feliz, my paternal grandmother, and myself

My father's tomb

My writer drove me to Dallas, Texas, where my father's side of the family resides. I met Maria Feliz, my paternal grandmother, my uncles Santos and Pablo, and other relatives and their old friends. My grandma felt right away that I was her son Jorge's daughter. At first my uncles doubted me because Reyna had told them that I was dead. I sat on the couch looking at all my relatives, not believing that I was actually among them. Thirty-three years have passed, but I always told myself that I would find my family.

Uncle Santos and other relatives came over that night. Uncle Santos asked one of the cousins to turn some music. Above the music, Uncle Santos raised his beer and started to sing along with the recording. I joined him in the singing. He hugged me. "Rosita, you sing the Mexican ranchera songs with heart, and you have a beautiful voice, reminds me of my brother Jorge's voice." He invited everybody to go outside, saying, "Rosita is going to sing for us."

The dark moonless night lit by bulbs, breathing the cool night fresh air, warmed by my blood relatives, I sang my song, "Soy la hija de nadie." Uncle Santos, the grandest of macho men, cleaned his tears. "Give us another one," he said. Another uncle chided in, "Yes, give us another one." My cousins also wanted another one. I was ready, but uncle Santos said, "Like the gringo says, 'Stop, stop.'" He raised his voice saying, "We are going to celebrate with beer bottles. This is for you, Rosita, for being so strong. To our attractive niece and all that she has battled to learn the truth about her family and the death of her father, Jorge." Uncle Santos look skyward, made the sign of the cross, raised his beer. "To you Jorge, my blood brother."

Uncle Santos, hugging me, said, "Jorge, you are up there in heaven, and part of your rib, your seed that you and Reyna planted, is here in my arms. The same daughter that you entrusted me with but couldn't find because of lies is here among us, her true family." He raised his beer and offered a toast to Jorge. "Yes, your daughter is beautiful, and we will toast her like you and I used to toast." My uncles grabbed their bottled beers and slammed them against each other. The bottles shattered into pieces; the beer splattered their hands but remained unhurt, no blood was shed. They shouted with gusto, and I started my song, "Que diren los de tu casa cuando..." We partied all night into the wee hours of the morning.

The following day, Tio Santos took me to where my father was laid to rest. My uncle hugged me and said to me, "Mija, I want to apologize here above your father's tomb for believing your mother, Reyna, when she told me that you were dead. After what she told me, I never continued to seek the truth. Now here you are, you never gave up looking for him or your family. Thank Dios for Don Felipe for telling you the truth and the Americanos that helped you get here. Thank you, my beautiful niece, because here we are in front of your father's tomb."

"Niña, I feel in my heart the happiness you have brought to your father, Jorge. You have wrestled with lies, you battled with your mother, and here you are with your father. His soul can now rest in peace. Niña, it doesn't matter that he is dead, I toast you and your father." He raised his beer and toasted my father and myself.

"My brother's soul and his blood is in you, Rosita, and now you are among your blood family." He said, "Like the gringo says...excuse me—" He blew his nose and swallowed his tears. "Niña, these tears are not those of a coward, rather of joy that you are of my same Bustos blood."

I knelt near my father's tomb and prayed. My feeling was mixed—first, sadness for not knowing him when he was alive, and happy that I had found the truth. I said, "Papa, my life would have been completely different if you were alive." The tears were mixed with sighs. I imagined myself in my father's arms. My uncle helped me to my weary feet. He cleaned my tears and helped me to the car.

My brother Marcelo came to my grandma's house to visit. We shared our past moments, we remembered when people used to tell us that we were siblings. I shared my life detailing what I had gone through. We discovered that Bolita is his uncle on his mother's side. Marcelo didn't disclose too much about his life in the United States. One item that he did disclose was that he was born in the States. He didn't learn that until he moved to el Norte. His mother had sold his birth certificate and social security and other papers to some unknown person when he was born. He was able to correct the situation.

My return trip to New Mexico was full of anticipation. I didn't feel alone anymore. I had found my family. I left all my papers with my author and headed back to California.

I kept in touch with my family. I made arrangements to go visit them again during Christmas. It was another dream come true, I would spend Christmas not alone, but with my family.

The afternoon of the day, Kim and I arrived in Dallas my uncles, my aunt, my brothers, and my grandma—all accepted me with open arms. Before supper, we were gathered in the living room talking. They asked about my book because they were very anxious to learn about my past life. I figured that it would be a good time to read them something that was contained in the book. I read the part where I thought they could relate to. When I finished reading part of it, Tio Pablo asked me if I wanted to meet that certain Bartolo, the one whose car I had washed as a little girl. "Sure, I would like to see him and wash his car again," I answered, smiling and half joking. "Maybe he'll give me another green dollar bill." Tio Pablo burst out laughing, accompanied by Grandma and the rest of the family in attendance.

"Rosita, would you also like to meet cousins, sons, and daughters of uncles on your mother's side of the family?"

"Yes, Uncle, I would like to meet them, would you take me to meet them?" The following day, he took me to meet and visit with them. The trip took about two hours. We came to a two-story, simple, nicely-built house. Tio Pablo pointed to the house. "That's where Bartolo lives." I met Tio Bartolo. He came out of the house to greet us. Tio Pablo and Bartolo greeted each other. Uncle Pablo turned to me and asked, "Bartolo, do you know this young lady?" He looked at me with a puzzled look in his face. "She looks familiar. Hmm, she reminds me of Jorge, your brother." I smiled when I heard him say that. "Tio Bartolo, do you have a car that I can wash, like the one I used to when I was a little girl? But this time you will have to give me two green norteño dollars."

"Don't bullshit me! You are Jovani? The daughter of Jorge and Reyna? You used to wash my car and sell me candies." He gave me a hug full of tears. My grandma and Tio Pablo couldn't stop laughing.

We entered his house, and he asked us if we wanted something to drink. Tio Pablo doesn't drink hard liquor, so he asked for a soft drink. Bartolo said, "Well, I do, and I'm going to drink a beer and toast Jorge's daughter, Jovani."

"Tio Bartolo, did you know that Jorge was my father?" He turned toward my grandma and Tio Pablo then toward me and said, "Jovani, you are Jorge's daughter. I know for a fact." Bartolo lifted his beer and toasted me; he said, "To the courageous daughter of Jorge." Afterward, my grandma asked Tio Bartolo if he knew that Jorge was my father, why had he not informed us? Tio Pablo asked the same thing. Tio Bartolo answered, "I didn't want to have problems with Reyna because she was known to have friends in the federal police department.

"My brother also knows a lot about the problems we'd have with Reyna. He also knows the problems Jovani faced when she was a little girl. However, we lost sight of Jovani. People were hearing that she was in a convent in Rome, others heard that she was dead. That's another reason that I didn't say anything. But now I can tell you anything you want to know."

I took out the few pages that had been written about my life, which would eventually become the story of my life. I showed Tio Bartolo the picture of me washing his car. Tio Bartolo proceeded to tell the story of the time I washed his car. He continued to rave about that big beautiful Americano car of his.

I realized that he is not my *tio*; why I referred to him as uncle goes back to my childhood. His sister is related to me by marriage. She married a son of my uncle, the brother of Reyna, my mother.

My cousins on my mother's side. One of the cousins is the one who used to give tacos made of goat's meat when I was a little girl. She'd see me selling my candies in the street and give the goodies.

Paternal Grandmother Maria's Birthday

MY GRANDMOTHER CELEBRATED HER BIRTHDAY (age undisclosed). My brother Cuco entertained everybody at his house. My paternal side of the family came to celebrate her birthday.

I left Dallas much happier knowing that I had attained a life-long dream. I was part of a family that loved me, a family that didn't doubt that I was a Bustos, the daughter of Jorge. I would no longer be alone.

For thirty-some years of my life, I have wrestled with my sickness, loneliness, with abuses, and unfulfilled promises. Currently, I feel that I have attained most of my lifelong dreams, desires, and purposes. I truly believe that my DIOSITO, MY CHUCHIN has been my guiding light. He has placed persons along the path of my life to help me.

About the Author

JERRY P. MARTINEZ HAS WRITTEN two other books. His second book, *Timely Conquest,* was awarded second place at the Los Angeles Times Festival of Books held at the University of Southern California (USC). He earned his undergraduate degree from College of Santa Fe and MBA from Loyola Marymount of Los Angeles.